The Renaissance of Lesbianism in Early Modern England

The Renaissance of Lesbianism in Early Modern England is the eagerly awaited study by the feminist scholar who was among the first to address the issue of early modern female homoeroticism. Valerie Traub analyzes the representation of female–female love, desire, and eroticism in a range of early modern discourses, including poetry, drama, visual arts, pornography, and medicine. Contrary to the silence and invisibility typically ascribed to lesbianism in the Renaissance, Traub argues that the early modern period witnessed an unprecedented proliferation of representations of such desire. By means of sophisticated interpretations of a comprehensive set of texts, the book not only charts a crucial shift in representations of female homoeroticism over the course of the seventeenth century, but also offers a provocative genealogy of contemporary lesbianism. A contribution to the history of sexuality, and to feminist and queer theory, the book views current theoretical preoccupations through the lens of historical inquiry. The book contains pictures from important documents and illustrations of the period and will be of interest to scholars and students of early modern English literature, women's studies and gay/lesbian studies, and English social history.

Valerie Traub is Professor of English and Women's Studies at the University of Michigan, Ann Arbor. She is the recipient of a National Endowment for the Humanities Fellowship, and author of numerous works on early modern, feminist, and lesbian/gay studies. Her book, *Desire and Anxiety: Circulations of Sexuality in Shakespearean Drama*, appeared in 1992 and a co-edited collection, *Feminist Readings of Early Modern Culture: Emerging Subjects*, appeared in 1996.

PELLISSIPPI STATE
LIBRARY SERVICES
P. O. BOX 22990
KNOXVILLE, TN 37933-0990

Cambridge Studies in Renaissance Literature and Culture

General editor
STEPHEN ORGEL
Jackson Eli Reynolds Professor of Humanities, Stanford University

Editorial board
Anne Barton, *University of Cambridge*
Jonathan Dollimore, *University of York*
Marjorie Garber, *Harvard University*
Jonathan Goldberg, *Johns Hopkins University*
Nancy Vickers, *Bryn Mawr College*

Since the 1970s there has been a broad and vital reinterpretation of the nature of literary texts, a move away from formalism to a sense of literature as an aspect of social, economic, political, and cultural history. While the earliest New Historical work was criticized for a narrow and anecdotal view of history, it also served as an important stimulus for post-structuralist, feminist, Marxist, and psychoanalytical work, which in turn has increasingly informed and redirected it. Recent writing on the nature of representation, the historical construction of gender and of the concept of identity itself, on theatre as a political and economic phenomenon, and on the ideologies of art generally, reveals the breadth of the field. Cambridge Studies in Renaissance Literature and Culture is designed to offer historically oriented studies of Renaissance literature and theatre which make use of the insights afforded by theoretical perspectives. The view of history envisioned is above all a view of our own history, a reading of the Renaissance for and from our own time.

Recent titles include

38. Ann Jones and Peter Stallybrass, *Renaissance Clothing and the Materials of Memory*

39. Robert Weimann, *Author's Pen and Actor's Voice: Playing and Writing in Shakespeare's Theatre*

40. Barbara Fuchs, *Mimesis and Empire: The New World, Islam, and European Identities*

41. Wendy Wall, *Staging Domesticity: Household Work and English Identity in Early Modern Drama*

42. Valerie Traub, *The Renaissance of Lesbianism in Early Modern England*

43. Joseph Loewenstein, *Ben Jonson and Possessive Authorship*

A complete list of books in the series is given at the end of the volume

Frontispiece Detail of Anthony Van Dyck, *Mirtillo Crowning Amarillis* (1631–32).

The Renaissance of Lesbianism in Early Modern England

Valerie Traub
University of Michigan, Ann Arbor

PUBLISHED BY THE PRESS SYNDICATE OF THE UNIVERSITY OF CAMBRIDGE
The Pitt Building, Trumpington Street, Cambridge, United Kingdom

CAMBRIDGE UNIVERSITY PRESS
The Edinburgh Building, Cambridge CB2 2RU, UK
40 West 20th Street, New York, NY 10011-4211, USA
477 Williamstown Road, Port Melbourne, VIC 3207, Australia
Ruiz de Alarcón 13, 28014 Madrid, Spain
Dock House, The Waterfront, Cape Town 8001, South Africa

http://www.cambridge.org

© Cambridge University Press, 2002

This book is in copyright. Subject to statutory exception
and to the provisions of relevant collective licensing agreements,
no reproduction of any part may take place without
the written permission of Cambridge University Press.

First published 2002

Printed in the United Kingdom at the University Press, Cambridge

Typeface Times 10/12 pt.   *System* LATEX 2_ε [TB]

A catalogue record for this book is available from the British Library

Library of Congress Cataloguing in Publication data
Traub, Valerie, 1958–
The renaissance of lesbianism in early modern England / Valerie Traub.
   p.   cm. – (Cambridge studies in Renaissance literature and culture; 42)
Includes bibliographical references and index.
ISBN 0 521 44427 6 – ISBN 0 521 44885 9 (pb.)
1. Lesbianism – England – History – 16th century.   2. Lesbianism – England –
History – 17th century.   3. Lesbianism in literature.   4. Lesbians in literature.
I. Title.   II. Series.
HQ75.6.E5 T73   2002
306.76′63′0942 – dc21   2001037954

ISBN 0 521 44427 6 hardback
ISBN 0 521 44885 9 paperback

To Brenda K. Marshall

Contents

List of illustrations	*page* x
Preface	xiii
Acknowledgments	xiv
Introduction: "practicing impossibilities"	1
1 Setting the stage behind the seen: performing *lesbian* history	36
2 "A certaine incredible excesse of pleasure": female orgasm, prosthetic pleasures, and the anatomical *pudica*	77
3 The politics of pleasure; or, queering Queen Elizabeth	125
4 The (in)significance of *lesbian* desire	158
5 The psychomorphology of the clitoris; or, the reemergence of the tribade in English culture	188
6 Chaste femme love, mythological pastoral, and the perversion of *lesbian* desire	229
7 "Friendship so curst": *amor impossibilis*, the homoerotic lament, and the nature of *lesbian* desire	276
8 The quest for origins, erotic similitude, and the melancholy of *lesbian* identification	326
Afterword	355
Notes	362
Subject index	472
Name and title index	480

Illustrations

Frontispiece: Detail of Anthony Van Dyck, *Mirtillo Crowning Amarillis* (1631–32). By permission of Graft von Schönborn Collection, Pommersfelden Castle, Bavaria.

1 Anthony Van Dyck, *Mirtillo Crowning Amarillis* (1631–32). By permission of Graf von Schönborn Collection, Pommersfelden Castle, Bavaria. *page* 2
2 Bartholomeus Breenbergh, *Amarillis Crowning Mirtillo* (1635). By permission of Bowes Museum, Barnard Castle. 4
3 Jacob Van Loo, *Amarillis Crowning Mirtillo* (1645–50). By permission of Instituut Collectie Nederland. 5
4 Funeral Monument of Mary Kendall (1710), Westminster Abbey, London. By permission of Flagg Miller. 71
5 Funeral Monument of Katharina Bovey (1727), Westminster Abbey, London. By permission of Flagg Miller. 73
6 Helkiah Crooke, *Microcosmographia* (1615). By permission of the Taubman Medical Library, University of Michigan. 91
7 Thomas Bartholin, *Bartholinus Anatomy* (1653/1668). By permission of the Folger Shakespeare Library, Washington, D.C. 92
8 Jacopo Berengario da Carpi, *Isagogae breves* (1522). Courtesy of the National Library of Medicine, Washington, D.C. 113
9 Andreas Vesalius, *Epitome* (1543); reproduced from *De Humani Corporis Fabrica*. By permission of the Historical Collection, Eskind Biomedical Library, Vanderbilt University. 114
10 Andreas Vesalius, *Epitome* (1543); reproduced from *De Humani Corporis Fabrica*. By permission of the Historical Collection, Eskind Biomedical Library, Vanderbilt University. 115
11 Thomas Geminus, *Compendiosa totius anatomie delineatio* (1545). By permission of The Wellcome Medical Library, London. 116
12 Giovanni Battista de Calivari, the Capitoline Venus, *Antiquarum Staturarum Urbis Romae* (1585). By permission of the Folger Shakespeare Library, Washington, D.C. 118

List of illustrations xi

13 Juan de Valverde de Humoso, *Anatomia del corpo humano* (1556/1560). By permission of the Taubman Medical Library, University of Michigan. 119
14 Helkiah Crooke, *Microcosmographia* (1615). By permission of the Taubman Medical Library, University of Michigan. 120
15 Helkiah Crooke, *Microcosmographia* (1615). By permission of the Taubman Medical Library, University of Michigan. 121
16 Juan de Valverde de Humoso, *Anatomia del corpo humano* (1556/1560). By permission of the Taubman Medical Library, University of Michigan. 123
17 Juan de Valverde de Humoso, *Anatomia del corpo humano* (1556/1560). By permission of the Taubman Medical Library, University of Michigan. 124
18 Armada portrait of Queen Elizabeth (attr. George Gower). By kind permission of the Marquess of Tavistock and Trustees of the Bedford Estates. 127
19 Portrait of Elizabeth as princess (attr. unknown, *c*. 1546–47). By permission of the Royal Collection © 2001, Her Majesty Queen Elizabeth II. 134
20 Darnley portrait of Elizabeth I (attr. unknown, *c*. 1575). By permission of the National Portrait Gallery, London. 135
21 Rainbow portrait of Elizabeth I (attr. Marcus Gheeraerts the Younger or Issac Oliver, *c*. 1600–03). By permission of the Marquess of Salisbury, Hatfield House. 136
22 *Elizabeth I and the 3 Goddesses* (attr. Hans Eworth or Joris Hoefnagel, *c*. late 1560s). By permission of the Royal Collection © 2001, Her Majesty Queen Elizabeth II. 138
23 Thomas Coryat, *Coryats Crudities* (1611). By permission of the Newberry Library, Chicago. 141
24 Christopher Saxton, *Atlas of England and Wales* (attr. Augustine Ryther, 1579). By permission of the Newberry Library, Chicago. 159
25 Justice and Prudence, Bolsover Castle. By permission of Flagg Miller. 161
26 Faith and Hope, Bolsover Castle. By permission of Flagg Miller. 162
27 Hendrik Goltzius, Justice and Prudence (from the *Allied Virtues*, *c*. 1578–82). Duke of Sutherland Collection, on loan to the National Gallery of Scotland. 163
28 Francesco Mazzola Parmigianino, from the *Fable of Diana and Acteon* (1523), Rocca Sanvitale, Fontanellato, Parma. By permission of Alinari/Art Resource, New York. 249

xii   List of illustrations

29 Titian, *Diana Discovering the Pregnancy of Calisto* (1559). By permission of the National Galleries of Scotland, Edinburgh.   271
30 Pieter Van der Heyden, Satirical print (late sixteenth century). By permission of the British Museum.   272
31 Peter Paul Rubens, *Jupiter and Calisto* (1613). By permission of Staatliche Kunstsammlungen, Gemäldegalerie, Dresden.   273
32 Jacopo Amigoni, *Jupiter and Calisto* (*c*. 1730s). By permission of the Metropolitan Museum of Art, New York.   273
33 François Boucher, *Jove, in the shape of Diana, surprises Calisto* (1744). By permission of the Metropolitan Museum of Art, New York.   274

Preface

The tension between history and theory evident throughout this book raises the question of its own placement within a historical narrative. I am aware, for instance, that many of the scholars whose work I most contest are themselves lesbian, and that many of them are of a generation whose scholarship made my own existence as a lesbian academic conceivable. A book dedicated primarily to the project of advancing lesbian theory or of historicizing contemporary lesbianism would articulate and analyze the social circumstances out of which such work arose.

This I have not done. Insofar as my focus is a genealogy of lesbianism, critics and theorists are employed as grist for my historical and analytical mill. I therefore wish to preface this book with an acknowledgment of the work of lesbian feminist scholars whose brilliance, courage, and grace made this book conceivable. When I wrote my undergraduate thesis on the novels of Jane Rule in 1980, the work of Carroll Smith-Rosenberg, Martha Vicinus, Adrienne Rich, and Lillian Faderman was my inspiration. But even then, in however nascent a way, I was trying to integrate their belief in the power and integrity of female love and eroticism with the genealogical project advanced by Michel Foucault.

As this book attests, I still am.

Acknowledgments

This book, written over a decade in two locales, has encumbered a large number of debts. Vanderbilt University and the University of Michigan underwrote this project with a variety of faculty research grants. A National Endowment for the Humanities fellowship at the Newberry Library allowed me the time to reconceive the project and begin to finish it. The Folger Library has been generous with short-term stipends, which made archival work possible.

Many more of my debts are intellectual and personal. A number of feminist scholars, whose work I esteem and whose friendship I treasure, have offered assistance and inspiration in amazing measure. Valerie Wayne unwittingly set the direction of my career by inviting me to contribute to her Shakespeare Association of America seminar; I have been the beneficiary of her care ever since. Susan Zimmerman likewise took a chance on an unknown scholar for her anthology, *Erotic Politics*, and the idea for this book was born; it could not have asked for a better midwife. Sue Lanser deserves special mention, not only for her thoughtful critique of a very rough typescript, but also for her ongoing intellectual engagement with my ideas and the friendship that has evolved out of our dialogue. In recognition of her brilliant advice and indefatigable support along the way, Jean Howard is herewith proclaimed my mentor. The friendship of Mary Beth Rose sustained me during my year in Chicago. Carol Batker remains an inspiration from afar. I look forward to many more years in the profession with the best possible peers, Dympna Callaghan, Fran Dolan, Lindsay Kaplan, Rick Rambuss, and Jyotsna Singh.

Although this book focuses on the unique pleasures implicit in connections among women, I am keenly aware that without certain men, it never would have been written. In negotiating academia with uncommon brilliance, humor, and generosity, Peter Stallybrass has been, and remains, my guiding light. Bruce Smith has sent to me so many archival treasures that I hesitate to leave his name off of the title page. Peter Erickson has pursued intellectual connections with an intensity and integrity I admire. The incisive reading of the typescript by the late, brilliant, and courageous Alan Bray, who evaluated my evidence with a charitable but rigorous historian's eye, made this book much better. Stephen Orgel's careful reading of the typescript and assurance of its import have been

Acknowledgments

no less crucial than his patience over the years it took to complete. Jonathan Goldberg has been an inspiring and challenging interlocutor. And Jeff Masten, whose own work on friendship has been a touchstone, has been a friend indeed, reading the typescript at an early stage with the analytical precision he brings to his own work.

Several members of the Vanderbilt English Department were generous with their support, guidance, and friendship, most especially Cecilia Tichi, Paul Elledge, Vereen Bell, and Jay Clayton. One could not ask for better colleagues, friends, and readers than Mark Schoenfield and Teresa Goddu, both of whom I still miss and always will. The hard work and good will of Carolyn Levinson, Lisa Cullum, Kathy Cody, and Janis May helped to keep my professional life in good order. During those years, Mona Frederick was a voice of sanity and humor and Marianne Varney was always willing to listen and advise.

My colleagues at the University of Michigan have been delightfully intelligent interlocutors, and I am particularly grateful to the early modernists, Linda Gregerson, Bill Ingram, Ejner Jensen, John Knott, Steve Mullaney, and Mike Schoenfeldt, for accepting me so warmly into their fold. Mike deserves special mention for his intellectual companionship and consistent support for my work and me, and Bill deserves special thanks for his help in deciphering early modern texts. P. A. Skantze and Carla Mazzio have been extraordinary comrades, whose unique capacities and brave life choices help me to think courageously about myself. Liz Barnes, Anita Norich, Yopie Prins, Suzanne Raitt, and Patsy Yaeger have provided a rare and much appreciated combination of intellectual and personal camaraderie; I am particularly grateful to Suzanne for her help in framing the Introduction. Through the First Draft club, Tobin Siebers has fostered an ongoing sense of intellectual companionship. David Halperin was an influence long before becoming a colleague and friend. Jan Burgess and Donna Johnston have kept my professional life on the up-and-up.

I have been blessed with the opportunity to work with extraordinary students whose own intellectual vitality has fostered mine. Some of them have, at one time or other, brought their insight and diligence to bear on this project. Misty Anderson, Jen Shelton, Adriane Stewart, Will Fisher, Amanda Eubanks Winkler, Elise Frasier, Gina Bloom, Maureen MacDonnell, Pavitra Sundar, Jennie Evenson, Holly Dugan, and Shana Kimball, have all, in ways great and small, affected the production of this book. A special thanks to Gina Bloom and Flagg Miller for being my spies on the ground in England, as well as to Angela Balla for her amazing help at the last minute. Theresa Braunschneider deserves particularly emphatic thanks for reading the typescript with her usual perspicuity and intelligence; my respect for her own work is recorded throughout the latter pages of this book.

I am grateful to Pat Simons for her rigorous critiques offered during the middle stages of this project. Al Young provided enthusiastic support from the standpoint of his own work on colonial America. Several scholars read and commented helpfully on individual chapters, including Carolyn Dinshaw, Valeria Finucci, Diana Fuss, Elizabeth Hageman, and members of the Folger Library Eighteenth-Century Studies Group. Doug Bruster, Dick Burt, Karen Newman, and Helmut Puff each led me to exciting new material. At a crucial time Sonja Rose and Carroll Smith-Rosenberg helped me to think through the parameters of the book. Likewise, the responses of Eve Sedgwick and Barbara Johnson led to new ways of framing questions and re-conceiving possible directions of inquiry. The staffs at the Folger Library and the Newberry Library offered their expertise and support; I would particularly like to thank Georgianna Ziegler. The Shakespeare Association of America has provided an important institutional welcome from very early on. And Josie Dixon and Vicki Cooper of Cambridge University Press have brought to this project a high degree of professionalism for which I am very grateful.

Brenda Marshall suffered through my ideas at their most confused, my prose at its most turgid, and my emotions at their most stressed. Nonetheless, she found the personal and intellectual wherewithal to engage, critique, edit, and support in all the ways that matter – which is only one of the reasons why this book is dedicated to her, with all my love.

NOTE

Unless quoting from a modern edition, I have retained early modern spelling, capitalization, and emphasis. For ease of comprehension, however, I occasionally have silently modernized *u/v*, *i/j*, and *i/y*; long *s* has been revised to *s*; y^e has been altered to *the*; and where a macron over a vowel indicates the suspension of *m* or *n*, I have added the letter.

Introduction: "practicing impossibilities"

> I will make their pains my pastimes, and so confound their loves in their own sex that they shall dote in their desires, delight in their affections, and practice only impossibilities.[1]

Imagine the scene. A man, thwarted in his desires and desperate for access to the woman he loves, disguises himself as a woman and follows her to a pastoral glade. His beloved, blissfully ignorant of his tormented passion, wiles the time away in the company of women. Her friends, mischievous and full of fun, decide to "practice" the art of kissing among themselves. To heighten their enjoyment, they declare a "kissing war." Having judged the shepherdess's mouth to be the fairest, they give her the role of judging whose kisses most please. The women begin to kiss. Enter the man, who takes his place in line.

The story is famous, the scene oft illustrated. A moment in the late sixteenth-century pastoral tragicomedy, *Il Pastor Fido* by Giovanni Battista Guarini, the story was the subject of multiple translations in many different languages, and over fifty artistic renditions before the end of the seventeenth century, including Dutch, Flemish, French, and Italian paintings, prints, tapestries, and wall panels.[2] *Mirtillo Crowning Amarillis*, painted by Anthony Van Dyck between 1631 and 1632, is one of the most celebrated visual interpretations of what is typically called the "crowning scene." (See frontispiece and figure 1.) It focuses on the moment when the disguised shepherd Mirtillo, having won the war and been crowned the victor, chivalrously places his floral crown on the head of his beloved, the shepherdess Amarillis.[3] Although in Guarini's play, as well as in the 1647 English translation by Sir Richard Fanshaw (*The Faithful Shepherd*), Mirtillo's gender identity is not revealed in this scene – indeed, Mirtillo languishes in unrequited love for much of the play – in Van Dyck's painting the reassertion of masculinity is superimposed on an implied declaration of heterosexual love. As a synchronic snapshot of a longer narrative, the moment of chivalrous crowning is presented visually as a consummation of both the story and Mirtillo's desire.

The fact that Mirtillo wins the "war" would seem to confirm the status of men as superior lovers, a status reinforced by the visual hierarchy of Van Dyck's

Figure 1   Anthony Van Dyck, *Mirtillo Crowning Amarillis* (1631–32).

composition: not only is the male–female couple positioned centrally in the group and their faces and pastoral crown located at the vanishing point of the canvas, but the postures of the nymphs and putti direct the viewer's gaze toward that focal point. The centralization of male–female eroticism is supported, too, by the manipulation of a racialized aesthetic, whereby the gesture of the one black nymph cuts laterally across the field of vision. Her dark, muscular arm, similar in color and shape to the limbs of the tree above, contrasts warmly yet decisively against all the pale, circular, connective activity conveyed by the postures of the other nymphs. Her left hand, grasping the palm of a nymph still engaged in kissing, links her to the circuit of female erotic contact even as she points to the reason for its interruption.

The painting's affirmation of the superiority of heteroeroticism, however, is destabilized by the narrative predicate of the story, as well as by the fact that Mirtillo's victory has not, apparently, stopped the war. What are we to make of an all-female kissing war? Is this standard sport among female rustics? And what exactly is a kissing *war*, anyway? Once we begin to ask these questions, the pairs of kissing nymphs come into sharper focus. Insofar as the sensual poses of the partially clad nymphs provide contrast and added *frisson* to the embrace of shepherd and shepherdess, heteroeroticism and its attendant pleasures seem to depend on the performance of a prior and idyllic homoeroticism, safely ensconced in a canopied bower. Furthermore, the degree to which Amarillis and Mirtillo embody stable gender positions is called into question by the use of crossdressing as the vehicle for Mirtillo's erotic access. How *hetero* is Amarillis's desire if, in the prehistory of the painting and more explicitly in the play, she has believed this fabulous kisser to be a woman?[4]

Other treatments of the story offer an array of interpretative possibilities. Bartholomeus Breenbergh's *Amarillis Crowning Mirtillo* (1635), for instance, enacts a strict spatial division between the crowning of Mirtillo and the nymphs engaged in kissing (figure 2). As two nymphs continue their amorous play off in a corner, an expanse of terrain quarantines them from the ritual festivities of a resumed heteroeroticism. In Jacob Van Loo's more domestic scene (1645–50), the expressions of Amarillis's companions are ambiguously rendered (figure 3). Do their looks of surprise indicate alarm over the fact that Mirtillo, still in the dress of a Dutch matron, has not yet revealed his masculinity? Or do they convey concern that he has so successfully crossdressed?[5]

Such representations and the questions they raise give us a means to contravene the standard critical orthodoxy, both gay and straight, regarding the invisibility of lesbianism in Western Europe prior to modernity. Representative statements from *The Gay and Lesbian Literary Heritage*, a 1995 reference work edited by Claude Summers and notable for its thorough and scholarly treatment of a vast range of topics, provide a convenient illustration of the historical vacuum into which women's erotic desires for one another so often continue to fall. Here are statements from three separate historical entries: "Lesbianism is a theme rarely treated in Latin literature ... [T]hough Ovid regards the love of boys as commonplace, love between females is *unthinkable* in his world." "[F]emale homosexual issues do not appear explicitly in medieval English literature ... For lesbians attempting to understand why they have been silenced for much of the English tradition, it is with the *silence* of medieval English texts that they should begin." "Lesbianism is almost *invisible* in the [English Renaissance]."[6] Such pronouncements, as mistaken as they are commonplace, have been proffered by some of the most esteemed scholars of early modern (male) homoeroticism. Literary critics and historians of contiguous periods largely have concurred. According to the authors of an influential study of female transvestism: "Until the end of the eighteenth century love affairs between women were not taken seriously, and perhaps not often even noticed at all ... [I]n the past lesbian love was inconceivable."[7] To many responsible, even ground-breaking scholars, female homoeroticism prior to the Enlightenment has seemed silent and invisible. Impossible.

Figure 2 Bartholomeus Breenbergh, *Amarillis Crowning Mirtillo* (1635).

Introduction: "practicing impossibilities" 5

Figure 3 Jacob Van Loo, *Amarillis Crowning Mirtillo* (1645–50).

Having pursued the silence, invisibility, and impossibility of early modern lesbianism for the last decade, I now want to propose a different way of engaging with the historical and interpretative problems it poses. I take my cue from the courtier-dramatist John Lyly's late sixteenth-century stageplay, *Gallathea*, performed by an all-boy troupe of actors in the private theaters. In this play, an impish Cupid titillates an audience of aristocratic ladies with a mischievous scheme he has devised. Referring to a group of Diana's virgin nymphs, he says, "I will make their pains my pastimes, and so confound their loves in their own sex that they shall dote in their desires, delight in their affections, and practice only impossibilities." Cupid's oxymoronic representation of what it means for women mutually to "dote in their desires" and "delight in their affections" extends to the love that develops between Gallathea and Phyllida, two girls crossdressed by their fathers to escape an annual ritual sacrifice of pretty virgins. This being a Renaissance romantic comedy, of course, disguise enables desire: Gallathea and Phyllida fall in love, and although each suspects the other to be female, they spend as much time as possible exploring and, as they put it, "mak[ing] much one of another" (3.2.56). Drawing on a long heritage of female–female relations as an *amor impossibilis*,[8] Lyly's play reproduces social orthodoxy: the prospect of women pursuing a loving and erotic life together simply cannot be. At the same time, by gesturing toward the enactment of erotic passion for one's own sex, by mining a tension between what can and cannot *be practiced*, *Gallathea* helps to make the impossible intelligible and the unintelligible possible.

I will return to Lyly's play in my final two chapters to explore the specific forms his representation of impossibilities take. For now, I want to propose that the notion of practicing impossibilities thematized by *Gallathea* neatly encapsulates the dilemma of lesbian representation in the early modern period. On the one hand, women's erotic desires for other women were considered improbable, implausible, insignificant, subject to all the force of negativity condensed within the early modern definitions of impossibility: that which cannot be, inability, and impotence. On the other hand, such desires were culturally practiced and represented in a variety of ways, although often according to a governing logic that attempted to reinscribe their impossibility. Adopting the paradox of practicing impossibilities as my framework for analysis, I attempt in this book not only to demonstrate the existence of a cultural awareness of women who desired other women in the early modern period, but to detail the complex and often contradictory modes of representation through which such desire was articulated. My guiding questions are these: How was same-gender female desire rendered intelligible? What tropes, what images, figured such desire? What strategies were employed to maintain the status of such desire as impossible? Were those strategies successful? And did those strategies change over time – specifically, over the course of the seventeenth century – as the emergence of new epistemologies and social practices generated unprecedented understandings of the body and the self? In addition to situating the representation of female homoeroticism in relation to other historical narratives, my book attempts to clarify the complicated intellectual and psychological investments of contemporary lesbians in the early modern representations we discover; it thus explores the ways that scholars harness history to concerns of the present. The puzzle of an impossibility that *can* be practiced functions not only as a useful metaphor for the way female–female desires gained intelligibility, but as an accurate measure of the scholarly task of rearticulating this occluded history. Practicing impossibilities thus is not so much a matter of how to make love to another woman, as Lyly's meddling Cupid would have it, but a description of the problem, both in the past and in the present, of how to represent women who would make such love.

My pursuit of impossibilities has emboldened me to argue that early modern England witnessed a *renaissance* of representations of female homoerotic desire. By this I mean three things. First, references to female–female desire in English texts increased dramatically over the sixteenth and seventeenth centuries. Beginning in the mid-sixteenth century, widespread social, intellectual, and economic changes fostered the production and dissemination of a variety of discourses alluding to the physical and emotional investments of women in one another. The circulation of classical texts in the vernacular, the rise of popular public and private theaters, the development of the secular visual arts, the emergence of illustrated anatomy books, travel narratives, and obscene texts, and the increase in female literacy all affected the number and kind of representations of women's desire for other women in English society. If these phenomena were not, strictly speaking, new, their interaction and the results of that interaction were unprecedented. Within the context of a pervasive belief in women's erotic intemperance – the insatiable lust that was woman's inheritance from Eve – these varied cultural developments generated an extensive array of detail about what it means for women to passionately love, and have sex with, other women.

Here is a partial list, in addition to Lyly, of English authors who contributed to such representations, both celebratory and condemnatory, from the mid-sixteenth to the end of the seventeenth century – or, to invoke the two female monarchs whose reigns mark the temporal boundaries of my study, between Queen Elizabeth and Queen Anne: Thomas Heywood, John Donne, Ben Jonson, Edmund Spenser, William Shakespeare, William Warner, Robert Burton, John Fletcher, James Shirley, George Sandys, John Crowne, Edmund Waller, Andrew Marvell, Margaret Cavendish, Katherine Philips, Aphra Behn, and several anonymous, possibly female poets. Add to their literary texts the medical works of anatomists and midwives who diagnose the medical problem of clitoral hypertrophy in terms of women's illicit "abuse" of their clitorises with other women; the many travel writers who claim to have witnessed illicit sexual contact among Muslim women in Turkey and North Africa; the lexicographers and lawyers who grappled with the meanings of the notoriously fraught terms "sodomy" and "buggery" and their applicability to women; the visual artists who depicted women in a variety of amorous poses, particularly when portraying pastoral and mythological themes; and the many continental writers whose own treatments of female–female love and erotic contact in romances, plays, poems, medical texts, and moral treatises were translated into English during this period, and you can begin to see why *renaissance* might be the appropriate word to describe this discursive proliferation.

Although some of the phenomena I will discuss were aspects of a manuscript culture (particularly the exchange of letters and the circulation of poetry among friends), it was the technology of print that fostered this proliferation of representations. I thus am making no quantitative claims regarding an increase in portrayals of female–female love and lust that are not true for countless other phenomena. Nor do I mean to elide classical or medieval discussions, whether they be in the form of allusions to female acts *contra naturam* in theology, penitential manuals, or convent rules, in references to tribadism in medical and astrological treatises, and in the desiring stances taken by women in their letters and poems.[9] Nor do I argue for a quantifiable increase in female–female sex, a "renaissance" of female erotic pleasure – indeed, I would not know how to measure it. I do contend that the increased availability of textual references to female intimacies, the graphic explicitness of some of these depictions, and the range of themes and tones expressed therein all initiate a profusion and variety of representations unique to the early modern era.

My use of "renaissance" also is meant to suggest that representations of female–female desire during this period depend heavily on classical antecedents for their modes of comprehension. It is through, quite literally, a rebirth of classical idioms, rhetorics, tropes, and illustrative examples that female homoeroticism gained intelligibility in early modern England. By renovating the discourses of the ancients, writers in the sixteenth and seventeenth centuries attempted to legitimize their own formulations, drawing on authoritative precedents such as Ovid, Martial, and Soranus for *risqué* or troubling ideas. To the extent that desire among women was a discursive phenomenon, then, it was fashioned primarily out of two rhetorics, both of which were revived from the ancient past: a medico-satiric discourse of the tribade, and a literary-philosophical discourse of idealized friendship. The classical discourse of tribadism tended to vilify female erotic transgression, while the classical discourse of *amicitia* – translated in early modern English as *amity* – celebrated ties among men. Both of these classical discourses were revised and reworked by early modern authors as they translated old stories into new contexts. I will say more about how these rhetorics were reborn and transformed later in this Introduction. For the moment what is important is that, in appropriating the term "renaissance" to describe both the amplified presence of, and the classical antecedents to, lesbian representation, I want to draw attention to the fact that portrayals of female homoeroticism in the early modern era are less a simple and inevitable precursor to distinctively modern erotic arrangements than an effect of the combination of classical terms and understandings with new knowledges and social formations. Arising in relationship to such different forces as the institutionalization of the "new science" and the ideology of companionate marriage, discourses about female–female desire make use of the classical past in order to create a specifically Renaissance mode of representation.

My use of the term "renaissance", finally, is meant to reclaim, ironize, and redeploy the meaning of the Renaissance itself. Since its nineteenth-century definition by Jacob Burckhardt in *The Civilization of the Renaissance in Italy* and its later formulation by Erwin Panofsky in *Renaissance and Renascences in Western Art*, the Renaissance has alluded to a rebirth that, in looking backward in time for its models, affiliations, and interests, synthesizes tradition and innovation, old forms and new social realities.[10] The Renaissance thus represents a revival of antiquity and a cultural efflorescence that is both an intellectual movement and a historical period. Burckhardt and Panofsky's understanding of a temporal period such as the Renaissance depended on their assumption of a culture's organic coherence and cohesion, made apparent through its intellectual and aesthetic achievements. With a single paradigm-breaking question, "Did women have a Renaissance?" Joan Kelly upset the picture of the Renaissance as a Burckhardtian epiphany of individual accomplishment, transforming it into a period of social and political retrenchment.[11] Since the publication of Kelly's essay in 1977, other commentators have argued that the Renaissance has stood for an implicitly masculine, humanist, elite culture that excluded most of the female and laboring population. The implications of Kelly's question have been debated with increasing sophistication and precision by feminist and social historians, yet the answer regarding European women as a whole, and English women in particular, still is a qualified "No." Whereas some elite, usually urban, women benefited from the expansion of humanist education and mercantilism, a variety of forms of social unrest, including Protestant reforms and the reaction they engendered, spurred a tightening of patriarchal controls.[12] If freedom for early modern women was defined as access to the public sphere, it was precisely in this sphere that women were losing traditional roles in professional and commercial life due to increased legal restrictions. Within the English context of recurrent inflation, land shortages, high population growth, widespread migration and poverty, there appears to have been, in the words of David Underdown, a "crisis of order," during which, if "patriarchy could no longer be taken for granted," it nonetheless developed new, and in some cases quite subtle, tactics for enforcing gender subordination.[13] Such tactics can be seen in the Crown's introduction of state-authored homilies, including sermons on marriage and adultery, which attempted to exert ideological control over an unruly populace, and the proliferation of conduct books, authored by men and women, that targeted the "middling sort" in their effort to inculcate patriarchal norms (in a manner seemingly congenial to many women).[14] Although the Protestant belief in the spiritual equality of men and women, as well as the active role women took in radical religious movements, accorded some women greater spiritual dignity and power, these gains did not translate seamlessly into economic, political, or social equality. Within the household and state, whether Protestant or Catholic, English or continental, the overall effect seems to have been, in the words of Lyndal Roper, a "resurgent patriarchalism" in education, religion, politics, and the family.[15]

Even as they demonstrate the complex strategies by which patriarchal authority re-exerted itself, feminist scholars increasingly have sought to resist the allure of a critical model of ideological containment, which tends to reinscribe patriarchy as monolithic and early modern women as powerless. Challenging the putative mastery of early modern ideology, ferreting out diverse instances of female agency and power, they have shown the manifold ways that women resisted the ideology of domestic confinement and the constraints of legal coverture, as well as their educational and political disenfranchisement. Scholars have turned our attention, for instance, to women's narrative strategies as religious poets and translators of others' works; to women's finesse in negotiating the perils of pamphlet debates about their rights; to the radical import of women's scaffold speeches, orated while awaiting execution for crimes committed against household and state authority; and to the freedoms that they may have experienced as consumers of theatrical entertainments.[16]

Few scholars, however, have granted female erotic desire (whether directed toward women or men) the same degree of power accorded to, for instance, female poets' articulation of a gendered voice, female dramatists' appropriation of strategies of male authorship, or female characters' disruption of the authority of fathers and husbands on the stage. Taking its place alongside two recent monographs, Elizabeth Wahl's *Invisible Relations: Representations of Female Intimacy in the Age of Enlightenment* and Harriette Andreadis's *Sappho in Early Modern England: Female Same-Sex Literary Erotics, 1550–1714*,[17] as well as a recent stream of articles and book chapters on seventeenth-century authors such as Katherine Philips and Aphra Behn, *The Renaissance of Lesbianism in Early Modern England* investigates the role women played as both subjects and objects of emerging erotic knowledges, from the anatomical "rediscovery" of the clitoris in 1559 to the explosion of "sapphic" narratives (literary, medical, and obscene) in the early years of the eighteenth century. In appropriating the term "renaissance" to refer to women's status as both subjects and objects of homoerotic representations, I do not mean to imply that women were the privileged recipients of intellectual, social, or economic favor, nor that they participated in a golden age of female intimacy. Rather than intimating the presence of cultural support, my use of "renaissance" is meant to convey the dynamic interactions of a range of knowledges about the anatomical and physiological body, about licit and illicit desires, and about prescribed and proscribed erotic practices. The renaissance of lesbianism arose when new discourses made certain interests in the body salient and innovative modes of investigation possible. During this period of discursive cross-fertilization, there also emerged a discourse of homoerotic desire articulated by women themselves. Although women did not originate the terms used to describe their desires, they did appropriate and revise prevailing tropes and rhetorics, participating in a cultural dialogue that put the meanings of same-gender love and eroticism under increasing scrutiny and pressure.

In *Epistemology of the Closet*, Eve Kosofsky Sedgwick proposes that many of the great artistic moments of the Western tradition – the Italian and English Renaissances, the New England Renaissance, and the Harlem Renaissance – depended on "gay desires, people, discourses, prohibitions, and energies." "No doubt," she comments wryly, "that's how we will learn to recognize a renaissance when we see one."[18] Whereas such renaissances mostly have been the purview of male authors intent on representing male desires (Michelangelo, Caravaggio, Shakespeare, Marlowe, Melville, Whitman, Cullen, McKay), postulating a renaissance of lesbianism allows us to consider the extent to which women's desires, bodies, and practices were ideologically contested and culturally productive sites of interpretation, knowledge, and power. The point, however, is not to restore lesbianism to visibility, as if the problems attendant upon its representation could be so easily dispatched. Rather, without exaggerating the claims of female homoeroticism on the cultural imagination, or underestimating the degree of patriarchal management exercised upon it, marking the parameters of this renaissance prompts us to reconsider the meaning of such culturally central terms as masculinity and femininity, friendship and marriage, reproduction and heterosexuality, visibility and invisibility.

How did early modern authors represent female–female love, desire, eroticism? To begin to answer that question requires resisting the truisms of the dominant orthodoxy which would foreclose the question by recourse to one of its own: *how do they do it?* Rather, our question becomes, how do *we* do it? Not how do we make love – notwithstanding *The Joys of Lesbian Sex*, books won't help us much here – but how do we know what is erotic? How do we know what is not? How did people in the early modern period "do it,"[19] and how do we recognize what "it" is? Through what interpretative procedures, for instance, do we construe as erotic the visual image of two naked nymphs embracing, a tale of shepherdesses engaged in an all-female kissing war, or an opera vocalizing ecstatic professions of devotion from a handmaiden to her mistress? To what extent is it appropriate to extrapolate presence from absence, cultural possibilities from asseverations of impossibility?

Beyond such questions of documentation and evidence lie methodological ones. Is our aim to construct a canon of lesbian authors? To offer close readings of literary texts that are attuned to homoerotic imagery? If our strategy is not to extrapolate homoerotic *motives* from the biographies of authors and artists, what authorizes as "homoerotic" the affect and effect of the texts, images, and sounds such persons have created?

Such hermeneutic questions blend into the historical. Is our aim to construct a new, homoerotic, literary history? To chart a chronology of changes in the cultural representation of female intimacy? How should the parameters of such histories be defined temporally, geographically, nationally, linguistically, and how do those choices affect larger periodizations? Do we claim for female homoeroticism an independent social status, or do we aim to demonstrate its embeddedness in, and mutual constitutiveness with, other social formations (such as heterosexuality, domesticity, status and rank, nationality, race)? Is the historiography we enact best done in conversation with women's history or with the history of gay men?

Although there are no easy answers to these questions, my approach, in both evidentiary and hermeneutic terms, has been to analyze a varied assortment of texts from numerous discursive domains to produce a thick associational field. Casting as wide a net as my training and resources have allowed, I have pursued traces of female–female eroticism in legal discourses, medical treatises, anatomy books, midwiferies, sexual advice books, travel narratives, poetry, stageplays, closet drama, music, and the visual arts. Although my focus is England, I have drawn from continental texts which would have been available to English readers, whether in Latin, in the European vernaculars, or in translation. I have bracketed the problem of the accuracy of such translations, focusing instead on their cultural availability. In a few cases, I have used non-English texts in modern translation to enable a comparative analysis or to introduce a question that otherwise would go unasked, but in general I have relied on early modern translations. At the beginning of my research, I suspended consideration of genre and discipline in order to ascertain those intertextual connections that exist across such domains – concentrating on the common play of metaphors, the assertion of analogies, the appropriations of one discourse by another. Because the formal boundaries between, for instance, travel narratives, medical treatises, and sexual advice manuals had yet to be rigidly codified, commonalities and repetitions occur as a result of their miscellaneous, encyclopedic character. As my research progressed, discursive disjunctions and genre distinctions accrued greater relevance, as did differences in authorship, audience, poetic and narrative conventions. The sensual pastoralism evident in Renaissance stageplays and paintings of mythological subjects, for instance, differs tonally, structurally, and thematically from the pseudo-scientific rhetoric of anatomy texts and treatises on hermaphrodites. The modes of personification in the lyric – consider the implications of the lyric voice and its purported relationship to subjectivity – contrast sharply to the reified stereotypes imposed by the language of satire and defamation. Continental law is far more condemnatory than medicine, and both are surpassed in salaciousness by obscene texts and courtly libels. Early modern discourses, in other words, do not speak with a unified voice. Just as there is no unified lesbian (or so the ensuing pages will argue), there is no univocal response to her cultural presence.

There are limits, of course, to this Renaissance plethora, including the deliberate obscurities introduced into texts discussing illicit sex. My collection of evidence, therefore, does not indicate a belief that evidence is "innocent" or simply waiting to be used – since any archive, in the words of Jeffrey Masten, is "precooked," that is, subject to prior modes of institutionalization, systems of classification, and hierarchies of value.[20] The use of disparate materials courts many dangers, the greatest two being the disservice done to each individual text or image *as a text or image*, and the lack of sustained engagement with the scholarly protocols of, and debates within, other disciplines. These potential problems, I hope, are counterbalanced by this book's generation of an archive and elucidation of a field of inquiry previously so occluded as to seem to have no place in history.

In the following pages, I attempt to show that it is precisely a historicized understanding of discourses of eroticism that allows us to claim certain representations as, if not exactly lesbian, then as crucial materials in a genealogy of female homoerotic desire. By claiming a variety of representations as erotic, I enact a lesbian-affirmative analytic, one that begins with the assumption of the worth and variety of female emotional and physical ties, and moves from there to explore the ways such ties are portrayed. By "desire," and more specifically "erotic desire," I mean, quite simply, intense emotional investment and compelling erotic attraction – that which the early moderns referred to as love, passion, appetite, lust. Manifestations of erotic desire among women took multiple forms: they include caresses, kisses, bodily penetration, and passionate verbal addresses expressing longing, loss, devotion, frustration, pleasure, and pain. Although some such manifestations of affection and tenderness appear to be indifferent to the genitals, I maintain that they are no less erotogenic, no less engaged with the pleasurable resources of the body, for that indifference. (Lest this formulation seem too anodyne, it may be useful to recall that the stated goal of many practitioners and theorists of SM is to locate non-genital potentials of pleasure and pain on the body's surface.[21]) My broadly inclusive view of eroticism strategically privileges a "universalizing" concept of erotic potential (the belief that homoerotic desire, variously manifested, pervades culture) over a "minoritizing" concept (the belief that such desire is salient only to specific individuals).[22] In the two representational figures with which this book is centrally concerned, the tribade and the friend, these contradictory (il)logics are crucially at work; as I trace the historical interaction of these figures, I show how the universalized concept is rendered susceptible to the prohibitions placed on the minority.

My lesbian-affirmative analytic thus resists the opening move of much lesbian scholarship, which begins by defining its central term: "a lesbian is x."[23] For several reasons, both epistemological and historical, such a definitional imperative functions as a straightjacket; it is both inappropriate and distorting. To address the epistemological problem first: notwithstanding its enabling, even life-affirming utility to countless individuals and collectivities, lesbian is a rather coarse and confining category of erotic identity. Lesbian not only implies a coherent and stable erotic orientation, but the achievement of this orientation through a developmental process of increasing self-awareness and self-expression – hence, the centrality of the metaphors of the closet and coming out. Yet, as Sedgwick has shown, such modern categories typically function in such a way as to occlude their constitutive incoherence: people simultaneously can hold diametrically opposed views about the ways in which lesbianism relates, for instance, to the physical body or gender roles, without recognizing the contradictions activated therein. The incoherences of erotic identities generally are papered over in an attempt to uphold binary gender as the privileged indicator of emotional affect and erotic desire. Despite the common-sense appeal of finding in the biological sex of one's erotic partner the prime indicator of "sexual orientation," desire, I believe, is not so easily oriented. Both desire and its related gender identifications can transit across identity categories and, following indeterminate trajectories, produce configurations of eroticism eccentric to the binaries of sex (male/female), gender (masculine/feminine), and sexuality (hetero/homo). Nor does the category of bisexuality lay to rest the conflicting identifications, investments, comforts, and satisfactions that together can comprise the erotic self. In addition, identity categories such as lesbian represent erotic orientation as much for the benefit of others as for the benefit of the self.[24] Even as lesbian is based on a concept of deviance, it functions as an externally ascribed designation with the power to create normative obligations; it is an injunction to which, it seems, one *must* respond. Finally, as a group identity, lesbianism ignores other components of social position – notably race and class, but also the specificity of erotic practices – in the interests of fashioning community. The recognition that such instabilities, conflicts, injunctions, and false unities are constitutive of modern erotic identities motivates my skepticism toward classifying schemes and definitions, and allies my work with some aspects of queer theory.[25] I share with Ed Cohen and other queer theorists the desire "to locate a point of intellectual entrée in terms of a *relation*, or more dynamically, a *process*," with the hope that such a strategy "might afford the local effectiveness of an identity – that is, provide a positioning from which to organize and channel movements of knowledge, while not confining the mobility of this positioning within any self-unified epistemological boundaries."[26]

These epistemological issues are redoubled when they are applied to the early modern era, for which the concept of erotic orientation was largely alien. Throughout this book, I explore the multiple ways that women who desired women were represented in a culture which, as Jonathan Goldberg puts it, did "not operate under the aegis of the homo/hetero divide."[27] Attentiveness to historical anachronism, however, need not take the form of dismissing the existence of female–female eroticism prior to modernity. It is one of my central arguments that certain social and epistemological changes in the late seventeenth century created the conditions of possibility for modern erotic identities.

Thus, to use the term lesbian when discussing early modern texts is prematurely to unify concepts that only began to come into contact, jostle, and intersect late in the period. Jeffrey Masten has used the phrase "queer philology" to describe "a new historical philology that investigates the etymology, circulation, transformation, and constitutive power of 'key words' within early modern discourses of sex and gender."[28] While not explicitly philological, my project tries to render the unfamiliar familiar by introducing to critical discussion the tribade (a woman alleged to possess an enlarged clitoris which she used to pleasure other women), as well as to render the familiar strange by demonstrating the erotic affects associated with the supposedly asexual friend.[29] *The Renaissance of Lesbianism* traces the separate yet eventually intertwined trajectories of these two figures, as well as some of the meanings left unarticulated by these keywords.

Throughout this book, then, "lesbian" refers to a representational image, a rhetorical figure, a discursive effect, rather than a stable epistemological or historical category. It is employed as an exceptionally compressed and admittedly inadequate rubric for a wide, and sometimes conflicting, range of affective and erotic desires, practices, and affiliations, which have taken different historical forms and accrued varied historical meanings. Whenever possible I have used the words and rhetorics of the past, and tried to make sense of them *on their own terms*, while resisting the pressure of the dominant ideology (both then and now) to define and delimit what such terms might be.[30] Five concepts have proven crucial to my investigation: *pleasure*, the somatic and psychological components of erotic enjoyment; *generation*, women's reproductive capacity and social responsibility to conceive and give birth; *chastity*, the ideology of bodily integrity that secures the meaning and viability of reproduction for the patriarchal order; *tribadism*, an activity that transgresses both chastity and reproduction through the misuse of body parts; and *friendship*, which in my study is the site where chastity and tribadism eventually mingle and collide. The proximity in this period of representations of tribadism to broader discourses of female erotic pleasure has prompted me to place considerable pressure on the meanings of chastity and friendship. The cultural mandate that women remain virginal until married and chaste within marriage does not address, much less exhaust, the possibilities of female bodily conduct if one is willing to consider erotic practices eccentric to phallic definitions of sexuality and the normative patriarchal life cycle (maid, wife, mother, widow). The potential for eroticism within chastity and friendship has been occluded by a frame of reference that assumes the phallus to be the primary signifier of sexuality, and penetration the only form of eroticism that counts.[31] My lesbian-affirmative analytic makes an end-run around the structures of visibility that have constrained the recognition of lesbian desire throughout history,[32] arguing that because certain forms of female affectivity and bodily intimacy did not threaten penetrative logics, they found a space for expression within the decorum of maidenly modesty.

This book thus enacts a double critical movement: maintaining an awareness of the difference between past and present while refusing to capitulate to prior ideas of what the past might have been. Whenever possible, I employ terms that are less implicated in modern discourses of identity than "lesbian" (or "heterosexual"). "Homoeroticism," while somewhat cumbersome and etymologically predicated on gender sameness, conveys a more fluid and contingent sense of erotic affect than either "lesbian" or "homosexual"; neither a category of self nor normatively male, homoeroticism retains the necessary strangeness and historical contiguity between early modern and contemporary forms of desire. The modifiers "homoerotic," "female–female," "same-gender," and "lesbian," when attached to such nouns as "love," "desire," "eroticism," "behaviors," and "practices," mark the subject of this book as a relation *to* an affective or bodily state.[33] However, because the nouns "lesbian" and "lesbianism" clearly are relevant to the histories, figures, and investments addressed herein, linking disparate phenomena as well as the past to the present, my solution, from this point on, is to italicize these terms. My hope is that the persistent typographical strangeness of *lesbian* and *lesbianism* will remind readers of their epistemological inadequacy, psychological coarseness, and historical contingency. (The one exception to this practice is when I refer to lesbian history, lesbian studies, or lesbian scholarship as institutional phenomena.) Throughout this book, *lesbian* functions as a strategic anachronism as well as an ongoing question: how does it function, what investments does it carry with it, what aims does it achieve?

What it means to be *lesbian*, of course, depends on what it means to make love; and what it means to make love depends on conceptualizations of the physical body. With the social construction of the body, as well as desire, in mind, my study takes as its point of historical origin the European rediscovery of the clitoris in the middle of the sixteenth century. Whatever information women possessed about their own bodies prior to the anatomical investigations of Gabriele Falloppia and Realdo Colombo, the rediscovery of the clitoris under the new science of dissection gave this organ an enhanced discursive presence. Described by Colombo as "the seat of woman's delight" – without which women would fail to conceive children – the clitoris medically and ideologically legitimized female erotic pleasure. At the same time, this scientific finding raised questions about the female body's potential autonomy: the "delights" of the clitoris, it was widely recognized, did not necessarily depend on the ministrations of men. Anatomical surveys of the size, use, and function of the clitoris invariably were followed by warnings about its misuse – or in the vernacular of the day, its abuse. Indeed, it is not accidental that accompanying, influencing, haunting every anatomical discussion of the clitoris and its pleasures was the monstrous figure of the tribade.

Tribade is a French term derived from the Greek *tribas* and *tribein*, to rub – and hence the Latin *fricatrix* and the English *rubster*. According to David Halperin,

> The female same-sex sexual practice that imperial Greek and Roman writers alike singled out for comment was 'tribadism', the sexual penetration of women (and men) by other women, by means of either a dildo or a fantastically large clitoris. The tribade makes memorable appearances, though not always under that name... she is represented as a shaven-headed butch, adept at wrestling, able to subjugate men and to satisfy women.[34]

Classical views on the tribade, however, were confined largely to learned Latin literature throughout the medieval period, until newly available Greek, Roman, and Arabic texts were translated in the fifteenth and sixteenth centuries. In chapter 5, I argue that the dissemination of classical literature and medical texts, concurrent with the anatomical rediscovery of the clitoris in the mid-sixteenth century, reintroduced the tribade to Western Europe. Indeed, I believe that the cultural rebirth of the clitoris and the reemergence of her ghostly yet monstrous twin, the tribade, inaugurated a crisis in the representation of female bodies and bonds. This crisis generated a discursive amplification of same-gender female desire: more texts, and more kinds of texts, began to speak of the enlarged clitoris and the lusty tribade, appropriating and extending one another's stories and tropes.

Although the figure of the tribade is represented as the outgrowth of a monstrous bodily morphology, insofar as she functions more generally as a metaphor for excessive and unruly female desire, she threatens to come into contact with, indeed to contaminate, women whose bodies do not produce legible signs of homoerotic desire. Much of what follows in this book is based therefore on the close contiguity expressed in medical texts between the legitimate and illegitimate use of female bodies. Whereas it would be a mistake to attribute too much social efficacy to medical treatises, or to make somatic experience overly dependent on advances in medical knowledge, the importance of such texts to the representation of female homoeroticism cannot be overstated. For it is a distinct feature of English society that although its legal professionals failed to consider the possibility of the erotic conjunction of female bodies, its medical practitioners seemed unable to refrain from seeing the possibility of such conjunctions at every possible turn.

It is within the context of such dangerous proximity that I approach the representation of intimate friendships among conventionally "feminine" women in Renaissance literature and the arts. The depiction of female emotional intensities, particularly those expressed through the figure of the eroticized, yet chaste, adolescent friend, occurs not only in Renaissance stageplays, but in closet drama, love lyrics, pastoral paintings, and opera. The popularity of such representations suggests that this figure provided artists and writers the opportunity to explore and exploit the sensuality of female bodies without crossing the boundaries of the licit. As in Van Dyck's painting, however, so too with many of these texts: often represented at the moment of its passing, female homoerotic desire and contact can be glimpsed only by attending to textual edges and margins. Particularly in the narrative forms of stageplays and prose, homoerotic friendship tends to be excluded, negated, overwritten, as it were, by the structural imperatives of marital alliance, in a process that generations of literary critics have naturalized as "comedic closure." Rather than assume the insignificance of female bonds or accede to the inevitability of such textual maneuvers, my analysis unpacks the ideological work involved in the repetition and enforcement of such "necessity."

Representations of intimacy among feminine women often derive from discourses of classical male friendship, whether they take the form of appropriations of male *amicitia* or reinterpretations of mythological and pastoral themes. In this respect, my study echoes in a female key two arguments made by recent scholars of male homoeroticism: that the cultural inheritance of mythology and the pastoral provided potent models for the figuring of homoerotic affect; and that no strict or secure boundary separates friendship from eroticism in Renaissance versions of *amicitia*.[35] Just as Greek and Roman mythology and the genre of the pastoral offered male writers and artists a homoerotic means of expression – evinced, for instance, in Michelangelo's painting of a pubescent Ganymede raised to heaven by the ardor of Zeus and Spenser's appropriation of Virgil's eclogues[36] – so too tales derived from Ovid offered early modern writers a means of figuring female intimacies. In early modern texts, Diana and Calisto, Iphis and Ianthe, and myriad anonymous nymphs are depicted touching, kissing, bathing, and sometimes even marrying one another.

Perhaps even more important than the affiliations of a homoerotic literary history is the way that understandings of the erotic have proven to be historically contingent. In this sense my study possesses a structural affinity to the work of Alan Bray, who has argued influentially that an ideological fissure separated a publicly condemned sodomy and a publicly idealized friendship in Elizabethan England: whereas sodomy was associated apocalyptically with criminality, calumny, and death, male friendship, the very basis of male homosociality and the patriarchal social order, enabled all manner of legitimate social ties and mutually beneficial obligations.[37] Bray argues, however, that the normative forms of male intimacy, embedded in relations of the household, service, and patronage, were pressured by the demise of the open-handed household.[38] With changes in prevailing modes of emotional and social ties, the line between legitimate and illegitimate types of male intimacy became difficult to discern. Particularly with the rise of molly houses in urban locales, male homoeroticism became, at least in London, more easily identified and prosecuted, attested by raids arranged by the Societies for the Reformation of Manners from 1690 to 1738.

Much influenced by Bray, Jeffrey Masten's *Textual Intercourse: Collaboration, Authorship, and Sexualities in Renaissance Drama* and George Haggerty's *Men in Love: Masculinity and Sexuality in the Eighteenth Century* both place love at the center of their analyses of male homoeroticism.[39] Analyzing the public expression of male–male love in manuscript and print sources, Masten and Haggerty emphasize the degree to which classical models of *amicitia* enabled male expressions of longing, emulation, and desire, particularly among social equals. In such representations, the intense unification of friends is an erotic encounter of the self with his mirror image, a form of erotic similitude. By emphasizing the extent to which the language of friendship is sutured to other discourses, Masten argues that to question the centrality of genitality to male–male eroticism is not to be sex phobic (or sex oblivious) but to pay attention to the historicity of the language of sexuality. In like manner, Haggerty maintains that "[l]ove as *eros* and love as *philia* cannot readily be distinguished in any culture, or indeed in many social situations, as well today as in the eighteenth century."[40]

It is a motive of the present study to demonstrate that the early modern representation of women's desires for intimacy and physical contact are likewise usefully understood to exist on the unstable boundary between *philia* and *eros* – or, to use the terms of some of the texts we will consider, in the interactions of amity and amour. By exploring the terms of female homoeroticism as figured in expressions of adolescent longing, in tropes of erotic similitude, in pastoral and mythological conventions, and in traditions of loving lament, my book illuminates what I call their (in)significance and places them in relationship to moments when female bodies and bonds attain special, even excessive, signifying power. My point, however, is not merely to demonstrate the existence of such discourses but, like Bray, to chart changes that occurred in the representation of female bodies and bonds over the course of the seventeenth century. I am especially interested in how the terms of visibility that permitted female–female eroticism to be interpreted as harmless friendship increasingly came into contact with new ideologies which reinterpreted female intimacy as a problem in need of social discipline. Whereas Bray emphasizes the decay of Tudor traditions of personal service as the factor leading to greater social scrutiny, as well as the providential millenarianism of groups that sought to clean up England after the libertinism of the Restoration, I argue that the intertextual circulation of anatomy books, midwiferies, travel narratives, obscenity, and other imaginative literature led to increasing suspicion about those forms of female intimacy previously considered chaste: the sharing of beds, kissing and caressing, and exclusive friendships. These behaviors, represented as unexceptional until the mid-seventeenth century, begin to be construed as immoral, irrational, a threat to other women as well as to men. In broadly schematic terms, my book thus charts how a discursive regime of impossibility is gradually displaced by a governing logic of suspicion and possibility. By the end of the century the chaste adolescent friend who expresses desire and love for her friend is implicated in the same nexus of transgression that formerly was attributed to her monstrous counterpart, the tribade. It is this "contamination" of the feminine woman by the phobias surrounding the tribade that, I argue, provides the condition of possibility for modern erotic identities, specifically for the range of female social "types" whose desires eventually were sutured to identity: masculine females, macroclitorides, female husbands, tommies, sapphists, inverts, female homosexuals, and *lesbians*.

By employing *figure* to describe the tribade and the chaste feminine friend, I mean to emphasize the extent to which these forms of embodiment are tropological. Whether conceived under the auspices of metaphor (a substitution based on resemblance or analogy) or metonymy (a substitution based on relations of cause and effect, contents and borders), the tribade and the friend are constructed by means of rhetorical, ideological, and psychological displacements. As tropological effects, the tribade and the friend function as emblematic personifications which nonetheless carry material weight. Providing the terms by which social beings are interpellated through strategies of inclusion and exclusion, they are infused with psychic energies and identifications while also being productive of social consequences.

In using *rhetoric* to describe the deployment of these figures, I mean to convey not only a highly organized mode of articulation, including the constitutive import of silence and lacunae, but also "the art of using language so as to persuade or influence others" (*Oxford English Dictionary*). The rhetorics of the tribade and friend participate persuasively in the fashioning of erotic bodies and psyches, rendering intelligible or unintelligible specific desires, longings, pleasures, and pains. Implicated differently in discourses of race, colonialism, and social rank, these two rhetorics also differ in their thematizations and modes of address. The rhetoric of chaste friendship thematizes the erotic position of white bourgeois European women who, by virtue of their fantasized location within a mythological or pastoral context, are both imaginatively referenced by, and socially excluded from, this erotic landscape. Directed toward an audience of literate women and men of middling or aristocratic status – people who attend plays, read drama aloud in the parlor, view and purchase visual art, travel to the continent – this discourse paradoxically provides a confirming, idealizing mirror for orderly Western women. At the same time, the rhetoric of chaste friendship hints at the possibility of intimate relations that could position daughters and wives outside of or against patriarchal authority. The rhetoric of the tribade, in contrast, focuses initially on the racialized bodies of women outside of Europe, and only gradually incorporates this exoticized figure into a European social landscape, where she emblematizes gender relations gone awry. The extent to which she remains racialized even after this incorporation, however, is not a given. No essential link obtains between the tribade and Europe's racialized others; rather, such racialization is part of the uneven and contradictory history of European colonialism. Early modern discourses of tribadism presume the reader's interest in medicine, travel, foreign peoples, and colonial and mercantile ventures – an interest which conceivably could extend from the lower middling ranks to the aristocracy. As for the producers of these discourses and texts, their social positions and relations to wealth, property, and the monarchy varied. Some were aristocrats or otherwise connected to the court. More were what we would now consider professionals: dramatists writing for the public stage as well as patronage; medical practitioners writing for a vernacular readership and career advancement; legal scholars and lexicographers publicizing the law; ambassadors and profiteers seeking political and mercantile gain. More important than their differences in social rank, I would argue, is their common relationship to, and exploitation of, the new modes of communication made available through a developing print culture and its networks of dissemination.

The renaissance of *lesbianism* occurred during a period when women's documented voices were largely silent about erotic acts. Although English women's literacy improved over the course of the seventeenth century and women increasingly contributed to the production of literary genres, few women wrote stageplays, love lyrics, or diary entries that allude explicitly to desire among women. Consequently, most – but not all – of the representations discussed in this book were created by men. Not surprisingly, they reveal a great deal of ignorance about, and suspicion of, female bodies and desires. Guided by an impulse to affirm the unique cultural contributions of women, some feminist historians might discount the relevance of these texts, judging them to be manifestations of anxiety, pornographic fantasy, or paranoid projections – in any case having little to do with women's actual lives. I believe, on the contrary, that male-authored discourses were an intrinsic, indeed, constitutive part of women's lived experience. They provided the images and idioms that women encountered, discussed among themselves, willfully appropriated, silently disavowed, and publicly contested. In addition, neither the masculine nor feminine signature is a reliable indicator of an author's stance toward female–female affectivity; many female-authored texts repeat, rather than interrogate, conventional, which is to say, patriarchal, understandings of homoerotic desire.

Articulating the embeddedness of homoeroticism within other social phenomena – the family, reproduction, kinship networks, friendship, modes of racialization, concepts of the unnatural – allows us to consider eroticism less as a self-evident category of behavior or identity than as a heuristic tool. Like gender, eroticism becomes *a category of analysis* rather than a self-contained object. Preeminently a form of negotiation of desire and the gendered body, eroticism also informs, and is informed by race, age, status hierarchies, and nationality. Like a kaleidoscope, it accrues different meanings with each shift in the angle of vision.

What might we deduce from the faultlines, to invoke Alan Sinfield's phrase, of dominant early modern erotic ideologies?[41] Renaissance theology and the law condemned women's inherent lustfulness while homilies and conduct books reiterated the importance of female chastity, providing examples of virtue rewarded and vice punished. Such repressive discourses not only registered anxiety that women were engaged in precisely the behaviors being negated rhetorically, but, by proffering negative exempla which became available to women for their own cognitive processing, contributed to women's ability to seize control of their own embodiment. Such unstable effects, which outdistance the intention of individual authors, provided women the opportunity to improvise a relationship to dominant ideologies that worked to their own advantage. The tribade, for instance, who became in this period a powerful model of female erotic transgression, functioned both as a cautionary tale and a figure for possible emulation. The prohibitive rhetoric of unmentionability, as well, that figures sodomy as the "unspeakable vice" or "mute sin," would seem to enforce a powerfully effective censorship; but it also afforded women opportunities to express their desires under the auspices of ideological conformity. Attending to such faultlines – discursive contradictions, lacunae, and misrecognitions – brings to the fore a range of homoerotic expressions existing in comfortable, even companionable, proximity to marital desire and reproductive alliance, existing within as well as outside the patriarchal household. To practice impossibilities, then, is to remain mindful of the ongoing tension between official prescriptions and resistant cultural practices, between the force of rhetorical negation and the uncertain effects of its proliferation, between the productivity of homoeroticism and the historical fate of heterosexuality.

As my use of the phrase "practicing impossibilities" should indicate, employing the terms of early modern rhetorics entails certain interpretative difficulties. Because Renaissance misogyny derived in part from anxiety about the female body, it is analytically imperative to develop methods that simultaneously disclose and resist orthodox constructions. Indeed, a primary obstacle to fashioning a *lesbian*-affirmative analytic is the difficulty of maneuvering around the cultural presumption in this period of women's erotic excess. After thirty years of feminist scholarship, this presumption is now a critical cliché, but it is useful to rehearse it, not only to recall its power, but to begin to move beyond it. The metaphysical tradition posited a coherence between woman, body, and earthly matter, a coherence that lent misogynist weight to medieval Christian suspicions about the pleasures of the flesh. Whatever feminine attributes may have been ascribed to the body of Christ, the foundation of sin in Eve's concupiscence fostered a view of earthly embodiment as irremediably fallen, a view that contributed, not incidentally, to the witchcraft persecutions of the late medieval and early modern eras. Indeed, the authoritative handbook on witchcraft, the *Malleus Maleficarum* (1487), concludes that "all witchcraft comes from carnal lust, which is in women insatiable."[42] Such a construal of "Eve's culpable flesh" motivates the late medieval visual motif of Eve being seduced by an insinuating female serpent, an image that silently yet provocatively locates female homoeroticism at the center of the Fall.[43] Woman's sinfulness, inferiority, and necessary subordination were believed to originate in her body, a body generally (though not inevitably) figured as inherently weaker, naturally cooler, more vulnerable to passion, and more resistant to reason than that of man – a construction used to justify the analogy between the body politic and the patriarchal household. Although Protestant reformers and humanists rejected the belief that women's bodies were inherently polluting, and actively extolled the virtues of marriage, women in the sixteenth and seventeenth centuries nonetheless continued to carry the burden of Eve's guilt: the presumption of sexual insatiability and extraordinary ability to incite male lust. Using biblical precedent as justification, sermons, homilies, conduct books, and popular pamphlets excoriated women for erotic acts deemed illicit or excessive; when they were judged guilty, women were punished severely by the ecclesiastical and secular courts.

It is one goal of this book to suggest that alongside such misogynist constructions of female concupiscence there existed other (albeit no less patriarchal) discourses that posited the female body as perfect in its own way and deserving of its own pleasure – the implications of which will be explored in chapters 2 and 3. Nonetheless, the widespread belief in women's weakness and carnality generated damaging, and in some cases lethal, constructions of female eroticism. The most common charge, of course, was that a woman was a whore. From the medieval period on, as Ruth Mazo Karras argues, the category of whore – and the related terms "prostitute," "harlot," "common woman," "strumpet," and "courtesan" – was deployed not only to signify the material exchange of sex for money, but as an ideological weapon to be used against any woman who ventured "out of place."[44] Karras's analysis of medieval attitudes resonates with early modern figurations, wherein "women, not men, bore the load of guilt for illicit sex... [and] women's virtue was premised entirely on sexual chastity."[45] The defamation of women for sexual misconduct only increased during this period of social unrest when more women turned to prostitution out of economic necessity. Stressing these material conditions, Jyotsna Singh notes that seventeenth-century discourses about prostitution obscure "the social displacements, poverty, and unemployment that led to the flourishing trade in female bodies";[46] instead, conduct books, homilies, ballads, and stageplays "transfer the burden of moral iniquity onto the 'immoral' women."[47] Whereas some Protestant leaders insisted that vaginal intercourse outside of marriage was equally sinful for husbands as for wives, in practice women were far more likely to be punished, whether by the church courts or later by the secular courts.[48] Within the context of a flourishing trade, the clients of prostitutes were prosecuted only intermittently, and were penalized with fines rather than the imprisonment enforced on women. The attempt to close brothels at different points after the Reformation paradoxically reinforced the sexual double standard. "Lust," as Lyndal Roper argues for Protestant Germany – and it was equally true for Protestant England – was "displaced on to woman," with the prostitute serving as "the Reformation's exemplar of evil womanhood."[49]

The displacement of lust onto women provides a core repertoire of the English Renaissance stage, which across genres was obsessed with the specter of the unfaithful woman. The accusation of whore traverses Renaissance tragedy, while city and romantic comedies mine the supposedly lighter side of women's axiomatic infidelity through the figure of the comic whore, cuckold jokes, and rituals of female humiliation. Conversely, the trope of psychical re-virgination, in which "polluted" female characters are killed metaphorically in order to be fantastically "reborn" as chaste and pure, indulges in a nostalgia for a female body untainted by wayward desire. Confinement, monumentalization, and death are the typical, and often quite spectacular, means the drama employs to transmute illicit female desire into acceptable form.

Because the tribade did not function, as the whore arguably did, as a social "type," she is far less familiar a figure. Although Bassa, infamous from Martial's Epigram 91, and Megilla, from Lucian's fifth dialogue, provided images of monstrous female predators, their stories through much of our period were confined largely to Latin (and hence elite) discourses.[50] The tribade is absent from David Underdown's three categories of rebellious women (the witch, the scold, and the domineering wife),[51] and she fails to appear in the language of sexual insult anatomized by Laura Gowing.[52] Although the term "tribade" is absent from prescriptive literature, occasional references to female–female lust occur in conduct books, witchcraft tracts, and sermons, generally as one example in a lengthy catalogue of illicit erotic practices.[53] Indeed, whatever association female–female eroticism had to witchcraft, it was as a symptom of women's erotic excess.

In fact, it is one of the ironies of *lesbian* history that the first recorded instance of a variant for tribade in English occurs at the turn of the seventeenth century, in a letter from one man to another, and that tribadism in this case figures a creative encounter between men. Apparently authorized by the tradition of the muses, T. W.'s verse letter to his friend John Donne celebrates "chaste & mystique tribadree" as the source of creative generation:

> Haue mercy on me & my sinfull Muse
> Which rub'd & tickled with thyne could not chuse
> But spend some of her pithe & yeild to bee
> One in that chaste & mystique tribadree . . .
> Thy Muse, Oh strange & holy Lecheree
> Beeing a Mayd still, gott this Song on mee.[54]

Here, the "chaste" – that is, non-penetrative – rubbing of two men's female muses enacts a tribadic model of generation: after the two muses rub and tickle, T. W.'s muse "spends her pithe" (ejaculates) while Donne's muse begets the song on the poet. Even as the bodily positions involved in this circulation of seed remain rather difficult to imagine, the erotic exchange between the muses provide the male poet with a novel means of appropriating female reproduction for his own creativity.

This linking of tribadism and literary creation is given a more nefarious cast by Ben Jonson who, drawing freely from his reading in classical literature, employed "tribade" and its variants to refer to female vice. In *Volpone* (1606), Lady Politic Would-be is called "a lewd harlot, a base fricatrice, / A female devill, in a male out-side" (4.2.55–56).[55] Closely associated with the tribade through the notion of sexual friction, "fricatrice" here seems to be a general term of opprobrium, consistent with whore and female devil, though carrying with it a veneer of masculinization. However, in the poem that begins "And must I sing? What subject shall I chuse?" Jonson revises T. W.'s equation between the tribade and "mystique" creation while drawing explicitly, as T. W. did, on the tribade's homoerotic signification. After rejecting a series of possible creative progenitors, including Pallas (termed a "mankinde maid"), to authorize his verse, the poet directs "light Venus" to either "Goe, crampe dull Mars" or "with thy *Tribade* trine, invent new sports." The rhyme concludes with the admonition: "Thou, nor thy loosenesse with my making sorts."[56] Whether "tribade trine" refers to the Graces or the triad of Venus, Juno, and Athena (made infamous by the Judgment of Paris), Jonson's rejection of their "new sports" implies that tribadism is an illicit form of contact that generates unacceptable forms of literary production.[57] The extent to which tribadic literary productivity is threatening is made even clearer in Jonson's epigram "The Court Pucell," where the poet caps off his denunciation of Celia Bulstrode's literary prowess (*pucelle* means both maid and whore) by terming it a "Tribade lust," violently forced upon a muse:

> Do's the Court-Pucell then so censure me,
> And thinkes I dare not her? let the world see.
> What though her Chamber be the very pit
> Where fight the prime Cocks of the Game, for wit? . . .
> What though with Tribade lust she force a muse,
> And in an Epicoene fury can write newes
> Equall with that, which for the best newes goes,
> An aerie light, and as like with as those?[58]

This linking of female literary accomplishment with tribadism figures the woman writer as an unnatural penetrator of the fount of creation, her misapplied pen a faulty penis: she must rape in order to produce, and the fruit of her womb is monstrous.[59]

Yet, Jonson's metaphoric use of the tribade for anti-feminist invective is unique in the early years of the seventeenth century; it reemerges only with the political obscenity that begins to be circulated during the Civil Wars. Far more common is Shakespeare's favored lexicon of insult: "whore," "witch," "hag," "strumpet," "harlot," "harpy." Cressida, Desdemona, and Hermione are defamed as whores, their faithful serving women denounced as shrews; and for all the vituperative curses Lear hurls at his daughters, the ailing king's imaginative reach does not extend to calling Goneril a tribade or accusing Regan of possessing a monstrous clitoris. (Indeed, within the Shakespearean corpus, whatever threat is embodied by women seems to be profoundly, definitively, *hetero*sexual – that is, a matter of women in relation to men, whether because of their differences *from* men, their propensity to act too much *like* men, or the things they do *to* men.)

By concentrating on the tribade and the friend, I do not mean to imply that these two figures comprehensively exhaust early modern typologies. Douglas Bruster and Mario DiGangi, for instance, have suggested the import of representations of relations among women that are more coercive than loving, aptly described by DiGangi as "the homoerotics of mastery."[60] The female procuress, who corrupts chaste young maidens by initiating them into the venereal arts, is of particular interest in this regard. Triangular relations among women and men are given a more innocuous cast by Michael Morgan Holmes, who traces in the poetry of Aemilia Lanyer the routing of female desires through Christ and, more broadly, through the language of religious devotion.[61] Although I touch briefly on the homoerotics enabled by various expressions of Christianity in the next chapter, for the most part I have limited my focus to the tribade and the friend, for they best enable me to make a historical argument about those changes that occurred over the course of the seventeenth century.

The Renaissance of Lesbianism in Early Modern England is simultaneously an act of historical recovery and a meditation on the difficulties inhering in such an act. My desire is to explore our historical differences from early modern women while showing how distant representations of female–female intimacy can be correlated, though not in a linear fashion, to modern systems of intelligibility. The methodological difficulty we face is not the absence of homoerotically desiring women, but tools adequate to crack the code organizing early modern conceptual categories. Once revealed, however, representations of female homoeroticism do not provide clear antecedents or stable historical ground for contemporary *lesbian* identities. Renaissance London is a far cry from San Francisco's Noe Valley, and however much we might see drag as a constitutive feature of both theaters, Shakespeare's Globe is not New York's WOW Café. In traveling back in time to ancient rhetorics and describing their re-configuration in the early modern period, my book does not push the birth of the *lesbian* back in time but, rather, pluralizes the notion of origins, multiplies sites of emergence, and traces various strands of influence. One result of this strategy is that instead of treating *lesbian* existence as the epiphany or "denouement of every argument,"[62] I resist the temptation to make historical inquiry culminate in a politics of identity. This is not to suggest that identity politics have no place in contemporary *lesbian* activism. As long as the lives of *lesbians* are constricted and destroyed by silences, misinformation, and hatred, the articulated self-presence and political agitation under the banner of identity will remain a crucial political strategy. Nonetheless, the politics of identity can operate as a stranglehold, limiting the questions one asks and thus the answers one finds. When identity politics are treated as the *sine qua non* of lesbian scholarship, when the modern category of "the subject" – whether conceived as a *lesbian* author, a *lesbian* character, or a *lesbian* poetic persona – governs the critical recognition of homoeroticism, often the claims one can make are reduced to the critical equivalent of "Look there! Look, there's another one!" I agree with Jeffrey Masten that "identifying Renaissance figures as gay – 'outing' them – seems the mildest of possible claims one might make,"[63] for such identifications effectively quarantine individuals from complex and interdependent systems of erotic affect and practice (not the least of which is heterosexuality) as well as isolate erotic systems from other social formations, such as race. One of the consolations my book offers to those looking for historical affirmations of gay identity is this: although we will not find contemporary *lesbians* in early modern England, neither will we find contemporary heterosexuals.

Even as I enact a critical method deliberately disengaged from questions of *lesbian* subjectivity, I recognize that the desire to discover *lesbians* in the past cannot be simply disavowed. In the college classroom and the public conference panel, no less than on the political stage, the claims of identity are revealed as deeply held investments that demand and deserve attention. In certain contexts, both pedagogical and political, the illumination of homoeroticism as a salient force in history and culture may necessitate temporarily suspending alterity in the name of transmitting vital cultural information, personal affirmation, homo life support. The needs are real, and nothing I advocate in this book is intended to minimize them. But in the context of scholarship, I have found it more enabling to work with and through, rather than concede, the intractability of our desire for a useable past. This desire can provide motivating energy at the same time that it can become an object of critique. By recovering and reclaiming a renaissance of *lesbianism*, I hope to show that analysis of female homoeroticism worthy of the complexity of the past obliges us to balance the supports of identity and the pleasures of identification with a recognition of the instability of these supports and the problematic nature of these pleasures.[64] In theoretical terms, my book pursues the implications of the radical incommensurability among erotic desires, practices, and identities, less in some abstract allegiance to queer theory than in the interest of *lesbian* specificity.

Rather than "looking for lesbians," then, this book explores what it means for women to inhabit specific categories of representation at particular moments in time. It takes the form of a genealogy, as I have striven not to recover the *lesbian* as a being with a discrete origin and stable meaning, but rather to examine the conditions of intelligibility whereby female–female intimacies gain, or fail to gain, cultural signification. As theorized by Michel Foucault, genealogy attempts not to establish historical truth or falsehood, but to reveal the discursive conditions that contribute to the construction of what comes to be regarded as true.[65] Jon Simons puts it succinctly: "[t]he genealogical approach provides historical rather than epistemological answers to the questions of what constitutes knowledge and truth."[66] My genealogy of *lesbianism* yields some of the structural determinants of past understandings of female desire and embodiment, as well as of current critical mappings (provided by feminism, psychoanalysis, the history of the family, New Historicism, lesbian and gay studies, and queer theory). Since a genealogy investigates a structure, it neither blames nor exonerates, seeking instead to unpack the logics of discourses and institutions which structure the possibility of knowledge. The effort to construct a genealogy of *lesbianism* without subsuming earlier figures under the sign of the *lesbian* has required a "strategic historicism," by which I mean a mode of historical inquiry attuned simultaneously to continuity and rupture, similarity and difference.[67] Aligned with Sinfield's exposition of ideological faultlines, the strategic historicism I advocate is committed to probing contradictions among multiple discursive domains. It subordinates many of the issues that have been axiomatic to much scholarship on the history of homosexuality: namely, whether eroticism in the early modern period is best understood through the paradigm of acts or identities; whether this history is primarily one of continuity or alterity; and whether the "birth" of the homosexual is a moment worth debating.[68] As several scholars now acknowledge, such debates, while initially productive, have become constraining – their conceptual divisions too crude, their polemics too unyielding.[69]

Problems of methodology are present in the work on sexuality in every historical period. Nonetheless, in my engagement with these issues, historical work on the eighteenth century has revealed most productively and dramatically certain problems endemic to the field as a whole. The current privileging of the eighteenth century as the time when certain social structures associated with male homosexuality became widely visible has no doubt exacerbated the issues involved, as historians of this period have had to confront, and in doing so have exposed the difficulties of evading, what Eve Kosofsky Sedgwick calls "The Great Paradigm Shift": the attempt to identify the precise historical moment when homosexuality, conceived as an identity, was born.[70] Cameron McFarlane, for instance, reiterates Sedgwick's critique of linear models of historical succession by referencing how "sodomite becomes molly becomes invert becomes homosexual becomes gay."[71] He queries the need of historians to emphasize "a radical conceptual shift," suggesting that their "aggressively teleological framework... carries with it the assumption that the preceding diffuse, more 'confused' structures of sexuality were eclipsed and rendered obsolete."[72] In an attempt to avoid this trap in his own historical practice, McFarlane deliberately deemphasizes diachronic arguments in favor of a synchronic reading of the figure of the eighteenth-century sodomite.[73]

Writing an inclusive history of sexuality that places the hetero in dialogue with the homo, Tim Hitchcock pursues the inverse of McFarlane's strategy, offering a diachronic chronology of the forces that led to the formation of modern sexual identities.[74] His commitment to a model of succession unfortunately reenacts the "aggressively teleological" format anatomized by McFarlane, particularly when he proposes a developmental schema which places at the beginning and end of the eighteenth century two opposed female figures: in the beginning, the tribade – hypersexualized and pseudo-male – who, under the domineering influence of medical discourse and marriage demographics, mutates into the asexual, passionless romantic friend. What this developmental schema leaves out, the rest of my book will suggest, is the long and complicated representation of chaste yet passionate eroticism among "feminine" women. These figures do not exist for Hitchcock, because the romantic friend must "evolve" out of the tribade in accordance with the growing importance of female passionlessness.

Hitchcock's reading of female sexuality relies heavily on the work of Randolph Trumbach, undoubtedly the most influential historian of eighteenth-century homosexuality. Due to his influence, I will take the liberty of quoting him at length. In a number of articles and more recently a monograph, he argues that

> A revolution in the gender relations of Western societies occurred in the first generation of the eighteenth century... Around 1700 in northwestern Europe, in England, France, and the Dutch Republic, there appeared a minority of adult men whose sexual desires were directed exclusively toward adult and adolescent males. These men could be identified by what seemed to their contemporaries to be effeminate behavior in speech, movement, and dress. They had not, however, entirely transformed themselves into women but instead combined into a third gender selected aspects of the behavior of the majority of men and women. Since a comparable minority of masculinized women who exclusively desired other women did not appear until the 1770s, it

is therefore the case that for most of the eighteenth century there existed in northern Europe what might be described as a system of three genders composed of men, women, and sodomites.[75]

For Trumbach, the central question for both male and female homosexuality is gender role, a role he defines in terms of erotic desire (for instance, the "third illegitimate gender" role is the "adult passive transvestite effeminate male or molly").[76] In tandem with his interest in the molly, when Trumbach turns to women, he elucidates the development of the "sapphist role":

[F]or women, the development of the sapphist role began slowly after mid-century, and could be seen enacted very clearly by some individuals in the last quarter of the century. In the first half of the eighteenth century, on the other hand, women who had sex with women also had sexual relations with men and were likely to use their hands for stimulation and to avoid penetration. Men speculated that women who did penetrate other women must do so either because their clitorises were enlarged or by using an artificial penis. It is likely that some women did in fact use dildoes, and that some of these women dressed as men and married women. But it is likely that most women who dressed and passed as men for any length of time, did not seek to have sexual relations with women, and this was probably true even of those who married women... Only at the end of the century did there appear women who sought to be sexually desirable by dressing in part as men, but who wished the eye of the knowing beholder to be a woman's and not a man's. These women dressed partly as men and partly as women, and their appeal lay in this ambiguity. They therefore differed considerably from the occasional passing woman who lived entirely as a man and may have married women and perhaps used an artificial penis. These new ambiguously gendered women were London's first sapphists of the modern kind, and their sexual taste was conceived to be the perversion of a minority and not a wicked sin to which any woman might be brought by the effects of great debauchery.[77]

Trumbach traces the development of the sapphic role by reference to hermaphrodites, female crossdressers, and sexual relationships, but despite his acknowledgment of such diversity, he repeatedly uses gender parallelism to organize his thinking about women: "By the end of the eighteenth century there is some evidence that there was beginning to appear *a role for women which was parallel to that of the molly for men.*"[78] Apparently, the sapphic role existed in some space reserved on the analogy to the molly. Due to women's enclosure within the private sphere and the paucity of opportunities for female autonomy from men, however, the sapphist (and the lower-class tommy) are belated, following in men's footsteps almost a century later.

The result of Trumbach's investment in parallel roles organized along different temporalities is that women are subsumed analytically under a historical rubric forged for men. Indeed, I would suggest that in his work the sapphist and tommy function as an analytical crutch and historical backformation: having caught up to the sodomite and molly, these female figures help to fix their revolutionary status. This subordination carries over into Trumbach's lack of appreciation that women are regulated *differently* than men, a factor that creates an interpretative brick wall when he considers those instances in which women's sexual acts were not prosecuted.[79] Most troubling is his contention that even those women who *did* have sex with women after the "new sapphist role had emerged, *could either know or not know the sexual content of their feelings*. Those who knew, were likely to be those who were stigmatized. But those who did not know were still likely ... to adopt some of the external characteristics of the sapphist role."[80] It is a very peculiar construction of female subjectivity that deems it possible for women to "not know the sexual content of their feelings." And it is a very peculiar construction of female sexuality that considers most important, not whether women *realize* they are having sex, but whether they adopt characteristics of a social role.

Notwithstanding their individual virtues, then, historical scholarship on eighteenth-century sexuality prompts several methodological cautions. Neither a reading of representation that brackets diachronic change nor a historical chronology of supersession nor a reading of *lesbianism* via a template devised for male homosexuality is adequate to the complexities of *lesbian* history. The strategic historicism I have adopted attempts to avoid precisely these pitfalls. Rather than cover over cultural contradictions and discontinuities with the force of teleology, I have probed contradictions and assessed uneven developments across different discursive domains.[81] Rather than elide differences between them or extrapolate from one domain to all others, I have tried to maintain awareness of their specificity. Each discourse evinces its own preoccupations and possesses its own form of cultural power. The church undertook as one of its main functions the regulation of erotic conduct, whether pursued through the Catholic confessional and ecclesiastical courts or the interiorization of authority in the form of Protestant piety and conscience. The secular courts drew upon long-standing legal precedents to police the body and restrain its passions, and over the course of a century appropriated much of the domain of ecclesiastical law. Medicine, increasingly empirical and systematizing, explored the body as a site of health and disease, and strove, particularly under the auspices of human dissection and anatomical inquiry, to conceptualize a normative bodily structure. Humanist education, especially in the form of prescriptive literature, took the unruliness of the body as its prime target, manifesting concern over bodily civility, and initiating new protocols for behaviors such as proper table manners and personal hygiene.[82] Stageplays performed in public and private theaters thematized and spectacularized gender relations and erotic desire, employing a variety of prosthetic devices (costumes, wigs, padding) to visually mark gender even as they confuted gender and erotic differences through the popular ploy of transvestism.[83] The poetry of love and friendship, circulating in manuscript and in print, created and sustained personal and political bonds, while the circulation of obscene literature exploited, celebrated, and sometimes satirized erotic misconduct. And the visual arts, particularly on the continent, reached new heights during this period in their imaging of sensual love, including that between women.

By tracing select discursive developments and crises, I have tried to bypass the methodological problems carried in the wake of scholars' emphasis on acts and identities. Although at certain points I stress the historical alterity of early modern understandings, I have not privileged alterity for its own sake, and instead have tried to explain the conditions contributing to historical difference. Balancing the claims of continuity and alterity within a historically specific study, I have tried to keep open the question of the relationship of present identities to past cultural formations – assuming neither that we will find in the past a mirror image of ourselves nor that the past is so utterly alien that we will find nothing usable in its fragmentary traces. Traces, indeed, are what we have inherited, and in this regard, my strategic historicism is informed by a theory of representation aligned, in some respects, with the more politically inflected forms of post-structuralism. As such, I have limited my claims to those that can be adduced from representations, and from the cultural potentials that recurring representations indicate. The one exception to this is chapter 1, where I use social and legal history to suggest how documented social practices might be used to inform our reading of figurative language. I have tried to resist the appeal of drawing out of textual materials conclusions unwarranted by the evidence, and in particular have resisted the urge to conflate figuration with lived experience, to project onto historical personages the thoughts and motivations that are bequeathed to us only in textual form. This is not to imply that representation can be firmly divorced from social reality; rather, it is to affirm that all historical knowledge is culturally mediated, that history is apprehensible to us primarily through representations which themselves participate in cultural processes. Nothing in my genealogy implies that desire among women is *merely* a discursive phenomenon. Rather, the reciprocal relations between cultural discourses and individuals reveal the faultlines of patriarchal dominion, and with them, both the explicit transgression of dominant ideologies and the quiet negotiation of their parameters.

Although genealogy is a historical mode of investigation, it is driven more by conceptual questions and the tracing of discursive conflict than by the mapping of chronology. Thus, my effort to evade the conceptual logjam of acts and identities has not resulted in a comprehensive work of social or intellectual history. My genealogy moves back and forth in time, following conceptual strands that, in the aggregate, contribute to an argument both historical and theoretical. In individual chapters, the accent sometimes falls on the exposition of a diachronic argument, sometimes on an intervention in contemporary theoretical or historiographic debates. Loosely described, the first half of the book is devoted to detailing aspects of the erotic system operating during the late sixteenth and early seventeenth centuries; the second half maps some of the forces that pressure that system after the period of the Civil Wars. Certain texts make repeated appearances, with the focus on different textual passages that pose new questions and invite additional arguments. Material that was published previously has been significantly revised and restructured; minor errors in transcription and dating have been rectified. This book, as is perhaps clear from the pace of this Introduction, begins slowly and deliberately in order to set the scene, as the title of chapter 1 puts it, for the more incisive arguments to follow. Likewise, the bibliographic apparatus is meant to bring to readers' attention the surprising amount of work that already has been done on this subject, as well as to affiliate my project with those fields whose perimeters have rubbed up against it. Rather than assume the reader's knowledge of, for instance, the history of medicine or queer theory, I have provided, both in the first two chapters and in the endnotes throughout, a conceptual roadmap that should prove helpful in exploring the territory that the rest of the book stakes out. How my genealogy coheres, or fails to cohere, with a "history of the subject" or "the history of the family," I leave to others. If scholars find in this book a challenge to constructions of, for instance, "the family, sex and marriage in England" and "the history of private life,"[84] I hope they also find much that will be useful to the creation of more inclusive histories and interpretations, as well as histories and interpretations focused on *lesbianism* – including how one might begin to look for them.

Throughout the writing of *The Renaissance of Lesbianism*, my aim has been to develop an analytical framework adequate to the complexity of the representations I have encountered and to the variety of issues they raise. To further this aim, certain concepts have been appropriated for new interpretative ends, and other terms have been coined: *amor impossibilis*, anatomical *pudica*, chaste femme love, erotic similitude, (in)significance, and prosthesis. Certain psychoanalytic ideas have been adopted and retooled: desire, anxiety, abjection, identification, melancholy, perversion, and psychomorphology. Together, these concepts and methodologies reveal and address a series of interpretative problems unique to early modern regimes of representation. The incoherences that structure modern homosexuality, giving rise to such paradigmatically modern tropes as coming out, the closet, and the open secret, do not correspond to the discursive structures through which early modern *lesbianism* was given meaning and form. Rather than being organized through concepts of in and out, secrecy and disclosure, oppression and liberation, the early modern representation of *lesbianism* is governed by tensions between visibility and invisibility, possibility and impossibility, significance and insignificance.

To a considerable extent, each of these contradictions revolves around the constitutive power accorded to the phallus in conceptualizations of sexuality. Within the scope of a masculine imaginary confident of its monopoly of gender and erotic prerogatives, the phallic standard, along with its corresponding visual economy, has imposed on to female bodies and desires a recalcitrant opacity: what DO *lesbians* do in bed? Insofar as this rhetoric of incredulity functions as a mechanism of prohibition, it differentiates the cultural illegitimacy of *lesbians* from that which they share with gay men: *lesbianism* is construed not only as ontologically impossible, but as epistemologically obscure. The force of this epistemological and ontological status has meant that *lesbianism* has functioned, in the words of Valerie Rohy, as "a repository for the failures of meaning inherent in figurality itself," as a symbol of "resistance to symbolization."[85] Likewise, Annamarie Jagose asks, "why is the problem of lesbianism so frequently a problem of representation?"[86] Jagose argues persuasively that a "consequence of the discursive production of the lesbian as invisible... has meant that the lesbian operates as a dense cipher for the limit conditions of cultural visibility. That is, the lesbian is not only constituted as a representation problem but equally stands as a potent figure for problems of representation more generally." Noting that "the diagnostic recognition of lesbian invisibility" is all too often "critically countered by attempts to negotiate for lesbianism a more straightforward relation to the cultural rubrics of legibility, as if the problems of lesbian invisibility might be shortcircuited by the reversal of that paradigm," she posits, on the contrary, that since "lesbian invisibility is precisely, if paradoxically, a *strategy of representation*... lesbian visibility cannot be imagined as its redress."[87]

Just as a phallic standard contributes to the "structuring mechanisms of lesbian invisibility,"[88] my analysis takes the clitoral body and the desires of the chaste friend, not as the essential truth of *lesbian* existence nor the rectification of *lesbian* invisibility, but as contested points of access to a dynamic, and historically changing, discursive field. My emphasis on the historical production of *lesbian* impossibility differentiates my study from work with which it otherwise has many affinities, namely, that which focuses on *lesbianism* as primarily a problem of figuration or narrative.[89] Nonetheless, my genealogy of the terms of *lesbian* representation is not pursued as a purely historicist aspiration, but as an intervention in contemporary understandings and opportunities. Although history will not provide the redress to *lesbian* invisibility, I do believe that its manifold complexities could render less dangerously presumptive the meaning of women's erotic desires and practices, both in the early modern period and our own time. Composed in the impassioned space of wanting, of longing, of imagining that *lesbians* can have a history without submitting to the deformations of identity or the double-binds of visibility, this book is offered in the name of history as well as in the name of a different futurity – of what Jonathan Goldberg has called "the history that will be."[90]

By prying apart the historical structures that have upheld the regime of erotic visibility, *The Renaissance of Lesbianism* contests the reign of the phallus over the domain of sexuality. It is not just, as Lacanians would have it, that the phallus can only do its job when veiled. Rather, the phallus isn't always the right tool for the job.

1   Setting the stage behind the seen: performing *lesbian* history

> ... Cupid's fiery shaft [was]
> Quench'd in the chaste beams of the wat'ry moon,
> And the imperial vot'ress passed on,
> In maiden meditation, fancy-free.[1]

Several years ago in Nashville, Tennessee, director Barry Edelstein staged a theatrical production of Shakespeare's *Twelfth Night* which comically highlighted the operatic dimensions of human passion. Although the performance closely followed Shakespeare's script, Olivia and Orsino, Aguecheek and Antonio all expressed their desires in over-the-top vocal performances that were observed, and wryly commented upon, by an earnest yet mischievous Viola/Cesario. My partner, at that time a theater critic for a local "alternative" newspaper, commended Tennessee Repertory Theater on its entertaining, witty, superbly acted production. She also praised the performance for its open exploration of the ways homoerotic attractions infused the interactions of Olivia and Viola, Orsino and Cesario, Antonio and Sebastian. Having sat through a number of plays in which closeted gay actors performed homophobic material, having spoken to actors anguished by their compromises with what some local directors deemed "the audience" – and aware that Tennessee at the time upheld a sodomy statute which criminalized consensual same-gender erotic acts – she considered this mainstreaming of homoerotic performance a momentous occasion.[2]

Momentous, indeed. The actress who had played Olivia with such passionate aplomb wrote a letter to the editor in horrified protest; the possibility of such an interpretation had never entered her mind. She did not play Olivia as "a homosexual"; nor did Shakespeare intend her to. Needless to say, her horror did not stem from a social constructivist view that the category of homosexual did not exist that far back in time. Vehemently, she declared she would never consent to play a part contrary to her personal ethics.[3] What about Medea or Salome? my partner wondered in response.

What happens when female–female desire is enacted today on the Shakespearean stage – in Nashville, New York, Stratford (England or Ontario)? Given that the trope of invisibility has governed discussions of *lesbianism* prior to 1800, what happens to Shakespeare (that icon of literary genius), to notions of the Renaissance (that icon of high culture), to actors and audiences in professional, community, and college theaters when women's homoerotic desires are granted a cultural presence? Insofar as theatrical and cinematic productions of Shakespearean drama are the primary medium through which most North Americans encounter "the Renaissance," how might directors, dramaturges, and actors intercede *now* in popular knowledge of what was possible, erotically speaking, *then*?[4]

Contemporary theatrical performance provides a point of departure for this chapter's consideration of how to recognize, interpret, and make manifest the cultural presence of *lesbianism* in the early modern period. Distinctively homoerotic representations of female desire in Shakespearean drama, and in Renaissance drama generally, can emerge from an awareness of the various historical discourses of female intimacy – from tribadism to female–female marriages to adolescent friendships. In order to set the stage for subsequent analyses, I first provide an overview of the theological, legal, and medical discourses that informed the social practices of female homoeroticism across Europe, and punctuate discussion of these discourses with examples drawn from selected literary texts. Using social and legal history to suggest new ways of reading representations, this chapter inverts the procedure of subsequent chapters, which will analyze representations to uncover the presence of social potentials heretofore unacknowledged by social history. My approach is deliberately schematic, synoptic, and synthetic, and unrestricted by the national, discursive, and temporal specificity that organizes the rest of the book. The second half of the chapter correlates these discourses, practices, and representations to a range of affective desires dramatized in one of Shakespeare's most frequently performed plays. My aim is not to provide a reading of *A Midsummer Night's Dream*, but to use its repeated, if tantalizingly brief, allusions to female intimacies to lift the curtain on occluded practices within early modern culture. Bringing together seemingly disparate phenomena, I argue that not only can history be brought to life through today's performances, but that theatrical companies could broaden their resources by attending to historical discourses of *lesbianism*.

The pun embedded in this chapter's title implies that visibility is a function of location: what is positioned *behind the scene* is denied visibility. Such a denial, my Introduction argued, has been the governing condition of early modern *lesbianism*. If we materialize the theatrical metaphor, however, we can recognize that what goes on behind the scene – the work, for instance, of stagehands, lighting technicians, directors, costumers, financiers – is also what makes the actors' performances possible. By appropriating this metaphor of constitutive but unacknowledged work, I propose that *lesbianism* has played a more important role in our cultural heritage than is commonly supposed.

I begin my investigation of cultural production through that canonical icon, "Shakespeare," because his name and the industry it now represents is a repository of cultural assumptions that I wish to vex and a site of cultural capital that I wish to employ.[5] As recent mainstream films of *Henry V*, *Richard III*, *Romeo and Juliet*, and *Titus Andronicus*, as well as films that allude to, cite, adapt, and revamp Shakespearean materials suggest, Shakespearean drama remains, even in a postmodern global economy, a privileged site of cultural production and interpretation. Despite its marginal status *vis-à-vis* other forms of television and cinema, Shakespearean performance, whether acted live or filmed, screened in an art house, the mall, or on TV, contributes in unique and pervasive ways to contemporary understanding of "high culture," "the arts," "human nature," and, perhaps most important for my purposes, "history." Even as contemporary production values update characters, clothes, and plots, making them "relevant" to today's viewers, "Shakespeare" remains one of the few cultural forms from which interpretations of the past are disseminated. Indeed, the cultural capital of the Shakespeare industry seems in direct proportion to its ability to proffer a fantasy of historical tradition and authority (or to contest it), whether through the means of period costume drama or postmodern pastiche. If, as the editors of *Shakespeare, The Movie* assert (after a spate of Shakespeare films in the 1990s), "just where the film industry will take Shakespeare seems quite up for grabs,"[6] the time seems right to grab what has been "behind" and to bring *lesbianism* onto center stage – not to enforce a politics of identity, but to destabilize some long-standing theatrical conventions and to activate the queer potential of today's global audience.

Theatrical and cinematic productions have many tools for dramatizing non-canonical interpretations of Shakespeare's plays, from the reinterpretation of character and reassignment of speeches to transpositions of time, place, and costume. But as progressive as the productions of some theatrical companies have been, not all the creative energies that can be brought to bear on Shakespearean performance stem from theatrical practitioners themselves. In this regard, contemporary performance has much to gain from the insights of feminist and queer criticism and theory. Often, however, the aims of feminist textual criticism and performance seem to be at odds. According to theater critic Lorraine Helms, "[p]erformance, like criticism, may either reproduce or reevaluate the ideology with which a dominant culture invests a play text. But if a production is to challenge the theatrical tradition... it must move from critique to revision." The problem with much feminist textual criticism of Shakespeare, Helms argues, is that it takes the form of critique rather than creative re-envisioning. Because the feminism of such criticism, she argues, often is "theatrically inert," "were it taken as the conceptual foundation for performance," it would unwittingly affirm rather than subvert "a misogynist interpretation."[7]

The aim of the present chapter is to begin to envision ways in which a *lesbian* analytic might make available to the stage (and cinema) new strategies for performing relations of gender and eroticism. By suggesting that a historical awareness of the range of female desires and bonds in the early modern period could profitably pressure how female characters are represented and erotic desire thematized, I do not mean to imply that contemporary Shakespearean production has totally avoided dramatizing homoerotic desire. Indeed, in response to contemporary politics – and sometimes in advance of academic theorizing – some theater companies have brought attention to, for instance, Antonio's love for Bassanio and the erotic relation between Salerio and Solanio, as in the New York Public Theater's production of *The Merchant of Venice*, or Orsino's attraction for Cesario, as in a recent Shakespeare Santa Cruz production.[8] Rather than invest certain characters with homoerotic desires in otherwise "straight" productions, other companies have queered the entire play by using male drag – as in Cheek by Jowl's all-male *As You Like It*, Theatre Rhinoceros's all-male *Twelfth Night*, Reginald Jackson's high camp *House of Lear*, and Shakespeare Santa Cruz's *A Midsummer Night's Dream*.[9]

The theatricalization of *lesbian* desire in Shakespearean drama occurs far less frequently. When it does occur, it tends to depend on cross-gender casting to parody or "modernize" Shakespeare. Cheek by Jowl's 1991 *As You Like It* portrayed Celia in love with Rosalind, but did so through the mediation of an all-male cast.[10] A 1996 Cornerstone Theater Company adaptation of *Twelfth Night*, committed to exploring the debate about "gays in the military," cast the love-sick Malvolio as a woman and set the action at a Southern California naval base.[11] Likewise, cross-gender casting animated Jill Dolan's 1991 University of Wisconsin production of *A Midsummer Night's Dream*, in which the forest was transformed into a gay disco, Oberon was played as a "fashionable, sexy, butch lesbian," and Demetrius, upon waking, discovered he was transformed into a woman – thus altering both his and Helena's erotic orientations.[12]

Cross-gender casting, parody, and modernization have their attractions, of course, including audience accessibility and appeal, as well as the communal joy of celebrating gay identity. And, there are several good reasons for the reliance of companies on male drag: the historically vibrant presence of transvestism in gay male culture;[13] the Renaissance theatrical tradition of using boy actors to play female roles;[14] and the theoretical import of drag as a performative subversion of identity.[15] But the problem with such strategies, when employed to the exclusion of other possibilities, is that they tend to reinforce the all-too-prevalent assumption that issues of erotic diversity are distinctively *modern* concerns. According to Susan Bennett, the attempt to resist or revise the Shakespearean text in theatrical or cinematic performance typically has meant to dehistoricize it.[16] While the use of Shakespeare for the purposes of multiculturalism or gay community-building implicates Renaissance drama in queer genders and sexualities, it tends to do so by highlighting meta-theatricality at the expense of early modern history. If directors and actors wish to demonstrate the contemporary relevance of Shakespeare's erotic plots, they need not feel limited to the strategy of modernization. Nor, if they wish to resurrect historical traditions, need they limit their approach to crossdressing and the use of boy actors. To what extent, for instance, do current productions employing drag register the actual tradition of passing women – women who crossdressed not only for economic advantage and/or freedom from patriarchal marriage, but to act on their erotic desires for other women, to cohabit with, and sometimes, to marry them? The goal in asking this question is not to forget the difference between stage representations and individual lives nor the absence of actual women from the Renaissance stage, but rather to investigate how theatrical drag registers – or fails to register – a specifically *lesbian* mode of representation. Such an investigation might ask which performance strategies beyond cross-gender casting and drag might make visible the full range of women's emotional and erotic attachments.[17] We do not need to laminate a *lesbian* presence *onto* Shakespeare's texts; once we begin to think historically about desires and practices, we can draw homoerotic meanings *out* of them. The point is not to deploy a discourse of authenticity to trump "trendy" postmodernism, nor to populate the Shakespearean stage with women whose desires are intelligible only in the idioms of the present.[18] To invoke if only to reconceptualize the title of the ground-breaking anthology, *Queering the Renaissance*: it is less a question of queering the past than of discovering the terms by which the past articulated its *own* queerness.[19]

If erotic desires and practices in the early modern period were not organized by an essential and exclusive division of homo- and heterosexual, how was eroticism organized? To begin with a critical commonplace: most aspects of women's lives were determined by their age, marital status, and position within the patriarchal household. Familial status relations (whether one was husband, wife, or child), along with hierarchies of social rank (whether one was master, mistress, servant, apprentice) established each person's opportunities and responsibilities. The legitimate social identities available to women – maid, wife, mother, and widow – were tied to marital status. Patriarchal authority and material necessity compelled most women to marry, and while daughters usually had the right to veto the recommendations of their fathers and advisors, in many espousals the hope was that women would come to love after, if not before, marriage. Noblewomen in particular were held accountable to considerable financial and political concerns, including the purity of genealogical lineage, inheritance of fortune and title, and consolidation of huge tracts of land. Daughters of the "middling sort" likewise were expected to make matches that helped the family's fortune by linking guildsmen and potential business partners, while daughters of the working poor may have had the least to lose or gain by the economic connections cemented by marriage.

The system of eroticism was organized in relation to patriarchal marriage, which was, as Isabel Hull argues,

the only framework for legitimate, socially approved sexual expression. This meant that marriage was a colossally overdetermined institution carrying an unsurpassed density of social meanings. Wealth, social standing, adulthood, independence, livelihood, communal responsibility, (for males) political representation, and sexual expression were all joined symbolically in this one estate, which meant that any one of these social meanings might stand for any other. The embeddedness of sex in this constellation, particularly its connection with property and marriage, constitutes its chief characteristic in the early modern period and also the main difficulty writers have had in interpreting it in its historical context.[20]

The dominance of marriage as a social and political institution does not negate the pervasiveness of illegitimate heteroerotic activity, including frequent adultery at the highest levels of society. The fact that England was ruled for almost half a century by a woman whose own legitimacy was contested suggests the extent to which the edicts of patriarchal marriage could be, and were, ignored. Nonetheless, the disproportionate conceptual weight accorded to marriage, combined with a phallic standard of sexuality and the absence of a concept of erotic identity, provided the conceptual and social framework for *lesbianism* across Europe. Within this framework, the treatment and semiotics of *lesbianism* were paradoxical. Authorities in all European societies were concerned about the threat posed by behaviors that crossed gender boundaries and/or the conjugal unit; thus, certain female–female erotic acts were met with harsh denunciation, punishment, and considerable publicity. Other behaviors that seem manifestly *lesbian* to twentieth-century minds, however, did not cause much social concern, and often were compatible with patriarchal marriage and alliance.

As Hull notes, the disciplining of illicit erotic acts was, in this time of nascent state formation, primarily a function of the church and community:

The church and the social nexus in which people lived – their family, neighbors, and fellow workers – exerted for a long time a stronger and more effective sexual discipline than the rudimentary state... The church set the basic framework within which the absolutist territorial state later exercised regulation. From the secular standpoint, the church's two most powerful contributions were the great significance it ascribed to sexual (mis)behavior and the paramount position it accorded to marriage as the only locus of accepted sexual expression. Following these principles (among others) the church carefully developed the hierarchy of sexual offenses that absolutist penal codes later adopted from canon law.[21]

Thus, even after secular statutes replaced ecclesiastical law, denunciation of non-reproductive erotic acts as "unnatural" was the universal aim of religious and secular authorities across Europe.[22] Paul's *Letter to the Romans*, in which he speaks of women who give up natural intercourse for unnatural, and of men who reject women and are consumed with passion for men, provided the primary biblical authority for condemning what was called the *crimen contra naturam*.[23] Although sodomy today is most often defined as anal penetration, in the early modern period sodomy functioned as a catch-all category for a range of erotic activities and positions: anal penetration (involving penis, finger, or other instrument, and engaged with men or women), masturbation, bestiality, rape, and child molestation.[24] Female–female eroticism was considered by medieval church fathers as one among a panoply of unnatural acts, included in penitentials and investigated in the confessional.[25] After 1550, legal statutes became more specific about the inclusion of female sodomy. By the sixteenth century in many European states, a woman's conviction for sodomy (whether enacted with women or men) resulted, like that of men, in the penalty of death.

Two essential paradoxes define the legal status of *lesbianism* throughout the sixteenth and seventeenth centuries: not all sodomy statutes explicitly mention female–female activities; and in those jurisdictions that criminalize female–female acts, prosecution is the exception rather than the norm. England is a prime example of the first paradox: in 1533 an Act of Parliament made buggery (the vernacular term for anal penetration) a secular rather than religious crime, and punishable by death; however, this statute, *25 Henry VIII, chapter 6*, did not mention women. In 1644, Sir Edward Coke, a prominent English interpreter of the law, proffered the opinion that if women committed buggery, it was by having sex with an animal.[26] Indeed, despite the fact that by the late seventeenth century vernacular dictionaries would include references to "woman with a woman" under the heading of "Buggerie," in reference to this crime Coke cites only an incident of "a great Lady [who] had committed Buggery with a Baboon, and conceived by it, etc."[27] In Scotland, however, Kirk Session records reveal one case of female sodomy in 1625, charged by the Glasgow Presbytery against two Egilshame parishioners, Elspeth Faulds and Margaret Armour; they were forced to separate from one another upon pain of excommunication.[28] The French seem to have more actively enforced their sodomy statute: the jurist Jean Papon documented the arrest and torture in 1533 of Françoise de l'Estage and Catherine de la Maniére in Toulouse (they were acquitted due to inadequate evidence);[29] Henri Estienne recounted the burning of a woman in 1535 for crossdressing and marrying a maid of Foy;[30] and in 1580 Michel de Montaigne recorded the execution of another crossdressed "female husband" who allegedly used "illicit devices" with her female partner in Montier-en-Der.[31]

In 1532, the Constitutions of the Holy Roman Empire made sex between women a capital crime.[32] Following suit, the city of Augsburg Discipline Ordinance of 1537 condemned "damned forbidden commingling" (referring to the provision of imperial law); however, no women seem to have been prosecuted under this ordinance.³³ Nonetheless, in Freiburg im Breisgau in 1547, Agatha Dietzsch was pilloried in an iron collar and banished for cross-dressing and marrying Anna Reulin.³⁴ Likewise, one Swiss woman was brought to trial and drowned in Geneva in 1568; and in 1647, Elsbeth Hertner was accused of both sodomy and witchcraft in Basel.³⁵

No sodomy bill was passed in the province of Holland until 1730 – and even then it did not mention women. However, in Leiden in 1606, Maeyken Joosten married Bertelminia Wale while dressed as a man; soon thereafter she was exiled from the city for life. In Leiden in 1688, Cornelia Gerrits van Breugel and Elisabeth Boleyn, who had been living together for a year, were married after Cornelia began dressing as a man; they both stood trial after Cornelia reverted back to female dress, and were exiled from the city for twelve years.³⁶ In Spain, the thirteenth-century legal code known as *Las siete partidas* (the seven laws) made "sins against nature" a capital crime, but it was not until the mid-sixteenth century that a legal gloss proposed extending the death penalty to women, and two Spanish nuns accused of using genital "instruments" were burned at the stake. Two other cases of women using genital instruments were reported in Seville; one couple was exiled while the other was hanged (for "robberies, murders, and audacity").³⁷ Whereas sodomy often was called the "Florentine vice," and throughout Italy the punishment for sodomy was burning at the stake, no executions of Italian women are documented.³⁸ Nonetheless, a Pescian nun, Benedetta Carlini, was virtually imprisoned for thirty-five years for heresy, a charge that stemmed in part from her mystical and physical union with another nun.³⁹

During the Moscovite period (fourteenth to eighteenth centuries), Russia was unique in Europe for failing to enact secular legislation prohibiting same-gender erotic activity (for men or women).⁴⁰ Of concern to Eastern Orthodox ecclesiastical authorities was the relative position of sexual partners: two women together (or two men) were no more sinful than a woman on top of a man. With homoeroticism considered a sin rather than a crime, the recommended penance was confession, prostrations, exclusion from communion, and dietary abstentions. When, in 1706, Russian laws penalized male sodomy, no mention was made of women.

In colonial North America, sodomy laws likewise differed by locale. A criminal code drawn up by John Cotton in 1636 for the Massachusetts General Court described sodomy as "carnal fellowship of man with man, or woman with woman," but the authoritative Body of Liberties omitted women from the final draft. Other New England colonies, with the exception of Rhode Island, took their cue from the Massachusetts Bay Colony, drafting codes without reference to female–female contact. New Haven included sex between women as a capital offense, its statute of 1656 being the most detailed and comprehensive in the colonies. The two known colonial cases in which women were charged with "unclean" behavior, however, invoked neither sodomy nor the draconian punishments typically associated with it: in 1642, "Elizabeth Johnson was whipped and fined by an Essex County quarterly court for 'unseemly and filthy practices betwixt hir and another maid, attempting To Do that which man and woman Doe,' and in 1648/49, Sara Norman and Mary Hammon of Plymouth Colony were publicly admonished for 'leude behavior each with other upon a bed.'"[41] In Virginia, an official inquiry into the anatomical sex of the crossdressing Thomas/Thomasine Hall may have been instigated by a rumor that Hall "did ly with a maid... called greate Besse," but the case was resolved without resort to capital punishment; Thomas(ine) was forced to adopt a hybrid form of dress and live a life devoid of erotic contact.[42]

This summary of patterns of legal prosecution reveals that, in contrast to the high incidence of prosecution of women for prostitution, adultery, bastardy, and witchcraft, comparatively few women in Europe and colonial North America were prosecuted for sodomy before the eighteenth century.[43] In fact, the official treatment of female–female erotic acts throughout the early modern era was somewhat incoherent, with the paucity of prosecutions at odds with the supposedly horrific nature of the crime. When read in the context of court testimony, the selective enforcement of sodomy laws suggests that the primary concern of authorities was women's appropriation of masculine prerogatives, whether in the form of crossdressing and passing as a man, the use of instruments of genital penetration (dildoes made of leather, wood, or glass), or other challenges to patriarchal authority. Some statutes specifically mandated harsher punishments for acts involving "material instruments" or devices for penetration.

When women were prosecuted for homoerotic acts, lawyers generally acted in concert with medical authorities, both physicians (exclusively men) and midwives (primarily women). Medical theorists and practitioners became involved in legal cases because, both in medicine and popular lore, women's erotic transgressions typically were read in relation to the dominant discourse of psycho-physiology, the humoral theory derived from the classical Roman physician, Galen. According to humoralism, the body is a dynamic, self-regulating process.[44] Each of the four humors (blood, choler, melancholy, phlegm) possesses two primary qualities: blood is hot and moist, choler is hot and dry, melancholy is cold and dry, and phlegm is cold and moist. Each has specific physiological functions: blood warms and moistens the body, choler incites the expulsion of various excrements, melancholy provokes the appetite, and phlegm nourishes the cold and moist organs such as the kidneys and the brain. The related doctrine of the four temperaments (also called complexion theory) diagnoses sanguine, choleric, melancholic, and phlegmatic temperaments as caused by the dominance of one of the humors. Temperament (and thus behavior) is a matter both somatic and psychic.

In humoral theory, physiological sex exists on a continuum: although typically men are hot and dry, some men are too moist; while most women are moist and cold, some women are too hot. Such variation in the humors explains the presence of manly women (dry and cold) and womanly men (moist and hot). Indeed, because medically (and theologically) women are considered imperfect versions of men, women occasionally – so it was said – turn into men. The spontaneous eruption of a penis from sudden motion or increased body heat is a logical extension of the belief that women's genital anatomy is merely an inverted (and imperfect) version of men's. Since nature always strives for perfection, virilization rather than effeminization is nature's preferred course.[45] Throughout the sixteenth and seventeenth centuries, instances of miraculous sex change were narrated among villagers and used as evidence of the devil's ability to use natural causes to work his evil. In answering the question "Whether by Witchcraft and Devil's Work the Sexes can be Interchanged," Francesco Maria Guazzo, for instance, lists several examples of women in Spain, Portugal, and Naples who spontaneously metamorphosed into men; some did so after years of marriage, some upon the onset of menses, some on their wedding night. All of them thereafter adopted the clothing and manners of men, several of them married women, and some were rumored to have fathered children.[46] In his treatise, *Des Monstres et Prodiges*, the influential French surgeon Ambroise Paré likewise provides a list of "memorable stories about women who have degenerated into men." In sixteenth-century scientific usage "*degenerer*" does not necessarily entail debasement, but rather registers a change from one species to another; according to Paré, the woman who is transformed into a man elevates her condition.[47] In one case, reported to Paré by the King's receiver of rents, a certain man at Reimes "was taken for a woman untill the fourteenth yeere of his age; for then it happened as he played somewhat wantonly with a maid which lay in the same bed with him, his members (hitherto lying hid) started forth and unfolded them selves."[48]

Whereas such cases of sex transformation pepper the literature on witchcraft and marvels, physicians and anatomists began to voice skepticism as anatomical investigation challenged the traditional homology of male and female reproductive organs. Over the course of the seventeenth century, medical writers increasingly denied the possibility of metamorphosis, arguing that such phenomena were attributable either to hermaphroditism or to unusual genital anatomy. In the latter case, the problematic "member" that made a woman look (and act) like a man was either a prolapsed vagina or, more commonly, an enlarged clitoris. In the latter case, such women were likely tribades, women who gained erotic satisfaction from rubbing against or penetrating other women's genitals with their "female yards." Helkiah Crooke, author of the English vernacular anatomy, *Microcosmographia: A Description of the Body of Man* (1615), for instance, summarized reports of sex transformation from the classical age forward for the purpose of arguing against its probability. He termed all such stories "monstrous and some not credible": persons alleged to have changed sex are either hermaphrodites or women who are "so hot by nature that their *Clitoris* hangeth foorth in the fashion of a mans member."[49] During the mid-seventeenth century, English medical popularizer Nicholas Culpeper was inclined to agree; but he hedged his bets, taking cover under the traditional adage that the size of the genitals correlates with the capacity for desire:

> Some are of opinion, and I could almost afford to side with them, That such kind of Creatures they call *Hermaphrodites*, which they say bear the Genitals both of Men and Women, are nothing else but such women in whom the *Clytoris* hangs out externally, and so resemble the form of a yard; I leave the truth or falshood of it to be judged by such who have seen them anatomised; however, this is agreeable both to reason and Authority, that the bigger the *Clytoris* is in Women, the more lustful they are.[50]

Culpeper's maxim, which correlates quantity of lust with size of genitals, exposes a powerful incoherence within the humoral dispensation. According to Galenic theory (and Biblical doctrine), women, weaker and more inconstant than men, are more subject to lust. However, if women's lust becomes excessive, they perversely and paradoxically threaten to become like men. Female insatiability generally is linked not to the genitals, but to a weak will and susceptibility to temptation; if, however, a woman's body evinces bigger (more manlike) sexual equipment, she is less likely than men to be able to control it.

I will discuss medical debates about clitoral hypertrophy in chapter 5. For now I want to stress the tight associations forged between sex transformation, hermaphroditism, tribadism, and sodomy in most European legal and medical practices. These associations derive from conflicting medical models of the causality of hermaphroditism as well as the pervasive tendency to read the tribade in terms of her bodily morphology. Early moderns tended to view sex, gender, and eroticism always in terms of one another; thus, the boundary was continually blurred between hermaphroditism (which we tend to consider an anatomical category) and tribadism (which we tend to consider a behavioral category). The line between the hermaphrodite and the tribade, for instance, proves to be a fine one in the chronicle of the count Froben Christop von Zimmern, who reports the following case:

> There was also at that time a poor serving-girl at Mösskirch, who served here and there, and she was called Greta... She did not take any man or young apprentice, nor would she stand at the bench with any such [i.e. work with them as husband and wife and sell his goods], but loved the young daughters, went after them and bought them pedlars' goods, and she also used all bearing and manners, as if she had a masculine *affect*. She was often considered to be a hermaphrodite or androgyne, but this did not prove to be the case, for she was investigated by cunning, and was seen to be a true, proper woman.

To note: she was said to be born under an inverted, unnatural constellation. But amongst the learned and well-read one finds that this sort of thing is often encountered among the Greeks and Romans, although this is to be ascribed rather to the evil customs of those corrupted nations, plagued by sins, than to the course of the heavens or stars.[51]

Because of her erotic behavior, Greta is considered by many to be a hermaphrodite; nonetheless, she is revealed as "a true, proper woman" after being "investigated by cunning." Such investigations into the truth of bodily morphology were serious, and sometimes highly public, occasions. Three separate medical commissions examined the case of Marie le Marcis, who in 1601 defended herself against charges of sodomy with her female lover, Jeane, on the grounds that she was a man. Pursued all the way to the Parlement of Rouen, this case of a chambermaid instigated a heated medico-legal debate between Jacques Duval, a provincial physician, and Jean Riolan, professor of anatomy and botany at the University of Paris. Their published disquisitions hinge on the ideological conflict between the Galenic/Hippocratic belief that hermaphrodites represent an intermediate sex (Duval's position), and the Aristotelian denial of true hermaphroditism and insistence that so-called hermaphrodites simply possess doubled or redundant genitalia (Riolan's position).[52] Whereas the Aristotelian model of reproductive anatomy tended to dominate, a mid-sixteenth-century resurgence of interest in Hippocratic theories redirected attention to the erotic possibilities posed by the hermaphrodite's gender ambiguity.[53] Within France, legal proceedings to determine the hermaphrodite's dominant sex increasingly focused on the possibility of sexual fraud and malfeasance; they thus depended more on the external testimony of medical experts than on the hermaphrodite's self-description or articulation of desires.

All of this is apparent in Marie's tale. Marie revealed to her lover, Jeane, that she was really a man. After consummating their vows, apparently to the mutual enjoyment of each, the couple sought public approval of their love. Marie changed her name to Marin, and began wearing masculine clothing. The two were subsequently arrested, tried, and condemned. The crime for which both were convicted was sodomy; despite Marin's claim that the terror of the trial had caused his penis to retract, the court maintained that Marie was a tribade. It was only upon Marin's appeal to the Parlement of Rouen, which appointed a panel of doctors, surgeons, and midwives to repeat a medical examination, that Duval applied pressure to Marin's organs, and found there "a male organ" which on second examination, "ejaculated" in a manner consistent not with woman's expulsion of seed, but a man's.

The difference between being judged a hermaphrodite or a tribade, then, was as crucial as it was uncertain. A further contribution to the confusion was the status of clothing as a signifier of identity. Discourses about hermaphrodites, tribades, female sodomites, and spontaneous transsexuals were also discourses about crossdressing. During this period of unprecedented geographical exploration, warfare, and colonization, many women took advantage of the rise in social status that a change in clothing could bring about. Under the cover of male dress, women's migration to urban centers, service as a soldier or shipmate, and immigration to the New World afforded them new opportunities for social advancement. Popular street ballads, broadsheets, and prose narratives extolled the exploits of female soldiers and sailors who accomplished heroic deeds while successfully passing as men – especially if they did so in order to accompany husbands or male lovers into battle.[54] However, despite avid interest in tales of passing women, in many continental countries crossdressing (legally considered a form of fraud) was a serious, even a capital, offense.[55] Although English sumptuary legislation regulated status boundaries rather than gender, and it is probably the case that very few women actually crossdressed, the anxiety that crossdressing would become a viable fashion was still evident: during the height of the pamphlet controversy about the nature of women in the early years of the seventeenth century, King James of England and Scotland instructed clergymen to preach against women wearing masculine accouterments such as doublets and swords.

Much of the social anxiety expressed about women's transvestism had more to do with concerns about their lewdness with men than with homoerotic transgressions. Most female crossdressers whose tales are recorded profess to have adopted masculine identities in order to pursue adventure, economic gain, or the men who had abandoned them. However, some of them were motivated by their own commitment to "female masculinity" and/or their attachments to other women.[56] Exposure was sometimes the result of a sexual liaison, as in an account published in *The Gentleman's Journal: Or the Monthly Miscellany* (April 1692), which speaks approvingly of an English soldier who

> served two years in the French Army in Piedmont as a volunteer, and was entertained for her merit by the Governor of Pignerol in the quality of his Gentlemen of the Horse; at last playing with another of her sex, she was discover'd; and the Governor having thought fit to inform the King his master of this, he hath sent him word that he would be glad to see the lady; which hath occasion'd her coming to Genoa, in order to embark for France: Nature has bestow'd no less beauty on her than courage; and her age is not above 26. The French envoy hath orders to cause her to be waited on to Marseille, and to furnish her with all necessaries.[57]

Other accounts from England, France, Germany, and the Netherlands document female crossdressers marrying women, and often attest to the wife's sexual satisfaction, as well as to her knowledge (whether before or after marriage) of her "husband's" sex. (Several such accounts will be analyzed in chapter 4.) The three "autobiographies" of Catalina de Erauso, a crossdressing Basque conquistador, as well as a play written about her, recount her amorous flirtations with Spanish ladies in the New World.[58] (Chapter 2 will begin with her story.) More prosaically, a London Consistory Court document details the annulment of a marriage contracted between Arabella Hunt and her "female husband," Amy Poulter (a.k.a. James Howard).[59] In her suit for annulment, apparently brought after six months of cohabitation, Hunt maintained that, when they married in 1680, Poulter had been legally married to a husband still living, that she alternated dressing as a woman and a man, and that she was "of a double gender." Although Poulter freely admitted the first two charges, and asserted that she had married Hunt on a lark, she flatly denied being a hermaphrodite – a denial supported by the five midwives who subsequently examined her. Because she was deemed "a perfect woman in all her parts" – that is, complete and without defect – she was not held liable for bigamy (two women could not contract a valid marriage) and neither she nor Hunt were charged with a crime. In fact, the court determined them free to remarry – as long as the husband was a man. Neither, however, did.[60]

Another English woman who crossdressed, allegedly in order to defraud young women of their dowries, was not so lucky; her story is briefly summarized by the Oxford antiquarian Anthony à Wood, who included the following anecdote in a letter to a friend in 1694:

Appeared at the King's Bench in Westminster hall a young woman in man's apparel, or that personated a man, who was found guilty of marrying a young maid, whose portion he had obtained and was very nigh of being contracted to a second wife. Divers of her love letters were read in court, which occasioned much laughter. Upon the whole she was ordered to Bridewell to be well whipt and kept to hard labour till further order of the court.[61]

Even though Wood shifts pronouns in order to narrate this episode – reserving the masculine pronoun for the person who had defrauded the maid of her portion – this "young woman in man's apparel" apparently did not present a forensic problem. Her clothes, rather than her anatomy, provided the visual sign of her masculinity; her "personation" of a man was a failed one. But when less clarity attended the accusation of hermaphroditism, sex transformation, sodomy, or tribadism, women were compelled to undergo a forensic medical examination. If the probing of a midwife or physician revealed the anatomy of "a perfect woman" (or "a perfect man"), she (or he) was reinserted into the traditional gender hierarchy (and sometimes subjected to further prosecution for erotic misdeeds). If found to possess both a penis and vagina, the now-confirmed hermaphrodite usually (though, as Thomas(ine) Hall's case makes clear, not inevitably) was allowed to choose a gender identity. As long as s/he did not switch back and forth, and gender-appropriate clothing was worn, s/he was allowed to marry.[62] Within Judaic law, marriage was permitted between an *androgunos* (one who possessed both penis and vagina) and a woman, but marriage of an androgunos to a man was prohibited – two penises, apparently, were considered too many in one marriage.[63]

These documents and narratives of female masculinity, tribadism, hermaphroditism, and sex transformation tell us little about the subjective experience of women's erotic desires and practices. In *Hunt vs. Poulter*, for instance, the ecclesiastical court was concerned with the legal status of their marriage, not their personal motivations. These texts do tell us, however, about some of the conditions under which women's erotic activities with other women were construed as a social problem. Such a construal, it is important to note, was not inevitable. Female–female eroticism was not universally or uniformly scandalous, or even criminal.[64] An informal allegation lodged against Susannah Bell, for instance, occurs only in the context of a proceeding against her previous husband, Ralph Hollingsworth, who was sued by his later wife, Maria Seely, in 1694 for bigamy. In his defense documented in the London Consistory Court, Hollingsworth describes Susannah: "now as to Susannah Bell: she knowing her infirmity ought not to have married; her infirmity is such that no man can lie with her, and because it so she has ways with women as well, as with her old companions men, which is not fit to be named but most rank whorish they are."[65] Whatever "infirmity" Susannah had (a small vaginal opening? an enlarged clitoris?) that prompted her to have "ways with women," she was not prosecuted for her behavior; her bigamist husband was.

It usually took some extraordinary circumstance to motivate a community to involve local officials or for such officials to embark on a legal proceeding. As Hull remarks of criminal prosecution in general: "The prosecution of sexual crimes was at the mercy of the local populace: they provided the original information for indictment, the testimony at the trial, and the audience for public punishments. If the parties to a dispute arising from sexual behavior could solve the problem among themselves, then the authorities might never hear of it."[66] It appears that female–female intimacy did not, on its own, generally occasion sufficient concern to warrant the involvement of authorities. Several court cases were initiated, not because of community outrage, but because one of the women sought a legal annulment, generally after several months, or even years, of cohabitation. Those women who *were* accused of sodomy, tribadism, or hermaphroditism seem to have gained local notoriety prior to their prosecution, whether through flagrant crossdressing, prostitution, vagrancy, or dissenting religious beliefs. Often they were strangers, wayfarers from other locales. Among those unfortunate women, it generally was the woman who crossdressed or used penetrative devices who received harsher punishment than her ostensibly more "feminine" partner – a system of punishment that both derived from and enforced a prevalent assumption that illicit female liaisons were governed by a logic of gender imitation.

To recognize the contingencies of prosecution is not to deny the lethal energies exercised against women who came to the attention of authorities, but rather, to insist that the history of *lesbianism* is not one of unrelieved oppression. Homophobia itself is a historically specific and variable phenomenon, deployed intermittently and under certain social conditions.[67] Many female–female couples may have lived unremarked by their neighbors and therefore unmolested by the law. In regards to a sodomy trial of 1477, for instance, Helmut Puff maintains that the "female husband" Katherina Hetzeldorfer had "shared at least part of her secret with individual members of Speyer's urban community."[68] The cohabitation of female couples may have been spoken about as different or strange, but may not have been a particular community concern. Such couples may have been subject to good-natured or ill-favored gossip, or to community harassment short of legal action. Even when subjected to official scrutiny, however, women were not censured uniformly. Whereas Elspeth Faulds and Margaret Armour were excommunicated by the Glasgow Presbytery, the London Consistory Court acted with indifference to the marital crossdressing of Amy Poulter/James Howard. Several female transvestites in sixteenth-century France and Spain were executed, while Catalina de Erauso was awarded a military pension for her colonial services by Philip IV and special permission from Pope Urban XIII to continue dressing as a man. Such conceptual and material contradictions suggest that there is no one history of *lesbianism* in early modern Europe and the Americas. Rather, there are multiple histories, each of them dependent upon complex and sometimes competing ideologies of gender, social status, and authority – not to mention the different personalities involved. Variations in local standards of morality and tolerances of diversity, contending medical cultures and contradictory "truths" about anatomy and physiology, and the evolving contests between the church and the state all had an impact on the construction and treatment of early modern *lesbianism*. Traversed by different discourses and subject to a variety of cultural investments, women interested in other women pursued erotic adventure, pleasure, and satisfaction by seeking modes of accommodation within the patriarchal landscape they inhabited.

Few women were directly affected by allegations of transvestism, tribadism, hermaphroditism, or sex transformation. Another discourse, however, had a direct if equivocal impact on the bodies of all early modern women. The ideology of chastity, an element of Catholic doctrine that continued in secular form after the Reformation, provided the *sine qua non* of women's social status. As the humanist educator Juan Luis Vives put it, "chastity is the principal virtue of a woman, and counterpeiseth with all the rest. If she have that, no man will look for any other; and if she lack that, no man will regard other."[69] Despite doubts among anatomists about the hymen's existence and its reliability as a sign of virginity, the intact hymen popularly was considered the guarantor of female virtue.[70] Yet, because the discourse of chastity figured the threat of phallic penetration as the only socially intelligible form of erotic congress – as the only erotic practice that *mattered* – a range of other erotic behaviors, technically chaste, might be pursued by adolescents and adult women. Adolescent Russian and Italian girls, for instance, regularly played mock wedding games, physically enacting the erotic positions and actions of husband and wife; because none of them possessed a penis or wielded a dildo, their erotic play was considered a harmless preparation for adult marital roles.[71]

I explore the faultlines within the ideology of chastity in several subsequent chapters. For now, I simply want to note that the contradictory social functions of chastity dovetailed with the material conditions of the early modern English household. As Lena Cowen Orlin makes clear, most house chambers, including bedchambers, were "communal and multipurpose," while beds themselves (relatively expensive household furniture) were located "in nearly every conceivable space – halls, parlors, stair landings, outbuildings, and kitchens, as well as bedchambers." Orlin's larger point – that boundaries between the private and public had not yet settled into their modern binary configuration – is supported by surviving floorplans and household inventories, all of which suggest "that privacy was not an object of the architecture of the period."[72] Nor was it the object of individuals, for, as Hull notes, "no one expected 'privacy' in the modern sense, where solitude is simultaneously a sign that the sexual act is nobody's business, that it is not social. Early modern Europeans assumed just the reverse; transparency was therefore not just the product of limited spatial resources (few separate bedrooms), it was positively desirable."[73] The architectural constraints on privacy and social expectations of communal life, congruent as they were with the ideology of chastity, insured that throughout Europe and across social rank, adolescent girls as well as married and unmarried adult women regularly shared beds with kinswomen, female friends, and servants. What Margaret Hunt says of laboring singlewomen in the eighteenth century is true for the earlier period:

Girls from poor and middling families generally began working very young ... At some point between about age ten and fifteen many of them were put out to service or (less often) apprenticeships ... The standard assumption was that they would save their money ... so as to be able to marry some time in their mid- to late twenties. During this lengthy period, often fifteen or more years, they habitually slept in the same bed with a succession of other girls or women, other female servants if there were any, the daughters of other women of the household, or not uncommonly, the mistress of the house herself ... Many female servants would have experienced the sleeping arrangements of half a dozen households before they turned thirty, and that during a period when they were lonely, often deprived of affection, and, at least part of the time, at a high libidinal pitch. The potential this system offered for risk-free, same-sex erotic activity was very great.[74]

With sharing beds a usual practice in households across the social spectrum, bodily intimacy conserved heat, fostered companionship, and enabled erotic contact.[75] We should not forget that the miraculous female-to-male sex transformation at Reimes reported to Paré supposedly occurred while the woman "played somewhat wantonly with a maid which lay in the same bed with him" – an activity that warrants no comment from Paré.[76]

The invitation to a woman to lie with her mistress or a noblewoman was considered a privileged sign of favor.[77] In a letter written in 1605 by Lady Anne Clifford to her mother, Anne apologizes for her inability to go "to Oxford, according to your Ladyship's desire with my Lady Arbella [Stuart], and to have slept in her chamber, which she much desired, for I am the more bound to her than can be, but my Lord would not have me go with the Court thither."[78] The sharing of beds with female intimates seems to have been an expected, yet nonetheless highly emotive, occurrence in Lady Anne's life. In her diary she records that, in punishment for having ridden horse alone with a man, her mother instructed that she should sleep alone in her room. This, Lady Anne writes, "I could not endure, but my Cozen Frances got the Key of my Chamber and lay with me which was the first time I loved hir so verie well."[79] "Loved hir so verie well" – Anne's affection for her kinswoman Lady Frances Bourchier, with whom she slept on other occasions, is expressed in the ambiguous, yet overlapping, terms of aristocratic kinship and passionate friendship.[80]

Further down the social scale – indeed, outside the household proper – the bedding down of two indigent women is briefly noted by Thomas Harman who, in his epistle dedication to the Countess of Shrewsbury in his *Caveat or Warening For Commen Cursetors*, describes the funeral of a gentleman:

at his buryall there was such a number of beggers, besides poore housholders dwelling there abouts, that unneath [with difficulty] they mighte lye or stande aboute the House: then was there prepared for them a great and a large barne, and a great fat ox sod out in Furmenty [wheat boiled in milk] for them, with bread *and* drinke aboundantly to furnesh out the premisses; and every person had two pence, for such was the dole. When Night approched, *the* pore housholders repaired home to their houses: the other wayfaring bold beggers remained alnight in *the* barne; and the same barne being serched with light in the night by this old man (and then yonge), with others, they tolde seven score persons of men, every of them having his woma*n*, except it were two wemen that lay alone to gether for some especyall cause. Thus hauing their makes to make mery withall, the buriall was turned to bousing *and* belly chere, morning to myrth, fasting to feasting, prayer to pastyme *and* pressing of papes, and lamenting to Lechery.[81]

In his analysis of Harman's censure of these "wayfaring bold beggars," Daryl Palmer points out that for Harman, "When plebeians take hold of hospitality, they overturn all, reversing every positive value... in an alliterative welter of 'pastime and pressing.' Even sexual preference submits to revision."[82] Of interest here is that whereas Harman condemns the beggars in general, no special condemnation is reserved for the two women. Whatever the "espeycall cause" for them to "lay alone to gether," it evidently is not one that much troubles Harman.

If, indeed, their motivation for "lay[ing] alone to gether" is mutual affection and desire (and not the need to sleep unmolested), Harman would not be alone in his indifference. Further up in the social scale and across the English Channel, Pierre de Bourdeille, Seigneur de Brantôme, urbane chronicler of the sixteenth-century French court, poses the question in response to a depiction by Martial: "if two ladies are amorous one of another, as one can find, for such pairs are today often seen sleeping together, in the fashion called in imitation of the learned Lesbian Sappho, *donna con donna*, can they be said to commit adultery and by their joint act make their husbands cuckolds?"[83] Whether one considers Brantôme's *Recuiel des dames* (*Lives of Fair and Gallant Ladies*) fiction or fact, gossip or history, this courtly chronicle provides important insight into the ways in which antique models provided a lexicon, and chastity offered an imaginative license, for female homoeroticism. Dedicating an entire section of his First Essay to this question, Brantôme ambles through a number of instances drawn from Martial and Lucian, repeats rumors about "such women and many Lesbians too, in France, in Italy and in Spain, in Turkey, Greece, and other places," and alludes to his own knowledge of elite French women. Alternating his discourse with "I have known" and "I have heard," Brantôme suggests that "where the women are recluses, and do not enjoy complete freedom, the practice is most developed," and that "[i]n our own France too such women are quite common" – although he repeats the xenophobic commonplace that "the fashion" was imported from "Italy by a lady of quality."[84]

Brantôme's urbane indifference stems in part from his estimation of such female pleasures as "merely the apprenticeship to the great business with men."[85] However, several of his examples belie his attempt to minimize the import of these liaisons, instead illuminating the lifelong homoerotic attachments of some women, as well as the ability of these relationships to intervene in marital fortunes. One woman, he maintained, "was [financially] supporting the girl in question and reserving her for her personal consumption alone."[86] More striking, Brantôme suggests that women pursue erotic liaisons with women because such affairs do not incur the social scandal of a premarital or adulterous affair with a man or the dangers of abortion or infanticide. Calling himself neither "their censor nor ... their husband," Brantôme maintains that "unmarried girls and widows may be excused for liking such frivolous, vain pleasures, and preferring to give themselves to each other thus and so get rid of their heat than to resort to men and be put in the family way and dishonoured by them, or have to get rid of their fruit." As for the homoerotic exploits of married women: "the men are not cuckolded by it."[87] Since women in lust are, in humoral psychophysiology, too hot, and thus in danger of upsetting their humoral balance, it makes sense to Brantôme that they relieve themselves of their excess heat in a manner that will not result in pregnancy.

Men are not cuckolded by *donna con donna* – despite the fact that Brantôme refers to Lucian's description of how such women "copulate like men, copulating with lascivious devices, far-fetched and monstrous, sterile things,"[88] and then describes how "these feminine love-makings are practised in two different ways": rubbing, which "does no harm," and using dildoes (or "godemichy"), which can cause loss of life by engendering unnatural growths in the womb. He includes an explicit description of two ladies of the court who were caught by a prince, "one with a big one between her legs, so neatly fastened on by little belts passing round the body that it looked like a natural member. She was so surprised that she did not have time to take it off, so much so, indeed, that the Prince persuaded her there and then to demonstrate how the two of them did it."[89] Brantôme concludes his chapter saying, "I could have gone on adding to endlessly, far more than I have done, for I have ample material and lengthy too."[90] The modern reader may resent Brantôme's attempt to reduce the significance of *donna con donna* even as he indulges in the titillation it offers. Nonetheless, his essay makes the case for the erotic potential of chastity quite dramatically. If erotic behaviors among women, including the use of dildoes, do not cuckold men, then it would seem that such pleasures fit within chastity's definitional embrace.

Brantôme's view, it must be said, was not widely articulated. Indeed, Montaigne, perhaps in reaction to the stories about tribades that he encountered during his travels, writes in a rather different vein. During a discussion of his delight in social intercourse with "beautiful and [B] honourable women," Montaigne remarks on the invidious deceptions of men in their quest of sex; he then glancingly refers to what women do in return: "Now from the regular routine treachery of men nowadays there necessarily results what experience already shows us: *to escape us, women turn in on themselves and have recourse to themselves or to other women*; or else they, on their side, follow the example we give them, play their part in the farce and join in the business without passion concern or love."[91]

The above discussion moves back and forth in time while traversing England, the European continent, and North America in order to present on a broad canvas the contours of female homoeroticism in the early modern period. Further archival research into local social conditions and controversies no doubt will nuance this synopsis, and enable more specific studies of temporal changes as well as comparative analyses of national, religious, political, and community differences. Wills, household itineraries, correspondence, and funeral monuments all need to be scrutinized with an eye looking for the many ways women lived and loved. But even with the expectation that our knowledge will change as such materials come to light, we know enough now to inform our reading, as well as future performances, of Shakespeare's plays.

The homoeroticism entailed in Shakespearean crossdressing has already been analyzed by several critics, myself included; indeed, interest in theatrical transvestism – whether that of the boy actor playing female roles or that of the crossdressed heroine – offered literary critics an initial point of access to the textualization of homoerotic desire. Let us consider briefly one crossdressing play that has figured centrally in critical discussions of Shakespearean gender and sexuality. In *Twelfth Night*, when Viola/Cesario confronts the implications of a love token sent to her by Olivia, she denounces her own masculine costume, describes disguise as a wickedness and herself as a "poor monster" (2.2.34). As many commentators have recognized, in condemning herself as a monster, Cesario employs the vernacular term for hermaphrodite,[92] while also indicating the "poor" nature of her sexual equipment. No critic, however, has pursued the erotic rather than gender implications of this association by taking up the historical point that hermaphrodites often were accused of being tribades and forced to undergo a medical examination. Similarly, Cesario's oft-cited bawdy joke just prior to being forced into a duel with Sir Andrew – "A little thing would make me tell them how much I lack of a man" (3.4.302–03) – has been interpreted as a comically abject *double entendre* that resounds against women's anatomy. Critics have neglected to notice that these repeated invocations of anatomical "lack" implicitly invite the audience to perform imaginatively the kind of scopic investigation a woman accused of tribadism might face. Cesario's allusion to the absence of a penis wittily avows the feminine nature of her body, but it also begs the question: why is this avowal necessary?

In contemporary criticism Cesario's self-indictment implicitly has served as a summation of early modern attitudes toward female homoeroticism: any woman desirous of another woman could only be viewed as monstrous. Yet, this orthodox position is precisely what much of the action of the play contests. The meaning of femininity has been called into question not only by Cesario's masculine costume – which, despite the audience's awareness of the ruse, is convincing enough to fool the other characters – but by her obvious delight in playing the erotic part of the man. Both the enjoyment with which she stands in for Orsino in wooing Olivia and the extent to which she elicits Olivia's desire carry a potent homoerotic charge. As a surrogate for the Duke, Cesario speaks some of the most beautiful love lyrics in the play. In response to Olivia's question about how she would love her, Cesario vows that she would

> Make me a willow cabin at your gate,
> And call upon my soul within the house;
> Write loyal cantons of contemned love
> And sing them loud even in the dead of night;
> Halloo your name to the reverberate hills,
> And make the babbling gossip of the air

Cry out "Olivia!" O, you should not rest
Between the elements of air and earth
But you should pity me! (1.5.263–71)

It is as object of another woman's desire that Cesario finds her own erotic voice. Olivia's response to this wooing – "You might do much" (272) – marks the moment when the mournful lady gives her heart to the woman she takes for a man.[93] The erotic tension between Cesario and Olivia (and the pleasure the audience takes in this tension) does much to explain why Cesario does not forsake her masculine costume when the confusions her impersonation have wrought threaten her with violence. What is more, the emphasis at the play's conclusion on finding Cesario's "women's weeds" (5.1.270) so as to reconfirm her female gender, gestures toward common legal practice regarding confirmed hermaphrodites.

Recognition of the eroticism entailed in moments that call attention to her gender-bending allows us better to understand Cesario's desire for Orsino, not in terms of her character's capitulation to romantic love (by which standards it is palpably incomprehensible, as many commentators admit), but in terms of the structural force of the courtship plot. Because marriage and service are presented as the only legitimate social currencies in this drama, the drive toward marriage (and out of service) overpowers the erotic play – and the erotic wit – that is so at the heart of *Twelfth Night*'s theatrical magic.[94] The erotic friction between Olivia and Cesario, which intensifies until Cesario is threatened with bodily harm, is resolved structurally rather than characterologically with the substitution of Sebastian for Cesario. In the course of the play's action, Shakespeare teases his audience with a culturally available, if implicit, association between crossdressers, hermaphrodites, and tribades; then, through the force of the marriage plot, the audience's attention ultimately is directed away from the specter of such erotic possibilities. Contemporary directors of *Twelfth Night* thus have a choice: they can dramatize the associations between Cesario's transgressions of gender and eroticism, or they can minimize such connections in a production shorn of the queerness of history.[95]

Let us next consider at greater length *A Midsummer Night's Dream*, one of Shakespeare's most popular,[96] and ostensibly one of his most heterosexual, plays.[97] Unlike *Twelfth Night*, *As You Like It*, *The Merchant of Venice*, and *The Two Gentlemen of Verona*, no crossdressing female character authorizes a homoerotic reading of this play. Rather, in its story of the Athenian lovers, *A Midsummer Night's Dream* depicts a close female friendship disrupted by jealousy and competition for men. But just as the gender politics of this play are fractured and inconsistent, presenting, as Louis Montrose has argued, early modern "precepts of domestic authority" as a matter of contestation and dispute, so too the erotic politics of this play convey a variety of affections and desires that must be rejected or elided for the courtship plot to conclude in patriarchal marriage.⁹⁸ If these alternative desires do not interrupt the structural movement toward the blessing of the bride-bed in the final act (indeed, one could argue that they provide part of the foundation for that movement), they nonetheless register, *behind the seen*, a range of female affiliations. Rather than offer a reading of *A Midsummer Night's Dream*, in what follows I employ the play heuristically, using its representational traces of female intimacy to speculate further about possible sites of homoerotic desire.

Both the possibility and structural elision of female intimacy are intimated early in the play when Hermia begins to unfold to Helena her plan to elope with Lysander: "in the wood where often you and I / Upon faint primrose beds were wont to lie, / Emptying our bosoms of their counsel sweet, / There my Lysander and myself shall meet" (1.1.214–17). The place where, day after day, these close friends chatted, relaxed, sought and offered advice, has now become the place of heterosexual assignation, as girlhood affections are displaced by the social imperatives of patriarchal marriage. But rather than simply reiterate the structural exigencies of the conventional courtship plot, and thereby reassert without question the force of dramatic and ideological orthodoxy, let us focus for a moment on the significance of the primrose *bed*. Although the phrase refers to flowers rather than a piece of furniture, it nonetheless is significant that beds are thematized elsewhere in Renaissance literature as an ambiguous site of hetero- and homoerotic contact, especially in the genre of romance. For instance, in Book Four of Edmund Spenser's *The Faerie Queene*, the crossdressed Amazon Britomart interacts so amorously with the lady Amoret that Dorothy Stevens writes, "Britomart dallies more with Amoret than she ever does with [the male knight] Artegall, and it is tempting to say that at this stage of the game, she mostly feigns [as a man] in order to flirt [with a woman]. By keeping her helmet on, Britomart can afford to raise the dialogue to a higher erotic pitch, engaging in a closer intimacy than would otherwise be allowable."⁹⁹ At the same time, Britomart's removal of her helmet is swiftly followed by an "innocent" invitation to Amoret's bed:

> And eke fayre *Amoret* now freed from feare,
> More franke affection did to her afford,
> And to her bed, which she was wont forbeare,
> Now freely drew, and found right safe assurance theare.
> Where all that night they of their loues did treat,
> And hard adventures twixt themselues alone,
> That each the other gan with passion great,
> And griefull pittie priuately bemoane.¹⁰⁰

As Stevens notes, this passage is highly if ambiguously erotic, for what, precisely, is the "right safe assurance" found between these women who "now freed from feare, More franke affection" show one another? How precisely "of their loues did [they] treat," and which "hard adventures twixt themselues alone" did they "gan with passion great"? The pronouns provide no sure anchoring of who is doing what to whom.

Just as Spenser maintains the chastity of this feminine sleep-over while exploiting its erotic ambiguity, so Sir Philip Sidney mingles eroticism with chaste intimacy in the *New Arcadia* (written for his sister, Mary Sidney, the Countess of Pembroke, and her circle). Lying in bed together, the sisters Pamela and Philoclea "impoverished their clothes to enrich their bed which for that night might well scorn the shrine of Venus: and there, cherishing one another with dear though chaste embracements, with sweet though cold kisses, it might seem that love was come to play him there without dart, or that, weary of his own fires, he was there to refresh himself between their sweetbreathing lips."[101] As Stephen Orgel remarks about this passage: "I do not think it can be argued that such a scene would not have been considered overtly sexual in 1590: Sidney's insistence that the embracements were chaste, the kisses cold, are surely there to contradict the inevitable assumption that they were, respectively, libidinous and hot."[102]

In the continental romance precursors to the *New Arcadia* and *The Faerie Queene*, *Orlando Furioso* and *I ragionamenti*, the shared bed also functions as an important site of female homoerotic attraction. In Ludovico Ariosto's tale, Bradamant (who had been crossdressed as a knight) is invited to share the bed of the love-struck Fiordispina (who knows Bradamant to be a woman). All through the night Fiordispina "wept and moaned, her desire ever mounting. And if sleep did occasionally press upon her eyelids, it was but a brief sleep charged with dreams in which it seemed to her that Heaven had allotted to her a Bradamant transformed into a preferable sex."[103] In Agnolo Firenzuola's *I ragionamenti*, the lady wrestling with such a desire gets just such a wish. Upon her husband's departure, the gentlewoman Lavinia "innocently" invites her new maid Lucia to share her bed. She "began to embrace and kiss Lucia most affectionately and, as may happen, her hand just strayed toward the side where one distinguishes a boy from a girl. Finding she was not a woman like herself there, she greatly wondered and drew her hand back," but eventually she "slipped under Lucia and began to excite the spot with those provocations that frolicsome girls willingly use on precocious young brats. With this game she assured herself that it was not a spirit bewitched and that she had not seen amiss, and she had such comfort from this as you yourself may imagine."[104] With the male Lucia crossdressed as a servant girl during the day and "innocently" sharing Lavinia's bed during the night, "[m]onths passed without anyone in the house becoming aware of anything."[105] Although the focus of Firenzuola's episode is on the secret fulfillment of male–female sex, it would be a mistake to gloss over his recognition that women's hands *do* stray when they embrace and kiss.

By the early seventeenth century in England, the pleasures of the shared bed are common enough currency to be explicitly debated in Thomas Dekker's stage play, *Satiromastix: or The Untrussing of the Humorous Poet* (1602).[106]

A gentlewoman asks her "bedfellow" why people bring "sweet hearbes and flowers" to weddings; the second gentlewoman responds: "One reason is, because tis – ô a most sweet thing to lye with a man." The first gentlewoman replies, "I thinke tis a O more more more more sweet to lye with a woman" – an effusion that incites the bawdy reply, "I warrant all men are of thy minde" (1.1.16–21). In Richard Brome's play, *The Antipodes* (1640), a similar reference to maids lying in bed becomes the means for emphasizing a married woman's sexual ignorance and an occasion for homoerotic bawdy.[107] Martha Joyless, suffering from a virgin's melancholy straight out of Robert Burton, is upset that her marriage has never been consummated: "He neer put child nor anything towards it yet / To me to making" (1.3). At the same time, she expresses ignorance about the actual means of making children:

> For were I now to dye, I cannot guesse
> What a man do's in child-getting. I remember
> A wanton mayd once lay with me, and kiss'd
> And clip't, and clapt me strangely, and then wish'd
> That I had beene a man to have got her with childe.
> What must I then ha' done, or (good now tell me)
> What has your husband done to you?

Barbara, her interlocutor, says in an aside, "Was ever / Such a poore peece of innocence, three yeeres married?" She then asks directly: "Does not your husband use to lye with you?" Martha's answer is full of earnest ignorance:

> Yes he dos use to lye with me, but he do's not
> Lye with me to use me as she should, I feare,
> Nor doe I know to teach him, will you tell me,
> Ill lye with you and practise if you please.
> Pray take me for a night or two: or take
> My husband and instruct him, But one night,
> Our countrey folkes will say, you London wives
> Doe not lye every night with your owne husbands. (1.3)

The focus throughout is on Martha's "simplicity" which leads her into unintentional puns; not only is she willing to expose her ignorance of sexual matters, but she is so eager for instruction that she would place both herself and her husband in Barbara's bed. Her lack of knowledge about the mechanics of intercourse is curiously accommodating to her memory of a "wanton mayd" who kissed, clipped, and clapped her. Indeed, this experience is depicted as Martha's only source of erotic knowledge, including the knowledge that women cannot impregnate one another. Modern editors have glossed "clipp'd and clapp'd" as "embraced and fondled passionately"[108] as well as "embraced and patted" – with the added suggestion that clapped "may imply something more firmly administered; 'slap and tickle' is a recent equivalent."[109] Such erotic language clarifies that the maid's wantonness defies modern gendered expectations of activity and passivity. Her behavior, which takes the form of aggressive, even forceful erotic play along with the desire to be penetrated and impregnated, provides a mirror to Martha's own ecumenical position regarding whether it be she or her husband to receive Barbara's erotic instruction.

In his analysis of the passage from *Satiromastix*, Mario DiGangi stresses how a "woman's desire for a woman can be more safely represented within the confines of a conditional statement that suggests her 'proper' desire for a man" – a description broadly applicable to the situations of the romance heroines discussed above. He reads the second gentlewoman's bawdy repartee as serving "to erase or subsume female homoeroticism by shifting the terrain away from any consideration of a female desiring subject towards the heteroerotic desire felt by 'all men.'"[110] This recognition of the move toward ideological containment is an accurate appraisal, from which any further analysis of the representation of homoeroticism must devolve. But the critical focus on the power of restraint also evacuates the agency of the characters and thus reproduces the containment it seeks to expose. While I agree that attempts to minimize and trivialize are a regular feature of representations of female erotic intimacy, from Brantôme to Brome, I am not convinced that this feature actually accomplishes what it sets out to do; in the very act of articulating alternatives, a faultline in the dominant ideology is exposed. The ideology of chastity depends on the belief that, although women may share beds, caresses, and kisses, such phenomena do not "count" as sex. Yet, what "counts" is precisely what is thematized in both of these plays – and however they may attempt to mitigate a homoerotic response (in either the dramatic character or the audience/reader) their efforts of containment are insecure. In *The Antipodes*, part of what is at stake in this private talk among women is knowingness about eroticism, including female–female sex. In *Satiromastix*, efforts to control behavior are undermined by the rhetoric of amplitude employed by the first gentlewoman. Her insistence that it is "more more more more sweet to lye with a woman" not only poses a challenge to the second woman's initial characterization of what is "most sweet," but does so through a quantifying idiom that appropriates and destabilizes the conventional patriarchal surety that phallic male (hetero)sexuality is the *more*, compared to the woman's *less*. In both cases, the overt bawdiness suggests a cultural awareness of the presence, as well as the ambiguous epistemological status, of female–female eroticism.

Such faultlines open at the level of textual editing as well. In the original 1640 edition of *The Antipodes*, the lines "Yes he do's use to lye with me, but he do's not / Lye with me to use me as she should, I feare," manifests a confusion at the level of pronoun, since the "she" of the second line grammatically refers to Martha's husband. Modern editors have handled this textual crux by amending "she" to "he,"[111] their editorial assumptions of foul case or foul copy buttressed by unacknowledged assumptions of a heteronormative syntax. But in the context of Martha's complaint about her husband's lack of sexual interest and her (fond?) memory of the kissing, clipping, and clapping of the "wanton mayd," such a confusion in the gender of the subject – such a queering, in other words – is thematically appropriate and characterologically consistent. The belated imposition of such heteronorms, as well as their instability, was brought home to me while reading my own library's copy of the 1640 edition. Here, an assiduous if overzealous reader had taken upon him/herself to meticulously block out the letter "s" with a neat column of pencil, thereby making the pronominal grammar conform to heterosexual expectations. Yet, in the very act of defacing the 1640 edition, this reader had left a palpable material trace of the very textual queerness s/he sought to eradicate.[112]

The fact that *The Antipodes*, *Satiromastix*, and *A Midsummer Night's Dream*, like their romance precursors, all use the trope of the household (or primrose) bed and the metaphor of "lying together" to represent the availability of female–female intimacies suggests that specific physical spaces provided women access to bodily intimacy away from the scrutiny of fathers and husbands. As recent work on place and space informs us, one's physical location within a specific locale or geography informs the subjectivity constructed therein; space is not just a backdrop for the subject, it helps to constitute the subject and her desires.[113] Approaching the history of *lesbianism* through spatial terms allows us to see the potentials for female–female intimacy that existed alongside the oft-noted trope of the female *hortus conclusus* or "the body enclosed."[114] For whereas the dominant ideology maintained that the closed door of the household contributed to a closed body and closed mouth,[115] certain enclosures *within* the patriarchal household – the bed, the bedchamber – might have been productive of female affectivity, where bodies and mouths sought and found their own pleasures. Thus, although we would err in conceptualizing early modern beds and bedchambers as private, they nevertheless seem to have functioned as a space *between* visibilities: their very "transparency," to invoke Hull, seems to have sanctioned an erotic architecture eccentric to patriarchal mandates. The *hortus conclusus*, in other words, may have functioned occasionally as a *locus amoenus*.

Certain enclosures located *outside* the household also may have permitted some women a space of independence and intimacy. One such locus was the convent. As "brides of Christ," nuns were relieved of many of the duties of patriarchal marriage, including reproductive labor. They experienced considerable opportunities for political, emotional, and erotic independence within a female community of work and support that, while marginal geographically and politically, nonetheless figured importantly even in a post-Reformation culture. The ambivalent relation of female monastic life to patriarchal culture has been explored by a generation of feminists; and although it is not my intent to claim the cloister as a *de facto lesbian* space, I do want to insist on its potential as a site for erotic contact.[116]

Martin Luther set the tone of much anti-Catholic polemic when he characterized Catholic monks as whores of the devil, the Pope as an arch whore, and the church as the whore's anus. Given Luther's association of popery with sodomitical vice, it hardly is surprising that anti-Catholic polemic alleged that nuns performed all manner of "unnatural vice." Although most frequently nuns were accused of fornication with monks and priests, the litany of debauchery was obsessively inclusive. In *Actes of the Englishe Votaryes*, for instance, the radical Puritan John Bale presents the nun as one among others who, with their "prodygyouse lustes of uncleanesse . . . leavying the naturall use of women . . . have brent in their owne lustes one to an other . . . man wyth man . . . monke with monke, nonne with nonne, fryre with fryre & prest with prest." In Bale's diatribe, chastity itself is "a fylthy Sodome," for the church of Rome is a "preposterus *amor*, a love out of order or a love agaynst kynde."[117] In this logic, same-sex transgressions are fostered by the innate hypocrisy of Catholics and the deprivations of sex-segregation: celibate, and therefore burning in lust, the wily nun is imagined to satisfy her lust either with other hypocrites like herself or, particularly egregious, with unsuspecting novitiates. In his colloquy, "Virgo misogamos" or "The Girl with No Interest in Marriage," Erasmus implies, but never directly states, a similar suspicion through the voice of his stand-in, Eubulus, who is attempting to dissuade the seventeen-year-old Catharine from entering a convent against her parents' wishes:

EUBULUS: What's more, not everything's virginal among those virgins in other respects, either.
CATHARINE: No? Why not, if you please?
EUBULUS: Because there are more who copy Sappho's behavior than share her talent.
CATHARINE: I don't quite understand what you mean.
EUBULUS: And I say these things in order that the time may not come when you do understand, my dear Catharine.[118]

The urbanity of Erasmus's tone and his recognition of Sappho's poetic talent do not moderate the force of his anti-monastic condemnation. Other literary texts continue to exploit the connection between women's eroticism, gender separatism, and heresy up through the religious upheavals of the seventeenth century. These associations provide a central trope, for instance, for Andrew Marvell's "Upon Appleton House," which figures the nun's "slippery tongue" as the agent of a religious and erotic apostasy, a kind of "spiritual cunnilingus,"[119] even as the nuns themselves bespeak their homoerotic desire in terms of chaste insignificance:

> Each Night among us to your side
> Appoint a fresh and Virgin Bride;
> Whom if our Lord at midnight find,
> Yet Neither should be left behind.
> Where you may lye as chast in Bed,
> As Pearls together billeted.
> All Night embracing Arm in Arm,
> Like Chrystal pure with Cotton warm.[120]

On a more positive note, the libidinal aspects of devotion, both Catholic and Protestant, may have provided access to homoerotic bonds, particularly within the experience of ecstatic mysticism.[121] Although erotic contact was prohibited by monastic rules that, for instance, barred nuns from sleeping together and mandated that a lamp burn in sleeping quarters, a series of ecclesiastical investigations of the Italian abbess, Benedetta Carlini, reveals homoeroticism to be at the heart of her mystic experience.[122] In addition, the import of devotional treatises about Mary (many of them dedicated to women patrons), the circulation of desire through a feminized Christ, and the iconography of the Virgin and female saints also may have furthered homoaffiliations.[123]

By the time Shakespeare began writing plays, English monasteries and convents had been dissolved by royal decree, and English Catholics had become a persecuted minority; hence, convent life was unattainable to any except the most elite of Catholic daughters, who were sent to the continent, particularly northern France, for education by their recusant families.[124] Nonetheless, the nunnery appears frequently in Shakespeare's plays, usually as a metaphor for bawdy (Hamlet's imperious command to Ophelia to "get thee to a nunnery" puns on the double meaning of "nunnery" as convent and brothel) or as an indication of perverse female willfulness (Isabella's determination to enter the novitiate in *Measure for Measure*). Women's religious vocation consistently is viewed by male characters as a fate worse than death, as when, in *A Midsummer Night's Dream*, Duke Theseus pronounces this edict on what will befall Hermia if she refuses to wed Demetrius:

> Either to die the death, or to abjure
> Forever the society of men.
> Therefore, fair Hermia, question your desires,
> Know of your youth, examine well your blood,
> Whether, if you yield not to your father's choice,
> You can endure the livery of a nun,
> For aye to be in shady cloister mew'd,
> To live a barren sister all your life,
> Chanting faint hymns to the cold fruitless moon.

> Thrice blessed they that master so their blood
> To undergo such maiden pilgrimage;
> But earthlier happy is the rose distill'd,
> Than that which withering on the virgin thorn
> Grows, lives, and dies in single blessedness. (1.1.65–78)

Despite Theseus's post-Reformation vision of a withered, barren virginity, the threat of abjuring "forever the society of men" and "enduring the livery of a nun" may not have been the correlative to death that he and scores of critics have made it out to be.[125] Hermia's appropriation of Theseus's rhetoric in her answer, "So will I grow, so live, so die, my lord" (1.1.79), resourcefully affirms the possibility of growth and life within a religious sisterhood. I am not suggesting that Hermia is represented as *wanting* to enter the novitiate; this character wants to marry Lysander. Yet, it is important to recognize that, faced with what Theseus figures as a kind of death, Shakespeare permits Hermia to imagine a kind of life. And monastic life, for thousands of actual women across Europe, undoubtedly meant that their most generative and sustaining bonds were found in the company of other women.

That Hermia has been the recipient of intense female affection is clear from Helena's reminiscence about their friendship:

> We, Hermia, like two artificial gods,
> Have with our needles created both one flower,
> Both on one sampler, sitting on one cushion,
> Both warbling of one song, both in one key,
> As if our hands, our sides, voices, and minds
> Had been incorporate. (3.2.203–08)

The terms of Hermia's appeal will be the subject of further analysis in chapter 4. For now, I merely want to echo Sylvia Gimenez's observation that *A Midsummer Night's Dream* associates female intimacies with all-female spaces that in various ways elude patriarchal control: in addition to the "primrose bed" and what Gimenez calls Helena and Hermia's adolescent "sewing circle," Hippolyta is queen of Amazonia; Titania and her votaress gossip on the Indian shore; Lysander's widowed aunt lives seven leagues from Athens; and an unnamed vestal virgin wings her way across the sky, away from Cupid's arrow.[126]

The mythical Amazons provided the prototype of female autonomy in this period. Their alleged military prowess, practice of male infanticide, and instrumental use of men for reproduction were considered the height of female insubordination; accordingly, Amazons often were viewed as embodying a dangerous and unnatural political self-sufficiency. According to Louis Montrose, "Amazonian mythology seems symbolically to embody and to control a collective anxiety about the power of the female not only to dominate or reject the male but to create and destroy him."[127] Both Montrose and Kathryn Schwarz imply that legends about Amazons at the margins of the known world are a repository of male castration anxiety: "Amazon myth plays out the fear that the object of desire, the body looked at or, in the case of the Amazon quest, looked *for*, may itself possess sexual agency: that all women might be sexually voracious, given half a chance."[128]

Given this emphasis on Amazons' agency and hostility to men (not to mention the European predisposition to view foreign women as unnatural in their sexual tastes), it seems worthwhile to ask whether Amazons ever were associated with same-gender desire. In general, Amazons seem not to have been interpreted routinely as erotic separatists. According to Schwarz, "the Amazons of English Renaissance texts are aggressively implicated in social structures; in narrative after narrative they are not lesbian separatists or ritualized descendants of goddesses but mothers, lovers, and in some cases wives."[129] In her most recent work, Schwarz modifies this account to note the presence of "a powerful and explicit Amazonian discourse of desire between women." "The catch," however, "is that one of the women is a man."[130] Yet, one masque performed in 1618 at the country house of Sir Thomas Beaumont suggests that the move from female separatism to erotic separatism was neither so far-fetched nor dependent necessarily on transvestism. Performed as a country-house entertainment celebrating the wedding of Lady Frances Devereux and Sir William Seymour, the Cole–Orton masque figures six female masquers representing the traditional feminine virtues.[131] With their masculine counterparts mysteriously imprisoned by Juno and Iris, the women masquers descend on stage while a song encourages them to enact "the precedencie of female virtue":

> Rejoice, all woman kinde,
> Juno haes her will of Jove.
> Each of you that list to prove,
> shall easie conquest finde.
> Be not, o be not blind,
> But know your strength & your own Vertues see
> which in everie Several grace
> of the mind, or of the face,
> Gives women right to have Prioritie.   (p. 334, lines 26–34)

The extraordinary suggestion that women not only deserve equality with men but possess more virtue, leads to the following song:

> Brave Amazonian Dames
> Made no count of Mankind but
> for a fitt to be at the Rutt.
> Free fier gives the brightest flames;
> Menns overawing tames
> And Pedantlike our active Spirits smother.

> Learne, Virgins, to live free;
> Alass, would it might bee,
> woemen could live & lie with one another! (p. 334, lines 35–43)

Penned during the apex of the pamphlet controversy over women's roles and explicitly staging social and amorous conflict between men and women, the Cole–Orton masque expresses in this song the fantasy of women living apart from men, taking one another as sexual partners, and making no account of men except for erotic pleasure (with a possible bawdy pun on "count" as cunt). The heavily conditional nature of the two final lines, however, attempts to undercut precisely this fantasy by reinscribing the conventional topos of impossibility; and, indeed, this portion of the masque concludes with a dance celebrating the equality and harmony of masculine and feminine virtues, figured through the trope of male–female coupling:

> Mix then and together goe,
> This be hers, and that be thine;
> All jarrs end by coupling so,
> 'Tis not long to Valentine. (p. 335, lines 30–33)

In this instance at least, mythological Amazons provided the masque audience with a titillating vision of a world in which women "could live & lie with one another," while also reasserting the impossibility of such a world. Amazons likewise are ascribed a female–centered eroticism by Brantôme, who registers his agreement with Martial that "it is much better for a woman to be virile, or a real amazon, or lubricious in this way, than for a man to be feminine... for the more mannish they are the more courageous they are."[132]

Hippolyta, of course, has been wooed by Theseus's sword, her love won by the injuries done to her (1.1.16–17). If her martial courtship renders Hippolyta's female separatism and possible erotic connections a thing of the past (a view reiterated by another Hippolyta in Shakespeare and Fletcher's *The Two Noble Kinsmen*), the faerie queen Titania carries the implications of her female intimacies into her marital present. In a speech both seductive and troubling, Titania describes her relationship to the mother of the "Indian boy," who is the ostensible cause of the conflict between her and Oberon:

> The fairy land buys not the child of me.
> His mother was a vot'ress of my order,
> And in the spiced Indian air, by night,
> Full often hath she gossiped by my side,
> And sat with me on Neptune's yellow sands,
> Marking th' embarked traders on the flood,
> When we have laughed to see the sails conceive
> And grow big-bellied with the wanton wind;
> Which she with pretty and with swimming gait

> Following – her womb then rich with my young squire –
> Would imitate, and sail upon the land
> To fetch me trifles, and return again,
> As from a voyage, rich with merchandise.
> But she, being mortal, of that boy did die.
> And for her sake do I rear up her boy;
> And for her sake I will not part with him.　　　　　(2.1.122–37)

This friendship, which has survived marriage, the bearing of children, and death, remains so compelling that Titania risks the wrath of Oberon by refusing to relinquish the child. That the "lovely boy" was "stolen" from his father, an "Indian king" (2.1.22), evidently at Titania's behest, makes clear that what is at stake in this domestic quarrel is Titania's assertion of female affection and autonomy over the authority of both father figures. Titania is psychologically threatening precisely to the degree that she upsets the homosocial "traffic in women" formally negotiated by Egeus and Theseus in the opening scene, and implicitly played out by Demetrius and Lysander in the forest.[133] By inverting the gendered relations of the homosocial triangle, Titania not only "effeminizes" the boy but usurps patriarchal power, fracturing Oberon's pretension to control. The child is the manifest link of a prior affection between women that is associated with their shared fecundity and maternal largess. With the repetition of the line, "And for her sake," and her later reiteration that she will not part with the boy, "Not for thy fairy kingdom" (2.1.144), Titania insists on the primacy and loyalty of female bonds. Her affront motivates Oberon's attempt to incapacitate Titania's body, to humiliate her erotically, to capture the boy, and secure him for martial, exclusively masculine, purposes.

Titania's bond with her votaress fails to occasion full admiration, however, for the pleasure she takes in her beloved friend is articulated through a mercantile rhetoric implicated in the colonization of both Old World and New. The Indian boy, after all, has been "stolen" from his homeland and his father. As Margo Hendricks notes in her reading of Titania's speech: "Titania evokes not only the exotic presence of the Indian woman's native land but also the power of the 'traders' to invade and domesticate India and, aided by the 'wanton wind,' return to Europe 'rich with merchandise.' In Shakespeare's 'poetic geography,' India becomes the commodified space of a racialized feminine eroticism."[134] It is the votaress who serves Titania's fancies, who fetches her trifles; and it is the faerie queen who steals the most fetishized piece of "merchandise" in the play, the dramatic structure of which depends upon a series of psychic and material exchanges (e.g., Lysander for Helena in Hermia's affection; Helena for Hermia in Lysander's attraction; Demetrius for Lysander in Helena's attraction; Lysander for Demetrius in Egeus's approval, etc.). Furthermore, the ease with which Titania stands in for the dead loved one, acting as a surrogate mother to the boy, enacts a dubious form of identification and substitution. At the exoticized Indian shore, in the "spiced Indian [night] air," racial differences, erotic possibilities, and gender identifications intersect in an ambivalent coding of bodies and bonds. If the reputed affection shared between Titania and her votaress complicates the relation between trading partners, their colonial dynamic equally problematizes their intimacy, even as it offers an alternative to the patriarchal structures of Oberon's faerie kingdom.

Perhaps the most provocative figure of female erotic autonomy and resistance to patriarchal affiliation in *A Midsummer Night's Dream* is the one about whom we know the least. As Oberon hatches his plan to humiliate Titania, he describes to Puck "a fair vestal throned by the west," whom Cupid attempted to pierce with his arrow. But "Cupid's fiery shaft / [was] Quench'd in the chaste beams of the wat'ry moon, / And the imperial vot'ress passed on, / In maiden meditation, fancy-free" (2.1.161–64). With her story narrated by Oberon as part of the prehistory of the dramatic action, this "imperial vot'ress" is an absent presence, never appearing on stage – she literally exists *behind the seen*. Yet, it is she who enables all of the subsequent action: her escape leads to the "wounding" of the "little western flower" whose magic nectar becomes the faerie potion Puck uses to wreak havoc among Titania and the Athenian lovers. The fact that the vestal virgin remains unpenetrated by Cupid's "fiery shaft" releases into the world a principle of uncontrolled libido. Her pharmaceutical ghostly presence disturbs the closure of the courtship plot, for not only do the lovers fall in and out of love based on the potion, but Demetrius is never freed from the effects of the drug.[135] That this figure of maiden integrity and self-sufficiency is connected in scholars' minds to another "imperial vot'ress," Queen Elizabeth, provides a point of entry into the chaste erotics of Elizabeth's court that will be explored in chapter 3.[136]

At the same time, this figure might have evoked more immediate associations. That a virgin might pass on, "in maiden meditation, fancy-free," was not all that unusual in Shakespeare's time. Although patriarchal ideology mandated the transfer of daughters directly from the governance of a father to the protection of a husband, and in practice marriage was the usual experience of most European women, demographic and legal research reveals that almost 20 percent of adult women in northwestern Europe never married. While reasons for this high rate of lifelong singleness are complex, and proportions varied across region, locale, and time, there were more singlewomen in northern than southern Europe, they were connected more often to poor than elite households, and their proportions grew over the sixteenth and seventeenth centuries.[137] Particularly in urban centers, singlewomen often worked outside the home, usually in domestic service or apprenticeship and sometimes in all-female guilds. Many such women lived in their fathers' or brothers' households; others lived together, often under the auspices of charitable communities (*Béguinages*, widows' hospices, houses for reformed prostitutes, hospitals for poor and immigrant women). In fact, at any given time, most adult women in England were not married (they were either widowed or never married); in addition, most widows did not remarry. Probably half of all singlewomen headed households or lived alone, and there were more of them doing so than singlemen.[138] In London for much of the seventeenth century, around 15 percent of households were headed by women; the proportion in rural areas hovered around 20 percent.[139] At any moment in time, the number of singlewomen could be significantly higher, if one includes widows and adult women who may have married later. Studies of two English communities at both ends of the early modern period demonstrate the high number of singlewomen: in Coventry in 1523, singlewomen made up at least 38 percent of the adult female population, while in Southampton in 1696, they comprised 35 percent.[140]

Two funeral monuments located in Westminster Abbey erected near the end of our period testify to the existence of unmarried women living together in terms that suggest the intensity of their friendships while also underscoring the compatibility of female intimacies to the early modern household.[142] The monument of Mary Kendall, commissioned by her cousin, Captain Charles Kendall, is located in the chapel of St. John the Baptist.[141] On her tomb, an effigy of Mary Kendall is shown kneeling in prayer (figure 4). Under her figure, the inscription reads:

This Monument was Erected by Capt. CHARLES KENDALL

Mrs MARY KENDALL,

Daughter of Thomas Kendall Esqr,	*These admirable Qualitys,*
And of Mrs Mary Hallet, his Wife,	*In which She was eqall'd by Few of her Sex,*
Of Killigarth, in Cornwall,	*Surpass'd by None,*
Was born at Westm^r. Nov. 8. 1677.	*Render'd Her every way worthy*
And dy'd at Epsome, March 4. 17$\frac{09}{10}$.	*Of that close Union & Friendship,*
Having reach'd the full Term	*In which She liv'd, with*
Of her blessed Saviours Life:	*The Lady* CATHARINE IONES;
And study'd to imitate	*And, in testimony of which, She desir'd,*
His spotless Example.	*That even their Ashes, after Death,*
She had great Virtues,	*Might not be divided:*
And as great a desire of Concealing them:	*And therefore, order'd her Selfe*
Was of a Severe Life,	*Here to be interr'd,*
But of an Easy Conversation;	*Where, She knew, that Excellent Lady*
Courteous to All, yet strictly Sincere;	*Design'd one day, to rest,*
Humble, without Meanness;	*Near the Grave of her Belov'd*
Beneficent, without Ostentation;	*And Religious Mother,*
Devout, without Superstition.	ELIZABETH *Countess of* RANELAGH.

Although Mary Kendall may have been married at one time – it is unclear if Mrs. is merely a title of respect – no mention is made of her husband; rather, her "close Union & Friendship" with Lady Catharine Jones is presented as

Setting the stage behind the seen

Figure 4 Funeral Monument of Mary Kendall (1710), Westminster Abbey, London.

the defining relationship of her life, one which she hoped to continue after death. At the same time – and this is crucial for our understanding of the meaning accorded to female intimacies in this period – the ties celebrated here are embedded firmly within larger social arrangements. The burial register for Westminster Abbey records not only Mary Kendall's burial on March 13, 1709/10, but also that of Lady Catharine Jones (April 23, 1740) and, as the tomb inscription would lead us to expect, other members of her Ladyship's immediate family: her mother, the Countess of Ranelagh (August 3, 1695); her father, the Right Hon. Richard Jones, Viscount and Earl of Ranelagh (January 10, 1711/12); her sister, Elizabeth the Countess Dowager of Kildare (April 22, 1758). All of them were interred in the small secluded chapel of St. John the Baptist, outside the choir screen on the north side of the high altar.[143] The monument extolling the relationship of Mary Kendall to Lady Catharine Jones is located, in other words, in what appears to be a family mausoleum of the Earl of Ranelagh. This, plus the fact that Mary Kendall's tomb was erected by Captain Kendall, Mary Kendall's residuary legatee (the son of a merchant, but a gentleman by virtue of his commission), suggests that more is at stake in the material presence of this monument than loving bonds between women. On the one hand, the rhetoric of the inscription, composed as it was by Captain Kendall, publicly marks the link of his family to the family of the Earl of Ranelagh; the "close Union & Friendship" lauded here is not only between two women, but between two families. On the other hand, the creation of a family mausoleum in a church was a practice that, through the payment of burial fees designated for the support of the poor, reenacted in death the social bonds that a household (ideally) was supposed to have had with the society around it. The embeddedness of Mary Kendall's tomb in a network of such obligations does not thereby lessen the import of her love for Lady Catharine, but it does tell us that such love was located, in death as in life, within the household of the Earl of Ranelagh. In this respect, Mary Kendall is lying in death in the same bed with Lady Catharine Jones as she might have in life: within the Earl's household.

The tomb of Katharina Bovey (d. 1727), also in Westminster Abbey, goes further in suggesting the possibility of independent female agency in the building of such memorials (figure 5). After extolling Katharina Bovey's virtues, the inscription concludes with the words, "This monument was erected With the utmost respect to her Memory and Justice to her Character, By her executrix Mrs MARY POPE Who lived with her near 40 years in perfect Friendship Never once interrupted Till her much lamented Death."[144] Several editors of *The Spectator* have linked Katharina Bovey to "the Perverse widow" who figures prominently in *The Spectator*'s issue 113, of July 10, 1711, and to whom Steele dedicated volume II of *The Ladies Library*. This fictional widow is beautiful, accomplished, scholarly – and profoundly uninterested in men. First encountered

Figure 5 Funeral Monument of Katharina Bovey (1727), Westminster Abbey, London.

during a court appearance regarding her dower rights, she is the cause of the "great Affliction" deriving from "a Disappointment in Love" of Steele's friend, "Sir Roger de Coverley."[145] According to Sir Roger, the widow's perversity resides in her desire to ensnare men's hearts only to dash them against the hard edge of her brain – all while her intimate female companion, described as her "malicious Aid," looks on.[146] In the words that Steele attributes to Sir Roger,

You must understand, Sir, this perverse Woman is one of those unaccountable Creatures that secretly rejoice in the Admiration of Men, but indulge themselves in no further Consequences. Hence it is that she has ever had a Train of Admirers, and she removes from her Slaves in Town, to those in the Country, according to the Seasons of the Year. She is a reading Lady, and far gone in the Pleasures of Friendship; she is always accompanied by a Confident, who is witness to her daily Protestations against our Sex, and consequently a Barr to her first Steps towards Love, upon the Strength of her own Maxims and Declarations.[147]

According to Donald F. Bond, editor of the Oxford edition, "Mrs. Catherine Bovey (or Boevey), the supposed original of this character, became a widow in 1692, at the age of twenty-two, upon the death of her husband William Bovey. She thereupon lived in retirement in the Manor of Flaxley, near Gloucester, devoting herself to religious and charitable works, in company with a friend, Mrs. Mary Pope of Twickenham."[148] If this identification is correct, it would seem that these companions established a self-sufficient household that was indifferent to the requirements, charms, or entreaties of men. Whether considered as "far gone in the Pleasures of Friendship" or as the beneficiaries of "near 40 years in perfect Friendship," Katharina Bovey and Mary Pope have, in the elegiac actions of Mary Pope, laid claim to the forms of public expression generally reserved for the marital bond.

Such public expressions, of course, are highly ritualized; they are organized not only by the conventions of marriage, but by the requirements of social ties extraneous to the bond itself. While memorializing private grief, they also perform and attempt to construct additional social obligations; their elegiac purpose guarantees that they express ideals which may or may not correlate with actual reality. Nonetheless, these funerary performances prompt me to look more closely at Lysander's description of his widowed aunt in *A Midsummer Night's Dream*:

> I have a widow aunt, a dowager
> Of great revenue, and she hath no child.
> From Athens is her house remote seven leagues;
> And she respects me as her only son.
> There, gentle Hermia, may I marry thee,
> And to that place the sharp Athenian law
> Cannot pursue us. (1.1.157–63)

As is made clear by her "great revenue" and her physical distance from Athens, Lysander's anonymous, childless, and householding aunt exists beyond the dominant structures of patriarchal alliance and marital reproduction. Given the oft-noted correlations between erotic desire and spatial geography in *A Midsummer Night's Dream* (Athens versus the green world), the widow's "remote[ness]" from the "sharp Athenian law" affiliates her less with the patriarchal order (from which she is now widowed) than with the other spaces of female intimacy I have mapped. We can no more speculate about the widow's erotic behavior than we can about Mary Kendall's, but the description of neither woman affirms heterosexuality. Without adducing a gay version of "How many children had Lady Macbeth?" we need to remember that the term "widow" signifies a woman's status *vis-à-vis* patriarchal marriage. It indicates absolutely nothing about eroticism practiced within her household after she becomes its head – its presence, its absence, its relation to men, its relation to women.

Shakespeare's characters and images in *Twelfth Night* and *A Midsummer Night's Dream* allow us to glimpse the presence of adult singlewomen, including an unmarried heiress, a widow, and nuns, living relatively unencumbered by direct masculine rule. Reading and watching these plays, we can witness the erotic complications occasioned by a female transvestite who elicits and enjoys the desires of another woman. We can hear the pained longings expressed by one character over the loss of her intimate friend, even as they both seek marriage. These understandings, I maintain, were available as well to members of Shakespeare's audience. That audience, as recent theater history has made clear, included significant numbers of women. Queen Elizabeth so delighted in plays that she overruled attempts by City of London authorities to quell disorder by closing the public theaters, countering their civic concerns with the monarchical rejoinder that players needed to rehearse for command performances at court. The Jacobean Queen Anne "was the prime mover behind the great series of masques that were the most distinctive feature of Jacobean Court entertainment,"[149] initiating the practice of the queen and her ladies silently dancing in masques.[150] Charles I's queen, Henrietta Maria, likewise "took command of the royal theatricals, commissioning plays themselves, and where necessary overruling the dramatic censor";[151] she and her ladies not only danced during the masques, but spoke during pastorals, thus incurring the notorious wrath of the Puritan polemicist William Prynne. Such courtly occasions were not uniformly decorous. Costume designs for masques by Inigo Jones, for instance, depict women with bare breasts,[152] and while we do not know if these costumes were used in performance, we do know that during a masque and pastoral of Queen Henrietta Maria, it was "the masculine dress of some of the ladies which raised the eyebrows."[153]

It was not only noblewomen who had access to theatrical entertainments, including plays from the public repertoire performed at court. Merchant wives, apple-wives, and fishwives also attended stageplays in the public amphitheaters and, after 1599, in the private theaters in even greater numbers.[154] Prostitutes were such a notable presence in the public theaters that women who attended unaccompanied by husbands, brothers, or fathers risked sexual harassment and moral censure; yet, some women defied these constraints on their behavior and, by the 1630s, groups of ladies and citizen wives arranged to view performances unescorted.

Taking into account the historical factors involved in the production and consumption of Renaissance drama, we can see the broad contours of a renaissance of *lesbianism* operating *behind the seen* of Shakespeare's creation of plot, character, location, and theme. Figures of female desire, affiliation, and affection, while not the center of dramatic action, are part and parcel of even his most heterosexually driven dramatic practice. As Montrose remarks about the gender politics of *A Midsummer Night's Dream*:

> It is obvious that theatrical productions and critical readings originating from beyond the cultural time and place of the text's own origin may work against the grain to achieve radically heterodox meanings and effects. But it may also be the case that the appropriative potential of such subsequent acts of interpretation *is enabled by Elizabethan cultural variations and contradictions* that have been sedimented in the text of the play at its originary moment of production.[155]

As we redefine the conditions of *lesbian* visibility, then, we might strive to enact in Shakespearean productions neither a realist reification of identity categories (e.g., Helena announces herself as a self-identified *lesbian*) nor a postmodern parody of them (the only available mode of homoeroticism is drag), but the staging of the contingency and historicity of such categories. Imagine, for a moment, a production of *A Midsummer Night's Dream* in which Titania's complex and implicitly colonialist affections for her votaress are not minimized but explicitly motivate her resistance to Oberon; in which Helena's anger over Hermia's betrayal is not an object of hilarity or ridicule but an impassioned expression of longing and heartbreak; in which the convent, the widow's house, the Indian shore, Titania's bower, and Amazonia exist as viable (imaginative and material) female spaces. Imagine a production that brings on stage the female affections rendered retrospective by the text, that gives temporary life to Titania's beloved votaress (perhaps even enacting *her* side of the relationship), and that shows us Helena and Hermia exchanging intimacies on their primrose bed, or sitting on one cushion, stitching one sampler. Imagine a production overseen, in other words, by the silent vestal virgin winging on, "in maiden meditation, fancy-free."

2 "A certaine incredible excesse of pleasure": female orgasm, prosthetic pleasures, and the anatomical *pudica*

> [A] certaine great and hot spirit or breath conteined in those parts, doth begin to dilate itselfe more and more, which causeth a certaine incredible excesse of pleasure or voluptuousnesse, wherewith the genitalls being replete, are spread forth or distended every way unto their full greatnesse.[1]

In 1620 in Guamanga, Peru, Catalina de Erauso, who had successfully disguised herself as a man for many years in Seville and the New World, was convicted of killing a soldier during a tavern brawl. In an attempt to escape capital punishment, she revealed her identity as a woman and a nun. Her tactic, a kind of strategic gender identification, was victorious. Three matrons were called in to examine her body; after they declared her to be a "virgin intact as the day [she] was born," the bishop stayed her execution, declaring that the viceregal court could not execute a nun, who was subject first to ecclesiastical law.[2]

Catalina de Erauso was an exceptional woman to have so adroitly manipulated gender to her advantage. Her adoption of masculine dress and behaviors enabled her to escape the confines of a Spanish convent and find adventure (if not fortune) in Peru. Hers was a virtuoso performance of female masculinity, as she engaged in the social roles of soldier, card-player, brawler, seducer, and protector of women. When her performance of masculinity posed an impediment, however, she insisted on the "fact" of her anatomical sex. Moving back and forth between genders amidst growing degrees of publicity, she became an unlikely cultural hero, the subject of three "autobiographies" and a play, *La monja alférez comedia famosa*, by Juan Pérez de Montalván.

Catalina de Erauso's escape from the Spanish authorities hinged on her body's "intact" status. The avowal of three matrons that her hymen remained unbroken not only provided evidence of her purity and virtue, but gave credence to her claim to be bound by the rules of the convent. (Although de Erauso had never taken orders, her association with monastic life protected her from the laws of civil society.) In the context of ongoing medical controversy about the existence and significance of the hymen, the "discovery" of an intact membrane could have been submitted to scientific dispute.[3] But it was not. Rather, the assertion of de Erauso's bodily integrity closed the book on the question of her gender.

The relevance of de Erauso's hymen to her erotic practices, however, is considerably less clear. By her own admission – and significantly aggrandized in her memoir and Pérez de Montalván's play – de Erauso not only delighted in other women's "pretty faces," but indulged in several erotic encounters with Spanish ladies in the New World.[4] While working for a wealthy merchant in Lima, for instance, de Erauso was asked to leave:

> the reason being that there were two young ladies in the house, his wife's sisters, and I had become accustomed to frolicking with them and teasing them – one, in particular, who had taken a fancy to me. And one day, when she and I were in the front parlor, and I had my head in the folds of her skirt and she was combing my hair while I ran my hand up and down between her legs, Diego de Solarte happened to pass by the window, and spied us through the grate, just as she was telling me I should go to Potosí and seek my fortune, so that the two of us could be married.[5]

Whereas de Erauso's intact hymen affirmed her virginity to the satisfaction of the colonial officials, it failed to signify the erotic activities she self-consciously, if obliquely, advertised, including her caressing of other women. Acting within the ideological constraints of chastity – and publicized through the exuberant narrative conventions of the picaresque – de Erauso, it appears, had a good deal of fun.[6]

We can gain some analytical purchase on de Erauso's behavior if we recognize that she, like her English counterparts, lived in a society that legally precluded female desire. Women "make no Lawes, they consent to none, they abrogate none," states *The lawes resolutions of womens rights*, a compendium of laws written to inform English women of their legal status. "All of them are understood either married or to bee married and their desires [are] subject to their husband, I know no remedy though some women can shift it well enough."[7] T. E., the compiler of this book, recognizes that, even as women's social identity is defined by marital status and their desires subject to their husbands, some women "shift it well enough."[8] Under certain conditions, he implies, patriarchal ideology might be torqued or tweaked to work in women's favor.

Taking my cue from de Erauso's infamous manipulation of a dominant discourse (chastity) and T. E.'s measured acknowledgment of women's ability to "shift it," I invert in this chapter the typical feminist strategy of detailing the workings of misogyny and then excavating female resistance. I first explore the extent to which women's erotic desires for men were licensed within patriarchal orthodoxy, and then consider how women's erotic bodies were implicated within a nexus of misogyny related to the production of cultural knowledge. As expressed in prescriptive literature and a range of medical writing, female erotic pleasure is a central component of reproductive, marital chastity, the discourse of which enjoins husbands to attend to their wives' desires in order to insure successful generation. I then turn briefly to several obscene poems that help us explore the faultlines of this erotic ideology. After locating the negotiation of female desire within the traditions of literary obscenity, I return to a crucial contradiction in medical texts: the tension between an investment in women's erotic pleasure and an aversion to female genitalia. My purpose is not merely to probe a contradiction in medical writing about women, or even to interject a feminist caution about the pervasiveness of misogyny; rather, this chapter uses the presence of ambivalence to examine the production of cultural knowledge (scientific and obscene) about women's eroticism. The gendered strategies by which medical writers handled the threat that their own texts might be judged obscene reveal that the female body performed a crucial service to scientific production: absorbing within her flesh the danger and ambivalence involved in unveiling and publicizing nature's secrets.

To what extent was the system of eroticism, as organized by patriarchal alliance, open to manipulation and "shifts"? Instances in which women deliberately (and sometimes quite flagrantly) flouted social dictates were not uncommon. Some women lied to parents about their suitors, maintained secret correspondence with the men they loved, and were adamant in their refusal of their parents' choices. One woman, literally obeying her mother's injunction not to see her suitor, met him with her eyes blindfolded.[9] When such strategies to enable the courtship of a preferred suitor failed, they sometimes were followed by secret elopements, in defiance not only of parents and guardians, but even of monarchs. Margaret Bagot married in secret, and her irate father had no choice but to give way; Ralph Josselin's attempts to control his daughter's choice of spouse ended in futility.[10] When Frances Howard was forbidden by Queen Elizabeth to marry the Earl of Hereford, she married him anyway. Arbella Stuart likewise risked the censure of her cousin and king, James I, when she cross-dressed in order to escape royal confinement and to join the husband forbidden to her.[11]

Defying the prerogatives of fathers and advisors was not the only means by which women could "shift" the erotic system more to their liking. English women married on average relatively late by European standards, and premarital erotic activity seems to have been fairly common across status lines. On the basis of church records from 1570–1640, Martin Ingram maintains that, allowing for variations among communities and changes over time, "at least a fifth of all brides were with child by the time they got married in church" and that "[v]ery little shame or disgrace seems to have attached to bridal pregnancy."[12] Ingram describes a cultural situation

> in which courting couples were customarily allowed a good deal of freedom not only to meet and talk but also to enjoy a measure of physical contact... A good deal of kissing and cuddling went on, often in private or semi-private, and couples sometimes spent

whole nights together, perhaps before the fire in the hall of the house where the woman lived with her parents or employers, in an inn or alehouse, or (in the summer) in the open air.[13]

After 1600, an increase in prosecutions against antenuptial fornication reflects, says Ingram, "a partial erosion of the more tolerant vein in popular thinking and a corresponding reinforcement of the ideal of premarital chastity," as well as the tightening economic factors that would lead, during the mid-seventeenth century, to a "hardening of attitudes towards sexual immorality" when it occurred outside the conjugal unit.[14] David Cressy, however, suggests that throughout the seventeenth century and despite religious and social prohibitions, "it was widely thought acceptable for a couple who had been 'made sure' by [spousal] contract to progress from kissing and fondling to full sexual intercourse. In the eyes of the law such premarital 'incontinence' was fornication, and might be punished if discovered. But a powerful cultural current permitted betrothed couples to risk each other's chastity in anticipation of matrimony."[15] Cressy reminds us of the proverb, "courting and wooing bring dallying and doing,"[16] and speculates that "half the couples who contracted to be married engaged in sexual congress."[17] By the late seventeenth century, Lawrence Stone maintains, "offenders were no longer liable to punishment as fornicators, but only as violators of an edict of the church prohibiting bedding before the spousals had been ratified by an open church wedding."[18]

It has become common to assert that northwestern Europe during the early modern period was what we might call a "sex-positive" culture. Whether the subject is the French "simple minded farmhand" innocently pursuing "inconsequential bucolic pleasures" in the caresses of little girls, as in Foucault's first volume of *The History of Sexuality*,[19] or the English "lusty widow" pursuing virile young men in the chapbook jests and ballads examined by Margaret Spufford,[20] scholars depict an ethos in which men and women, both within and outside the conjugal bed, desired and actively sought a variety of forms of erotic contact. In advancing his argument about the stereotype of female sexual voraciousness, for instance, Anthony Fletcher suggests that in England, the "drama and ballad literature of the sixteenth and seventeenth centuries has a consistent vein of bawdy which reflects a spontaneous rather than a guilt-ridden attitude to sexual pleasure."[21] Citing William Gouge, who suggests in *Of Domesticall Duties* that there might be an equality in sexual relations ("for the wife [as well as the husband] is therein both a servant and a mistress, a servant to yield her body, a mistress to have the power of his"), Fletcher suggests that the "normal rules of patriarchy . . . did not apply behind the chamber door . . . this piece of prescriptive advice . . . seems to mean that the strict and reproving husband was being told to transform himself into a democratic and mutual lover."[22] Angus McLaren likewise has argued that this period evinced an "earthy attitude towards sexuality"; that "the bed was one place at least in which men and women were more or less equal"; and that "from the sixteenth to the eighteenth centuries it was commonly assumed that women not only found pleasure in sexual intercourse but that they positively had to if the union were to be a fruitful one."[23]

Spontaneous, pleasurable, earthy, equal – these are some of the terms used by scholars, some of them extremely influential, to describe early modern women's experience of eroticism. Such assessments of heterosexual conduct derive primarily from descriptions embedded in the prescriptive literature and vernacular medical writing brought into critical prominence by social historians. I now turn to conduct books and medical texts to scrutinize their depictions of the female erotic body, asking whether the celebratory narrative of bodies and pleasures promoted by scholars is an accurate portrayal of the representations found therein.

Erotic activity clearly was legitimated by sixteenth- and seventeenth-century humanists and Protestant moralists as an essential aspect of the conjugal bond.[24] As one tenet of their vision of companionate marriage, the erotic union of husband and wife – always in the proper position, of course, and always pursued in moderation – provided a potent emblem of marital harmony. Henry Smith called upon ancient rhetoric in his *Preparative to Mariage*: "Marriage is called Conjugium, which signifieth a knitting or joining together."[25] His fellow writers of prescriptive literature applied this dictum quite literally, arguing that it was during lovemaking that two became one. According to Patricia Crawford, Gouge

> urged his readers to "Read the Song of Songs," where they would find in the affection of Christ for his spouse their own model for marital love. Other divines cited the example of Isaac sporting with his wife Rebekah in private as showing God's approval of marital sexual pleasure. As the physician Lemnius pointed out, good sex made for domestic harmony. Good sexual relations were thus a central part of married life.[26]

David Cressy concurs: "Single people were supposed to remain continent, but married couples were supposed to make love."[27]

In his *Christian Œconomie*, William Perkins explicates three ways for spouses to express the "due benevolence" that "must be shewed with a singular and entire affection one towards another," the first of which is "the right and lawfull use of their bodies, or of the marriage-bed, which is indeed an essentiall dutie of marriage. The marriage-bed signifieth that solitarie and secret societie, that is betweene man and wife alone."[28] Likewise, William Whateley concludes his discussion of marital chastity in *A Bride Bush* by referring to "the due and lawfull enjoyment of marriage": "it is a principall meanes of living purely in this estate, to enjoy it moderately and holily."²⁹ In his discussion of "due benevolence," Whateley moves from the kindness owed to the spouse to the terms of erotic engagement:

The married must not provoke desires for pleasures sake, but allay desires, when they provoke themselves. They must not strive by words and gestures, to enflame their passions, when were it not for such inforcements, they would be coole enough. But when such passions are of themselves moved, then must they take the benefit of their estate to asswage them, that for want of just satisfaction, they may not be troublesome to them in the duties of religion, and of their callings.³⁰

With the medieval concept of the marriage debt modified into a gesture of due benevolence, the marital obligation is overwritten with a tone of Christian charity. And, with the practice of this good will marked as an aid to religious devotion and productive labor, Whateley defines marital eroticism as "the benefit of their estate." Indeed, Whateley's rhetoric employs the term "marriage" as a synonym for erotic activity:

In a word, *marriage must be used as seldome and sparingly*, as may stand with the neede of the persons married: for excesse this way doth weaken the body, and shorten life: but a sparing enjoyment would help the health, and preserve the body from divers diseases in some constitutions... If the fancy, and imagination, and corruption provoke desires, the body not needing, nor inforcing them; not *marriage*, but prayer & humiliation must heale this disease: but when the motions arise from the bodily temper or fulnesse, the marriage bed was ordained for a remedy against sin, & to that end must be enjoyed.³¹

In addition to the widespread meaning of marriage as an entry into a lifelong condition of wedlock and the performance of a ritual ceremony, marriage in Whateley's text becomes the act of making love. Indeed, the marriage bed becomes a synecdoche for marriage itself.

Whateley's view of the purpose of marriage was widely shared. When he includes a spouse's withdrawal from the conjugal bed as a possible reason for dissolving the bonds of matrimony, for instance, he reflects common legal practice: one of the few grounds for annulment was permanent impotence or frigidity.³² Annulment left the partners free to remarry, although the consequences for women could be harsh since their dower rights were annulled as well. Even in colonial America one of the few permissible grounds for divorce was male impotence. According to Mary Beth Norton,

New Haven statutes made explicit what was implicit in the jurisprudence of the other colonies. As that province's divorce law delicately put it, if a woman "needing and requiring conjugall duty, and due benevolence from her husband" found "after convenient forbearance and due tryall" that he "neither at the time of marriage, nor since, hath been, is, nor by the use of any lawfull means, is like to be able to perform or afford the same," she could sue for divorce and permission to marry.[33]

The emerging doctrine of due benevolence, then, elevated conjugal eroticism to the very heart of what it meant to be married.

Whateley's assertion of the healthful benefits of moderate erotic activity within marriage was founded on good medical authority, for it was widely believed that orgasm (or, in contemporary parlance, the emission of seed) provided a necessary excretion, purging the bodies of men and women alike of evil humors. Regular and satisfying erotic activity for adults was a basic health requirement, a key to the vitality of both individuals and the human race. Although the underlying assumption of all these prescriptions is that the primary purpose of erotic congress is procreation, procreation itself takes a back seat in these descriptions of the performance of conjugal love.

The idea that orgasm purges the body of harmful humors derives from a central understanding underlying all humoralism: that bodies and behaviors translate easily into one another. The cold and moist complexion of women, for instance, explains simultaneously menstruation and female timidity.[34] With physiological functions and somatic features merging continually into psychological states and bodily behaviors, any corporeal deviation or upset is readable as an index to moral character. The apparent reciprocity of mind, body, and spirit led natural philosophers to develop complex schemes in which the various passions are shown to influence the humors and temperaments, and vice versa, in what philosopher John Sutton calls "continual reciprocal causation."[35] According to Thomas Wright, author of *The Passions of the Minde in General*, "Passions ingender Humours, and humours breed Passions."[36] Along with the internal organs, the "animal spirits" further inform the constitution of affective states, including erotic desire. Intention and action likewise are assigned a corporeal function, with virtue and vice located materially within a taxonomy of internal organs and members.[37] Erotic desire, we should note, is a sanguine passion, associated with the humor of blood.

In their encyclopedic intent to systematize corporeal phenomena, sixteenth- and seventeenth-century medical writers drew freely from Platonic and Christian theories which, thrown into the conceptual pot with humoralism, the Hippocratic corpus, and in some cases, medieval astrology, resulted in a materialist mechanics that consistently reached toward ethical explanations of embodiment. Thus, in his treatise on love melancholy, Jacques Ferrand considered erotic love to be, in the words of his modern editors, simultaneously "an endogenous disease conditioned by the complexions of the body" and "a passion of the soul that begins in an act of misguided volition."[38] Synthesizing Platonic, Christian, and Galenic understandings, Ferrand believed that the depraved judgments and imaginations of lovers came about as the result of the cloudy spots and vapors generated by the adustion of humors, for it was the burning by the passions that provoked the decline into states of depression or mania. Yet it was the fixing of the will upon the beloved object that first stamped the imagination, imprinting it with an image that displaced all other considerations, that dried and chilled the brain and brought on the illness. Any definition of love must involve both the mechanisms of perverted reason and the mechanisms of the body whereby the corruption is spread throughout the physical organism.[39]

With these beliefs about the psycho-physiology of eroticism in mind, we can better understand why medical writers advised women suffering from greensickness or suffocation of the womb to marry, confident that the expulsion of seed that accompanied orgasm would expel evil humors and restore humoral balance.[40] When marriage prospects were not imminent, midwives were encouraged, on the authority of Galen, to manipulate manually their patient's genitals. In *The Woman's Doctour*, a mid-seventeenth-century textbook for English doctors and lay readers, Nicholas Fontanus cites Galen's example of how "the abundance of the spermatick humour was diminished by the hand of a skilfull Midwife, and a convenient oyntment, which passage will also furnish us with this argument, that the use of *Venery* is exceeding wholsome, if the woman will confine her selfe to the lawes of moderation, so that she feele no wearisomnesse, nor weaknesse in her body, after those pleasing conflicts."[41] The "hand of a skilfull Midwife," associated with the "wholsome" "use of Venery," is on the same level as "a convenient oyntment." Erstwhile writer, compiler, and popularizer Nicolas Culpeper in his *Practice of Physick* likewise prescribed for greensickness first, marriage, and, if marriage were unavailable, the manual ministrations of a midwife. In Culpeper's rhetoric, we begin to see a glimmer of concern about the legitimacy of female–female bodily contact: "the genital Parts should be by a cunning Midwife so handled and rubbed as to cause an evacuation of the over-abounding sperm. But that being a thing not so allowable, it may suffice whilst patient is in bath to rub her belly in the Region of the Womb."[42] It no longer being "so allowable" to venture toward the genitals, the hand of the midwife should attempt to bring off an orgasmic "evacuation" by rubbing the patient's lower abdomen.[43]

Orgasm, then, was one way to maintain a healthy body. However, when Whateley considered the conditions that might incite desire, he took pains to clarify the difference between what he called "mutuall dalliances for pleasure sake" which was "a fault, even betwixt yoke-fellowes, unlesse it fall out, that the ones necessitie require the other to pay the debt of due benevolence," and "naturall desires" which are "the temperate enjoyment of Gods ordinance, as for a man to drinke, when labour or other occasion hath made him thirstie."[44] His distinction between those "desires" provoked by the "fancy, and imagination," and those "motions" arising from "bodily temper" was derived from the humoralism of medical practitioners. Such practitioners, however, were more permissive than Whateley and other writers of conduct books in specifying the means of erotic stimulation. Whereas it might seem reasonable for a midwife, whom a woman might consult for infertility, to describe ways to maximize the chance of conception, such explicitness about sexual technique was no less the purview of the anatomist, the physician, or popularizers such as Culpeper and Fontanus.[45] Concern about women's successful conception, pregnancy, delivery, and nursing of children authorized a good deal of latitude in examining and articulating women's perceived physiology and psychology. Thus, when speaking about the need to arouse women through careful lovemaking, medical authors demonstrate a thorough appreciation of the fact that such arousal was not accomplished by phallic penetration alone. Conception, everyone agreed, depended upon both male and female emission of seed. And such emission, everyone knew, would not happen without giving women what they wanted – or, at least, what men thought they wanted.

Thus, Thomas Johnson's 1634 translation of the 1549 treatise of French surgeon Ambroise Paré urges husbands to spend time arousing their wives:

When the husband commeth into his wives chamber hee must entertaine her with all kinde of dalliance, wanton behaviour, and allurements to venery: but if he perceive her to be slow, and more cold, he must cherish, embrace, and tickle her, and shall not abruptly, the nerves [penis] being suddenly distended, breake into the field of nature [vagina], but rather shall creepe in by little and little, intermixing more wanton kisses with wanton words and speeches, handling her secret parts and dugs, that she may take fire and bee enflamed to venery, for so at length the wombe will strive and waxe fervent with a desire of casting forth its owne seed.[46]

The quality of lovemaking was crucial, not only because mutual pleasure was necessary for the emission of seed, but because generation linked the individual to God. By paying proper physical attention to what provident Nature, in her divine wisdom, had mandated for the human body, including its potential to "wax fervent with desire," individuals fulfilled God's ingenious plan for reproduction. If one believes, along with Helkiah Crooke (whose compilation, *Microcosmographia: A Description of the Body of Man* [1615], was the preeminent English anatomy in the early seventeenth century) that Nature is the name "under which ... I always understand the wise administration of Almighty God," then microcosm and macrocosm met under the sheets of the conjugal bed.[47]

Medical knowledge in early modern England was constructed largely out of a Latin continental tradition that itself was heavily indebted to Greek, Roman, and Arabic models. The reintroduction of ancient medical thought to the Christian West is a complex phenomenon that is usefully summarized by Nancy Sirasi:

[T]he sequence of reception provides one kind of chronological framework for the development of medicine in medieval and Renaissance western Europe: thus, in the early Middle Ages, scanty knowledge in the West contrasted with the much fuller reception and understanding achieved in the Muslim world. The balance was redressed to some extent by the new translations of Greek and Arabic medical works that began to appear, first from Constantinus Africanus in southern Italy in the late eleventh century and then from the circle of Gerard of Cremona in Spain in the twelfth century. These works formed the basis of a new Latin medical learning that was developed and refined in the milieu of the universities from the thirteenth to the fifteenth centuries. In yet another phase of transmission and reception, Latin medicine provided the conceptual and often the textual basis for a growing vernacular European medical literature produced from the late fourteenth until the sixteenth century. Finally, the endeavors of a handful of medical humanists in the late fifteenth and the sixteenth centuries produced a full knowledge of the surviving texts of Greek medicine in the original language as well as in a fresh round of translations into Latin.[48]

Renaissance anatomy, in particular, generated out of empirical methods of observation including human dissection, gained greater currency with the publication of Andreas Vesalius's widely influential *De Humani Corporis Fabrica* of 1543. The dissemination of continental anatomies in the latter half of the sixteenth century prompted not only the development of vernacular English anatomy, but an increase in the number of English midwiferies and obstetric manuals (previously based primarily on the texts of Soranus and Trotula) as well.[49] All of these works, dependent as they were on humoral and Arabic models, emphasized the importance of women's pleasure, for Arabic treatises were equally concerned with the relation between orgasm and conception. According to Danielle Jacquart and Claude Thomasset, Arabic treatises included detailed instruction for cures for sexual frustration, impotence, and infertility, including coital remedies; they cite one author who wrote: "Men should take their time over playing with women... They should caress their breasts and pubis... [t]hey should watch out for the moment when the woman clings more tightly, when her eyes start to go red, when her breathing becomes more rapid and she starts to stammer."[50]

Prior to the seventeenth century, medical writers were preoccupied with two issues about women's anatomy and physiology: "is she an imperfect version of the male, and does she produce fertile semen?" Anthony Fletcher agrees with Ian Maclean that by 1600, "the vast majority had answered the first question by replacing the notion that woman was less perfect than man with the argument that she was 'equally perfect in her own sex.'"[51] Early modern writers, however, were unwilling to forsake completely the notion of female deficiency. Crooke, for instance, argues in 1615 that "the female sexe as well as the male is a perfection of mankinde," the main difference being that man is "a creature begetting in another" whereas a woman is "a Creature begetting in her selfe." On the one hand, he asserts that "as the soule of a woman is the same divine nature with a mans, so is her body a necessary being, a first and not a second intention of Nature, her proper and absolute worke not her error or prevarication."[52] On the other hand, he also maintains:

> wherefore a woman is so much lesse perfect then a man by how much her heate is lesse and weaker then his; yet... this imperfection turned unto perfection, because without the woman, mankinde could not have been perfected by the perfecter sexe. The great Maister workman therefore of set purpose, made the one halfe of mankinde imperfect for the instauration of the whole kinde, making the woman as receptacle of the seede of which a new man was to be created.[53]

"[I]mperfection turned unto perfection," of course, did not mean equal – and no medical writer attempted to argue, on the basis of anatomy, for women's social, moral, intellectual, or political equality. Nonetheless, by the late seventeenth century, the philosopher Poulain de la Barre would write, in the polemic entitled *The woman as good as the man, of the equality of both sexes* (first published in France in 1673 and translated into English in 1677):

> God willing to produce men in dependence, one upon another by the concourse of two persons, for that end framed two bodies which were different, each was perfect in its kind... It is then without reason that some imagine that women are not so perfect as men and that they look upon that (in them) as a defect, which is an essential portion of their sex: without the which it would be useless for the end for which it hath been formed: which begins and ceases with fecundity, and which is destined for the most excellent use of the world: that is, to frame and nourish us in their bellies.[54]

Few medical writers waxed as expressive in support of women as Poulain de la Barre. However, his basic assertion of female reproductive equality was widespread, and in England was popularized not only by Crooke, but by the other prolific publishers of vernacular medical texts in the seventeenth century, Thomas Bartholin, Nicolas Culpeper, and Jane Sharp.

What made possible the shift from the widespread belief in the sixteenth century in female imperfection – anatomical, physiological, and psychological – to this more moderate view that (while consigning woman to an inferior social position) recognized the perfection of her bodily structure and function "for the end of which it hath been formed"? One part of the answer surely must be the (re)discovery of the clitoris. For, although others have minimized the ideological impact of this event,[55] I want to suggest that the (re)introduction of this third term into the traditional homology of penis and uterus meant that the Galenic truism that posited the female as an inverted and imperfect version of the male could no longer hold.

The Renaissance discovery of the clitoris was, as Katharine Park makes clear, a rediscovery:

Although the clitoris as an anatomical organ (rather than a general locus of female sexual pleasure) had been well known to late Greek writers on medicine and surgery, that knowledge had been lost to medieval European medical authors. Misled by the linguistic imprecision of their Arabic sources, exacerbated by the uncertain terminology of Latin translators, they tended either to identify it with the labia minora or, following the eleventh-century Persian medical authority Avicenna, to think of it as a pathological growth found only in a few women. In the middle decades of the sixteenth century, however, European anatomists rediscovered the clitoris through a rereading of the ancient Greek works, supplemented by their own anatomical researches on female cadavers.[56]

Several anatomists seem to have been approaching a recognition of the independent status of the clitoris around the same time, although it was not until the publication of Colombo's *De re anatomica* in 1559 that its role in producing pleasure was clearly expressed.[57] In England, the royal physician Thomas Vicary refers to an organ at the mouth of the vagina as "tentigo," or tenseness, a word that had an erotic overtone at the time, in his *Profitable Treatise on the Anatomie of Mans Body*, published in 1548. Vicary, however, did not attribute to the tentigo any pleasurable function: "it hath in the middest a Lazartus pannicle, whiche is called in Laten Tentigo. And in the creation of this Pannicle is founde two utilities: The first is, that by it goeth forth the urin, or else it should be shed throughout the Vulva: The seconde is, that when a woman doth set hir thies abrode, it altereth the ayre that commeth to the Matrix for to temper the heat."[58] In France, Charles Estienne described the clitoris as part of woman's "shameful member" (*membre honteux*) and "a little tongue [*languette*]... at the place of the neck of the bladder" in his *La dissection des parties du corps humain*, published in Latin in 1545 and in French the following year. Although he included a visual illustration of the clitoris in one of his plates of female reproductive anatomy, Estienne, like Vicary, related the function of the clitoris to urination rather than sexual response. According to Park, "his observation made no discernible impact," for in Venice Gabriele Falloppia celebrated what he considered his own discovery of the clitoris in his *Observationes anatomicae*, written around 1550.[59] Because Falloppia did not publish his finding until 1561,

Realdo Colombo tried to appropriate it, staking his own claim in his treatise *De re anatomica* (On anatomy), which he brought out two years before his rival's work, in 1559. While later writers generally discounted Colombo's assertions of priority, they nonetheless acknowledge him as the first to emphasize its role in female sexual pleasure. "It is the principal seat of women's enjoyment in intercourse," he wrote, "so that if you not only rub it with your penis, but even touch it with your little finger, the pleasure causes their seed to flow forth in all directions, swifter than the wind, even if they don't want it to."[60]

In the translation provided by Laqueur, Colombo continues: "Since no one has discerned these projections and their workings, if it is permissible to give names to things discovered by me, it should be called the love or sweetness of Venus."[61] As the seat of woman's enjoyment or delight, responsive to both the touch of the finger and the penis, the clitoris entered anatomical discourse as the enabling source of female reproductive vitality. According to the *OED*, the noun "seat" has three primary meanings extant in the early modern period: (1) "Action or manner of sitting" (as in a horsewoman's seat); (2) "Place or thing to sit upon" (like a chair); and (3) "Residence, abode, situation." It is this third sense that is employed by Colombo, for in this period it includes the additional meaning: "The thing (esp. the organ or part of the body) in which a particular power, faculty, function or quality 'resides'; the locality of a disease, sensation, or the like." The seat of woman's delight is, in short, the primary residence of female erotic pleasure.

Admittedly, it is difficult to take seriously the thrill of discovery accompanying the inclusion of the clitoris by Colombo and Falloppia into anatomical discourse. The problem is succinctly addressed by Audrey Eccles, who asserts that "it would be naïve to imagine they actually discovered it, or that their statements that it was the chief seat of sexual pleasure in women came as a great revelation."[62] However, whereas Eccles's assertion of women's prior experience of their bodies is well taken – one's experience of erotic pleasure does not depend on comprehending the anatomy and physiology underlying it – her irony elides the fact that it is only under the auspices of anatomical investigation that the clitoris is given a name; and only with a name does the clitoris come into being as a discrete spatial dimension with a specific function, that is, as an *organ*. Despite the historical blindness to female embodiment retrospectively evinced by the anatomists' rediscovery, and despite the intersection of knowledge, power, and misogyny manifested in the debate over the clitoris's existence – Andreas Vesalius, contemporary of Colombo and Falloppia and the reigning authority on anatomy, for instance, disputed its existence – the incorporation of this organ within a specific domain of "modern" knowledge gave female erotic pleasure a new articulation and heightened cultural capital.

Colombo's influential formulation, repeated virtually verbatim by medical writers for two centuries, stresses that without sufficient attention paid to the clitoris, a woman neither conceives nor desires to conceive, for it alone governs the expulsion of female seed. By 1615, the existence of the clitoris was so well established that Crooke's *Microcosmographia*, the first English anatomy to discuss the form, function, and role of the clitoris, did so at some length:

[The clitoris] commeth of an obscoene worde signifying contrectation [to handle] but properly it is called the womans yard. It is a small production in the upper, forward . . . and middle fatty part of the share [genitals], in the top of the greater cleft where the *Nymphes* [labia] doe meet, and is answerable to the member of the man, from which it differs in length, the common passage and the want of one paire of muscles; but agrees in scituation [*sic*], substance, and composition. For it consisteth of two nervous bodies (which *Laurentius* cals ligaments) round without, hard and thick; but within spongy and porous, that when the spirits come into it, it may bee distended and grow loose when they dissipated, these bodies, as those of the mans yarde, are full of blacke, thicke, and sprightfull blood... The head is properly called *Tentigo* by Juvenall, which is covered with a fine skin made of the conjunction of the *Nymphae* as it were with a fore-skinne. It hath an entrance but no through passage; there are vesselles also running along the backe of it as in a mans yarde; and although for the most part it hath but a small production hidden under the *Nymphes* and hard to be felt but with curiosity... The use of this part is the same with the bridle of the yard; for because the Testicles of the women are far distant from the yard of the man, the imagination is carried to the spermaticall vessels by the motion and attrition of this *Clitoris*, together with the lower ligatures of the wombe, whose orignall toucheth, cleaveth and is tyed to the leading vessels of the seede, and so the profusion of their seede is stirred up for generation... wherefore although by this passage their seede is not ejaculated, yet by the attrition of it their imagination is wrought to call that out that lyeth deeply hidden in the body.[63]

It is with refreshing, though by no means uncharacteristic, irony that Crooke follows Colombo in calling the clitoris "*aestrum Veneris & dulcedo amoris*" and "the especiall seate of delight in [women's] veneral embracements, as *Columbus* imagineth he first discovered."[64] Providing an illustration of female reproductive anatomy that, drawn in the Vesalian fashion, positions the clitoris on top of a penis-like vagina, Crooke's *Microcosmographia* seems uneasily perched between the old Galenic homologies and a newer dispensation that attends to what the eye, with the help of the scalpel, can see. (Figure 6; clitoris marked by letter *m*.) His text held sway as the preeminent vernacular anatomy in England until mid-century, when the Latin anatomy of Caspar Bartholin was translated and updated under the auspices of his son, Thomas.[65] Bartholin's anatomy includes an even more detailed description of the clitoris (which will be discussed in chapter 5). Whereas his illustrations of vaginal and uterine anatomy remain Galenic, his realistic illustration of the woman's surface anatomy clearly labels the clitoris amid the labial folds. (Figure 7; clitoris marked by letter *a*.)

Despite the slow move away from Galenic homologies in the visual illustration of female genitalia, from Vicary to the anonymously authored and best-selling *Aristotles Master-Piece* (*c*. 1684), the clitoris typically was described as the conceptual equivalent of the penis, "suffer[ing] erection and falling in the same manner."[66] This functional homology of the male and female "yards" existed, initially without too much contradiction, alongside the traditional Galenic homology between the penis and the uterus.[67] Eventually, however, as the uterus became the defining characteristic of womanhood – likewise perfect in its own way – the clitoris alone carried the conceptual burden of penile equivalent. By the time of Bartholin's anatomy, the structural homology between male and female reproductive anatomy began to collapse under its own weight: "some

"A certaine incredible excesse of pleasure" 91

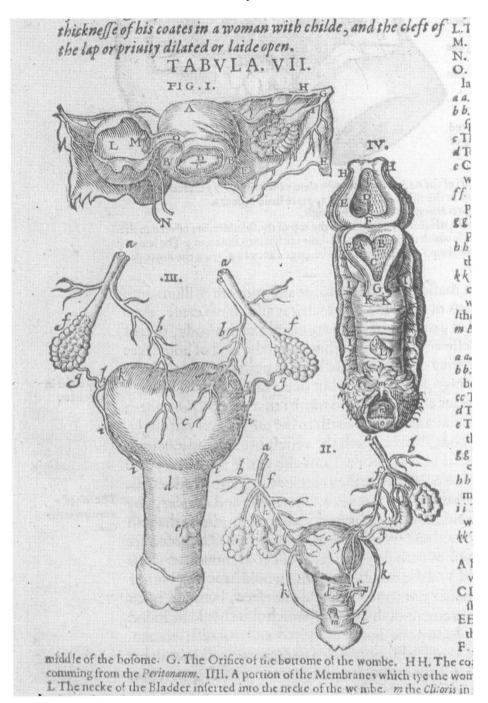

Figure 6   Helkiah Crooke, *Microcosmographia* (1615).

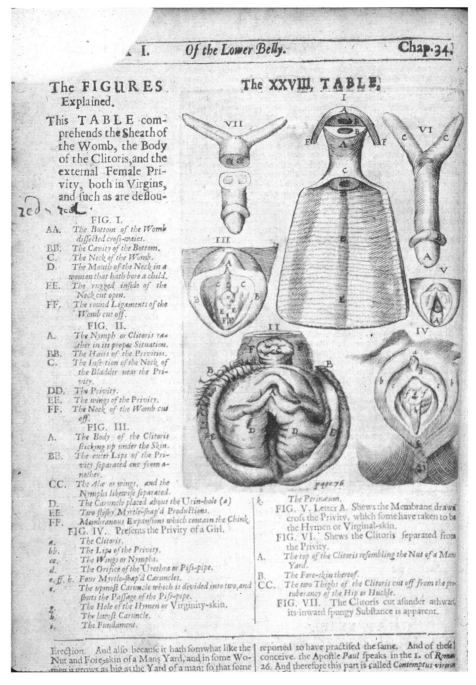

Figure 7 Thomas Bartholin, *Bartholinus Anatomy* (1653/1668).

liken the Womb to the Cod [testicles] of a Man, and some to the Nut of the Yard. Some will have the Neck of the Womb [vagina] to answer the Mans Yard, and others will have the Clitoris. Which Conceits falling to the ground by their own weakness, I shall proceed to explain the Parts." Some of those parts, Bartholin asserts, "agree after a sort with those of Men, as the spermatick Vessels, the Stones, and the *Vasa deferentia*, or Vessels that carry away the Seed. Others are wholly different, as the Womb with its Bottom, Orifice, and Neck, the Hymen, the Myrtle-shap'd Caruncles, the Vulva with its Wings, the Clitoris, and the little Hillocks."[68] As we shall see, however, even as the structural homology between penis and clitoris fell apart, their functional equivalence remained strong.

From the mid-sixteenth through the end of the seventeenth century, all the English commentators agree: women's clitoral pleasure is significant because, and only because, the physiology of reproduction requires it. In the context of significant medical controversy – whether the hymen exists, whether women can transform spontaneously into men, whether the womb contributes a material "efficient cause" to the fetus, whether the womb can wander, whether women are anatomically perfect or deficient – on this one matter, at least, for over one hundred and fifty years, there was no controversy: the clitoris "is that which causest Lust in women and gives delight in Copulation, for without this a woman neither desires Copulation, or hath pleasure in it, or conceive by it."[69] This etiological observation, repeated again and again, is the *sine qua non* of early modern erotic ideology. The belief that erotic friction produces heat, that heat is necessary for the emission of seed, and that women's seed is crucial to conception underpins every piece of medical commentary about female erotic activity until the eighteenth century. It authorized the judgment that women experience twice the physical pleasure of man – "For as the Delight of Men in Copulation, consists chiefly in the Emission of the Seed, so Women are delighted both in the Emission of their own, and the Reception of the Man's"[70] – and that "big-bellied Women find more pleasure in Coition, than others, because the Seed is then discharged by a longer Passage."[71] It underlay the widespread belief that, because there is no pleasure in sexual violence, "there never comes Conception upon Rapes"[72] – a view used to discount women's claims of sexual assault – as well as the idea that "[w]ives are more healthfull than Widowes, or Virgins, because they are refreshed with the mans seed, and ejaculate their own, which being excluded, the cause of the evil is taken away."[73] It provoked debates about whether simultaneous orgasm was necessary for conception (Crooke thought not, although he argued that simultaneous orgasm would hasten the mingling of seed).[74] It informed advice given to parents not to force their children to marry against their inclination, for fear of barrenness. It authorized physician

Hugh Chamberlain's belief in women's nocturnal emissions "merely by the Force of *Imaginary* VENERY."[75] It led writers to advise women suffering from greensickness or suffocation of the womb to marry. And the observation that in the clitoris "lies the chief pleasure of loves delight in Copulation" supported midwife Jane Sharp's puncturing of romantic ideals: "were not the pleasure transcendently ravishing us, a man or woman would hardly ever die for love."[76]

The emphasis on female pleasure within this politics of reproduction entailed contradictory effects. On the one hand, it authorized women to enjoy a range of erotic activities, including those that have been termed since the eighteenth century "foreplay."[77] The tropes used to describe the experience of arousal and satisfaction throughout the early modern period are not particularly linear or even penetrative; rather, arousal for both men and women is an itching, a biting, a tickling, and orgasm is an "extasie" or "a little Epilepsie."[78] This is because the physiology of lovemaking, as Paré in the sixteenth century makes clear, is governed by humoral processes, combined with the action of the spirits and organs:

nature hath endued the genitall parts with a far more exact or exquisite sense than the other parts, by sending the great sinewes unto them, and moreover she hath caused them to be bedewed or moistened with a certain whayish humour... this moisture hath a certaine sharpenesse or biting, for that kinde of humour of all others can chiefly provoke those parts to their function or office, and yeeld them a delectable pleasure, while they are in the execution of the same. For even so whayish and sharpe humours, when they are gathered together under the skinne, if they waxe warme, tickle with a certain pleasant itching, and by their motion infeere delight: but the nature of the genitall parts or members is not stirred up or provoked to the expulsion of the seed with these provocations of the humours, abounding either in quantity or quality onely, but a certaine great and hot spirit or breath conteined in those parts, doth begin to dilate itselfe more and more, which causeth a certaine incredible excesse of pleasure or voluptuousnesse, wherewith the genitalls being replete, are spread forth or distended every way unto their full greatnesse.[79]

Because of the importance of the humors and spirits, if a woman is not feeling aroused, Paré recommends heating with aphrodisiacs:

it shall be necessary first to foment her secret parts with the decoction of hot herbes made with Muscadine, or boiled in any other good wine, and to put a little muske or civet into the neck or mouth of the wombe: and when shee shall perceive the efflux of her seed to approach, by reason of the tickling pleasure, shee must advertise her husband thereof, that at the very instant time or moment, hee may also yeeld forth his seed.[80]

In Paré's vision of copulation, men and women have mutual, if asymmetrical, responsibilities: he to arouse her and she to communicate her arousal to him.

Like Paré, Laurent Joubert's *Erreurs Populaires* (1578) views sexual activity as a kind of play or entertainment; but Joubert is as likely to see it initiated by the erotic organs of women as the penile itchings of men; in his words, "the womb begins to wriggle, feeling like some love games."[81] Joubert compares the lovemaking technique of old men, "now that the youthful fury has run its course," to that of young men, "because when their irons were hotter, they never stopped beating them on their anvils and never did anything right." (Beating on their anvils does not here refer to masturbation.) The old man "most often is contented with kissing his wife's nipples, tickling her belly, and indulging in other amorous caresses, delicacies, and entertainments," a healthful situation that leads to "the sperm, staying longer in its vesicles" being "more elaborated and refined," thus enhancing the old man's ability to beget sons.[82] Joubert's criticism of young men "beating on their anvils" implies that early modern medicine judges phallic penetration to be just one technique among many. "Love games" also include kissing breasts, tickling bellies and pudenda, and various "other amorous caresses, delicacies, and entertainments."

Joubert's assumption of the desirability of male progeny, of course, registers the weight of patriarchal privilege. Equally weighty is Crooke's assertion that

[t]he woman was ordayned to receive and conceive the seede of the man, to beare and nourish the Infant, to governe and moderate the house at home, to delight and refresh her husband soreswunke with labour, and well-nigh exhausted and spent with care and travell; and therefore her body is soft, smooth, and delicate, made especially for pleasure, so that whosoever useth them for other doth almost abuse them.[83]

It is in such phrases as "made especially for pleasure" that we begin to apprehend the flip side of the discourse of women's pleasure: by wholeheartedly endorsing male sexual demands, it leaves little moral or medical refuge for those women for whom vaginal intercourse with men was not enjoyable, or who faced ill health and even death from the repeated trials of childbearing. On a conceptual level, the location of female pleasure within a paradigm of reproduction conflates three separate experiences: the pleasure and heat of erotic arousal; the orgasmic emission of seed; and the moment of conception. Any analytical divorce of arousal and orgasm from conception – a separation that might legitimate a variety of sexual positions and activities – is unthinkable within the terms of this paradigm. The subordination of women's pleasure within a politics of generation, then, must qualify the narrative of early modern "sexual liberation," whether it be the "earthy attitude towards sexuality" celebrated by McLaren or the "spontaneous rather than guilt-ridden attitude" toward sex found by Fletcher. The asymmetries of gender ideology permeate such "attitudes," rendering them structural as well as psychological. Indeed, although men's pleasure also was legitimated from within a politics of reproduction, the sexual double standard was alive and well.

There is, in short, a defensiveness to these medical affirmations of female pleasure, a defensiveness that covers over certain anxieties: about the female body, as well as the potential autonomy of women's eroticism. This recognition, however, need not lead us to replace the story of woman-as-man's-equal-in-bed with the familiar narrative of woman-as-victim-of-misogyny. Male anxiety about women exists as one of several discursive threads circling around female bodies and eroticism, threads that also include concerns about physiological health, successful reproduction, male sexual performance, and the social legitimacy of those persons who make bodies their business. We thus need to attend to the faultlines of early modern erotic ideology, which licensed certain bodies and pleasures in the name of reproduction or health, vilified others as disgusting or unnatural, and could slip from one position to the other with astonishing ease.

Such faultlines are exposed in England's most explicit "obscene" native literary product of the late sixteenth century, Thomas Nashe's "The choise of valentines."[84] In this bawdy verse narrative of amorous pursuit, male sexual inadequacy leads to a woman's "choise" of a dildo, the "valentine" or sweetheart of the poem's title. This ribald fabliau ventriloquizes female desire in terms that would have been familiar to any reader of early modern medical texts. The assumption of the need for erotic mutuality as well as the value of simultaneous orgasms are articulated both through the voice of "mistris Francis" and her hapless lover, the narrator, Tomalin. Having gone in quest of his supposedly virtuous mistress only to discover her in a local brothel, Tomalin and Francis proceed to make passionate love. In the midst of vigorous erotic intercourse, Francis cries, "Oh not so fast" (line 179), and then proceeds to give her lover further sexual instruction:

> Togeather lett our equall motions stirr
> Togeather lett us live and dye my deere
> Toge[a]ther lett us marche unto content,
> And be consumed with one blandishment.   (lines 183–86)

Acquiescing to this tutelage, Tomalin reports, "As she prescrib'd, so kept we crotchet-time, / And everie stroake in ordre lyke a chyme" (lines 187–88).

Nashe's representation of the need for sexual intercourse to proceed through unity (the repetition of "togeather"), pacing, and harmony ("in ordre lyke a chyme"), however, is less in the service of celebrating erotic mutuality than in reproducing the Renaissance topos of female insatiability. The passionate togetherness desired by Francis, it turns out, proves to be beyond the capabilities of Tomalin. As she demands further erotic play, Tomalin – whose name, incidentally, means "little Thomas" – finds himself not up to the job, a failure that leads to his ignominious dismissal by his sexually demanding lover:

> Adiew unconstant love, to thy disporte,
>   Adiew false mirth, and melodie too-short.
> Adiew faint-hearted instrument of lust,
>   That falselie hast betrayde our equale trust.
> Hence-forth no more will I implore thine ayde,
>   Or thee, or men of cowardize upbrayde.
> My little dilldo shall suplye their kinde:
>   A knave, that moves as light as leaves by winde;
> That bendeth not, nor fouldeth anie deale,
>   But stands as stiff, as he were made of steele,
> And playes at peacock twixt my leggs right blythe,
>   And doeth my tickling swage with manie a sighe;
> For, by Saint Runnion he'le refresh me well,
>   And never make my tender bellie swell.   (lines 233–46)

Inverting a tradition of female complaint, Francis bids goodbye to that "faint-hearted instrument of lust, / That falselie hast betrayde our equale trust," and turns instead to her proud and steely dildo, that never folds or bends and, what's more, has no reproductive consequences. Despite the claims of "equale trust" on male and female sexual partners validated by this poem, its aim is not to celebrate woman's assertion of erotic autonomy. Rather, Nashe's verse conveys, albeit comically, a cautionary tale to men, while also assuaging male anxiety about erotic performance by displacing any blame for male inadequacy onto the frivolous woman who would make use of such "unnatural" devices. The idea that the instrument of female pleasure could be divorced from male genital anatomy first leads Tomalin to despair – "Curse Eunuke dilldo, senceless, counterfet, / Who sooth maie fill, but never can begett" (lines 263–64) – and then to a lengthy description of this diminutive "dwarf." Described as a "youth almost tuo handfulls highe, / Streight, round, and plumb," the dildo is imaged simultaneously as a little child and a mechanical device, both attired and nourished by its loving owner. It is a figure shot through with ambivalence: on the one hand, it rides magisterially on a "charriot of five wheeles" (the hand); on the other hand, it is condemned as a "blinde mischapen owle" (lines 266–88), a miniature grotesque. Much in the way that cuckold jokes function in Shakespearean comedy,[85] Tomalin's description of the dildo defends against his own physical limitations while bonding with other men over their common lot:

> I am not as was Hercules the stout,
>   That to the seaventh journie could hould out.
> I want those hearbe's and rootes of Indian soile,

> That strengthen wearie members in their toile;
> Druggs and Electuaries of new devise
>   Doe shunne my purse; that trembles at the price.
> Sufficeth, all I have, I yeald hir hole,
>   Which for a poore man is a princelie dole.   (lines 301–08)

Francis's "choise" of a dildo ends up legitimating the sexual apparatus of the common "poore man" who is not Herculean in his sexual prowess and who commonsensically shuns new-fangled accouterments and aphrodisiacs. Rather than metonymizing woman's autonomous desires, the dildo figures an absurd, artificial, costly knick-knack, grotesquely detached from the body of natural man.

Insofar as this attempt to dismiss the dildo positions Nashe as an apologist for the phallus, which *should* be sufficient to please, it gives an added dimension to the alternative title of the poem, "Nash *his* Dildo" (emphasis mine). The poem concludes with the speaker claiming that he wrote it "onelie for my self," an admission that suggests it was written both to vent frustration and to create an alternative ego-ideal. Indeed, throughout the poem, the dildo functions as a fetish, not, as one might expect, of female desire, but of the male bodily ego. Enacting a logic of substitution – first the dildo replaces Tomalin's inadequate penis, then his newly imagined "sufficient" penis replaces the "new devise" – this poem registers not only fears about male subordination to female sexual demands, but also anxieties about the expendability of the penis. Both the dildo in the poem and the poem itself function as substitutes for a lost object of desire, the all-powerful penis. Akin to the mixture of misogyny and pleasure that informs medical advice in the early modern period, "Nash his Dildo" condenses within its central image the contradictions of early modern erotic ideology: assumption of the need for erotic mutuality, fear of female sexual voraciousness, and anxiety about male erotic performance and phallic substitutability. Exposing the faultlines of pleasure, anxiety, and misogyny that run throughout the early modern erotic landscape, "Nash his Dildo" unwittingly acts as a wedge, prying female erotic pleasure apart from the apparatus of reproduction (and the body of man) that confers upon women's desire its social legitimacy.

As the only known piece of obscene literature of its kind circulating in sixteenth-century England, this poem by "the English Aretino" is something of an aberration.[86] Imitating and parodying the fabliaux of Chaucer, the voyeurism of Spenser, and the sensuality of Ovid, it inaugurates something new. In the words of David Frantz, "no other poem of the Elizabethan era is so explicit... It purports no moral end; it does not say that it is trying to teach by negative example; it does not condemn lust. It appeals frankly to those who have an itching to be scratched."[87] Whether that appeal is successful is a matter of some debate.[88] Critics have registered varying levels of confidence in the masculine reader's response to Nashe's "voyeuristic sexual comedy,"[89] primarily because it is not a utopian "pornotopia" populated with erect phalluses that perform "cum shots," but a nightmare of male sexual dysfunction. Granted, the point of this dysfunction is prophylactic: to express and allay the anxieties of the common man, whose ordinary penis should be more than enough. Nonetheless, Nashe's portrayal of a fallible phallus has more in common with Shakespeare's Ovidian "Venus and Adonis" – where, as Richard Halpern argues, "the strategic absence of Adonis' erection locates the ontological lack structuring the literary artwork" – than with later licentious writing.[90]

Indeed, the accepted history of the rise of pornography in England suggests that Nashe's poem lacked the hard satiric edge that would dominate obscene literature by the late seventeenth century. During and after the Civil Wars, a more graphic, scurrilous, and polemical obscenity, often alleging licentious behaviors on the part of the aristocracy, increased in manuscript and print. With the libertinism of the 1660s, the satiric offensiveness of, for instance, *Newes from the New Exchange, or the Commonwealth of Ladies* (1649) – which purports to reveal the sexual proclivities of certain aristocratic ladies who, "casting off the intolerable yoke of their *Lords* and *Husbands*, have voted themselves the *Supreme Authority* both at home and abroad"[91] – was heightened by the in-your-face debauchery of the poems of John Wilmot, Earl of Rochester (1647–80).[92] Obscene invective remained the norm until the aim of licentious and obscene literature shifted from political attacks to narrative strategies designed to produce sexual arousal.

This critical emphasis on scurrility and politics – authorized, no doubt, by the social import of the Civil Wars – leaves out, however, other trends in obscenity. A bawdy poem entitled "The Violin," published in 1655 in *Wits Interpreter, The English Parnassus* by the compiler John Cotgrave, for instance, carries on Nashe's lineage:

> To play upon a Viol, if
> A Virgin will begin,
> She first of all must know her cliff,
> And all the stops therein.
> Her prick she must hold long enough,
> Her back-falls gently take;
> Her touch must gentle be, not rough,
> She at each stroak must shake.

For the first two stanzas, the central image of the viol functions as a synecdoche of the woman's body (exploiting analogies between the shape of a woman and a violin).[93] Offering up a fantasy of masturbatory pleasure, these lines suggest that the virgin's enjoyment requires a process of tutelage: a virgin must know her own "cliff" and her own "stops." As the verse continues, however, the viol begins to take on the shape of a man:

> Her body must by no means bend,
> But stick close to her fiddle;
> Her feet must hold the lower end.
> Her knees must hold the middle.
> She boldly to the bowe must flie.
> As if she'd make it crack;
> Two fingers on the hair muw lie,
> And two upon the back.

The autoeroticism of the first stanzas merges into a posture of shared music-making. But even as the poem stabilizes its image of intercourse, it takes pains to present the woman's degree of control:

> And when she hath as she would have,
> She must it gently thrust,
> Up, down, swift, slow, at any rate
> As she her self doth list.

It is only in the final four lines, which obliquely imply that the outcome of erotic activity will be a child, that heterosexuality is ultimately secured:

> And when she once begins to find
> That she growes something cunning,
> She'l nere be quick in her mind,
> Untill she find it running.[94]

Just as the image of the viol enables a vision of both masturbation and intercourse, so too the prick and bow can refer to a penis, a dildo, or the virgin's own finger. Lingering over the virgin's body as she learns her lesson, "The Violin" is as interested in woman's pleasure – both that she takes in her own body and in the body of another – as in the gratification of men. Indeed, female fulfillment, whether autoerotic or heteroerotic, is at the center of this poem's vision of sexual knowledge.

Perhaps because its erotic ambiguity is so obliquely rendered, the voyeuristic spectacle of sexual pedagogy in "The Violin" expresses none of Nashe's anxiety about the substitution of a dildo for a penis. In light of these different attitudes toward prosthetic pleasures, I want to turn briefly to a bawdy song from the turn of the seventeenth century. "My Thing is My Own" presents a catalogue of male come-ons in the voice of a female persona who joyfully resists men's assaults on her chastity:

> I a tender young Maid have been courted by many,
> Of all sorts and Trades as ever was any:
> A spruce Haberdasher first spake me fair,
> But I would have nothing to do with Small ware.
> *My thing is my Own, and I'll keep it so still,*

Yet other young Lasses may do what they will.
A sweet scented Courtier did give me a Kiss,
And promis'd me Mountains if I would be his,
But I'll not believe him, for it is too true,
Some Courtiers do promise much more than they do. *Refrain*
A fine Man of Law did come out of the Strand,
To plead his own Cause with his Fee in his Hand;
He made a brave Motion but that would not do,
For I did dismiss him, and Nonsuit him too. *Refrain*
Next came a young Fellow, a notable Spark,
(With Green Bag and Inkhorn, a Justices Clark)
He pull'd out his Warrant to make all appear,
But I sent him away with a Flea in his Ear. *Refrain*
A Master of Musick came with an intent,
To give me a Lesson on my Instrument,
I thank'd him for nothing, but bid him be gone,
For my little Fiddle should not be plaid on. *Refrain*
An Usurer came with abundance of Cash,
But I had no mind to come under his Lash,
He profer'd me Jewels, and great store of Gold,
But I would not Mortgage my little Free-hold. *Refrain*
A blunt Lieutenant surpriz'd my Placket,
And fiercely began to rifle and sack it,
I mustered my Spirits up and became bold,
And forc'd my Lieutenant to quit his strong hold. *Refrain*
A Crafty young Bumpkin that was very rich,
And us'd with his Bargains to go thro' stitch,
Did tender a Sum, but it would not avail,
That I should admit him my Tenant in tayl. *Refrain*
A fine dapper Taylor, with a Yard in his Hand,
Did profer his Service to be at Command,
He talk'd of a slit I had above Knee,
But I'll have no Taylors to stitch it for me. *Refrain*
A Gentleman that did talk much of his Grounds,
His Horses, his Settling-Dogs and his Grey-hounds,
Put in for a Course, and us'd all his Art,
But he mist of the Sport, for Puss would not start, [*sic*] *Refrain*
A pretty young Squire new come to the Town,
To empty his Pockets, and so to go down,
Did profer a kindness, but I would have none,
The same that he us'd to his Mother's Maid Joan. *Refrain*
Now here I could reckon a hundred and more,
Besides all the Gamesters recited before,
That made their addresses in hopes of a snap
But as young as I was I understood Trap,
My thing is my own, and I'll keep it so still,
Until I be Marryed, say Men what they will.[95]

Employing to comic effect the trope of male trades, "My Thing Is My Own" mocks eleven male stratagems, from those of the courtier to those of the tailor, through the voice of a knowing female. Like "The Violin," this jaunty "catch" figures the female body as a fiddle. Like "Nash his Dildo," it pokes mild fun at male ineptitude (e.g., haberdashers with "Small ware" and courtiers who "promise much more than they do"), while ventriloquizing female knowledge about sex. Even as it gives voice to the dominant ideology of chastity (chastity is a "Free-hold' to be defended), however, this song assertively maintains that "my thing is *my* own." Rather than promoting a narrow notion of female purity, it defers its mention of marriage until the final version of the refrain, which "saves" the song from total illicitness. Implying that the experience of chastity might involve its own pleasures, "My Thing Is My Own" neatly conflates separate aspects of female embodiment – virginity, vagina, clitoris – into "my thing."

The potential pleasures of chastity will be explored in the next and subsequent chapters. For now, I want to suggest that the erotic imaginaries of these three texts play a more important role in the evolution of the genre of sexual obscenity than has previously been thought. By the early eighteenth century, pornography, with the "self-conscious aim of arousing sexual desire in the reader,"[96] was thriving on English soil, rivaling the output of the French and Italians rather than, as had been true before, primarily translating them. It has been noted by critics that these later texts inherit from their predecessors the formal strategy of articulating female desire *as if* from the female perspective.[97] Female volubility is tied intimately to another popular pornographic convention, the character of the female prostitute or courtesan.[98] As Kathryn Norberg suggests,

From the Renaissance to the French Revolution, the courtesan fills libertine literature; her life and loves form the very stuff of many pornographic texts. The whore biography or confession is exceedingly common in the genre and, usually, the whore herself narrates the story. From *La Puttana errante* to *Fanny Hill*, from Margot to Juliette, the prostitute's chatter simply *is* much of Western pornography, and no other character, male or female, pimp or rake, can dispute her dominance in the world of the obscene.[99]

The illusion of an overheard "privacy" among women enables writers to portray an elder prostitute's tutelage of a novice whore or two neophytes comparing sexual technique. But the loquaciousness of whores is not limited to descriptions of past or future sexual encounters with men. Female characters also frankly describe their own pleasures to each other – including how they like it with men *and women*. More often than not, such intimate talk leads to intimate action, whether in the form of an educational "how to" or in a more candid pursuit of gratification. The depiction of homoeroticism in Restoration and eighteenth-century English pornography is amply demonstrated by Emma Donoghue, and is parenthetically noted in most accounts of the genre.[100] Given that in many cases the women eventually become frustrated by the absence of a penis and turn to men for fulfillment, most commentators view representations of women pleasuring one another as a stabilizing fantasy geared toward the delectation of male readers – just one more titillation leading up to the exhibition of male sexual prowess. As prostitutes, after all, these characters are defined in terms of their sexual service to men. In many feminist accounts of contemporary porn, a similar line of argument is sustained: images of *lesbianism* – so frequent in both soft and hard-core porn – are judged to be in the service of male commodification of women. Donoghue, however, challenges the phallocentrism of this account, reminding us that such images may also have been available to at least some women readers, providing them with valuable information, food for fantasy, and a sense of erotic possibility. Brantôme, for instance, describes a French noblewoman who "kept a figure of Aretino in her room... [for] 'books and other devices had served her well.'"[101]

The interpretation of prostitution as always in the service of men has kept us from seeing the role of women's autonomous desire in the development of the genre. From the ventriloquization of female pleasure in Nashe to the sexual play among women in Cleland, pornography relies on women's ability to say what they want, and want what they say. It also relies, if we take the titles of Nashe's "Dildo," "The Violin," and "My Thing is My Own" seriously, on a materialization of female desire in the form of prosthetic objects: a dildo, a violin (that both is and is not one's own body), my "thing." In forging a link between female desire, the articulation of women's erotic prerogatives, and the pursuit of autonomous pleasures, these texts bequeath to posterity an ambivalent legacy that would inform and also destabilize the obscenity of the future: the image of women taking pleasure, literally, into their own hands.[102]

Most scholars of early modern pornography and medical writing at some point find themselves meditating on the fine line between licentiousness and science. The genre of medical advice in this period is widely acknowledged to skirt the edges of the obscene. From historians of medicine (Roy Porter and Robert Martensen)[103] to historians of pornography (Roger Thompson) to historians of *lesbianism* (Emma Donoghue and Susan Lanser), scholars agree that not only do some medical manuals exhibit a titillating tone, but that genuinely obscene works attempted to authorize themselves by association with medical works. As a result, vernacular medical texts were regarded as objects of suspicion and, as Thompson observes, there is a "detectable defensiveness on the part of authors of serious or pseudo-serious medical works on these sensitive topics about the motivation of some of their readers." The association of medicine with obscenity is registered, as Thompson reports, in *The Practical Part of Love*, which refers to the "library of 'Love's University,'" which "contains along with blatantly dirty books, such titles as *Culpepper's Midwife*, *The Compleat Midwife* and *The Birth of Mankind*."[104]

Given the permeable boundary between obscenity and medical writing in this period, it makes sense to ask whether the thematic strategies pursued in obscene poems bear some relation to the strategies of those English medical texts that include explicit descriptions of genital anatomy and sexual functioning. Vernacular medical writers were keenly aware of the censorship of sexually explicit materials. The same year that saw the rediscovery of the clitoris had witnessed the first papal index of forbidden books – an edict of which Aretino's works ran afoul. And such efforts to censor were not the purview solely of the Roman Catholic church. It is a peculiarity of the history of English censorship that "The choise of valentines" was not burned alongside other obscene, scurrilous, and satiric texts in London during the Bishop's Ban of 1599 – perhaps because it had not yet come to the attention of the authorities.[105] Facing charges of obscenity that Nashe's poem somehow escaped, medical writers had more in common with Nashe than they might have preferred to think, for their treatments of gynecology articulate similar connections among women's desire, their legitimate erotic needs, and the possibility of their autonomous pleasures. In doing so, medical texts negotiated the same terrain of misogyny and anxiety that obscene poems exposed to comic effect.

Such a negotiation, I want to argue, is particularly evident at the point when medical texts move from discussions of the clitoris to a more general description of the female genitals. As we have seen, the view that the female body was weaker, colder, more prone to disease and more difficult to cure than the bodies of men was pressured in the seventeenth century by growing beliefs in women's own special form of perfection and purpose in God's design. Despite this theological and ideological advance, however, throughout the seventeenth century the vagina and uterus continue to be considered aesthetically unpleasant, annoyingly difficult to access, and – apparently self-evidently – loathsome. A scatological disgust seethes from descriptions of the female genitals across the early modern period. Paré set the tone in the mid-sixteenth century:

But out of all doubt unlesse nature had prepared so many allurements, baits, and provocations of pleasure, there is scarce any man so hot or delighted in venereous acts, which considering and marking the place appointed for humane conception, the loathsomnesse of the filth which daily falleth downe unto it, and wherewithall it is humected and moistened, and the vicinity and nearenes of the great gut under it, and of the bladder above it, but would shun the embraces of women.[106]

Crooke, writing in the early seventeenth century, concurs: "For were it not that the God of Nature hath placed heerein so incredible a sting or rage of pleasure, as whereby wee are transported for a time as it were out of our selves, what man is there almost who hath anie sense of his own divine nature, that would defile himselfe in such impurities?"[107] Crooke reiterates this sentiment after describing the clitoris and the excretion of seed: "And indeed this sting of pleasure was very necessary, without which man especially the one sexe in scorne and detestation of so bruitish and base a worke, the other for feare of payne and trouble, would have abhorred this woorke of Nature." He also says of the womb: "we are bred of a brittle & perishing substance betweene the excrements and the urine, and must moulder againe into earth and dust," and calls the "orifice of the necke" (the vagina) "too obscoene to look upon."[108]

Likewise, James McMath, writing *The expert midwife* in the late seventeenth century, reports that people copulate "chiefly, from that signal *Delite*, and enchanting *Pleasure* found therein... For else how could man, so noble a *Creature*, make any attrection of these *Obscoene parts*, which (for being so *Foulsome*, are turned down into the *Vilest Room*, in a manner the *Sink* of the *Body*) much less court, accept, or indulge to this *Embrace*, so filthy a *Fact*."[109] Even Thomas Bartholin, staunch supporter of female reproductive integrity, poses the question: "Why therefore should we be proud who are bred between Dung and Urin?"[110] This formulation is modified somewhat by Jane Sharp, who describes the neck of the womb standing "betwixt the urinary passage and the right Gut, which are the two great sinks of the body that vain Man should not be over proud of his beginning."[111] Shifting the emphasis away from the site of "Dung" and "Urin" to the vanity of man, Sharp subtly overwrites masculine disgust: the vagina represents not the abjection of the female, but the overweening pride of mankind.

Just as the purpose of sex for men and women is the same, so too are the basic mechanics identical, as Crooke attests:

that there might bee a mutuall longing desire between the sexes to communicate with one another, and to conserve their stockes together for the propagation of mankinde, beside the ardor and heate of the spirits conteyned in their seeds, the parts of generation are so formed, but there is not onely a naturall instinct of copulation, but an appetite and earnest desire thereunto, and therefore the obscoene parts are compounded of particles of exquisite sense, that passion being added unto the will, their embracements might be to better purpose.[112]

Despite this identity of purpose and process, a difference is introduced when the meaning of erotic pleasure is addressed, for the logic of this scatological disgust and the compensation that pleasure provides are structured symmetrically along gender lines: in all of these texts, pleasure propitiates men for contaminating contact with female genitalia; while women, punished by the curse of Eve, are compensated for their future childbirth labor. As Crooke asks: "what woman would admit the embracements of a man, remembering her nine moneths burthen, her painefull and dangerous deliverance, her care, disquiet and anxiety in the nursing and education of the infant."[113] The idea that woman is blinded by pleasure was anticipated by Paré: "Nor would any woman desire the company of man, which once premeditates or forethinkes with her selfe on the labour that shee shall sustaine in bearing the burthen of her childe nine moneths, and of the almost deadly paines that she shall suffer in her delivery."[114] This line of reasoning is vulgarly affirmed by Joubert: "This is why the woman, driven by this lustiness, quickly forgets the vows and protestations she uttered, racked with pain, during childbirth when she had to vomit back the pleasure received previously."[115] And it is reiterated more respectfully by McMath: "What Woman also, would else impair her *Health* . . . in *Breeding, Bearing* and *bringing* up of *Children*, if not bewitched to this incredible pleasure excited in *Coition*."[116] Ferrand uses the concept of compensation to settle the old question of which sex has greater pleasure during intercourse: "the woman experiences more violently this brutal desire, and not unreasonably so, since nature owes her some compensating pleasures for the suffering she endures in pregnancy and childbirth."[117]

The logic that women are condemned to the horrors of childbirth while men are condemned to the horrors of female anatomy is conventional enough to comprise a *Leitmotif* of early modern medicine. The symmetry of this logic only underscores the asymmetry at its core: women's genitals pose a threat to man, a threat that apparently is assuaged only by the extraordinary pleasure of the "little epilepsy" of male orgasm. It is the rare writer who does not correlate a woman's physical pain with a man's aversion to women, who does not judge them both as compensated by orgasm, and who does not, in making this argument, differentiate between the female "sink of the body" and the "seat of woman's delight." Poulain de la Barre is one exception. Writing in the late seventeenth century, he argues that women pay dearer for sexual contact than do men, "but their pain and trouble ought not to be prejudicial to them and draw upon them contempt in place of esteem."[118] Thomas Raynald, author of *The birth of mankind, otherwise named The Womans Booke* (1545), is another, and extremely early, example, since he may have been the first to refute the concept of women's imperfection.[119] The preface of his 1626 edition disputes that men who read of female anatomy "shall conceive a certaine loathsomnesse and abhorring towards a woman," arguing

I know nothing in woman so privie ne so secret, that they should neede to care who know of it, neither is there any part in woman more to be abborred, then in man. And if the knowledge of such things which commonly be called the womens privities, should diminish the hearty love and estimation of a woman in the minde of man, then by this reason, Physitians & Chirurgians wives should greatly be abhored and misbeloved of their husbands.[120]

Raynald's text presents women's pleasure as recompense for childbirth, but without making invidious comparisons to men:

For if that the God of nature had not instincted and inset the body of man and woman such a vehement and ardent appetite and lust, the one lawfully to company with the other, neyther man ne woman would ever have been so attentive to the works of generation and the increasment of posterity, to the utter decay in short time of all mankinde. For yee shall heare some women in time of their travaile, moved through great paine & intollerable anguish, forswere and vow themselfe never to companie with a man againe: yet after that the panges passed, within short while, for entyre love to their husbandes, and singular naturall Delight betweene man and woman, they forget both the sorrow passed, and that that is to come.

The explanation here of the purpose of pleasure – that a mutual "singular naturall Delight" provides a means of insuring procreation – is superseded by the logic of compensation articulated by most writers over the following century.

Why and how this change in logics occurred can only be ascertained from a more comprehensive, diachronic examination of medical texts. My purpose in drawing attention to the near consensus of seventeenth-century medical writers on men's need for compensation is to mark the tonal contrast between their celebratory treatments of the clitoris (the "seat of women's delight") and their venomous representations of the vagina and uterus (the "sink of the body"). Although the "sink of the body" is used in anatomical treatises to describe the location in both sexes of urinary and excremental evacuation, the trepidation articulated when this image is associated with the female genitalia is not attributable to a phobic reaction to bodily waste in early modern culture. Given the emphasis in humoral medicine on the healthful benefits of excretion and purging, early moderns approached urination and defecation primarily through a discourse of internal regulation and management.[121] As employed in gynecological discussions, the "sink of the body" seems to mark the way the female body merges excremental, reproductive, and sexual functions. This condensed image of a female "sewer" does not make the bowels sexual, but rather, renders the genitals excremental. It communicates less a fear of being swallowed or enclosed, than a fear of one's body part being contaminated and then expelled. Since H. R. Hayes explored from the perspective of cultural anthropology the theme of the *vagina dentura*,[122] scholars have examined the ramifications of the vagina as the gate of entry into life, a critical tradition culminating for many scholars of the early modern period in the brilliant psychoanalysis of male fears of engulfment by Janet Adelman.[123] But the misogyny of early modern medicine does not encompass the female body *tout court*; rather, medical texts differentiate the site of male anxiety from the site of female pleasure. Contrasting the horror of the one to the equanimity of the other not only suggests that such fears are historically specific, it also reveals an important and heretofore under-theorized fissure in early modern erotic ideology. This fissure will be mined further in subsequent chapters which focus more on the clitoris than the vagina, more on the possibility and practice of woman's erotic autonomy than on the recurrence of male anxiety.

The contradictions of medical writing, and the compensations constructed in the wake of such contradictions, inform the strategies medical writers pursue when negotiating the peril of revealing nature's or women's "secrets,"[124] or of representing the "obscene" parts of the body in the vernacular. In response to the risks involved in publishing texts directed beyond a social or scientific elite, including the risk of censorship, medical writers pursue apotropaic strategies to appease the censors and ward off criticism. In particular, they attempt to protect themselves from the vulnerability of exposure by projecting the potential charge of obscenity onto the body of woman. Countless medical prefaces – and many tangents in gynecological discussions – confront the problem of "Englishing" an academic knowledge previously expressed in Latin, as writers acknowledge the responsibility they bear for the illicit uses to which their vernacular texts might be put. In 1578 John Banister, a reader in anatomy who published *The Historie of Man*, declined to describe the female genitalia, invoking the indecency of lifting "up the veil of nature's secrets in woman's shapes."[125] In his "Epistle to the Chirurgians," he claims that he has "endeavoured to set wyde open the closet doore of natures secretes, whereinto every Godly Artist may safely enter, to see clearly all the partes, and notable devices of nature in the body of man. From the female, and that (as I suppose) for sundry good considerations, I have wholly abstained my penne: least, shunning Charibdis, I should fall into Scylla headlong."[126] The "Prologue to the women Readers" in the 1604 edition of Raynald addresses the problem first by praising knowledgeable midwives and castigating ignorant ones, and then concluding,

And this do I say, because that at the first comming abroad of this present boke, many of this sort of Midwives, moved either of envie or els of malice, or both, diligented and endeavoured them very earnestly, by all wayes possible, to find the means to suppresse and abrogate the same, making all of their acquaintance (whom they thought to have any knowledge thereof) to beleeve that it was nothing worth, and that it should be a slaunder to women, for so much as therein was descried and set foorth the secrets and privities of women, and that every boye and knave had of these bookes, reading them as openly as the tales of Robin hood, &.

Apparently under attack from midwives for having exposed the "secrets and privities of women" to "boyes and knaves" who might read the book "as openly as the tales of Robin hood," Raynald asks of his "gentle readers ... that if they finde any thing therein interpretable to divers sense, to accept onely that which may make to the best, according to my meaning." Rhetorically attempting to construct chaste readers, Raynald positions certain ignorant midwives as the conservative rearguard of women's reproductive health while simultaneously treating those midwives who would read "according to my meaning" with intellectual generosity. The revised preface in the edition of 1626 states that "there is nothing under heaven so good, but that it may be perverted and turned to an evill use, by them that be evill & naught themselves"; thus, "it shall be no great wonder, though this little book also, made, written and set foorth for a good purpose, yet by light and lewde persons be used contrary to godlinesse, honestie, or the entent of the writer thereof."[127] The condemnation of "light and lewde persons" is taken up by Nicolas Culpeper, best-selling compiler and translator of several books of physic and midwifery, who is even less sanguine about his readers, more convinced that, whatever his godly intentions, his words will be put to lascivious use. After debating the problem of hermaphroditism and the possibility of "mutation out of one Sex into another," for instance, Culpeper concludes with the problem of the vernacular: "Perhaps it may be judged by some, to have been more decent that these things should have been delivered in the Latin, than in the Vulgar Tongue, that so the secrets of Nature might not have been prostituted to every unworthy Reader that makes use of such things, only for a mockery, and a May-game, and to promote idle and lascivious discourse." He justifies the publication of his midwifery by appealing to the deaths of women and infants in childbirth, arguing that the concealment of Nature's secrets "had been much more inexcusable, than the publishing can be."[128] Taking refuge in the surety that his publications will relieve misery and save lives, Culpeper does not so much attempt to construct a chaste reader as shame the "prostituting" reader who would use his text for a "mockery and a May-game." Since Jane Sharp's entire text of 1671 is devoted to unveiling the secrets of generation, her Introduction, "Of the necessity, and Usefulness of the Art of Midwifry," constructs her authorial persona as "desiring the Courteous Reader to use as much modesty in the perusal of it, as I have endeavoured to do in the writing of it, considering that such an Art as this cannot be set forth, but that young men and maids will have much just cause to blush sometimes, and be ashamed of their own follies, as I wish they may if they shall chance to read it, that they may not convert that into evil that is really intended for a general good."[129]

Vernacular medical writers had good reason to be concerned. In the sixteenth century the renowned French surgeon Ambroise Paré had been put on trial, ostensibly for publishing his complete works without authorization; but the rhetoric of his defense makes clear that he believed the problem to be the openness with which he described in French rather than Latin reproductive functions and erotic transgressions. Under pressure from the Parisian Faculty of Medicine, he excised from the third edition of *Des Monstres et Prodiges* his discussion of tribades (drawn from Leo Africanus) which had appeared in the second edition, replacing it with a brief reference to the capital trial of two French women for sodomy; eventually he removed the entire passage on the female genitalia. When Johnson's seventeenth-century English translation of Paré's *Workes* arrives at the clitoris, the text refers briefly to Colombo and Falloppia, and then defers responsibility: "Because it is an obscene part, let those which desire to know more of it, read the Authors which I cited."[130] Nonetheless, Johnson elsewhere includes a defense of medical explicitness to preface Paré's discussion of "atheists, Sodomites, Out-lawes" who "have not doubted to have filthy and abhominable copulation with beasts":

That which followeth is a horrid thing to be spoken; but the chaste minde of the Reader will give mee pardon, and conceive that, which not onely of the Stoikes, but all Philosophers, who are busied about the search of the causes of things, must hold, that there is nothing obscene or filthy to be spoken. Those things that are accounted obscene may bee spoken without blame, but they cannot bee acted or perpetrated without great wickednesse, fury and madnesse; therefore that ill which is in obscenity consists not in word, but wholly in the act.[131]

Laurent Joubert, like Paré, was forced to revise the second edition of his *Erreurs populaires* due to accusations that his work might incite lascivious thoughts or behaviors in girls better kept in ignorance.[132] In a more radical case of censorship, the royal Parisian physician Pineaus had his books on gynecology and obstetrics confiscated because of his discussion of the loss of virginity.[133]

The situation was no different in England. When Crooke proposed to publish *Microcosmographia*, the London College of Physicians called him to account for his description of the reproductive organs. According to Jonathan Sawday, portions of the text were in circulation when John King, Bishop of London, reported being affronted by Books 4 and 5, on the "parts belonging to generation." The Bishop influenced the President of the College of Physicians to condemn the book and to inform the printer, William Jaggard, that if published without alteration, it would be destroyed.[134] In his 1615 preface to the Barber-Surgeons, Crooke answered several objections, including his inclusion of anatomical illustrations, which had been judged "as obscoene as Aretines" – "a shamelesse accusation," he retorts, since the figures are drawn from the most eminent anatomists, and had already been included in English works dedicated to "three famous princes, the last a Mayden-Queene." (Perhaps in recognition that an allusion to Pietro Aretino, whose obscene sonnets had circulated with Guilio Romano's sixteen postures might heighten rather than lessen illicit connotations, this passage is deleted in the second edition of 1631.) Referring to the authority of other wise men as well as the king, Crooke says, "[f]or my adding the History of the partes of Generation, I have already given account, partly to his Majesty, partly in my Prefaces to the fourth and fift bookes."[135]

Indeed, the preface to the Fourth Book, "Of the naturall Parts belonging to generation, as well in Men as in Women," is a lengthy peroration which dramatizes Crooke's dilemma. He admits to having "entred into deliberation with my selfe":

whether I were best silently to passe it by, or to insist upon it . . . I conceived my labour would be but lame if it wanted this limbe, and a great part of my end and ayme frustrated, it being to exhibit the wonderfull wisedome and goodnesse of our Creator, which as

"A certaine incredible excesse of pleasure" 111

in all the parts it is most admirable, so in this (if perfection will admit any degrees) it is transcendent. The whole body is the Epitomie of the world, containing therein whatsoever is in the large universe; Seed is the Epitomy of the body, having in it the power and immediate possibility of all the partes ... Adde hereto, first that the diseases hence arising, as they bee most fearefull and fullest of anxiety especially in the Female sexe, so are they hardest to be cured: the reason I conceive to be, because the partes are least knowne as being veyled by Nature, and through our unseasonable modesty not sufficiently uncovered.¹³⁶

Invoking the prestige of those anatomists who, "even in their mother tongues" had "received allowance in all ages and Common-wealths," Crooke maintains:

there was onely one obstacle; to reveyle the veyle of *Nature*, to prophane her mysteries for a little curious skil-pride, to ensnare mens mindes by sensuall demonstrations, seemeth a thing liable to hevy construction. But what is this I pray you else but to araigne vertue at the barre of vice? Hath the holy Scriptue it selfe (the wisdome of God) as well as in the old Law particularly, as also in many passages of the new, balked this argument? God that Created them, did he not intend their preservation, or can they bee preserved and not known? Or knowne and not discovred? Indeede it were to be wished that all men would come to the knowledge of these secrets with pure eyes and eares, such as they were matched with in their Creation: but shall we therefore forfet our knowledge because some men cannot conteine their lewd and inordinate affections?¹³⁷

Admitting the "hevy construction" to which he knows he is liable, Crooke rehearses the dangers attending his effort to "reveyle the veyle of Nature." Lifting the veil threatens to "prophane" it, a problem he handles by displacing it: the issue is not obscene pictures and descriptions, but "some men" who cannot contain their "lewd and inordinate affections." If this displacement does not suffice to quiet the reader's fears, "we have so plotted our busines, that he that listeth may separate this Booke from the rest and reserve it privately unto himselfe."¹³⁸ Crooke ends his preface by advising "no man to take further knowledge then shall serve good instruction."¹³⁹ Clearly anxious about the efficacy of his cautions, Crooke one page later again appeals to the reader to approach his description of "these parts of generation" with "as chaste heart to reade as wee did to write,"¹⁴⁰ thereby banking his trust on the reader's identification with the writer.

Crooke's efforts to construct a chaste reader, however, take a curious turn in his conclusion to his chapter on the "yard." Here Crooke expresses the hope that, while he has "bin indeed as particular as the Anatomicall History did require," he "shall finde pardon, because the Reader may perceive (at least if he have any knowledge) that I have pretermitted many secrets of Nature, which I could and would heere have somewhat insisted upon, if I had imagined that all into whose hands this worke should come had bin competent and fit Auditors for such kinde of Philosophy."¹⁴¹ Coyly refusing to fully "reveyle" the "veyle of Nature" when it covers the male member, Crooke constructs the reader as someone who, if only sufficiently knowledgeable, would know which secrets remain hidden.

In an effort to maintain the chastity of his readers, Crooke simultaneously entices the reader with, and chastises him for, his desire for further knowledge. In other words, he strategically gives and withholds, discloses and obscures. This strategy, I want to suggest, is not adequately interpreted as a manifestation of an emerging culture of politeness, but rather must be viewed in relation to the institutional practices of early modern science, including the growth of male medical practitioners and, in particular, their appropriation of those aspects of gynecology and obstetrics that previously had been the purview of female midwives.[142] We can gain some analytical purchase on the intertwining of anatomy, obscurity, modesty, and misogyny, as well as the problem of censorship, by looking more closely at anatomical illustrations themselves.[143] For in his simultaneous commitment to display and concealment, Crooke performs rhetorically what anatomy books perform visually. If, in their prefaces and apologies, medical writers attempt to overwrite the female body as always already modest, securely placed in the epistemological and social service of man, in their use of images of the naked yet chaste woman they shift the burden of concern about "lifting the veil of nature" onto the female body. The tensions between scientific inquiry and illicit titillation that surface in addresses to the reader are mirrored in the tension between modesty and exposure evinced in anatomical engravings of women.

Throughout the early modern period, such illustrations focus primarily on the female reproductive organs, as women are employed as the reproductive supplement to generic man.[144] In Berengario da Carpi's *Isagogae breves* (1522), the female figure reveals her organs of generation in a triumphant lifting of Nature's veil[145] (figure 8). Like da Carpi's male figures, who also perform exuberant self-demonstrations, these female figures advertise delight in the new knowledge born of empirical inquiry. But the concept of revelation would become more complex and more gendered with Vesalius's *Epitome* of 1543. Here nude male and female figures illustrate surface anatomy through the medium of the classical antique – in accord with Vesalius's belief that "the body employed for public dissection be as normal as possible according to its sex and of medium age, so that you may compare other bodies to it, as if to the statue of Policletus"[146] (figures 9 and 10). Referring to Polykleitos, the antique sculptor who developed a canon of human proportions, Vesalius proposes the purpose of anatomy as the revelation of an ideal measure; the figures of his *Epitome* correspondingly demonstrate surface perfection, proper proportion, and harmonious form. Rather than gleeful self-demonstration, however, the female figure of the *Epitome* enacts feminine modesty, her hand placed protectively over her genitals. The Vesalian figure is part of a lineage of the "Venus *pudica*" (the modest Venus) derived from Praxiteles's *Knidian Aphrodite*, sculpted in the fourth century, BCE. As the "first monumental cult statue of a goddess to be represented completely nude," the *Knidian Aphrodite*

Figure 8   Jacopo Berengario da Carpi, *Isagogae breves* (1522).

Figure 9 Andreas Vesalius, *Epitome* (1543); reproduced from *De Humani Corporis Fabrica*.

was, in the words of Nanette Salomon, the inspiration of "countless Hellenistic and Roman copies, adaptations and derivations."[147] In a state of both "complete nudity and self-conscious nakedness," Praxiteles's Aphrodite draws attention to her genitals in the act of protecting them; she is "vulnerable in exhibition" and the condition of her display is precisely that she "does not wish to be seen."[148]

"A certaine incredible excesse of pleasure"   115

Figure 10   Andreas Vesalius, *Epitome* (1543); reproduced from *De Humani Corporis Fabrica*.

116 The renaissance of lesbianism

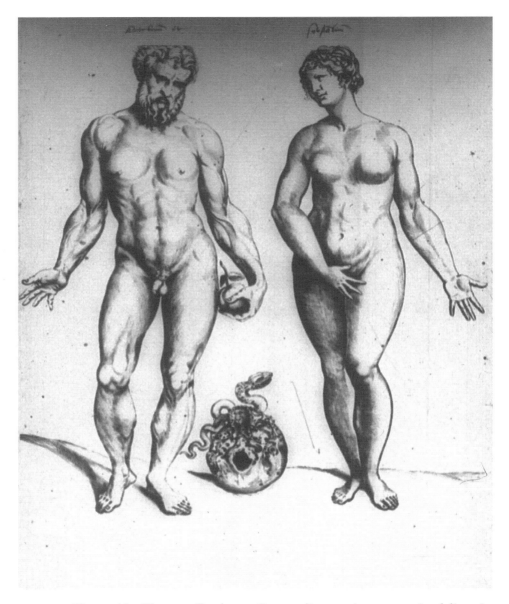

Figure 11 Thomas Geminus, *Compendiosa totius anatomie delineatio* (1545).

Vesalius's figures from the *Epitome* were quickly pirated by Thomas Geminus, a Flemish printer, who united them in his English *Compendiosa totius anatomie delineatio* of 1545[149] (figure 11). By bringing the two figures together, relocating the skull, and adding a serpent and an apple, Geminus transfigured the Vesalian antique into Adam and Eve.[150] Geminus's use of images of biblical progenitors to illustrate the book that would open the body operates simultaneously in two directions: alluding to the Fall of man, it registers the potential danger of anatomical investigation, while also insisting on the Christian authority of the knowledge gained thereby – no mere pagan knowledge this. With the advent of Adam and Eve as anatomical figures, the tension between modesty and exposure evident in the *pudica* pose is heightened.[151]

In antique sculpture, the Venus *pudica* evolved into a conventionalized posture: as in the most oft-cited derivation, the Capitoline Venus (a Roman copy of a Hellenistic original, *c*. 120 BCE), she protects her genitals with one hand while touching her breast with the other (figure 12). It is this image that would prove to be particularly enabling for early modern anatomy. With her ambivalent gestures of both modesty and revelation, the Venus *pudica* replaced Eve as the dominant trope for anatomical illustration of the female body, employed throughout the sixteenth and seventeenth centuries on title pages and frontispieces. First depicted in Juan de Valverde de Humoso's *Anatomia del corpo humano* (1556), what I call the anatomical *pudica* provides, through the directional siting of her hands, a visual correlation between breast and womb, food and infant, economically representing the purpose of female anatomy and physiology[152] (figure 13). At the same time, the act of covering the pubis visually dramatizes the question faced by medical writers: how to unveil the body without venturing into obscenity.

Etymologically, *pudica* derives from words for modesty and shame; Crooke's definition of the woman's "privitie," for instance, is "pudendum muliebre" or the "woman's modesty."[153] Through the visual tradition of the *pudica*, the associations between the female genitals, feminine modesty, and the shame of exposure are harnessed to the anatomical project. Indeed, as the anatomical *pudica* comes to function as a figure for the anatomical endeavor more generally, she becomes the means by which anxiety about obscenity is parlayed. Crooke, for instance, used an Englished version of Valverde's figure to represent not only the reproductive interior (figure 14) but, positioned alongside venous man, the anatomical project itself (figure 15). Subsequent illustrations employing the anatomical *pudica* are reiterated on anatomical plates and frontispieces throughout the seventeenth century, including André Du Laurens's influential *Opera omnia anatomica et medica*.[154] Whether used to demonstrate the exterior of the flesh or the interior reproductive organs, the anatomical *pudica* embodies the tension between chastity and obscenity, scientific inquiry and illicit knowledge, that vexes anatomy in the vernacular.

Given the way the female body was deployed to negotiate such questions of epistemology, it is difficult not to see in Jane Sharp's assertion that "we women have no more cause to be angry, or be ashamed of what Nature hath given us than men have, we cannot be without ours no more than they can want theirs" a defensiveness born of over a century of gynecological ambivalence.[155]

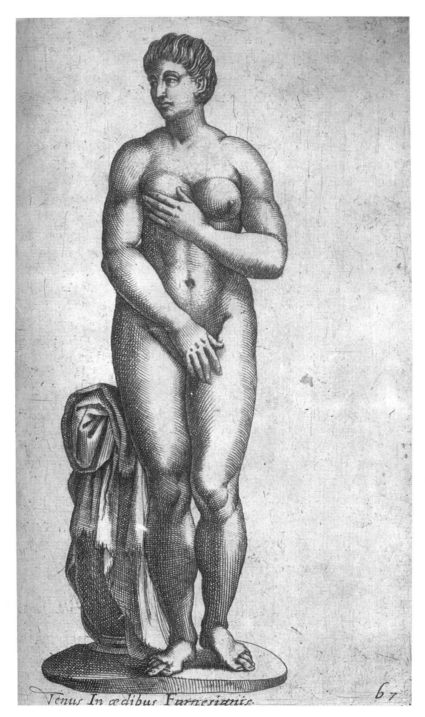

Figure 12   Giovanni Battista de Calivari, the Capitoline Venus, *Antiquarum Staturarum Urbis Romae* (1585).

"A certaine incredible excesse of pleasure" 119

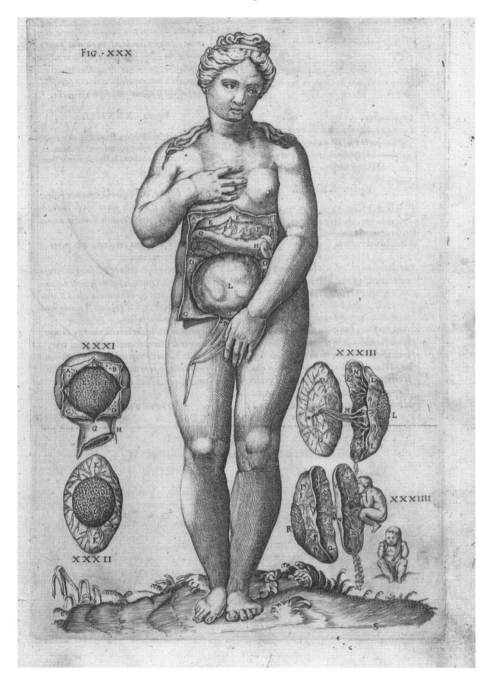

Figure 13   Juan de Valverde de Humoso, *Anatomia del corpo humano* (1556/1560).

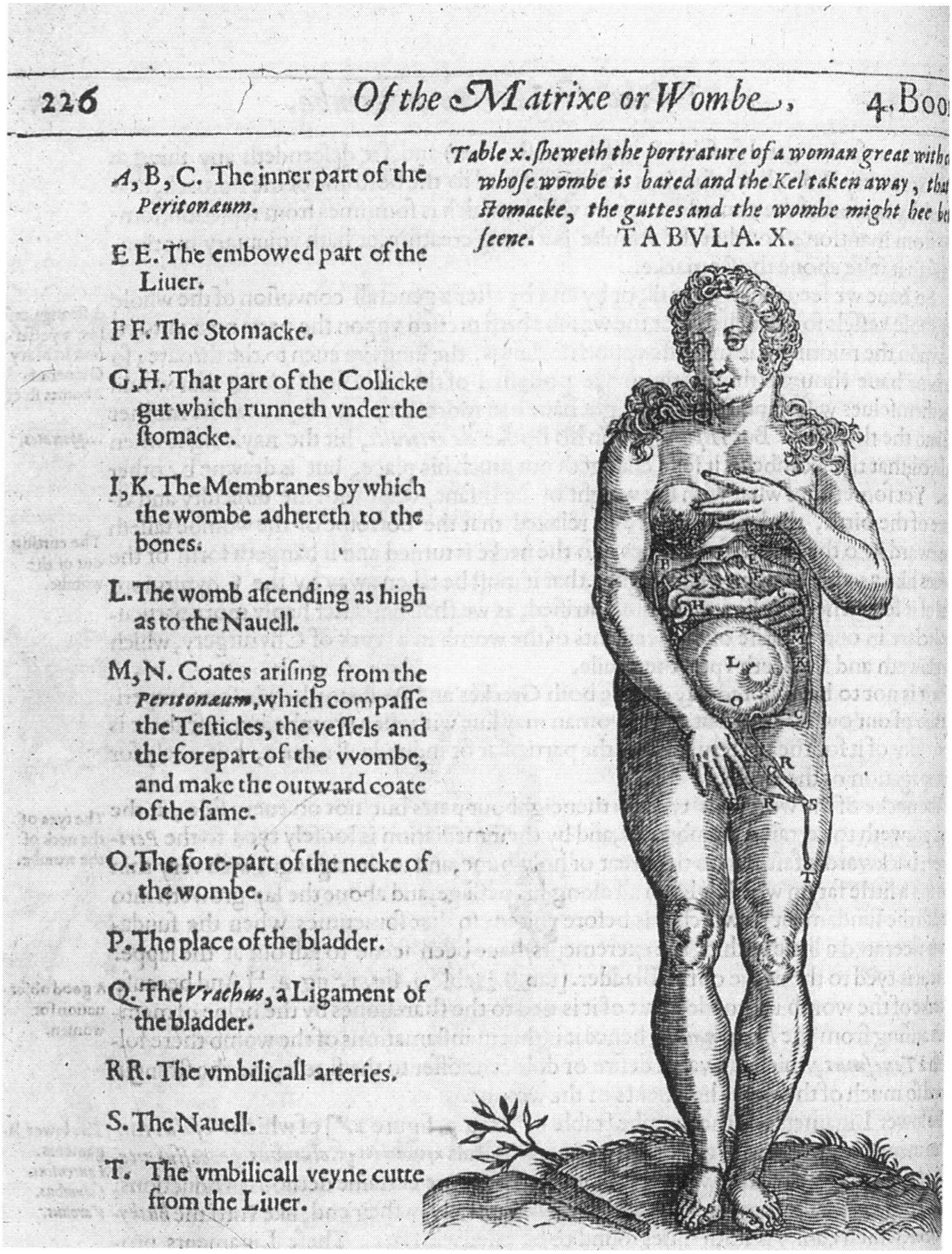

> 226 Of the Matrixe or Wombe, 4. Boo
>
> Table x. sheweth the portrature of a woman great with [child]
> whose wombe is bared and the Kel taken away, that
> Stomacke, the guttes and the wombe might bee [better]
> seene. TABVLA. X.
>
> A, B, C. The inner part of the Peritonæum.
>
> E E. The embowed part of the Liuer.
>
> F F. The Stomacke.
>
> G, H. That part of the Collicke gut which runneth vnder the stomacke.
>
> I, K. The Membranes by which the wombe adhereth to the bones.
>
> L. The womb ascending as high as to the Nauell.
>
> M, N. Coates arising from the Peritonæum, which compasse the Testicles, the vessels and the forepart of the wombe, and make the outward coate of the same.
>
> O. The fore-part of the necke of the wombe.
>
> P. The place of the bladder.
>
> Q. The Vrachus, a Ligament of the bladder.
>
> R R. The vmbilicall arteries.
>
> S. The Nauell.
>
> T. The vmbilicall veyne cutte from the Liuer.

Figure 14 Helkiah Crooke, *Microcosmographia* (1615).

Intervening in her culture's assumptions of female inferiority, and explicitly altering the debate about which sex bears the greater burden of shame, Sharp attempts to level the gender playing field by comparing Nature's bequest to men to that of the abjected female body. By rewriting the meaning of *pudica* on

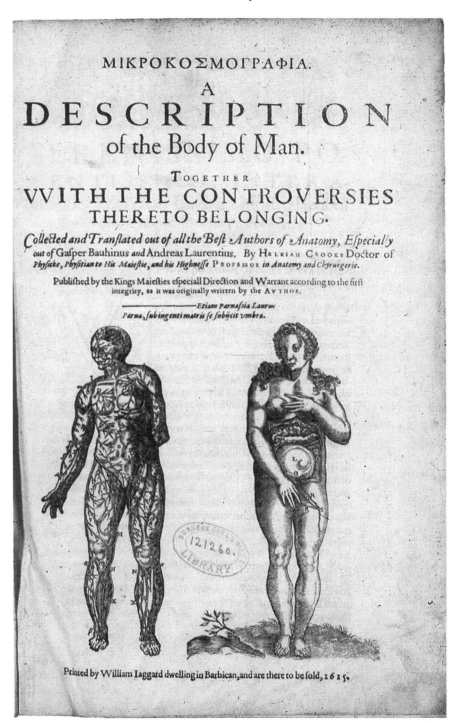

Figure 15   Helkiah Crooke, *Microcosmographia* (1615).

behalf of the integrity of women, Sharp also rearticulates, no doubt unintentionally, the ambivalent logic structuring anatomical knowledge in the vernacular. The scatological disgust about the female genital interior both enables, and is enabled by, anatomy's ability to shift its burden of concern. For a medical profession unsure of its prerogatives, the danger and ambivalence involved in unveiling Nature's secrets are figuratively borne by women.

This displacement of obscenity onto women reminds us of the extent to which misogyny remained a powerful force in the imaging of the female body – which had, after all, been equated with intransigent matter (*materia*) by classical philosophers and medieval theologians. But far from confirming such fears of women as essential and transhistorical – or, indeed, confirming that misogyny could serve as an adequate mode of explanation in and of itself – the strategies of medical texts demonstrate that misogyny is not a simple matter of oppressing or excluding the "inferior sex." Rather, misogyny is a flexible, productive, and historically specific phenomenon, mobilized in relation to particular social institutions (such as the emergence of "modern" medical science and the social regulation of its corps of professionals), and manifested through particular material practices (such as the use of print technology for anatomical illustration). Like Nashe's unfortunate Tomalin, whose misogyny is elicited by the experience of phallic inadequacy and who rails unsuccessfully against the prosthetic device that supplants his own insufficient body, early modern medicine exposes its own vulnerabilities in its efforts to manage them. The similarity of the strategies employed by reputable (scientific) and disreputable (obscene) knowledges when they confront the epistemological questions of female corporeality and desire thus reveal a complex and contradictory cultural calculus. This calculus is born not only of an investment in patriarchal reproduction, recognition of women's clitoral physiology, and dread of the female genital interior; it also is the product of historically specific anxieties about male impotence and exposure, sexual and textual, literary and scientific. By means of this calculus, the female erotic body is deployed as the abject figure for what it means to know – and to pursue knowledge of – the body itself.

The exculpatory strategies of medical texts demonstrate that misogyny, whatever form its mobilization takes, is radically unstable. For, if fear is what renders the body of woman available as the abject figure for what it means to know, this strategy uncannily turns back on men. In her transfer from the pages of the book of generation to the frontispieces of works with subtitles such as *A Description of the Body of Man*, the anatomical *pudica* becomes an inverted mirror image of the male medical writer. The abjection written over and through the anatomical *pudica* is in fact the abjection of men, uncertain about their own complicity in defiling Nature's body. We can see this uneasy identification across gender most clearly in Crooke's "pretermitting" of information about the male genitalia,

"A certaine incredible excesse of pleasure" 123

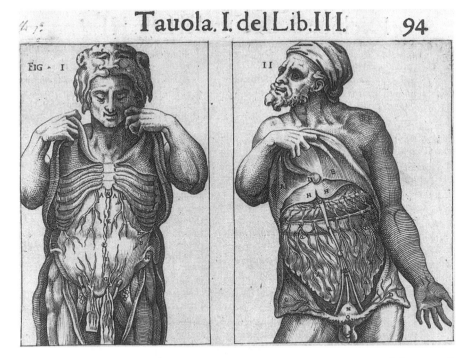

Figure 16 Juan de Valverde de Humoso, *Anatomia del corpo humano* (1556/1560).

hiding knowledge of the masculine member, as it were, behind his own knowing, coy, self-protective hand. Nonetheless, Crooke's gesture makes legible what is implicit in the anatomical project more generally: that the anatomical *pudica* is a cross-gender identification of men's fears about their own pursuit of scientific knowledge. Worthy of a tradition that previously had mitigated anxieties about its empirical practices through such ambivalent and deconstructive images as the self-demonstrating corpse (figure 16) and the anatomist anatomized (figure 17), the figure of the anatomical *pudica* destabilizes, even as she is employed to confirm, masculine pretensions to knowledge.

As it extols the virtues of regular and satisfying sex, then, early modern medicine does not so much liberate the female erotic body as appropriate it as a figure for its own situation *vis-à-vis* the production of new scientific knowledge. As a central figure in the renaissance of corporeal knowledges in the early modern period, the female erotic body carries with it the burden of the illicit, the disgusting, the abject and, as subsequent chapters will show, the unnatural. But in protecting her genitals, the anatomical *pudica* also points to the instabilities of the regime of knowledge that seeks to mediate its own anxieties in and through

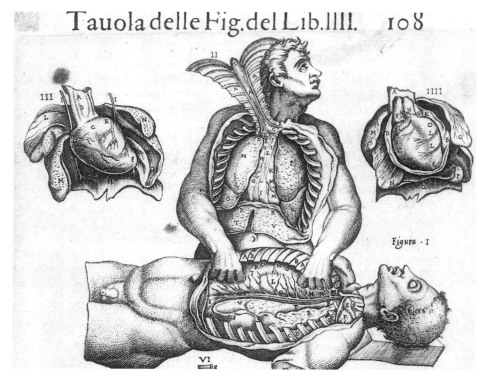

Figure 17 Juan de Valverde de Humoso, *Anatomia del corpo humano* (1556/1560).

her. Given my reading of obscenity, we might wonder whether such a gesture of self-protection might also be interpretable as an act of self-pleasure.[156] It is this possibility that connects the renaissance of bodily knowledges I have examined thus far to the renaissance of *lesbianism*. Without replicating the patriarchal assumption that *lesbianism* is merely masturbation, we will next pursue the possibility that, like Catalina de Erauso, female bodies carry with them their *own* pleasures – clitoral, prosthetic, and otherwise.

3 The politics of pleasure; or, queering Queen Elizabeth

> ...the links between a specifically female eroticism and chastity...are always implied in Elizabethan iconography: a female body in touch with itself.[1]

Within the context of the English Reformation and emerging discourses of companionate marriage, the rediscovery of the clitoris and the dominant humoral dispensation promoted paradoxical understandings of women's eroticism: on the one hand, medical, prescriptive, and obscene discourses were acutely attuned to female psycho-physiology, going so far as to authorize erotic mutuality and equality; on the other hand, these discourses were committed to the subordination of women (as well as the pleasures they might experience) within a resolutely patriarchal, reproductive economy. This ambivalence, exploited for titillating effect by writers of obscenity, proved equally enabling for medical writers, who assuaged their anxieties about the explicit nature of their vernacular texts by displacing onto the female body the very meaning of obscenity. In the present chapter, I continue to explore the potential for female erotic agency from within the confines of patriarchal ideology by shifting my focus from the presumption of marital reproduction toward women who resisted marriage. I thus turn to the famously virginal Queen Elizabeth I, whose body has been interpreted largely through the hermeneutic of the mythological virgin, Astrea or Gloriana.[2] In contrast to this critical tradition, I follow in the steps of Philippa Berry, who emphasizes the import of an iconography of female community for understanding Elizabeth's complex performance of chastity.[3] Rather than place Elizabeth within the context of Diana and her nymphs, as does Berry, I use the contradictions revealed by the anatomical *pudica* as my point of departure. The anatomical *pudica*, I have argued, is the visual epitome of the contradictory position of woman in anatomy and gynecology. Certain representations of Queen Elizabeth, I now suggest, function as one of the *pudica's* more positive avatars. Like the anatomical *pudica*, these images of Elizabeth perform feminine modesty while also calling attention to erotic potential. While the anatomical *pudica* is vulnerable in her exhibition, protectively covering her genitals as a precondition for her display, Elizabeth's self-presentations perform a more complex and dynamic allegory of revelation and concealment. Representations of the Queen reveal the investment in female erotic pleasure endorsed by the medical regime, even as they hint at the autonomous pleasures a virginal (and exceptionally powerful) woman might enjoy.

As an icon of queenship, Elizabeth has become central to our notions not only of the era graced by her name, but the Renaissance itself. Symbolizing the life's blood and destiny of the nation, her dynastic body was the most cathected in the realm, closely watched by courtier and commoner alike. With her lack of progeny posing the problem of succession, any possible erotic entanglement was scrutinized, advocated for, and argued against in the court, Parliament, homes, and pubs. Despite considerable pressure to marry, Elizabeth resisted encroachments on her power, instead manipulating gendered idioms of virginity, maternity, and kingship to enhance her royal prerogative,[4] while using her status as a marriageable monarch to finesse her relations with courtiers and princes. The courtships of Elizabeth thus have been of considerable interest to historians and biographers, who focus invariably on her marital diplomacy or her "failure" or "resistance" to marry.[5] For most scholars, the question of Elizabeth's eroticism is overwritten by the ideology and iconography of chastity. Certainly it is the case that, with the exception of the Virgin Mary, nowhere in England was chastity so elegantly elaborated as in the panegyric cult of Elizabeth. Interpreted in light of the familiar dichotomy of virgin and whore, Elizabeth's chastity corresponded perfectly to the intertwined terms of sexual polarization and religious conflict in the late sixteenth century. A powerful rhetorical weapon, the dichotomy of virgin and whore reached a peak after the Queen's death, when numerous elegies figured Elizabeth as a bride of Christ. As significant as such binarisms were, however, virgin and whore were not the only modes of intelligibility for female eroticism in the early modern period. Elizabeth's self-presentation as an object and subject of erotic interest occurred, not in contrast to the image of chaste virgin, but in terms of it. By entertaining the proposition that Elizabeth manipulated not only discourses of virginity but also of erotic pleasure, I hope to unpack the semiotics of chastity while gaining access to erotic possibilities that extend far beyond Elizabeth's body.

I begin by applying some analytical pressure to an image of Elizabeth that already has elicited a good deal of scholarly commentary: the "Armada" portrait (1588) (figure 18). An exemplary, but by no means isolated, manifestation of the translation of Elizabeth into an ideological and aesthetic icon, this painting in homage to the defeat of the Spanish Armada demonstrates the sophisticated ways in which representations of gender and eroticism are embedded in, and reproduce relations of, cultural and monarchical power. In an influential argument that elucidates the political efficacy of virginity, Louis Montrose reads across the painting's canvas to focus on the apex of Elizabeth's stomacher, where a white bow against a black, triangular background spectacularly figures Elizabeth's "virgin knot":

The politics of pleasure

Figure 18   Armada portrait of Queen Elizabeth (attr. George Gower).

In the appropriate spot, at the apex of the inverted triangle formed by her stomacher, the beholder's attention is drawn to an ostentatious bow. Resting upon it are a rich jewel in an elaborate setting and a large teardrop pearl pendant, both of which are attached to a girdle that is also composed of jewels and pearls. This demure iconography of Elizabeth's virgin-knot suggests a causal relationship between her sanctified chastity and the providential destruction of the Spanish Catholic invaders.[6]

In the context of the other representations of power in the painting – the crown to Elizabeth's right, her hand resting atop the globe, the background tableaux of the defeat of the Spanish fleet and the victory of the English navy – the virgin knot, metaphorically referencing her body on top of her clothes, announces Elizabeth's chastity as the origin, justification, and exemplum of her sovereign omnipotence.

In the years since Montrose's essay appeared, the Armada portrait has been subject to a number of readings focused on the portrayal of the Queen's body. Whether arguing, as do Andrew Belsey and Catherine Belsey, that the painting "subdue[s] her sexuality in order to proclaim her power,"[7] or as does Susan Frye, that it offers a representation of the Queen's self-empowering, "self-possessed female virginity,"[8] critics tend to agree that the portrait figures a body whose power depends on a repudiation of eroticism.[9] Correlatively, virginity is understood to require no definition or explanation. I want to contest the assumptions about eroticism that inform such interpretations, not just to offer an alternative reading of Elizabeth's "resistance" to marriage, but to analytically divorce chastity from asexuality. In analyzing how representations of the Queen's body destabilize conventions of modesty, my objective is not a biographical study of Elizabeth's erotic behavior. My strategy in this chapter is deliberately heuristic and instrumental, intended to open up a question upon which my ensuing arguments will depend: What might it do to our paradigms and histories of female eroticism were we to read the Queen's chastity, fetishized both in her day and in ours, as temporally and ideologically *proximate* to cultural ideas about female erotic pleasure?

Much of Elizabeth's power, both personal and political, was located in her ability to say No. Yet, before she could deny or defer the desires of others, she first needed to incite them.[10] One of the means available to her was in the performance of her body's desirability. In this regard, the cultural elaboration of a cult of chastity is compensatory, mediating anxieties about the Queen's potential or alleged sexual profligacy. At the same time, Elizabeth's own apparent preference for the single life was articulated consistently throughout her reign. To Sir Thomas Pope, she said before her coronation that she would like "to remayne in that estate I was, which of all others best lyked me or pleased me ... I so well like this estate, as I perswade myselfe ther is not anie kynde of liffe comparable unto it ... though I were offered the greatest Prince in all Europe." To her first Parliament in 1559 she announced: "I happelie chose this kynde of life, in which I yet lyve which I assure yow for myne owne parte, hath hitherto best contented my self." To an imperial envoy she stated: "If I am to disclose to you what I should prefer if I follow the inclination of my nature, it is this: beggar-woman and single, far rather than Queen and married!" And to the Parliament of 1576 she fantasized: "if I were a milkmaid with a pail on mine arm, whereby my private person might be little set by, I would not forsake that single state to match myself with the greatest monarch."[11] Although Elizabeth's refusal of the offers of several princes was certainly an aspect of her domestic and international policy, such remarks hint that her abiding preference for the single state was not exclusively a result of *Realpolitik*.[12]

In Montrose and in subsequent readings, the Armada portrait is shown to yield an emerging discourse of nationalism and imperialism, figured not only in the image of the destroyed Spanish fleet, but in the fantasy of world dominion, powerfully imaged by Elizabeth's hand over the globe. In such monarchical portraits, says Peter Stallybrass, "the conjunction of imperial virgin and cartographic image ... constitute together the terrain of Elizabethan nationalism."[13] But how, specifically, does the conflation of monarchical body and body politic work – at least, according to the logic of contemporary analysis? First, the metaphoric coherence of impenetrable virgin and inviolable nation assumes and reproduces a phallic frame of reference: phallic penetration implicitly is defined as what counts as sexuality. Second, within these terms of reference, the portrait's tightly knotted ribbon figures the female genitalia *tout court*. But let us pause at the metaphorical genitalia and ask whether the signifiers displaced on top of Elizabeth's robes are so uniform and seamless in their signification? The distinction drawn in medical texts between the vaginal "sink of the body" and the clitoral "seat of woman's delight" adduced in the previous chapter compels my gaze downward: what about the drop pearl dangling just below the virgin knot?

Glistening in ostentatious splendor, this jewel is not closely analyzed by Montrose, perhaps because it does not contribute much to an argument dedicated to exposing the political efficacy of Elizabeth's impermeability. Whereas Montrose emphasizes the way the portrait draws all lines of power back to Elizabeth's chaste body, I am struck by its ambiguous enticement of the viewer's gaze, as it teases with an image not only of self-containment, but self-assertion. It does not seem to be stretching the properties of visual mimesis too far to see in the pearl's shape and location a glimmer of the "tentigo," or tensile property of erection, that was asserted from the mid-sixteenth century on to be "the seat of woman's delight."[14] I do not mean to imply that the pearl represents the clitoris in a one-to-one correspondence of signifier and signified. It is doubtful that the mid-century treatises of Italian anatomists had yet permeated English medical circles, or that Elizabeth or her painters were familiar with such scientific rediscoveries. Nonetheless, the social investment in women's venereal delights was articulated in Elizabethan England prior to the disputations of anatomists. And one need not posit the clitoris as the source of this image to see in the drop pearl a metonymy of female pleasure.

The quest for self-enjoyment is precisely what is charged against Elizabeth by her detractors. When William Allen, expatriate Cardinal working to place Philip II of Spain on the English throne, signed a 1588 polemic against Elizabeth, he explicitly accused her of using sexual profligacy to overthrow her own nobles and gentlemen:

she hathe abused her bodie, against Gods lawes, to the disgrace of princely majestie & the whole nations reproche, by unspeakable and incredible variety of luste, which modesty suffereth not to be remembred, neyther were it to chaste eares to be uttered how shamefully she hath defiled and infamed her person and cuntry, and made her Courte as a trappe, by this damnable and detestable arte to intangle in sinne and overthrowe the yonger sorte of the nobilitye and gentlemen of the lande . . . [she] promised mariage to sum of the nobillity at home, makinge many of them in single lyfe to the danger of their soules, and decay of their famelies, to attend her pleasure: & no lesse depelie dallied & abused by dissembly almost all the great personages of Europe, to whom aswel by letters, as by sollemne Embasses, she proffered herselfe, to the mockery & finall delutio of them all, to her owne infamy, and the daunger of her people, and specially of late yeares she hathe most pittifuly and devilishly abused, the late noble brother of France, by manifold hope and promise of her mariage and croune, by which baite, and her deceitefull suggestion, the poore yonge gentleman was driven into those dangerous actions and dishonerable affaires of Heretikes and rebells, to his great dishonor, and likelie shorteninge of his daies.[15]

This is what comes, Allen implies, of (Protestant) women taking erotic, marital, political, and spiritual matters into their own hands: a ruinous dissipation of the nobility. Hawking her body across Europe, abusing others' bodies, she abuses as well the patriarchal system of alliance that, as Christian monarch, she is entrusted to uphold. With the Elizabethan religious settlement hardly settled, and concern about the succession growing, the nation's patrimony rests uneasily, for Allen, in a prostitute's pleasure-seeking hands. Nor was such rhetoric used only by militant defenders of the Catholic faith; the Puritan John Stubbs's *The Discoverie of a Gaping Gulf whereinto England is Like to be Swallowed by an other French mariage* (1579) employed similar tropes to dissuade Elizabeth from marrying the duc d' Alençon.[16] As Ilona Bell puts it, Stubbs "plays upon the gender unconscious – inciting fears that the Queen's body is threatening the social order."[17]

Within this discursive context, the drop pearl in the Armada portrait emblematizes the erotic self-assertion of the most powerful woman in the realm, figuratively announcing Elizabeth's sovereign right to her own pleasures. This self-assertion is reinforced by the painting's composition, which utterly defies any logic of penetration. Centralized and static, Elizabeth's symmetrically foregrounded figure is flattened and stretched across the canvas in a visual address that simultaneously solicits and prohibits the spectator's access. Enveloped in a French costume – voluminous velvet gown, long decorated sleeves, and lace collar – her body is completely hidden. Translucent pearls, gold embroidery, and pink bows stud multiple accent points across its surface, while her tiny, luminous, and emphatically white face and hands emerge from this gorgeous and prohibitive enclosure.[18] The physical encasing of the Queen's body serves as a barrier to the viewer's gaze that is reproduced in the painter's stylistic technique. The tight, smooth, linear application of pigment on the canvas; the invisibility of the brush strokes that obscure the painting process; the creation of a flat, decorative surface – all render the representation of the Queen opaque and two-dimensional. As Elizabeth's figure merges with her clothing, throne, and draperies, the viewer is unable to lift the body visually from the background. Succumbing to the flat, continuous visual plane, the spectator's eye is forced to gloss over the monumental body, compelled to appreciate not its vitality and movement and depth, but its status and stasis and sheen. With ornamental surface privileged over implied interior, Elizabeth's "real" body, like the pudendum of the anatomical *pudica*, is protected from view. Visually and ideologically, this painting offers an erotics of visual and tactile surfaces rather than physical and emotional depths. As the viewer's gaze moves across the portrait, pleasure inheres less in the attempt to pierce, examine, or chart its interior, than in visually fondling the rich, textured bodily surface. The tactile address and appeal of Elizabeth's body are strikingly coincident with the physiology of female arousal as elucidated by early modern medical texts. The dispersion of smaller pearls across the Queen's costume enhances this diffuse erotic effect, bringing to mind the "tickling pleasure[s]" of erotic contact, "wherewith the genitalls being replete, are spread forth or distended every way unto their full greatnesse."[19] As if in anticipation of feminist philosopher Luce Irigaray, who reclaims female pleasure from its post-Enlightenment diminishment – "woman has sex organs more or less everywhere"[20] – this portrait of Elizabeth proclaims a profusion of pleasure points.

The impenetrability of this glossy, monumental surface leads many viewers of Elizabeth's portraits to misconstrue them as essentially bodiless. With the one exception of Scrots's portrait of Elizabeth as princess (which, David Howarth contends, "is the only image which shows her with breasts and as an attractive adolescent on the verge of her sexual potential"), portraits of Elizabeth, most critics assert, banish "images of flesh and blood" and "tend to underplay any sense of her physical presence and the ravages of time."[21] Belsey and Belsey argue that the Armada portrait effaces "all other indications [besides face and hands] of a human body," as they chart the progressive abstraction of the representation of the Queen to the point that she becomes "pure geometry."[22] It is true that the dominant aesthetic of Elizabethan portraiture was non-illusionist and emblematic, and that Elizabeth's "mask of youth" attempted to banish the "ravages of time." But this does not mean that Elizabeth's corporeality is absent from her portraits; rather, a simulacrum of her body is manifested on top of, and as an integral part of, Elizabeth's clothes. The metaphorical displacement of the genitals on top of Elizabeth's dress calls attention to two bodies in the Armada portrait: the corporeal body which is implied but obscured under clothing; and the representational body which is offered up for display. Both the "real" and representational bodies are textualized: the former is "real" merely in the sense that it has a human referent which is available only to the viewer's imagination. But the difference between these two bodies creates ambiguity: Elizabeth's body is both present and absent, centralized and displaced, seductive and protected. Like the anatomical *pudica*, she enacts modesty and revelation, with one crucial difference: she is both erotic subject *and* object.

In fact, there are not two bodies in this painting, but three. Elizabeth is turned slightly away from the only other figure in the frame: a small statue of an exquisitely carved "mere-maid," whose genitals are effaced by the smooth and continuous impenetrability of her aquatic appendage. In Renaissance typologies of the monstrous, the hybrid bodies of mermaids, like those of sirens and nereides, defy what Ambroise Paré calls the "confusion and conjunction of seeds," that is, the reproductive potential that is every woman's lot.[23] The mermaid's vagina is precisely a point of non-entry, overwritten by the fantasized space of a mythical marine topos. No line separates her torso from tail; surfaces overlap, in an eerie reminder of Elizabeth's dress. Representing genital impossibility, the mermaid is endlessly desirable: like the sirens, she lures men into the boundless sea of desire; but because her body is devoid of a genital opening, the psychic threat of "erotic drowning" is displaced away from her body and onto the sea that is her element. The mermaid thus reiterates several aspects of the Queen's self-presentation: seductive display, erotic self-containment, ultimate inaccessibility.[24] That the unavailability of the erotic object had by 1588 become one of Elizabeth's strategies of state suggests that the mermaid's presence is simultaneously erotic and political. Within the Armada's frame, then, are three of the most significant early modern emblems of female eroticism: seduction, announced by the mermaid; chastity, figured by the virgin knot; and autonomous pleasure, glimmering in the shape of the pendulous pearl. Together, they rewrite the dynamic of self-protection and display constitutive of the anatomical *pudica* as a matter of female volition. Together, they represent erotic desirability, bodily integrity, and female-centered pleasures. Together, they pronounce the Queen to be both object and subject: as erotic object, she solicits the viewer's appreciative gaze; as erotic subject, she asserts her sovereign power.

Given the legacy of the Venus *pudica* and the use of the anatomical *pudica* as the primary anatomical emblem of the female body, how is it that this representation could be, within a Christian and patriarchal world view, unencumbered by shame? How do we account for the publicity of the pearl, its visual *ostentatio genitalium*, its hieratic appeal? Do these paintings become less regal, less persuasive as imperial propaganda, more, in a word, obscene, once their erotic command is acknowledged? The answer, I believe, is no, primarily because of the happy confluence of the portrait's fantasies of dominion and the strategies by which they are inscribed: on the one hand, an imperial cartography of England; on the other hand, a metaphorical anatomy of Elizabeth.[25] The pearl is answerable to a politics of the monarchical body which finds its mirror image in the Queen's hand resting confidently atop the globe – the assertion of an imperial monopoly over the bodies of her realm and, with the help of English naval power, over the entire world. Just as the globe cartographically metonymizes the Queen's national and imperial power, the pearl anatomically metonymizes Elizabeth's erotic stance; together, they allegorize and authorize Elizabeth's erotic pleasure in terms of sovereign power. The logic of this sovereignty is recursive: fantasies of imperialism authorize the Queen's erotic pleasure while the fiction of omnipotent pleasure promotes England's imperial claims. Cartography and anatomy work together to advance an absolutist and imperial eroticism: all bodies and pleasures are subject to Elizabeth's will.

By simultaneously invoking the virgin knot and the seat of women's delight, the Armada portrait represents and reconciles cultural tensions between chastity and pleasure, bodily integrity and self-assertion, modesty and obscenity. It is only our privileging of the phallus as the *sine qua non* of early modern eroticism that renders the clitoral body asexual. An ideological backformation, this privileging is one way to override an erotic system that paradoxically was more open to female pleasure than the erotic regimes subsequent to it. With our acceptance of the assumption, sexuality = phallic penetration, we have fundamentally misconstrued the meaning of chastity in the early modern period. It is the clitoral body of Elizabeth, not the imagined threat of the phallus, that reigns over the Armada portrait.

The erotic address of this painting is not unique; other state portraits thematize the proximity of chastity to pleasure through the use of a variety of compositional strategies. In the first known painting of Elizabeth as princess (formerly attributed to William Scrots, *c.* 1546–47), she is represented as an attractive but modest young lady, carrying a small prayer book as she stands next to an opened Bible (figure 19). In a reiteration of the *pudica* gesture, she covers her genitals with the prayer book, thereby analogizing maidenly decorum to spiritual knowledge. This equation is destabilized subtly, however, by the two fingers inserted between the pages of the book. In a reversal of the Armada portrait's displacement of body part on top of the gown, this portrait covers the pudendum, only to allude through the fingers' directional siting to the maiden's hidden genital interior.

This simultaneous covering and indexing of the genital area is reiterated, with a difference, in the "Darnley" portrait (*c.* 1575), where a full fan of multicolored ostrich feathers replaces the closed book (figure 20). The fan both covers and intimates the pudendum, with the tactile sensuality of the feathers simulating human hair. If this portrait seems less erotic than the Armada, it is in part because the visual focus is split between the elaborate fan and Elizabeth's eyes, which directly address the spectator, humbling spectator desires in accordance with the Queen's royal station. With crown and scepter merging into a dark background, this portrait fashions a semblance of mature interiority that quietly invites and imperiously commands.

As a group, these three portraits move temporally toward increased erotic explicitness: in the 1546 princess portrait, the genitals are covered by a prayer book; in the 1575 Darnley portrait, the genitals are covered by the pudendum-like fan; in the 1588 Armada portrait, the covering is, in a sense, cast aside in favor of the metonymy of virgin knot and pearl. Despite this continuity, however, none of these portraits has generated readings focused on Elizabethan eroticism – a fact all the more interesting because another portrait has spawned

134 The renaissance of lesbianism

Figure 19 Portrait of Elizabeth as princess (attribution unknown, formerly attributed to William Scrots, *c.* 1546–47).

so many. The "Rainbow" portrait (attributed variously to Isaac Oliver and to Marcus Gheeraerts the Younger, *c.* 1600–03) depicts a mythologized and elaborately accoutered Elizabeth delicately holding in her hand an arching rainbow (figure 21). Her torso feminized by a bodice, the sensuality of her figure is

Figure 20 Darnley portrait of Elizabeth I (attribution unknown, *c.* 1575).

Figure 21 Rainbow portrait of Elizabeth I (attr. Marcus Gheeraerts the Younger or Issac Oliver, *c.* 1600–03).

heightened through the layering of robes, the exposure of her upper bosom, and the tactile contrast of cold jewels against warm skin. Even as this notoriously enigmatic painting interweaves a complex skein of religious and political allusions, two aspects of its iconography are particularly relevant to our consideration of Elizabethan eroticism: the disembodied eyes, ears, and mouths arrayed on top of her clothes, and the colorless rainbow in Elizabeth's hand. Increasingly, the rainbow is interpreted not only as a royal scepter but as an ambivalent image of phallic power (bent, not erect), while the open mouths, ears, and eyes, along with the folds of the mantle itself, have been viewed as disturbingly vaginal. For Susan Frye, these body parts "form a disquieting suggestion of vaginal openings,"[26] while Joel Fineman calls attention to the "salacious ear that both covers and discovers the genitals" of the Queen.[27] For Daniel Fischlin, the "ambiguous folds, in combination with the vaguely phallic rainbow and the string of pearls looped suggestively round Elizabeth's genital area, image an erotic potential complicit with the sovereign vitality the portrait projects."[28] Elizabeth's metaphorical embrace of the phallus, whether construed as an assimilation and erasure of masculine power or a prosthetic supplement to her own body, confirms her status as actively desiring, erotically commanding, and self-pleasuring. The relative position of rainbow and hands enhances this reading: just as the visual line of the rainbow fades toward the genital area, the thumb and bent index finger of Elizabeth's left hand are inserted into the folds of her mantle. As Fischlin remarks, the "subtle visual and figurative resonances of the fold" intensify the female-centered bodily imagery, insinuating a masturbatory erotics that "rescripts the sovereign's potency in terms of both masculine and feminine agency."[29] Grasping the phallus and touching herself, Elizabeth would seem to possess doubled access to pleasure.

As eroticized as the "Rainbow" portrait is, perhaps the most assertive of erotic meanings in Elizabethan portraiture is figured in a narrative painting that does not call visual attention to the genital area. *Elizabeth I and the 3 Goddesses* (attributed to Hans Eworth or Joris Hoefnagel, *c*. late 1560s) illustrates the classical myth in which Paris awards the golden apple to the goddess whom he judges to be the most beautiful (figure 22). The usual interpretation, promulgated by Roy Strong and Frances Yates, and reproduced recently by Rob Content, is this: "In this monumental painting, Elizabeth is glorified as the true winner in a contest with Juno, Minerva, and Venus... The queen is depicted trumping the individual virtues of the goddesses with the rarer combination of her own."[30] But a different, and potentially more subversive (albeit unknowing), interpretation was offered by Christopher Lloyd, official Surveyor of the Queen's Pictures, in 1991: "The queen plays the part of Paris... This conceit refers not only to Elizabeth I's abilities as a ruler, but also to her role as a woman as she is seen to combine the virtues of all the goddesses."[31] If the Queen not only "trumps" the goddesses by her combination of virtues, but also "plays the part of Paris," then she simultaneously enacts both masculine and feminine roles. Traversing gender boundaries, she transplants the desiring male subject, impersonating him with her own female body. As the Queen's self-sufficiency is elaborated in the threefold image of the goddesses, the corporeal "virtues"

Figure 22 *Elizabeth I and the 3 Goddesses* (attr. Hans Eworth or Joris Hoefnagel, *c.* late 1560s).

incorporated in the Queen are arrayed on a continuum – from the ruler covered to the neck by a heavy, layered brocade to the nude and gleaming Venus. As the direction of Elizabeth's walk and gaze propels the viewer's eyes from dark to light across the allegorical spectrum, they come to rest appreciatively on Venus's spectacularly naked body.[32]

There is nothing given about which part of the body will elicit symbolic elaboration. I have focused on representations of the genital area in order to draw to the surface the eroticism implicit within the chaste body. It was not, however, Elizabeth's clitoris that elicited comments from those who observed her – at least as far as the documentary record reveals. What this record divulges instead is the repeated allegation by foreign dignatories conducting business at court that the Queen exposed her breasts. Excerpts of their ambassadorial letters and reports are reproduced in many biographies of Elizabeth, but the account provided by Janet Arnold in *Queen Elizabeth's Wardrobe Unlock'd* is particularly revealing of the power of such reports to elicit scholarly anxiety. Invested as she is in the "magnificent, regal figure of Gloriana,"[33] Arnold discredits the comments of foreign visitors whenever they would appear to impugn the Queen's modesty, insisting instead on alternative explanations for the Queen's alleged exhibitionism. Arnold includes numerous accounts of Elizabeth's manipulation of her clothing, but two descriptions from the private journal of André Hurault, Monsieur de Maisse, Catholic ambassador of King Henri IV of France, are representative:

She excused herself because I found her attired in her nightgown... She was strangely attired in a dress of silver cloth, white and crimson, or silver "gauze", as they call it. This dress had slashed sleeves lined with red taffeta, and was girt about with other little sleeves that hung down to the ground, which she was for ever twisting and untwisting. *She kept the front of her dress open, and one could see the whole of her bosom, and passing low, and often she would open the front of this robe with her hands as if she was too hot.* The collar of the robe was very high, and the lining of the inner part all adorned with little pendants of rubies and pearls, very many, but quite small. She also had a chain of rubies and pearls about her neck. On her head she wore a garland of the same material and beneath it a great reddish-coloured wig, with a great number of spangles of gold and silver, and hanging down over her forehead some pearls, but of no great worth. On either side of her ears hung two great curls of hair, almost down to her shoulders and within the collar of her robe, spangled as the top of her head. *Her bosom is somewhat wrinkled as well as [one can see for] the collar that she wears round her neck, but lower down her flesh is exceeding white and delicate, so far as one could see.*[34]

During a second audience, Elizabeth appeared

clad in a dress of black taffeta, bound with gold lace, and like a robe in the Italian fashion with open sleeves and lined with crimson taffeta. She had a petticoat of white damask, girdled, and open in front, as was also her chemise, in such a manner that *she often opened this dress and one could see all her belly, and even to her navel.* Her head tire was the same as before. She had bracelets of pearl on her hands, six or seven rows of them. On her head tire she wore a coronet of pearls, of which five or six were marvellously fair. *When she raises her head she has a trick of putting both hands on her gown and opening it insomuch that all her belly can be seen.*[35]

What is manifest here, Arnold argues, is not the Queen's exposed skin, but the Frenchman's inadequate command of English, particularly his ignorance of the English names for wardrobe items and body parts: "This curious description may be a confusion of terms made in transcription and translation. It is unlikely that the Queen's women would have been so careless as to allow her to appear in public without fastening her clothes properly... It would have been easy for any man, particularly a foreigner, to confuse the terms for different parts of an Englishwoman's dress... Even the names for the parts of the body may be misleading."[36] Displacing the responsibility for bodily exposure away from Elizabeth, first to her ladies-in-waiting and then to the ambassador, Arnold strives to protect the Queen's modesty.

Arnold is not unique in her attempt to explain away de Maisse's observations. From a feminist perspective dedicated to retrieving female agency, Lisa Jardine revisits de Maisse's journal entries in order to dispute Louis Montrose's use of them in his description of Elizabeth's erotic appeal. Taking up Montrose's assertion that Elizabeth's "conspicuous self-displays were ... a kind of erotic provocation," Jardine counters that any "erotic provocation" belongs to de Maisse's "text, and its cultural conventions – the shaping in the telling which refracts and intensifies 'experience' into expression – not to the event (that is, to any of the Queen's many public appearances)."[37] Insisting on the breach to decorum that Protestant female rule would signify to de Maisse, Jardine disputes that Elizabeth actually laid bare her bosom, arguing parenthetically and in her endnotes that the problem stems not from the ambassador's misunderstanding of English, but a later mistranslation of de Maisse's original French.[38]

Whether the crux of the problem is in the Frenchman's faulty English, his Catholic sensibilities, or an inaccurate modern translation is less important to me than why this eroticized portrayal of the Queen has elicited such dismissive argumentative strategies, unifying scholars invested in, and resistant to, the iconic status of the Virgin Queen. Even more curious is why other critics have skated over this allegation of extreme *décolletage* with a minimum of commentary, thereby implying that exhibiting one's breasts was, in Elizabethan England, typical behavior, at least for unmarried women. Montrose, for instance, asserts that "Elizabeth's display of her bosom signified her status as a maiden," while Hannah Betts proposes that "[t]his gesture, a form of self-display made available to a limited audience, had a political currency as the dramatization of the queen's youth and virginity."[39] They might be banking on the authority of Paul Hentzner, who said of the sixty-five-year-old Queen that "her bosom was uncovered, as all the English ladies have it, till they marry."[40] Whether the Queen had a preference for dishabille, we probably will never know. Given the indeterminacy of the documented references, accusations as well as defenses of the Queen miss the point. Whatever this ambassador and others saw (or thought they saw), at stake are not only interpretations of Elizabeth's erotic behavior, but more importantly, our understanding of Elizabethan eroticism. Certainly it strains credibility to believe that Elizabeth routinely attended court topless. Yet, if the exposure of her breasts was one of the Queen's royal prerogatives, it seems important to explore what a bare bosom signified: whether a virgin's chastity, a prostitute's immodesty, or a sovereign's prerogative, the naked female breast allows us further access into the semiotics of early modern eroticism.

Changes in the gendering of clothing style are central to the eroticization of the breast in the early modern period. As Phyllis Rackin remarks, "[u]ntil the late middle ages, men and women had worn similar long, loose robes. In Shakespeare's time, however, clothing was designed to produce embodied sexual difference. Men's robes had been shortened to reveal their legs, and the codpiece had been invented. Women wore tight bodices that altered the shape of their breasts and low-cut gowns to display them."[41] References to bare breasts occur regularly in comments about contemporary fashion.[42] If there is any truth to descriptions of travelers and polemicists, it would seem that the fashionable ladies of France and Italy were particularly prone to exhibitionism. In his travel narrative of 1494, the Canon Pietro Casola, for instance, records that "Venetian women, especially the pretty ones, try as much as possible in public to show their chests – I mean the breasts and shoulders – so much so, that several times when I saw them I marvelled that their clothes did not fall off their backs."[43] Over a century later, the Englishman Thomas Coryat likewise asserts of Venice that "[a]lmost all the wives, widowes and mayds do walke abroad with their breastes all naked."[44] The titlepage to *Coryats Crudities* (1611), an elaborate frontispiece with a cameo portrait of Coryat surrounded by three women (representative of "Gallia, Germania, and Italia") depicts the Italian woman with her bust fully exposed[45] (figure 23). Such commonplaces provide grist for invidious cross-cultural comparisons. The French humanist and anti-Catholic polemicist Henri Estienne, for instance, defends Frenchmen who, he says, "would have a hard conceit of a woman that should go up and downe the streets with her breast laid open, shewing halfe her dugges: whereas in some places of *Italie* (especially at *Venice*) not so much as old filthy hanging dugs but are set out (as it were) to shew and sale."[46] Even so, in 1585 the Franciscan friar Antoine Estienne Mineur inveighed against French bare-breasted fashions, which he saw as part of the "dissolute adornment" pursued by all manner of Frenchwomen "seeking curiously after new inventions, and being miserably led astray by your carnal passions."[47]

Certain scholars suggest, on the basis of social polemics, that the fashion of bare breasts was popular in England during the reigns of Elizabeth and James I. Under his entry for "Naked paps," for instance, James Henke suggests "[i]f we are to take the fulminations of contemporary social critics at face value in the late 16th c., such gowns were becoming fashionable with a variety of 'honest' madams," not just among prostitutes. He cites several instances in which the style of bare breasts was satirized by critics such as Thomas Nashe, Stephen Gosson, and Richard Braithwaithe, and cites as well a fashion historian who notes that "[e]xtreme *décolletage* exposing the breasts was a fashion for unmarried women (1605–1650)."[48] Perhaps, then, it was her marital status that led to the disapproving comment about Margaret Cavendish, Duchess of Newcastle, who allegedly attended a performance of her husband's play, *The Humorous Lovers*, in 1667, in extreme *décolletage*. A letter describing the event portrays the Duchess's sumptuary style in salacious detail: "Her brests all laid out to view in a play house with scarlett trimd nipples."[49] In *Anthropometamorphosis* (1653), that international catalogue of bodily abuses wrought by artificially meddling with nature, when the indefatigable John Bulwer arrives at "Pap-Fashions" and "Breasts and Waste" he asserts that "the *chief use of the Breasts*" is "the *generation of milke*," whereupon he rails against those who "*do forfeit this principall use of these excellent parts, and make them*

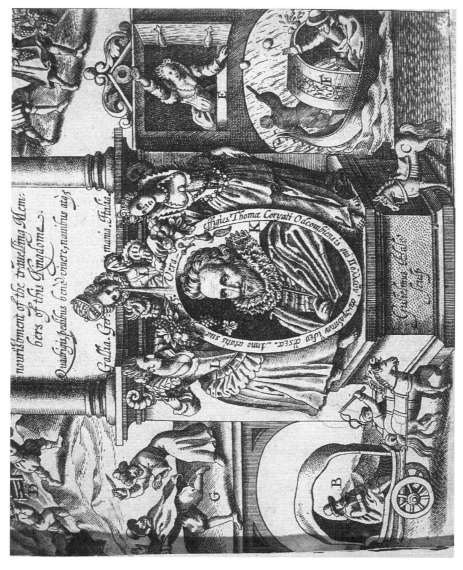

Figure 23 Thomas Coryat, *Coryats Crudities* (1611).

only Stales, or Bawds of Lust, as too many Ladies amongst us do, who by opening these common shops of temptation, invite the eyes of easie Chapman to cheapen that flesh which seemes to lye exposed (as upon an open Stall) to be sould."[50] A naked bosom not only connotes whoredom and cheap commerce; it also manifests female desire: *"There being good reason in Nature why women should have a modest regard of them, and not so openly expose them; because the consent between the Breasts and Wombe is very great, in so much as the only contrectation [handling] of them provoketh Lust."*[51] Bulwer here appropriates the language of anatomy. Laurent Joubert, for instance, affirms that "when the nipples are tickled, the womb takes delight in it and feels a pleasant titillation. Also, this small button on the breast is highly sensitive because of an abundance of nerve endings; and this is so that, even here, the nipples will have an affinity with the reproductive organs."[52] Given this affinity between breasts and womb, lactation and lust, we can understand better why the Virgin Mary's bosom also became a site of controversy,[53] calling for lengthy defenses against its appropriation for immodest purposes, as in *The Overthrow of the Protestants Pulpit-Babels* by the Jesuit John Floyd.[54]

Polemicists are unreliable witnesses to social practices, but their lack of restraint in declaiming against social ills helps to reveal the faultlines of bodily decorum. Clearly, women's naked breasts were eroticized objects throughout the early modern period, subject to social discipline, lascivious comments, and loving appreciation.[55] Renaissance poets consistently lauded their attractions, from Thomas Lodge's idealizing "Her paps are centres of delight / Her breasts are orbs of heavenly frame," to Andrew Marvell's coy promise to his coy mistress that, if he had "world enough and time" he would devote "two hundred [years] to adore each breast."[56] Perhaps no poet lavished more attention on women's breasts than Robert Herrick, whose verse about his imagined "mistresses" in *Hesperides* (1648) return again and again to breasts as an object of complexly entangled specular, tactile, and oral fascinations.[57] Unlike Marvell's or Donne's poems of seduction – which perform their rhetorical strip-teases with phallic end always firmly, if somewhat edgily, in sight – Herrick's verse enacts a poetics of polymorphous perversion: it dallies and defers, playing out its fantasies across the surface of the female body without feeling the need to come to a point. The orality, tactility, and scopophilia of Herrick's verse is imaged partly through his obsession with small objects – dainty, discrete, delectable. Bits of clothing (lace, cuffs, shoelaces), morsels of food (almonds, cherries, fragrant spices), diminutive features of the natural world (dew and blossoms), and precious gems (rubies and pearls) clothe, flavor, scent, and adorn his poetry, creating a "bodyscape" of sensual pleasure whose appeal to the senses is heightened by his frequent use of diminutives: niplet, nervelet, rubulet, thronelet. Even Julia's sweat and breast milk are the subject of encomiums, suggesting the lengths to which Herrick will go in dwelling appreciatively on the female body and constructing his fetishism of body parts. If Herrick's "microphilia," as Alastair Fowler terms his penchant for the diminutive,[58] is excessive and no doubt says much about a desire for control, Herrick's imaginative resources were not that unusual. His fetishistic lexicon and imaginary, in fact, are constitutive elements of the Renaissance blazon. Compare Herrick's "Upon the Nipples of Julia's Breast" –

> Have ye beheld (with much delight)
> A red-Rose peeping through a white?
> Or else a cheerie (double grac't)
> Within a Lillie centre plac't?
> Or ever mark't the pretty beam
> A Strawberry shewes half drown'd in Creame?
> Or seen rich Rubies blushing through
> A pure smooth Pearle, and Orient too?
> So like to this, nay all the rest,
> Is each neate Niplet of her breast.

– to this less aesthetically proficient, but no less fetishistic encomium to Queen Elizabeth by George Puttenham: "Her bosome sleake as Paris plaster, / Helde up two balles of alabaster, / Eche byas was a little cherrie: / Or els I thinke a strawberrie."[59] So conventional are the images that we tend to overlook the particular pleasures they inscribe. Breasts are likened to strawberries, cherries, and apples, alabaster, rubies, and pearls;[60] they are served up on a plate and offered as exotic ware. Such images express the possibility of a *simultaneity* of different and diffuse oral, visual, and tactile pleasures. In a society in which fornication and adultery were crimes defined by phallic penetration, it is not surprising that looking, touching, and sucking would play a major role in the erotic imagination. The "immaturity" so often ascribed by critics to Herrick's verse seems not to be peculiar to his individual biography (e.g., a "bachelor," "regressive," "incestuous"),[61] but is shared by others of his contemporaries. The pleasures of kissing and caressing are evident, for instance, throughout the diary of Samuel Pepys, multiple entries of which attest to his repeated fondling of his housemaids. It would seem, then, that Herrick's verse expresses, remarkably unselfconsciously, the polymorphous perversity of some forms of early modern eroticism.

Modern assumptions about what constitutes adult sexuality, dependent as they are upon a teleology of foreplay, consummation, and orgasm, and bolstered by the developmental taxonomies of Freud (oral, anal, and phallic fixations), are not much use in accessing the appeal of these early modern fantasies. Furthermore, it is not just common convention nor a phallocentric psychology that has kept us from considering this fetishism of body parts from a less normalizing perspective. Feminist emphases on the deleterious effects for women of the anatomical blazon have focused our attention on the pernicious aspects of the blazon's strategy of bodily fragmentation.[62] Valuable as this work has been, it is time to bring a queer perspective to the erotic appeal of "the body in parts."[63] Strange as it might seem, my critical point of reference is the aggressively heterosexist critic William Kerrigan who, in an essay on kissing in Herrick's poetry, not only skewers the condescension of Herrick's detractors, but makes a number of valuable observations about sex. "Kissing," Kerrigan contends, "is consummation's supplement, differing from orgasm in its capacity for limitless increase, and deferring orgasm by virtue of that increase."[64] He continues: "As is not the case with intercourse, the orifices joined in kissing have no gender differences. Both have lips, and both have tongues, and both are, if you will, *both*. Mouths joined in kissing fit like the halves of an equation."[65] He accurately notes the mutability of body parts in Herrick's poetry: they seem to migrate, transmute, and absorb each other's functions. Analyzing the complex erotics of "The Vine," for instance, Kerrigan suggests

> The vine is superior to the penis because it is not a penis merely, but a penis fused with a tongue . . . just as the vagina for Herrick is not a vagina merely, but a vagina fused with a breast. Kissing is meant to divert erotic energy from the consummation of intercourse. But a classic psychoanalytic fate intervenes: deny one of life's formidable masters, such as genital sexuality, and it will reappear in the very terms set forth to deny it. Intercourse reemerges in the dream of "The Vine" as cunnilingus, for Herrick a forbidden and shameful kiss that would regain in the clitoris the first oral object, the nipple of the breast.[66]

Setting aside much that is objectionable in Kerrigan's interpretation (including the relentlessly teleological model he affirms, the description of "genital sexuality" as "one of life's formidable masters," and the seamless equation between the nipple and clitoris), we can be alerted by him to the transitivity of Herrick's imagined body parts: unmoored by gender, the vagina, clitoris, and breast attach and mutate into each other in a profusion of allied pleasures. If, indeed, the nipple is the original (and originary) infantile object of desire, in Herrick, it would seem, this object remains the favored, but by no means exclusive, emblem of adult eroticism. In contrast to the genitally driven narrative of penetration and climax, Herrick's poetry privileges mouth and eyes (like the "Rainbow" portrait), touch and sight (like the "Darnley" and "Armada" portraits), clitoris and breast (like the "Armada" portrait and Elizabeth's reputed behavior). Indeed, microscopic delectation often merges into taste as the visually replete body becomes food, as in the four-line lyric, "Upon Julia's Breasts": "Display thy breasts, my Julia, there let me / Behold that circummortall purity: / Betweene whose glories, there my lips Ile lay, / Ravisht, in that faire Via Lactea." In the similar oral fantasy of "Fresh Cheese and Cream," to the question, "Wo'd yee have fresh Cheese and Cream?" the answer is, "*Julia's* Breast can give you them: / And if more; Each *Nipple* cries, / To your Cream, here's *Strawberries*." Scopophilia, often interpreted as protecting masculine ego boundaries in the face of a feminine threat, gives way to fantasies of incorporation; bodily boundaries are dissolved as bodies become food that is ingested. The indolence of lying "ravisht" between Julia's breasts or sating oneself on her mammary cream provide a gloss to the final lines of Herrick's most celebrated poem, "To the Virgins, to make much of Time," which, in conventional *carpe diem* fashion, enjoins virgins to "GAther ye Rose-buds while ye may": "For having lost but once your prime, / You may for ever tarry." Tarrying and dallying are, in fact, the end of much of Herrick's verse – in part, as the poem "Julia's Petticoat" implies, because there is no necessity that bodily pleasure end. Enthralled by the movements of Julia's petticoat, Herrick's poetic persona describes its freedom to move toward, away, and against Julia's body: "Sometimes away 'two'd wildly fling; / Then to thy thighs so closely cling, / That some conceit did melt me downe, / As Lovers fall into a swoone: / And all confus'd, I there did lie / Drown'd in Delights; but co'd not die." Continuing to gaze, enraptured at the sight, he does not mourn or curse his inability to come, but hopes only "t'ave seene of it my fill." That he never will be filled is made clear by the extraordinary fantasy of another four-line poem, "Upon Sibilla": "With paste of Almonds, Syb her hands doth scoure; / Then gives it to the children to devoure. / In Cream she bathes her thighs (more soft then silk) / Then to the poore she freely gives the milke." Transforming the Marian figure of Charity into a bathing nursemaid, this poem sensualizes the provision of food while locating it in a freely circulating, never-ending plentitude of oral and tactile pleasures.

Herrick's versification of the female body provides access to the erotics of the early modern period in one further way. His oft-noted personification of clothing, generally treated as an aesthetic matter, merits his place in anthologies for undergraduates. Yet, his personification of clothing has much more than aesthetic significance. "Julia's Petticoat" follows the agential movements of the "azure Robe" not only in order to eroticize Julia's body, but to eroticize clothing itself. The same is true of the widely anthologized poem, "Delight in Disorder," which attributes to an "erring Lace," a "Cuffe neglectfull," a "tempestuous petticote," and a "carelesse shooe-string," the very "wantonnesse" and "wilde civility" that the poetic persona most admires in women. Significantly, the wantonness of clothing inheres in the inability of ribbons to stay tied or robes to cover fully. Just as "Ribbands...flow confusedly" in "Delight in Disorder," Julia's petticoat is "erring here, and wandring there, / Pleas'd with transgression ev'ry where." The eroticization of clothing is maximized in "Upon Julia's Clothes," which projects onto robes the liquidity of desire, the attributes of melting, swooning, dissolving, that form the essence of Herrick's vision of erotic pleasure: "WHen as in silks my *Julia* goes, / Then, then (me thinks) how sweetly flowes / That liquefaction of her clothes." The repetition of the O sounds punctuates the exclamation of the final line: "Next, when I cast mine eyes and see / That brave Vibration each way free; / O how that glittering taketh me!" Rather than signifying an ejaculation, the O in Herrick's vision of Julia's clothes sounds out the fantasized state of continually, repeatedly, being "taken," "ravisht," "drowned."

That Herrick and other poets might have drowned in the delights of the female body is hardly surprising, given the complex economy of bodily orifices and oral pleasures that form our common inheritance as infants born of and fed by the bodies of women. It may come as more of a surprise to note that within several early modern texts, female breasts are represented as the objects of female appreciation and desire. Such, at least, is suggested by "To a Friend for her Naked Breasts" by the anonymous poet, "Eliza." The poem begins as an eulogy in praise of a woman's partial nakedness:

> Madam I praise you, 'cause you'r free,
> And you doe not conceal from me
> What hidden in your heart doth lye,
> If I can it through your breasts spy.
> Some Ladies will not show their breasts,
> For feare men think they are undrest,
> Or by't their hearts they should discover,
> They do't to tempt some wanton Lover.
> They are afraid tempters to be,
> Because a Curse impos'd they see,
> Upon the tempter that was first,
> By an all-seeing God that's just.
> But though I praise you have a care
> Of that al-seeing eye, and feare,
> Lest he through your bare brests see sin,
> And punish you for what's within.[67]

Marilyn Yalom and Germaine Greer assure us that the title of the poem is ironic, and that the lyric reproduces the self-evident sinfulness of female nakedness.[68] Certainly the poem, one of over a hundred "divine offerings" by a self-consciously Protestant poet, is written within the terms of Christian theology: for a woman living under the curse of Eve, to bare her bosom is to expose the truth hidden within the heart. But even as it participates in a cultural discourse against hypocrisy, this epideictic verse seems to take pleasure in her friend's "free" display, particularly insofar as it conveys an intensified bond of female friendship.

The representation of female intimacy through the exhibition of breasts is evinced as well in Edmund Spenser's *The Faerie Queene*. This epic encomium to the Queen's special powers of chastity and seduction repeatedly invokes the voyeuristic appeal of female "paps," as Spenser tends to call them. In a manner similar to Herrick's manipulation of a "sexual curiosity" that is, as Lillian

148   The renaissance of lesbianism

Schanfield puts it, "aroused by parts that are hidden rather than exposed,"[69] Spenser exploits, in David Miller's terms, "alternations of concealment and display or invitation and delay."[70] Acrasia, for instance, "fairer seemes, the lesse ye see her may; / Lo see soone after, how more bold and free / Her bared bosome she doth broad display."[71] Such voyeuristic scenes ostensibly are in the service of a desiring male viewer, whether it be the questing male knight of the canto or the implied male reader whose identifications are so much at stake in the narrative address of this poem. One of the more extended of such moments, however, complicates the heterosexual appeal of the naked bosom by representing an exchange of gazes and touches between women.[72] As Guyon, erstwhile Knight of Temperance, prepares to enter Acrasia's bower of bliss in Book 2, canto 12, he is arrested by a beguiling sight:

> Two naked Damzelles he therein espyde,
> Which therein bathing, seemed to contend,
> And wrestle wantonly, ne car'd to hyde,
> Their dainty parts from vew of any, which them eyde.
> Sometimes the one would lift the other quight
> Above the waters, and then downe againe
> Her plong, as over maistered by might,
> Where both awhile could covered remaine,
> And each the other from to rise restraine;
> The whiles their snowy limbes, as through a vele,
> So through the Christall waves appeared plaine:
> Then suddeinly both would themselves unhele,
> And th'amarous sweet spoiles to greedy eyes revele.   (stanzas 63–64)

The glimpse of these two damsels "wrestling wantonly" as they bathe in supposed privacy causes the watching Guyon to "relent his earnest pace" while his "stubborne brest gan secret pleasaunce to embrace" (stanza 65). There is nothing, however, in the previous stanza to suggest that the women themselves are not enjoying "th'amarous sweet spoiles" of each other's bodies, deliciously covered and uncovered by the water as they splash, lift one another, and "plong" (plunge). Certainly, as the episode progresses, it is Guyon's "greedy eyes" that become the narrative focus. But this shift occurs during a temporal suspension of the narrative, as the two women gaze back at Guyon, united in their subjective knowledge of the meaning of his hungry eyes: "The wanton Maidens him espying, stood / Gazing a while at his unwonted guise" (stanza 66). Only after the women return his gaze does the narrative turn decisively toward heteroerotic exchange.

As if to enact the opposed roles of chastity and lasciviousness, one of the maids, "abasht," ducks under the water, while her shameless companion "rather higher did arise, / And her two lilly paps aloft displayd, / And all, that might his melting hart entise / To her delights, she unto him bewrayd: / The rest hid underneath, him more desirous made" (stanza 66). Then, as if responding to a silent invitation from her brazen friend,

> ... the other likewise up arose,
> And her faire lockes, which formerly were bownd
> Up in one knot, she low adowne did lose:
> Which flowing long and thick, her cloth'd arownd,
> And th'ivorie in golden mantle gownd:
> So that faire spectacle from him was reft,
> Yet that, which reft it, no lesse faire was fownd:
> So hid in lockes and waves from lookers theft,
> Nought but her lovely face she for his looking left. (stanza 67)

The female body, it seems, has its own method of concealment which also, paradoxically, is a mode of further revelation: the long, thick hair that clothes the naked ivory body in a golden mantle makes the watcher more keenly aware of what lies underneath. In this complicated play of revealing, concealing, and further revealing, it is the intimation of female intra-sex communion and communication, hovering around and infusing what amounts to a visual *ménage à trois*, that heightens Guyon's and the reader's pleasure. As the women laugh, blush, and merrily beckon to the knight, in whose face "the secret signes of kindled lust appear" (stanza 68), it is the intrepid Palmer who "much rebukt those wandring eyes of his" (stanza 69), turning Guyon back to the task at hand, the goal of Book 2: the destruction of Acrasia's bower.

Spenser's poetics of voyeurism and delay allegorizes the dangers of lust to the male reader being schooled by Spenser's Palmer and epic poem. But this threat is not contained by *The Faerie Queene*'s structure of address, any more than the bower of bliss can be destroyed once and for all.[73] Female readers might enjoy the visual spectacle of the wanton damsels, appropriating the part of Guyon, just as Queen Elizabeth impersonated the part of Paris. To do so would implicate them as subjects in the complex choreography of exposure and concealment enacted by Spenser's nymphs. This choreography, I want to suggest, is uncannily similar to the actions attributed to Queen Elizabeth by de Maisse. His account not only suggests that Elizabeth's breasts were exposed, but calls attention to her act of opening (and presumably closing) her garments: "She kept the front of her dress open, and one could see the whole of her bosom, and passing low, and often she would open the front of this robe with her hands as if she was too hot... [S]he often opened this dress and one could see all her belly... When she raises her head she has a trick of putting both hands on her gown and opening it insomuch that all her belly can be seen." It appears that Elizabeth treated her clothing as erotically as Herrick imagined the petticoats of Julia. Even more strikingly, she seems to have performed a "trick" of display and concealment similar to that narrated in Spenserian romance – and captured in the visual composition of her own portraits.

It thus does not seem strange that a further performance of self-conscious display should be noted regularly of Elizabeth. Giovanni Michiel, Seigneur de Maurier, and Seigneur de Maisse all record that Elizabeth had beautiful hands, which she habitually showed off with much pleasure.[74] In his travel journal, Paul Hentzner, a tutor traveling with a young German nobleman, describes the Queen's mannerisms: "Whoever speaks to her, it is kneeling; now and then she raises some with her hand. While we were there, William Slawata, a Bohemian Baron, had letters to present to her; and she after pulling off her glove, gave him her right hand to kiss, sparkling with rings and jewels, a mark of particular favour."[75] Generally bedecked with costly jewels, Elizabeth apparently drew attention to her long, graceful fingers by drawing her gloves off and on over the course of an interview. Even Arnold admits of Elizabeth that, while "taking her gloves on and off so many times during an audience seems more like a nervous habit . . . it certainly attracted attention to the beautiful white hands."[76] In a culture where so much of the body is often hidden from view, the hands, clasped shut or held invitingly open, easily could be fetishized in the manner of the breasts – providing yet one more object of visual and tactile delight. Within the context of polymorphous pleasures we have adduced thus far, Elizabeth's habit of pulling her gloves on and off mimics the performance of revelation and concealment that played such a constitutive role in the repertoire of early modern eroticism.[77] There is, I want to suggest, something *queer* about all of this – determinedly fetishistic, delightfully polymorphous, and slyly destabilizing to the putatively straight line separating chastity from eroticism.

In "Of Chastity and Violence: Elizabeth I and Edmund Spenser in the House of Busirane," Susan Frye significantly advances our understanding of Elizabeth's chastity by describing it as a "counterheterosexual" strategy.[78] Like Montrose, Frye reads the Armada portrait to demonstrate Elizabeth's use of "an empowering virginity," but she moves beyond Montrose by emphasizing how Elizabeth resists the patriarchal logic of female definition and by highlighting the import of the pearl: "the artists have represented Elizabeth's chastity in the bow and single dangling pearl – her 'jewel,' generally connoting the female genitalia – hanging directly over her genital area."[79] Frye does not specify the erotic nature of that resistance, however, and thus implies a more unitary understanding of female eroticism than her own term, counter-heterosexuality, might suggest. If "empowering virginity" is signified by a pearl, then how does this signifier function? What is the logic that governs its intelligibility? Frye's conflation of Elizabeth's "jewel" with the inclusive "general connotation" of "female genitalia" inadvertently elides the erotic specificity of the clitoris, which, I am arguing, specifies a crucial erotic difference *within* the terms of female embodiment.

The question of erotic specificity is obscured as well in Frye's term "counter-heterosexual." Does Elizabeth's chastity stand *against* heterosexuality or is it an alternative form *of* heterosexuality? In broaching such questions, I hope to extend Judith Bennett's inquiry into the terms of "lesbian-like" existence, a phrase that Bennett uses to describe "women whose lives might have particularly offered opportunities for same-sex love; women who resisted norms of feminine behavior based on heterosexual marriage; women who lived in circumstances that allowed them to nurture and support other women."[80] Similarly, Theodora Jankowski argues that adult female virginity might function as the site of queerness in early modern culture, insofar as queerness is characterized by a rejection of normative systems of alliance, the male-headed household economy, and reproductive sexuality.[81] If there are good reasons to resist applying the modern terms "lesbian" and "queer" to early modern women, there are equally good reasons to pursue the range of alternatives that both "lesbian-like" and "queer" are meant to invoke. Even as I strive to specify the analytical space between "lesbian" and "like" that Bennett's use of a hyphen risks eliding, wariness of historical anachronism need not preclude the question: to what extent is Elizabeth's virginity accurately considered *hetero*sexual?[82]

Such a question arises in relation to the account of the Spanish ambassador, Guzman de Silva, in which Elizabeth remarks that she would like to meet the widowed Princess Juana: "how well so young a widow and a maiden would get on together, and what a pleasant life they could lead. She (the Queen) being the elder would be the husband, and her Highness [the princess] the wife. She dwelt upon this for a time . . . "[83] Carole Levin, for one, asserts that "[w]e are not meant to take this request seriously, and it is clear that neither Elizabeth nor de Silva did at the time . . . This is not to suggest that Elizabeth wished for a female partner."[84] Here I echo Frye in her review of Levin's book, "Why not?"[85] What – other than an ideology of normative heterosexuality that, ensuing chapters will argue, postdates Elizabeth's reign – authorizes the wholesale dismissal of this possibility? As Laurie Shannon perceptively notes about Elizabeth's remark,"[w]hat is . . . clear is that female marriage presented so logical (if not practical) a solution to her dilemma that she cannot have failed to think of it . . . what is more stunning about the fantasy is its apparent utterability in such a context and the completely unvexed account of it de Silva provides."[86]

Shannon employs Elizabeth's comment less to press for a recognition of homoerotic desire than to argue for a recognition of multiple norms within early modern culture, which make it impossible to reduce "the queen's affective strategies" to "a question of ideological conformity or resistance."[87] Although her point is well taken, it is important not to lose sight of the fact that the dominant ideology of patriarchal alliance *was* being resisted, if not by Elizabeth's musings about Princess Juana then by her refusals of marriage to men. Indeed, Elizabeth's resounding No to this system opens a space for us to refuse the collateral imperative to privilege courtship and marriage (or adultery) as the only available avenues for tracking desire. Elizabeth's articulation of a fantasy of female–female alliance – whether construed as political, emotional, or erotic, or some mix thereof – clearly and unhesitatingly bespeaks a desire not adequately accounted for within a strictly heterosexual syntax. This recognition is especially crucial given that critics have argued that the pathway for patronage and promotion was by way of masculine desire and eroticized submission to the Queen.[88] So important was this ritualized form of submission that by the 1570s, "to court" meant both "to curry favor at court" and "to woo"; "being a courtier" and "playing the lover" came to mean the same thing during Elizabeth's reign.[89] Yet, what would limit such "courting" to a circuit between the Queen and her male favorites? In addition to princes, diplomats, courtiers, and petitioners, Elizabeth was surrounded by her ladies of the Bedchamber, kinswomen, and friends. As Frye notes, Elizabeth seems "to have preferred the pleasures of her life in the company of selected women."[90] As Philippa Berry reminds us, "at the heart of this cult [of Elizabeth] were numerous depictions of a woman *with other women*."[91] The monarch's interference in the erotic liaisons of her ladies-in-waiting – often dismissed as feminine jealousy or political machination – is notorious. Given the eroticized courtly milieu, Elizabeth's self-presentation – both her actual behavior and the visual representations authorized by her – may have elicited complex, contradictory fantasies on the part of the women and men over whom she had so much control.[92]

By presenting Elizabeth's lifelong erotic autonomy in relation to contemporaneous discourses of female bodily pleasures, I have sought less to rewrite her biography than to denaturalize the semiotics of chastity. Like the lower-class conquistador, Catalina de Erauso, Elizabeth manipulated the ideology of chastity in pursuit of her own complicated, oft-times spectacular, and finally inscrutable ends. Her success at this manipulation, which spawned countless eulogies and the manufacturing of the Queen into an icon, has been so complete that the specific manner in which it occurred has escaped notice. It takes a historical perspective on the polymorphous eroticism evident elsewhere in early modern discourses to recognize the sheer complexity of Elizabeth's politics of pleasure. If it is true, as Montrose argues, that "the pervasive cultural presence of the Queen was a condition of ... imaginative possibility" for *A Midsummer Night's Dream*,[93] then, given the homoerotics that suffuse that play (as I argued in chapter 1), perhaps it is time that we reexamine the image of the "imperial votaress" who, from Frances Yates to contemporary editors, is considered one of Shakespeare's few allusions to his Queen.[94] Perhaps it is time, in other words, to take a closer look, not only at the politics and poetics of heterosexual desire enabled by Elizabeth, but the homoerotics as well.[95]

Such an examination need not uphold Elizabeth as singular or unique. Jonathan Goldberg usefully cautions against viewing the Queen's gender performance as "anomalous" because of the normalizing assumptions such a judgment of exemplarity tends to carry in its wake. Refusing Elizabeth the status of exception, he challenges the assumption of a seamless operation of a patriarchal hegemony to which all other women are subject: "To treat her as 'anomalous' is to assume that biological sex and gender are unproblematically sutured in 'ordinary' cases and that heterosexuality assigns men and women to stabilized and opposing positions... Elizabeth's refusal of marriage was not the ordinary thing for a woman in the period. Yet, I would argue, the possibility of the gender positions she occupied was not that anomalous either."[96] Like other scholars, Goldberg's point of departure is the Queen's appropriation of masculine symbols and stances; unlike those scholars, he perceptively argues that Elizabeth's gender transitivity enables the non-normative desires of others: "she is the place where those desires could meet and cross without necessarily becoming identified one with another, without either of them ever assuming the position of male/female desire as it is supposedly controlled by the institution of marriage."[97] Goldberg implies that when scholars analyze Elizabeth's adoption of masculine imagery – emphasizing, for instance, her androgyny – they tend to presume that the only way for an early modern woman to be powerful was to imitate men, and that any sexuality therein expressed must be masculine.[98] In a problematic confusion of desire with identification, such scholars read Elizabeth's lack of sexual intercourse *with* men as an attempt to *be* a man and vice versa. (Conversely, when Elizabeth's gender identification is assumed to be feminine, all too often her heterosexuality tends to be read as frivolous, manipulative, or coy.) By introducing into the discussion those desires enabled by Elizabeth's performance of masculinity, Goldberg disrupts this binary, using the transitivity of identification to deconstruct the normativity of desire.

Although allied with Goldberg's aims, my approach is to highlight not Elizabeth's performance of masculinity but the female specificity of her performance of eroticism, and thus, to destabilize from a different angle the undertheorized binary of gender and sexuality operating in readings of her majesty. We do not need the rubric of masculinity to see in Elizabeth's self-presentations an erotic position eccentric to patriarchal marriage. We need only attend closely to the terms of gender manifest in her angry words to Robert Dudley, Earl of Leicester: "I will have here but one *mistress* and no *master*."[99] As a "masterless" woman who "mistressed" herself, Elizabeth took full advantage of the corporeal spectacularity of the early modern court. She dallied, erotically and politically, with nobles, foreign princes, her own subjects and advisors. She may have bared her breasts on at least a few state occasions, and not just to maternal effect. She played the role of object of desire in courtly entertainments performed in her honor. She lived her life surrounded by other intelligent and seductive women, reserving the right to procure husbands for them (and to forbid undesirable liaisons), thereby appropriating the patriarch's role.

Rather than assume Elizabeth's heterosexuality and, more importantly, the coherence and stability of heterosexuality itself, we need to examine the ways that such a category was produced *retroactively* as the sole mode of possibility for a self-identified Virgin Queen. As Peter Stallybrass has argued, "the concept of transgression is liable to smuggle in the notion that boundaries are somehow just *there*, waiting to be transgressed... To understand transgression, we need to understand the formation of boundaries."[100] We therefore need to ask, not just whether Queen Elizabeth was "counter-heterosexual" or "queer," but what were the (anatomical and ideological) boundaries of early modern women's bodies, and how were they formed? What were the discourses that informed that boundary-making and how effectively did they operate? Elizabeth's politics of pleasure – her ability to use a female-centered eroticism as one ground of her sovereignty – was historically contingent and politically circumscribed. In some ways, it began the moment that she did, born out of the contradictions between her father's programmatic promiscuity and her mother's execution on charges of adultery and incest. Elizabeth's chaste erotics, in no small measure a result of lessons learned from the body politics of Henry VIII (who banked his own sovereignty on his personal powers of seduction), was a virtuoso re-signification of her paternal and maternal inheritance. Yet, as the seventeenth century progressed, the self-pleasuring female ruler, commanding and flouting the spectator's gaze, would become increasingly untenable. She was replaced first by the determinedly patriarchal self-representations of James I, who sought to supplant the cultural memory of Elizabeth by promoting himself as father of his people and husband of his realm: "What God hath conjoined, then let no man separate. I am the husband, and the whole isle is my lawful wife; I am the head and it is my body," James proclaimed to Parliament in defense of his Union of Crowns.[101] If James's self-presentation was first and foremost patriarchal (albeit vulnerable to charges of sodomy), his son's was resolutely conjugal. After a rocky start, the marriage of Charles I and Henrietta Maria was idealized as a model of harmony, and "his affection for his family provided the perfect antidote to his cold public persona."[102] The power of the royal couple's affectivity, fertility, and domesticity was enhanced by the Queen's adoption of the courtly culture of the "précieuses,"[103] a power that, nonetheless, was rendered impotent by subsequent political events.

After the political upheavals of mid-century, celebratory representations of national eroticism would no longer be drawn easily from the monarch's body. As Paul Hammond argues, after 1660 "any notion of sovereignty which was founded upon the royal body had to take account of two scandals: firstly the execution of Charles I, the literal dismemberment of the king's body as a deliberated judicial and symbolic act; secondly the sexual exploits of Charles II, the involvement of the king's body in highly publicised promiscuity."[104] While royalists may have viewed Charles as saving the nation from repression, with multiple mistresses and fourteen illegitimate children he was hardly an icon of royal integrity. Even as he attempted to represent his Restoration rule as the relation between an ardent lover and mistress, this image was compromised by his bestowal of favor on actresses and politically powerful elites such as the Duchess of Portsmouth.[105] Like Elizabeth, whose sexual body occasioned satiric obscenity as well as praise, Charles's absolutism was analogized by some as a tyrannical attempt to debauch his people, and he was travestied for treating his scepter like a penis.[106]

No longer could the body politic be subsumed under the monarch's body, hidden, as in the off-reproduced Ditchley portrait, under the Queen's skirts. Rather, the nation would begin to represent itself as an aggregate of multiple bodies, accorded civil form through the increasingly powerful houses of Parliament and, by the end of the century, by the two political parties, the Whigs and Tories.[107] In such a pluralist polity, the burden of representing the link between eroticism, sovereignty, and nationhood, so eloquently represented in the Armada portrait as inhering in a centralized seat of power – the "seat of women's delight" – would thereafter be dispersed throughout the populace. As Hammond argues,

> the person of the king could no longer be an acceptable symbol of sovereignty now that the nation had learned other ways of representing itself. Even if Charles II had been chaste, or at least discreet, the king's body could not have occupied the same place in the national discourse which it had been granted before the Civil War... The Exclusion Crisis, which was generated by the failure of the king to produce a legitimate heir for the crown, occasioned a fundamental debate over the way subjects exist in a legal relationship with the sovereign. A literal failure of patriarchy occasioned a crisis in the constitutional system which took paternity as its practical basis and its legitimising rhetoric.[108]

Subsequent to the Exclusion Crisis, patriarchy could not function as a "completely persuasive figure of the relation between prince and people."[109] Changes in the ideology of the family also pressured the patriarchal analogy between household and state: marital sexuality was becoming more private, and predatory male sexuality more offensive. Just as marriage was turning more "companionate," so too, in a sense, was the relation between rulers and ruled. If "contract" was the term that would come to signify this mode of participatory government, it is no accident that the same word would, over the course of the next century, be the contested term in the discourse of marriage and women's rights as well.[110] Attempting to locate the mechanisms of the shift from early modern aristocratic patriarchalism to modern patriarchy, Michael McKeon notes in a discussion of Robert Filmer's *Patriarcha* that "the onset of political crisis in the seventeenth century" meant that

> the analogy between familial and political order had to be rationalized, and people were obliged to concretize both terms and acknowledge what was problematic in the comparison. The apparent integrity of patriarchal authority in the family was found in fact to consist of several distinct authorities – that of the father, the husband, and the master – whose compound complexity deviated from the simplicity of the model of

absolute royal prerogative. In this sense, Filmer marks not the triumphant ascendancy of patriarchal thought, but its demise as tacit knowledge, the fact that it is in crisis.[111]

In the declaration of Princess Mary of Orange "to renounce the crown to William, should she inherit it, on grounds that a wife must obey her husband," direct rule by women temporarily was forsworn in favor of activity behind the scenes.[112] At the same time, the imagery of marriage was "exploited to defend William III's right to the throne."[113] In this context, the wedding of the monarch to the people proclaimed not the force of aristocratic privilege, much less monarchical absolutism, but a system of mutually negotiated and carefully legislated bonds. When the government passed to Anne, she accepted the contractual nature of these bonds and repudiated the concept of hereditary succession. Proving herself effective in balancing the factions that circled around her, she did so not by manipulating her chastity, much less by flaunting her desirability, but by transmuting the history of her seventeen (ultimately futile) pregnancies into a compensatory emblem of maternal obligation to her realm. I can only surmise that it was in response to the debilitating reproductive politics of her own body, and hence, as a retrospective form of wish-fulfillment, that she adopted Elizabeth's grammatically inflected feminine motto of chastity, *Semper Eadem* (always the same), and occasionally dressed in imitation of Elizabeth's portraits.[114]

It is thus more than ironic that, unlike Elizabeth, whose detractors likened her to a whore, Anne was the monarch whose intimacy with female friends first became a matter of public debate. Charges levied against her by a prior intimate, Sarah Churchill, Duchess of Marlborough, circulated both in private correspondence and published pamphlets. Childhood friend and the Groom of the Stole and Keeper of the Privy Purse, the Duchess for many years had been Anne's favorite. After her fall from favor, Churchill began to cast suspicion on Anne's relationship to Abigail Masham, the poor relative who had replaced Churchill in the Queen's affections. Letters from Churchill to the Queen, as well as between Churchill and her secretary, insinuate "unnatural" affections to Anne and Abigail, while ballads and pamphlets (probably commissioned by Churchill and penned by her secretary) were more explicitly scandalous:

> Whenas Queen *Anne* of great Renown
>   *Great Britain's* Sceptre sway'd,
> Besides the Church, she dearly lov'd
>   A Dirty Chamber-Maid.
> Oh! *Abigail* that was her Name,
>   She starch'd and stich'd full well,
> But how she pierc'd this Royal Heart,
>   No mortal Man can tell.
> However, for sweet Service done
>   And Causes of great weight,

> Her Royal Mistress made her, Oh!
>   A Minister of State.
> Her Secretary she was not,
>   Because she could not write;
> But had the Conduct and the Care
>   Of some dark Deeds at night.[115]

Although this scandal figures prominently in biographies of the Queen, the charges generally are dismissed as the hysterical vindictiveness of a power-hungry Duchess, with Anne coming off somewhat the worse as weak and emotionally dependent. Rather than speculate, as other critics have, that Queen Anne was a *lesbian*,[116] I submit that these charges mark the advent of a new point of public access to the Queen's body in an era of growing explicitness. However much it was intended to do political harm, Churchill's attack was not the result of a fevered imagination, the defensive homopanic of a "latent homosexual," or the bitterness of a spurned lover. It was the result of a transformation in discourse, wherein intimate female friends, including matronly monarchs with seventeen pregnancies behind them, could be interpreted as purveyors of sexual vice. The public censure of the "unnatural affections" of a reigning female monarch who modeled herself on the Virgin Queen is one measure of the historical parameters of the renaissance of *lesbianism* in early modern England. It is to the details of this renaissance that the rest of my book turns.

4 The (in)significance of *lesbian* desire

> We, Hermia, like two artificial gods,
> Have with our needles created both one flower,
> Both on one sampler, sitting on one cushion,
> Both warbling of one song, both in one key,
> As if our hands, our sides, voices, and minds
> Had been incorporate. So we grew together,
> Like to a double cherry, seeming parted,
> But yet an union in partition;
> Two lovely berries molded on one stem;
> So, with two seeming bodies, but one heart.[1]

In an essay devoted to the interpretation of gendered representations of royalty, Stephen Orgel calls attention to an allegorical Peace and Justice embracing one another in a cartouche placed above Queen Elizabeth on the frontispiece to Christopher Saxton's *Atlas of England and Wales* (1579) (figure 24). Orgel perceptively reads this image in terms of Elizabethan imperialism, religion, and eroticism. Contextualizing the bodily comportment of these figures by means of literary references to Nashe's "The choise of valentines," Sidney's *Arcadia*, and T. W.'s verse letter to Donne, he suggests that " '[c]haste and mystic tribadry' ... may well be an element in the impresa that hangs above Elizabeth's head."[2] Orgel's larger arguments – that early modern iconography was extremely labile, even profligate, that female–female sexuality was conceivable in this period, and that this image in particular "is characteristically Elizabethan in its determination both to include and to disarm the realities of lust and conquest within the concept of imperial power"[3] – are, I believe, incontestable, and indeed have informed my own analysis throughout this book. Nonetheless, I want to suggest that it is precisely *not* as a tribade – at least not as a tribade as understood within the dominant discourses of the day – that Saxton's impresa allegorizes Elizabethan (homo)erotic power. T. W.'s lyrical reference to "chaste and mystic tribadry" in his private letter to Donne (discussed in my Introduction) suggests that the language of tribadism could be appropriated for a variety of ends, including playful ones among highly literate men. (The same could be said of the urbane use of the term "sodomy.") Nonetheless, it remains the case that throughout

The (in)significance of *lesbian* desire

Figure 24 Christopher Saxton, *Atlas of England and Wales* (attr. Augustine Ryther, 1579).

the early modern period, tribadism referred primarily to an extreme of female erotic transgression. Given this, an iconographic reference to tribadism probably would call to mind not only anatomical but moral monstrosity – hardly the appropriate image to publicize the Queen's authority over her newly surveyed realm. But if tribadism is unlikely to be used to describe Elizabeth's erotic stance, then how do we understand the impresa's iconography? How is the image of a naked Peace sitting on the lap of an armored Justice a suitable emblem for the Queen as patron of a national geography?

The allegory enacted in this cartouche, that of the "Virtues Reconciled," was a popular trope throughout the early modern period.[4] It alludes to the Parliament of Heaven, where the conflicting claims of Justice (or Righteousness) and Mercy over the fate of Man are argued.[5] Truth stands with Justice, and Peace allies with Mercy; their reconciliation is achieved when Christ offers himself as redeemer. Together these four "daughters of God" personify the "Reconciliation of the Heavenly Virtues," as stated in Psalm 85: "Mercy and truth are met together; righteousness and peace have kissed each other."[6] The theme appears in all manner of medieval and Renaissance cultural production.[7] It was used as a papal emblem for Pope Julius III, and it is inscribed on the inner wall of St. Paul's Cathedral. Righteousness (with sword) and Peace (with olive branch) appear arm in arm on the frontispiece of the Cambridge Bible of 1629. Perhaps in imitation of Saxton's popular atlas, the frontispiece to Book 5 of Georg Braun and Franz Hogenberg's comprehensive city atlas, *Civitates Orbis Terrarum* (Towns of the World) depicts Peace and Justice holding one another in a delicate embrace.[8]

Because of the nudity of Peace and the addition of the putto holding the scales of Justice, Saxton's frontispiece is more erotic than most other renditions of this theme. As Orgel notes, a "naked woman accompanied by a putto inescapably suggests Venus and Cupid; and indeed, one's first impression of the impresa is that it represents the more commonplace coupling of Venus and Mars – in the topos, the armed woman, Pallas or Bellona, has replaced the god of war."[9] But Saxton was not alone in eroticizing the female Virtues, particularly as biblical iconography was appropriated and adapted for secular decorative arts. A sensuous series of Virtues Embracing adorn the interior of Bolsover Castle, one of the homes of William Cavendish, Duke of Newcastle (the husband, from 1645 until her death in 1673, of Margaret Cavendish). A self-consciously Cavalier pleasure palace, Bolsover Castle was built by Sir Charles Cavendish and his son William during the early years of the seventeenth century.[10] One of its three buildings, the "Little Castle," is a fantastical "blend," in the words of Timothy Raylor, "of romance, chivalry, and pageant merged with classical myth and legend," which functions as a "witty apologia for its owner – and perhaps even as a site for the pursuit of his amours."[11] The interior of this three-floor palace is sumptuously ornamented with paintings on wall and ceiling panels;

The (in)significance of *lesbian* desire

Figure 25   Justice and Prudence, Bolsover Castle.

they include emblematic depictions of the temperaments, the senses, Hercules's labors, saints, prophets, apostles, gods and goddesses. According to Raylor, the eclectic interior is tied together organizationally through the theme of the reconciliation of pleasure to virtue, with Ovidian pleasure and Christian and classical virtue consistently held in dynamic and self-aware tension. It is of some consequence, then, that in the "Marble Closet," a public chamber on the second floor, personified female Virtues are portrayed with a good deal of focus on the sensual pleasures of their embrace. Three wall lunettes depict classically proportioned nude female figures amorously entangled[12] (figures 25 and 26). These pairs were copied from Hendrik Goltzius's series of engravings of the *Allied Virtues* (figure 27), which merges the classical themes of Fortitude and Prudence with the Christian iconography of Hope and Faith.[13] Rather than Truth allied with Justice, Cavendish's lunettes show Justice with her scales passionately kissing a snake-wielding Prudence, Fortitude holding onto a column as she kisses Patience, who carries a press, and a gavel-bearing Faith receiving the kiss of Hope tied down in bondage. Located on the upper walls of the Marble Closet, this series of pastoral nudes reiterates the union of pagan sensuality and Christian virtue evinced throughout the ambience of the Little Castle, while also enacting a very particular form of voyeurism – one that indulges not only in the

162 The renaissance of lesbianism

Figure 26 Faith and Hope, Bolsover Castle.

visual delight of female nudity, but in the *frisson* of female hands caressing and mouths kissing. Indeed, sensuality wins out over virtue in the lunettes' design. Completely intent on clasping and kissing, these figures hold the emblems that announce them as "Virtues" off to the side. Given the play of light and shadow, the spectator's eye is drawn to the place their bodies meet, while their accompanying attributes fade into the darkened background. Authorizing the figures' interactions, the accouterments apparently are necessary but unimportant; the visual focus is on the women's beauty, nude proximity, and ardent interaction.

Self-knowing, even sly, Cavendish's lunettes call out for erotic interpretation. And yet, like Saxton's impresa (until Orgel's analysis), their eroticism has been overlooked, either processed through (and subsumed under) the emblematic lens of allegory or disregarded in favor of a description of the seducing or post-coital Venus and Mars, Omphale and Hercules, Daphne and Apollo, who grace the walls of the "Elysium Room" on the third floor.[14] Why has the eroticism attendant upon these beautiful Virtues Embracing been so easily ignored? The rest of this chapter suggests one answer.

In her trenchant analysis of the regulation of sexuality in Germany prior to the eighteenth century, Isabel Hull summarizes "several features common to

Figure 27   Hendrik Goltzius, Justice and Prudence (from the *Allied Virtues*, c. 1578–82).

the early modern organization of sexual life as people lived it, rather than as ideology might have it." In its broad contours, her description of Reformation Germany pertains equally to the English situation:

First, sex was completely embedded in the socioeconomic circumstances of their lives; it was not a thing-in-itself, nor did it have value or meaning except in its various contexts. Second, because of its centrality in organizing socioeconomic life, marriage also exercised a kind of conceptual monopoly over sexual expression; that is, not only was marriage frequently held to be synonymous with sexual expression altogether (because it was the only framework for legitimate sexual activity), but "illicit" sex also tended to be judged by its relation to marriage (the threat it posed, for example). Third, because the system was so strongly social, people's attention tended to focus on the relational aspects of sexual behavior, on *who* was being linked, rather than on *what* they were doing. This meant that acts with few social-relational consequences (not ending in the production of a child, not ending in a long-term relationship, not with a person at all) tended to disappear from view as insignificant.[15]

Erotic acts come to signify, as Hull's book on their regulation makes clear, through a complex and continual social process. Taxonomies of significance, whether explicit or implicit, formal or informal, are developed out of a heterogeneous mix of local conditions, conflicts between contesting authorities, and the weight of social tradition. The remaining chapters of *The Renaissance of Lesbianism* are devoted to exploring conditions of significance and insignificance, the way that certain bodies and bodily acts accrue meaning and intelligibility *as sexual*. I begin with the observation that nowhere is social significance more visibly and forcibly marked than in the disciplinary apparatus of the law. The ongoing process of interpreting, attributing, and reevaluating *what matters* to a particular society temporarily comes to a halt in the formation of legal statute, which thereafter carries with it the force of legal precedent. By beginning with this legislative resting point, my aim is less to document social practices than to anatomize the silence about female–female eroticism within English law. I then turn to the rather different play of insignificance in early modern drama, where female affections and bonds are not so much marked by invisibility and silence, as harnessed to a dramatic trajectory that renders them simultaneously crucial and insignificant to their romantic plots.

Early modern law was formed out of the accretion of previous cases, commentaries, judicial decisions and challenges to them. However strong was the attachment to, and reliance on, legal precedent during the early modern period, however, the interaction with past decisions and values was neither simple nor absolute. Although legal historiographers analyzed the law in terms of the past, they also exposed ancient law as unfamiliar and alien, in a dynamic Debora Shuger describes as the "*duplicity* of the ancestral past during the Renaissance – its double status as mirror and other."[16] This cultural negotiation between past ascriptions and present values is evinced in popular and scholarly texts that sought to authorize and explain English law, particularly legislation concerned with regulating sexual conduct, as the progressive fulfillment of a historical process. We can see this tendency most clearly in texts published in the early eighteenth century, which attempt to stabilize and disseminate the meanings of legal statutes as they developed through the Reformation, the Civil Wars, and the Restoration. In 1729, for instance, Giles Jacob, a prolific writer of popular legal books, published a vernacular law dictionary to make legal terms, statutes, and the derivation of legal precedent available to "Barristers, Students, and Practicers of the Law, Members of Parliament, and other Gentlemen, Justices of the Peace, Clergymen, &c."[17] Jacob's *New Law Dictionary* defines sodomy, for instance, with reference to its etymology, relevant statutes, and record of punishments:

Buggery, or *Sodomy*, comes from the Italian *Buggerare*, to *bugger*; and is defined to be a *Carnalis copula contra Naturam, & hoc vel per confusionem Specierum, sc.* a Man or Woman with a brute Beast; *vel Sexuum*, a Man with a Man, or Man with a Woman. 12 *Rep.* 36. This Sin against God, Nature, and the Law, 'tis said was brought into *England* by the *Lombards. Rot. Parl.* 50 *Ed.* 3 *numb.* 58. Stat. 25 *H.* 8. *cap.* 6. And in antient Times, according to some Authors, it was punished with Burning, though others say with burying alive: But at this Day it is Felony excluded Clergy, and punished as other Felonies. 25 *Hen.* 8. *cap.* 6 and 5 *Eliz.* 17. And it is Felony both in the Agent and Patient consenting, except the Person on whom committed be a Boy under the Age of Discretion; when 'tis Felony only in the Agent. For many Years past, the Crime of *Buggery* has been greatly practiced in this Kingdom, without any exemplary Punishments of the Committers of it; till *Anno* 12 *Geo.* a great Number of these Wretches were detected of the most abominable Practices, and three of them put to Death; which seasonable Justice seems to have given a Check to the before growing Evil.

Linking the punishments of "antient Times" to the "seasonable Justice" practiced "at this Day" to check "the before growing Evil," Jacob's careful discriminations balance the synchronic with the diachronic in order to demonstrate the rightness of current judicial practice. Attachment to historical precedent is further enacted in his faithful recapitulation of Edward Coke's mid-seventeenth-century definition of "Copulation Against Nature," where bestiality is subsumed under sodomy as a parallel crime against nature. Although he is more exhaustive than Coke was in *Institutes of the Lawes of England*, Jacob's summary develops his predecessor's exemplary gendered logic of penetration and physical position. What links the "confusion of species" with "confusion of sexes" is neither species nor sex *per se*, but the nature of the orifice and the relative position of the partners. Men can unnaturally penetrate beasts, other men (including boys), and women; and women can seek to be penetrated by either men or beasts. But, locked into a position of receptacle, woman cannot – in English law – penetrate another woman.

In the same year that Jacob published his *Dictionary* (1729), his contemporary, John Disney, published *A View of Ancient Laws Against Immorality and Profaneness*. A practicing magistrate and an Anglican divine, Disney reviewed ancient vice laws from the perspective of "a warm supporter of the societies for the reformation of manners," the activist reform group responsible for periodic raids on molly houses.[18] Beginning his compendium of sexual sins with a chapter entitled "Of the Incentives to Vice, ill company, obscene Talk, and lewd Books or Pictures" and proceeding to such matters as "Of Polygamy," "Of Incestuous Lewdnesse," and "Of Rape," the ten chapters of Section One exhaustively order people and behaviors according to their alleged deviations from nature. In the final chapter, "Of Sodomy and Bestiality," not only are these two manifestations of the unnatural linked in a strained narrative of causality, but, as is true in Jacob's *Dictionary*, no mention is made of female–female acts. Explicitly defining sodomy as "the unnatural Conjunction of Men with Men or Boys," Disney treats age as a salient index of the unnatural,[19] but elides the possibility of an unnatural conjunction of women with women. His elucidation of Romans 1: 20–28, which mines the rhetoric of unspeakability, likewise fails to directly address the possibility of female–female sex:

These Lewdnesses are so detestable, that nothing needs be said to increase their Horror: for Nature suffers almost as great a violence in *hearing* of them, as in the perpetration.

It is wonderful, indeed, how it ever came into the thoughts of *Men* to commit them: but, as the Apostle says, (*Rom*. I. 20–28) when they gave them-selves up to Idolatry, God gave them up to vile Affections; and the Devil put them upon going as much out of the way for wickedness, as he had brought them to do for their Religious Worship. They had changed the glory of the incorruptible God into Images of corruptible Men and Beasts, for Adoration: and therefore He left them to debase *themselves*; and turn the Channel of their Lusts, as well as their Devotions, from what was natural, to what was abhorrent from Nature; to their own Sex, and to brute Beasts.[20]

Although Disney's use of biblical rhetoric alludes to a specific verse in which women are condemned, his strategy of indirection contrasts profoundly with the rhetoric in his two chapters focused on women's sexual transgressions: "Of Common Whores" and "Of What the Roman laws called Stuprum; the Lewdnesse of (or with) unmarried Women, who are *not* Common Whores" (emphasis mine). Here, his exacting division between those women who are lewd with men for money and those who are lewd with men for free provides a negative template against which we can measure his attempt to articulate a discourse of lewdness (pecuniary or not) between women. In his discussion of prostitution, Disney conventionally cites the condemnation of temple prostitution in Deuteronomy 23:17, "*There shall be no Whore of the Daughters of Israel; nor a Sodomite of the sons of Israel*," parenthetically inserting "a whoremaster" after "sodomite" and registering his incredulity that "How our [biblical] Translators came to think of a *Sodomite* here, is hard to say."[21] The quote continues:

The words in the Hebrew that mark out the Criminal, in both clauses of this text of *Deuteronomy*, being apparently the same, (with the difference only of a feminine termination in the former,) have a visible and natural relation to each other; as *Adultera* and *Adulterer*, *Moecha* and *Moechus*, and the like. If, therefore, the former signifies a *whore*, (as all agree it does;) the latter, (tho' in some places where it stands single, without any such relative feminine, it may be put for a sodomite,) must in this place signify a *whoremaster*, or one that accompanies with such women.[22]

Indeed, Disney, along with Seldon in *Uxor Ebraica*, is verified in his belief by the Geneva Bible, which had translated the original Hebrew *kadesh* as "whorekeeper" (reading it symmetrically to *kadesha*, or "whore"). In their attempt to record faithfully historical meaning, modern scholarly translators render this verse even more symmetrical in order to impart gender neutrality: "None of the daughters of Israel shall be a temple prostitute; none of the sons of Israel shall be a temple prostitute."[23] Presumably, as part of their ritual practices, both male and female temple prostitutes engaged in sodomitical acts – that is, acts that involved "unnatural" orifices or positions. But for Disney, the biblical sodomite must refer to a pimp, not to a male prostitute – and this, despite the fact that the marginal gloss on "whore" in the King James Bible is "sodomitess."[24] Disney's conceptual dependence upon discrete, mutually exclusive categories of sexual sin gives his treatise an acute definitional clarity: not only can women not be sodomites; men cannot be whores.

We know, however, that men *could* be whores. Male–male prostitution was a thriving trade in London, as elsewhere on the Continent, and was satirized from the late sixteenth century on by vociferous social critics.[25] Anti-theatrical tracts and satires describe in detail the dress, gait, and manners of boys and men involved in sex work, obsessively articulating the anxiety that men or boys will use their "feminized" bodies as loose women do.[26] Stageplays employ "whore" and its variants to describe male characters, as when Thersites labels Patroclus "Achilles' male varlet," his "masculine whore," and Hamlet refers to himself as "a very drab, / A stallion."[27] A specific vocabulary of male sexual types – catamite, ingle, ganymede, hermaphrodite – is used to convey the unnatural use of the male body for money or favor. And at the end of the seventeenth century, the Society for the Reformation of Manners attempted to purge London of sodomites and male prostitutes, two social ills it viewed as indistinguishable. Indeed, in the early modern conflation of the (male) sodomite and the (male) whore we find precisely the interpenetration of categories that Disney's treatise so assiduously denies.

In their efforts to trace the historical lineage of vice and vice law, Disney and Jacob construct taxonomies of significance deeply indebted to earlier orthodoxies of gender and eroticism. If we recognize in the logic of their treatises not the idiosyncrasies of individuals but the discourse of a culture, we gain a point of access into the historical obscurity of early modern women's erotic desires for one another. For if the whore was not exclusively female in the early modern period, other forms of illicit eroticism may not have been as rigidly defined as Disney and Jacob would have us believe. *A View of Ancient Laws Against Immorality and Profaneness* and *A New Law Dictionary* partake of an Enlightenment impulse to stabilize, codify, and delimit precisely those desires and practices that are conceptually unstable, resistant to codification, and defiant of limits. Such attempts, of course, did not originate in the eighteenth century; indeed, the Puritan divine and Justice of the Peace Thomas Beard had issued a less systematic, more anecdotal historical compendium of sins and punishments, ominously entitled *The Theatre of Gods Judgements*, in 1597. With chapters on adultery, rape, prostitution, unlawful marriage, incestuous marriage, unlawful divorce, incest, drunkenness, and the greediness of lust, Beard's "collection of Histories out of Sacred, Ecclesiastical and Profane Authors" includes a long, apocalyptic chapter on "effeminate persons, Sodomites, and other such like Monsters," tightly linking the erotic deviation of sodomy to the gender deviation of effeminacy. Women, however, are excluded from his account of sodomy.[28] The crucial point is this: whether these "histories" take the form of miscellany, dictionary, or encyclopedia, whether they derive from scholarly or vernacular traditions of theology or law, whether their focus is the judgment of

God or the jurisprudence of man, these influential treatises, divided by a century and a half, either ignore or refuse to admit the possibility of female–female sex.

What is peculiar about this refusal is that English theology, biblical commentary, and church practice *had* admitted such a possibility in the medieval period. Although it was not described with the frequency of references to male sodomy, female–female eroticism nonetheless was one among many unnatural acts that were referred to in penitential manuals and investigated in the confessional. In addition, continental legal statutes, with which Jacob, Coke, and Disney must have been familiar, make specific mention of female–female contact as an act *contra naturum*. And some early modern English men *were* including sex between women in their catalogues of vice. In his description of sodomy, for instance, Robert Burton mentions bestiality, male–male sex, anal and oral sex, masturbation, and "wanton-loined womanlings, Tribades, that fret each other by turns, and fulfil Venus even among Eunuchs with their so artful secrets." To the classically trained Burton, "Tribades" refers to women who are so masterful in the secrets of venery that their rubbing can satisfy not only other women, but even eunuchs.[29] And Jacob's lexicographical precursor, Thomas Blount, a barrister of the inner Temple, included "woman with a woman" under the category of "buggery" in the second edition of his vernacular dictionary *Glossographia* of 1661, despite the fact that the legal authority he cites is none other than Sir Edward Coke. He repeated his definition, adding relevant statutory information, in his law dictionary of 1670.[30] So, too, *The Ladies Dictionary: Being a General Entertainment for the Fair Sex* included "Woman with a woman" in its definitions of "Buggarie."[31] A survey of dictionaries published between 1538 and 1704 suggests, however, that these were the exceptions.[32] The overwhelming tendency of lexicographic, legal, and theological texts from the mid-sixteenth to the early eighteenth century was to remain silent on the matter of female–female sex.[33] Theology and the law, of course, are only two social discourses, and not necessarily the most revealing of popular understandings or behaviors. Nonetheless, the invisibility ascribed to *lesbianism* in many contemporary critical discussions seems to stem precisely from the tendency to privilege the legal-theological category of sodomy. Because the discourse of law has stood as arbiter of social fact, the possibility of analysis has been precluded: if no Englishwoman was brought to trial under the sodomy statute, *ipso facto* no women practiced such behaviors.

In order to dissolve this critical cliché, we can gain direction from Hull's characterization of the "organization of sexual life as people lived it, rather than as ideology might have it" in the seventeenth century:

[B]ecause desire is created out of so many different strands of necessity, not all of which tend in the same direction, it can develop at odds with the prevailing social or erotic system ... [W]hatever the forces sustaining conformity, the early modern popular sexual systems had room for idiosyncrasy ... [I]mportant were the places of structural refuge within the system, *the large tracts of social irrelevancy* where certain manifestations of sexual desire seem to have been relatively underinterpreted, such as masturbation, positions, bestiality, possibly rural same-sex relations that remained undiscovered, genital touching, and so on. This is a difficult subject to research and one should be wary of confusing silence with tolerance. *Nonetheless, the early modern sexual map had sufficient white space to accommodate errant wandering, some of which would not even have been classified by contemporaries as sexual.*[34]

It is the aim of the present chapter to explore some of that "white space" on the early modern English map, deliberately abandoning the law and theology as the appropriate point of access to representations of female homoeroticism. If we look for the inscription of English women within the confines of the legal-theological category of sodomy, we will find only absence, hear mostly silence. Margaret Hunt contends that the relative indifference of the law to *lesbianism* registers the strength and effectivity of "an already well-established set of precepts, practices, and discursive conventions at both the elite and popular levels" already dedicated to the regulation of female bodily conduct.[35] But if that is the case, why do other discourses over the course of the seventeenth century increasingly take up the issue of female–female eroticism with growing explicitness? By shifting our gaze toward these other discourses, we discover, as the previous chapters have begun to illustrate, rhetorics of desires and acts that not only can be articulated but correlated with our modern understanding of diverse erotic practices among women. These rhetorics are not, at least in the first instance, authored by women; and even when they carry a female signature, they are mediated by patriarchal protocols. At the same time, in their particular representations of female desire, and in their expression of anxiety (or, perhaps more significantly, *lack* of anxiety), these rhetorics illuminate the conventions, idioms, and figures according to which desire among women was rendered intelligible. The purpose of this and subsequent chapters, then, is to delineate the content and parameters of these rhetorics and to evaluate their various ideological effects.

Heretofore, the primary means of access into early modern *lesbianism* for literary scholars has been the transvestite heroine of Renaissance literature. As many critics contend, crossdressing temporarily accords female characters in the genres of drama and romance the linguistic and social resources of men (although many critics also emphasize the eventual containment of female power ensured by the device of disguise and the use of boy actors).[36] Other critics suggest that, within the metamorphic economy of desire that structures so many literary texts, female transvestism registers and assuages cultural anxieties about the potential instability of gender.[37] And others, spurred by the treatment of *lesbianism* in social histories of transvestism, have argued that crossdressing provides a means of erotic opportunity for women with women. The bawdy banter between Rosalind and Phebe in *As You Like It*, for instance, depends precisely on the mix of femininity and masculinity that Rosalind's impersonation of Ganymede effects. Such an equivalence among clothes, masculine prerogatives, and erotic potential gives an embodied meaning to the understanding of female transvestism as a strategic appropriation of the phallus.

Nonetheless, I want to suggest that we err when we treat crossdressing, whether literary or social, as the exemplary instance of female homoeroticism in the early modern period.[38] The problems with remaining complicit with this assumption are several. First, to the extent that transvestism seems the *only* means of access into female erotic intimacy, other points of access are overlooked. Second, social orthodoxy, which would condemn female masculinity if, at the conclusion of the narrative, the character's "real femininity" fails to shine through, continues unchallenged. Despite the confusions wrought by a change of clothes, the status of a normalizing gender, mapped on to a normalizing eroticism, remains.[39] And third, insofar as crossdressing implies that homoeroticism has to be physically disguised to be articulated, it unwittingly brings to bear the "epistemology of the closet," to invoke Eve Sedgwick, on a world prior to closets (or, as chapter 8 will argue, a world where the closet was more a space of religious devotion than sexual secrecy). In an effort to move beyond these impasses, we need to ask, were there other ways of registering *lesbian* affects than transvestism, ones that were equally capable of dispelling the anxieties such expression might elicit?

Such other ways, in fact, compose an important tradition in early modern literature. From William Shakespeare's *A Midsummer Night's Dream* (1594–95) and *As You Like It* (1599) to his collaboration with John Fletcher on *The Two Noble Kinsmen* (1613) to James Shirley's *The Bird in a Cage* (1632–33), what we might call, anachronistically but nonetheless advantageously, "femme–femme" love is registered as a viable and dramatically compelling, if ultimately untenable, state. After the Civil Wars, the love and desire between two conventionally "feminine" women is depicted by women writers as well: by Katherine Philips, whose erotic friendship poems of the mid-seventeenth century will be analyzed in chapters 7 and 8, and by Margaret Cavendish, Duchess of Newcastle, who thematized such desire in several works, but most notably in her drama, *The Convent of Pleasure* (1668).

As noted in chapter 1, *A Midsummer Night's Dream* presents two female friends whose erotic investments in each other do not depend on crossdressing or the performance of female masculinity. Conventionally and symmetrically "feminine" in their outward demeanor, Helena and Hermia are unconventional only in the lengths they are willing to go to attain their heart's desires. When Hermia compares the "primrose beds" where she and Helena "were wont to lie" (1.2.215) to the meeting place, and later the bedding place, of Hermia and

Lysander, we are encouraged, in the context of a culture in which the sharing of beds was common, to notice a repetition and displacement of one bedmate for another. Indeed, this play, so thoroughly concerned with the tension between unity and duality, merger and separation, oneness and twoness, presents Lysander's seductive come-on, "One heart, one bed, two bosoms, and one troth" (2.2.42) as no different – qualitatively, emotionally, physically – from Helena's pained admonition:

> Is all the counsel that we two have shar'd,
> The sisters' vows, the hours that we have spent,
> When we have chid the hasty-footed time
> For parting us – O, is all forgot?
> All school-days friendship, childhood innocence?
> We, Hermia, like two artificial gods,
> Have with our needles created both one flower,
> Both on one sampler, sitting on one cushion,
> Both warbling of one song, both in one key,
> As if our hands, our sides, voices, and minds
> Had been incorporate. So we grew together,
> Like to a double cherry, seeming parted,
> But yet an union in partition;
> Two lovely berries molded on one stem;
> So, with two seeming bodies, but one heart;
> Two of the first, like coats in heraldry,
> Due but to one and crowned with one crest. (3.2.198–214)[40]

Helena concludes this passionate appeal with the question, "And will you rent our ancient love asunder . . . ?" (3.2.215)

So too, Celia's speeches to Rosalind in *As You Like It* are as emotionally and erotically compelling as anything spoken in the heteroerotic moments in these comedies. Even before Rosalind's incarnation as the saucy youth, Ganymede, it is the "feminine" Celia who urges Rosalind to "love no man in good earnest" (1.2.26) and who asserts, "We still have slept together, / Rose at an instant, learn'd, play'd, eat together, / And wheresoe'er we went, like Juno's swans, / Still we went coupled and inseparable" (1.3.71–74). In Ovid, swans accompany Venus, goddess of love, not Juno, goddess of marriage; Celia's transposition thus conflates erotic love and marriage in the service of female amity. Their love is presented as both exceptional in quantity and unexceptionable in type: "never two ladies lov'd as they do" (1.1.107–08) says Charles, and Le Beau describes their love as "dearer than the natural bond of sisters" (1.2.266). Helena's sense of betrayal is reiterated by Celia, who complains, "Rosalind lacks then the love / Which teacheth thee that thou and I am one. / Shall we be sund'red?" (1.3.94–96).[41] Helena and Celia's poignant questions, which echo the rhetoric of the Anglican marriage ceremony, "Those whom God hath joined together, let no man put asunder," ask us to recognize female unity as parallel in its emotional intensity and physical closeness to that of marriage.[42] Indeed, Helena's reference to "Two of the first" heightens this comparison, as it refers to the first quartering in a coat of arms which occurs when two houses are joined through marriage; like the separate coats of arms of a marital pair, she and Hermia have been not only emotionally unified, but materially and symbolically conjoined, "crowned with one crest."[43]

That these dramatic texts formulate the divorce of female unity in such similar terms substantiates James Holstun's contention that female homoerotic desire was figured in seventeenth-century poetry primarily in an elegiac mode.[44] Nostalgia circumscribes the possibility, in particular, of "feminine" female intimacy, limiting it to a mournful expression of what *was* rather than what *is* or *might be*. As Holstun makes clear in his treatment of the poems of Marvell and Donne, this elegiac strategy is a conventional topos of Renaissance literature. It is reproduced in the requiem for female affection that Shakespeare wrote in collaboration with John Fletcher in *The Two Noble Kinsmen* (1613). Even as the love of Duke Theseus and the general Pirithous is allowed passionate expression up to the eve of Theseus's marriage to Hippolyta, Emilia's love for Flavina takes the form of a mournful eulogy for the "playfellow" who "the grave enrich'd . . . when our count / Was each aleven" (1.3.50–54). To her sister, the now-vanquished Amazon queen, Emilia says:

> You talk of Pirithous' and Theseus' love:
> Theirs has more ground, is more maturely season'd,
> More buckled with strong judgment, and their needs
> The one of th' other may be said to water
> Their intertangled roots of love, but I
> And she (I sigh and spoke of) were things innocent,
> Lov'd for we did, and like the elements
> That know not what nor why, yet do effect
> Rare issues by their operance, our souls
> Did so to one another. What she lik'd
> Was then of me approv'd, what not, condemn'd,
> Nor more arraignment.   (1.3.55–66)[45]

As her encomium of this childhood friendship picks up steam (in passages that will be analyzed in chapter 8), Emilia characterizes their bond of amity as a "rehearsal" (1.3.78), a word that anticipates a subsequent (heteroerotic) performance. But as if to subvert this teleology, Emilia concludes her speech with a passionate avowal that challenges the priority of the marital bond: that "true love 'tween maid and maid may be / More than in sex dividual" (1.3.81–82).[46] Remarking on Emilia's emotional "high-speeded pace," Hippolyta offers her interpretation of the comparison: "That you shall never (like the maid Flavina) / Love any that's call'd man." Hippolyta's ambiguous syntax doubles the negative: like Flavina, Emilia will never love a man; Emilia will never love any man as well as she loved Flavina. To both assessments Emilia replies decisively, "I am sure I shall not" (1.3.83–85).

Emilia's self-knowledge and steadfastness motivate Laurie Shannon to read *The Two Noble Kinsmen* as resistant to the elegiac mode that Holstun and I have argued dominates the terms of "feminine" homoeroticism in early modern drama. In a perceptive reading of the intertwined erotics and politics of the play, Shannon connects Emilia's emotional resolution to a political principle of self-rule coextensive with a concept of chastity as a primary bond between women. As a votaress of Diana and sister to the Amazon queen, Emilia espouses faith in female autonomy and amity not only as a personal preference, but also as a political challenge to Theseus's tyranny, which would compel political and erotic submission. In thus articulating a reasoned alternative to the sovereign's politics of compulsion and degree, Shannon argues, Emilia's resistance to marriage, her doctrine of chastity, and her preference for the company of women move beyond elegy: "female homoerotics [move] from utopia into the realm of political contest... its apparent defeat by marriage is marked by funerals rather than celebration... the 'inevitability' of a female homoerotics pressed into the past tense is just what Shakespeare and Fletcher qualify and recast as political injustice."[47] On the eve of Emilia's espousal to the unknown victor for her hand, Shannon notes, Emilia may be "bride-habited," but she remains "maiden-hearted" (5.1.150–51).

Arguing further that "serious female association is linked to a proprietary space and not just a matter for nostalgia," Shannon invokes the Ovidian trope of the garden, the *locus amoenus*, as a "zone of feminine autonomy... [which] gives female friendship an even more marked sense of place than idealized male friendship enjoyed." Acknowledging that the "seclusion of women within the garden and domestic space has a primarily regulatory purpose," Shannon posits that such regulation "also generates an anxiety about their conduct within the women's quarters."[48] She then reads as flirtatious the playful scene in the garden between Emilia and her Woman, as they pick flowers and bawdily banter about the attractions of men and of chastity. At the end of this scene, Emilia remarks, "I am wondrous merry-hearted, I could laugh now," to which her Woman replies, "I could lie down, I am sure." Emilia retorts, "And take one with you?" The Woman answers, "That's as we bargain, madam." To which Emilia concludes, "Well, agree then" (2.2.150–52). According to several editors, "laugh and lie down" was a card game replete with sexual meanings. This allusion, plus the ambiguity of the bargain struck in the context of the flirtatiousness of the entire scene, lead Shannon to suggest "that these final lines refer to a sexual encounter between Emilia and her Woman."[49]

I agree that an elegiac poetics does not fully comprehend the erotic politics of *The Two Noble Kinsmen*, which exploits the associational bonds of chastity as a matter of affective and political volition. Concentrating on the erotic potential of chastity thus leads to a fuller recognition of female agency than a focus on elegy allows (and in this respect, is a reading strategy similar to the one I employed in chapter 1). Nonetheless, I would argue that even as Emilia articulates her homoerotic desire as a present condition, the structure of *The Two Noble Kinsmen* positions it in the past. Character and plot are at odds here, and even when read as a tragedy, this play drives toward the marital alliance that Shakespearean comedy presents as woman's inevitable lot. As was true for the loving female dyads of earlier Shakespearean plays, the unity, mutuality, and affection of Emilia and Flavina are idealized and portrayed as a foil to male–female antagonism; at the same time, these bonds are represented as temporary, firmly located in childhood or adolescence, and necessarily giving way to patriarchal marriage. Presented as always already in the past, and hence irrecoverable, or so impossible an undertaking as to never partake of a future, female homoerotic desire simultaneously is acknowledged *and mastered* by male writers. Or, in my reworking of Holstun's terms, symmetrical, "feminine" homoerotic desire is granted signification only in such terms that would render it insignificant.

It is important to recognize the implicit power asymmetry that, with the notable exception of Emilia, constitutes the homoerotic pair: the relative power of each woman is aligned according to her *denial* of homoerotic bonds. Generally, it is the female rather than the male characters of these plays who, by their silent denial of another woman's emotional claims, position homoerotic desire in the past. And if neither Rosalind nor Hermia directly answers the charges of betrayal articulated by Celia and Helena, *As You Like It* and *A Midsummer Night's Dream* nevertheless stage a violent repudiation of female allegiance: Rosalind nastily mocks Phebe's expression of erotic interest, while Helena and Hermia come to physical blows. Femme–femme love is thus figurable in terms not only of the always already lost, but the always about to be *betrayed*. And the incipient heteroeroticism of the woman who is recipient rather than enunciator of homoerotic desire comes to stand as the natural telos of the play.

The gendered and erotic scenarios enacted in all of these texts do not exemplify psychosexual necessity – that is, a developmental movement through progressive erotic stages – but an economic, political imperative: as each woman is resecured in the patriarchal, reproductive order, her desires are made to conform to her "place" (and if, like Emilia, she refuses to conform, she is married anyway). Despite the fantasized typology of Amazonia in *A Midsummer Night's Dream* and Emilia's Amazonian resistance to Theseus, the female characters in these plays are not suspected of being unmarriageable. Their "feminine" gender performances ensure that their homoerotic desires exist comfortably within the patriarchal order – at least until the onset of courtship and marriage. It is only with the social imperative of cementing male bonds through the homosocial exchange of women that women's independent desires become a focus of male anxiety and retribution.

In Shakespeare's and Fletcher's plays, an originary, prior homoerotic desire is crossed, abandoned, betrayed; correlatively, a desire for men or a marital imperative is produced and inserted into the narrative in order to create a formal, "natural" mechanism of closure. Loosely associated with a pastoral environment aligned with the emotionally expansive Shakespearean "green world," female homoeroticism is thus part of an Ovidian heritage of metamorphosis that authorizes a temporary suspension of social order and fleeting indulgence in polymorphous desire. I will discuss the resource Ovid offers to representations of female–female desire more fully in chapters 6 and 7. For the moment, I want to stress that Renaissance drama's use of pastoral repeats and enhances the temporal dynamics of elegy. This is no accident, for elegy is one of pastoral's primary modes.[50] The combined effect of pastoral and elegy in these plays is to render "feminine" homoeroticism insignificant by situating it safely in a spatially and temporally distant golden age.

Over the course of the seventeenth century, the elegiac pastoralism of these Elizabethan and Jacobean plays was supplanted by representations that locate female–female desire in the present tense. Emilia's mature commitment to female separatism in *The Two Noble Kinsmen* anticipates these later plays, which exploit the sensuality of adult homoeroticism while situating these desires in female-governed spaces that remain marginal to the social polity. Transported to an even more bounded enclosure, female–female eroticism paradoxically is given freer, more explicit, rein. At the same time, the dramatic focus on the loving female couple is loosened, as homoerotic pleasures are explored within a community of women.

Satirically dedicated to the Puritan polemicist William Prynne, who attacked women actors as "notorious whores" in *Histrio-mastix: The Player's Scourge or Actor's Tragedy*, James Shirley's *The Bird in a Cage* (1632–33) is a defense of Queen Henrietta Maria, patroness of the Cockpit players for whom Shirley was principal dramatist.[51] Just weeks before Prynne's publication, the Queen and her ladies had performed speaking parts at court in Walter Montague's pastoral extravaganza, *The Shepherd's Paradise*. Prynne's alleged libel against the Queen gave the authorities the chance they had been looking for to imprison him, inflict corporal punishment, and suppress his book.[52] The gender and erotic consciousness expressed in *The Bird in a Cage* thus implicitly refers to the material reality of a queen displaying her body and speaking in theatrical spectacle. The play's role in this contemporary controversy pushes its meaning toward a social referent and verisimilitude. At the same time, its attempts to distance homoeroticism are somewhat less effective than the elegiac pastoralism of the previous generation.

The "bird in a cage" refers extra-theatrically to Prynne languishing in prison, and within the play to both the princess Eugenia, confined with her ladies to a tower by her overly zealous father, and to her beloved Philenzo, who secretly enters her chamber disguised as a bird in an enormous cage.[53] During their confinement, the ladies decide to pass the time by staging an "interlude," the story of Jupiter's "seduction" of Danaë, which replicates in miniature the themes of the main plot: Eugenia acts the part of Danaë and her lady, Donella, plays Jupiter. In the view of Sophie Tomlinson, Shirley's attempt to exonerate the queen's acting is contradicted by

> the clashing tone of the interlude itself... The scene might be read as legitimizing this kind of recreational activity for women, were it not for the fact that the extempore play takes the form of a riotous burlesque, fusing imaginative release with sexual excitement in a way which wholly confirms Prynne's epithet: "I have known men have been insufficient," declares one of the princess's ladies, "but women can [always] play their parts" (416). While the behaviour and language of the princess are impeccable, her maids are cast in the comic mould of lustful court women, speaking lines such as, "Now would I give all my jewels for the sight of a pair of breeches though there were nothing in them" (415).

The upshot of the "Ladies interlude" is that, in Tomlinson's estimation, Shirley's "play actually illustrates Prynne's notorious equation."[54]

Yet, despite her recognition of the double entendres animating the interlude, Tomlinson seems unaware that much of the bawdy refers not to the physical attributes of men, but to the attractions of women. Donella's impersonation of the unbridled Jupiter, performed without recourse to crossdressing, is a remarkable performance of femme–femme desire. Playing Jupiter, her twenty-eight line amorous speech to the sleeping Danaë ends with a self-admonition to forego poeticizing and begin *acting*: "But I rob my selfe of Treasure, / This is but the Gate of Pleasure. / To dwell here, it were a sin, / When *Elizium* is within. / Leave off then thes flattering Kisses, / To rifle other greater Blisses" (4.2. sig H2v, 24–29). The threatened rape is interrupted by a bell announcing the surprise arrival of the bird cage and, by means of this device, Philenzo's "rescue" of Eugenia. Donella's response to this interruption is explicit and confused disappointment: "Beshrew the Belman, and you had not wak'd as you did Madam, I should ha' forgot my selfe and play'd *Jupiter* indeed with you, my imaginations were strong upon me; and you lay so sweetly – how now?" (sig H2v, 32–35).

With her imaginations strong upon her, Donella implies that in playing the part of Ovidian seducer, she has discovered something of her own desires. Given Prynne's condemnation of the theatrical imagination and Shirley's implicit counter-argument in favor of it, Donella's erotic "imaginations," I submit, are homoerotic. Her female-oriented desire is affirmed by another gentlewoman, Cassiana, who earlier remarked upon Jupiter's entrance: "now comes *Jupiter* to take my Lady napping, we'l sleepe too, let the wanton have her swinge, would she were a man for her sake" (sig H2r, 36–sig H2v, 1). That the "wanton" simultaneously *is* Donella and Jupiter is suggested by Cassiana's retention of female pronouns, which helps to materialize the pun embedded in Donella's wish: to play Jupiter in *deed*. In light of this, it would not stretch erotic allusion too far to see in Donella's earlier response to Cassiana's impromptu poeticizing the presence of a bawdy joke about the physiology of female arousal. Cassiana begins: "Thinke Madame all is but a dreame, / That we are in – Now I am out – beame, creame. / Helpe me *Katerina*, I can make no sence rime to't." To which Donella puns: "Creame is as good a Rime as your mouth can wish, / Ha, ha, ha" (sig. H1r, 34–38).[55]

The two rapes with which Eugenia is threatened invert conventional expectations. Whereas Donella's erotic approach first seems to exist only in the realm of her imagination, and conversely, the disguised Philenzo's erotic demands appear as a real threat to the Princess's safety, it soon becomes clear that it is Donella who actually is so transported with desire as to force herself upon her mistress and that Philenzo has adopted the guise of rapist as a manipulative ploy.[56] And whereas the stage directions tell us that Philenzo "discovers himselfe" to the Princess (sig. I1r, 11–12), Donella seems to have "forgot" her "selfe" (sig. H2v, 33) in precisely the way Prynne and other anti-theatricalists feared. Nonetheless, despite the strength of Donella's "imaginations," the dramatic process of Shirley is, like that of Shakespeare and Fletcher, to pose eroticism between women as an enticing option, only to displace it through the force of a seemingly "natural," ultimately more powerful attraction to men. The dominant economy of desire that these plays endorse, however, does not cancel out the erotic attraction expressed among female characters; rather, such desire is represented as a distinct, if temporary and physically bounded, possibility.

When Margaret Cavendish, Duchess of Newcastle, wrote her plays, prose romances, and utopian fantasies, she had at her imaginative disposal some strong precedents for the figuring of female–female desire.[57] In *The Convent of Pleasure* (1668), Cavendish explicitly explores the attractions of homoeroticism among women, only to reaffirm the necessity of marital alliance as the price of a harmonious dramatic conclusion.[58] She does so, in a fashion faithful to Shakespeare (whom she had dreamed of marrying when a girl), by exploiting the eroticism afforded by transvestism, making particular use of *Twelfth Night*, where the crossdressed outsider, Viola / Cesario, gains access to a desirable heiress who has forsworn the company of men. Like Shakespeare's Olivia, Lady Happy has just inherited her father's estate and is thus a suitable object of matrimonial designs. But rather than negotiate access to the lady by means of a messenger, Cavendish follows in Shirley's footsteps, enclosing her characters within the formidable walls of an aristocratic, all-female cloister – not an imprisoning tower, but a convent of pleasure – that is penetrated, not by a bird in a cage, but by a foreign prince disguised as a princess. The brainchild of Lady Happy, who is called a "Votress to Nature" (2.1. p. 11), the convent of pleasure is her solution to the "inslave[ment]" of women in marriage; she decrees that a world without men need not be a world without pleasure or freedom: "I will take so many Noble Persons of my own Sex, as my Estate will plentifully maintain . . . to live incloister'd with all the delights and pleasures that are allowable and lawful" (1.2. p. 7). With women's physical needs and emotional desires ruling every decision, Lady Happy creates an environment in which theatrical interludes, dancing, and singing are the pastimes of choice.

Unlike Shirley's play-within-the-play, which is a risqué retelling of a canonical myth, the ten scenes acted for the benefit of Lady Happy and her friends derive from the tradition of female lament, giving powerful voice to female discontent. Physical abuse at the hands of alcoholic husbands, poverty caused by male gambling and whoring, and the horrors of repeated childbirth and infant mortality are represented as the plight of married women in a series of vignettes that ends with the pronouncement, "*Marriage is a Curse, we find / Especially to Women kind: / From the Cobler's Wife we see, / To Ladies, they unhappie be*" (3.10. p. 30). In addition to their boldness in assigning responsibility for the misery of womankind to the actions of men, these vignettes attain dramatic power from their status as the theatrical, crossdressed version of a "real world" that happily has ceased to exist with the exclusion of men from Lady Happy's domain.

Cavendish's metatheatrical strategy is not wholly dedicated to feminist polemic. Whereas segregation from men removes temporarily the threat of marital oppression, eroticism remains ever present, not only as an aspect of the sensual environs, but in the entertainments and eventually in the behaviors of Lady Happy and a mysterious stranger. As if in homage to the pastoral of Shakespeare and Lyly, much of the homoeroticism of the play arises out of the amorous pastime of pastoral "Recreations" in which "some of [the] Ladies do accoustre Themselves in Masculine-Habits, and act Lovers-parts" (3.1. p. 22). Pastoral in this play does not promote an elegiac distancing of homoerotic bonds, but further enables transitive gender and erotic exploration through playing the parts, for instance, of a shepherd and shepherdess or Neptune and a sea goddess. It is while she is costumed as a shepherd that the foreign Princess, "a Princely brave Woman truly, of a Masculine Presence" (2.3. p. 16), begins to woo Lady Happy, herself dressed as a shepherdess. The amorous freedom associated with pastoral, combined with the gender fluidity of transvestism, lead to an expression of love:

PRINCESS: Can Lovers love too much?
LADY HAPPY: Yes, if they love not well.
PRIN: Can any Love be more vertuous, innocent and harmless then ours?
LADY H: I hope not.
PRIN: Then let us please our selves, as harmless Lovers use to do.

LADY H: How can harmless Lovers please themselves?
PRIN: Why very well, as, to discourse, imbrace and kiss, so mingle souls together.
LADY H: But innocent Lovers do not use to kiss.
PRIN: Not any act more frequent amongst us Women-kind; nay, it were a sin in friendship, should not we kiss: then let us not prove our selves Reprobates. *They imbrace and kiss, and hold each other in their Arms.*
PRIN: These my Imbraces though of Femal kind, May be as fervent as a Masculine mind.

(4.1. pp. 32–33)

Having aligned female virtue, innocence, and lack of harm with the "feminine" pleasures of talking, embracing, kissing, and mingling souls, the Princess reasserts their erotic power by characterizing these actions as "fervent" as those of men. Kissing, the natural and frequent sign of female friendship, is explicitly eroticized as something continuous with, yet more than, friendship. Embracing is an action categorized as both "of a Femal kind" and "Masculine." To the Princess's declaration, "May I live in your favour, and be possest with your Love and Person, is the height of my ambitions," Lady Happy responds, "I can neither deny you my Love nor Person." But to the Princess's complaint, "In amorous Pastoral Verse we did not Woo / As other Pastoral Lovers use to doo," Lady Happy responds, "Which doth express, we shall more constant be, / And in a Married life better agree." Pastoralism promises to give way to marriage with the Princess's declaration: "We shall agree, for we true Love inherit, / Join as one Body and Soul, or Heav'nly spirit." Their mutual vows are celebrated by communal dancing around the may-pole, after which festivities the pair is crowned "King and Queen of all the Shepherds and Shepherdesses" (4.1. pp. 37–38).

Unlike Shakespeare, who establishes the "femininity" of his heroines before allowing them to don masculine dress, Cavendish withholds the gender of the Prince(ss) until the final unveiling scene. The extent to which the relationship between Lady Happy and the Princess is one of two femmes, then, relies on the reader's (or auditor's) lack of knowledge of the cross-gender disguise. Certainly, Lady Happy believes herself to be in love with a woman who, however "masculine" her presence, fits comfortably and companionably in with the other women (some of whom also dress as shepherds). The play's homoerotic effect is further intensified, as Misty Anderson has shown, by the play's indulgence in the sensuality of tactile pleasures which were increasingly associated, both philosophically and culturally, with the "feminine."[59] In the sumptuously decorated apartments of the convent, the walls are hung with silk, the floors are strewn with flowers, and each chamber is adorned with "a great Looking Glass... that we may view our selves and take pleasure in our own Beauties" (2.2. p.14). The environment is possessed of endless variety, as the tapestries, carpets, plate, perfumes, linens, and gardens change with the seasons. Cavendish's "convent" is no "shady cloister" where "barren sisters... chant... faint hymns to the cold fruitless moon," as scornfully conjured by Theseus in *A Midsummer Night's Dream*. Rather, in her vision of an environment appropriate to women, aristocrats pursue elite pleasures surrounded by the material means to do so, employing a contented retinue of female physicians, surgeons, apothecaries, brewers, bakers, and swineherds.[60]

Whereas Cavendish's overall design owes much to the conventions of those dramatists who preceded her, her representation of female homoeroticism revises their models, pushing them as far as they will go without overstepping the bounds of female decorum. Licensed through the artifice of the pastoral, explored through the strategy of transvestism, and supported by a sororal community, "feminine" homoeroticism appears as part and parcel of the pleasures Lady Happy deems a noblewoman's natural right. Having created a vital and generative, if spatially marginal and socially elitist, world of female amity, Cavendish nevertheless reimposes marital alliance as the necessary outcome of female affectivity. Lady Happy and her Prince marry in church, their nuptials celebrated by dancing and feasting, and the Prince has the final say about the fate of the convent. Despite having articulated the question, "since there is so much folly, vanity and falshood in Men, why should Women trouble and vex themselves for their sake?" (1.2. p. 4), Cavendish reasserts the force of aristocratic alliance and the mystifications of romantic love. However far away from men her imagination can roam in pursuit of female pleasures, Cavendish returns to men as the apparent price of formal closure. Implicit in her fantasy is the hope that the Prince has learned something of marital responsibilities from his masquerade, and something of women's desires from luxuriating among the convent's many pleasures.[61] As if in unconscious discomfort with this return to "necessity," Cavendish continues the gender bending outside the frame of the play; in the *Dramatis Personae* placed at the end of the text, Lady Happy's beloved is listed as *The Princess*.

In Cavendish, Shirley, Fletcher, and Shakespeare, the displacement of the homoerotic by the heterosexual happens so "naturally" that the tension between the two modes of desire is erased. But are these in fact *two separate* modes of desire? The sum of these dramatic representations suggests that in the minds of certain playwrights, such a contiguity existed between female homoerotic and heteroerotic desires that the direction of "object choice" hardly mattered at all. At least for female *characters* who did not challenge conventional gender roles – who did *not* crossdress, who did *not* wear swords, who were not anatomically "excessive" and who did not use "illicit devices," whose gendered "femininity" belied the possibility of "unnatural" behaviors – desire is depicted as flowing relatively freely between homo and hetero modes. What is true of stage representations may indicate possibilities for individuals, and it is with this potential in mind that I suggest, further, that for *women* who did not challenge the dictates of gender, desire may have been allowed to move in multiple directions as well.

Such texts suggest that what is at issue in feminine homoeroticism, both on the stage and off, is less eroticism or even gender *per se* than the upholding of marital alliance, with social and biological reproduction at its core. As the next chapter will demonstrate, it is not a woman's desire for other women or any nongenital acts she might pursue that raise alarms, but rather her usurpation of male prerogatives. The chaste friend's desire is ultimately untenable not because it is viewed, as is the tribade's, as imitative of masculine prerogatives and hence monstrous, but because it fails to contribute to the reproduction of patriarchal authority, including the social structures of the early modern household and the transmission of property and wealth through the bodies of legitimate heirs. Through their narrative trajectories these plays suggest that female–female desire becomes an issue – becomes significant – only when the time comes for the patriarchal imperative of marital alliance, and with it the transmission of property and the reproduction of children, to be enforced. Woman's social role within a system of procreation relies not only on her biological capacity to give birth, but on her willingness to perform that labor and to enter into the lifelong social bonds with men that legitimate maternity. Only when women's erotic relations with one another threaten to become exclusive and thus endanger the fulfillment of their marital and reproductive duties, or when they symbolically usurp male sexual prerogatives, are cultural injunctions levied against them.[62] It is precisely the cultural anxiety that women will fail to comply with their socially mandated role to become wives and mothers that these dramatic texts obsessively articulate and assuage. It is hardly incidental that female homoerotic liaisons are dramatized only within the context of heteroerotic courtship plots (rather than, for instance, the genres of the history play or tragedy), for one purpose of comedy is to naturalize the expulsion of undesirable social relationships in order to resecure the social order. The eradication of the feminine homoerotic position to desire, in other words, is precisely what must be *staged*. These five plays also imply, however, that *if* same-gender erotic practices *could* exist coterminously with the marriage contract and husbandly authority, there would be little cause for alarm. Posing no threat to the organization of socioeconomic life, they would, in the words of Hull, "disappear from view as insignificant."

Viewed as a group, then, these dramatic texts encourage us to recognize how utterly conventional, even routine, was the eroticization of female friendship. The re-citation of femme–femme love in texts throughout the seventeenth century suggests the extent to which these representations provided reassurance to a patriarchal culture in a continual state of crisis about female autonomy, social and erotic. Although transvestites, tribades, and female sodomites necessarily performed a certain amount of "gender trouble," femme–femme couples seem to have posed very little gender trouble at all. Within the terms of social orthodoxy, this absence of trouble marks out their particular social function: able to simultaneously elicit and elude erotic meanings, femmes embody the fantasy of women loving women *to minimal social effect*.

Perhaps this explains why, in continental legal practice, the femme involved with a tribade generally was perceived as the not-altogether-innocent victim of another woman's lust; her crime was correspondingly minor, her punishment less severe. Indeed, as will be discussed in greater detail in the next chapter, when early modern law included female–female eroticism within its purview, it viewed the erotic practices of tribades and femmes as radically discontinuous: it was assumed that only the tribade penetrated or "abused" her partner, that femmes were passive recipients of an asymmetrical lust. But here we stumble across a circularity of definition: it is, after all, the use of a dildo or an enlarged clitoris that in the sixteenth and seventeenth centuries defines the sodomite or tribade, and it is the "feminine" woman's status as penetrable that defines her as a woman. This bifurcation points again to an underlying reason for the absence of animus against femme–femme love. For, if we have not interpreted the language of Helena, Celia, Emilia, and Donella (or the images of Virtues Embracing) as homoerotic, it is not only because of our internalized homophobia, or because of our formalist inclinations to privilege the heterosexual teleology of dramatic plots, but because the palpable "femininity" of these characters blinds us – and, I suspect, may have blinded many of their contemporaries as well – to the eroticism evident in their language of desire. Existing in an eccentric relation to the representational nexus of sodomy and tribadism, bodily supplementation and gender appropriation, these plays suggest that "feminine" homoerotic desires were dramatized precisely because they did not signify.

To what extent, then, can early modern women's relationships with one another be perceived as resistant, oppositional, or transgressive? To the extent that they existed coterminously, companionably, with patriarchal prerogatives, perhaps not at all. They only *become* oppositional when perceived as a threat to the reproductive designs of marital alliance or to the exclusive masculine prerogative over phallic power. Whereas the tribade and sodomite functioned as magnets for cultural fantasies and fears – about gender, reproduction, nature, monstrosity, and the ultimate instability of all such cultural categories – the femme, who challenged neither gender roles nor reproductive imperatives, seems to have been unworthy of special notice.

Except, that is, when the female community, rather than the loving couple, becomes the focus of concern. To the extent that a femme–femme liaison contributes to, or is supported by, a community of like-minded women, to the extent that this sodality is envisioned not as a temporary phase or far-off place, but as an institutable social formation, it could indeed represent a potential threat in the early modern period. It is just such an alternative sociality, wherein chastity represents not merely an individual vow but a primary affective bond among women, that I analyze in chapter 6.

In the years since an early version of this argument was published, some readers have taken my proposition of the (in)significance of *lesbian* desire to mean that female–female eroticism was unthinkable, meaningless, or successfully ideologically contained. Given the essay's commitment to analyzing representations of femme–femme love, interpretations that attribute to me an impulse to dismiss *lesbianism* are a bit puzzling. My deconstructive apparatus should have made clear that my interest is in the ways in which bodies that don't signify nonetheless *do matter*. The confusion seems to have stemmed from my use of "(in)significance," a locution that was meant to encapsulate the paradox of "feminine" homoeroticism in this period. The parentheses function as diacritical markers of a problem, a tension – between signification and significance, between patterns of articulation and ascriptions of value – that historically has governed the predicament of conventionally "feminine," homoerotically desiring women.[63] As it turns out, a greater number of early modern texts refer to femmes than I first realized – all of which strengthens my conviction that the failure to signify is, like all such truisms, an ideological operation, and thus, a problem to be investigated.[64] But rather than pursue such an investigation, some readers have rewritten the dynamic of (in)significance as simple insignificance, while others have misinterpreted an argument specific to one gender performance – conventional femininity – as a global pronouncement on all forms of *lesbianism*. Bent on declaring the fact of *lesbian* existence in the early modern period – that it *did* exist and *did* matter – they neglect to examine why femme–femme love in particular failed to register much static on the conceptual screen.

The most insightful critique comes from Laurie Shannon who, in her effort to explore how an episteme of "homonormativity shapes the licit," suggests that my "strategy of reading ... associates 'signification' per se with 'transgression' and so declines to take up the ways textual or discursive phenomena participate in 'established' structures of thought."[65] Astute as this critique is in its awareness of a prior binary structuring my account, it neglects to note that my "strategy of reading" associates absence not with a lack of desiring women but with a lack of social concern. Insignificance is thus allied to precisely the performance of female intimacies that we both investigate (retrospectively) as significant. Indeed, in arguing that such intimacies did not signify as transgressive in the early modern period, my position is not far from Shannon's own that "[p]rinciples of likeness ... exert greater controlling powers than a classificatory view of sexual practices does in the Renaissance naming of desire and affects."[66] As will become clear in chapters 7 and 8, the close link I observe between discursive signification and social significance is founded on precisely the "'established' structures of thought" that she analyzes: resemblance, similitude, and likeness.

Let me affirm, then, that for actual early modern women, "feminine" homoeroticism may not have been insignificant at all. Nonetheless, all we have at this point is piecemeal and irreducibly textualized evidence for such a supposition. A case in point is provided by the material traces of early modern correspondence. By the seventeenth century, many women of the gentry and aristocracy were prolific correspondents; their epistolary activities were not only a source of information and news; they also positioned women within a broader social network than that made possible within a father's or husband's household. The exchange of letters among friends often took the form of the "familiar" letter, a conventional form characterized by benevolent wishes for the friend's welfare and ardent hopes for reciprocal feeling.[67] Although those persons most likely to write such letters would be the ones least likely to need epistolary models (having learned such social niceties by virtue of their social status), for the less fortunate, models were available in the form of published collections. One such collection, *Hobsons Horse-load of Letters* (1617), compiled by the hack writer, Gervase Markham (also author of popular manuals on huswifery, horse husbandry, angling, and gardening), presents stock characters in stock situations, and offers to those persons aspiring to gentility appropriate templates of rhetorical style. In one letter, entitled "From one Gentlewoman, to another Gentlewoman," the writer adopts the persona of one pining for her absent friend:

My onely friend, not all the pleasures of a Country house . . . can make up that content I parted withall when I left thee: It doth mee good, retiring my selfe many times into my selfe, to call to minde our being together, our discourse and pritty harmelesse pastimes; My best companion here is my Arcadia . . . I like better here our thick Groves then large Plaines; for there being alone, as I always being without thee, the trees seeme to be my companions, who better please mee with their silence, then our rude youth with their vaine speeches. And truth I tell thee, even those of mine owne fere least delight me, such is their boldnesse, and manly carriage; if it bee fashion and comelinesse, I shall better content my self with mine owne homelinesse, and rather with want of maners then want of modesty: I stay unwillingly from thee, but must pay the obedience I owe to a father, with forcing my mind to content my selfe in it selfe, and flatter it with promise of enjoying thee, which till I do, I am but halfe my selfe, and rest wholly in thee. Ever thine, S.T.[68]

Her "correspondent" in the city responds in an equally melancholy mode:

My worthy choyce, how miserable may I then account my selfe, who have here nothing but houses to looke on, which can neither delight nor take away any thing from my discontentment. To you, the flowne fields, pleasant meadowes, silver rivers, spacious plains, thicke groves, high mountaines and humble vallies may well entertaine and steale away much tediousnesse from the slow-footed houres. My owne thoughts which were wont to accompany mee, growe now aweary of themselves, finding no comfort but in forgetting sleepes, as if since you were gone, all other objects prove matter rather of griefe then content. I have been pittifully troubled, since your departure, with a raging in my teeth, and am beholding to thy memory for much ease, my minde dulled with thy losse, being not so sensible of the extremity of paine: I pray thee write often and long to me; for wherein can I better bestow my selfe, then in reading thy storie, written by thine owne hand. Though I am almost fallen out with all mankinde (the ruine and shame of our Sexe) yet I could wish my Sexe changed for thy sake, from whose sweetnesse and vertue the world may expect large hopes, pitty they should either be buried in thy maiden Sepulchre, or lost in the wildnesse of mens frenzies. For my part no husband shall take me from thee, but while I live, I will be th' admirer of thy chastity and doting lover of all thy perfections.[69]

These letters, it must be said, are utterly conventional. At the same time, we would do well to scrutinize the terms of their conventions. Beyond the sympathetic regard for her friend's welfare, the first correspondent discreetly expresses a desire to "enjoy" her friend and finds Ovidian license to do so while walking alone in thick rural groves (her own pastoral Arcadia) and, one surmises, reading Sidney's *Arcadia*. The second letter-writer heightens the rhetoric by registering her appreciation of her friend's perfections in distinctly erotic terms. Both writers express a growing aversion to men (an aversion, it must be noted, that in this period rarely was ascribed to women by men); characterizing men as "the ruine and shame of our Sexe," determined that no husband will interfere in their loving bond, they articulate a critique of men and marriage ("the wildnesse of mens frenzies") worthy of the players in the vignettes of Cavendish. Yet neither embarrassment nor furtiveness accompanies their expression of love. Rather, they imagine sex transformation to be the utopian solution to social impediments.

Whether these letters were written by Markham for the edification of female readers or by two long forgotten gentlewomen whose correspondence somehow came into Markham's hands; whether, if they were living persons, the authors of these letters married or actively resisted marriage, we probably will never know. We do know, however, that the rhetoric evinced here was used by at least some early modern women. An equally passionate expression of love for a female friend is evinced in a letter of a sister to her brother, as she describes to him her affections for his bride-to-be. In 1636 Constance Fowler, wife of Walter Fowler, wrote to her brother, the Hon. Herbert Aston, a lengthy letter chiefly concerned with Katherine Thimelby, with whom she has been in correspondence:

For I believe I am blest with the most perfectest and constant lover as ever woman was blest with. Oh, if you would know the story of our affection, you must come hither and read volumes of it, afore you can be able to understand half the dearness of our love. I keep them apurpose for your sight, and no creature breathing but my self ever saw them

186   The renaissance of lesbianism

or knows of them else. You will say, I am certain, when you peruse them that there was never any more passionate affectionate lovers than she and I, and that you never knew two creatures more truly and deadly in love with one another than we are . . . For after I had made known to her by letters how infinitely I honoured her, and how I had done so since I first saw her here, she writ me the sweetest answers, that from that very hour I confess I have been most deadly in love with her as ever lover was.[70]

After relating "that many letters having passed between us of only complimental friendship" (suggesting awareness of gradated degrees of genteel intimacy), Constance describes the ladies' chance meeting at a dinner at Tixall, where they "converse" by "silent expressions." She then entreats her brother to continue his courtship of Katherine, described as "the only wonder of this age," in terms that reverse, and render explicitly passionate, the terms of the more usual homosocial triangle:

For in the success of your affections depends the happiness of my life; for I have nothing in this world that I can receive contentment in, if this prosper not as I wish. For you two are dear partners in my heart, and it is so wholly divided betwixt you, that I have so much ado to get leave of it to place any other friend of mine there . . . [D]o what you can to compass that happiness for yourself which I so thirst after, that my dearest friend and you being united in one, your hearts may likewise be come one, and so I may keep them with more ease in my breast than now I can, they being divided . . .[71]

With her own heart divided between Katherine and Herbert, Constance feels their division internally; it is only their unification that will allow her to keep them "with more ease" in her own breast. After contemplating the possibility that some obstacle will prevent the unity she seeks, she remarks that "all the world could not have invented a more killing news than this will be to me . . . For I speak it to you with my eyes drowned in tears; I think, nay, I am certain the grief of it would kill me . . . "[72] Rhetorically emphasizing the extremity of her feelings – "truly and deadly in love with one another," "deadly in love with her," "a more killing news," "the grief of it would kill me" – Constance expresses her belief that her happiness, indeed her life, depends on her brother's marriage to Katherine.

How do we assess the rhetoric and sentiments of such letters? How could Herbert Aston bear to be the recipient of such effusions, which seem to have been adopted out of the likes of *Hobson's Horse-load of Letters*? One part of the answer, of course, is that the languages of friendship, kinship, and love overlapped in meaning; Constance Fowler, after all, signs her letter to her brother "Your dear affectionate *lover*." Such linguistic flexibility alluded to, and enabled, a spectrum of genteel relations among women. But a further and more substantive answer is that the rhetorical affects expressed in these letters fit comfortably in the pattern of (in)significance accorded to femme–femme love. Viewed as a temporary stage of female affectivity, a "rehearsal" to the "natural" conclusion of marriage, such desires among women are rendered intelligible from within the protocols of chastity. Even an aversion to men could be construed as a manifestation of maidenly modesty. As long as "the obedience" that such women "owe to a father" governed their lives, their desires for their friends would have been considered neither transgressive nor unorthodox. Rather, their love – like that of Helena, Celia, and Emilia – would have failed to signify.

5 The psychomorphology of the clitoris; or, the reemergence of the tribade in English culture

> We have long realized that in women the development of sexuality is complicated by the task of renouncing that genital zone which was originally the principal one, namely, the clitoris, in favour of a new zone – the vagina.[1]

Thus far in this book I have examined discourses, representations, and figures for the unintentional warrant they may have offered to early modern women's pursuit of erotic pleasure. Such license was indirectly conceded within the ideological confines of three distinct representational topoi: the ideological embrace of reproductive marriage; the regal prerogatives of a queenly absolutism; and the imagined golden age of female intimacy. But neither women's homoerotic affections nor the clitoris itself were consistently the subject of tolerance, benign neglect, or enthusiasm. Anatomists and medical writers were concerned about the misuse – or abuse, to use their terminology – of the clitoris, a misuse that was universally associated with women's attempt to usurp male sexual prerogatives.

In this chapter I analyze that concern. Before turning to early modern writers, however, I shall frame my analysis with reference to an issue of particular relevance to contemporary constructions of *lesbianism*. For it seems more than a historical accident that the apprehension of early modern writers was reiterated and elaborated in the work of the major modern theorist of sexuality, Sigmund Freud. As my chapter epigraph illustrates, Freud considered the clitoris a problem. This is hardly a startling revelation. From Anne Koedt's early feminist critique, "The Myth of the Vaginal Orgasm," to Thomas Laqueur's "Amor Veneris, Vel Dulcedo Appeletur," many critics have elucidated the strategies whereby Freud attempted to reconcile women's physiology with a heterosexual imperative.[2] His theory – that in the oedipal phase the female child must renounce clitoral stimulation in favor of vaginal penetration – is widely acknowledged to be an attempt to secure phallic privilege by imposing a cultural solution on what he deemed a biological problem. Such psychosexual adaptation is enabled by Freud's equation between the clitoris and the penis, an equivalence that simultaneously is physiological (the clitoris and penis are analogous in structure and function), psychological (both organs indicate an active masculine aim), and metaphorical (during the infantile "phallic" stage, "the little girl is a little man").[3]

For Freud, the clitoris also is linked inextricably to *lesbianism*. Female resistance to foregoing pleasure in the clitoris is associated with an inability to replace the first object of desire, the mother, with the more proper object, the father. Just as vaginal satisfaction is the developmental sign of mature heterosexuality, clitoral attachment is the symptom of a recalcitrant, immature homoerotic desire. From a retrospective viewpoint, every woman moves through a psychosexual stage in which her clitoris threatens fixation on homoerotic objects; *lesbians* fail to follow the dictates of culture, narcissistically remaining attached to "anatomy" and "mother," and projecting their envy of the male organ onto their own "phallic" genitality. A Freudian system of equivalencies, whereby the penis = the clitoris = *lesbianism* = penis envy, sets up a smooth continuity among terms, the effect of which is a transposition of bodily organs by psychic states. The circularity of this equation despecifies female erotic experience by referring woman's body and desire back to the phallus – in modernity, the privileged term that links sexuality to identity. The formalization of two incommensurate object choices (homo and hetero) based on two separate genital "zones" (clitoral and vaginal) moderates the more radical implications of Freud's theory of bisexuality and polymorphous perversity, and resecures the direction of female desire toward men, toward reproduction, and, if all goes well and there is no slippage of identification within heterosexuality, toward the reproduction of patriarchal culture.[4]

Within psychoanalysis, then, the clitoris and the *lesbian* have been mutually implicated in a sisterhood of shame: each is the disturbing sign (and sign of disturbance) that implies the existence of the other. Underlying the perversion of *lesbian* desire is not only the polymorphous perversity of the infantile body and the inherent bisexuality of all drives, but also a female anatomical organ that transcends age, gender identification, or sexual orientation. Joined through the imperative of repression, the clitoris and the *lesbian* together signify woman's erotic potential for a pleasure outside of masculine control. At the same time, Freud's binary (and teleological) model of incommensurate pleasures (clitoral *or* vaginal, not clitoral *and* vaginal) produces a bodily schema of *lesbian* eroticism that obscures the range of erotic activities, including vaginal penetration, historically performed by women with women.

Freud's views have exerted enormous influence on modern understandings of homosexuality. Indeed, even when emphasizing the agency of gay people, most historians of sexuality attribute to psychoanalysis, sexology, and related epistemologies such as criminology and anthropology an originary, constitutive force in the construction of the "homosexual subject."[5] However, the system of equivalencies between the penis, the clitoris, and same-gender female desire predates Freud by several centuries. Sixteenth- and seventeenth-century

European anatomists, physicians, and midwives regularly employed a penis–clitoris analogy as part of a system of representation that asserted the homologous yet hierarchical relation between male and female bodies. Likewise, the association between the clitoris and tribadism has an equally long cultural history. Such analogies are less an *effect* of the modern construction of female "homosexuality" than the cultural material out of which such a category was created.

The present chapter details the conjunction of the clitoris and the tribade during the early modern period in which both were given their first sustained articulation as objects of anatomical inquiry. Building on my analysis of the rediscovery of the clitoris in chapter 2, I argue that a circular, self-referential relation – whereby the clitoris and the tribade imply, necessitate, and support one another – structures the terms of intelligibility that governed an influential representation of female homoerotic desire in the early modern period. Indeed, the structural link between the clitoris and the tribade has operated historically as one primary condition of intelligibility for such desire. Freud's recapitulation of this paradigm both reformulates and occludes this link; in his hands, what was previously conceptualized as a spatial, metonymic connection between body and body part becomes the symptomatic sign of a psychosexual phase.

This shift in logic from spatial (metonymic) to temporal (developmental) is less of an advance than it might at first appear to be. Under the guise of explorer of the psyche, Freud appropriated and converted earlier paradigms of scientific discovery, imposing a teleological narrative of psychosexual development onto a preexisting map of the female body. The map Freud redrew was born of protocolonialist and patriarchal imperatives that instigated and invigorated the quests of early modern science. Likewise, his narratives of space and time depended on a form of analogical thinking prevalent in the early modern period that forcibly fused body part to erotic behavior. Freud solicited the authorizing power of discourse that, in its replay of the "discovery" of the clitoris through the invention of clinical psychoanalysis (and the invention of the vaginal orgasm), materially affected the pleasures and possibilities of the modern female body. At the same time, the prior conceptual paradigms to which Freud was indebted were obscured by the institutional power of psychoanalysis. Peter Hulme's assertion regarding colonialist discourses that "the gesture of 'discovery' is at the same time a ruse of concealment" is true not only of Freud's reconstitution of earlier spatial metonymies, but also of the extent to which those earlier maps themselves concealed alternative conceptualizations of the female body.[6]

The terms of embodiment that have governed the construction of the clitoris as the metonymic, material sign of same-gender female desire were engendered by a complex cultural interplay of psychic and material forces. As chapter 2 intimated, when the clitoris was rediscovered in the mid-sixteenth century, it immediately was subjected to cultural expectations, fantasies, and fears. In the present chapter, I examine the specific anxieties about the illicit uses to which the clitoris might be put. By means of this analysis, we gain better access not only to the morphology of the clitoris, but to its *psychomorphology* – by which I mean the extent to which this bodily structure cannot be separated from the ideologies that constitute it. The psychomorphology of the clitoris highlights the historicity of the terms by which Freud contributed to the modern consolidation of *lesbian* identity – that is, as an essential, and essentially pathological, subjectivity.

The point is not simply to historicize Freud or to refute his narrative of *lesbian* pathology. Rather, my aim is to demonstrate the extent to which feminist figurations of *lesbian* desire and subjectivity are implicated within the same psychomorphology that gave rise to Freud's mapping of the *lesbian* body. In the critique of Freud that pervades contemporary *lesbian* scholarship, a logic of reversal structures analytic resistance to the psychoanalytic narrative; rather than pathologize, as Freud does, the equation between the *lesbian* and the clitoris, many theorists and critics celebrate (and unwittingly reify) this analogy as the enabling truth of *lesbian* existence. In rejecting the self-evident nature of the clitoris–*lesbian* connection, I want to suggest that metonymies that presume the commensurability of body parts to erotic desires and practices, whether presented in spatial or temporal terms, continue rather than challenge the history from which modern terms of female embodiment evolved.

The most historically detailed and analytically elaborated account of the cultural representation of female genital anatomy is the work of Thomas Laqueur. In *Making Sex: Body and Gender from the Greeks to Freud* and the essay "Amor Veneris, Vel Dulcedo Appeletur," Laqueur reconstructs a history of the female body that shows how anatomical knowledge is developed through the coordinates of gender ideology.[7] Fashioning an epistemic model derived from the archaeology of Michel Foucault, Laqueur upsets the presumed naturalism of the body, demonstrating the degree to which eroticism and the body partake of, and are knowable only through, discursive formations. Laqueur argues that the anatomical rediscovery of the clitoris in the sixteenth century drew from and reinforced the view of the two sexes as isomorphic: whereas the vagina visually resembled the penis, the clitoris *functioned* like the male organ, becoming erect when aroused and emitting seed during orgasm. According to Laqueur, the apparent conceptual contradiction involved in women having two penises (vagina and clitoris) while men possessed only one did not trouble the prevailing medical paradigm, dedicated as it was to a Galenic one-sex model in which difference was inconceivable: "Thus, the elaboration in medical literature ... of a 'new' female penis and specifically clitoral eroticism, was a re-presentation of the older homology of the vagina and penis, not its antithesis."[8]

Even as Laqueur brilliantly reveals the force of social construction on "biology" and even as he resists teleological narratives of causality, the epistemic quality of his work results in an unduly unifying rubric of explanation. Intent on demonstrating the sudden shift from a one-sex to a two-sex body, Laqueur argues that medical literature up to the eighteenth century speaks cohesively and insistently of gender isomorphism. Discarding conventional periodizations (the Renaissance, the Enlightenment, modernity), Laqueur replaces them with a binary model organized along the temporalities of the *before* and *after* – before the one-sex model gave way to the two-sex model, after the two-sex model initiated the regime of oppositional difference. That which is conflicted and contested within and among different discourses is subordinated to a master rubric that is statically organized along the temporal axes of the pre- and the post-. To put this another way, Laqueur constructs a diachronic narrative of historical change that nonetheless carries with it vestiges of a structural model of how change happens. The result is that, within each axis, contest is translated into uniformity, struggle into consensus. The multiplicity of discourses – their differences, discontinuities, and dialogic character – is transformed into a homogeneity that gains its existence from one overarching mode of intelligibility. What is lost is the specificity by which human actors experience their relationship to different discursive formations, as well as a more precise diachronic charting of the advent and processes of change.

Laqueur has been critiqued, by Katharine Park among others, for his silencing of those medical voices in the sixteenth and seventeenth century that do not concur with the paradigm of the one-sex body.[9] Though he records some of these alternative voices in *Making Sex*, he does so only to assert their ineffectiveness in challenging the dominance of the Galenic model. In particular, Laqueur's contention that the rediscovery of the clitoris had no impact on the one-sex model is refuted by Park, who argues that knowledge of the clitoris pressured the paradigm of homology, and helped to initiate, much earlier than Laqueur suggests, the shift to a model of two diametrically opposed genders.

I would add that two further problems, both of them linked to his epistemic commitments, trouble Laqueur's account. Just as his focus on dominant discourses elides cultural contestation, so too his commitment to rearticulating these discourses constrains the distance he might achieve from them. In his effort to demonstrate the stranglehold of Galenism, he analytically "visibilizes" the female body *only in relation to* the male – either as homologous or as oppositional; he thus reiterates the conceptual bias he purports to analyze and ends up eliding the specificity of the female body.[10] Second, endorsing Foucault's contention that the appearance of the "homosexual" as a category of identity became available only after the rise of a modern disciplinary apparatus, Laqueur argues that "[l]esbianism and homosexuality as categories were not possible before the creation of men and women as opposites," that is, before the two-sex model.[11] At this moment the elision of female specificity and the elision of Renaissance homoeroticism converge: references to tribades in Laqueur's account become merely gestural, as the focus is more on the social construction of an anatomical part (the clitoris) than the varied uses to which that part could be put. Resistance to examining the specificity of same-gender female eroticism prior to the inauguration of "homosexuality" then allows Laqueur to describe and reaffirm a male-oriented paradigm in which the only erotic possibility is homoeroticism between men: "When among themselves, [these Renaissance authors] seem to be saying, women rub *their* penises together... Indeed, all sex becomes homoerotic."[12]

Each of us makes interpretative choices. Laqueur has read the clitoris-as-penis analogy in terms of a model of masculine imitation; by extension, tribadism becomes male homoeroticism. Because Laqueur can see in the enlarged clitoris only a simulacrum of the penis, its potential to challenge the Galenic paradigm is subsumed under the ideological weight of the one-sex body. In this acquiescence to the logic of homology/imitation, he is joined by Stephen Greenblatt, whose influential essay, "Fiction and Friction," helped bring to visibility the importance of the transvestite and the tribade to Renaissance literature. Consider, for instance, the following anecdote with which Greenblatt begins his essay:

In September 1580, as he passed through a small French town... Montaigne was told an unusual story that he duly recorded in his travel journal. It seems that seven or eight girls... plotted together "to dress up as males and thus continue their life in the world." One of them set up as a weaver... fell in love with a woman, courted her, and married. The couple lived together for four or five months, to the wife's satisfaction, "*so they say.*" But then, Montaigne reports, the transvestite was recognized... "the matter was brought to justice, and she was condemned to be hanged, which she said she would rather undergo than return to a girl's status; and she was hanged for using *illicit devices* to supply her *defect* in sex."[13]

I recall Greenblatt's use of Montaigne's anecdote about this weaver of Vitry in order to suggest that, although there existed an official discourse about this case (the trial and execution took place just days before Montaigne's visit to the French town where the story was narrated to him), desire among women is revealed less in that official discourse than in the multiple voices of the community, whose members were sifting the controversy through their own understandings of appropriate gender roles and their curiosity about the variety of erotic practices. That popular discourse is apparent in those ambivalently coded, anonymously referring words of Montaigne's, "so they say," which follow the widespread community affirmation of "the wife's satisfaction." People in that small French town were talking, and talking publicly enough for a stranger to overhear the details of the couple's conjugal relations, including their four or five months of apparently mutual erotic pleasure.

As this and other accounts noted in chapter 1 suggest, in France – as well as in Spain and throughout the Holy Roman Empire – sodomy for women generally was associated with the use of illicit sexual devices, devices which, as

Greenblatt later remarks, "enable a woman to take the part of a man."[14] Indeed, we possess a historical record of such cases not primarily because the women desired or seduced other women, but because their prosthetic use of implements of penetration, when it came to the attention of the community, set in motion a defensive legal apparatus. French sodomy, it would seem, typically is defined by penetration; legal discourse demanded rigorous delineations of proof, and dildoes met that forensic test. By means of this legal process, an implicit distinction is set up between, on the one hand, sinful *desires* and criminal *acts* and, on the other hand, those sexual practices that do not involve penetration and those that do.[15] Neither a French woman's desire for another woman nor any non-penetrative acts she might commit were necessarily crimes (although, depending on other opportunistic factors, they could become so). Rather, within the early modern logic of crime and punishment, the prosthetic supplementation of a woman's body, when used to penetrate the body of another, was unambiguous grounds for execution.

This concern about the supplementation of women's bodies crossed the Channel in those French and English gynecological texts that repeatedly refer to female sexual organs growing beyond "normal" bounds. First (re)articulated in French medicine by Ambroise Paré, and then in England by Helkiah Crooke in *Microcosmographia* (1615), an enlarged clitoris was believed to cause "unnatural" desires in a body already defined as sexually excessive:

[S]ometimes [the clitoris] groweth to such a length that it hangeth without the cleft like a mans member, especially when it is fretted with the touch of the cloaths, and so strutteth and groweth to a rigiditie as doth the yarde [penis] of a man. And this part it is which those wicked women doe abuse called *Tribades* (often mentioned by many authors, and in some states worthily punished) to their mutual and unnatural lusts.[16]

The reference to tribadism in the context of discussions of clitoral enlargement is a crucial aspect of the history of *lesbianism*, and I will examine this association in some detail in a moment. For now, I simply want to point out that the reference to tribadism in the discourse of gynecology complicates the operation of sodomy as a legal, if not moral, category. Indeed, the asymmetrical prosecution of French and English women under sodomy statutes brings to light an irregular fracturing of the early modern conceptual and geographical terrain. Yet, when we forego our myopic focus on legal categories, we find a previously undetected structural coherence unifying the French and English divide: both gynecological tribadism and statutory sodomy depend upon a logic of supplementarity for their condition of possibility, with tribadism functioning through anatomical rather than artificial means. The discursive shift from a legal concern with instruments of penetration to a medical focus on clitoral hypertrophy enacts only a slight distinction within an overall economy of the supplement. Despite the rhetorical focus on penetration, both discourses actually fail to distinguish carefully between specific sexual acts: vaginal or anal penetration, rubbing of clitoris on thigh or pudendum, and autoerotic or partnered masturbation. Instead, as in Crooke's passage above, they employ vague analogies to male sexual practices. Whether employing a dildo or her "female yard," a sodomite's or tribade's body becomes, in the gendered discourse of both nations, "masculine." In both senses of the phrase, the woman *takes the part* of a man.

And yet... the terms by which such supplementation have been defined both in early modern and contemporary critical discourses not only describe but *reproduce* dominant gender ideologies. In the passages by Greenblatt cited above, for instance, his methodology and rhetorical style, like that of Laqueur, collapse any distance that might obtain between early modern discourses and a feminist understanding of female-centered erotic acts. His methodological commitments (in this case, to the transvestite stage) allow him to see only a male body, while his adherence to dominant discourses leads to a failure to articulate the varied and dissonant meanings that erotic acts can express. In particular, he obscures whatever meanings the use of "illicit devices" may have signified for the women involved. Within Greenblatt's rhetoric, as within the rhetoric of early modern authorities, the commingling of two female bodies is subsumed by an androcentric narrative: female penetration signifies an *imitation* of male (body and role-defined) "parts." Whatever independent agency is expressed in the performance of such erotic acts is rendered invisible at the same time it is resecured into a patriarchal economy. Gaining no metacritical distance on the problems of representation and power posed by the "conjunction" of female bodies, Greenblatt implicitly, if unintentionally, preserves gender as an essence – it can be imitated, but not, ultimately, subverted.

The fact that the model of imitation was favored by early modern legal, theological, and medical authorities prompts my search for a more dynamic and heteronomous understanding of the ways erotic pleasure was conceived, pursued, and achieved outside the limits of social orthodoxy. For although we have inherited no first-person accounts that we know were written by self-identified tribades or female sodomites, the actions of women who were so nominated are, in theoretical terms, circumscribed by a logic of neither imitation nor originality. If the tribade exists as a constructed, disciplined object of knowledge, she also glimmers in the conceptual distance as an elusive reminder of female erotic autonomy. Taking place within a system of signification that precedes her, her erotic practices are molded by a set of conventions and contingencies for possible action; but this frame does not exhaust the meanings such practices might signify to and for her and her lover. Constructing erotic opportunities out of the conceptual materials at hand, such women practiced a resourceful *bricolage*; in so doing, they were neither psychologically deluded "failed men" nor politically inauthentic upholders of patriarchy.

If, as Judith Butler argues, gender is not only a representation, but a performance staged within the enclosure of cultural coordinates,[17] and if masculinity is not an essential attribute but a cultural production, then what these women perform is, in the words of Jonathan Dollimore, a "transgressive reinscription" of gender and erotic codes.[18] At once repetition *and* transgression, such reinscription displaces conventional understandings from *within* dominant systems of intelligibility. Claiming the right to bodily pleasure in the face of an ideology that denies that right outside of patriarchal marriage, and fulfilling male fears of female hypersexuality while also fulfilling their fears of male insufficiency, the tribade performs the work of the "supplement" in Derridean terms. The supplement as deconstructive instrument breaks open, exposes, and refigures the gender codes that have delimited the terms by which tribadism and sodomy are interpreted. Derrida employs the notion of supplementarity as that which both adds to *and* replaces the original term; an instance of *différance*, the supplement deconstructs the putative unity, integrity, and singularity of the subject (in this case, its gender and erotic position), and registers these as always internally *different* from themselves.[19] Early modern women's prosthetic supplementation of their bodies is, I would argue, both additive and substitutive: as a material addition to the woman's body and as a replacement of the man's body *by* the woman's, prosthesis not only displaces male prerogatives, but exposes "man" as a simulacrum, and gender as a construction built on the faulty ground of mutually exclusive binaries. Indeed, in the authorities' discourse, the enlarged clitoris and the dildo become objects of cultural *fantasy*. Which is not to imply that there did not exist epistemological confusion about the status of, and differentiation between, male and female "yards," but it is to suggest that the meanings attached to the clitoris exceed the anatomical. It is not scientifically established anatomical norms and measures (what, after all is the size of a normal clitoris, or, for that matter, penis?), but gender expectations that manifest themselves in descriptions of tribades. Indeed, erotic variation is readable in this culture only through the lens of gender; conversely, what is exposed in anxieties about erotic difference is the instability of gender, the disconcerting ability of women to act successfully like men. I would go so far as to argue that the enlarged clitoris and the dildo take on in these rhetorics the quality of a fetish, a stand-in for a lost object of desire.[20] The question is, whose desire is being represented in these accounts? What the official discourse reveals is less the desire of the women than the authorities' desire for the (always already missing) phallus, which would stabilize gender precisely at the moment of its literal displacement. Contemporary critical accounts that rely on a logic of imitation tacitly repeat this gesture by focusing on the replacement of the lost object rather than the pleasures afforded by the performance of erotic supplementarity. By neglecting to insert a wedge between their rhetoric and that of early modern writers, by employing without demurral descriptions of the tribade such as "taking the man's role in lovemaking" and "playing the man's part during intercourse,"[21] they preserve the privilege of the phallus even as they would appear to deconstruct it.

The idea that a dildo-wearing or -wielding woman imitates the actions and anatomy of a man itself functions as a discourse of containment, a way of enjoining insignificance and immateriality onto performances of (for lack of a better term) female masculinity. We can resist this containment by noting the ways in which the tribade displaces and supplements masculine privilege, exposing it as nothing more (or worse) than a simulacrum. Further, we can do so by attending to the specific historical circumstances in which the tribade was constructed, without, however, reproducing the dominant ideology. Rather than reinscribe the logic of imitation and the gender hierarchy this logic upholds, I ask: what is at stake in the cultural effort to disavow the gender specificity of the clitoris and of erotic acts among women? By analyzing Renaissance discourses about the clitoris from the angle of female specificity, we will see how the rediscovered clitoris upsets prevailing accounts of Renaissance sexuality and the historical narrative of homosexuality derived from them. The representational crisis that took place around the rediscovery of the clitoris provided one of the conditions of emergence *for* modern identity categories. *Lesbians* did not arrive on the modern scene as fully formed social objects; nor did the ascendancy of a two-sex anatomical model ensure their arrival. The category of the *lesbian* was fashioned only after available rubrics for understanding and assimilating erotic variation failed to account adequately for activities women had been pursuing – under widely divergent conceptual systems – at least since Sappho.

Just as the "birth" of the *lesbian* is not a discrete social occurrence, the emergence of anatomy as a field of knowledge production is not a singular scientific phenomenon. Rather, anatomy as a separate epistemology was consolidated in concert with the development of other domains of knowledge, and it was enabled by the ability of anatomists and popularizers of medical texts to appropriate and reformulate the knowledges of other genres, including natural histories, herbals, Latin commentary on Greek and Roman literature, and travel narratives. Early modern travel accounts, in particular, contribute significantly to the construction of the contours and meanings of the early modern body. Generated at the same historical moment and governed by similar tropes of exploration and discovery, anatomies and travel narratives share a common imperative to chart, catalogue, and colonize the body.[22] Both genres synthesize received authority, observation, and invention as they commit highly interpretative acts under the guise of disinterested description.[23] Their narrative strategies and cultural functions are allied closely: both are dedicated to rendering intelligible and distinct that which appears chaotic, primitive, or previously unknown by employing strategies of description, nomination, and classification. Metaphorically, anatomical texts act as a discourse of travel, visually traversing the body in order to "touch" and reveal a cosmically ordained corporeal whole, while travel narratives observe and dissect peoples and countries, interrogating and reaffirming their place in the cosmic order. Together, their exploratory gazes create the possibility of looking "inward" and "outward," as they formulate the contours of bodily, social, and geographical boundaries.[24] Their processes fashion two sides of the same coin: whereas the dissection of the corpse and its textual reconstitution create a normative, abstracted body whose singularity encompasses and signifies all others, travel accounts compose an exoticized body which often, though not inevitably, reveals the antithesis of (Western) normativity. Locating bodies within prevailing epistemic hierarchies by charting corporeal cartographies, anatomies and travel narratives not only function as colonialist discourses but urge colonialism into being.[25]

Whether primarily concerned with commerce or conquest, Western European travelers to foreign lands chart a cultural anthropology that functions like a physical geography. Describing the New World, Africa, and the East, narrators obsessively remark upon those cultural practices that distinguish native inhabitants from Europeans, often employing rhetorics of gender and sexuality as explanatory tropes.[26] Marriage rituals, dowries, divorce, and polygamy excite Western curiosity and provide travelers to Africa and Arabia, in particular, a means of deploying the sexual status of indigenous women as a primary marker of cultural definition and civility.[27] A spatial geography of erotic behavior constructs women (and by implication, the nation) as beautiful and chaste (for instance, Persians) or hideous and loose (black Africans). The assumption of female lasciviousness gains self-evident power through the structure of a cross-cultural polarity: whereas the partial nudity of women in various African nations authorizes readings of female incontinence, the practice of Muslim purdah constructs the woman whose body is hidden as a highly desirable (and also desiring) object. Although same-gender female eroticism rarely is mentioned in these accounts (unlike charges of male sodomy), its presence routinely is associated with certain locales. Travelers to Turkey, in particular, curious about Muslim attitudes toward cleanliness and intrigued by the Ottoman segregation of women, typically relay rumors about women pleasuring one another – or themselves – within all-female spaces.[28]

Ogier Ghiselin de Busbecq, a Flemish ambassador to the Sultan, explains to a fellow ambassador why women are segregated from men:

The Turks are the most careful people in the world of the modesty of their wives, and therefore keep them shut up at home and hide them away, so that they scarce see the light of day. But if they have to go into the streets, they are sent out so covered and wrapt up in veils that they seem to those who meet them mere gliding ghosts. They have the means of seeing men through their linen or silken veils, while no part of their own body is exposed to men's view. For it is a received opinion among them, that no woman who is distinguished in the very smallest degree by her figure or youth, can be seen by a man without his desiring her, and therefore without her receiving some contamination; and so it is the universal practice to confine the women to the harem.[29]

A narrative by Robert Withers, published in 1587, which describes the architectural arrangements regulating the women in the sultan's seraglio, suggests that the practice of confining women entails certain problems:

Now, in the Womens lodgings, they live just as the Nunnes doe in their great Monasteries; for, these Virgins have very large Roomes to live in, and their Bed-chambers will hold almost a hundred of them a piece: they sleepe upon *Sofaes*, which are built long wise on both sides of the Roome, so that there is a large space in the midst for to walke in. Their Beds are very course and hard, and by every ten Virgins there lies an old woman: and all the night long there are many lights burning, so that one may see very plainely throughout the whole Roome; which doth both keepe the young Wenches from wantonnesses, and serve upon any occasion which may happen in the night.[30]

Keeping "young Wenches from wantonnesses" involves taking precautions with their provisions:

Now it is not lawfull for any one to bring ought in unto them, with which they may commit the deeds of beastly uncleannesse; so that if they have a will to eate Cucumbers, Gourds, or such like meates, they are sent in unto them sliced, to deprive them of the meanes of playing the wantons; for, they being all young, lustie, and lascivious Wenches, and wanting the societie of Men (which would better instruct them) are doubtlesse of themselves inclined to that which is naught, and will be possest with unchast thoughts.[31]

The idea that cucumbers would be used by women on themselves or with one another is reiterated in many subsequent narratives, including one published almost a hundred years later by the French baron, Jean-Baptiste Tavernier. Despite calling the cucumber tale a "Fabulous Story" in *A New Relation of the Present Grand Seignor's Seraglio* (1677), Tavernier nonetheless extends the range of women's practices of "abominable Vice" beyond Constantinople to far-flung provinces. This generalization seems to be authorized by the practice of male sodomy which was widely thought to "infect" Muslim culture, and which, according to Tavernier, Turkish women then imitate:

[T]heir unvoluntary restraint forces them to the same unseemly actions amongst themselves, as the brutish Passions of those Young Men engages them in, whenever they can find the opportunities to commit them. And this presumption has no doubt given occasion to the Fabulous Story, which is related of their being serv'd up with Cucumbers cut into pieces, and not entire, out of a ridiculous fear least they should put them to undecent uses... But it is not only in the Seraglio, that that abominable Vice reigns, but it is predominant also in the City of *Constantinople*, and in all the Provinces of the Empire, and the wicked Example of the Men, who, slighting the natural use of Women-kind, are mutually enflam'd with a detestable love for one another, unfortunately enclines the Women to imitate them.³²

Reversing the narrative of Romans 1: 26–27, where it is the men who follow the unnatural example of women,³³ Tavernier's story is more invested in the ubiquity of the sodomitical Turk than in the culpable flesh of woman.³⁴

As Withers's account demonstrates, the sultan's harem generated comparisons to convents which, in anti-Catholic polemic, were reputed to be a haven for "unclean" behaviors. But whereas associations with the nunnery led to a focus on sleeping (and eating) arrangements, the communal nudity of the *hannam*, or Turkish bath, occasioned even more explicit comment about women's bodily behaviors. Nicholas de Nicholay's *The Navigations, Peregrinations, and Voyages, Made into Turkie*, translated into English in 1585, depicts typical procedures involved in visiting the public baths, and concludes his description of female bathers in this way:

[They] do familiarly wash one another, wherby it cometh to passe that amongst the women of Levan, ther is very great amity proceding only through the frequentation & resort to the bathes: yea & sometimes become so fervently in love the one of the other as if it were with men, in such sort that perceiving some maiden or woman of excellent beauty they wil not ceasse until they have found means to bath with them, & to handle & grope them every where at their pleasures, so ful they are of luxuriousnes & feminine wantonnes: Even as in times past wer the Tribades, of the number whereof was Sapho the Lesbian ... ³⁵

Other travelers reproduce such rumors. De Busbecq, for instance, writes in his third ambassadorial letter:

The great mass of women use the public baths for females, and assemble there in large numbers. Among them are found many girls of exquisite beauty, who have been brought together from different quarters of the globe by various chances of fortune; so cases occur of women falling in love with one another at these baths, in much the same fashion as young men fall in love with maidens in our country. Thus you see a Turk's precautions are sometimes of no avail, and when he has succeeded in keeping his wives from a male lover, he is still in danger from a female rival! The women become deeply attached to each other, and the baths supply them with opportunities of meeting. Some [men] therefore keep their women away from them as much as possible, but they cannot do so altogether, as the law allows them to go there. This evil affects only the common people; the richer classes bathe at home.³⁶

De Busbecq augments this description of a class-specific eroticism with an anecdote about an elderly woman who, having fallen in love with a young woman, crossdresses as a man, obtains permission to marry, and is foiled only upon being recognized by her betrothed as someone she encountered at the baths.³⁷ Thomas Glover, secretary to the English ambassador, concludes his description of Turkish baths with this terse condemnation: "Much unnaturall and filthie lust is said to bee committed daily in the remote closets of the darkesome Bannias: yea, women with women; a thing uncredible, if former times had not given thereunto both detection and punishment."[38]

The seraglio and the *hannam* are not the only locales that engender anxiety about same-gender female activity. In *The History and Description of Africa*, translated into English in 1600, Leo Africanus describes the erotic practices of fortune-tellers in Fez:

But the wiser and honester sort of people call these women *Sahacat*, which in Latin signifieth *Fricatrices*, because they have a damnable custome to commit unlawfull Venerie among themselves, which I cannot express in any modester termes. If faire women come unto them at any time, these abominable witches will burne in lust towards them no otherwise then lustie yoonkers [young men] doe towardes yoong maides, and will in the divels behalfe demaunde for a rewarde, that they may lie with them: and so by this meanes it often falleth out, that thinking thereby to fulfill the divels command they lie with the witches. Yea some there are, which being allured with the delight of this abominable vice, will desire the companie of these witches, and faining themselves to be sicke, will either call one of the witches home to them, or will send their husbands for the same purpose: and so the witches perceiving how the matter stands, will say that the woman is possessed with a divell, and that she can no way be cured, unlesse she be admitted into their societie. With these words her silly husband being persuaded, doth not onely permit her so to doe, but makes also a sumptuous banket [banquet] unto the damned crew of witches: which being done, they use to daunce very strangely at the noice of drums: and so the poore man commits his false wife to their filthie disposition.[39]

These exoticizing tales, most of them written during the period when the Ottoman Empire posed a viable military and religious threat to Western Europe (and, incidentally, during the period when, according to Leslie Pierce, "high-ranking women of the Ottoman dynasty enjoyed a degree of political power and public prominence greater than ever before or after"[40]), enable a number of observations about the rhetorics and figures of female–female eroticism in the early modern period. First, even though these texts attempt to create an illusion of eye-witness veracity, they are extremely intertextual; they draw freely from one another, often quote each other verbatim, and blithely neglect to cite original sources.

Second, these texts treat eroticism among women as a real and present danger – albeit one that is located outside of Christian Europe – that is made intelligible largely through signifiers of an ancient past. A specific vocabulary – the Greek *tribas*, Latin *fricatrice*, and Arabic *Sahacat* – provide the historical lexicon and the authorizing lens through which to condemn the bathers of Turkey and the witches of Fez. The repetition of these terms conveys a consistent manner of naming women erotically engaged with other women, who, even if they are unaware of it, are allegedly following the classical example, as de Nicholay puts it, of "Sapho the Lesbian."

Third, no consensus regarding the cause of female–female eroticism emerges from these accounts. All of the writers attest to the inherent wantonness of women, and all of them judge women's desire as boundless; but they variously attribute the catalyst for the commission of "unnatural acts" to the segregation of women from men, to witchcraft, and to emulation of male sodomites.

Fourth, much like the spatialization of female–female eroticism noted in literary texts in chapters 1 and 4, an architectural logic structures these accounts, as certain physical locales enable female contact. As spaces originally built to block male access and protect female chastity, the harem and the bath are described as enabling the circulation of desire enclosed within. And as one of the few places that women could congregate in public, the bazaar brings into contact modest wives with "abominable witches," who then invade the patriarchal household. Emerging out of the colonial imaginary is a sexual geography not unlike that of Ovid and Shakespeare.

Fifth, such narratives assume not only that women willingly deceive their husbands or masters, but that homoerotic pleasures, once experienced, prove to be irresistible. The "burning lust" that de Nicholay and others figure as flowing indiscriminately through the waters of the Turkish bath is represented by all the narrators as undermining the patriarchal authority of the harem or household. Although it is occasionally aligned with male sodomy (and thus implicitly judged an act *contra naturam*), female–female eroticism is more often viewed as an affront to husbandly authority. When it comes to the erotic transgressions of women, concerns about "nature" seem to be subsumed under patriarchal imperatives.

Sixth, despite their ostensibly descriptive purpose, and despite their convenient use of ready-to-hand labels, these travelers employ what seems to modern ears to be a vague, euphemistic rhetoric: "commit unlawful Venerie," "burn in lust," "inclined to that which is naught," and "handle and grope them everywhere." Leaving the precise nature of erotic acts unspecified, these narratives both assume and occlude the reader's knowledge of "deeds of beastly uncleannesse."[41]

Finally, and most importantly for my argument about early modern England: notwithstanding gossip about aristocratic women such as that penned by Brantôme, each of these travelers assumes that African and Muslim women are uniquely (if amorphously) amoral in their erotic desires and practices. As befits the conventions of travel narration, female homoeroticism is located somewhere *else*.

The elsewhere of the "exotic" is produced through a cultural exchange – psychic, material, rhetorical – between self and other. It thus is perhaps unnecessary to aver that, despite their assertion of eye-witness authority, these travel accounts are hardly empirical, truthful reports of the activities of Middle Eastern and African women. It is possible, of course, that throughout the Islamic world the seraglio and *hannam* may have enabled female homoeroticism. According to Kathryn Babayan, early modern Persian women during the Safavi empire often exchanged vows of sisterhood and, in the enclosure of the harem, developed intimate friendships, some of which formed the basis for political unions, some of which were erotic. In addition, according to male-authored texts, women would speak freely about sexual matters within the space of the bath. One woman is said to have declared that "whenever differences occurred between husbands and wives, the wife needs to speak about it. It is permissible if all her female companions join in and talk about their own sexual organs and laugh about it."[42] My project, however, is not to write a social history of female affectivity within the Muslim world,[43] but to focus on the way the protocolonialist imperatives of travel narratives ultimately contribute to the erotic representation of Englishwomen. Jane Sharp alludes to the dissemination of travel accounts as she describes clitoral enlargement in *The Midwives Book* (1671): sometimes the clitoris "grows so long that it hangs forth at the slit like a Yard, and will swell and stand stiff if it be provoked, and some lewd women have endeavoured to use it as men do theirs."[44] "In the *Indies*, and *Egypt*," she says, such incidents "are frequent"; but she goes on to assert that illicit contact among women occurs primarily beyond England's borders: "I never heard but of one in this Country." She then concludes with the ambiguous statement, "if there be any they will do what they can for shame to keep it close," an admonition that, in conflating the enlarged clitoris with the use to which it could be put, could refer either to keeping genitals hidden or illicit erotic practices secret.[45] In a later passage, she writes:

> I told you the Clitoris is so long in some women that it is seen to hang forth at their Privities and not only the Clitoris that lyeth behind the wings [labia] but the Wings also... In some Countries they grow so long that the Chirurgion cuts them off to avoid trouble and shame, chiefly in *Egypt*; they will bleed much when they are cut, and the blood is hardly stopt; wherefore maids have them cut off betimes, and before they marry, for it is a flux of humours to them, and much motion that makes them grow so long. Some Sea-mem [*sic*] say that they have seen *Negro* Women go stark naked, and these wings hanging out.[46]

Although Sharp does not marginally gloss these passages describing clitoral hypertrophy and clitoridectomy, she does cite Leo Africanus elsewhere in her book. I want to suggest that neither her minimizing of the frequency of Englishwomen's "unnatural" contacts nor her displacement of these practices onto foreign women is adequately understood as a conventional English effort to refer the origin of unwelcome behaviors, physical disorder, and disease elsewhere.[47] Sharp's gesture is more than an instance of the colonial imaginary that, as Jonathan Goldberg has shown, "is particularly prone to a desire to other its own desires."[48] Cultural contact not only involves a response to the "other," but creates new possibilities and compensations for viewing the subjects of "home." Sharp's strategy of displacement is a failed one, for her anxieties about foreign bodies inadvertently rebound back onto figurations of English women.

Increasingly esteemed by feminist scholars as a heroine of seventeenth-century English midwifery, Sharp is judged to perform a crucial service in contesting the growing dominance of male-midwives and challenging male-dominated medical knowledge through the publication of her own book. As noted in chapter 2, Sharp attempted to counter male disgust about the female genitals and, as part of her effort to undermine misogyny, even poked fun at male sexual dysfunction. She relays, for instance, the story of a French man who complained "sadly, that when he first married his Wife, it [the vagina] was no bigger nor wider than would fit his turn, but now it was grown as a Sack; Perhaps the fault was not the womans but his own, his weapon shrunk and was grown to little for the scabbard."[49] Turning military metaphors against men, Sharp here, as elsewhere, wittily defends women's sexual integrity.

However, as Eve Keller notes, Sharp's text "contains much that is normative, much that enforces the prevailing gender assumptions."[50] Sharp's discussion and condemnation of tribadism, like every other seventeenth-century anatomy and midwifery, immediately follows the description of the clitoris and its possible enlargement. Thus, if it is the case, as Keller argues, that Sharp's rhetorical strategies, which propose the female body as the norm as frequently as the male, undercut the male dominance of the Galenic model, then it is all the more significant that Sharp rehearses conventional wisdom in regard to "some lewd women [who] have endeavoured to use it [the clitoris] as men do theirs." In her effort to reorient the traditional masculine hierarchy of perfection and to assert the unique structure and function of the female body, Sharp positions the tribade as foreign, shameful, and expendable.

I have already argued that the incorporation of the clitoris within the domain of scientific knowledge gave female erotic pleasure a new, albeit ambivalent, articulation. With that articulation, I now want to suggest, came a representational crisis. This crisis stemmed less from the rancorous disputes among anatomists regarding the clitoris's existence than from the fact that anatomical representation of the clitoris became a focal point for the expression of anxieties about the cultural meanings of the female body. As anatomical plates and texts from Italy, France, Spain, and Germany made their way into England, as English physicians and midwives contributed their own methods of textually communicating the "new science" of anatomy, strategies of accommodation – of, quite literally, in-corporation – were developed. The trajectory of these strategies suggests that this clitoral "age of discovery" was a pivotal moment in the cultural history of English women, of their embodiment and eroticism. Over the next century, as information about this "new" anatomical organ was incorporated into, and helped to refigure, an old corporeal framework, a discourse evolved that increasingly fixed on the clitoris as the disturbing emblem of female erotic transgression.

We need only return to Crooke's conclusion of his description of the clitoris in *Microcosmographia* to recognize the contours of this crisis. When he says, for instance, that it is an enlarged clitoris that "those wicked women doe abuse called *Tribades* (often mentioned by many authors, and in some states worthily punished) to their mutuall and unnaturall lustes," and then marginally glosses his text with "*Tribades odiosae feminae*,"[51] Crooke draws from prior authority, citing Caelius Aurelianus (a fifth-century Latin translator of Soranus) and Leo Africanus. When Falloppia laid claim to his discovery of this organ in 1561, he likewise had referred back to the authority of classical and Arabic writers:

Avicenna makes mention of a certain member situated in the female genitalia which he calls *virga* or *albathara*. Albucasis calls this *tentigo*, which sometimes will increase to such a great size that women, while in this condition, have sex with each other just as if they were men. The Greeks call this member *clitoris*, from which the obscene word *clitorize* is derived. Our anatomical writers have completely neglected this and do not even have a word for it.[52]

Intent on proclaiming the existence of this organ, Falloppia focused on its nomenclature and only vaguely described the practices to which it could be put. Later in the sixteenth century, André Du Laurens, however, used the name for the women who, so endowed, engaged in libidinous behavior: "I have become aware of the use of this, whereby after being rubbed all over it excites the sluggish faculty. It increases in some people to such an inappropriate extent that it hangs outside the fissure the same as a penis; women then often engage in mutual rubbing, such women accordingly called *tribades* or *fricatrices*."[53] Jacques Daléchamps, professor of medicine at the University of Montpellier, describes in his 1570 *Chirurgie françoise* a troublesome large "nymphe," pervasive among Egyptian women as well as "some of ours, so that when they find themselves in the company of other women, or their clothes rub them while they walk, or their husbands wish to approach them, it erects like a male penis, and indeed they use it to play with other women, as their husbands would do."[54] If here the surgeon reproduces the medieval confusion about whether it is the clitoris or the labia that enlarge, he nonetheless connects hypertrophy to tribadism. As Katharine Park notes in her examination of Daléchamps' sources, "Daléchamps seems to have fabricated the connection between clitoral hypertrophy and female homoeroticism by consolidating what were in fact two separate topics in his ancient texts and then to have authorized his construction by projecting it back onto those texts. The amalgamation of these two separate ideas became standard in French."[55] Indeed, this conflation became definitive in English texts as well.

Drawing from previous authorities to bolster his claims of knowledge, Crooke makes specific use of both medical and "anthropological" texts. And yet something crucial changes as we move from travel narration to anatomical treatise: none of the travel writers of the late sixteenth century mention the "abuse" of a particular body part. Though the words *tribade*, *fricatrice*, and *Sahacat* are used, and cucumbers and public baths loom large, no enlarged clitoris haunts their accounts; rather, there is simply a boundless, deceitful desire of which all foreign, non-Christian women presumably are suspected. As anatomical descriptions of the clitoris absorb and revise the representations of travel accounts, however, the site of transgressive female eroticism subtly shifts away from the behavioral excesses of Mediterranean climes to the excessive endowment of female bodies.

This is not to suggest that the strategies of travel literature and anatomical texts are all that different. Indeed, the anatomical articulation of clitoral hypertrophy carries with it lineages from medieval accounts of "marvels" and "wonders," a genre from which travel literature itself evolved. As Mary Campbell notes,

> The "wonders" are the most extreme and exquisite projections of European cultural fantasy: it is against their iconographic background of grotesque similes that a responsible literature of travel will develop, and it is among their images that Europe will find nourishment for its notions of "monstrous" savagery. The model (which finds its authority, though not its origins, in Pliny) of a world normal at its (European) center and monstrous at its (Asian and African) margins is easy to see as the self-image of a culture quite literally scared of its own shadow.[56]

Campbell further remarks, "[t]he features of the organic marvels manifest characteristically grotesque principles: hyperbolic dimensions, multiplication of body parts, and fusions of species."[57] Likewise, "The marvelous is marginal, biologically and culturally, although it may be used as a figure for central and interior desire. The marvelous is also, in part, a rhetorical phenomenon. A brief enough description, especially when communicated as a distortion of the familiar rather than as something *essentially* different, produces a marvel."[58]

The tribade is not literally a marvel or wonder of nature. Although her behavior regularly was described in moral terms as monstrous and *contra naturam*, in ontological terms her being was not *praeter naturam*, outside the ordinary course of nature. She does not appear in the medieval typologies of the monstrous races derived from the natural history of Pliny or the geography of Strabo, although she is included, at least initially, in Paré's discussion of monsters and marvels (alongside hermaphrodites and sex transformations).[59] Once expelled from Paré's subsequent editions, however, the tribade demonstrates that her relation to a discourse of teratology is moral rather than ontological, and thus a matter of continuing negotiation. To take up Campbell's terms, the tribade is a marvelous "distortion of the familiar," produced rhetorically as a marker of gender and erotic norms. She may not *be* a marvel, but, with her hyperbolic clitoris and allegedly grotesque efforts at coupling, she functions *like* a marvel. Indeed, it is through a diffusion of the rhetorical operations of the marvelous into anatomy that the tribade, as a phenomenon knowable to modern science, was discursively born.[60]

Hyperbole and the grotesque, of course, are socially constructed categories, drawn, according to one theorist, from the proportions of the body. In her meditation on the role of the miniature and the gigantic in modern culture, Susan Stewart notes that the "body is our mode of perceiving scale and, as the body of the other, becomes our antithetical mode of stating conventions of symmetry and balance on the one hand, and the grotesque and the disproportionate on the other."[61] Although her focus is on how the miniature functions as "a metaphor for the interior space and time of the bourgeois subject," while the gigantic is "a metaphor for the abstract authority of the state and the collective, public, life," Stewart's examination of the cultural meaning of hyperbole is useful in considering the tribade's clitoral enlargement. She notes that

exaggeration takes place in relation to the scale of proportion offered by the body. Although this body is culturally delimited, it functions nevertheless as the instrument of lived experience, a place of mediation that remains irreducible beyond the already-structured reductions of the sensory, the direct relation between the body and the world it acts upon. Yet once the abstractions of [social] exchange are evident, exaggeration must be seen in relation to the scale of measurement, and thereby the scale of values, offered by a more abstract domain of social convention – and that social convention achieves its ideological force by virtue of the powers of authority.[62]

Viewed through a cultural scale of values, the discourse of the enlarged clitoris and the tribade are revealed to be part of the anatomical attempt to construct a normative body and normative erotic practice.[63] This normativity ultimately gains "its ideological force by virtue of the powers of authority." The repetitive tropes circling around the clitoris suggest that the scale of measurement used to define a normative clitoral morphology depends upon a specter of monstrosity, hyperbole, and the grotesque – in short, a psychomorphology.

By the early seventeenth century, under the auspices of anatomical research, a paradigm of women's boundless *desire* present in travel literature is transmuted into a paradigm of discrete and empirically verifiable bodily *structure*. In the emerging terms of early modern medicine, it is not the tribade's inconstant mind or sinful soul, but her uniquely female yet masculinized *morphology* that either propels her to engage in, or is itself the effect of, her illicit behavior. Clitoral hypertrophy is posited as one cause of early modern tribadism, but perhaps more importantly, early modern tribadism increasingly is inconceivable without clitoral hypertrophy. Anatomy provides a map of this connection.

The early modern mapping of the tribade's body produces and is produced by an anatomical essentialism – the riveting of body part to behavior – that continues to underpin modern discourses of sexuality. Such essentialism is the result not of empirical fact, but of a strategy to organize and make intelligible the plurality of corporeal structures and behaviors within the conceptual confines of Renaissance cosmological and earthly hierarchies. The early seventeenth-century production of anatomical essentialism is related to other intertextual shifts: as the discourse of anatomy early in the century appropriated the tropes of travel narratives, the racialized "anthropology" born of a proto-colonialist imperative was first used to authorize anatomical investigation of erotic transgression, and then was displaced momentarily in favor of an articulation and consolidation of normative bodily form. This is not to suggest that cross-cultural, anthropological comparisons were no longer relevant; after all, colonialism was gathering, not losing, steam. Rather, the aims of anatomy and travel discourse, linked as they were to distinct institutional and material practices, began to diverge in the seventeenth century. As anatomy defined its project as the construction of a normative bodily schema, the myriad forces of colonial expansion expended their material, financial, and ideological energies in an unprecedented exploration of otherness. The temporary displacement of anthropological concerns by anatomy is evident in *Microcosmographia*: figuring tribadism as a "mutual lust" that is "often mentioned by many authors" and "worthily punished" in other nations, citing Leo Africanus but failing to locate illicit practices in any particular nation or locale, Crooke's medical treatise is uninterested in making explicit cultural comparisons. One effect of this lack of concern is that Crooke ignores the possibility of tribadism in England.

The unspoken assumption of tribadism's foreign otherness that gives Crooke's account such an air of unflappability begins to break down by mid-century. Thomas Bartholin's English translation and expansion of his father's Latin anatomy draws on Crooke for his entry "Of the Clitoris," and then proceeds to recontextualize "tribadic" practices. After terming such women "*Confricatrices*" or "Rubsters," Bartholin introduces a reference to the "lascivious Practice" of "Philanis and Sappho." Then, after citing Romans 1:26 ("for this cause God gave them up unto vile affections: for even their women did change the natural use unto that which is against nature"), he asserts that such lascivious practices cause the clitoris to be called "*Contemptus viorum*" or "the Contempt of Mankind" (an ambiguous construction that fails to specify whose contempt is thereby invoked).[64] Bartholin continues in this vein as he discusses clitoral size:

> Its *Size* is commonly small; it lies hid for the most part under the Nymphs in its beginning, and afterward it sticks out a little. For in Lasses that begin to be amorous, the Clitoris does first discover it self. It is in several persons greater or lesser: in some it

hangs out like a mans Yard, namely when young Wenches do frequently and continually handle and rub the same, as Examples testifie. But that it should grow as big as a Gooses neck, as *Platerus* relates of one, is altogether praeternatural and monstrous. *Tulpius* hath a like Story of one that had it as long as half a mans finger, and as thick as a Boys Prick, which made her willing to have to do with Women in a Carnal way. But the more this part encreases, the more does it hinder a man in his business. For in the time of Copulation it swells like a mans Yard, and being erected, provokes to Lust.[65]

By morphologizing the tribade, anatomy paradoxically moves her closer to home: the erotic excess that was attributed to foreign women now can be found on the Christian bodies of "Lasses" and "young Wenches" who handle themselves as well as each other. This Englishing of anatomical rhetoric, which attempts to make the incommensurate seem commensurable,[66] implies that it is not merely the clitoris's enlargement that might "hinder a man in his business," but women's erotic interest in their own and other women's bodies.

Bartholin's "Englished" anatomy includes the first non-Galenic anatomical illustration of the clitoris in an English book, where it is shown to be the "commonly small" outgrowth of a normative body (see Figure 7, p. 92). But despite this visual schematization of an anatomical norm, and despite Bartholin's ambiguous rejection of Platerus's story as "praeternatural" (does Bartholin mean impossible or simply monstrous?), the discursive exaggeration of the clitoris and its association with tribadism continued unabated. In France earlier in the century, Jean Riolan had repeated Platerus's story of the goose's neck and offered two accounts of the clitoris "as long and thick as my little finger."[67] Nicholas Culpeper's *Complete Midwife's Practice Enlarged* states that the clitoris "hath been observed, to grow out of the body the breadth of four fingers."[68] The reiterated link between what must have been proportionately insignificant physical aberrations to what was in all likelihood a small number of erotic transgressions indicates an anxiety less about the body unnatural than the unnatural use to which *any* female body might be put. As the potential measure of *all* female bodies, clitoral hypertrophy metonymizes women's supposedly inordinate capacity for pleasure. As anatomies like Bartholin's begin to invoke cautionary references and biblical citation (assuming more and more frequently the function of conduct books), and as the anatomist's repudiation of women's pleasure grows more insistent, the specter of the enlarged clitoris looms larger: if not as big as a "Gooses neck," yet as big as a "Boys Prick."[69]

Market exigencies within the print industry no doubt played a part in this discursive amplification as well. In the genre of marital advice books that developed out of the intersection of anatomy and conduct literature, hyperbole promoted sales. Nicholas Venette's immensely popular *Conjugal Love, or The Pleasures of the Marriage Bed*, for instance, first describes the size of a typical clitoris as "longer more or less than half a finger," then terms the clitoris "the fury and rage of love," and finally asserts:

This part lascivious women often abuse. The *lesbian Sappho* would never have acquired such indifferent reputation, if this part of her's had been less. I have seen a girl eight years of age, that had already the *clitoris* as long as one's little finger; and if this part grows with age, as it is probable it may, I am persuaded it is now as long as that of the woman mentioned by Platerus, who had one as big and long as the neck of a goose.[70]

With the clitoris of most women measured at the length of "half a finger," it is perhaps less fantastical that within a Renaissance economy that correlates quantity of lust with physical size, the clitorises "abused" by "lascivious women" could be asserted to attain the length of a goose's neck. It is, I believe, the discursive amplification of the threat posed by this ever-growing female "prick" that motivates Jane Sharp to resurrect the colonialist imperative, rise to a sisterly defense of Englishwomen, and exile the tribade from England. Her efforts were for naught. Thomas Gibson's *The Anatomy of Humane Bodies Epitomized* (1682) translates the Greek term for the clitoris as "that [which] signifies lasciviously to grope the *Pudendum*," and then reports:

In some, it grows to that length as to hang out from betwixt the Lips of the Privity: yea there are many stories of such as have had it so long and big as to be able to accompany with other Women like unto Men, and such are called *Fricatrices*, or otherwise Hermaphrodites; who it is not probable are truly of both Sexes, but only the *Testes* fall down into the *Labia*, and this *Clitoris* is preternaturally extended. But in most it jets out so little as that it does not appear but by drawing aside the *Labia*.[71]

Even as the normal clitoris is deemed to jet out just a little, and the existence of actual hermaphrodites is disputed (she becomes the woman whose "testes" fall down into her labia and whose "clitoris is preternaturally extended"), it is the woman who is "able to accompany with other Women like unto Men" who becomes the object of medical fascination. Daniel Tauvry's *New Rational Anatomy* (1701) likewise reports of the clitoris that it "sometimes shoots it self out to that degree, that Women may employ it to a wrong use; upon which account 'tis call'ed, *Paenis Faeminaeus*."[72] During this period of changing medical theories, in which the structural homology between clitoris and penis (and thus, the term "female yard") slipped out of use, the enlarged clitoris remains invested with masculinity: it alone is dubbed the female penis because it "shoots it self out," usurps the masculine prerogative, and is employed "to a wrong use."

From Falloppia and Du Laurens to Crooke, Culpeper, Bartholin, and Sharp, the clitoris and the tribade are positioned paratactically as mutually constitutive forms of female matter. The tribade functions as the abject other against which a normative female body is defined,[73] and the clitoris comes into representation as the metonymic sign of the unnatural, transgressive tribade. The logic of these anatomies and midwiferies suggest that the description of the one phenomenon would be incomplete without the other. Despite the sense of inevitability structuring this logic, however, the actual meaning of tribadism and the precise acts this term was supposed to denote were less than clear. Katharine Park follows Lillian Faderman in reserving the use of the term "tribadism" for the activity of rubbing, claiming that "French writers made a clear distinction between female homoerotic behavior that involved rubbing the genitals... and any activity that involved the penetration of one woman by another."[74] Certainly it is true that penetration (with any object) was widely construed as the most readily recognized transgression and also the crime most harshly punished. But the medical, theological, moral, and legal texts on which Park and Faderman base their assertions are not exhaustive measures of the range of meanings circulating in early modern culture. Thus, rather than interpret writers' "exceedingly clear distinctions," as Park does, as a sign of clarity, I propose that we read for the cultural anxiety embedded within the effort involved in making such distinctions; whatever success such texts may have achieved was by virtue of an ideological backformation, imposed after a considerable amount of confusion and contestation.

Indeed, it is at the end of the early modern period, in a continental text that articulates precisely the cultural logic implicit within earlier (and English) discourses about the tribade, that we can most clearly see the expenditure of effort involved. In 1700, the Italian friar Ludovico Sinistrari sought to stabilize boundaries between various erotic acts in his treatise, *De Delictis et Poenis*. Sinistrari's goal, to help confessors understand how to classify and appropriately punish sexual sin, finds an unlikely authorization in the anatomy of Thomas Bartholin:

All Moralists treat of this filthy vice between women and declare that real Sodomy is committed between them. But as to how this takes place, nobody that I have seen explains. Yet to know this or to be ignorant of it must not be thought a thing of no importance or idle curiosity. In practice, this knowledge is necessary for Confessors, that they may be able to determine, when women, by their mutual touches, have brought on but voluntary pollution, and when they have fallen into the crime of Sodomy: now that they may be able to form a just notion of the grievousness of the sin, now find out when they can or can not absolve them, in the parts reserved for *Sodomy*. More than once I have consulted very learned men, perfect adepts in the administration of the Sacrament of Penance: they all candidly confessed they held even with the common of Moralists, that Sodomy is committed between women: but that they were completely ignorant as to how it can differ from the pollution, produced by rubbing their privy parts together.[75]

Thereafter addressing the problem of female–female eroticism from a variety of angles, and refusing the definitions of a number of authorities, Sinistrari argues, on the basis of Bartholin's anatomy, for a theological distinction between "mere pollution" and "genuine sodomy" based on clitoral activity.[76] If a woman rubs her clitoris against another woman, her sin is simply pollution, and she can be absolved by her confessor. But if she penetrates another woman with her clitoris, then the sin is sodomy, and she cannot be absolved. Such distinctions between penetrative and non-penetrative sex accord easily with the pervasive understanding of penetration as a definitively masculine privilege. However, Sinistrari parts company with dominant discourses by distinguishing between penetration performed by the clitoris, the finger, or "some tool of glass, wood, leather, or other material."[77] In contrast to the legal authorities of most European nations, Sinistrari argued that the use of a dildo is not sodomy, because it is a senseless tool, a dead thing, and not a part of the body; absent the conjunction of the genitals – "those parts of the body by which male and female become two in one flesh" – no genuine copulation can occur.[78] Nor does the use of a finger meet the definition of copulation. Rather, the only form of "genuine sodomy" is that performed by a clitoris.

Sinistrari proceeds to draw cross-cultural comparisons, again supposedly based on Bartholin's anatomy:

In Ethiopia and Egypt, says Bartholinus, all women have it out, and it hangs just like a yard. And as soon as babes are born, midwives are wont to burn their clitoris with a red-hot iron, lest it should grow too long and hinder a conjunction with a male. The Abyssinians, adds the same author, make a ceremonial circumcision on this part of women. But, in Europe, the clitoris breaks out only in some women, those, for instance, who from plenty of heat and seed have strong seminal spirits, which swell the clitoris and stretch it beyond the nymphs; and those who, out of precocious and prurient wantonness, meddle in girlhood with their privy parts. While in some women the clitoris is the size of one's middle finger, in others it is larger; so much so that there was at Venice a courtesan whose clitoris was the size of a gander's neck.[79]

In Sinistrari's appropriation of Bartholin, all Ethiopian and Egyptian women possess clitorises the size of a penis, the "commonly small" clitoris of Bartholin's original description of "some women" grows to "the size of one's middle finger," and the story of a goose transmogrifies into the story of a gander.

Sinistrari is deadly serious. Once accused of sodomy, he maintains, the defendant must be medically examined by a jury of matrons: "For, if these find the clitoris, and it be proved the women lay together, and the matrons' corroborations side with the crime, there is a presumption that they made use of it for the heinous delinquency... Hence it is necessary to have recourse to torture, that the Judge may find out whether the unmentionable crime was committed."[80] Any anatomical aberration in a woman accused should be taken as a presumption of guilt. If the text qualifies this presumption with the need to prove that the women "lay together," Sinistrari's synoptic "Contents of Matters" is far less cautious: "If a woman is accused of Sodomy, she must be inspected. Should the clitoris hang out in a woman, it is presumed she made use of it."[81]

My point in detailing the labyrinthine but nonetheless lethal logic of this early modern friar is simply this: once aberrant anatomy is deemed a presumption of guilt, once possession of an anatomical means of penetration is *ipso facto* evidence for the prosecution, then whatever conceptual distinction may have obtained between rubbing and penetration, so carefully parsed out into pollution and sodomy, in fact breaks down. Sinistrari's sustained focus on clitoral hypertrophy helps us to see that the term "penetration" can be used in such a way as to render moot, indeed, to dissolve into irrelevancy, exactly what action a clitoris performs. In addition, despite Sinistrari's rigorous effort to distinguish between pollution and sodomy, rubbing and penetration, such differentiations would be difficult enough to ascertain during confession, much less to maintain during sexual acts. An enlarged clitoris could be an instrument of friction or entry or something in between; and, as my quotations throughout this chapter demonstrate, authors of anatomies and travel literature seem unconcerned to delineate the difference. Whereas the evolution of ecclesiastical and state jurisprudence demanded, and thus created, ever more precise terms and definitions, the artificiality of such pseudo-precision, as well as the ideological exertion involved in constructing it, may have been palpably evident to those whose bodies were most intimately involved.

Whether denounced as sodomy or mere pollution, whether condemned by an Italian friar or described by an English physician, the tribade's activities represent a non-reproductive misuse of female anatomy. Or more accurately, *abuse*. The rhetoric of use and abuse permeates anatomical discussions of the female body from the late sixteenth to early eighteenth century, as Theresa Braunschneider has shown.[82] Following the trope of the enlarged clitoris up to 1741, when it is given the label "Macroclitoride" by James Parsons, Braunschneider demonstrates that it is through the repeated rhetorical figure of *abuse* that medical texts tie the tribade and the clitoris together.[83] From the Latin source, *ab-use* ("away from use"), the meanings of abuse in early modern dictionaries range from misuse and misorder to impropriety and deceit. In contrast to the modern meaning of "to harm," abuse, when applied to the tribade, suggests not something malicious done to someone else, but rather a form of "agency gone awry."[84] Within a cultural lexicon in which "use" is a common term for sexual intercourse – especially something that men do to women[85] – the tribade's clitoral "abuse" comes to stand for all that is wrong with her social behavior, even as its vagueness obscures exactly what women do with one another.

Seemingly content with the euphemistic yet efficient way that "abuse" figured the tribade's transgressions, medical writers throughout the seventeenth century neglected to ascribe a definite cause to tribadism. They all agreed that clitoral size correlates with quantity of desire, and that both body parts and emotions are governed by humoral heat. Anatomists also agreed that some kind of motion (whether internal humoral flux, as suggested by Sharp, or external "fretting" by clothing or fingers, as suggested by Crooke and Bartholin) could cause the clitoris to grow.[86] Due to excessive bodily heat, the clitoris becomes engorged with fluids and gravitates outward, imitating the extension of the penis and, seeking, almost with a will of its own, to penetrate other bodies. Other than locating such growth within a humoral economy, however, medical writers failed to distinguish whether an enlarged clitoris incited unnatural lust or sexual "abuse" of the clitoris caused it to grow monstrously large. Although different authors implied different interpretations based on the details they selected, none of them definitively asserted a causal explanation, and none of them posed the question as foundational. This indifference is partly due to the model of reciprocal causality endemic to early modern psycho-physiology, the ease of slippage in humoralism between body and behavior. Nonetheless, even within the Galenic model it would make sense to pursue questions raised by the correlation of quantity of lust, size of organ, and tendency toward illicit behavior. For instance, if the clitoris is the female yard, is it governed, as the penis is, by an involuntary mechanics of erection? Does it possess, as anatomists alleged of the penis, a will of its own? Or is the tribade's will, and not her unruly organ, to blame?

Such questions, occulted as they are within medical discourse, constitute a crucial crux of early modern erotic ideology. As a logical extension of the terms of medical discourse, they are necessarily implied, but within those terms, they are utterly unanswerable. For the tribade's morphology is also a psychomorphology: both cause and effect, originator and result. Despite the confident descriptions of a range of classical, medieval, and Renaissance authorities; despite the precise discriminations of crime and punishment achieved by forensic theologians like Sinistrari; and despite the insertion of local color by Thomas Bartholin, no one knew what caused tribadism – and that, precisely, was the trouble. Every woman possessed the necessary clitoral equipment as well as a predisposition to immoderate lust. Given the inherent instability of the humors and the capriciousness of female desire, then, any woman's genitals might grow to monstrous proportions. In contrast to later periods, when a woman's lust for another woman signified primarily a deviation of gender (and thus was intelligible within a paradigm of inversion), in the early modern period, despite the imitative masculinity ascribed to the tribade, her behavior was a logical extension – indeed, a confirmation – of femininity in all its heavenly ordained intemperance.

The implications of this nexus of gender are important to our understanding of the various interpretative matrices imposed on early modern eroticism. One might have thought that the tribade's clitoral hypertrophy – described as a long-term somatic condition correlated with a specific erotic predisposition – would confer upon her a coherent erotic identity. Foucault, after all, described the "nineteenth-century homosexual" as "a type of life, a life form, and a morphology, with an indiscreet anatomy and possibly a mysterious physiology." The anatomy of the early modern tribade was nothing if not indiscreet; her body was, above all, defined as an excessive morphology. But even as the tribade was understood in such minoritarian terms, she always was in danger of being universalized. In the absence of an unambiguous boundary between the size of a "normal" clitoris and the size of a tribade's, in the absence of scientific measurements that could adjudicate between a "commonly small" organ and one the length of a man's finger, clitoral hypertrophy threatened, at the level of unspoken ideology, to become hyper*typic*.

Anatomists hid their confusion regarding causality behind the standard correlation of quantity of lust with size of the genitals. Medical and theological authority represented women as more vulnerable to lust than men, yet, within the contradictory Renaissance logic of sex transformation described in chapter 1, a woman's excessive lust paradoxically threatens to make her into a man. Physical metamorphosis, in other words, provided a satisfying cultural narrative that massaged the links between anatomy and gender, and both of these to erotic desire. But as medical science became more committed to empiricism, and as disbelief about the viability of spontaneous sex transformation grew over the seventeenth century, the (putatively cohesive and transparent) logic of anatomy, gender, and eroticism previously expressed through narratives of metamorphosis sought an alternative mode of articulation.

It was found in the fantasy of the enlarged clitoris. Belief in the possibility of women metamorphosing into men initially was contested and pressured by the anatomical possibility of genuine hermaphroditism (as argued in chapter 1). Nonetheless, the *coup de grâce* of sex transformation was the construction of the tribade. For a long time, the hermaphrodite (the person with ambiguous or doubled genitalia) and the tribade (the woman who used her enlarged clitoris to penetrate other women) were confused and conflated. But whereas the medical controversy over the distinction between tribadism and hermaphroditism continued into the eighteenth century, the concept of sex transformation died out. It is not that cultural fears about the mutability of gender altered, or that anatomy's role as adjudicator of such fears lessened. Rather, such fears of gender instability and transgression, previously articulated through concepts of sex difference, began to be refracted through a tendentious description of erotic practices. From Crooke to Sinistrari, the tribade is what disrupts the prior model. Sinistrari is adamant in his disbelief about sex transformation:

Now, unsexing [sex transformation] is utterly impossible, seeing that the generative organs are so widely different in make, shape, substance and situation in males from the organs of females, as those with even a very slight knowledge of anatomical experiments are aware. Therefore the girls looked upon as changed into males were those whose clitoris, as we have said, broke out; and it is owing to this transformation in their sex [the enlargement of their clitoris] that persons unacquainted with anatomy thought they had turned males... An accident of this kind happened to a nun in her fourteenth year's profession, in the Convent of the Passion, at San Feliz de los Galegos, in the diocese of Ciudad. She consulted Barbosa about her case. But I suppose he had not read this

216   The renaissance of lesbianism

doctrine on the clitoris. Because if he had glanced over what modern Anatomists write about it, he would have boldly asserted that this nun was not at all unsexed [transformed into a man]; that she was consequently bound to keep her vows and cloister, but that care should be taken to prevent her from being able to carry on any obscene practices with the nuns.[87]

Unlike the woman who spontaneously transforms into a man, the creature endowed with ambiguous genitalia fails to provide a reassuring cultural narrative. To the contrary: she exposes the strains in the linkages among erotic practices, gender identity, and anatomical sex. In the body of the tribade, gender is perceived less as a function of anatomical sex than as an effect of an erotic behavior authorized by a particular anatomy. In the historically contingent and mutually constitutive triad of anatomy, gender, and eroticism, the accent increasingly falls on the latter term; eroticism becomes the primary diacritical marker, the thing that matters most.

The seriousness with which anatomists took the tribade's behavioral "imitation" of men is evinced in the rhetorical linkages forged in their work between anatomy, eroticism, and surgery. Since the narrative trajectory of these texts monotonously moves from a description of normative genitalia to a discussion of clitoral hypertrophy, and from there to censure of the tribade, it perhaps comes as no surprise that the narrative often ends with a recommendation of genital amputation. Paré, who in his early discussion of tribadism confuses the clitoris with the labia, recommends labial amputation;[88] and Bartholin approvingly cites the practice of female circumcision of ancient and Eastern nations. Culpeper goes one step further in his *Fourth Book of Practical Physick* (published in 1662 after his death with his best-selling *A Directory for Midwives*), providing precise if erroneous instructions for how to excise both the enlarged clitoris and the labia.[89] *The Chyrurgeons Store-house* (1674), an English translation of *Wundarztneyishes Zeughaufs* (1665), a surgical textbook by Johannes Scultetus, includes a pictorial depiction of an adult clitoridectomy as a treatment for "the unprofitable increasing of a Clitoris."[90] Whereas none of these writers explicitly recommends eradicating the social phenomenon of tribadism through clitoridectomy, the narrative logic of their entries makes clear that, if clitoral hypertrophy causes problems, surgical intervention is available.[91] Within this hypertropic discourse, whether the clitoris or the labia are cut off, what is excised *ideologically* is an agency and a pleasure that grow beyond their own abjection.[92]

The discursive appropriation by anatomy of the descriptions and preoccupations of travelers demonstrates the emergence of a social *conflict* about the terms by which female desire, pleasure, and embodiment were to be represented. Such a conflict is the result of a psychomorphology – the fantasies that structure and the structures that fantasize – of the clitoris in the sixteenth and seventeenth centuries. I am not suggesting that such a conflict did not previously exist, nor do I mean to occlude the prehistory of the tribade in the ancient and medieval periods. The association of the clitoris with immoderate desire, and of clitoral hypertrophy with the putative tribadism of African women, crops up in the medical works of classical and medieval Arabic authors, and is one source of early modern accounts.[93] References to tribades can be found as well in Latin literature from the second century BCE through the second century CE, as well as in occasional religious commentary.[94] This prior history, however, situates the tribade primarily in the Mediterranean. Discussion of the tribade in northwestern Europe was impeded by the instability of textual transmission and linguistic differences in an era of religious and political conflict.

Nor, in concentrating on medical and travel accounts, do I mean to imply that they are the only genres relevant to the understanding of early modern eroticism. The work of Judith Hallett and Harriette Andreadis demonstrates the extent to which intimations of female–female eroticism remained alive within the Latin literary tradition, particularly as continental commentary on Ovid's *Heröides* was supplemented by English translations of Ovid and Martial.[95] As the references to Sappho by the physician Bartholin and the traveler de Nicholay evince, this literary heritage was appropriated to bolster the judgmental commentary of their respective texts. However, it was the early modern interaction between travel literature and anatomy, with their shared cartographical impulse to chart the bodies of both self and other, that revived the category of the tribade and invested it with new implications in England.

Under the auspices of emerging epistemologies and under pressure from new cultural exigencies, an ancient linguistic and social category was revived and transfigured, giving rise to specifically early modern significations. The convergence of anthropological and medical discourses in seventeenth-century England was not solely a function of the routes whereby knowledge was transmitted, but of social processes that granted a renewed relevance to concerns about female erotic transgression. As the ancient logic of sexual activity and passivity that gave rise to the Greek *tribas* survived in early modern Galenic medicine,[96] it interacted with new conceptual schemes for figuring gender, erotic, racial, and cultural difference. The early modern tribade was a product of the negotiation not only between modern and ancient modes of knowledge, but between various epistemological domains that sought to map the early modern body. In this sense, the English tribade is not a creature of exotic origins imported to Europe by travel writers, but rather is the discursive effect of travel writers' transposition of ancient and medieval categories of intelligibility onto foreign "matter," and of anatomy's appropriation and refashioning of these "travel maps."[97]

In "Sappho in Early Modern England," Andreadis argues that "prurient interest in the clitoris was evidently continuing to increase" in the mid-seventeenth century, and she locates a discursive shift in English representations of tribadism "in or around the mid-seventeenth century. The language of literature and respectable society seems to have become more evasive as the existence of lesbianism was increasingly acknowledged by other dimensions of public discourse."[98] Andreadis goes on to argue that this bifurcation of discourse – "the evasiveness and eventual silence of 'respectable' society" versus "the transgressiveness and prurience" of medicine, literature, and pornography – led to a corresponding splitting off of a language regarding forbidden sexuality from the language employed by romantic friends, in particular that used by women writers who sought to distance themselves from scurrilous images.[99] I agree that by the end of the century, anatomical discourse, as well as related discourses such as travel accounts and marital advice books, imparted to female–female eroticism not only a name and a morphology, but an increasing opprobrium. So too, the emerging conjunction of obscene texts with medical literature invited a corresponding cultural pressure to differentiate legitimate from illegitimate desire.

My next two chapters will argue, however, that whatever the efforts of female friends in the late seventeenth century to ward off suspicions about their affections, rather than effectively protecting themselves from the transgressive signification associated with the tribade, such friends increasingly were in danger of being interpreted from within the terms of tribadism. These chapters also will argue that the increased circulation of discourses about the tribade was in part a function of an intensifying social investment in the erotic desire of the conjugal couple or, as I call this ideological formation, *domestic heterosexuality*. Yet, heterosexual desire did not assume its new significance alone. It is partly through women's common clitoral inheritance – an inheritance that is as much historical as biological – that the oppositional dyads of modernity (homo/hetero) develop. If the clitoris comes into representation accompanied by the tribade, and the tribade only takes up residence in England when endowed with an enlarged clitoris, and the clitoris must be threatened with removal whenever the tribade appears, then these associations provide some of the raw material out of which modern erotic identity categories would begin to be constructed. The inauguration of "the heterosexual" as the original, normative, essential mode of erotic behavior is haunted, from its first recognizably modern articulation, by an embodiment and practice that call the conceptual priority of heterosexuality into question. In historical terms, *lesbianism* is not, as Freud's developmental narrative would have it, the preoedipal embryo of an adult heterosexuality, but rather the troubling potential that accompanies and threatens to disrupt heterosexuality. In the psychomorphology that our clitoral inheritance inaugurates, *lesbianism* is less an alternative to female heterosexuality than its transgressive twin, "born" into modern discourse at the same ambivalent cultural moment.

This assertion challenges the adequacy of several analytical models currently circulating in lesbian studies. My effort to produce a nuanced account of erotic discourses prior to 1700 takes exception to the presentist bias of much recent work, particularly that which implies that little can be said of same-gender female eroticism before the inauguration of modern discourses of identity. One example of such presentism, as well as a lesson in the dangers of wholesale adoption of Laqueur's thesis, is found in an essay on clitoridectomy in Victorian Britain by Ornella Moscucci:

> Throughout the sixteenth and seventeenth centuries, it was accepted that the clitoris was the seat of woman's sexual pleasure; medical writers were not worried about the potential of the clitoris for lesbianism or masturbation, nor about its size, which was seen positively, as a healthy mark of female lustfulness. By the end of the eighteenth century, however, the clitoris had become much more problematic. As the emerging notion of two opposite sexes made heterosexual coupling "natural," the capacity of the clitoris for homo- and autoeroticism was increasingly perceived as a threat to the social order.[100]

Moscucci follows Laqueur's lead in homogenizing a range of early modern discourses, constructing them as univocal and unambivalent about female erotic power; she fails, however, to follow his example of attention to historical specificity, instead condensing his analysis of the early modern period to a series of sound bites. To anatomize adequately the gender and racial dynamics informing the practice of clitoridectomy in the mid-nineteenth century requires a historical gaze that looks beyond the "enlarged clitoris and labia of the Hottentot" which became such "an important criterion of racial classification" by the late eighteenth century.[101] The eighteenth-century imperialist construction of a "torrid zone," a geography of the equatorial regions of the globe as well as of the female body that, as Felicity Nussbaum argues, was "formative in imagining that a sexualized woman of empire was distinct from domestic English womanhood," owes much to the earlier discourses of the clitoris and the tribade I have been tracing.[102] (Considering the seventeenth-century dynamic between racialized and Englished versions of the tribade also might dispel the prevalent notion that the tribade was always-already and uniformly racialized.) So too, the nineteenth-century sexological understanding of inversion – a deviation in gender produced under special circumstances and marked by geographical otherness – has a long and involved colonial prehistory, which can be traced from the ambassadorial letters of de Busbecq to Richard Burton's *The Book of The Thousand Nights and a Night*.[103] Indeed, these traditions emerge in one of the most notorious accusations of tribadism in the early nineteenth century, the libel trial of Marianne Woods and Jane Pirie, during which one of the justices used classical sources to argue, much like Jane Sharp, that the "imputed vice has been hitherto unknown in Britain."[104]

Although late nineteenth-century psychoanalysis, sexology, anthropology, and criminology solidified erotic identities, the critical tendency to subsume early modern eroticism under modern categories obscures the indebtedness of modern discourses to prior discourses and conflicts. This presentist tendency thwarts inquiry both into the construction of the homo/hetero divide and the regulatory function of identity. The early modern reinvention of the tribade demonstrates that several aspects of the modern formation of *lesbianism* – in particular, its anatomical essentialism and colonial imaginary – are not original to the Enlightenment regime of "the subject"; rather, they predate and help to constitute such modern formations.[105] That is, under the auspices of protocolonialist discourses a new nexus of modern knowledge about female bodies was produced. Within the logic of this emerging epistemology were some of the primary terms by which certain female bodies subsequently would be pleasured as reproductive capital, while others would be condemned for their usurpation of masculine prerogatives and their pursuit of autonomous pleasures. If the regimes of Enlightenment knowledge inaugurated the category of "the subject" out of which a *lesbian* identity would be generated (by Freud among others), then such epistemologies inherited from early modern travel narratives and anatomies the bodily contours of that subject.

Inherited, but not without significant change. Tribades were not *lesbians*; tribades were constructed out of an anatomy, physiology, and epistemology of desire that only intermittently and incoherently map on to contemporary understandings. And, whereas the early modern mapping of the tribade's body provides a means of understanding historical antecedents to modern identities, it does not reinscribe such identities as historically invariable or self-evidently knowable. How is the tribade *not* like a contemporary *lesbian*? Or more precisely: how does the early modern discourse about tribades differ from dominant (and thus, often homophobic) discourses about *lesbians*? *Lesbians* today are not assumed to be marked by an anatomical deviation. (Such marking, rather, is reserved for a discourse of intersexuality.) Their erotic practices are not assumed primarily to take the form of vaginal penetration. (Quite the contrary; oral sex is widely assumed to be "what *lesbians* do.") Nor are *lesbians* believed to be more lustful than heterosexual women. (Even within the *lesbian* community, jokes about "lesbian bed death" abound.) Most importantly, according to the logic of modern homophobia, *lesbians* hate (or fear) men; in contrast, according to the Renaissance psychomorphology of the clitoris, the tribade enacted that sincerest form of flattery: emulation.[106]

In making these distinctions, my study contravenes the (re)essentializing account currently making a resurgence in lesbian studies, perhaps most influentially in *The Apparitional Lesbian* by Terry Castle. While insightfully demonstrating that female homoeroticism has been a central, if ghostly, presence in Western culture since the eighteenth century, she denies the importance that history might make in *lesbian* definition. Her attempt to bring the "apparitional lesbian" into visibility prior to 1900 assumes the cohesion of *lesbianism* not only with the Enlightenment, but with all of human history. The first postulate of Castle's "A Polemical Introduction" proclaims of the lesbian (no scare quotes, no italics) that "She is not a recent invention" – by which she means neither recent nor constructed.[107] If one of the pleasures of reading *The Apparitional Lesbian* is that it demonstrates the centrality of *lesbianism* to modern Western culture, one of the disappointments is that Castle does so without formulating the historical terms of the *lesbian's* ghostly centrality. The absence of historical specificity allows Castle to make the misguided proclamation that "By its very nature... lesbianism poses an ineluctable challenge to the political, economic, and sexual authority of men over women [and] implies a whole new social order."[108] I hope to have called into question the idea that *lesbianism* has any such transhistorical "nature." Furthermore, Castle's empiricist, "common-sense" assumption that one knows, in an "ordinary," "vernacular" sense, what a *lesbian* "is," that this meaning is to be found in dictionaries,[109] and that on the basis of such tautologies one can forge stable connections across time and culture, obscures the recognition that such knowledge is less a position from which one can make autonomous claims than the result of normalizing discourses, the history of which I have been tracing.[110]

A related problem mars Andreadis's reading of representations of Sappho in literature, mythology, and medicine. Her valuable essay seeks "to recover some aspects of public discourse about female sexuality in sixteenth- and seventeenth-century England – before a language of lesbian sexuality as we know it became available."[111] Attempting to negotiate between "the Scylla of essentialist, transhistorical meanings and the Charybdis of feminist controversies between a 'lesbian continuum' of romantic friendship and the necessary sexualizing of female erotic relations,"[112] Andreadis identifies three primary modes of representing Sappho in early modern England: the heterosexual figure of suicidal abandonment found in the tradition of Ovid's *Heröides*; the originary exemplar of female poetic excellence; and the much maligned representative of tribadism. But although Andreadis pays careful attention to the specific investments of different discourses, her implicit (and parenthetical) definition of "same-sex eroticism" as "sapphism" leads her to the conclusion that "lesbianism as we know it, with Sappho as its chief exemplar, had entered vernacular discourse in England by the middle of the seventeenth century."[113] With this reference to "lesbianism as we know it," Andreadis implies that whereas the language of *lesbian* sexuality may have changed, the meanings of *lesbianism* have not. Citing Bartholin's reference to "rubsters" as initiating "the language through which what since the early twentieth century has been called lesbianism originally entered verbal consciousness in the vernacular," Andreadis charts philological change only to conflate *lesbianism* with "sapphism."[114] Although "Sapho the Lesbian" was decried as a tribade by anatomists and travel writers, as a cultural phenomenon, sapphism is not tribadism: rather, as chapter 7 will discuss, sapphism is born of a different (and later) nexus of textual and social conditions.

As Andreadis's explication of discursive traditions demonstrates, "Sappho" has proven to be a remarkably unstable signifier historically. Nor do the contradictory yet overlapping meanings of Sappho end with the seventeenth century. Charting the multiple ways in which Sappho's name has functioned to authorize lyric poetry, Yopie Prins in *Victorian Sappho* argues that in the nineteenth century Sappho became "exemplary of lyric" as well as exemplary of the process "of lyric reading."[115] She dedicates her book to the project of deconstructing the "logic of lyric reading that has produced" various figures of Sappho, including the "conversion of Sappho of Lesbos into a lesbian Sappho."[116] Refusing to mediate between the "homoerotic Sapphism of Michael Field," the sadomasochistic "rhythms of Swinburne's Sapphic imitations," and the "overdetermined heterosexual identification" of Victorian Poetesses with a Sappho "doomed to die for love,"[117] Prins reads the Sapphic fragment as a "structure for shifting identifications, rather than the fixing of an identification."[118] This deconstructive move is offered not to delegitimate *lesbian* appropriations of Sappho, but to demonstrate that all such appropriations are effects of the legacy of (lyric) fragmentation to which Sappho (and we) are heir.[119]

Prins's analysis of identification via the problematics of a Sapphic voice and signature suggests that the subject of lyric poetry, and, by implication, the identity of those "named" by Sapphism, are specular – an idea that I will explore further in my final chapter. At this point, I simply want to suggest that the variety of identifications gathered under the name of Sappho (within Renaissance culture and Victorian poetics) disrupts the attempt to create a smooth continuity of *lesbianism* across the centuries. Further differences between the Renaissance tribade from the modern *lesbian* have been usefully, if somewhat schematically, described by Barbara Creed, who uses Laqueur's epistemic paradigm to undergird her analysis:

In the one-sex model, the tribade is guilty of assuming the male role which she is seen as perfectly capable of doing because she is already potentially a man; in the two-sex model the lesbian is deemed ultimately as incapable of even assuming a pseudo-male position because, like all women, she signifies an irremediable lack. Her genitals are not in danger of falling through her body and transforming her from male to female, nor does she possess a clitoris that might be taken seriously enough by a judge or medical doctor to suggest she might adopt an active, rubbing role in sex – she signifies only castration and lack.[120]

The modern psychoanalytic discourse of *lesbianism* recuperates and refigures the seventeenth-century psychomorphology of the clitoris, accepting the analogy between penis and clitoris, yet reading that analogy through the developmental narrative of castration. The indebtedness of modern discourses to preexisting corporeal maps, then, impels us not only to question the provenance of definitional tautologies ("lesbianism as we know it"), but to query the adequacy of the trope of metonymy to organize our understanding of the relation between bodies, identities, and desires. If the psychomorphology of the clitoris demonstrates the extent to which the clitoris and the *lesbian* are mutually constituted by a colonialist and patriarchal dynamic (which represses as much as it reveals same-gender female desire), then perhaps we can recognize the impact of this history on our attempts to think beyond the pathologies inscribed by Freud. In particular, we can trace the lineages of this occluded history in current feminist strategies to displace the phallus by a female corporeal imaginary; for, as important as this displacement of the phallus by the labia has been in refiguring female sexuality as something other than lack, the theoretical recourse to female genitals tends to reiterate the logic of metonymy through which same-gender female desire has been anatomized and colonized.

The problem with such feminist strategies extends beyond the inability to conceive of the pleasures for *lesbians* of vaginal penetration (by fingers, penis, tongue, or dildo) or the possibility of a non-phallocentric heterosexuality – although these are crucial issues as well.[121] In her attempt to counter the intense vaginal focus of modern discourses, Paula Bennett, for instance, recognizes that female sexuality is not limited to clitoral stimulation; and yet she concludes her essay on clitoral imagery in nineteenth-century poetry by asserting that "[w]ithout the clitoris, theorists have no physical site in which to locate an autonomous sense of female sexual agency... With the clitoris, theorists can construct female sexuality in such a way that women become sexual subjects in their own right... No longer married... to the penis or the law, they can become... by themselves healthy and whole."[122] Locating the possibilities of psychic health, wholeness, and agency in the clitoris seems a lot to ask of any one organ, particularly if women's embodied experience of desire, pleasure, and orgasm is, according to many testimonies, more fragmented and diffuse than unitary. But more is at issue here than the humanist basis of such claims: for the elevation of the clitoris (or labia) as the *sine qua non* of *lesbian* sexuality not only overvalues the genitals as a source of pleasure, but overestimates the power of bodily metonymy to represent that pleasure.

In 1611, the lexicographer Randle Cotgrave defined the clitoris as "a womens Privities," thus making explicit the metonymic logic animating early modern thinking about the female genitals.[123] If the clitoris stands, as it were, for the privities, then it functions not only as "the seat of women's delight," the residence or site of woman's erotic pleasure, but also as the synecdochal part for the genital whole. Oddly enough, the assertion of metonymy advanced by Cotgrave continues to exert such a stranglehold on feminist thinking that we can trace its impact among a diverse set of feminist theorists and critics. The radical feminist critique of patriarchy promulgated by Andrea Dworkin and Catherine MacKinnon, for instance, posits a seamless equation between male domination and heterosexuality; their critique of female subordination extends outwards in many directions to encompass almost all aspects of contemporary life, and yet the source of subordination is found to reside in the genitals, with the opposition of phallic violence to vaginal vulnerability condensed by Dworkin in the term *intercourse*.[124] The critique of compulsory heterosexuality advanced by Audre Lorde and Adrienne Rich focuses less on women's victimization than the ability to reclaim the female body as a source of self-knowledge, authenticity, and power, but this reversal nonetheless operates by way of a metonymic logic that results in an idealization of the *lesbian* body as a privileged locus on the continuum of female identification and bonding.[125] More recently, the tendency to spatialize the female body through a logic of metonymy underpins Ruth Vanita's focus on genital metaphors (mainly gems and flowers) in her quest for "sapphic" representations in nineteenth-century British literature.[126]

But by far the most sophisticated expression of a metonymical mode of interpretation is that of Luce Irigaray. By situating a mechanics of fluids against the specular economy of the phallus and mobilizing a labial logic characterized by multiplicity, movement, fluidity, and tactility, Irigaray challenges the humanist tradition of phallomorphic logic, with its emphasis on singularity, unity, and visibility. Irigaray's invocation of vaginal and facial "lips" that "speak together" disperses the singularity of the signifier into a plurality of pleasures, zones, and sites of articulation:

> [W]oman's pleasure does not have to choose between clitoral activity and vaginal passivity... The pleasure of the vaginal caress does not have to be substituted for that of the clitoral caress. They each contribute, irreplaceably, to woman's pleasure... Among other caresses... [f]ondling the breasts, touching the vulva, spreading the lips, stroking the posterior wall of the vagina, brushing against the mouth of the uterus, and so on... *[W]oman has sex organs more or less everywhere.*[127]

Supplementing the clitoris with the labia, the vagina, and the breasts, Irigaray charts a "geography of feminine pleasure" which would seem to bypass and subvert the history of analogies between penis and clitoris that I have been tracing.[128]

Or does it? Does Irigaray's "vulvomorphic geography" actually sustain the deconstructive project she announces in *This Sex Which Is Not One*? Or does Irigaray's labial morphology reenact the anatomical essentialism that links body part(s) to erotic desire, and then enforces this link through the identification (and abjection or celebration) of a social type? I submit that the metonymic association of female bodily organs (no matter how plural) with an erotic identity (no matter how "deviant") does not so much refigure female desire as reproduce the contours of the colonialist geographies and anatomies out of which *lesbian* identity emerged.

To respond to Irigaray in this way is not simply to rehash the problems of essentialism and referentiality that have dominated the reception of this theorist's work in the North American academy.[129] As Diana Fuss and Jane Gallop have argued persuasively, Irigaray's bodily aesthetic can be read as a strategic *composition*, a *poiesis*, rather than a referential *reflection* of the female body.[130] Nonetheless, this strategy of reading Irigaray rhetorically and performatively fails to take into account the extent to which the terms of that (re)composition carry with them a particular history. This ignorance of historical terms is evinced by Gallop: "Vulvomorphic logic, by *newly* metaphorizing the body, sets it free, if only momentarily." Although Gallop recognizes that "as soon as the metaphor becomes a proper noun, we no longer have creation, we have paternity," she nonetheless asserts: "Metaphor heals."[131]

I propose to read Irigaray's bodily poetics, not from the perspective of philosophy, but from the angle of genealogy. Lineages of a colonialist history of embodiment become evident if we recognize *This Sex Which Is Not One* as an effort to articulate not only a specifically "feminine" voice and desire, but also a *lesbian* subject. This subject is brought into being by a textual progression of chapters within *This Sex Which Is Not One* that asserts the commensurability of body part(s) to erotic identity under the guiding auspices of metonymy. To read Irigaray genealogically, in other words, means to move from the problem of ontology (the task of defining what a woman "is") and mimesis (the adequacy of the signifier to denote the real) to the problem of metonymy and synecdoche (the adequacy of the part to stand for the whole). It is metonymy that enables Irigaray's valorization of a tactile over a visual economy, that allows her to envision the possibility of a touch unmediated by culture and bodily difference. And it is metonymy that enables, over the course of her text, the supplanting of the category "woman" by the category "*lesbian*." In chapter 2, "This Sex Which Is Not One," the two lips that cannot be parted (except through phallic violence) represent the inherent autoeroticism and self-sufficiency of the female body – and this image functions as her central metaphor throughout. Which makes it all the more striking that in chapter 11, "When Our Lips Speak Together," the two lips become the lips of (at least two) women erotically pleasuring one another. What began as an assertion of bodily self-sufficiency ("she touches herself in and of herself without any need for mediation"[132]) ends in a poetics of female merger: "You? I? That's still saying too much. Dividing too sharply between us: all."[133] In a move reminiscent of Rich's *lesbian* continuum but devoid of Rich's acknowledgment of differences along that spectrum, Irigaray slides from celebrating a unique female positivity to lauding the special effects of homoerotic desire. Negating the difference between one and two (bodies, subjects, erotic practices), Irigaray collapses the labia, the female voice, and *lesbian(s)* into a unified expression of feminine *jouissance*. If Irigaray's strategic "concentrism" is a reversal and displacement of phallocentrism, it nonetheless constructs *lesbianism* through the terms bequeathed by phallocentric models of the subject: preoedipal desire for the mother, autoeroticism, and narcissism. As if she is performing her own thematics of merger, Irigaray conflates these psychic affects and desires, in the name of an Imaginary plenitude which is both prior to and beyond the Symbolic.[134]

Where this correlation positions women who are not *lesbian*,[135] just where the exteriority of *lesbianism* is located, how *lesbians* may relate psychoanalytically to their mothers, and the extent to which *lesbians* may not enact a transgressive politics, are questions left unanswered by Irigaray's bodily composition. But, more importantly for my argument, Irigaray's conflation of body part(s) and erotic identity maintains the psychomorphology of the clitoris by positing body part(s) as a sufficient sign of desire, and desire as adequately expressed through the rubric of (constructed) identity.[136] Although the specific terms of embodiment have changed, the logic of metonymic equivalence still holds: if not penis = clitoris = *lesbian*, then labia = *lesbian* desire = *lesbian* identity. My point is not to dispute the connection between body parts and erotic pleasure, but to highlight the extent to which body parts and pleasures are employed to anchor erotic identity. Despite the erasure of phallomorphism from the equation, the underlying structure of commensurability secured by the phallus remains: body part = embodied desire = erotic identity. The phallus remains secure because this metonymic logic enacts and reinforces the power and propriety of naming. Indeed, one reason the relational structure I have described is so resistant to alteration is that it functions as a meta-narrative of legitimation.[137] Although the clitoris is no longer posited as an equivalent to the penis, female genitals are still invested with the power conventionally attributed to the phallus: they serve as the authorizing signature, the "proper name" of erotic desires, practices, and identities.

The problem with these bodily metonymies, then, is the synecdochal presumption that a part *can* stand for a whole, and that there is in fact a whole to be represented. I do not mean to imply that bodily metonymy invariably is colonialist. As a performative strategy, metonymy may be as good a strategy as any: one continually is in the process of narrativizing one's own body, and the more rhetorical figures at one's disposal the better.[138] (Such was the case, I argued in chapter 3, for Queen Elizabeth.) However, the particular metonymies that organize the *lesbian* body have functioned hegemonically as a master narrative that occludes not only its own historical construction, but the (anatomical) emergence of the body it purports to represent. My genealogy thus confirms, and in some ways departs from, certain of the theoretical arguments advanced by Judith Butler. Her contention that the abject "is the excluded and illegible domain that haunts" intelligibility, "the spectre of its own impossibility, the very limit to intelligibility, its constitutive outside," could have been written about the early modern tribade.[139] However, although Butler recognizes that "regulatory schemas are not timeless structures, but historically revisable criteria," her work, albeit genealogically motivated, is written more with an eye toward the future than the past.[140] In this, she reiterates the predisposition of much feminist theory which, regardless of important differences among its central terms – patriarchy (Dworkin and MacKinnon), compulsory heterosexuality (Rich), phallocentrism (Irigaray), the heterosexual matrix (Butler) – tends to avoid submitting these structures to historical investigation. This indifference to history is of particular concern in regard to Butler's astute analysis of "the lesbian phallus and the morphological imaginary." She argues that *lesbians'* appropriation of the phallus not only exposes "the synecdochal logic by which the phallus is installed as the privileged signifier" but, through its detachability and transferability, could be deployed in the service of a new sexual imaginary.[141] Her greatest advance is in recognizing that the detachability of the phallus could release the body from the logic of identity altogether. As much as I applaud this utopian project, my genealogy interjects a caution: even as the tribade challenged patriarchal edicts, performing through her "prosthetic" bodily acts a fair amount of gender trouble, insofar as her appropriation of the phallus was interpreted through the rubric of masculine imitation, it comprised part of a colonial, patriarchal history of abjection that helped give rise to the very logic of erotic identity that Butler would deconstruct.

As long as this metonymic logic of legitimation holds steady, female–female desire will be caught within the coordinates of a colonialist and patriarchal history. What finally is most troubling about the strategy to refigure the *lesbian* as a body composed of multiple lips or (to a lesser extent) the celebration of the *lesbian* phallus, is the way it allows us to forget the centuries-long material processes that have pathologized those female psyches and bodies that desire other women. Insofar as Irigaray is working within the terms of a psychoanalytic paradigm that elides history in the name of the psyche, she cannot help but reiterate these material processes; insofar as Butler's appeal for a different morphological imaginary is a response to Irigaray, it pushes against, yet to a certain extent remains caught within, some of these prior terms. The reason for their imprisonment, my genealogy has tried to show, is this: the very intelligibility of *lesbianism* has devolved from the recitation of a past that exerts its power precisely because it is so rarely self-consciously cited.

Our task now is not to revise or reject the psychoanalytic narrative of *lesbian* pathology; these and other scholars already have done so brilliantly.[142] Rather, in order to resist the overdeterminations of history, we need to acknowledge the force of the psychomorphology that contributed not only to the psychoanalytic narrative of *lesbian* pathology, but to the feminist counter-narrative of *lesbian* identity, health, and wholeness. As two sides of the same identity coin, both narratives offer the *lesbian* body as the diacritical marker of female subjectivity, even though the values they confer on that body differ dramatically. As someone who is called, interpellated, identified by that name, I protest: *lesbianism* neither *is* the problem of female desire nor *solves* the problem of female desire. Rather than simply repudiate or disavow that version of *lesbianism* (a strategy that remains caught within an oscillating prison of identification/disidentification) I suggest that we pry apart the terms – the equation of body part and embodied desire, of embodied desire and erotic identity – through which the metonymic logic of anatomical essentialism continues to delineate, define, and discipline erotic possibility. Only by disarticulating these links can we extend the meanings of same-gender erotic desires beyond the geographies and anatomies that would circumscribe them; only by articulating the incommensurability of desires, bodies, and identities can we move beyond the history from whence, inscribed, abjected, and unintelligible to ourselves, "we" came.

6 Chaste femme love, mythological pastoral, and the perversion of *lesbian* desire

> Let's go kiss each other, yes, yes.
> All hours of this day make our hearts happy,
> Let's not delay in enjoying the hours in sweet bliss,
> To kisses, to kisses.[1]

In chapter 4 I explored the ways in which the genre of Renaissance pastoral combined with a poetics of elegy to formulate the terms of *lesbian* (in)significance. Through this combination of generic forms, adolescent female affections are rendered temporary by a dramatic structure that colludes with the ideology of marital alliance. In the present chapter, I return to Renaissance pastoral (in particular to that inspired by Ovidian mythology), to further investigate pastoral's resources for imaging female–female love. Classical mythology and pastoral conventions have been intertwined from the beginning of what Douglas Bush calls the "new mythology" of the Renaissance: translations of Ovid's *Metamorphoses*, *Amores*, and *Heröides*, and the literature inspired by Ovidian motifs.[2] From Venus and Adonis to Hermaphroditis and Salamacis, Ovid's depiction of bodily metamorphosis licensed Renaissance writers' depiction of desire's endless variety.[3] In addition, the *Idylls* of the Greek poet Theocritus and the *Eclogues* of his Roman successor, Virgil, provided powerful inspiration for representations of male homoerotic desire via a pastoral mode.[4] Although the distinctly urban poetry of Martial and Catullus articulated a more overt sexualization of male–male desire, it was the pastoral that influenced the poems and romances of Edmund Spenser, Richard Barnfield, and Christopher Marlowe, as well as Renaissance artists' mythographic representations of homoerotic liaisons between gods and mortals.[5]

The pastoral representation of female homoeroticism is derived not from Theocritus or Virgil but Ovid. Like its male counterpart, it often begins with retirement from city or court and, as chapter 4 argued, often employs elegy. The imagery of nature, however, is drawn less from the shepherd's flock than from secluded bowers and grottoes, while the activities are less those of shepherds and shepherdesses than of the huntress, Diana, and her band of separatist nymphs. In chapter 7 I will examine Renaissance reworkings of the Ovidian tale most often recognized as the Ur-story of *lesbian* desire, that of Iphis and Ianthe. In the present chapter I argue that another story derived from Ovid functioned as an equally crucial site for the negotiation of the meaning of female–female desire in the late sixteenth and seventeenth centuries. My aim is not merely to highlight the import of mythological pastoral in the imaging of female homoeroticism, but also to extend the analysis, broached in chapter 4, of the "femme," a homoerotic figure who, until quite recently, has been effaced from the historical account. Defined primarily as *lack*, the blank space made intelligible only by the implied presence of the tribade or the butch, the femme has operated, both historically and in contemporary culture, as an erotic cipher.[6] The elision of the femme is not simply the result of ignorance or bias; rather, as chapter 4 argued, her inability to signify has been a structural condition of her intelligibility. Figured either as the invisible, if antithetical, complement to a masculinized tribade or as a reflective mirror to her equally insubstantial feminine partner, the femme embodies a logical contradiction within past and present systems of gender and sexuality. Conventionally feminine and yet not (exclusively) heterosexual, her presence quietly disarticulates the presumed equation between (feminine) gender and (hetero)sexuality that has governed the terms of female embodiment. Yet, insofar as her sexual deviance is interpreted through the terms of her gender performance, it generally fails to signify, and thus solicits silence rather than censure. The contradictions that suffuse this figure seem to result in a representational impasse: always conceived relationally, signaled by the presence of others, the femme is rarely discernible as a presence in her own right. These terms of invisibility, lack, and insignificance have been perpetuated in contemporary *lesbian* discourse which, in analyzing modern butch–femme couples has until recently focused on the more visibly transgressive butch style or, conversely, repudiated all roles in the name of an utopian vision of feminist partnership that often seems emptied of eroticism. Although a discourse is emerging in which contemporary femmes begin to speak on their own behalf,[7] a corresponding historical discourse which would ground contemporary expressions and distinguish them from the past remains obscure.

In my analysis of (in)significance, I offered a historical anachronism, femme–femme love, to call attention to the homoeroticism suffusing the relations of conventionally feminine friends. To label such women femmes is to mark the importance of their gender performance (conventional femininity) to their articulation of erotic desire. In the present chapter, I modify the terminology slightly in order to shift the interpretative focus away from the issue of gender performance and onto that of erotic performances within an all-female community. My concern here is how the eroticism of the femme, like that of Queen Elizabeth's self-presentations discussed in chapter 3, occurs under the auspices of the ideology of chastity, as well as how the female sodality we can only glimpse in the historical record of Elizabeth is conceptualized within a literary domain. Whereas most critical discussions of chastity examine the protection of women's bodies from masculine assault,[8] my reading of chaste femme love among women reveals the erotic license that the paradigm of chastity enables, particularly when it forms the basis of a community forged through female affections. As I trace the treatment of female–female eroticism within revisions of Ovid's tale of Calisto from the late sixteenth to the late seventeenth century, I argue that there occurred a historical shift in the terms of female embodiment: as the femme's erotic potential increasingly is articulated, the conventions of chastity are pressured; and as the terms of her representation intersect with changing ideologies of marriage, a transformation of erotic definitions resounds throughout the system of gender and eroticism.

Together, chapters 5, 6, and 7 point to the mid-seventeenth century as an inaugural period in the construction of the erotic meanings of modernity: a moment when particular negotiations of significance and insignificance, articulation and negation, brought to the fore the terms by which erotic identity would be conceived. Crucial to the emergence of conditions that would give rise, in the eighteenth century, to a recognizable "sapphic" subject was the collapse, over the course of the seventeenth century, of what previously seemed to be two mutually exclusive modes of embodiment, the tribade and the friend. Throughout the sixteenth and seventeenth centuries, the tribade was associated with somatic and moral monstrosity; her excessive bodily morphology was mimetic of her excessive lust and she often was accused of using instruments of penetration. Anatomy texts, in particular, implied that once the pleasures of tribadism are discovered, they become a way of life. The chaste female friend, by contrast, was interpreted largely through the lenses of behavioral and bodily femininity; her chastity and innocence generally were regarded as unimpeachable, and her affection for women was judged a temporary, natural phase. Kisses and caresses, rather than penetration, were the forms of intimacy associated with her, and they were imagined to be experienced under the covers of a shared bed or under the shade of a pastoral bower. The present chapter argues that, by the final years of the seventeenth century, the chaste friend began to absorb into her figure the behaviors previously attributed to the "unnatural" tribade. It is this historical process, not a psychosexual proclivity, that I term the historical perversion of *lesbian* desire. This process of perversion brought into confused contact the attributes of innocence and vice, femininity and monstrosity, and called into question behaviors, such as kisses and embraces, that previously had been indices of feminine virtue. The result of this more explicit articulation of feminine homoeroticism was the demonization of a greater range of female bonds.

In classical mythology, Calisto, a virgin nymph attending the goddess Diana, was raped and impregnated by a crossdressed Jove; when her pregnancy was revealed, she was banished from Diana's circle. Her tale provided writers and artists with ample opportunity to depict popular pagan and Christian themes: the promiscuous "loves of the gods," metamorphosis and transcendence, and stories of origins, whether of the heavenly constellations or the nation.[9] Above all, her story has been portrayed as an allegory of chastity. Recent studies of both classical and Renaissance figurations of Diana demonstrate that the goddess's personification of chastity is built on complex and ambivalent codes: whereas her bodily integrity signified a prelapsarian natural world, hidden divine mysteries, and the inviolable sanctity of the state, it could also generate anxieties about woman's ability to elude masculine control.[10] Such tensions between celebration and condemnation are even more evident in the figure of Calisto who, while similarly chaste, embodies an erotic connection to her mistress that belies the presumed asexuality of Diana's virgin order.

Although Apollodorus, Hyginus, and Euripedes all narrate Calisto's story,[11] the major source for early modern English readers was Ovid's *Metamorphoses* (Book 2, fables 5 and 6), available in the original Latin and in popular verse translations by Arthur Golding (1565–67) and George Sandys (1621–26; 1632),[12] both of whom sought to demonstrate the morality of Ovid by reconciling his amorous tales to Christianity.[13] Jove first meets the beautiful Calisto in Diana's forest while surveying the destruction the Earth had sustained in Phaeton's attempt to guide the chariot of his father.[14] In Golding's version, Jove, upon sight of Calisto, immediately

> ... counterfeiteth *Phebe* streight in countnance and aray,
> And says O virgine, of my troope, where dist thou hunt to day?
> The Damsell started from the ground and said hayle Goddesse deare,
> Of greater worth than *Jove* (I thinke) though *Jove* himself did heare.
> Jove heard hir well and smylde thereat, it made his heart rejoyce
> To heare the Nymph preferre him thus before himselfe in choyce.
> He fell to kissing: which was such as out of square might seeme,
> And in such sort as that a mayde could nothing lesse beseeme.
> And as she would have told what woods she ranged had for game,
> He tooke hir fast betweene his armes, and not without his shame,
> Bewrayed playnly what he was and wherefore that he came.
> The wench against him strove as much as any woman could:
> I would that *Juno* had it seene: for then I know thou would
> Not take the deede so heynously: with all hir might she strove:
> But what poore wench, or who alive could vanquish mighty *Jove*?
> *Jove* having sped flue straight to heaven.[15]

From the moment of dressing in Diana's clothes to his flight back to heaven, Jove's rape of Calisto takes a mere sixteen lines. The deed itself is described euphemistically: Jove "[b]ewrayed playnly what he was and wherefore that he came" and, "having sped," flees. The prior moment of "seduction" – the moment which in subsequent versions allows us access to attitudes toward female–female contact – is not much more explicit: "He fell to kissing: which was such as out of square might seeme, / And in such sort as that a mayde could nothing lesse beseeme."[16] After the rape, Calisto returns to Diana's band, her spirit crushed, her voice muted:

> Oh Lord how hard a matter ist for guiltie hearts to shift,
> And kepe their countnance? from the ground hir eyes scarce durst she lift.
> She prankes not by hir mistresse side, she preases not to bee
> The foremost of the companie, as when she erst was free,
> She standeth muët: and by chaunging of hir colour ay,
> The treading of hir shooe awrie she plainely doth bewray.   (lines 555–60)

Calisto's "guiltie heart" is mirrored in the guilty issue growing in her belly. Nine quick months later, Calisto's pregnancy is revealed. The location is a "coole and shadie lawnde," where a "shallowe brooke with trickling streame on gravell bottom glide" (lines 566–67). Stripped by the other nymphs, Calisto, "with hir naked body straight hir crime was brought to light" (line 574). Diana, furious that her edict of chastity has been violated, banishes Calisto from the woods: "Fie beast (quoth Cynthia) get thee hence thou shalt not here defile / This sacred spring, and from hir traine she did hir quite exile" (lines 576–77). Juno, Jove's jealous wife, compounds Calisto's problems by vengefully transforming the nymph, now the mother of Jove's son, into a bear. For fifteen years, as her son Archas grows up unaware of the fate of his mother, Calisto roams the forest. Just when Archas is about to shoot his mother with an arrow, Jove transforms both figures into a constellation: "And there did make them neighbour starres about the Pole on hie" (line 629).[17]

Golding's version is brief, euphemistic in its sexual language, and it locates blame squarely on Calisto. Sandys's version, just as economical, is only slightly more explicit. "Inflam'd" with the sight of Calisto's beauty, Jove assumes Diana's form and begins his seduction. Immediately, "His kisses too intemperate grow; / Not such as Maids on Maidens doe bestow. / His strict imbracements her narration stay'd; / And, by his crime, his owne deceit betray'd."[18] The illicit nature of Jove's kisses is conveyed coyly through gender difference: "Not such as Maids on Maidens doe bestow." Women don't kiss women with the intemperance of men. Phallic penetration simultaneously reveals Jove's dual crimes: deception and sexual assault. But the guilt falls on to Calisto: "Ah, how our faults are in our faces read! / With eyes scarce ever rais'd, shee hangs the head: / Nor perks shee now, as shee was wont to doe, / By *Cynthia's* side, nor leads the starry crew. / Though mute shee be, her violated shame / Selfe-guilty blushes silently proclaime" (pp. 91–2). "Selfe-guilty," Calisto's "violated shame" reappears at the moment of bathing, both in her blushing display of her "offence" and in the reactions of the other nymphs:

> *Calisto* blusht: the rest their faire lims strip.
> And her perforce uncloth'd, that sought delayes;
> Who, with her body, her offence displays.
> They, all abasht, yet loath to have it spy'd,
> Striving her belly with their hands to hide. (p. 92)

The narrative emphasis on guilt is allegorized in Sandys's commentary, appended to the 1632 edition, which interprets Jove as "a common father," who "cannot order his owne affections." His deception of Calisto is credited to the fact that "Vice is ashamed of vice: and so ugly, that it cannot deceave but under the pretext of Virtue." Juno is "Jealousie ... unplacable." Calisto "signifies beauty: the more beautifull the more perspicuous their blemishes." The moral of the entire story is unambiguous: "So loose they their faire figures, and resemble deformed beasts, who abandon their chastities" (p. 70).[19]

Subsequent writers who mined the Ovidian narrative, similarly concerned to overwrite the sensuality of the pagan original with Christian allegory,[20] intensified or muted the themes of sexual violence, female resistance, guilt, and shame as they saw fit. Using Jove's transvestism to explore the performance of masculinity and Diana's separatism to explore female resistance to men, certain writers, freed from the creative confines of translation, also exploited the moment of Jove's seduction, indulging in voyeurism for the female nude, and revealing the possibilities of and limits on female–female intimacy. William Warner's *Albion's England* (1586), for instance, presents an erotically explicit version of the tale embedded within his versified chronicle that extends from the birth of Jupiter through Brutus to the monarchs of England. Supposedly dedicated to describing how the kingdom of Pelasgis was named Arcadia, chapter 11 of Book 2 presents "Calisto" as an inset tale.[21] Like Golding and Sandys, Warner imparts religious significance to Diana and her domain: Calisto is described as an Arcadian nun, Diana's domain is a nunnery or cloister, Calisto's room is a cell where she is "seated in religion." Virginity is rendered intelligible through a religious discourse of sainthood, and throughout, the female cloister is contrasted to Jove's licentious court. Unlike Golding and Sandys, Warner's jaunty iambic septameter verse expands on the details of Jove's desire, his attempt at seduction, and the eventual rape. Despite the fact that the story is about rape, Warner turns Ovid's tale of woe into a romantic comedy, with Calisto ending up as a rival to Juno in Jove's court after being saved fortuitously from her savage son. Her tale proper begins after Jove vanquishes her father, King Lycaon, in battle:

> *Calisto* was as faire a Maide, as faire as faire might bee,
> Her father King *Lycaon* fled, *Jove* chaunced her to see,
> And seeing liked, liking loved, and loving made it knowne

> To her (sweet lasse) for fathers losse that maketh then her mone.
> Take patience, wench, said *Jupiter*, with thee shall all be well,
> Thy fathers deeds have their deserts, but thou in peace shalt dwell.
> I am his Victor, but thy selfe art Victoresse of mee:
> Doe graunt me love, my zeale is more then fatherly to thee ...
> Of hartie Love this kisse (he kist) an happie hansell bee. (p. 49)

Calisto pleads virtuously that he kill her and, failing that, "Graunt that among *Dianas* Nunnes a Votarie I go:/For neither fits it now to love, or ever shall it so." Jove, bent on seduction – "What viewed *Jupiter* this while not pleasing to his sight?/Or what unviewed did he gesse, not adding to delight?" (p. 50) – grants her wish and, after dressing as a woman, he quickly follows her to the forest. Insinuating himself into Diana's circle and Calisto's affections, Jove works wool, performs women's chores, and adopts the quintessentially feminine activity of chatting: "Yet chieflie to *Calistos* vaine he formed life and limme, / And Sisterlike they single oft, and chat of many things, / But that *Calisto* mindeth love no likelihood he wrings" (p. 51). Until one day, Calisto, weary from hunting, "resteth in the Thicks." Jove spies his chance:

> Nymph-like he sits him by the nymph, that tooke him for no man,
> And after smiles, with neerer signes of Loves assault began.
> He feeleth oft her Ivorie breasts, nor maketh coy to kisse:
> Yet all was well, a Maiden to a Maiden might doe this.
> Then ticks he up her tucked Frocke, nor did *Calisto* blush,
> Or thinke abuse: he tickles too, no blab she thinks the Bush.
> Thus whilst she thinkes her Sister-Nunne to be a merrie Lasse,
> The wanton did disclose himselfe, and told her who he was. (p. 51)

Despite its narrative description as "Loves assault," Jove's behavior is not thought to be offensive, unusual, or, in the poem's terms, "abuse." Kissing, caressing, tickling, feeling Calisto's breasts and lifting up her dress, Jove is judged to be "a merrie Lasse." In accord with the terms of chaste insignificance, "all was well, a Maiden to a Maiden might doe this." It is not until Jove "disclose[s] himselfe" (and one suspects that the disclosure is simultaneously phallic and linguistic) that Calisto becomes alarmed; at this point, chastity becomes a matter of fortifying herself against "Loves assault." Once more attempting persuasion, Jove offers to live with her in disguise in Diana's cells, arguing that "there in beds, in bushes heere (My fainings fit so well)/We may enjoy what love enjoynes, and none our scapes shall tell" (p. 51). Then, in two wonderfully economic lines, Warner narrates the rape: "She would not love, he could not leave, she wrangleth, and he woeth / She did resist, he did persist, and sport denied dooeth" (p. 51). Having sought sport from the beginning of the poem, Jove finally has had his way with her, a resolution that is underscored by the merger of the narrator's voice with that of Jove and, presumably, of Calisto:

> That done, which could not be undone, what booteth discontent?
> As good bee pleas'd as not be eas'd: away *Calista* went
> To Cloyster, *Jupiter* to Court: nor much she did repent.
> Untill her growing wombe disclosde an anti-cedent fault,
> Then in the Chapter house she told of *Jupiters* assault. (pp. 51–52)

Presenting Calisto as secretly fulfilled by her sexual encounter, the narrator maintains that it is only once the pregnancy discloses "an anti-cedent fault" that Calisto is forced to reveal the truth. Outraged, Diana discharges Calisto from her cell, and the nymph, seeking to hide, huddles in a cave, there to await the birth of her child. Arcas grows up – wild, hairy, and savage, the unfortunate result of his social isolation. Without cause, he torments his mother on an hourly basis. One day, his anger propels him to pursue her into the city, where he wreaks havoc until

> ... out came *Jupiter* in armes, whom, when *Calisto* knewe,
> Help *Jove* (she cryde) for loe thy sonne his mother doth pursue.
> He knew his Leiman at the first, and joyed of her sight:
> Then kisse they, when the Savage boy by force did leave to fight. (p. 52)

Her secret desire fulfilled once again, Calisto is restored to a position by Jove's side and the story comes to a close, with Jove in happy possession of a wife in Olympus and a "Leiman" in the city:

> *Calisto* lived Lady-like, yea, *Junos* Rivall now,
> And *Arcas*, nobly mannaged, such vertues him indow,
> That (*Jove* consenting) him for King Pelasgis did allow.
> A sonne well worthy such a Syer, and for his prowes and fame,
> Pelasgis then, of *Arcas* tooke Arcadia to name. (p. 53)

Calisto is twice called "the hansell of this love," a word which pulls together many related meanings: lucky omen, auspicious gift, foretaste of good things to come, a first installment on a payment. Calisto is the fitting prize for Jove who, Warner asserts, is not to blame for getting carried away. Calisto, after all, is his very first love: "Blame *Jupiter* of other Loves, of this doe set him cleere. / It was his first, and first is firme, and toucheth verie neere" (p. 50).

The romantic guise of *Albion's England* influenced Thomas Heywood who in the early years of the seventeenth century wrote no fewer than three treatments of Calisto's rape.[22] His first rendition, part of his episodic stageplay, *The Golden Age, Or the Lives of Jupiter and Saturn, with the Deifying of the Heathen Gods* (performed at the reopening of the Red Bull theater in 1609), dramatizes Jupiter's attempt to seduce Calisto in the context of other escapades of the Gods.²³ Like *Albion's England*, *The Golden Age* augments Ovid's story by providing a narrative of Calisto's life prior to joining Diana's circle and including details about the internal operations of Diana's female realm. At this stage, however, Heywood seems less proficient a writer than Warner: his characterizations are flat, the dialogue terse, the language unembellished, and the meter inconsistent. Upon Calisto's refusal of Jupiter's precipitous offer of marriage, she flees her father's kingdom and joins Diana's band; hot in pursuit, Jupiter disguises himself as a "stout Virago" and successfully infiltrates Diana's cloister. According to the rule of her order, Diana's "princesses" are paired off in monogamous couples. When Diana welcomes and prepares to accommodate Calisto, she asks her attendant Atlanta:

DIANA: Is there no princesse in our traine,
   As yet unmatch'd, to be her Cabin-fellow,
   And sleepe by her?
ATLANTA: Madam, we are all cuppled
   And twin'd in love, and hardly is there any
   That will be wonne to change her bed-fellow.
DIANA: [To Calisto:] You must be single till the next arrive:
   She that is next admitted of our traine,
   Must be her bed-companion; so tis lotted.²⁴

With the state of being single or "cuppled" commensurate with the state of one's sleeping arrangements, with coupling presented as a state of being "twin'd in love," the eroticism of Diana's realm is subtly authorized under the idiom of chastity. Indeed, Jupiter must take an oath of chastity, which is explicitly defined as protection of one's hymen from phallic penetration:

ATLANTA: You never shall with hated man attone,
   But ly with woman or else lodge alone...
   With Ladies you shall onely sport and play,
   And in their fellowship spend night and day...
   Consort with them at boord and bed,
   And sweare no man shall have your maiden-head.

To which Jupiter eagerly responds: "By all the powers both earthly and divine, / If ere I loos't, a woman shall have mine." This bawdy double entendre, spoken directly to Diana, prompts the huntress to applaud Jupiter's speech – "You promise well, wee like you, and will grace you" – and to grant him Calisto as his bedmate. The reiteration of the concept of women lying in bed, "consorting" together as "bed-fellows" and "bed-companions," explicitly and matter-of-factly poses "sport and play" between women as a chaste alternative to penetrative sex with "hated man." With their emphasis on being "match'd," "cuppled," "twin'd in love," Diana's nymphs pose monogamous, erotic virginity as the appropriate expression of love between women.

When Jupiter attempts to capitalize sexually on his inclusion into Diana's circle, Calisto first lacks the sexual awareness to understand his actions, and when understanding dawns on her, resists. Yet the text fails to indicate whether the cause of her resistance is due to an aversion to passion between women, to Jupiter's haste and aggressiveness, or to some inchoate suspicion regarding Jupiter's coercive designs:

JUPITER: O how I love the, come, let's kisse and play.
CALISTO: How?
JUPITER: So a woman with a woman may.
CALISTO: I do not like this kissing.
JUPITER: Sweet sit still,
    lend me thy lippes, that I may taste my fill.
CALISTO: You kisse too wantonly.
JUPITER: Thy bosome lend.
    and by thy soft paps let my hand descend.
CALISTO: Nay fye what meane you?

Jupiter ambiguously responds: "Pre'the, let me toy, / I would the Gods would shape thee to a boy, / Or me into a man." That Calisto's transformation into a boy would help Jupiter's plight adds the further titillation of male homoeroticism to a plot already full of erotic possibilities. Throughout, the play capitalizes on the erotic potential of an all-male theater (Jupiter's lewd invitation, "Lend me your hand, / And freely taste me, note how I will stand," is only one example). This playful homoeroticism, authorized by two male actors dressed as women, is, however, shunted aside when rape becomes Jupiter's sole aim. In this period in which rape was quintessentially a matter of male domination over women (male–male rape was considered a form of sodomy), Jupiter's act of carrying Calisto offstage forcefully reinserts gender difference. The contrast between Jupiter's sexual assault and the loving ministrations of Diana's circle could not be clearer. And the ramifications for Calisto are, as we know from Ovid, tragic: eight months later, her pregnant evidence of intercourse with a man leads to banishment from Diana's society.

Heywood's stageplay is not as sexually explicit as Warner's epic. Nonetheless, their renditions share certain textual strategies for managing the representation of female–female desire. By disguising Jupiter not as Diana (as happens, for instance, in Sandys), but as a member of her order, Heywood and Warner promote an image of the goddess apart from and undefiled by association with Jupiter's sexual coercion. By representing rape as an act of sexual aggression, they contrast the loving bonds between women to the invasive, violent desires of men. The terms and meanings of Diana's kingdom – physical and emotional autonomy from men, physical and emotional connections among women – are represented matter-of-factly, without censure or shame. There are subtle differences, of course: in Warner, the narrator asserts along with Jove that "a Maiden to a Maiden might doe this"; in Heywood, Calisto resists Jove's assertion that kissing is something "a woman with a woman may" do. In Warner, Calisto is presented as secretly desiring Jupiter's affection; in Heywood, Diana and Calisto figure the moral center of a world disrupted by a willful, if godly, masculine self-assertion. Nonetheless, both writers depict love between women as the unproblematic, "natural" state of Diana's order.

Troia Brittanica: Or, Great Britaines Troy (1609), Heywood's epic poem of thirteen thousand lines, includes, as the title page announces, "many pleasant Poeticall Tales" in addition to its chronicle of Troy from the world's creation through the sacking of the city to the consolidation of the English monarchy.[25] Two cantos of over one hundred stanzas are dedicated to Calisto's story, rendered as a chronicle of courtly love. The first half of Canto 2 primarily concerns the war between the kingdoms of Pelagia and Epire, which leads to a supposed truce. On an embassy to collect hostages, Jove, representing his guardian, the King of Epire, attends a banquet to which Lycaon, King of Pelagia, has invited him. Lying on the table is the dismembered body of an Epirean hostage, roasted, salted, and baked. Angrily bearing away the mangled body, Jove takes to the streets to orate the monstrous deeds of the "bloody Tirant" (stanza 29). An uprising ensues, leading to Lycaon's flight to the forest, where he is metamorphosed into a wolf, "[t]rans-formed in body, but not chang'd in mind" (stanza 34).

After the victorious Jove is crowned king, he discovers Calisto, prostrate with grief for her father on the floor of her chamber. The military hero turns chivalric, falling in love at first sight: "The youthful Prince whom Amorous thoughts surprise, / With comfortable words the Lady cheeres, / Supports her by the arme, intreats her rise, / And from her bosome to remove her fears" (Stanza 39). Addressing her in the rhetoric of courtly love, Jove attempts to console her, to no avail:

> By many faire perswasions the *Prince* moves her,
> To stint her passion, and to stop her teares,
> He whispers in her eare how much he loves her,
> But all in vaine, his tongue he idly weares:
> By all Rhetoricke and Art he proves her,
> Which makes her at the length lend her chast eares,
> And thus reply: I cannot love, untill
> You one thing grant me, the Prince sweares he will.　　　(stanza 47)

Having obtained his promise to not break his oath, Calisto asks that she may become "a consecrated maide" (stanza 51). Seeking to dissuade her, Jove pulls out all the stops; the next five stanzas present various arguments of seduction, gradually gathering steam as they move from her beauty, the claims of nature, and the reproduction of the species,[26] to the destruction of mankind, infanticide, and murder:

> Yee wish to see the long-liv'de world at end,
> And in your hart you mankinde would destroy,
> For when these lives no further can extend,
> How shall we people th' Earth? Who shall employ
> The Crowns we win? The wealth for which we strive?
> When dead our selves, we leave none to survive. (stanza 55)

He then accuses her of infanticide – "You might as well kill children" (stanza 56)[27] – and ends by invoking the son they *could* have had (stanza 57). Unmoved by his hyperbole, Calisto finally is granted permission to join those other "Daughters of Princes, they that late were seene / In Courts of kings" who are now followers of Diana (stanza 62).

Far from being the promiscuous and imperious seducer of mythological tradition, the courtly Jove of *Troia Brittanica* is a heartsick and steadfast lover:

> Being alone, *Calistoes* shape imprest
> So deepely in his heart, lives in his eie;
> Shee's lodg'd both in the Forrest, and his brest...
> He haunts the Forrests and those shadowy places,
> Where fayre *Dyana* hunteth with her Mayds,
> And like a Hunts-man the wilde Stag he chases,
> Onely to spy his Mistresse mongst the shades:
> And if he chance where bright *Calisto* traces,
> He thankes his fate, if not his Starres upbraids,
> And deemes a tedious Summers day well spent,
> For one short sight of her, his soules content. (stanzas 73–74)

Skulking in the forest to catch sight of Calisto, Jove is more courtly than heroic. As if to compensate for the effeminacy of Jove's love melancholy, the narrator's description of Jove's training in the arts of femininity focuses on the distasteful nature of women's chores and behaviors. As "he makes speed to where the Virgins stay,"

> ...by the way his womanish steps he tride,
> And practis'd how to speake, to looke, to stride.
> To blush and to make honors (and if need)
> To pule and weepe at every idle toy,
> As women use, next to prepare his weed,
> And his soft hand to Chare-workes to imploy:
> He profits his practice (heaven him speed)
> And of his shape assumed graunt him joy,
> Of all effeminate trickes (if youle beleeve him,)
> To practice teares and Sempstry did most greeve him. (stanzas 77–78)

With the narrator cheering him on, Jove's self-tutelage in "effeminate trickes" progresses. Twice he doubts his ability to perform convincingly, but his masculine pride prevents him from giving up: "I am *Jove* (quoth he) and shall I then / Of women be affraide, that feare no men" (stanza 79). His efforts are rewarded for, upon gaining entrance into Diana's gate, he gazes delightedly on a "multitude of beauties" (stanza 83), among whom Calisto is the most beautiful: "So many sparkling eyes were in his sight, / That hedg'd the sacred Queene of Virgins round, / That with their splendor have made noone of night" (stanza 84). These splendid women are firmly ruled by an appraising queen:

> *Diana, Jhove* in every part surveyes,
> Who simpers by himselfe, and stands demurely,
> His youth, his face, his stature she doth praise,
> (A brave *virago* she suppos'd him surely)
> Were all my trayne of this large size (she saies)
> Within these Forrests we might dwell securely:
> Mongst all, that stand or kneele upon the grasse,
> I spy not such another Manly Lasse.   (stanza 85)

Accepted into the band, Jove quickly develops a familiarity with all of the maidens, who "teach him how to Sow, to Card, and Spin" (stanza 86). As in *The Golden Age*, "The beautious Virgins were by couples matcht" (stanza 91), and Jove is permitted to choose Calisto as his bedfellow: "With her all day he works, at night he lies, / Yet every morne, the mayde, a Mayde doth rise" (stanza 86). Here Heywood elaborates on his theme of Calisto's resistance to Jove's maidenly familiarity:

> For if he glaunst but at a word or two
> Of Love, or grew familiar (as Maydes use)
> She frownes, or shakes the head (all will not doe)
> His amorous parley she doth quite refuse:
> Sometime by feeling touches he would woo;
> Sometime her necke and breast, and sometimes chuse
> Her lip to dally with: what hurt's in this?
> Who would forbid a mayd, a Mayde to kisse?
> And then amidst this dalliance he would cheere her,
> And from her necke, decline unto her shoulder,
> Next to her breast, and thence discending nearer
> Unto the place, where he would have bin boulder:
> He finds the froward Gyrle so chastly beare her,
> That the more hot he seem'd, she showed the colder,
> And when he grew immodest, oft would say:
> Now fie for shame, lay by this foolish play.   (stanzas 87–88)

Other maidens apparently speak "Of Love" and grow "familiar." Although Calisto allows her friend to caress her neck, shoulder, breasts, and although she recognizes that it would be churlish to "forbid a mayd, a Mayde to kisse," ultimately she stops this "foolish play," becoming the personification of cold chastity. The narrator's sympathy is all with fiery Jove:

> Alas (poore *Prince*) thy punishment's too great,
> And more than any mortall can endure,
> To be kept hungry in the sight of meat,
> And thirsty, in the sight of Waters pure. (stanza 89)

When the moment of "seduction" finally arrives, the amorous Jove confronts a sweetly resistant Calisto: "Now with his Love, he once more gins to play, / But still she cryes; nay prethe (sweet) away" (stanza 94). Jove's persistence is presented in detail:

> He gins t'unlace him, she thinkes tis for heate,
> And so it was for heate, which only she,
> And none but she could qualifie: His seat
> He changde, and now his dalliance growes more free,
> For as her beauty, his desire is great,
> Yet all this while no wrong suspecteth she:
> He heaves hir silke-coats, that were thin and rare,
> And yet she blust not, though he see her bare. (stanza 95)

With a "free" "dalliance" authorized by the paradigm of chastity, the unsuspecting Calisto allows herself to be unburdened of her "silke-coats." She is neither ashamed by her nakedness nor, despite her dislike of love-talk, concerned about her companion's intentions. Her trust is rapidly betrayed:

> *Jhove* takes th' advantage, by his former vow
> And force perforce, he makes her his sweete prize:
> Th' amazed Virgin (scarce a virgin now)
> Fils all the neighbour-Goves with shriekes and cries,
> She catches at his locks, his lips, his brow,
> And rends her garments, as she struling lies:
> The violence came so sudden and so fast,
> She scarce knew what had chaunst hir, till was past. (stanza 96)

"Calisto defloured," this stanza is marginally glossed – and indeed, the passage conveys in quick fashion what apparently happens quickly. Nonetheless, just as Heywood lingered over Jove's attempts at seduction, he conveys in considerable detail the subjective experience of sexual assault:

> As when a man strooke with a blast of Thunder,
> Feeles himselfe pierst, but knowes not how, nor where,
> His troubled thoughts confusd with paine and wonder,
> Distracted twixt amazednesse and feare,
> His foote removes not, nor his handes doth sunder,
> Seemes blind to see, and beeing deafe to heare,

> And in an extasie so farre misled,
> That he shewes dead alive, and living dead.
> Even so this new-made woman, late a mayde,
> Lyes senslesse after this her transformation,
> Seeing in vaine she had implor'd heavens ayde,
> With many a fearefull shrike, and shrill Oration,
> Like one intranc't upon the ground shees layde,
> Amazde at this her sudden alteration:
> She is she knowes not what, she cares not where,
> Confounded with strange passion, force and feare. (stanzas 97–98)

Struck with the phallic thunderbolt of Jupiter, Calisto is "distracted," "intranc't," "senslesse," "amazde," and "confounded." Her "transformation" is not, as in the other versions, presented as the moment of being metamorphosed into a bear or a star, but rather – as the emphasis on this "virgin (scarce a virgin now)" and this "new-made woman, late a mayde" brings home – her sexual passage from maidenhood into womanhood. Jove offers her marriage, but "she weeping sweares, / To tell *Diana* of his shamefull deed" (stanza 100).

Like *Albion's England*, *Troia Brittanica* focuses primarily on Jove's desires in the context of a chronicle of nation-building; in so doing, it attempts to rewrite Ovidian tragedy as chivalric romance. Although the tragic subjectivity allotted to Calisto momentarily threatens to undermine Jove's status as chivalric hero, the resumption of the narrative about England's destiny reorients the focus. Even though Heywood briefly returns in the next canto to Calisto, "[w]hose sorrow with her swelling belly growes" (Canto 3, stanza 10), he does so only to indulge in voyeurism over Diana's bathing nymphs, even inserting himself into the narrative as they begin to undress:

> Now all at once they gin themselves t'unlace:
> (Oh ravishing Harmony) had I bin by them,
> I should have thought so many silken strings,
> Tutcht by such white hands, musicke fit for kings. (stanza 11)

His rendition of Calisto's unveiling takes the side of patriarchal convention:

> But when her vaile beneath her navell fell,
> And that her belly shew'd so plumpe and round,
> They little need to ask if she transgrest,
> *Calistoes* guilty blush, the act confest. (stanza 15)

Her pregnant body read as sexual confession, Calisto's previous "shriekes and cries" are reinterpreted as an act of transgression. The narration, which never again attempts to enter into Calisto's experience, takes the disapproving Diana's part by interjecting a stanza eulogizing the similarly firm judgments of Queen Elizabeth:

> So did our *Cynthia* Chastity preferre,
> The most admired Queeene [*sic*] that ever rained,
> If any of her Virgin traine did erre,
> Or with the like offence their honors stained
> From her Imperiall Court she banish her,
> And a perpetuall exile she remained. (stanza 18)

As in Warner, the wild Archas pursues his terrified mother into the city. She, spying Jove, throws herself at his feet and he, seeing in Archas his own lineaments, acknowledges him as his son. Although "[t]he strife betwixt the mother and the childe, / Is by the father and the husband ended," Calisto's story remains tragic. Rather than live as his lover, she scorns "the grace that *Jove* to her extended: / She hies her to the groves and forrests wilde," when she finds herself transformed into a bear, terrified of her own shape (stanza 23–25). As chivalric romance, *Troia Brittanica* is steadfastly masculinist.

Similarly invested in the male hero's romantic chivalry is *The Escapes of Jupiter* (*c.* 1622), a manuscript play by Heywood which, as far as we know, was never performed. Cobbling together a number of scenes from *The Golden Age* and *The Silver Age*, reusing some of the best rhetorical moments of *Troia Brittanica*, and pirating freely from his theatrical and poetic predecessors, Heywood offers a sensationalistic pastoral dramatization of Jupiter's "seductions" of Calisto, Danaë, Semele, and Alcmena.[28] Each act ends with an interjection by Homer, whose narration swiftly moves the action on to the next seduction. Beginning with a discussion of the exchange of hostages after "Lonnge warre and much effuse off bloodd" between the kingdoms of Pelagia and Epyre (line 1), the play continues in the vein of *Troia Brittanica*, representing tyranny in the figure of King Lycaon and courtly honor and justice in Jupiter. Emissary to the King of Epyre, Jupiter is affronted first by King Lycaon's ignorance of his birth and stature, and then more so when the head and "martyr'd limbs" of the Epyre Lord he has bargained for are served at a banquet (line 58). With the tyranny of Lycaon established, a "Confused ffray" quickly ensues (line 72), the upshot of which is that Jupiter is crowned King by the "ffree and uncompeld" Lords of Pelagia (line 92). Again, Jupiter falls in love at first sight of Calisto (who represents beauty): "what [strnng] rare dejected bewty's this / that on the suddeine hath Intranced mee / and made mee sick wth passion?" (lines 128–30). As in *Troia Brittanica*, the aim seems to be to join together the two meanings of "courtly" – to be a courtier and to woo. As before, Jupiter's wooing takes the form of mouthing many of the arguments of Renaissance love poetry and, in the tradition of *carpe diem*, he urges Calisto to submit to his desires. Although he never accuses her of murdering unborn children, he does lay at her feet the specter of the end of the world: "shoold all women / bee off your strict [per strict perversnes] and peevish abstinence / Posterity shoold ffayle and mankinnd Cease" (lines 216–18). To all entreaties, Calisto is "deaff" (line 229); having committed herself to Diana, she leaves, prompting Jupiter to ask, "whats that Diana?" (line 232). Upon hearing the huntress described, he devises his plot to make "my selff one off her Trayne" and, swiftly dispatching the "state busines" pressed upon him by his lords (lines 243–44), he follows Calisto to the forest.

Calisto is given a majestic welcome by Diana who, in the fashion of Duke Senior in *As You Like It*, extols the virtues of the forest over the court; unlike the Duke, Diana asks the newcomer to commit herself to "chast virginity" (lines 280–84). Calisto eagerly "professe[s]" herself a "seperatist/ffrom all Earths pompe and mundane vanty/Coort pleasures, Citty Curiosityes" (lines 291–93), and disclaims all "Alliance" from the "Loathd society off man" (lines 297–98). The subsequent discussion of Calisto's bedmate is drawn almost verbatim from *The Golden Age*, including Atlanta's description of female amity: "all our Cupples are so sweetly matcht/and twin'd in love amongst us theres scarce one/that Can be [moved] woon to Chandg her bedffell<o" (lines 323–25).

Jupiter enters, concerned, as in *Troia Brittanica*, with his performance of femininity: "nay: that stryde was somwhat too lardge," he says, and he resolves "To lispe, and simper" (lines 336, 341). He likewise is nervous about what will befall him should his masculinity be revealed; imagining himself rather in the image of Acteon, he bemoans the possibility of dying "lyke a stagge and bee shott to death [v.th] wth theire arrowes" (lines 345–46). His anxiety that Diana's handmaidens will set him "to spin to sowe, or any such ffemall/follery" (lines 357–58) is unfounded: these strapping virgins are more interested in the enjoyments of the hunt than in carding and spinning (lines 420–29).

Pleased with the stranger's narration of her birth and fortunes, as well as her large stature, Diana welcomes Jupiter into her circle in terms lifted from *The Golden Age*:

DIANA: you never shall wth hated man attone,
 but lye wth woman, or elce lodge alone ...
 All your societye shall bee wth vestalls.
 Enterd (as you) Into our sisterhoodd ...
 Consort wth them att boord and bedd
 And sweare no man shall have your madenhead.
JUPITER: By all the gods boath Earthy and devyne
 Iff [I] eare I loo'st, a woman shall have mine. (lines 396–406)

The frisson of the subsequent "seduction" scene hinges on just how far Calisto will allow her bedmate's hand to stray:

JUPITER: ffayre bedffellowe thyne hand
CALISTO: There.
JUPITER: what have I ffelt, unlesse blanch't snowe off substanc'e n'ot to melt
 Temperd wth llyvely warmth
CALISTO: you gripe too hard.

JUPITER: howe sweetely coold I rest
 Iff my faint head [wh] weare pillowed on your bres<t
CALISTO: leane on mee then,
JUPITER: so might the weight thereoff
 perhapps offend your youthffull tendernesse,
 o how I love thee; letts toye kisse and play
CALISTO: howe;
JUPITER: so one woman wth another may
CALISTO: this kissinnge I lyke not
JUPITER: nay sweete lye still, and let mee tast your lippe,
CALISTO: [oh ffy] howe wantonly you kisse,
JUPITER: you woold say lovinngly: lett mee glove my hand
 [In your] beetwixt your Ivory brests.
CALISTO: o ffy what meane you,
JUPITER: ffor your sake only I coold wishe' the gods woold
 by altrinnge nature make' mee maskuline
CALISTO: To bee a man?
JUPITER: let not that startle you [ffor] wee are farr ffrom such
 Lye downe again your ffoout I oft have praysd
 Ey and your legge, nay mownt yr skyrt a little
 Il measure ffor the wager off a ffall
 wch hath the greatest great, or smallest small
CALISTO: you are too wanton, and too ffree your hand.
JUPITER: you neede not blush att what a woman sees.
 mee thinks you shoold bee ffatt pray lett mee feele.
CALISTO: o ffye you tickle mee,
JUPITER: proove mee wth your hand
 You shall not ffinde me so,
CALISTO: your Coortshipp is scarce modest, and It tasts
 Too much off man. (lines 464–99)

Extending the voyeurism of the scene, Heywood licenses Jupiter's roving hands, allowing them to move from Calisto's hand to breasts to foot to thigh, proceeding with a request to Calisto to lift her skirt, and ending with an invitation for her to touch in return. There is no question but that this cross between a poetic blazon and a strip-tease functions primarily in the service of *hetero*eroticism. Nonetheless, Jupiter's insistence that such actions are permissible among women – "you need not blush at what a woman sees" – suggests that a fair amount of visual pleasure and bodily contact are the purview of chaste women. The question is, when does the behavior Jupiter describes as "lovingly" become what Calisto calls "wantonly"? When does modesty spill over into immodesty? The answer, it turns out, is a tautology: it does so, in the words of Calisto, when it "tasts / too much off man." Chastity is only assaulted when a man (or a woman) acts like a man. But the difference between the actions of men and women is none too clear in this play, where the term "Coortshipp" can be applied equally to women's and men's caresses of women. When Calisto threatens to "ryse, / and wth my Clamours ffill the neighboringe groves" (lines 502–03), Jupiter refigures himself as the victorious hunter – "heare stands one ready that must stryke a Doe / and thou art shee" (lines 506–07) – and bears his doe offstage.

In Heywood's hands, Calisto's story reveals several anxieties about women.[29] Jupiter's hyperbolic arguments against chastity, especially the injunction to procreate to prevent the end of the world, sound remarkably like modern homophobia. His uneasiness about performing femininity and his trepidation about being shot like a stag seem compensatory, indicating a fear that Diana's "cloister" is less an innocuous nunnery than an Amazon fortress. Indeed, it might not be off the mark to describe Jupiter's fears as revealing a "castration anxiety" specifically elicited by women's rejection of men. Calisto's use of the noun "separatist" to describe herself gestures toward a total commitment to female alliance, while Diana appropriates the language of chivalry in suggesting that a virago as large as Jupiter "shalbee Championes<s to all our wronged Ladyes" (lines 386–87). Even as Heywood maximizes the potential of Jupiter's sexual assault to titillate, he does so in terms that draw attention to the very fine line that divides licit from illicit desires among women.

In revisions of Ovid's story after the middle of the century, the eroticism exploited by Heywood literally is brought onto center stage; there, the faultlines between female modesty and transgression are exposed and female intimacies rendered problematic. The opera of Pier Francesco Cavalli and Giovanni Faustini, *La Calisto*, first performed at the *Teatro San Apollinaire*, Venice, in 1651, intensifies the plot's eroticism, making female intimacy more sensual and also more contested within Diana's order.[30] The new Venetian opera was one of the most popular entertainments in the seventeenth century, performed not only in other Italian cities and towns, but throughout the Continent.[31] Its representations of women were ambivalent, reflecting faultlines in the gender ideology of Venice itself: on the one hand, Italian women were strictly governed by the institutions of the Catholic church and the family; on the other hand, the carnival city of Venice licensed a thriving sex industry.[32] Adding non-Ovidian characters to enhance his erotic plot, Cavalli ups the ante on female intimacy by having Jove assume the guise, not of some stranger to the order, but of Diana. Calisto, believing that her mistress's caresses grace her with unique favor and love, eagerly responds to the disguised Jove and, indeed, wholeheartedly commits herself over to passion. The duet, "*Sien mortali o divini*," sung by Calisto and Jove after he, crossdressed as Diana, has discovered her in the forest, is imbued with a rapturous eroticism that the musical intermingling of voices amplifies (the original Italian is supplied in the notes):

JOVE AS DIANA: Now make up for the bitterness of your absence with the sweetness of your kisses.
CALISTO: As many as you want shall be given to you,
shall be offered to you by my devoted lip[s]
which are accustomed always to invoking your divinity.

JOVE AS DIANA: In a shadier spot, in a leafier place,
with the murmuring made by the falling waters of a spring
even clearer than this one, let's go kiss each other's mouths,
beloved follower.
BOTH SING TOGETHER: Let's go kiss each other, yes, yes.
All hours of this day make our hearts happy,
Let's not delay in enjoying the hours in sweet bliss,
To kisses, to kisses.[33]

Only the audience "knows" that the figure whom Calisto believes to be a woman is a man. Although it is unclear whether the part of Jove originally was sung by a man or woman, the possibility that it was the latter adds another homoerotic layer to these performances.[34]

Calisto's passion, unambiguously directed toward a feminine object, is expressed by means of an oral economy of desire. She refers to the "pleasant and sweet honeycombs" of Diana's mouth, the "heavenly rubies" of her lips.[35] In Cavalli's opera, kissing seems, to summon the words of William Kerrigan, to differ "from orgasm in its capacity for limitless increase... [W]ith kisses the market is always up, always gaining,"[36] and also to allude to a feminine bodily imagery much like Luce Irigaray's invocation of "two lips which speak together."[37] (The opera's imagery, however, is not implicated in the equation of eroticism and identity that, I suggested in chapter 5, Irigaray's philosophy unintentionally enacts.) With all hours of the day dedicated to pleasure, the atemporal nature of the sensuality celebrated here is augmented by the resistance of such pleasure to quantification, as the following lines, sung by Calisto, attest: "Clear and pure springs, to the sounds of your gurglings, my goddess and I, a beloved and dear couple, will kiss each other endlessly. And we will sing gentle melodies, here where Echo answers with several voices, and where the sound of kisses merges with the sound of the water."[38] With the melodies of their voices echoed by another nymph, Echo, and with the sound of their kisses merging with the gurgling of the water, the experience of sensual love becomes an endlessly recursive circle of mutual pleasures, celebrated joyfully by animate nature. Jove's invitation to retire to "a shadier spot, in a leafier place" further associates the damp and shadowy natural world with the female genitalia, as both become the proposed site of erotic contact.

The femininity of these thematizations is enhanced by the pastoral idiom itself, which depends on an early modern vocabulary of the female body. During this period, the word "nymph" conveyed connotations of female nakedness, tactile pleasures, and even the genitalia itself. These associations are evident in the visual tradition, from medieval woodcuts to Renaissance frescoes to mannerist paintings, that portrays Diana and her naked nymphs bathing. In addition, as Patricia Simons has discussed, such depictions of the bath of Diana often show women, naked or partially clothed, fondling one another's bodies.[39]

Figure 28 Francesco Mazzola Parmigianino, from the *Fable of Diana and Acteon* (1523), Rocca Sanvitale, Fontanellato, Parma.

Given the nexus of associations embedded in this visual tradition, the location of Parmigianino's 1523 fresco of two naked nymphs embracing one another on the wall of an Italian noblewoman's private bathing chamber at the Rocca Sanvitale in Fontanellato, Parma seems particularly apt (figure 28). The association of female bodily intimacies within the context of bathing nymphs is present as well in the Porte Dorée in Fontainebleau: decorated throughout with images of Diana, its Appartement des Bains (1541–47; destroyed in 1697) included a fresco cycle by Francesco Primaticcio, with lunettes depicting Jupiter and Calisto and Diana discovering Calisto's pregnancy.

The association between nymphs, the naked female body, and water is linguistic as well. In early modern English dictionaries and anatomical treatises, the labia, thought to protect the body from the passing of urine, are termed the "nymphae."[40] Helkiah Crooke offers an etymological connection, noting that the nymphae

> leade the urine through a long passage as it were betweene two walles, receyving it from the bottome of the cleft as out of a Tunnell: from whence it is that it runneth foorth in a broad streame with a hissing noise, not wetting the wings of the lap in the passage; and from these uses they have their name of Nymphes, because they joyne unto the passage of urine, and the necke of the womb; out of which, as out of fountaines

(and the Nymphes are sayed to bee presedents or dieties of the fountaines) water and humours do issue: and beside, because in them are the veneriall delicacies, for the Poets say that the Nymphes lasciviously seeke out the Satyres among the woods and forrests.[41]

Jane Sharp also describes the "privy parts" in terms that resonate with pastoral language: "At the bottom of the womans belly is a little bank called mountain of pleasure near the well-spring... Under this hill is the spring-head, which is a passage having two lips set about with hair as the upper part is."[42] This association is present in Italian as well: one of the definitions of "ninfa" is "the small lips of the vagina."[43] Given this linguistic context, Cavalli's placement of female erotic contact by "the murmuring made by the falling waters of a spring even clearer than this one" and "where the sound of kisses merges with the sound of the water" creates a further link between the female genitals, water imagery, and oral pleasures.[44] With these images in mind, the significance of the opera's opening lament about how the earth has become scorched by Phaeton's chariot becomes clearer. Jupiter, having descended to earth to survey the destruction of Arcadia, discovers Calisto lamenting the drying up of the spring; his first act of largesse is to cause the water to spurt forth. Reiterated throughout the opera, these associations of pleasure and liquidity create a sustained effect of erotic anticipation and fulfillment.

The celebration of fluid abundance is countered, however, when the "real" Diana overhears Calisto singing of the sensual pleasure she has just enjoyed:

CALISTO: Your sweet lips distilled immense and dear joy into my breast. Those kisses that you gave me, oh gentle goddess, were, oh god, sweet. But my mouth gave you compensation in return...

DIANA: Silence, lascivious girl, silence! What obscene delirium has clouded your reason? How immodest! How could you profane that breast by introducing into it such foul desires? What wicked harlot could, shameful girl, say worse things? Leave the forest, and no longer dare to speak to my chaste and virginal followers, out-of-control harlot: Contaminated by the senses, go, flee, and in fleeing on winged foot may the blush of your sin accompany you.[45]

Diana's judgment of Calisto's pleasure as "obscene delirium" and "foul desires" introduces a novel vocabulary of condemnation toward chaste femme love. It is a vocabulary previously reserved, in other discursive domains, for the tribade. Censuring Calisto's desires – not only are they unreal, a manifestation of Calisto's delirium, but they are obscene and sinful, on par with the language of prostitutes – Diana registers the belief that female–female eroticism is beyond the pale of reason, modesty, and religion.

Revising Ovid, whose Diana is an avatar not only of chastity but female self-sufficiency and self-rule, Cavalli positions the goddess as the primary spokesperson against all-female love. It is not Calisto's pregnancy – and thus her presumed rebellion against the circle's vows – that dictates her banishment in the opera, but Diana's fear and disgust at being implicated in Calisto's fantasies. In Calisto's memory of their lovemaking, she was "gathered on a beautiful breast, embraced, and kissed... She took me to a pleasant cave and kissed me many times as if she were my beloved, my groom."[46] Misrepresented as the erotic pursuer of her handmaid, Diana defends herself by exiling the one who threatens to malign her. Indeed, Cavalli's Diana is not a self-sufficient erotic separatist, but rather is suffering the pangs of what she fears to be unrequited love for the astronomer shepherd, Endymion; hypocritically deceiving the members of her order, Diana represents the ostensibly independent woman who is betrayed by her own desires. As one of the minor characters, the Little Satyr, sings about Diana: "At last, she who is so severe, she who is the empress and tyrannical leader of the virgins, turns out to be just like other women, who are subject to their frail senses."[47] Cavalli's depiction of Diana's realm verges on parody: not only are Diana's handmaidens all ill-content with their female companions, longing for the caresses of men, but Linfea in particular (a comic rendition of the conventional bawdy older companion) aggressively pursues a husband, sings an aria in praise of men's sweetness, and judges Calisto's senses to be clouded and her reason to have abandoned the proper path.

When Juno descends to earth, she discovers Jove's adultery and commands the Furies to torture Calisto; they transform her into a bear who is borne skyward in a torturous crescendo. Later turned back into human shape by Jove, Calisto is finally made immortal, her apotheosis transfigured by Cavalli into a Christian allegory: "Oh king of the universe I feel born again by the sound of your divine voice... I am your maidservant. Dispose, as you like, king of the spheres, of her whom you created, and whom, with happy fraud, oh my great Fate, you deigned to gather into your blessed breast."[48] Transmogrified into God's grateful servant, Calisto's stellification depends on the sublimation of eroticism. As her soul ascends to heaven and is reunited with God, Calisto is applauded by the chorus, "Heaven smiles on the happy creatures who have faith in almighty god,"[49] thereby transforming Jove's original act of deception into an act of grace.

The sensuous celebration and subsequent condemnation of Calisto's passion in Cavalli's opera stage a crucial turn in the history of representations of female–female desire. Suturing Christian dogma to Greek mythology and translating rape as an act of divine favor had been common strategies since the late medieval *Ovide Moralisé*. But before *La Calisto* allegorizes Calisto's plight into spiritual transcendence, it disciplines her homoerotic desire by condemning it as perverse. The bodily bliss of Diana's kisses is replaced with and corrected by a consecration to a disembodied patriarchal love. Having displaced homoerotic agency from Ovid's Diana to Calisto, Cavalli suppresses it all the more forcefully. By 1651, at least in Venice, the same love that partook, in Heywood's and Warner's versions, of kisses and playful sport, the same love that moments earlier in the opera was sensually celebrated in explicitly erotic terms, suddenly elicits charges of madness and immodesty, and fears of contamination. Anxiety about homoeroticism is reiterated when, after Endymion mistakes Jove for his beloved goddess, Mercury begs Jove to stop parading around as Diana lest he start attracting men: "Throw off these deceptions and these disguises, my lord, because, if you do not, instead of beautiful girls, you will find husbands!"[50] Paradoxically, it is only in the increasingly conventionalized "trouser-role" – in this case, the character of Endymion – that homoerotic desire between women is granted (mediated) expression.

In *La Calisto*, erotic love between women is performed precisely to be reviled and contained. It is as if the explicit, rather than muted, vocalization of an all-female passion necessitates a defense against that representation: the figure who embodies such desire is literally disembodied. Rather than sitting by Jove's side at court or even ranging wild in the forest as a bear, Calisto is metamorphosed into a glimmering constellation. At the same time, the contradiction between enactment and containment destabilizes the opera's narrative construction of perversion: the condemnation of Calisto's vision of bliss has required a greater, more precise articulation of the erotic pleasures being defended against.

This dynamic of articulation and negation, I want to suggest, registers the contradictions attending the historical emergence of a conceptual divide between hetero- and homoerotic desire. Although I will explore this tension more fully in the next chapter, for now I want to suggest that in the stellification of Calisto we can see a defensive reinscription of the ideology of chastity, a reinscription made necessary because it was coming under pressure. As I have argued, the ideology of chastity not only attempts to construct and maintain women's sexual purity, but defines female bodily integrity through a phallocentric understanding of what counts as sexual. At the same time, the cultural fetishization of the hymen obscures the array of erotic activities open to, and deemed pleasurable by, women. It thus is of some historical importance that before Cavalli's opera transports its purified emblem of chastity to the heavens, it subjects chastity itself to suspicious scrutiny. Jove defends his pursuit of the nymph to his wife in these terms: "Kissing is not denied to chaste lips. A pure and modest mouth can kiss without shame, her shepherd friend without shame." To which Juno replies: "Yes, but it is not permissible to take young girls to caves and then give them a certain pleasure, as you have done."[51] Exactly what it is that Jove (as Diana) has done to Calisto is rendered inexpressible, for when Juno inquires of the nymph, "Tell me, what else besides kisses took place between your goddess and yourself?" Calisto reiterates the phrase, "A certain pleasure that I wouldn't know how to describe to you."⁵² This "certain pleasure," whether performed orally, manually, through bodily rubbing or penetration, although seemingly inexpressible, is not depicted as an impossibility. It is precisely the idea that Jove-as-Diana could pleasure Calisto while the nymph believes herself to be making love to a goddess (there are no shrieks and cries here), that introduces female–female sex as a distinct possibility. With this possibility, however inchoately envisioned, the terms that have governed female–female eroticism begin to shift: the absence of male penetration no longer assures the chastity of the female body. Indeed, for Jove's female disguise to remain convincing to Calisto, any *penetrative* pleasures that might have been performed would have been enacted as a form of tribadism.

The fetishization of chastity tends to appear whenever there is a fear that women are *not* refraining from erotic contact – either with men or with each other. This diacritical dynamic is as true for England as for Italy. The cult of chastity during Elizabeth I's reign, for instance, celebrated the Queen's intact hymen and defended it against the specter of violation – all in the context of widespread rumors about the Queen's promiscuity (as well as rumors about her hymen's pathological impenetrability, supposedly so tough it needed to be penetrated surgically). The phantasmagoria of chastity – in both its celebratory and defensive guises – operates in a compensatory fashion, blurring and assuaging the anxiety that chastity might not be locatable in a physical sign. Animating both medical texts and the drama, this fear of hymenal insufficiency also undercuts the sufficiency of the phallus as the flag that marks virgin territory. Once the recognition takes hold that vaginal penetration is not the only, or necessarily preferred, erotic activity conducted by women, the moment is ripe for the destabilization of chastity's reign.

In 1662, Lorenzo Magalotti, agent of Prince Cosimo de Medici, recorded a commission of the newly restored Charles II to the court painter Sir Peter Lely: "The King is having him do a very beautiful picture, which represents an Arcadia where all the most beautiful ladies of the court and of London will be depicted life size dressed as nymphs." Although the painting apparently was never executed, and the project itself may have fragmented into a group of individual portraits known as the "Windsor beauties," Magalotti writes, "I have seen the sketch, which is very beautiful." He takes further note that "Lady Castlemaine did not wish to be in it saying that she would be mixed with so many women without a single man."⁵³

Barbara Villiers Palmer, Countess of Castlemaine and Duchess of Cleveland, was the first of several mistresses of Charles II. As an influential member of the King's entourage, she was the subject of numerous portraits by Lely and his associates. Clearly her disinclination toward the proposed project did not stem from an aversion to sitting for portraits. What was offensive about an all-female composition? Why was a man required? After all, the project was the brainchild of her lover and monarch. Soon to be displaced in the King's bed by Louise Renée de Kéroüalle, Duchess of Portsmouth, Lady Castlemaine may have harbored suspicions of other women. But female jealousy does not adequately address her need for a group of ladies to be augmented by a man.

Perhaps it was not merely the male absence, but that absence in the context of the Arcadian motif that displeased the Countess. What signification did a group of nymphs convey in the licentious atmosphere of the Restoration court? Is it possible that the anxious morality articulated in Cavalli's opera had made its way to the courtly milieu of Charles II? One means of access into that question is through what "was probably the most elaborate production staged at Whitehall during the entire Restoration period,"[54] John Crowne's court masque, with music by the Master of the King's Musick, Nicholas Staggins. *Calisto: Or, The Chaste Nimph* was performed at court on February 22, 1675, as well as in March and April.[55] Part of the theatrical vogue of the mid-1670s, this masque was commissioned by the King in an attempt to resurrect the Stuart tradition of lavish entertainments as well as to integrate French styles, such as the French overture, opera, and *ballet de cour*, into his court. In the words of Andrew Walkling, *Calisto* was "a magnificent and well-attended extravaganza,"[56] costing well over £5,000. One hundred and eleven actors, dancers, and singers, courtly and professional, rehearsed throughout the winter in order to perform for an audience of nobles, gentry, and foreign dignitaries. The principal role of Calisto was acted by thirteen-year-old Princess Mary, eldest daughter of James II, then Duke of York (she later ruled as consort to William III). Her sister, Anne, then aged eleven and the future monarch, played Calisto's sister Nyphe, while ten other ladies had speaking roles and eight gentlemen danced in the prologue.

In the tradition of Tudor and Stuart masques, *Calisto* linked the performance of chastity to the performance of royal authority. Princess Mary's role as Calisto, in the words of Carol Barash, represents "both a symbolic heir to Elizabeth's 'chaste' rule, and allegorically a reign free from the violent assaults on monarchy associated with the civil wars and their aftermath."[57] Barash rightly notes that the masque reshapes political vulnerabilities as failed sexual transgressions, and suggests that the force of the central allegory is "lessened by references to lawless sexuality at Charles II's court."[58] In interpreting all of the erotic innuendoes in the masque as heterosexual, however, Barash fails to apprehend the crucial difference between Elizabeth's allegorical counterpart, the powerful goddess Diana, and Calisto, the handmaiden who could be depicted as believing herself to be in love with her mistress.[59] Given this distinction within the allegorical terms of chastity, we might, following Elizabeth Bellamy, read the deployment of chastity in Crowne's masque as a symptom, that is, as the return of the repressed.[60] Crowne's elaborate restaging of Calisto's story reveals the difficulty of achieving a satisfactory representation of chastity in a social milieu in which its meaning is under pressure.

In his address to the reader, Crowne disclaims responsibility for his masque's quality, complaining that he was summoned by the king's men to produce play, prologue, and songs in less than a month. Although the performance was deferred to allow time for rehearsals, Crowne insists that he finished his part within the time first allotted, despite a further constraint placed upon him: "I was also confined in the number of the persons; I had but seven allowed me... those seven to be all ladies, and of those ladies two only were to appear in men's habits."[61] Why *Calisto* was to be an all-female production and why, despite the willingness to employ transvestite costume, there was a restriction on the number of crossdressed players, remains a mystery. Crowne defends his choice of the Calisto myth largely on the basis of his haste, but then explains the challenge to decorum his decision entailed:

> I employed myself to draw one contrary out of another; to write a clean, decent, and inoffensive play on the story of a rape, so that I was engaged in this dilemma, either wholly to deviate from my story, and so my story would be no story, or by keeping to it, write what would be unfit for Princesses and Ladies to speak, and a Court to hear. That which tempted me into so great a labyrinth, was the fair and beautiful image that stood at the portal, I mean the exact and perfect character of Chastity in the person of *Calisto*, which I thought a very proper character for the princess to represent; nor was I mistaken in my judgment, the difficulty lay in the other part of the story, to defend chastity was easy, the danger was in assaulting it; I was to storm it, but not to wound it; to shoot at it, but not offend it; my arrows were to be invisible, and without Piles; my guns were to be charged with white powder; the bullets were to fly, but give no report.   (p. 237)

Expressing the difficulty involved in representing the female body as both erotically inviting and physically inviolate, Crowne shows the terms that define appropriate courtly feminine behavior to be under strain: erotic desirability is subject to an articulation and a staging that simultaneously must silence and refuse to stage. Thus, all of the eroticism performed in Crowne's pastoral is subsumed, monitored, and contained under "the exact and perfect" guise of "Chastity." In order for his production to be "a clean, decent, and inoffensive play on the story of a rape," Crowne makes Jupiter unsuccessful, not only in his repeated efforts to seduce, but in his ability to rape. Both when disguised as Diana and in his own form, Jove elicits from Calisto only a firm (and undramatic) resolve to maintain her purity. Calisto's bodily integrity is so inviolate and static that she neither gives birth to a son nor voices homoerotic passion for Diana. The use of chastity as a metonym for monarchy seems to require that any glimmer of homoeroticism be excluded.

Through his resistance to staging male erotic aggression and female homoeroticism, Crowne diverts erotic attention away from the adolescent girl and woman who were to perform the roles of Calisto and Jupiter/Diana. In a related move that foregrounds his strategy of displacement, Crowne creates a subplot whose sole purpose is to censure female amity. His addition involves Mercury's erotic pursuit of Psecas, described in the *Dramatis Personae* as "an envious Nymph, Enemy to Calisto," whose story intertwines with that of Juno's jealousy. Psecas assists Juno in her jealous rage against Calisto and is rewarded with Juno's promise to make Psecas the goddess of the woods. Psecas then devotes herself to Juno in a manner reminiscent of Diana's handmaids. It is this mutual devotion that becomes the object of Jupiter's scorn:

> A most harmonious friendship this must prove!
> The fates designed 'em for each other's love.
> For none love them, and they have love for none;
> Their kindness centres on themselves alone.
> And they are so exactly of a make
> Each may the other for herself mistake. (p. 320)

Juno conventionally was considered the goddess of marriage and helper to women, an association that augments the effect of her husband's sarcasm, which serves to marginalize women whose emotional connections are primarily to one another. The displacement of anxieties about eroticism onto Juno and Psecas further registers the historical transformation of the imaginative context for such bonds: the loving choice of bed and playmate in Heywood's sequestered community is replaced by a pair of spiteful women who deserve one another. Their dyad is depicted as a lonely narcissism, in which neither truly loves the other because she desires only her own image in the other. The aural pun on "make/mate" brought about by the final couplet suggests the extent of "mistaking" that may be inferred from this love: each woman not only mis-takes the other for herself, but their "mating" is itself a mistake.

In contrast – and in deference not only to the presumed virginity but the sibling relationship of the Princesses Mary and Anne – Calisto is given not a son, but a sister, Nyphe; together they manifest a properly secured feminine dyad, a couple eternally linked yet devoid of erotic connection:

> Accept the small dominion of a Star.
> There you and beauteous Nyphe may dispense
> With cooler beams your light and influence.
> On the great ceremony Hermes wait,
> Let all the Gods give their appearance straight.
> These virgins' consecration nought debars,
> I'll in full assembly crown 'em stars. (p. 320)

The gift of celestial dominion, an ideologically fitting conclusion to a masque in which the central characters are played by royalty, hypostatizes female chastity; by figuring "their virgin consecration" as an eternal state of (dis)embodiment, the vulnerable female body – so much at issue in Crowne's apology – is permanently positioned beyond the threat of rape and the possibility of erotic affiliation. As Bellamy says of the Lady's chastity in Milton's masque, *Comus*: she "cannot *do* anything."[62] Dispensing their "light and influence" with "cooler beams," Calisto and her sister become static emblems of erotic sublimation. In Crowne, the temporal progression of demonization and idealization evident in Cavalli's opera is divided structurally into two complementary movements: while the separation and isolation of Juno and Psecas marginalizes their alliance, the cool communion of Calisto and her sister disembodies and de-eroticizes women's mutual love.

The revisions of the Calisto story from Warner and Heywood to Cavalli and Crowne register an increasingly anxious reaction to chaste femme love. Within these different genres – epic poems, stageplays, opera, and masque – feminine figures who were at one time represented as unexceptional begin to be construed as immoral, irrational, a threat to other women. The chaste femme who expresses homoerotic desire becomes implicated in the same nexus of transgression that formerly was attributed solely to her monstrous counterpart, the tribade. The relation of these figures to one another correlates to the early modern bodily canon of the classical and grotesque, a pervasive dualism that provides one conceptual axis for the terms of women's embodiment in this period.[63] Upon these axes are located such conceptual divisions as receptive/aggressive, dutiful/transgressive, orderly/disorderly, civilized/uncivilized. The absorption by the femme of those traits formerly associated with the tribade signals a correlative shift along these axes: from feminine love as the sign of the idealized classical body (enclosed, impermeable, perfect) to the same love as transgressive, grotesque, perverse. Correspondingly, the disciplining of the newly grotesque femme body involves a strategy of reclassicization: the errantly desiring Calisto becomes a star, a shining beacon of an eternally disembodied, allegorically fixed "Chastity."

As a historical narrative, these treatments of the Calisto myth exhibit a process of cultural abjection, a ritualized expelling of that which threatens to disrupt the security of a cultural order. They also reveal the construction of abjection – of horror and shame – at the level of the individual and collective female psyche. In staging the terms by which abjection occurs, these texts expose those cultural energies and strategies that are occluded in the representation of the tribade, whose otherness is so naturalized in travel narratives and anatomy texts that her demonization is a matter-of-course. The ideological work involved in the Calisto narratives allows us to see the inauguration of chaste femme love as perverse, and with that perversion, the inauguration of a newly applicable construction of shame. The *impudicia* that earlier writers located in Calisto's pregnancy is transferred to her expression of desire for another woman.[64]

Although the temporal coordinates of their abjection differs, neither the tribade nor the femme embodies a preexisting threat (which early modern texts and cultures then seek to domesticate). Rather, their particular embodiments are *produced* as a threat through a process of representation that has as its aim the containment of a wide range of female erotic possibilities. As with the tribade, so with the femme: "lesbianism," does not, as many scholars have argued, pose "by its very nature ... an ineluctable challenge to the political, economic, and sexual authority of men over women," a challenge presumably constant throughout history.[65] The historical relation of the tribade to the femme demonstrates that *lesbianism* has no such "nature," unity, or inherent transgressiveness; rather, the meanings of female homoerotic desire are continually negotiated in relation to other discourses of gender and eroticism, including chastity, marriage, reproduction, and friendship.

The process by which the femme becomes invested with the (historically prior) abject status of the tribade is what I call the perversion of *lesbian* desire. Although this transformation did not necessarily progress uniformly, over time it inaugurated what would come to be the dominant ideology regarding female bodies and bonds. Perversion is defined as "an act of perverting" as well as a "preference for an abnormal form of sexual activity" (*OED*). In using this term to describe a historical process, I intend not only to destabilize the meaning of perversion by insisting on its social construction, but also to suggest that the cultural project of delimiting certain desires as perverse occurs within particular temporalities and by means of discernible strategies. As Jonathan Dollimore has argued, the history of perversion often involves a displaced abjection whereby that which is marginalized in fact originates in that which has the power to repudiate.[66] One of his most potent insights is that abjection can be rooted as much in a terror (and disavowal) of *similarity* as of difference. It is not just fear of the diametrically opposed other, but anxiety about the proximate, the adjacent, the familiar, that can initiate the historical mechanisms of perversion. Dollimore's account helps us to see that because the femme inhabits an ideological site proximate to conventional femininity, she poses a different kind of threat to patriarchal relations than does the tribade. Dollimore does not, however, explore the historical forces that set off the mechanisms by which the proximate becomes threatening. In chapter 4 I argued that intimate friendships between feminine women failed to signify erotically in late sixteenth- and early seventeenth-century England. In chapter 5 I proposed that, with the increased dissemination in England of anatomies, midwiferies, and travel narratives, there occurred a discursive amplification about the proper and improper use of the female body. My reading of the Calisto materials enables me to join these two arguments together: not only does the femme begin to pose a threat in the late seventeenth century, but she does so because the meaning of heterosexuality itself has begun to change.

Or, perhaps more accurately, a particular form of heterosexuality has begun to be produced. The perversion of *lesbian* desire revealed in the textual progression from Warner to Crowne is inextricably linked to an intensified cultural interest and investment in the mutual erotic desires of men and women. Since the 1970s, when historians first began to address the structure and function of marriage and the family, scholars have debated the social role and meanings of intimacy between men and women, with the sixteenth and seventeenth centuries often figuring importantly in their discussion. According to certain historians, widespread social, economic, demographic, and religious dislocations in England during the Reformation and Civil Wars prompted a decisive change in familial relations. They argue that the emerging capitalist mode of production (and the rhetoric of possessive individualism that accompanied it) rendered the economic function of the dynastic family less crucial to the success of the bourgeois individual than the ability to accrue wealth through individual labor. The fact that financial stability and upward mobility did not necessarily depend upon familial resources meant that marriage could be conceived less as a dynastic transaction across a horizontal social plane than a working partnership primarily between two adults. Even though a decline in cottage industries and guilds may have resulted in a greater emphasis on dowry and inheritance, a shift away from contact with family, kin, and community involvement in all aspects of the marital economy brought about, they argue, an increasingly privatized construction of conjugal life. At the same time, material changes in the architecture of the household – the kitchen, the bedroom, the closet, corridors – derived from and augmented growing expectations of privacy.[67] Both in response to and as a spur to these changes, theologians, humanists, and writers of prescriptive literature produced an outpouring of writing and legislation about a variety of marital matters, including the reintroduction of clerical marriage; the recognition of children's rights to choose their mates (and a corresponding conservative reaction asserting the rights of parents to approve their children's choices); descriptions of the proper management of a pious household; advocacy and refutation of legal divorce; and debate about appropriate punishments for "domestic" crimes such as petty treason, wife and husband beating, adultery, and bastardy.

Most importantly for my purposes, they argue that these interrelated changes in the nature of property, individualism, kinship, and the household contributed to the development of an ideology of "companionate marriage," in which the conjugal unit was promoted as a locus of domesticity, spiritual equality, and companionship. Conveyed to households by the marketing of a wide array of conduct books, the ideal of companionate marriage promulgated the belief that husbands and wives were intended by God to be companions and helpmeets, each with his or her own distinct realm of labor and contribution to family welfare. Accompanying rising expectations of mutuality and friendship between spouses was a growing concern about children's nurturance, religious instruction, and education, which resulted in an emphasis on emotional closeness as a perquisite of family life. The overall effect of companionate discourses was to construct the family as essentially private, autonomous, and affective, rather than public and permeable to kin and community.

The companionate marriage thesis, most often attributed to Lawrence Stone but advocated by many others,[68] has been much contested. At issue is not whether an ideology of companionate marriage ultimately prevailed; most historians would agree that expectations of emotional compatibility and the separation of spheres became the reigning ideology, if not necessarily the dominant practice, by the eighteenth century. Rather, the conflict is over periodization, causality, and the correspondence between official doctrines and social practices. When did changes in marital structure and affectivity occur, and in which classes of people? To what extent can other social changes be correlated to the form and meaning of marriage? Do textual expressions accurately reflect actual practices?[69] Concurrent with the exploration of these questions, the history of the family has grown into a complex sub-field, defined not only by its object of study, but by spirited critiques and defenses of a variety of historiographic methods (including historical demography and social, economic, and legal history). Peter Laslett and Alan Macfarlane, in particular, set many of the terms of subsequent debate with their criticisms of Stone's methodology, their efforts to demonstrate the "nuclearization" of the family in the late medieval period, and their advocacy of historical demography.[70] Ralph Houlbrooke added his voice to confirm that "the elementary or nuclear family typically occupied a central place in the life and aspirations of the individual between 1450 and 1700 as it still does today... furthermore... the momentous developments of this period, though certainly affecting family life, brought no fundamental changes in familial forms, functions and ideals."[71] It might not be exaggerating too much to say that the dominant historiographic establishment in Britain, associated with the Cambridge Group for the History of Population and Social Structure, considers the matter closed, with the proponents of essential historical continuity from the fifteenth to the eighteenth centuries prevailing over the proponents of significant early modern change.[72]

I want to suggest that any notion of consensus is premature. Historians and literary critics on both sides of the Atlantic continue to pursue questions of change and, in so doing, are beginning to link the study of family life to the history of subjectivity, to issues of female agency, and to the history of the emotions. In venturing into this terrain in the section that follows, my aim is neither to resurrect Stone nor to critique historical demography, but rather to illuminate some of the issues occulted in the discussion as it has been conducted by advocates on both sides. If, as should be clear, my reading of the historiographic literature and historical texts is allied with those who deduce a significant transformation in the ideology of marriage over the course of the seventeenth century,[73] my goal is less to join their ranks than to refine the ways gender analysis is deployed in these debates and to demonstrate the payoff to be had in integrating the study of homoeroticism into the history of the family.

The controversy about the historicity of marriage and the family has been conducted around a remarkably stable set of terms. Historians have analyzed patterns of family size, composition, and relation to kinship; the definition of the family and household;[74] the effects of humanist, Reformation and Puritan discourses;[75] the role of private property, individualism, and the market; the privatization of the family *vis-à-vis* the larger community; the treatment of children and servants, including the emotional climate of family life and the use of discipline; the degree of parental control over a child's choice of spouse; the role of romantic love and the sexual double standard; and the subordination of wives within the patriarchal household. These foci, as important and diverse as they are, have, in their very centrality (and our overinvestment in them) served to conceal other considerations of the meanings and functions of family. This occlusion is only furthered by the passionately argued methodological issues fracturing the field. Fueled by disputes about historiographic method, by different rules for evaluating evidence, by the division of scholarship into opposed camps, and by the tendency for both sides to make grandiose claims (nothing changed between the fourteenth and the eighteenth century; everything changed), the debate has blinded us to the import of other questions. If the choices between change and continuity, between a family lacking in intimacy and one full of love, between male domination and spousal equality, are, as several historians have begun to note, too blunt, they also call out for examination from a different angle. One such angle, I propose, is that provided by a focused inquiry into the role and meanings of erotic desire. It may come as a surprise to hear that despite historians' remarks on the presence or absence of romantic love, their interest in courtship rituals and premarital sexual contact, and their quantification of rates of sexual intercourse and illegitimate births, they rarely treat the *meanings* of erotic desire, and the bodily practices such desire involves, as subject to historical specificity. The reason, I suggest, is because the naturalness of heterosexuality (in contrast, for instance, to family size or courtship rituals) is presumed to be self-evident. Although historians have analyzed the social practices that contribute to the "performance" of marriage – from handfasting and gift-giving to bundling and feasting – and thereby implicitly acknowledge the contingency of its social expression,[76] for the most part they have not queried the assumption that underlies the very definition of marriage: that it is a union exclusively of two people of different genders.

Rather than examine the processes by which men and women are interpellated to engage in an alliance that "naturally" combines property, reproduction, the emotions, and eroticism, historians have tended to approach the issue of intimacy through "quality of life" issues: the degree of love and attraction motivating the choice of a spouse, the emotional texture of conjugal life and, given women's subordination within the patriarchal household, the balance of hierarchy to love. Most early modern people, historians have shown convincingly, probably were propelled into marriage by some combination of compatibility, affection, and erotic attraction, with a potential mate's suitability being the result of a mix of material, emotional, and erotic considerations. The precise mix no doubt was influenced by social rank, as Keith Wrightson maintains in his analysis of sixteenth-century marriages:

Among the landed elite, a variety of criteria governed matchmaking, but considerations of rank and estate necessarily took first place in determining eligibles. For the "middling sort" parity of wealth and status was an important matter, but their less elevated social position, together with the greater freedom allowed young people in seeking prospective partners, gave enhanced significance to the element of personal attraction, which could, in the final analysis, prove decisive. Of the propertyless we know much less... [but it] seems probable that more attention was paid to personal qualities and individual attraction.[77]

Equally of interest is how the mix of material, affective, and erotic interests played out during marriage. Erotic impulses and material interests might clash, passion might be overruled by calculation, but the ideal was that personal inclinations could be reconciled with practical necessities. There is ample evidence from diaries, letters, and wills from the sixteenth century that husbands and wives could and did speak affectionately and passionately to and about one another.[78] As Ralph Houlbrooke sums up contemporary portrayals of marriage: "expectations were high, emotional demands extensive, mutual involvement deep, and shared interests and sense of humour very important."[79]

Like many other historians who emphasize the degree of companionability present in the sixteenth-century household, however, Houlbrooke minimizes the impact of patriarchal ideology. His summary represents the views of many: "In practice the real distribution of power within marriage was very often determined to a great extent by personal character, and actual partnerships could be much less patriarchal than ideal images might suggest."[80] Emphasizing individual character and choice, such historians imply that patriarchy was less a structure permeating all aspects of life than a matter of good or bad will. The issue of female subordination is complicated by Stone, who argued that companionate discourses weakened patriarchy by granting husband and wife equal roles (the eighteenth-century "egalitarian family" also was adduced by Randolph Trumbach and Edward Shorter). Most feminist scholars, however, point out that companionate marriage had paradoxical effects on women's status; while granting women greater respect, it helped shore up male dominance by locating women, through their affections, more firmly within the domestic household.

As Valerie Wayne notes, "[w]hile the subject position of a wife was given a degree of respectability that it had not previously achieved, wives were defined so that the more they loved, the more they were to subject themselves to their husbands' desires. In theoretical terms, the wife who became a subject through this ideology of marriage was increasingly subjected to a husband who was supposed to appropriate her agency."[81]

Just as women did not have a Renaissance, then, companionate discourses did not replace a notion of gender hierarchy with meaningful equality. The issue is further muddied by the notion of "emotional modernization," the view that family life prior to the eighteenth century was cold and unforgiving. This is an idea that has proven particularly noxious to feminists. As Amy Erickson remarks, citing other feminists, "the idea of emotional modernization amounts to little more than a 'male generosity theory' of increasing status for women and children, 'a great self-serving myth of the modern world.'"[82] Intent on disabusing us of such myths, feminist historians have tended to emphasize the continuing presence of patriarchal power connecting the sixteenth to the eighteenth century. In the words of Patricia Crawford and Laura Gowing, "[t]he romantic ideal of the eighteenth century did not replace patriarchal marriages with more equal relationships; nor was the sixteenth- and seventeenth-century model of patriarchal order incompatible with ideals of companionship and intimate, loving marriages. For most early modern people, marriage necessarily involved both partnership and hierarchy, love and mastery."[83] In another study of early modern women written in collaboration with Sara Mendelson, Crawford concludes by observing that "[o]ne of the most fundamental insights which has emerged from our study is the remarkable degree of stability sustained by the patriarchal gender order throughout the whole of our time-period." At the same time, they caution that stability "does not denote stasis ... but rather the dynamic ability to compensate for change, to adapt the gender order to a new equilibrium position."[84]

The need to stress the historical continuity of female subordination is understandable. Yet, in doing so, I would argue, feminist scholarship has become vulnerable to those who would appropriate it to buttress their claims about the essential continuity of family forms. Given this potential problem, the work of Anthony Fletcher, which seeks to synthesize feminist insights with more traditional scholarship on the family, contributes something particularly important to the discussion. Acknowledging that the eighteenth-century ideal of companionate marriage was no less patriarchal than the institutions and ideologies that preceded it, Fletcher argues, *pace* Susan Amussen and David Underdown, that seventeenth-century patriarchy itself was in crisis. His diagnosis of the cause and effects of this crisis begins with the assertion that gender relations in the sixteenth century, underpinned by traditional religious morality, were profoundly unstable, founded as they were upon men's perception of their sexual vulnerability to the women whom they constructed in contradictory terms (e.g., lacking in reason yet competent household managers). Beset with such contradictions, patriarchy nonetheless proved to be extremely resilient, able to adapt to the opening up of intellectual, social, and political life during and after the Civil Wars and, in effect, to reconsolidate its power. If the Restoration gave rise to such proto-feminist voices as Mary Astell and Margaret Cavendish, it also saw the failure of their plans for female education, an erosion of women's legal and civic rights, and a crackdown on the public roles women played in religious and political dissent. Over the long term, Fletcher argues, traditional "scriptural" patriarchy collapsed, and by 1800 its negative, misogynist model of womanhood was transformed into "something less demonised and more positive." A more secular "world picture" based upon "ideas of human progress" meant that "women were desexualised... but, at the same time, their moral, intellectual and spiritual qualities received much more open and evident validation and acknowledgment."[85] This more secular patriarchy was enabled by a domestic ideology that had at its core "the romantic notion that a woman fastened her emotion upon a married partner, idealised him and projected the course of her life in terms of her mission to sustain and care for his needs and salve his every emotional wound."[86] At the same time, "the very essence of companionate marriage," Fletcher maintains, "was the subordination of women."[87]

By accommodating feminist insistence on the continuing reality of patriarchal power to a narrative that incorporates the idea that change in some areas did occur, Fletcher disentangles threads that were previously skewing the historical account. By shifting the companionate marriage debate away from a focus on family size, structure, and economic function, and by nuancing the treatment of emotion as more than a question about the absence or presence of affection, Fletcher brings to the table a set of interrelated topics previously ignored by most historians of the family. Ideas about the nature of female erotic desire, changing attitudes toward the purpose of chastity, the social function of the sexual double standard, and the meanings of affection and eroticism all are shown to interact crucially in the construction of gender – for men as well as women. Importantly for the argument of this chapter, Fletcher demonstrates that changing understandings of women's eroticism affected the meanings of chastity. In the sixteenth century, under the influence of the misogynist topos of women as sexually insatiable, chastity was something that "women had to learn by hard graft against the direction of their whole being"; in the eighteenth century, as "chastity became interpreted... as an inner virtue based upon lack of sexual desire," chastity became an internalized ideology, "the essence of [women's] natural innocence."[88]

It is not irrelevant that Fletcher draws heavily on what we might call "literary" evidence – not only poetry and drama, but conduct literature and medical texts.

In this respect, his method is akin to that practiced by many literary critics, particularly those associated with the New Historicism and cultural materialism, who also tend to see fundamental ideological changes occurring over the seventeenth century. It is from within these disciplinary parameters, and particularly from a perspective on the power of ideology, that my own argument evolves. My contribution is to suggest that we further shift the terms and angle of vision in three ways. First, we need to recognize that the term "companionate" has tended to be conflated with "egalitarian," while "romantic love" stands in not only for "affection" but "erotic desire." The problems with such misrecognitions, particularly the normalizing assumptions about gender and eroticism that they enforce, should be clear to anyone who has read thus far. Second, we need to reorient the history of the family, wresting its gaze away from its traditional preoccupations, and demanding that it attend to the history of sexuality. By refusing to position marriage as the stable point of origin for all analysis, we can address with greater flexibility the varying relations of eroticism to the social structures within which it has been expressed and regulated (examining not just "courtship," for instance, or "prostitution," but all erotic contact, prescribed and proscribed). Third – and this both inspires and develops out of my second point – we need to take up the implications of the proposition, argued throughout this book, that the meanings of eroticism between women changed significantly over the course of the seventeenth century. If this is so, then we need, correlatively, to entertain the hypothesis that the meanings of eroticism between women *and men* might have been affected by shifts in erotic ideology.

But if, as I have suggested, historians of the sixteenth century have demonstrated persuasively that personal attraction motivated many espousals and rendered at least some marriages emotionally satisfying, then what, precisely, changed over the subsequent hundred years? It is in order to address this question that the rest of this section elucidates the construction of what I call *domestic heterosexuality*. As an alternative formulation to companionate marriage, domestic heterosexuality foregrounds those aspects of conjugal affection evident in the sixteenth century, but augments that understanding with the assertion of the intensifying importance of eroticism within marriage. Domestic heterosexuality, I suggest, is a form of conjugal relation that *demands* the melding of love and erotic desire. It does not merely privilege emotional connections, a sense of privacy, and the separation of the domestic from the public sphere; it also intensifies the erotic relation between spouses. Under the regime of domestic heterosexuality, erotic desire for a domestic partner, in addition to desire for a reproductive, status-appropriate mate, became a *requirement for* (not just a happy byproduct of) the bonds between husband and wife. We can observe this shift in the rhetorics by which the roles of husbands and wives were characterized, which increasingly emphasized erotic desire as the presumed basis for the experience of family itself. Not only did eroticism become constitutive of marital expectations and aspirations, it also became a primary means by which the family was interpreted as meaningful.

I gain support for this hypothesis by the analysis of heterosexuality recently advanced by the work of literary critics Rebecca Bach and Catherine Belsey. Bach historicizes the functioning of what she calls the "heterosexual imaginary" of modernity, suggesting that early modern England had "lots of marriage but no heterosexuality."[89] Marriage was compulsory for most people, but "heterosexuality," in the sense of emotionally endowed erotic desire, was not. Divorcing sexual practices from marriage in order to better apprehend the historicity of each (as well as their changing relations to class and patriarchal power), Bach argues that romantic love is a modern backformation, projected onto a very different system of gender and sexuality.[90] Bach's genealogy of heterosexuality, focused primarily on men, augments Catherine Belsey's analysis of masculine anxiety about conjugal life as expressed in conduct books, literature, and material culture. Whereas Belsey accepts as a starting point C. S. Lewis's assertion of a broad transition from "the medieval romance of adultery" epitomized in courtly love to "the Renaissance romance of marriage," she highlights "the difficulty with which the ideal is defined in the period, and the degree of uncertainty that attends the institutionalization of love."[91] Even within the celebration of conjugal love there remains an identification of marital desire as dangerous. Judging this apprehension of marital danger to be "a structural anxiety" that continues through the late seventeenth century, Belsey analyzes representations of marital jealousy, particularly that of men.[92] Her refinement of the account of the affective family translates the question of desire from an issue of relative warmth and coldness into an issue of men's erotic *dependency*.[93]

As a corollary to her historicization of the problems attending heterosexual desire, Belsey argues that love and lust, which in the early sixteenth century appear to operate as "synonyms for desire, each innocent or reprobate according to the context," slowly if unevenly are dissociated from one another. In this "new taxonomy" of erotic desire, love comes to signify appropriate, marital desire, whereas lust "lose[s] its innocence," coming to express an "exclusively sexual and specifically reprobate" emotion, manifested in those forms of "lechery" performed outside of marriage: fornication, adultery, incest, rape.[94] Love is not emptied of eroticism but, rather, becomes the metaphor for eroticism within marriage. Belsey locates this shift in taxonomy within the emerging conditions of companionate marriage:

the celebration of love as the foundation of a lifetime of concord, and the inclusion of desire within the legality of marriage, brought with it an imperative to distinguish between true love, which would lead to conjugal happiness on the one hand and, on the other, appetite, which was the worst possible basis for a stable social institution. True love was sexual, but it was also companionable; lust, by contrast, was precipitate, inconsistent, turbulent, and dangerous.[95]

The emergence of a distinction between love and lust correlates with changes both in prescriptive literature and medical paradigms. The prescriptive literature and medical texts discussed in chapter 2 all advocated compassionate, companionate lovemaking as the best way to insure offspring. But the physiology underwritten by this reproductive imperative was, at least initially, in some conflict with understandings of the proper household hierarchy expressed in conduct literature. Most writers of conduct manuals in the late sixteenth century promulgated the belief that women's erotic desire should be subsumed under that of her husband. In *The Flower of Friendship*, first published in 1568 and republished in seven editions through 1587, Edmund Tilney advises husbands on their role in the management of their wives' desires: "[T]he wise man maye not be contented onely with his spouses virginitie, but by little and little must gently procure that he maye also steale away hir private will, and appetite, so that of two bodies there may be made one onelye hart, which she will soone doe, if love raigne in hir."[96] Mirroring the legal logic of coverture, Tilney's advice erases the wife's private will, her individual volition, as well as her appetite, her erotic desire. And in *The Mother's Blessing* (1616), Dorothy Leigh reiterates the theme, adding to it a gloss of female gratitude: "Thy desire shall be subject to thy husband. As if God, in mercy to women, should say, You of your selves shall have no desires, onely they shall be subject to your husbands."[97] Later texts, however, emphasize the mutuality of erotic desire in the conflation of marriage and sexual contact – as noted in chapter 2's discussion of William Whateley's *A Bride Bush* (1623). By 1638, when Robert Crofts published *The Lover: or, Nuptiall Love*, the rhetoric and tone of the discussion had altered significantly: "there is no pleasure in the world like that of the sweet society of Lovers, in the way of marriage, and of a loving husband and wife. Hee is her head she commands his heart, he is her Love, her joy, she is his honey, his Dove, his delight."[98] In Croft's description, pleasure, lovers, and marriage all inform and define one another. As Belsey notes, this "rhapsodic account of the romantic and companionable happiness of married love and family life" explicitly affirms mutual erotic pleasures. Indeed, "Crofts sees no reason why married lovers should not have recourse to the arts of love to enhance their pleasure, and he advises husbands to talk to their wives about love and its value or to tell them love stories, both happy and sad."[99] By the mid-seventeenth century, marital desire had begun to be viewed not as the imposition of the husband's desire onto his wife, but as a mutual sharing, enhanced not only by the caresses advocated earlier by Paré, but the love stories advocated by Crofts.

The medical theories that supported attention to women's desires also were undergoing change during this time. With the gradual acceptance of Harvey's ovum theory, mention of the agency of female seed slowly disappeared in medical texts.[100] By the late seventeenth century, medical professionals no longer believed that a woman's seed contributed anything to the fetus. With the demise of the two-seed theory, the function of women's orgasm became irrelevant to medical views of conception. It took some time for the diminishment of female erotic pleasure to filter down into the populace, especially since popularizing medical texts and marital advice books continued to express outdated ideas. But by the end of the seventeenth century, the agency of reproductive eroticism had begun to be viewed as a special masculine prerogative:

But that this passiouate [sic] desire might strongly opporate, as well in sensual felicity as on the imagination. God has firmly impressed it in all Creatures subject thereto, both Male and Female; *but more especially on man*, and least it should prove unruly in him and not easily subdued: he has thought it convenient to prescribe him bounds, in granting him the use of the Matrimonial Bed.[101]

Male orgasm remained vital to men's physiology, whereas female pleasure began to be psychologized: "[t]he Venerial Appetite also proceeds from different causes, for in Men it proceeds from a desire of Emission, and in Women from a desire of Completion."[102] Eventually, medical disinterest in female erotic pleasure would contribute to the doctrine of female passionlessness. But before it did – and as if to compensate for the replacement of the orgasmic seed by the indifferent egg – the conflation of emotional affect and erotic activity became a central tenet of marital life.

The development of a new marital regime in which erotic desire became the *sine qua non* of conjugal life did not happen overnight. The social upheaval of mid-century, the public presence of women in religious and political dissent, and the social backlash that accompanied the Restoration all contributed to anxieties that probably subtended rising expectations of marital intimacy. In addition, the family is not simply a passive vehicle for transmitting social expectations and values; an "agent" in the historical process, it also contributes its own values and behaviors to other social formations such as gender and class.[103] Domestic heterosexuality was the result of a variety of discourses and cumulative changes that occurred unevenly throughout the social polity. Nor was it installed securely. Because heterosexual desire itself is socially contingent, subject to contestation and negotiation, a cultural commitment to heterosexuality never can be achieved completely. Nonetheless, domestic heterosexuality appears to have been a transitional ideology of gender and sexuality, posed temporally between the sixteenth-century ideology of female voraciousness and male victimization to female lust, and the late eighteenth-century ideology of female passionlessness, idealized maternity, and male sexual predation.[104] In contrast to both the earlier and later regimes, domestic heterosexuality is predicated on the belief that the conjugal unit is the appropriate place for men and women to have mutually satisfying sex. By differentiating love from lust, domestic heterosexuality promoted a self-conscious ideal of romantic love within marriage.

Given the growing irrelevance of certain social and economic supports for marriage, it might not be pushing my argument too far to say that under the regime of domestic heterosexuality, heterosexual desire was constructed in order for marriage itself to remain socially desirable.[105]

To the extent that historians characterize their stance on companionate marriage as advocacy either of essential historical continuity (of the emotions, of family forms) or of emotional modernization, they obscure a fundamental point: that men and women across status lines were enjoined to invest more of their emotional life into their domestic partners, and to express it through sex. Whether individuals or whole classes submitted to such interpellation seems less important to me than the fact that a host of social discourses urged them to do so. Domestic heterosexuality expressed a greater inclination than did previous marital regimes to articulate explicitly those bonds which might be deemed antithetical to conjugal success. By further differentiating martial eroticism from the intimacies of non-marital friendship, the production of domestic heterosexuality had a crucial impact on the renaissance of *lesbianism*. On the one hand, as Ruth Vanita notes, the "idea of companionate marriage, seen by some feminist historians as liberatory for women, may equally be read as involving the institutionalization of compulsory heterosexuality in a more definite form and the persecution or downgrading of other alternatives, including celibacy, same-sex eroticism, and friendship."[106] On the other hand, accompanying an intensified social investment in the desire of the conjugal couple was a concern that chastity was not a sufficient means to differentiate legitimate from illegitimate desires. Prior to the development of domestic heterosexuality, only those relations that had threatened the stable transmission of property and lineage were considered unchaste; but once the traditional supports for marriage were loosened and the domestic couple eroticized to its core, chaste femme love became a potential threat to marital bonds. Thus, we might speculate that the history of the femme has been obscured, not because she posed no threat, but because, during a time of crucial changes within the ideology of heterosexuality, the danger she posed was considerable.[107]

My effort to recalibrate the history of the family from the measure of erotic desire thus upsets the supposition, implicit throughout the historiography of the family, of a preexisting divide between homo- and heterosexuality. (Even as astute a historian as John Gillis, who places his description of courtship in the context of a widespread preference for homosocial friendship, views heterosexuality and homosexuality as utterly distinct.[108]) In neglecting to correlate the histories of homo- and heterosexuality, historians not only exile homoeroticism to preconfigured minority space, but misunderstand the processes by which modern heterosexuality itself is formed.[109] Given this, certain methodological implications derive from the hypothesis that domestic heterosexuality emerged as the terms of female–female desire began to be contested, implications important not only for historians of the family but for historians of sexuality. Primary among them is this: valuable as a conceptually distinct history of *lesbianism* has been, such methodological separatism may fail to accurately reflect the historical position of both *lesbianism* and heterosexuality in the early modern period. *Lesbianism* and heterosexuality have operated historically as mutually constitutive forces, together helping to constitute broad regimes of knowledge and power. Given that in order to signify, a desire must be posited in opposition to other desires, heterosexuality becomes meaningful only by way of that which seems to oppose it. Likewise, it only becomes possible to read the Calisto narratives as *lesbian* once we possess a notion of transgressive female desire that itself was produced through these narratives. We need to explore further the possibility that not only is the deviant inconceivable without the norm, but that the concept of a norm may be a backformation from the concept of deviance.[110] One of the greatest theoretical challenges facing historians of *lesbianism*, then, is not the elision of *lesbians* from history – a small but significant body of work is starting to fill that gap – but the elision of heterosexuality from *lesbianism*.[111]

The specific terms by which modern *lesbianism* (and heterosexuality) would come to be defined were not put into play until there existed, among other things, a concept of Enlightenment subjectivity that could accommodate the inclusion of sexual identity and the growth of connections among persons self-identifying as eccentric to dominant systems of desire and affiliation. Nonetheless, the conceptual divide between homo and hetero did not appear on the scene fully formed. The historical perversion of *lesbian* desire suggests that neither the nineteenth-century discourses of sexology, psychoanalysis, and criminology, nor the women who were their objects of study, invented the categories of inversion and perversion *tout court*. Even at the beginnings of their modern elaboration, these categories carried with them the lineages of a prior cultural contest: meanings and morphologies that are the ambivalent bequest of such "innocent" cultural materials as Ovid's story of Calisto.

The perversion of *lesbian* desire raises the question of periodization. Although this question will be my point of departure for the next chapter, I want to acknowledge that the exposition of my last two chapters has been relatively chronological, positing a historical shift in the discourses of companionate marriage, anatomical knowledge, and chaste femme love. Despite the development of new cultural prohibitions about female–female intimacy, however, these prohibitions were enacted unevenly across various discursive domains. Because different discourses vary in their social investments and means of transmission, they will articulate their concerns differently; in addition, what is permitted in one medium or cultural context may be censored in another.

The lack of straightforward development is particularly evident in the temporal distinction between textual and visual renditions of Calisto's story. Visual

Figure 29 Titian, *Diana Discovering the Pregnancy of Calisto* (1559).

artists continued to treat her from within the terms of chaste insignificance long after the seventeenth century came to a close. Mythographic treatments primarily have focused on three aspects of her tale: Jupiter's seduction, the bathing of Diana and her nymphs (sometimes conflated with the story of Diana surprised by Acteon), and Calisto's discovery and expulsion. The depiction of Calisto's shame and Diana's admonishment, usually treated within the context of bathing, are the subject of treatments by, among others, Paris Bordone (*c.* 1545), Bonifazio de' Pitati (1553), Titian (1559), Annibale Carracci (1598–99), and Agostino Tassi (*c.* 1626), with Titian's perhaps the best known (figure 29). These scenes of bathing and expulsion reproduce the dichotomy present in the literary tradition between erotic innocence and chastity, on the one hand, and sexual knowledge, violation, and shame (*impudicia*), on the other. Calisto is an emblem of what will befall the woman who surrenders, willingly or not, her virginity. It thus is not surprising that the theme of *impudicia* could also be parlayed into political satire. Titian's design, for instance, was appropriated for one of the more notorious depictions of Queen Elizabeth I, an

272 The renaissance of lesbianism

Figure 30 Pieter Van der Heyden, Satirical print (late sixteenth century).

unauthorized print by Pieter Van der Heyden (figure 30). Grasping a shield bearing the Tudor coat of arms, Elizabeth in the guise of Diana points to a pregnant Pope sprawling on the ground, his stomach bared by Father Time. The gynecological inspection of the Pope's defiled body reveals not only a lack of virginity, but a grotesque pile of monstrous births tumbling below.[112]

As the mythographic tradition developed over the course of the seventeenth century, artists tended to accentuate the pastoral sensuality of the story of Calisto's seduction. A 1613 painting, attributed to Peter Paul Rubens, signifies Jupiter's masculine presence through the ominous positioning of an eagle, whose posture mimics that of the crossdressed Jove (figure 31). But just as often, the erotic pleasures of the encounter are rendered in distinctly feminine terms. Jacopo Amigoni (*c.* 1730s) and François Boucher (1744), for instance, depict Jupiter's seduction of the nymph by minimizing the masculine iconography[113] (figures 32 and 33). The success of Jupiter's seduction – and the success of the paintings' visual seduction of the viewer – depends on the complete translation of his masculine presence into the feminine body of Diana,

Chaste femme love 273

Figure 31   Peter Paul Rubens, *Jupiter and Calisto* (1613).

Figure 32   Jacopo Amigoni, *Jupiter and Calisto* (*c*. 1730s).

Figure 33 François Boucher, *Jove, in the shape of Diana, surprises Calisto* (1744).

whose sensual form is surrounded by her talismanic crescent moon, her bows, arrows, and hounds.

The pictorial conventions of visual pleasure, particularly the tradition of female nudity, appear to have authorized a more overt (if nonetheless subtle) articulation of female–female eroticism than would have been possible, for instance, on the seventeenth-century stage. That which appears in the visually mediated form of painting as romantic pastoralism might, if performed on stage, be deemed obscene. Rather than employ strategies of visibility in order to condemn, those paintings that focus on the seduction of Calisto by Diana/Jove suspend moral imperatives in the interest of the pleasures of looking. Exploiting the formal and erotic possibilities of female nudity inherent in the pictures of Diana and her nymphs bathing, they zoom in, as it were, onto a detail of that all-female space, foregrounding the sensual pleasures manifest in the physical proximity of two partially nude women. The effect is simultaneously one of chaste insignificance and erotic titillation – a combination that has offered an influential legacy to the visual arts.

7 "Friendship so curst": *amor impossibilis*, the homoerotic lament, and the nature of *lesbian* desire

> Ovid's Iphis & Ianthe
> no longer seems out of Possibility.[1]

In 1661 Thomas Blount, lexicographer and barrister of the Inner Temple, included "woman with a woman" under his entry for "Buggerie" in the second edition of his revised vernacular dictionary, *Glossographia*. The first edition of 1656 had provided definitions of sodomy, sodomite, sodomitical, ingle, and ganymede, but included no reference to female–female acts. Blount added this definition despite the fact that the legal authority he cites, "My Lord Coke," had elided this possibility from his interpretation of statutory law.[2] Blount repeated and augmented his entry in his *Law Dictionary* of 1670, adding as statutory precedent *Statute 25 Henry VIII, chapter 6*.[3] As the first English compiler of a "hard word list" to consider women as possible buggerers, Blount silently (if perhaps unwittingly) contravened not only his nation's preeminent judicial scholar, but actual statutory precedent. No female sodomy cases had come to court in the seventeen years between Coke's 1644 *Institutes of the Lawes of England* and Blount's effort to make difficult words and the labyrinthine law more accessible to his countrymen.

Blount's lexicon did not definitively replace Coke's authoritative *Institutes*, which continued to be republished throughout the eighteenth century. It is worth noting, for instance, that the only known case of female–female marriage brought before an English court in the seventeenth century – Hunt vs. Poulter of 1680 – involved not an accusation of sodomy or buggery, but charges of male impersonation, hermaphroditism, and bigamy. Nonetheless, Blount's intervention gestures toward a shift in the logic of intelligibility that, over time, would prove to be crucial to the formation of *lesbianism* as a category of identity in England. This shift is heralded by the process of vernacularization, reflected in and furthered by the publication of dictionaries and hard word lists. Although no sixteenth- or seventeenth-century dictionary included "tribade" or "fricatrice," once "woman with a woman" was defined as a species of buggery, the lexicon of female homoeroticism could no longer be confined to learned texts. Regardless of its impropriety, the possibility of illicit sex between women was on its way to becoming a widely recognized – and recognizable – phenomenon. And with the publication of other reference works – such as *The Ladies Dictionary: Being a General Entertainment for the Fair Sex*, which in 1694 included as part of its "entertainment" the phrase "woman with a woman" in its definition of "buggarie"[4] – it threatened to become more so.

The publication of dictionaries and hard word lists was part of an effort to codify and fix meanings that had been in cultural circulation, at least in certain discursive domains, for some time. But codification would happen slowly and erratically: terms like "tribade" and "fricatrice" continued to retain some of their old significations, while new terms (macroclitoride, masculine female, sapphist, tommy, romantic friend, female husband), new circumlocutions (the game of Flats), and possible codes (queer, singular, whimsical) emerged over the course of the eighteenth century.[5] In short, long before sexologists turned their attention to the invert, a vernacular taxonomy of female–female eroticism had evolved. The development of this nonce taxonomy was uneven, however, as lexicographers used varying criteria to measure the relevance of a word, its meaning, and use. Giles Jacob, for instance, neglected to include female buggery or tribadism in his *New Law Dictionary* of 1729. Even with the massive undertaking of the *Oxford English Dictionary* in the nineteenth century, lexicographers were unable or unwilling to survey the entire discursive terrain: despite its coinage in the 1860s, "homosexual" did not make it into the *OED* until the 1960s. The early modern linguistic field was even less coherent. The oft-used word "tribade" failed to make it into dictionaries; "buggery," a term almost never used for women, was redefined sporadically so as to include them.

Through such choices the lexicographers enacted, rather than reconciled, the fissures of signification that I have charted throughout this book. These are the contradictions we confront as we try to pry a history of *lesbianism* out of the textual relics of the English past: the law fails to include women within its sodomy statutes and neglects to prosecute women for homoerotic acts; and dictionaries, those presumably reliable repositories of cultural signification, fail to convey accurately the range of meanings available. The presence of such faultlines demonstrates that the discursive development of *lesbianism* – by which I mean the amplification of a vocabulary, the emergence of a forensic taxonomy, the eventual pathologization, and the consolidation of a self-conscious identity – was neither direct nor inevitable.

Since the conclusion of chapter 3, when I contrasted the rhetorics of monarchical eroticism available to Queens Elizabeth and Anne, each of my chapters has registered transformations in representations of female–female eroticism over the course of the seventeenth century. Each chapter has ended with an allusion to how these trends set the stage for Enlightenment attempts to link erotic desire and practices more tightly to gender and to personal identity. The last chapter, in particular, argued that by the end of the seventeenth century, chaste feminine love had begun to be imbued with associations of tribadism. The convergence of the tribade and the friend was gradual and uneven, but it was nonetheless decisive. After making discursive contact, the attributes associated with these figures would never again be easily disentangled. Attempts to separate them would entail, at specific historical moments, different representational strategies, new ideological work. By the end of the eighteenth century, as my epigram from Hester Thrale Piozzi's diary entry of 1778 attests, "Ovid's Iphis & Ianthe no longer seems out of Possibility." Once considered so unlikely as to be routinely denied, female–female eroticism, this diarist suggests, is on the representational rise; indeed a diary entry of 1795 states: "'tis now grown common to suspect Impossibilities – (such as I think 'em) – whenever two Ladies live too much together."[6]

The various ways that such "impossibilities" are placed under suspicion during the eighteenth century have been analyzed insightfully by Susan Lanser and Elizabeth Wahl. According to Lanser, modern patriarchy is formed not simply through an ideology of sexual difference (as argued by Thomas Laqueur and Michael McKeon), but through an ideology of *hetero*sexual difference; the historical effect of the conflation of gender and eroticism is conveyed by her use of the term *heteropatriarchy*. Attending carefully to differentiations of discursive domain (literary, medical, legal, obscene), narrative genre, and social class, she describes an unprecedented proliferation of discourses about female intimacies, beginning early in the century and reaching greatest intensity in the 1740s and 1750s. By the end of the eighteenth century, the tribade and chaste friend had been joined by the female husband, the romantic friend, the sapphist, and the "homo-adventurer" (a term coined by Lanser).[7] The increase in discourse about these figures, she contends, correlates with a shift in the understanding of female anatomy, as hermaphroditic models of explanation give way to models based on the legibility of "masculine" attributes such as clothing, manner of walking, a loud voice. As the explanatory model based on anatomical deviations hidden beneath the clothes is replaced by a model of fashion accouterments worn on the surface of the body, an important reconfiguration of female homoeroticism occurs. With a new emphasis on public legibility, the social markers of class and race become increasingly pertinent – one effect of which is that women of gentry status who presented themselves as devoted lifetime companions were protected by an armor of virtue. Insulating themselves from the taint of deviance through their display of innocence, such intimate friends could be viewed as performing a social role compatible with notions of British nationhood.[8]

Such intimate friendships, however, are, as Thrale Piozzi attests, *susceptible* to interpretations of immorality. There seems to have developed an ideological continuum structured along the axes of innocence and suspicion, a continuum complicated by the fact that some "virtuous" friends participated in cultural practices associated with the "immoral" women from whom they attempted to distance themselves. (The decorous "Ladies of Llangollen," for instance, wore masculine riding habits above their skirts.) It is in part through these complicated processes of identification and disavowal that an identifiable social *type* was born: the sapphist, a woman whose transparent legibility as a lover of women meant that she could be publicly identified by any savvy viewer. Whereas crossdressing women in the earlier period were more likely to be interpreted as whores than tribades, by the end of the eighteenth century, sapphism became one of the primary meanings of female masculinity. The sapphist, in other words, occupied a social role; she embodied a publicly recognizable identity.

How did the discourse of impossibility change from indicating a benign to a suspect category of female behavior? Elizabeth Wahl argues that an important ideological shift started, first in France then in England, as "sexualized" models began to be associated with "idealized" models of female intimacy. Moving between English and French representations of female conduct in juridical and medical texts, libertine and obscene literature, the writing of the *précieuses* and English women, Wahl argues that the boundaries between idealized and sexualized models began to blur, with the effect that "the idea of female homosexuality was gradually acquiring the ambiguous status of an 'open secret.'"[9] In the present chapter, I provide my own reading of the cultural transformations already broached in chapters 5 and 6, and thus construct a bridge between my discussion of tribadism and chaste friendship and the phenomena analyzed by Lanser and Wahl. In so doing, I complicate the binary model I have used thus far to structure my historical chronology. Having already considered the historical perversion of the chaste friend by the tribade, I turn back to the trope that accompanies this perversion and that, in fact, haunts the entire renaissance of *lesbianism*. As Thrale Piozzi's remark attests, the trope of impossibility, signified by Ovid's story of Iphis and Ianthe, epitomizes the fate of female–female love up to the end of the eighteenth century.[10] The *amor impossibilis* is not reducible to a discursive figure like the friend or the tribade, but rather functions as a thematic convention within a long literary heritage. Related to both the rhetoric of idealized love in the friendship tradition and the convention of sex transformation in the discourse of tribadism, the *amor impossibilis* is, like them, derived from classical models and, like them, undergoes substantial transformation during the renaissance of *lesbianism*.

The *amor impossibilis* also is directly linked to the concept of Nature, a concept that implicitly undergirds most early modern thematizations of *lesbian* love. Nature remains a stable conceptual ground for such representations until the middle of the seventeenth century. By the eighteenth century, however, Nature itself had been subjected to intense scrutiny, and this could not help but affect the meaning of female erotic contact. The reconsideration of the meaning of Nature was one aspect of Enlightenment thought which, as Lanser reminds us, was important to the general cultural milieu of sapphism:

By questioning the foundations of the natural, by valuing private pleasure and personal happiness, by challenging conventional religious and political authorities, Enlightenment inquiry opened up new ways to think about same-sex desire; it is no accident that Diderot's famous proclamation, "Nothing that exists can be against or outside nature," appears within one of the century's most radical discourses on sexuality, the "Suite de l'entretien," which legitimates both masturbation and sex "with a like being [,] male or female."[11]

Glimpses of concern about the meaning of Nature can be seen in the recognition of Nature's multiplicity and creativity in the natural philosophy of Bacon and Newton.[12] They also can be seen, more warily, in seventeenth-century medical discourse, where Nature is deployed as a powerful ideological constraint, mediating concepts of the female anatomical body while legitimating the production of scientific knowledge about it. As discussed in chapter 2, when medical texts (nervously) advocate "lifting the veil" of Nature, they construct Nature as an intrinsic, material phenomenon that can be empirically revealed, described, and classified. Each of these discourses of the "new science" attempts to wrest Nature away from the theological terms set in place when sodomy was first formally condemned by the third Lateran Council of 1179. By 1250 concepts of Nature were firmly entrenched in medieval canon law, part of the church's attempt to expel sodomy as the *crimen contra naturam*.[13] A fourteenth-century commentator, for instance, stated that "whenever humans sin against nature, whether in sexual intercourse, worshipping idols, or any other un-natural act, the church may always exercise its jurisdiction . . . For by such sins God himself is offended, *since He is the author of nature*."[14]

Theology, medicine, and natural philosophy, however, do not address the role of Nature from the standpoint of female–female desire. Indeed, Lanser notes that despite the protest against capital punishment for (male–male) sodomy in the texts of the *Philosophes*, female homoeroticism is hardly mentioned at all. In contrast, a long literary heritage explicitly links female homoeroticism to the constraints of Nature. Faced with the impossible nature of their love, female characters – from translations of Ovid's story of Iphis and Ianthe and the reincarnations of his tale in Renaissance drama, through the romance tradition of Ariosto and Sidney – appeal to Nature for help in a soliloquized lament of distress. In her continuation of this romance tradition, Margaret Cavendish puts the concept of Nature under extreme pressure while devising a unique (and from the perspective of *lesbianism*, unsatisfying) compromise with social convention. Katherine Philips's passionate poems of female friendship likewise address the terms of Nature; but rather than directly confront Nature in the course of lamenting an *amor impossibilis*, Philips refigures Nature in the course of celebrating her love and laments the folly of an uncomprehending world.

Philips's mid-seventeenth-century reformulation of the terms of female desire occurs within the context of an increasingly voluble literary discussion about the nature of female bonds. Several poems written between 1645 and 1730 contextualize Philips's intervention. While some poems carry on the tradition inaugurated by Philips by recommending love between women as preferable to that between women and men, other poems bemoan the exclusivity of female intimacy and attempt to interrupt it through the forceful persuasions of a would-be male lover. Recognizing that the proclivity for female bonds may not disappear naturally after adolescence but could prevail as an adult resistance to men and marriage, these lyrics seek to fashion in their addressees a heteronormative relation to desire. The Renaissance rubric under which feminine women were represented as naturally, developmentally, without any visible effort, moving from intimacies with girlhood friends to marriage with men was slowly replaced by a conceptual paradigm in which women would need to be *told* to do so.

Thus the "friendship so curst" of my title. A line from John Hoadley's admonitory lyric of 1730, it gestures simultaneously toward either end of the historical spectrum and the literary tradition surveyed in this chapter. Initially, the concept of a "friendship so curst" indicates the self-articulation of a female speaker who, in a dramatic moment of "private" self-expression, laments the unnaturalness of her love. Whether expressed by a crossdressed female speaker who concedes that fulfillment is impossible, or by a character who discovers that her male lover is really a woman in disguise, the speaker grieves having been cursed by Nature, and anticipates only a magical solution to her dilemma. By the end of the seventeenth century, "friendship so curst" literally refers to a male poet's cursory summation of the horror of female bonds; it is a curse thrown back onto women by men all too aware of their exclusion from female intimacy.

Discourses about female homoeroticism in the late seventeenth and early eighteenth centuries drew from and expressed prior understandings of female bodily intimacy, even as those understandings mutated under changed cultural circumstances. Late medieval continental romances, in fact, set the stage for future confrontations with the meaning of Nature.[15] Many of these texts resolve the predicament of the *amor impossibilis* by the miracle of sex transformation. For instance, *Yde et Olyve*, a thirteenth-century continuation of the epic poem, *Huon de Bordeaux* (translated into English in 1543), depicts the marriage of the crossdressed heroine Ide (somewhat against her will) by the Holy Roman Emperor to his daughter, Olyve. Feigning illness to avoid consummation, Ide spends the next fifteen days "clippying and kyssyng," after which she confesses privately to her wife that she is a woman. Olyve responds:

My right swete lover, discomforte not yourselfe / for ye shall not be bewrayed for me nother to no man nor woman livinge / we are wedded togyther, I wil be good and trewe to you syn ye have kept youre selfe so trewly / with you I will use my time and passe my destany syn it is thus, for I se wel it is the pleasure of our lord godde.

When the Emperor discovers Ide's secret, he decrees that she should be burned, "for he sayd he wold not suffre suche boggery to be used." Ide is saved by being magically transformed into a man.[16]

Olyve's advice to her "husband" – "discomforte not yourselfe" – proves to be an ironic exception to the literary tradition that evolves, in which the narrative spirals into a heart-felt lament that fulfillment is unattainable. As a variation within the tradition of female complaint, the homoerotic lament of the *amor impossibilis* functions as a governing convention until the mid-seventeenth century. In Ariosto's *Orlando Furioso* (1516; translated into English in 1532), for instance, the Spanish princess Fiordispina, in love with the crossdressed Bradamant, pours out her distress in an apostrophe to Love:

Never was any torment so cruel... but mine is crueller. Were it a question of any other love, evil or virtuous, I could hope to see it consummated, and I should know how to cull the rose from the briar. My desire alone can have no fulfillment. / If you wanted to torment me, Love, because my happy state offended you, why could you not rest content with those torments which other lovers experience? Neither among humans nor among beasts have I ever come across a woman loving a woman; to a woman another woman does not seem beautiful, nor does a hind to a hind, a ewe to a ewe. / By land, sea, and air I alone suffer thus cruelly at your hands – you have done this to make an example of my aberration, the ultimate one in your power.[17]

Perceiving herself to be the original "woman loving woman," Fiordispina compares her state to those of hinds and ewes. Moving rhetorically from a description of the beasts of Nature to other illicit loves, she judges her folly to be the greater, as decreed by a personified "Nature, who is all-powerful." Hoping to trick herself if not Nature, Fiordispina costumes Bradamant in female attire, under the expectation that seeing her beloved in feminine dress will abate her desire. This attempt at self-deception fails: as the women share a bed that night, "How many prayers and vows did she not offer that night to Mahomet and all the gods, asking them to change Bradamant's sex for the better by a clear and self-evident miracle!"[18] Her predicament is resolved by the appearance of Bradamant's twin brother who, in a homoerotic twist, gains her affection through his own crossdressed impersonation of his sister.

The rhetoric of lament, the litany of beasts, and the fantasy of a miraculous sex-change (achieved literally in *Huon of Bordeaux* and metaphorically through the introduction of a brother in *Orlando Furioso*) are indebted to a classical precedent, which has proven to be the most influential depiction of *lesbian* love in the Western literary tradition: Ovid's story of Iphis and Ianthe from the ninth book of his *Metamorphoses* (lines 666–797).[19] Crossdressed from infancy by her mother to protect her from her father's decree that any female born to his wife be killed, the adolescent Iphis is betrothed by her unsuspecting father to the maiden Ianthe. Both girls are deeply in love with each other. Nonetheless, Iphis cannot see her way toward marriage. In William Caxton's 1480 manuscript translation of Ovid's tale, the lament of Iphis is expressed as an issue of right reason:

Iphis loved her wel. but herof she was moch descomforted whiche supposed never to have mow enjoye her ne acowple to her. This was the thyng that moste entreated her ardeu [ardor] & sorow. And the more she embraced her the more she was abasshed & moch pytously complayned oftymes wepynge. Alas what sorrow said she. What couseil shal I holde. What shal I do and to what ende may I com. Who sawe ever happene to fore me that setted hys entente in so folysshe beaulte. I am nothynge worthy of suche love. Yf the goddes had ben to me propice they hade wel kepte me from this folye. Alas they dystroye me by this fowle ameros [amorous] rage, Which is not covenable to me nomore than one kowe [cow] to desyre another. A shep [sheep] femele desyreth the masle [male] & engendre togeder And a kowe assembleth her to a bulle Every femele by ryght requyreth his masle. Ther is no femele that desireth to acowple her to another femele. And I a femele requyre as masle agaynst raison. I hade lever not to be born than to have so folisshe hope. Yet said Yphis out of Crete yssueth al mescheaunce Pasyphae was therein born whych was eschauffed with the love of a bulle. And as wood decyved him & Ioyned her self to hym. but yet passeth my love heeris [hers] in folye. For she loved better in ryght than I doo. For I may not become a masle ne she nether that abydeth for me.

The love of Iphis for Ianthe is judged a folly, a foul amorous rage, and the impossibility of enjoying Ianthe is depicted as absolute. The sorrowful Iphis accepts these terms of impossibility, proclaiming that "every femele by ryght requyreth hir masle" and articulating a bestiary of sex prohibited by Nature: a cow doesn't love a cow nor a female sheep a female sheep. Comparing her love for Ianthe to other monstrous loves wrought by the gods, Iphis notes that even the love between human and bull is "better in ryght"; at least *it* has a means of satisfaction.

Arthur Golding's 1567 verse translation likewise emphasizes the unnaturalness of Iphis's love:

> Herself a Mayden with a Mayd (ryght straunge) in love became.
> Shee scarce could stay her teares. What end remaynes for mee (quoth shee)
> How straunge a love? how uncoth? how prodigious reygnes in mee?
> If that the Gods did favor mee, they should destroy mee quyght.
> Or if they would not mee destroy, at leastwyse yit they myght
> Have given mee such a maladie as myght with nature stond,
> Or nature were acquainted with. A Cow is never fond
> Uppon a Cow, nor Mare on Mare. The Ram delyghts the Eawe,

> The Stag the Hynde, the Cocke the Hen. But never man could shew
> That female yit was tane in love with female kynd. O would
> Too God I never had beene borne.[20]

Describing her love for Ianthe as strange, uncouth, and prodigious (a term that signified monstrous), Iphis amplifies upon the bestiary theme: ewe, hind, hen all love their male counterparts who, in the natural order of things, are called by masculine names. Her strange love is beyond the "acquaintance" of Nature, an unnatural form of endogamy. Even though both heavenly and earthly authorities have consented to her marriage, she concludes, "But nature stronger than them all consenteth not theretoo. / This hindreth mee, and nothing else" (lines 891–92). It is Nature that forbids her marriage; and Nature, at least in Iphis's mind, is stronger than the gods. Iphis's mother, knowing of her daughter's plight, prays to the goddess Isis on the eve of the wedding. Isis, it turns out, proves to be stronger than Nature:

> The temple doores did tremble like a reede.
> And hornes in likenesse too the Moone about the Church did shyne,
> And Rattles made a raughtish noyse. At this same luckie signe,
> Although not wholy carelesse, yit ryght glad shee [her mother] went away.
> And *Iphys* followed after her with larger pace than ay
> Shee was accustomd. And her face continued not so whyght.
> Her strength encreased, and her looke more sharper was too syght.
> Her heare grew shorter, and shee had a much more lively spryght,
> Than when she was a wench. For thou O *Iphys* who ryght now
> A moother wert, art now a boay. (lines 920–29)

Magically transformed as she makes her way to the church, Iphis takes on the physical attributes of masculinity: a longer stride, a darker face, shorter hair. Stronger and more lively than when she was female, "*The vowes that Iphys vowd a wench, he hath performd a Lad*" (line 933).

Even as the Ovidian *amor impossibilis* thematizes the unnaturalness of female–female love, the predicament of the lamenting lover is presented in romantic, grief-stricken terms. Spokeswomen for an outrageous love, Iphis and Fiordispina nonetheless are depicted sympathetically in texts that dramatize the satisfaction of love's desire. In George Sandys's popular verse translation and commentary (1632), Iphis's lament explores the paradox that social impossibility intensifies erotic desire: "Poor Iphis loves, despaires; despaire ejects / Farre fiercer flames: a maid, a maid affects." She goes on to ask:

> What will become of me (she weeping said)
> Whom new, unknown prodigious loves invade!
> If pittifull, the Gods should have destroy'd:
> Or else have given what might have beene injoy'd.
> No Cow a Cow, no Mare a Mare pursues:

> But Harts their gentle Hindes, and Rammes their Ewes.
> So Birds together paire. Of all that move,
> No Female suffers for a Female love.
> O would I had no being! Yet, that all
> Abhord by Nature should in *Creet* befall;
> *Sol's* lust-incensed daughter lov'd a Bull:
> They male and female. Mine, ô farre more full
> Of uncouth fury! for she pleas'd her blood;
> And stood his errour in a Cow of wood:
> Shee, for her craft, had an adulterer.
> Should all the world their daring wits confer:
> Should *Daedalus* his waxen wings renue,
> And hither fly; what could his cunning doe!
> Can art convert a virgin to a boy?
> Or fit *Ianthe* for a maidens joy?
> No, fixe thy minde; compose thy vast desires:
> O quench these ill advis'd and foolish fires!
> Thinke of thy sex, or even thy selfe abuse:
> What may be, seeke; and love as femals use.
> Hope wings desire: hope *Cupids* flight sustains:
> In thee thy Sexe this deads.[21]

Certain that "No Female suffers for a Female love" and that her love is "Abhord by Nature," Iphis vacillates between bemoaning impossibility and indulging in the "hope" that "wings desire." During this vacillation, she articulates a number of possible outcomes to her impossible plight. Turning first to the magical powers of art – "Can art convert a virgin to a boy?" – she then contemplates self-abuse (autoeroticism) as a better alternative to her miserable situation. But these possible solutions come to nothing, and she returns to the problem of Nature as the prohibition on her satisfaction:

>   No watch restraines
> Our deare imbrace, nor husbands jealousies,
> Nor rigorous Sires; nor she her selfe denies:
> Yet not to be injoy'd. Nor canst thou bee
> Happy in her; though men and Gods agree!
> Now also all to my desires accord:
> What they can give, the easie Gods afford;
> What me, my father, hers, her selfe, would please,
> Displeaseth Nature; stronger then all these.
> Shee, shee forbids. (p. 421)

The two "shee"s repeated in the final line could refer sequentially to Ianthe then to Nature, or to an emphatic negative attributed to Nature. The absoluteness of Nature's displeasure echoes throughout the rest of the lament, which ends plaintively, "We both are Brides: but where is the Bride-groome?" (p. 422).

In his moralizing commentary, Sandys focuses not on the unnaturalness of Iphis's love but on her articulation of hope. Glossing the magical remedy of transsexuality, Sandys converts Iphis's confrontation with Nature into a tale of spiritual faith: "By this the Ancient declared, that men should despaire of nothing; since althings were in the power of the Gods to give; and give they would what was justly implored." He goes on to assure the reader skeptical of sex change: "Nor shall wee be hardly induced to believe that women have beene changed into men, if we give any credit to Authors either ancient or moderne," citing numerous authorities, from Pliny to Montaigne, describing instances of women turning into men. Sandys concludes on a note indebted to the medical commentators of his day: "But it is with out example that a man at any time became a woman. From whence we may derive this morall, that as it is preposterous in Nature, which ever aimes at perfection, when men degenerate into effeminacy; so contrarily commendable, when women aspire to manly wisdome and fortitude." Secure that Nature has the final say in legislating gender and its mutability, Sandys represents Iphis's desire to be changed into a man, not as a dangerous transgression, but a praiseworthy "aspiration" toward "manly wisdome and fortitude" (pp. 449–50).

Ovid's tale of misplaced desire and gender mutability motivated not only the continental romances of Ide and Olyve, Fiordispina and Bradamant, but many English romances and stageplays as well. In Sir Philip Sidney's *New Arcadia* (1590), Philoclea is anguished by her erotic attraction for the woman she believes to be Zelmane (in actuality, the crossdressed male knight Pyrocles). Languishing within the labyrinth of the *amor impossibilis*, she picks up Iphis's cue that impossibility intensifies desire:

[I]t is the impossibility that doth torment me: for unlawful desires are punished after the effect of enjoying, but unpossible desires are punished in the desire itself. O then, O ten times unhappy that I am, since where in all other hope kindleth love, in me despair should be the bellows of my affection; and of all despairs the most miserable which is drawn from impossibility. The most covetous man longs not to get riches out of a ground which never can bear anything. Why? Because it is impossible. The most ambitious wight vexeth not his wits to climb into heaven. Why? Because it is impossible. Alas, then, O love, why dost thou in thy beautiful sampler set such a work for my desire to take out, which is as much impossible?[22]

Invoking "impossibility" and "impossible" six times within nine sentences, Philoclea contrasts her desire not to those of beasts but to those of covetous and ambitious men – and her fate is worse than theirs for they do not attempt to possess what they cannot attain. Focused less on Nature than on the nature of desire, her lament implicitly reframes the issue of Nature. Noting a difference between unlawful and impossible desires, she finds a different form of punishment appropriate to each: with despair the "bellows" of her "affection," her desire is punished at its very inception, prior to any "effect of enjoying." Nor is she particularly satisfied with the option bequeathed to her from the Ovidian heritage. She has come to "wish either herself or Zelmane a man, that there might succeed a blessed marriage betwixt them. But when that wish had once displayed his ensign in her mind, then followed whole squadrons of longings that so it might be, with a main battle of mislikings and repinings against their creation, that so it was not."[23] With the words "against their creation," Philoclea seems to register an ambivalence about bodily metamorphosis. With her longing "that so it might be" warring against her misliking "that so it was not," Philoclea implies that there is something wrong with sex transformation as a solution to her dilemma. Rather than resolve these plot issues in the traditional manner, Sidney focuses on the subjective experience of desire, its recursive intensification of torment and despair.

In his dramatic retelling of Ovid's tale in *Gallathea*, John Lyly's crossdressed Phyllida confronts her love for the crossdressed Gallathea in a rhetoric similar to that of Iphis: "Poor Phyllida, what shouldst thou think of thyself, that lovest one that I fear me is as thyself is?.... If it be so, Phyllida, how desperate is thy case! If it be not, how doubtful! For if she be a maiden, there is no hope of my love; if a boy, a hazard."[24] Enhancing the dramatic conflict of disguised identities with a subplot rivalry between the goddesses Venus and Diana, Lyly positions the goddess of love, as the magician of sex change, against Diana, the spokesperson for Nature. Although the play leaves unspoken which girl will be transformed into a boy, it makes clear that such a transformation is the only means for a happy conclusion:

DIANA: Now, things falling out as they do, you must leave these fond, fond affections. Nature will have it so, necessity must.
GALLATHEA: I will never love any but Phyllida. Her love is engraven in my heart with her eyes.
PHYLLIDA: Nor I any but Gallathea, whose faith is imprinted in my thoughts by her words.
NEPTUNE: An idle choice, strange and foolish, for one virgin to dote on another and to imagine a constant faith where there can be no cause of affection. How like you this, Venus?
VENUS: I like well and allow it. They shall both be possessed of their wishes, for never shall it be said that Nature or Fortune shall overthrow love and faith... Then shall it be seen that I can turn one of them to be a man, and that I will.
DIANA: Is it possible?
VENUS: What is to love or the mistress of love unpossible? Was it not Venus that did the like to Iphis and Ianthes?   (5.3.125–46)

In response to Diana's arrogation of the terms of Nature and Neptune's assumption that, absent a penis, "there can be no cause of affection," Venus takes matters, quite literally, in hand. Rewriting Ovid's Isis with her own name,[25] and disdaining the possibility that mere Nature should overthrow love, Venus trumps Diana by maintaining that nothing is "unpossible" to the mistress of love. With this move against her rival, Venus begins to disengage the terms of the *amor impossibilis*, for love or *amor* is precisely what makes the consummation of these desires possible.[26]

Like the model letters published by Gervase Markham discussed in chapter 4, sex transformation in these texts is promoted as the imaginative means to elude impossibility: "Yet could I wish my Sexe changed for thy sake," writes the second correspondent to her beloved in the country, then her friend's "sweetnesse and vertue" need not be buried in a "maiden Sepulchre, or lost in the wildnesse of mens frenzies." Disposing of a future imagined as either a barren virginity or a continual rape, this writer's indulgence in a transsexual fantasy concedes, as does each of these texts in the Ovidian tradition, that only differently sexed bodies can be joined in the social compact of marriage, and thus experience "consummation." This impediment – to which the texts give the name of Nature – is initially viewed as absolute. Nonetheless, with a little divine aid, the body can be changed, betrothals celebrated, matrimony solemnized, and erotic longing fulfilled. All of which suggests that from the perspective of romance, the problem posed by the *amor impossibilis* is less desire itself than the intractability of the physical body and the body's social function as a legible marker of gender within the patriarchal organization of reproduction. If the body could be brought in accord with the *social* dictates of Nature, then all would be well. The solution of sex transformation mandates neither the eradication of desire nor its redirection toward a different object, but a change in the desiring subject's body. Even as it concedes to a system of eroticism linked to gendered binaries, it performs, if unwittingly, an implicit disarticulation of the body from desire.

All of these utopian longings – the temporary separation of desire from the body, the wish for a marriage based on desire, and the fantasy of bodily metamorphosis – hinge on a direct confrontation with the claims and orders of Nature. Yet, the attitude toward Nature in these laments is not uniform. In Golding's and Sandys's translations, Nature functions primarily as a taboo, prohibiting certain couplings. In Sidney's romance, the question of Nature seems subordinated to the more psychologically complex crux of the origin of desire and its modes of intensification. In Lyly's drama, the reign of Nature is judged to be inadequate, for homoerotic desire questions the ways and means of love. Love, at least when personified by a powerful goddess, can conquer Nature.

The utopian aspirations articulated in these laments are given powerful expression in a Middle Scots poem known only as Poem XLIX in *The Maitland Quarto Manuscript* (1586).[27] In this lyric a female speaker contemplates the perfection of her female beloved and proclaims herself to have been ravished by their affection for each other. The speaker then compares the quality of their love to that of a series of famous male pairs – Perithous and Theseus, Achilles and Patroclus, David and Jonathan – arguing that women love with more constancy. Appropriating the classical discourse of idealized male *amicitia*,[28] Poem XLIX renegotiates the possible terms of female–female amity by invoking a historical precedent for such liaisons – Ruth and Naomi – and implicitly envisioning a world in which women can marry. Recognizing that such a world does not yet exist, the speaker envisions the next best thing: an Ovidian metamorphosis. Asking God to transform her into a man, the speaker confidently asserts, "No brutus then sould caus ws [us] smart / as we doe now vnhappie wemen / Then sould we bayth [both] with Ioyful hairt / honour and bliss ƺe [the] band of hymen." Such divine intervention would create heaven on earth:

Then our mair perfyte amitie	Then our more perfect amity
mair worthie recompence sould merit	more worthy recompense should merit
In heaven eternal deitie	In hevin eternall deity
amang the goddis till Inherit ...	among the gods to inherit ...
freindschip and amitie sa suire	friendship and amity so sure
with sa greit feruencie and force	with so great fervency and force
Sa constantlie quhilk sall Induire	So constantly which shall endure
That not bot deid sall ws divorce ...	That not both death shall us divorce ...
no troubill / torment / greif / or tein	no trouble / torment / grief / or sorrow
nor erthlie thing sall ws disseuer	nor earthly thing shall us dissever
Sic constancie sall ws mantein	Such constancy shall we maintain
In perfyte amitie for euer.	In perfect amity forever.

Even as it appropriates the magical conclusion of Ovidian prose and verse narrative, Poem XLIX refuses to accede to the unnaturalness of its *amor*, refuses to mourn its own impossibility. This break from the Ovidian tradition is enabled through a change in form: as lyric utterance, the temporality of this poem stays with, and in the experience of, desire. Regardless of the fact that it cannot inhabit that future *now*, it elaborates the utopian aspirations of the poetic persona, who despite her willingness to be metamorphosed into a man, remains gendered female. Narrative and dramatic structure, and their usual accompaniments – sequence, causation, temporality, teleology – are left behind.[29] Her female voicings stay in the present moment of desire, even as she proleptically articulates a vision of human love existing outside human time. The poem's temporal grasp is expansive, balancing the voice of present longing ("as we do now unhappy women"), the construction of an authorizing past (the biblical Ruth and Naomi), and the anticipation of a radically different future ("perfect amity forever"). In its incorporation of a past and present desire in an eternal present, Poem XLIX comes very close to imagining that future into being.

Given the importance of the trope of Nature to the tradition of homoerotic lament, it is remarkable that Poem XLIX attempts to leave the constraints of Nature behind. Instead of rehearsing the prohibitive Ovidian catalogue of beasts,

Poem XLIX offers an enabling canon of great homoerotic loves. Instead of bemoaning what cannot happen, it focuses on what can and has. Rewriting human history, it elides Nature as a governing force. It then lays claim to the institution of marriage and bolsters this claim with a healthy dose of religious devotion.

In appealing for a sex change to make female marriage possible, Poem XLIX returns to conventional terms of intelligibility. But it does so with a difference. Imbued with the energy of its present-tense desire and articulated through the lyrical voice of a homoerotic persona, this poem attempts to construct for female–female love a place *within* culture. Surpassing Helena's elegiac invocation of the Anglican marriage ceremony, this lyric insists on the right of women to form a socially and religiously legitimized conjugal pair. If a divinely administered sex change is imagined as the only means by which such a possibility can be materialized, then, according to this poem, so be it: desire, rather than gender or the body, is what counts.

Poem XLIX offers a model of lyric expression that can guide us in our efforts to understand the modes through which the homoerotic lament is negotiated by subsequent female writers. Margaret Cavendish clearly draws from this tradition when, in *The Convent of Pleasure* (1668), Lady Happy mourns her attraction to the Princess:

My Name is *Happy*, and so was my Condition, before I saw this Princess; but now I am like to be the most unhappy Maid alive: But why may not I love a Woman with the same affection I could a Man?
No, no, Nature is Nature, and still will be
The same she was from all Eternity. (4.1. p. 32)

Condensing Iphis's lament to the brief question, "Why may not I love a woman?" and answering with an emphatic negative, "No, no, Nature is Nature," Lady Happy finds herself in a bit of a quandary. Determined to worship the "Goddess Nature" and all the pleasures she allows, Lady Happy now finds herself beseeching Nature to come to her aid: "O Nature, O you gods above, / Suffer me not to fall in Love; / O strike me dead here in this place / Rather than fall into disgrace" (4.1. p. 40). Whereas Iphis wished never to have been born (implying the desire to have saved herself from the torment of desire), Lady Happy wishes to be struck dead rather than face the social opprobrium she assumes would accompany a homoerotic union. When the Prince(ss) asks, "My dearest Mistress, do you shun my Company? is your Servant become an offence to your sight?" Lady Happy replies in such a way as to position Nature against her homoerotic love: "No, Servant! Your Presence is more acceptable to me than the Presence of our Goddess Nature, for which she, I fear will punish me, for loving you more than I ought to love you" (4.1. p. 32).

Earlier in the play, Monsieur Take-Pleasure smugly reports that if Lady Happy is, as she says, "a Votress to Nature, she must be a Mistress to Men" (2.1. p. 12), thus making a bawdy joke that depends on the heterosexual and procreative bias of Nature. In keeping with this bias, Madame Mediator, the voice of female anxiety in the play, admonishes, "you know Womens Kisses are unnatural, and me-thought they kissed with more alacrity then Women use, a kind of Titillation, and more Vigorous" (5.2. p. 48).[30] Yet, as mentioned in chapter 4, the Prince(ss) convinces Lady Happy to kiss precisely by invoking the naturalness of women's kisses. These competing claims about the nature of female kissing reveal that the two interpretations were simultaneously available and either could be applied to a "feminine" lady like Lady Happy.

What does Nature mean if identical behaviors can be deemed both natural and unnatural? *Is* Nature, in fact, natural? *The Convent of Pleasure* reiterates the tradition I have surveyed insofar as Nature continues to govern the possibility of homoaffiliation. At the same time, the terms by which Nature is understood have changed since the late sixteenth century. Nature is not self-evidently natural in an environment so obviously fashioned to accord with women's wishes. Laura Rosenthal points out that "[i]n the convent, nature is *not* nature but, like everything else, a performance"[31] – artificial, consciously constructed, designed to intensify seasonal variety within the convent's walls. Cavendish's amplification of the charms of the natural world denaturalizes Nature, and this denaturalization is mirrored in the fluidity of gender roles and the playful pastoralism of female shepherds and shepherdesses discussed in chapter 4. Nature is, at least temporarily, in female hands. This feminine usurpation of Nature is abandoned, however, when Cavendish exposes the Princess as a Prince, taking recourse in the metaphorical transformation of sex and thereby conceding to the conventional requirements of Ovidian closure.

This tension between a homoerotic resistance to the heteroerotic bias of Nature and a capitulation to Nature's social demands is a hallmark of Cavendish's work.[32] The disarticulation of desire from the body, on the one hand, and the marital injunctions of Nature, on the other, are dramatized, for instance, in Cavendish's play, *The Presence*. A Princess selects a sailor as her ideal mate, much to the chagrin of her father, who condemns the sailor to death for his presumption against rank. But before he can be hanged, the sailor is revealed to be a woman and therefore "in no wayes capable of Marrying your Princess; for this Person is not only a Woman, but a Princess her self; being Daughter to the Emperor of *Persia*."[33] When the Princess is asked if her "Melancholy Passion of Love" is now over, she replies, "My Melancholy is past, but not my Love; for that will live so long as I shall live, and will remain pure in my Soul, when my body is dead and turn'd to dust" (p. 84). Although marriage between women is impossible, *The Presence* suggests, an enduring love of one woman for another is not. The plot is resolved with a conventional romance doubling, as the sailor with whom the Princess fell in love turns out to be not the Persian Princess, but her male twin. Although such multiplications of identity enable Cavendish's drama to reach a marital conclusion, they do not undercut the homoeroticism of the plot, which is made explicit by the Fool: "Lady, you speak extravagantly, talking of Chast Love, when as never Lover was Chast, for they commit Adultery either in Mind or Body" (p. 86). Chaste love for another woman, it would seem, is inherently impossible – not because it is the epitome of the *amor impossibilis*, but because *all* lovers, whether chaste or not, commit erotic acts, either imaginatively or physically.

In Cavendish's prose romance, *Assaulted and Pursued Chastity* (1656), another Princess falls in love with a crossdressed heroine, initially an unnamed Lady who later takes on the names of Affectionata and Travellia. As the personification of chastity, this Lady's ostensible goal, however much she roams the world, is to maintain her virginity; the major threat to her bodily integrity is the Prince of the Kingdom of Sensuality, a married man who falls in love with and seeks to conquer her. Early in the story, the Lady, upon being shipwrecked during a journey, is held captive in the Kingdom of Sensuality, where she is subjected to a conventional and highly suspect lecture on Nature by a bawd masquerading as a "virtuous mistress":

her mistress began to read her lectures of Nature, telling her she should use her beauty whilst she had it, and not to waste her youth idly, but to make the best profit of both, to purchase pleasure and delight; besides, said she, Nature hath made nothing vainly, but to some useful end; and nothing merely for itself, but for a common benefit and general good, as earth, water, air and fire, sun, moon, stars, light, heat, cold and the like. So beauty with strength and appetites, either to delight her creatures that are in being; or to the end, or ways to procure more by procreation; for Nature only lives by survivors, and that cannot be without communication and society. Wherefore it is a sin against Nature to be reserved and coy, and take heed, said she, of offending Nature, for she is a great and powerful goddess, transforming all things out of one shape and into another.[34]

Ventriloquizing the standard trope of *carpe diem* (and echoing, in the process, Jupiter's rhetorical seductions in Heywood's *Troia Brittanica* discussed in chapter 6), the Bawd defines the "great and powerful" Nature as pro-heteroerotic and pro-procreation. Nature's power to transform "all things out of one shape and into another" works, in this case, not to authorize sex change but to "procure more [creatures] by procreation." Procuring and procreation, it would seem, are one and the same natural activity. The bawd's arguments, specious though they be, do not offend the Lady, for were it not for the bawd's pecuniary designs on her chastity, these arguments would represent a common sentiment of the seventeenth-century love lyric.

The Lady escapes from the bawd, as well as from the more threatening clutches of the Prince of Sensuality, by disguising herself as a man and taking to sea. Under the physical guise of masculinity, and under the symbolic guise of chastity, Travellia, as she now calls herself, is adopted by an old man, with whom she travels to an unnamed kingdom of colorful heathens. There, Travellia proves herself to be a powerful orator and converts the heathens to Christianity. A series of misadventures takes her to the shores of the Kingdom of Amity where, because of her intrinsic nobility, she becomes military general to the female ruler. The Queen of Amity, at war with the King of Amour (a result of having denied his offer of marriage), quickly falls in love with the disguised stranger. A series of battles ensue, some on the plain, some in the heart. At one point, the Queen of Amity is taken prisoner and Travellia, "was high enraged, which choler begot a masculine and courageous spirit in her; for though she could not have those affections in her for the Queen as a man, yet she admired her heroic virtues, and loved her as a kind and gracious princess to her, which obligations made her impatient of revenge" (p. 95). The Queen, it turns out, has fewer compunctions about loving a woman. It is the Prince of Sensuality, still hot on Travellia's trail, who sees through her disguise and takes it upon himself to give the Queen the bad news:

I must tell you, you are in love; and those you love, although there is a society of all excellencies, yet cannot return such love you desire; for you have placed your affection upon a woman, who hath concealed her sex, in taking the habit of a man, and might more confirm your mistake by the actions of a soldier. I know not . . . how kind you have found her, but I have found her cruel[;] then telling the story from the first time he saw her until that present.

When the Queen had heard his relation, her colour came and went, moved by her mixed passions, anger and love; angry that she was deceived, *yet still did love, as wishing she had been a man.* (p. 112, emphasis mine)

As in the previous tales, the revelation of the beloved's sex does not alter the nature of her desire; nor, with the Prince's recognition of the possibility that Travellia has been kind to the Queen while cruel to him, is that desire presented as beyond the pale. In contrast to the traditional prayers for sex transformation, however, Cavendish's Queen prays to Cupid for a rather different change – of her heart:

> *Thou powerful God of Love, that shoots from high,*
> *One leaden Arrow in my breast let fly,*
> *To quench that scorching heat thou mad'st to burn,*
> *Unless a Woman to a Man can turn.*
> *With that the God of Love did pity take,*
> *Quenched out the first, and did a new Fire make;*
> *Yet was it weak, as being made but new,*

> *But being kindled, it much better grew.*
> *At last, the Flame got hold upon the King,*
> *Which did much Joy unto each Kingdom bring.* (pp. 112–13)

The ambiguous syntax of "[u]nless a Woman to a Man can turn" suggests simultaneously the ability to turn toward and to turn into a man. Either way, what is important is that, despite the fantastical imaginings (including purple-skinned people) that animate her stories, sex transformation is excluded from Cavendish's allegorical romance. Instead, the Queen of Amity prays for her love to be directed toward her former enemy, the King of Amour, and with this magic accomplished, the realms of Amity and Amour are united, satisfying simultaneously the basic requirements of an allegory of companionate marriage and royalist reunification. As for the Prince of Sensuality, his abandoned wife is finally and conveniently dead; and Travellia, her chastity now safe, has come to love her former tormentor. The Queen gives permission to General Travellia to marry, saying to the Prince of Sensuality, "I have promised your mistress to protect her against your outrageous assaults; but since your suit is just, and your treaty civil, I will yield her to you, upon that condition you carry her not out of my kingdom; for since I cannot marry her, and so make her my husband, I will keep her if I can, and so make her my friend" (p. 114). As befits the Queen of *Amity*, she ends up not only with a masculine *Amour*, but with a female *friend* who, with her gender transitivity still intact, becomes Viceroy in the Kingdom of Amity. In a mutually beneficial compromise, love and friendship are triangulated between the King, the Queen, and her best friend. For Travellia's part, in her own negotiation of the claims of Sensuality and Amity, she tells the Prince "that he should govern her, and she would govern the kingdom" (p. 116).

This ending, which resolves in quick order what have been represented throughout the tale as intractable problems, is as complex as it is neat. The reconfiguration of the beloved as a friend finesses the Ovidian heritage by providing an alternative compromise and mode of compensation. Both in terms of the literary heritage it reworks and the trajectory of its narrative, *Assaulted and Pursued Chastity* displaces the trope of the partner-who-changes-sex (or the beloved-replaced-by-her-brother) with a triangular model of domestic heterosexuality and feminine friendship, and in the process converts erotic attachments into friendly political alliances. The emotional affects associated with Travellia are split in two: within the context of companionate marriage, Cavendish seems to imply, the only thing that differentiates a husband from a friend is sex.

The incompatibility of this fantasy of symmetrical male and female companions with the plot is registered in the narrative's title: assaulted and pursued chastity hardly promises a future of conjugal bliss. Nonetheless, having converted the problem of the *amor impossibilis* from one of Nature, desire, and the body into one of domestic harmony and carefully parsed hierarchy, Cavendish offers a seventeenth-century form of feminism in which men can personally subject individual women as long as women govern the social polity. Domestic heterosexuality, in this fantasy kingdom, turns out to be congruent with a royalist feminist politics born out of Cavendish's experience of social upheaval during the Civil Wars. As a lady-in-waiting to Queen Henrietta Maria during the exile of the royal household, and as wife to one of Charles's less successful military commanders, Cavendish experienced firsthand the political yearnings of women and the political failures of men.[35] She seems to have translated this experience of female companionship and royalist aspiration into her vision of the amicable relations among love, sensuality, amity, and political rule. But the cost of her compromise among marriage, friendship, and politics is, from a *lesbian* point of view, very high: indeed, in Cavendish's work, the articulation of female–female love seems to have hit an impasse, subordinated to dreams of companionate marriage and a utopian political order.

"[W]e may generally conclude the Marriage of a Friend to be the Funeral of a Friendship; for then all former Endearments run naturally into the Gulf of that new and strict Relation, and there, like Rivers in the Sea, they lose themselves for ever."[36] So wrote Katherine Philips, in a letter to her literary friend, Sir Charles Cotterell, rejecting precisely the compromise between friendship and marriage that Cavendish's *Assaulted and Pursued Chastity* so miraculously achieved. Wed at age sixteen to a man of fifty-four, Philips not only sets up an opposition between these two forms of relatedness, but does so in terms that emotionally privilege friendship (the flowing River of an Endearment) while admitting ruefully the superior social power of that strict Relation, the marital Gulf or Sea.

Philips's radical expression of the opposed claims of friendship and marriage registers, from the vantage of historical hindsight, a huge ripple in the waters of female love and friendship. Lauded posthumously as "the Matchless Orinda" (the subtitle of the 1667 edition of her poems as well as the title of Webster Souers's 1931 biography),[37] Philips authored over fifty poems addressed to a succession of women, many of them passionate lyrics of love. Long relegated to an obscurity unknown in her lifetime, Philips has been reclaimed by feminist literary critics as an icon of seventeenth-century women's writing.[38] This status is based partly on Philips's masterful appropriation and revision of masculine poetic conventions and partly on the communitarian impulse of her aesthetic practice. In the 1650s, she instituted a Society of Friendship in order to foster political, literary, aesthetic, and affective bonds among women (as well as select men). This circle of friendship (some aspects of which may have begun during her boarding school years) continued until her death in 1664. Self-consciously appropriating the imaginative resources of pastoralism, she and her coterie adopted pastoral names, wrote and circulated amongst themselves poetry extolling the virtues of friendship, and, in Philips's case, explored a range of intense emotions toward women.

Many scholars have attempted to define the precise nature of Philips's attachments to the various women with whom she was intimately involved, both during her adolescence and after her marriage, by analyzing the homoerotic content of her verse.[39] Although biographical criticism has predominated, critics also have demonstrated Philips's indebtedness to a discourse of classical male *amicitia*, to the genre of pastoral, and to the conventions of heterosexual love poetry, particularly the metaphysical conceits of John Donne. What is striking about all of this scholarship is that it seems to assume that no prior literary traditions of female homoeroticism existed. But Philips clearly was working within and through the tradition of *amor impossibilis* and homoerotic lament. Her attraction to pastoral was not simply a measure of her indebtedness to neoclassicism, as many critics contend, nor was it merely the means by which she merged concepts of Platonic love with heteroerotic conventions to ennoble female friendship. Rather, her appropriation of pastoral conventions interrupts and reconfigures the tradition of the *amor impossibilis* which, from Iphis and Ianthe to *The Convent of Pleasure*, had confronted the claims of Nature while remaining caught within a marital resolution. Philips's *Poems*, published four years before *The Convent of Pleasure*, breaks the *amor impossibilis* apart into a diverse set of themes, including emotional longing, ecstasy, heartbreak, anger, bitterness, and betrayal. Central to her lyric repertoire is a homoerotic lament which focuses not on the self-evident unnaturalness of female–female desire, but on the physical absence of the beloved and the inadequacies of a what she calls the "rough, rude world."

Philips's translation of the *amor impossibilis* from a cry of pain about the body, desire, and Nature into a mournful negotiation of the lover's absence marks an alteration in aesthetic sensibility, strategy, and subjectivity. Cavendish's characters, for instance, are cardboard spokespersons for abstract concepts: Amity, Amour, and Sensuality operate like figures on a chessboard, and even Lady Happy functions more as an allegorical personification than a character possessing interiority. In contrast, despite her often allegorical language, Philips's lyrics of female love cut much closer to the bone. Part of the reason is her choice of genre. Like Shakespeare, Sidney, and Spenser, Philips contributed to the construction of a lyric tradition that, at least since the Romantics, has been read under the auspices of the subject: as the exemplary expression of a subject's interiority, as the authentic revelation of inward thought, as the immediate outpouring of intimate desire. Read within these terms, the lyric tends to be viewed as a fictionalized private utterance, as soliloquy or dramatic monologue or, in the words of Virginia Jackson's critique of this concept, "privacy gone public."[40] The result is that poetic voice, persona, and author tend to be conflated at the same time that all three are sundered from history (and thus, the "individual voice" is rendered timeless and universal).[41]

Philips's production of a compelling homoerotic subjectivity, however, is not best understood as "self-expression" at all, but rather as a "subjectivity effect." I appropriate this phrase from Joel Fineman's account of Shakespearean literary subjectivity to force a wedge between Philips as author and "Philips" as lyric voice and persona.[42] Such a dissociation Philips herself would have resisted, as she was passionately invested in her literary subjectivity ("Orinda" functions within her pastoral coterie as a proper name, a passionate identification, not a pseudonym or cover). Nonetheless, this disarticulation is crucial if we are to apprehend the extent to which Philips participates in a series of conventions that precede and define the terms within which, and against which, she writes. According to Fineman's analysis of Renaissance poetry, the literary formation of the self occurs in the slippage between self-presence and representation; it is only through such slippages that the voicings of the lyric subject are interpretable as expressing a deeply interiorized desire. Although this fiction of self-presence is in fact predicated on loss and self-distance, it is no less powerful or constitutive for that. My appropriation of Fineman's argument is both homage and critique. For, in Fineman's relentlessly masculine and heterosexualizing account of Shakespeare, eroticism and subjectivity are always that of the male subject, whose desire is achieved only by misogynistically erecting a distance between himself and "woman," the figure who thematizes the deceptiveness of literary language. Fineman's rigid geometry of gender and sexuality, which apprehends the presence of sexuality only within the articulation of (gender) difference, necessarily elides *as sexual* Shakespeare's poems to the young man, which are judged instead as "ascetic."[43] By suggesting that Philips manipulates in her epideictic poetry the terms of similitude that Fineman sees governing Shakespeare's sonnets to the young man, I insist on the erotic power of what Paula Blank has called in another context, "homopoetics."[44] Philips's love poetry attempts to articulate a homoerotic subject through the fictions and temporalities of lyric expression, deploying the lyric voice to disrupt those relations between ideology, causality, and sequence that, in the drama and prose narrative, propel the plot teleologically toward a marital conclusion. Moving beyond the thematic strategies adopted by Poem XLIX (and that of her contemporary, Cavendish), Philips bypasses the tradition of miraculous transformation (or the fortuitous replacement of a woman by her brother), crafting instead a strategy of legitimation that is at once profoundly confrontational and conventional: in addition to the idealizing similitude which she ascribes to her loving relationships, over and over again she insists that her love for other women is "innocent."

Assertions of innocence in Philips's poetry generally have been read by critics as an elevation of *lesbian* love into the spiritually lofty realm of Platonic friendship; proof positive that she did not carnally desire her friends; a phobic disavowal of the fact that she *did* desire her friends; or a strategic cover for a *lesbian* not yet ready to come out of the closet. None of these interpretations, I believe, adequately accounts for Philips's appropriation of innocence as the proper term for passion among women.

We can gain some purchase on Philips's deployment of a rhetoric of innocence by noting the way certain discriminations are negotiated in those masculine discourses of *amicitia* which Philips so deliberately regenders. The *locus classicus* for the uneasy if productive proximity of masculine friendship to eroticism in the early modern era is Michel de Montaigne's "*De l'amitié*." Eulogizing with a keen sense of loss his intense friendship with Etienne de LaBoëtie, Montaigne idealizes the bonds of sympathy and equality among men. But while drawing on a web of classical allusion, Montaigne nonetheless distinguishes his concept of *amitié* from "that alternative licence of the Greeks" which "is rightly abhorrent to our manners; [C] moreover since as they practised it it required a great disparity of age and divergence of favours between the lovers, it did not correspond either to that perfect union and congruity which we are seeking here."[45] The distance Montaigne would erect between his own pure, equal love and that of the licentious and hierarchical Greeks, however, does little to dispel the erotic force animating those passages articulated through somatic metaphors, as when Montaigne describes how "the same affection [was] revealed each to each other right down to the very entrails," or through the use of penetrative tropes:

This friendship has had no ideal to follow other than itself; no comparison but with itself. [A] There is no one particular consideration – nor two nor three nor four nor a thousand of them – but rather some inexplicable quintessence of them all mixed up together which, having captured my will, brought it to plunge into his and lose itself [C] and which, having captured his will, brought it to plunge and lose itself in mine with an equal hunger and emulation. [A] I say "lose myself" in very truth; we kept nothing back for ourselves: nothing was his or mine.[46]

Despite Montaigne's own effort to delineate between the passion of men for women (which he describes as "active, sharp and keen"; "rash . . . fickle, fluctuating and variable") and the love of men for men (a "general universal warmth, temperate moreover and smooth, a warmth which is constant and at rest, all gentleness and evenness, having nothing sharp nor keen"),[47] the salient difference seems to be less the gender of the beloved object than the relative state of ease experienced by the desiring subject. For as soon as "sexual love," which is but "a mad craving for something which escapes us,"

enters the territory of friendship (where wills work together, that is) it languishes and grows faint. To enjoy it is to lose it; its end is in the body and therefore subject to satiety. Friendship on the contrary is enjoyed in proportion to our desire: since it is a matter of the mind, with our souls being purified by practising it, it can spring forth, be nourished and grow only when enjoyed.[48]

In Montaigne's ecology of desire, it is less that male–male love is not of the body than that male–female love is not of the mind. Linking friendship to a desire that can never be sated, that is nourished and grows through its enjoyment, Montaigne's metaphors for male friendship thoroughly eroticize it.

Such eroticized friendship is, as Alan Bray's *The Friend* makes clear, one aspect of a widespread network of affects and obligations among men.[49] Tracing the rituals of sworn brotherhood through a variety of medieval and early modern documents and artifacts, Bray provides an archeology of masculine friendship that demonstrates its utility to other social institutions, including the family. Indeed, Bray's research suggests that the early modern family, rather than providing the only basis of social cohesion, subsists within larger structures of relation, including the "voluntary kinship" of intimate male friends.

Both the discourse of *amicitia* and the practices of voluntary kinship were predominantly masculine prerogatives. Montaigne provides one of the most potent ideological expressions of female insufficiency in this regard:

women are in truth not normally capable of responding to such familiarity and mutual confidence as sustain that holy bond of friendship, nor do their souls seem firm enough to withstand the clasp of a knot so lasting and so tightly drawn. And indeed if it were not for that, if it were possible to fashion such a relationship, willing and free, in which not only the souls had this full enjoyment but in which the bodies too shared in the union – [C] where the whole human being was involved – it is certain [A] that the loving-friendship would be more full and more abundant. But there is no example yet of woman attaining to it [C] and by the common agreement of the Ancient schools of philosophy she is excluded from it.[50]

But women could be friends – not least of which among themselves. They formed their own alliances among kinswomen, regularly visited with neighbors, and pursued long-distance epistolary correspondences.[51] Yet, there was little public discourse about the virtues and possibilities of friendship between women, and what discourse did exist had none of the elevated social standing accorded to Montaigne's essays.[52] Nor did female friendship function as effectively as did men's to create and maintain legal, economic, and familial advantages. In this context, women's friendships were unmarked, naturalized, as little subject to scrutiny as to celebration.

It is of no little import, then, that Katherine Philips laid explicit claim, in life as in poetry, to both *amicitia* and voluntary kinship in the mid-seventeenth century. Indeed, her life expresses the tension between submission to dynastic marriage (undertaken for the sake of kinship, politics, religion, wealth) and the quest for personal happiness which men were licensed to find outside of the nuclear family. In this sense, Philips's Society of Friendship functioned as an alternative form of voluntary kinship.[53] There is no question that Philips felt herself to be kin to Anne Owen (the "Lucasia" of her poetry): she commemorated the deaths of Owen family members in eulogies; she spent a full year away from her husband while accompanying the newly married Anne Owen, Lady Dungannon, to Ireland; and when she wrote a poem about the burial place of her husband's ancestors, "Wiston Vault," it is not her anticipated inclusion in her husband's patrimony that she versifies, but the more lasting "monument" provided by Lucasia's love:

> But after death too I would be alive,
> And shall, if my *Lucasia* do, survive.
> I quit these pomps of Death, and am content,
> Having her heart to be my Monument:
> Though ne'er Stone to me, 'twill Stone for me prove,
> By the peculiar miracles of Love.
> There I'll Inscription have which no Tomb gives,
> Not, *Here Orinda lies*, but, *Here she lives*.[54]

Just as the desire that friendship could be on equal par with marriage is demonstrated throughout her life, so too Montaigne's trope of souls "mingled and confounded in so universal a blending that they efface the seam which joins them together"[55] is adopted by Philips as her signature *cri de cour*. By deploying an idiom of idealized *amicitia* heretofore reserved for men, Philips not only usurps some of that tradition's symbolic capital, but also makes manifest the homoerotic potential lodged within all those chaste female friendships we have surveyed, from Iphis to Calisto.

When literary critics move beyond the issue of whether Philips's *oeuvre* is legitimately viewed as homoerotic, they tend to focus on the emotional affects expressed in her poems. Harriette Andreadis, for instance, defines Philips's "sapphic platonics" via poems that celebrate the ecstatic merger of the beloved with the self. Focused on the issue of power relations, Elaine Hobby interprets certain poems as expressing sadomasochistic desire. Carol Barash and Elizabeth Wahl implicitly mediate between these views when they argue that a tension emerges in Philips's poetry between, in the words of Wahl, an "abstract or 'programmatic' rhetoric of friendship that Philips uses to describe an egalitarian relationship of mutual sympathy and a mystic transformation of two selves into one soul and a more 'courtly' rhetorical strain in which she adopts the hierarchical relation between a male suitor addressing his female beloved to woo a particular woman in the name of friendship."[56] Rather than focus on the two poetic modes, platonism and courtly love, within which Philips worked, or the two erotic stances, merger and aggression, authorized by these modes, my strategy is to read Philips's thematizations of Nature from a *lesbian*-affirmative perspective. How does Nature look, even in those poems not addressed to the female beloved, when viewed from the perspective of someone whose desires have been, in the prior literary tradition, defined as outside or against it?

Philips typically invokes Nature via pastoral associations, as in her meditation on the moment of separation, "Lucasia, Rosania, and Orinda parting at a Fountain, July 1663":

> Here, here are our enjoyments done,
> 	And since the Love and Grief we wear
> 		Forbids us either word or tear,
> And Art wants here expression,
> See Nature furnish us with one.

Forbidden by love and grief to cry or speak their sorrow, the women appropriate the image of the pastoral fountain nymph whom Nature has kindly provided to mimetically enact their grief:

> The kind and mournful Nimph which here
> 	Inhabits in her humble Cells,
> 		No longer her own sorrow tells,
> Nor for it now concern'd appears,
> But for our parting sheds these tears.

Her own concerns forgotten, the fountain nymph sheds watery tears *for them*; her sorrow articulates and authorizes their grief. With this conceit of mutual identification, "Orinda" mediates the pain of parting by forging a link between the pastoral victims of classical tales – Iphis, Calisto, Diana's nymphs – and the losses felt within her own loving circle.

Whereas here Orinda authorizes her emotional affects by placing them comfortably within a homoerotic pastoral tradition, in "To my Lucasia," a poem that repudiates the new empirical philosophy for its mechanistic understanding of the universe, she more directly contests the putative priority of Nature:

> . . . he
> That Nature's harmony intire would see,
> Must search agreeing Souls, sit down and view
> How sweet the mixture is, how full, how true;
> By what soft touches Spirits greet and kiss,
> And in each other can complete their bliss.

Invited to witness "Nature's harmony intire," the male reader is instructed to search "agreeing Souls." He should "sit down and view" female spirits greeting and kissing, touching softly and mixing sweetly. Mildly voyeuristic, this poem echoes the sensual intimacies enjoyed in Cavendish's convent of pleasure as it transports the loving couple to a *locus amoenus*; but with complete "bliss" offered as the epitome of Nature's "harmony intire," the distance could not be greater from Lady Happy's resigned tautology, "Nature is Nature."

Indeed, in other poems Philips makes clear that Nature is something to be manipulated. In "To Mr. Henry Lawes," Philips ends her encomium to the man who set her and other poets' verses to music by invoking his power over Nature:

> Live then, great Soul of Nature, to asswage
> The savage dulness of this sullen Age.
> Charm us to Sense; for though Experience fail,
> And Reason too, thy Numbers may prevail.
> Then, like those Ancients, strike, and so command
> All Nature to obey thy gen'rous hand.
> None will resist, but such who needs will be
> More stupid than a Stone, a Fish, a Tree.
> Be it thy care our Age to new-create:
> What built a World, may sure repair a State.

Philips's reformulation of Nature, I want to suggest, is an integral part of a poetic stance which, at least in these poems, conflates rather than separates the spiritual and the bodily. Although some of Philips's poems assume and work within the opposition between the platonic and the courtly, the spiritual and the fleshly, other poems rhetorically merge these affective registers. In these latter poems, the aim is not to elevate the spiritual in a transcendence of the body, but to reject the opposition. Orinda, for instance, mediates both the meaning of her desire and the anguish of parting from her beloved through the willful assertion of spiritual merger. Often elegiac, these poems seek to overcome the absence and loss of the beloved's presence through a determined negation of difference and distance. "To Mrs. M. A. at Parting," for instance, begins with the disclosure:

> I have examin'd and do find,
>   Of all that favour me,
> There's none I grieve to leave behind
>   But only only thee.
> To part with thee I needs must die,
> Could parting sep'rate thee and I.

The point, of course, is that parting cannot separate her from Mary Awbrey (Rosania), for their "mingled Souls are grown / To such acquaintance ... That each is in the Union lost," a spiritual unification so extraordinary that it will "teach the World new Love" and "Redeem the Age and Sex." Anyone who thinks that women are inferior to men in performing the rites of friendship will be proved wrong.

Nonetheless, "the tedious smart / Of absent Friendship" is, in "Parting with Lucasia: A Song," a rather more physical pang. What's more, "absent Friendship" is the victim, not of Nature but Necessity:

> Yet I must go: we will submit,
>   And so our own Disposers be;
> For while we nobly suffer it,
>   We triumph o're Necessity.

Having dutifully performed the rites of separation – "that rigid thing / Which makes Spectators think we part" – but in reality having triumphed over physical absence through the mingling of souls, these beloved friends look forward to a future meeting:

> Nay then to meet we may conclude,
>   And all Obstructions overthrow,
> Since we our Passion have subdu'd,
>   Which is the strongest thing I know.

Structured by an enabling paradox, this poem implies that even as their passion is suppressed, it overcomes all obstacles. Yet sometimes Orinda's passion cannot be subdued, and we gain a glimpse of the effort expended in the attempt. As she says in "To my Lucasia": "But Bodies move in time, and so must Minds; / And though th'attempt no easie progress finds, / Yet quit me not, lest I should desp'rate grow, / And to such Friendship adde some Patience now." Asking for Lucasia's patience as she attempts to control her feelings, Orinda places herself in the position of supplicant, Lucasia in the position of power. Indeed, the absence of Lucasia calls forth a lament that draws all its mournful force from Orinda's utter dependence on the love object. In "Orinda to Lucasia parting October 1661. at London," she bids her love goodbye: "Adieu, dear object of my Love's excess, / And with thee all my hopes of happiness." Just as unrestrained and despairing is the epideictic "Orinda to Lucasia" which, after a stanza based on the conventional conceit of the Sun's necessity to the natural world, ventures a hyperbolic comparison:

> Thou my *Lucasia* art far more to me,
> Than he to all the under-world can be;
>   From thee I've heat and light,
>   Thy absence makes my night.
> But ah! my Friend, it now grows very long,
> The sadness weighty, and the darkness strong:
>   My tears (its dew) dwell on my cheeks,
>   And still my heart thy dawning seeks,
> And to thee mournfully it cries,
>   That if too long I wait,
>   Ev'n thou may'st come too late,
> And not restore my life, but close my eyes.

Becoming the sorrowful nymph of the fountain, Orinda tearfully grieves that the "heat and light" she derives from Lucasia's presence are the Nature she needs:

the "dawning" that her "heart" "seeks" in a love melancholy that threatens her very life.

By the use of such conceits, Orinda appropriates and reconstitutes the image of Nature bequeathed to her by the tradition of homoerotic lament: no longer the taboo forbidding female love or the ground against which perversion is defined, Nature becomes the *means* of homoerotic expression. Inverting the terms of this tradition, Orinda positions Nature as fully *continuous* with female desire, a continuity intensified by Philips's use of images of pastoral retreat as the proper home for passionate women. What women alone together possess, she makes clear in "To Mrs. M. Awbrey," is precisely what the "factious World" has "lost":

> Let the dull World alone to talk and fight,
> And with their vast Ambitions Nature fright;
> Let them despise so Innocent a flame,
> While Envy, Pride and Faction play their game:
> But we by Love sublim'd so high shall rise,
> To pity Kings, and Conquerours despise,
> Since we that Sacred Union have engrost,
> Which they and all the factious World have lost.

Proceeding by a series of oppositions – the dull, factious World versus frightened Nature; vast Ambitions versus innocent Flame; Envy, Pride, and Faction versus Love – Orinda aligns female–female love with a frightened but innocent Nature while aggressively elevating the "Sacred Union" of women above the kings she pities and the conquerors she despises. Blaming men for the loss of her royalist World, she evinces a tone of condescension and denial that is amplified in "A Retir'd Friendship. To Ardelia," a lyric that disdains "the boisterous World," confident that the pleasures enjoyed in the all-female seclusion of a "Bower" is "what Princes wish in vain." As the salvific antidote to what she repeatedly calls the "rough, rude world" and the "dull angry world,"[57] Philips's pastoralism echoes the sentiments of those Cavalier poets who, as Warren Chernaik remarks, were "constantly drawing magic circles that will shut the world out, seeking to find an autonomous realm of love and art, a court immune to change."[58] But unlike that of the Cavaliers', Philips's retreat is exclusively female; and like the representations of Diana's virgin circle, the pleasures of Orinda's conclave are repeatedly contrasted to the violent, intemperate, and phallic world of men. Indeed, in her "Articles of Friendship," Philips appropriates from a "Goddesse" the power to "perform the rite" of friendship, which is explicitly compared to the "knitting together" or "conjugiam" of marriage: "The Soules which vertu hath made fitt / Do of themselves incline to knitt; / Yet wedlock having priests, allow / That I be friendships Flamen now." The rite which she performs is not only a "simulacrum of holy wedlock,"[59] but a repetition of Diana's injunction to her coupled nymphs: "If you these terms do disapprove, / Ye cannot, or ye wil not love. But if ye like these lovely bands, / With them join hearts, & lips, & hands!"

As Carol Barash has argued, Philips's love poetry, especially her poetry of retreat, is embedded in the political turmoil of mid-century England: "Orinda's Society of Friendship is not merely about community among women, but also about how, through the 'mutual love' of friends, one can soar into heaven with one's political allies, leaving one's opponents in the dust."[60] Barash provides a fascinating account of the changes in Philips's love poetry as the political climate altered. Prior to the Restoration, Charles I functions as "the absent third party in these poems, making them not only about the relationship between Orinda and Lucasia, but also about their mutual longing for the material presence of the king."[61] After the Restoration, "the relationship between Orinda and Lucasia comes to be situated more specifically in relation to literal marriage. Lacking a referent outside the women themselves, friendship, as symbol, loses its mystical potential. In this context, the two women's friendship proves a real – indeed, a sexual – threat."[62] Without a masculine and royalist third term to mediate their intimacy, the meaning of their love is made newly subject to suspicion and condemnation.

For Barash, the restored monarch contextualizes this change. But as my last chapter argued, other mid-century phenomena had a significant impact on female–female eroticism as well, particularly the ideology of domestic heterosexuality. Changes at the level of patriarchal alliance directly and recursively pressured the terms of female homoeroticism. Once friendship becomes a goal of marriage for men and women, female friendship begins to look a lot like companionate marriage. At the same time, when female–female love becomes, as I've argued, increasingly available as an imaginative and social reality, the burden on women *to choose* to bond with men increases.[63] It is in the context of this amplified discourse on female choices that I suggest we read Orinda's repeated assertions of innocence. For instance, in "Friendship in Embleme, or the Seal. To my dearest Lucasia," Orinda dissociates the heart from the pull of "lower ends": "The Hearts are free from lower ends, / For each point to the other tends. / They flame, 'tis true, and several wayes, / But still those Flames do so much raise, / That while to either they incline / They yet are noble and divine." Self-consciously acknowledging the presence of erotic heat, admitting that their hearts are aflame and that these flames move in "*several* wayes," this poem nonetheless refutes the notion that such flames are anything but "noble and divine." Their nobility depends, I believe, not on their dissociation from erotic passion, but from a studied awareness of passion's proper end: as in companionate marriage, erotic love should be selfless, directed toward the other, and hence ultimately inclined heavenward.

Such sentiments are reiterated in "To my Lucasia in defense of declared friendship," wherein Orinda figures the body as the necessary site of merger she desires. "O My *Lucasia*, let us speak our Love," the poem exultantly begins, moving through a description of a friendship that would fail to claim enough of its due: "If this be all our Friendship does design, / We covet not enjoyment then, but power: / To our Opinion we our Bliss confine, / And love to have, but not to smell, the flower." The wish to inhale rather than simply hold the flower, to experience its full promise of "enjoyment" and break out of that which would "confine" "our Bliss" is followed by an extended simile that rewrites, in the name of pleasure, Philips's imagery of the victory of marriage over friendship: "And as a River, when it once hath paid / The tribute which it to the Ocean owes / stops not but turns, and having curl'd and play'd / On its own waves, the shore it overflows." Materializing female passion as an ever-swirling wave, curling and playing on and around itself, Orinda then appropriates this physical image of self-reflexive pleasure to describe the amorous soul: "So the Soul's motion does not end in bliss, / But on her self she scatters and dilates, / And on the Object doubles till by this / She finds new joys which that reflux creates." The soul's motion does not, has no, end; rather, "she" continually scatters and dilates, both on herself and on the "Object." This process of "reflux creates" "new joys" which the loving soul then "finds." Such joys cannot be "contained" by the Soul, however, and the poem returns to the metaphors of ear and speech which it has worked throughout: "But then because it cannot all contain, / It seeks a vent by telling the glad news, / First to the Heart which did its joys obtain, / Then to the Heart which did those joys produce." Speaking first to oneself and then to the beloved, the Soul must use a "vent" – or, as she says in the eighth stanza, since the Soul is imprisoned by the Flesh, "There's no way left that bondage to controul, / But to convey transactions through the Ear."

The erotic imagery of this poem is simultaneously atemporal and spatially incontinent. Able to overflow boundaries, desire is figured in the humoral terms of female orgasm: a dilation, swirling, and scattering of fluids. Yet such erotic imagery is not always without ambivalence for Philips. As Wahl argues,

As much as Philips tries to limit or deny any connection between her love for Lucasia and the bodies through which that attraction is mediated, her recourse to a rhetoric of transcendence continually finds its spiritual images contaminated by erotic, carnal resonances that reinforce the reader's sense that Philips cannot exclude the physical world from her desire to create a union of hearts and minds, and on some level may not even wish to.[64]

Barash, likewise, reminds us that the terms of female friendship were socially contested, that Philips felt the need to reassert the innocence of her passion, and that "Against Pleasure" (set to music and appearing in many manuscript miscellanies) is "an indictment of Orinda's desire for Lucasia as part of what she calls the 'fruit of *Sodom*'":

> For by our Pleasures we are cloy'd,
>   And so Desire is done;
> Or else, like Rivers, they make wide
>   The Channel where they run.

Suggesting that "'Rivers' enlarging the 'Channel where they run' enact female ejaculation, as if desire, whether admitted or not, becomes overpowering liquid, like semen,"[65] Barash notes Philips's use of similar images in many other poems.

How, given the repeated use of such erotic imagery, do we interpret Philips's assertions of innocence? Wahl argues that "the very overdetermination of these qualities of 'innocence' and 'transparency' paradoxically contributes to the reader's sense that Philips does feel that she has something to hide and betrays her anxiety that such relations might be viewed as morally or sexually suspect despite all her protestations to the contrary."[66] Barash, while suggesting that the language of politics makes "possible the innocently expressive language of heroic women,"[67] also acknowledges that there is an ongoing struggle here:

> Philips resolves her relationship with [Anne] Owen by making the terms of its "Innocence" explicit – it is friendship not idolatry, religious duty not pagan sensuality. But the "funeral of Friendship" happens no more permanently in *Poems* (1664) than it did in fact. As in the manuscript version of the relationship, Lucasia returns, and the "Innocence" of the love between the two women must be "declared" yet again.

"Why," Barash asks, "does Philips insist upon this repetition of elegies for friendship – elegies which refuse to be elegies because their object will not die or disappear?"[68]

The answer, it seems to me, is that Philips's professions of innocence draw from and manipulate prior conventions of chaste female intimacy even as they reformulate Nature to newly authorize such bonds. It thus is a mistake to read Philips's expressions of innocence solely in terms of her own struggle to overcome erotic feelings or as part of a strategy of coding, masking, or disguising a desire that is not yet ready to "come out of the closet."[69] Read in the context of the literary traditions explored in the last two chapters and the historical discourses of eroticism analyzed throughout this book, Philips's recourse to innocence is apprehensible neither as the "truth" of her closeted desire nor proof of her disinterest in genital contact. Rather, innocence is the historically accurate word that Philips appropriates from the literary heritage of chaste femme love. It is the same innocence that had been conferred regularly onto such characters as Helena and Hermia, Rosalind and Celia, Emilia and Flavina. The difference, however, is that Philips attributes this innocence not to adolescent "maids," but to mature, even married, women. In addition, having silently absented men (and in large part patriarchal marriage) from her representation of loving friendship, Philips's consistent imagery of the "rough, rude world" suggests that the world of men is one of intrusion, intemperance, and conflict, both political and sexual.

In contrast, the vision of intimacy in her verse is one in which relationships are governed – indeed, governed is precisely the word, as we can see the careful effort involved in formalizing female relations through ritual – by the desire (whether it is fulfilled or not) for an eroticized merger of body and soul. I will say more about Philips's vision of female bliss in the final chapter. For now, I close my discussion of Philips with the suggestion that her poetry, indebted as it is to a prior tradition of chaste female friendship – including the *amor impossibilis*, the homoerotic lament, and the elegiac pastoralism of Renaissance drama – simultaneously registers, as Wahl and Barash suggest, changed social conditions. As such, the verse of Philips functions as a symptomatic break: between the Renaissance discourse of chaste, innocuous insignificance, on the one hand, and the increasingly public discourse of illicit desire that carries with it the stigma of significance, on the other.[70]

In a commendatory poem to the 1667 posthumous edition of Philips's poetry entitled "To the Excellent *Orinda*," an anonymous speaker, Philo-Philippa (lover of Philips), sings the praises of a long line of women who, by virtue of their intellectual and physical prowess, demonstrated their equality with men. In the course of this encomium, Philo-Philippa invokes the plight of Iphis and Ianthe in order to dismiss the necessity of a sex transformation: "Ovid *in vain Bodies with change did vex, / Changing her form of life*, Iphis *chang'd Sex*." Judging Ovid's imposition of a sex change to be not only a means to "vex" Iphis, but ultimately "in vain," Philo-Philippa rejects the miraculous finale (based as it is on the presumption of masculine superiority), in favor of a philosophy of female equality.[71] Philo-Philippa's feminist stance is echoed and furthered in "Chloe to Artimesa. 1700," an anonymous manuscript poem collected in a miscellany around 1701. It takes the form of a verse letter which, in its mode of address, implicitly creates a loving colloquy of two:

> Madam.
> While vulgar souls their vulgar loves pursue,
> And in the Comon way themselves undoe,
> Impairing Health and Fame, and risquing life,
> To be a Mistress, or what's worse a wife,
> We, whom a nicer tast has rais'd above
> The dang'rous folly of such slavish Love,
> Despise the Sex, while in ourselves we find
> Pleasures, for their gross Senses too refin'd.
> Let Brutish men, made by their weakness vain,
> Boast of the easy Conquests they obtain,
> Let the poor Loving Wretch do all she can
> (And all won't please th' ungratefull Tyrant, Man.)
> We'l scorn the Monster, and his Mistress too,
> And shew the world, what women ought to do.[72]

The persona of this poem separates herself and her addressee not only from man (reduced to "the Sex," an "ungratefull Tyrant," and a "Monster"), but from the "poor Loving Wretch" or "Mistress" who is under his sway. Instead, she revels in the "Pleasures" found in her own sex which are deemed "too refin'd" for the "gross Senses" of "brutish Men." Her "nicer tast" raises her and her friend above the vulgar, shameful, and harmful pursuit of a husband or consort, for whom one's love could only be "slavish." Discarding the conventional privilege of matrimony over whoredom – indeed, inverting that hierarchy – this speaker considers all forms of sexual congress with men to risk women's health, reputation, and life. Although this poem is less inflected with eroticism than is Philips's verse, it implies that gender equality enables and requires female–female love: divorcing themselves from men and indulging in all-female pleasures is "what women ought to do."

What women ought to do is an issue as well in the entry on friendship in *The Ladies Dictionary*, which, as previously noted, includes "Woman with a Woman" in its 1694 definition of "Buggarie." In response to the question, "Friendship contracted by single Persons, *may it continue with the same Zeal and Innocence if either Marry?*" the answer is this:

It *may*, tho Ten to One if it *does*; since in those Circumstances there will be a great *hazard*, that either the *Innocence* will spoil the *Zeal*, or the *Zeal* the *Innocence* . . . The worst on't seems to be here. – That seeing *Friendship* can be only in the *heighth* (as we have formerly describ'd it) *between* two, how shall it remain with *equal Zeal* and *Innocence*, at least *Justice*, when *one* is *Marry'd*? For either there must be *more* or *less tenderness* for the *Friend* than for the *Wife* or *Husband*, – If more, 'tis *Injustice*; for People ought not to *Marry any*, but such as are fit to make *Friends*; if less, the *former Friendship* must be diminish'd, as if the *Marriage* be *happy*, it *generally* perhaps *always* is. If I amn't mistaken, the *pinch* is here, and the *Solution* accordingly, *That if the Friendship between the Persons Marry'd have but the ascendant, and if that be continued with the highest degree of* Zeal, *any lower measure of that and* Friendship *may innocently remain where it was before planted.*[73]

Although the question and answer presumably are posed in regard to friends of either sex, in this book addressed expressly to ladies, it is not surprising that the terms by which the conflict between friendship and marriage is explored are derived from the tradition of Cavendish and Philips. Like Cavendish, this entry asserts the dictum of companionate marriage that "[p]eople ought not to Marry any, but such as are fit to make Friends." Like Philips, it also ruefully acknowledges that "Ten to One," marriage will win out over friendship. But should friendship continue after marriage, then the "hazard" to be confronted is the ratio of innocence to zeal: "either the Innocence will spoil the Zeal, or the Zeal the Innocence." Since zeal in this period referred to "ardent love or affection" as well as to "ardent, earnest, or eager desire" (*OED*), it is safe to assume that *The Ladies Dictionary* recognizes such love and desire to exist in both friendship and marriage. By failing to employ gendered referents, the entry implies that the balance of zeal to innocence is as relevant to intimacy among women as to that between women and men. The problem is similar to the one posed by Philips: how best to express love and desire for one's friend within the terms of a marital economy. Like much of Philips's verse, this issue becomes particularly acute only after one of the friends has married. Unlike Philips, who manipulates innocence to her own ends, the *Dictionary*'s recommended "Solution" here is caution, for, whatever else happens, "the Friendship between the Persons Marry'd" must have priority. As long as marriage is the site of the greater zeal, then friendship "may innocently remain." Even as it asserts this conservative conclusion, *The Ladies Dictionary* acknowledges that a "pinch" is felt when married people experience greater intimacy in the company of those to whom they are not wed.

The negotiation of zeal and innocence, friendship and marriage, expressed in the prose of Cavendish, the verse of Philips, Philo-Philippa, "Chloe to Artimesa. 1700," and *The Ladies Dictionary* occurred within a larger social debate about marriage, female equality, and separatism during the turn of the seventeenth century, a debate that produced such polemics as Mary Astell's feminist *Reflections on Marriage* (1700) and Bernard Mandeville's *Virgin Unmask'd* (1709). Both of these tracts, as Susan Lanser notes, laid "positive grounds for a separatist singleness." At the same time, widespread resistance to ideas of reform implies that the "spectre of wellborn, accomplished women opting out of marital systems was . . . particularly and newly worrisome . . . by the turn of the eighteenth century."[74] Ros Ballaster likewise notes that public discourse about the courtly women who surrounded Queen Anne indicates that there was a "fear about women's proximity to power and the exclusion of men from political life, imaged through their exclusion from sexual contact with them."[75]

Yet, the terms of intimate female friendship had been strained for half a century before Anne's reign, hinting that such pressure was not solely dependent on women's increased participation in politics or public life. In the 1590s, Shakespeare's Le Beau describes the love of Celia and Rosalind in *As You Like It* as "dearer than the natural bond of sisters" (1.2.266); despite the fact that his words imply that their love is *more dear* than is natural, his tone is admiring, and presumably no one would have raised an eyebrow. By the 1650s, however, this might not be the case. Edmund Waller's lyric, "On the Friendship betwixt Sacharissa and Amorett" (1645), begins to sound the note of warning, as his male persona strikes a pained rejected lover's pose in response to the exclusionary intimacy of female friends:

> Tell me lovely loving paire,
> Why so kinde, and so severe?
> Why so careless of our care,
> Onely to prove selves so dear?

Privileging one another (and, in the mimetic logic of this poem, oneself) over men, the "lovely loving paire" is "careless" of the care of men:

> By this cunning change of hearts,
> You the power of love controul,
> While the boyes deluded darts,
> Can arrive at neither soul.
> For in vain to either breast
> Still beguiled love does come,
> Where he findes a forrain ghuest [*sic*],
> Neither of your hearts at home.

Controlling the power to love, these female intimates delude the beguiled Cupid, who arrives at the female breast only to find that her heart has absconded to strange lands, leaving some foreign guest in residence. Harsher criticism follows:

> Debtors thus with like designe,
> When they never mean to pay:
> That they may the Law decline,
> To some friend make all away.

The women's exchange of hearts is like the stratagem used by a debtor who protects his possessions by giving them to a friend. Dishonest, never intending to pay back what they owe, these female friends keep their hearts off the market, rejecting the validity of the "Law" of marital reproductivity. Nonetheless, they remain thieves of men's hearts, for their attractiveness to men seems to grow in proportion to their unavailability:

> Not the silver Doves that flie,
> Yoak't in *Citharea's* Car,
> Not the wings that lift so high,
> And convey her son so far.
> Are so lovely, sweet, and fair,
> Or do more enable love,
> Are so choicely matcht a pair,
> Or with more content to move.[76]

The language here is at once admiring and resentful. On the one hand, this "lovely, sweet, and faire" dyad calls forth from the poetic persona an obvious delight in their ability to "enable love." Even more beautiful than the coupled doves who drive Citharea's carriage, these women, so "choicely matcht," mirror one another in their beauty.[77] Similitude, lovely in itself, is even more so when each half of the pair is so lovely. The equanimity of this tautology is disrupted, on the other hand, by the fact that this "choicely matcht" pair excludes men. Moving past the conventional address to a lady in retirement (evident in Waller's "Go, Lovely Rose" and "To a Lady in Retirement," both of which seek, in typical *carpe diem* fashion, to convince the beloved of the necessity of giving way to man's desire), the message of "On the Friendship betwixt Sacharissa and Amorett" is urgent and clear: women should stop being "severe" and "careless" of men's "care."

When the first verse of Waller's lyric was set to music at the turn of the century, the composer emphasized through repetition several words: "Tell me love – ly, love – ly, love – ly pair; why, why, why, why so kin–d and so severe? why, why, so careless, care – less of our ease? on – ly to your selves, your selv – es so dear: By this cunning, this cunning change of hearts, you, you the pow'r of love can rule, while the Boy's, de – Inded, de – In – ded darts, can arriv – e, can ar – rive at neither, neither, neither, neither, Soul."[78] Highlighting the loveliness of the pair, obsessively repeating the question "why," and concluding with a quadruple negative that redounds on the loving couple, this musical version emphasizes the indictment of carelessness and solipsism intimated in Waller's poem.[79]

If we move forward thirty years, we can see this indictment of female intimacy take on added force. Rather than a plaintive "Tell me," John Hoadley's similar poem, "On the Friendship of two young Ladies, 1730," begins on a deceptively lofty and affirmative note:

> HAIL, beauteous pair, whom Friendship binds
>   In softest, yet in strongest ties,
> Soft as the temper of your minds,
>   Strong as the lustre of your eyes.
> So Venus' doves in couples fly,
>   And friendly steer their equal course;
> Whose feathers Cupid's shafts supply,
>   And wing them with resistless force.

Employing Waller's image of female friends as coupled doves, Hoadley further intimates that their feathers provide materials for Cupid's unerring shafts. After this transformation of forms of female intimacy into the materials of heteroeroticism, the poem strikes a more condescending and hostile tone:

> Thus as you move Love's tender flame,
>   Like that of Friendship, paler burns;
> Both our divided passion claim,
>   And friends and rivals prove by turns.

Attempting to contain the potential autonomy of female bonds, the male persona advises: don't limit yourself to being friends; be rivals for the affection of men as well.

> Then ease yourselves and bless mankind,
>   Friendship so curst no more pursue:
> In wedlock's rosy bow'r you'll find
>   The joys of Love and Friendship [t]oo.[80]

Friendship between women is "curst" because it excludes men and keeps women from their "ease" – presumably, the ease one finds in the economic, emotional, and sexual advantages of conjugal union. The retreat to "wedlock's rosy bow'r" will not only prove a blessing to mankind, but will provide women with double their pleasure. In such a way that would meet with the approval of *The Ladies Dictionary*, Cavendish's attempt to triangulate marriage and friendship is renegotiated by Hoadley as a more singular joy, with love and friendship collapsed into the lone figure of husband.

These poems of masculine anxiety draw from and revise the seventeenth-century tradition of *carpe diem*, which figures the attempt to seduce women as a matter (indeed, an index) of poetic persuasion. From Donne's "Elegy 16: To His Mistress on Going to Bed" to Herrick's "To the Virgins, to Make Much of Time" to Marvell's "To His Coy Mistress," the rhetoric of *carpe diem* presumes the naturalness of male–female attraction, underscores this naturalness with the use of pastoral imagery, and seeks only to bypass the conventional temporal sequence of marriage before sex. Sex in the *carpe diem* tradition requires seduction in the form of persuasive argumentation, but the argument is not about women's attraction to men. Confidently assuming the existence of female desire for men, lyrics asking women to seize the day confront feminine reluctance in order to convince their addressees to accede to male sexual demands *now*. The poems of Waller and Hoadley, in contrast, seem unable to take women's desire for men for granted.

Concurrent with the genteel poetry of Waller and Hoadley, which thematize the dangers of female intimacies within the public sphere of courtly and bourgeois discourse, a more satiric, "scandal" literature circulated similar anxieties without the patina of respectability. This literature was written by both women and men. Delarivier Manley's scandal novel, *The New Atalantis* (1709), for instance, depicts a "female cabal" linked to Whig politicians whom Manley sought to embarrass. What the members of the cabal practice is, according to the satiric narrator, Lady Intelligence, an "excess of amity":

Two beautiful ladies joined in an excess of amity (no word is tender enough to express their new delight) innocently embrace! For how can they be guilty? They vow eternal tenderness, they exclude the men, and condition that they will always do so. What irregularity can there be in this? 'Tis true some things may be strained a little too far, and that causes reflections to be cast upon the rest.[81]

While Lady Intelligence archly manipulates the discourse of female amity in tongue-in-cheek fashion, the naive Astrea attempts to reaffirm boundaries between friendship and marriage, the natural and the unnatural: "If only tender friendship, inviolable and sincere, be the regard, what can be more meritorious or a truer emblem of their happiness above?... But if they carry it a length beyond what nature designed and fortify themselves by these new-formed amities against the hymenial union...'tis wrong and to be blamed."[82]

The gently mocking tone expressed in *The New Atalantis* takes on a rougher edge in a mock-heroic satire attacking Frances Brundenell, Countess of Newburgh, published pseudonomously by the Jacobite William King in 1742. Originally entitled "The Hermaphrodite" but subsequently known as "The Toast," this long, vituperative work included "An Ode to Myra" in the first edition. "Myra" – a name derived in part from "a Corruption of *Myrrhina* a famous Courtesan of *Athens*, who first practis'd and taught in that City *Sappho's* Manner and the *Lesbian* Gambols" (or so the "Notes and Observations" assures us) – is accused of all manner of vice, including hermaphroditism and tribadism.[83] King appropriates the poetic image of female doves to bring the discourse of female friendship squarely into the realm of the obscene:

> What if *Sappho* was so naught?
> I'll deny, that thou art taught
> How to pair the Female Doves,
> How to practice *Lesbian* Loves:
> But when little A———n's spread
> In her Grove or on thy Bed,
> I will swear, 'tis Nature's Call,
> 'Tis exalted Friendship all. (p. 85)

With "Nature's Call" satirically invoked as a justification for practicing "*Lesbian* Loves," and with "exalted Friendship" equated with the practice of spreading A———n's little body, the terms of female friendship are radically destabilized. No matter whether in a grove or on a bed, the image of women lying together is made graphically explicit and, as such, can no longer be taken for granted as chastely insignificant.

Just a few years later in 1749, an anonymous pamphlet, *Satan's Harvest Home*, records a new phrase for this form of female intimacy:

Sappho, as she was one of the wittiest Women that ever the World bred, so she thought with Reason, it would be expected she should make some Additions to a *Science* in which Womankind had been so successful: What does she do then? Not content with our Sex, begins *Amours* with her own, and teaches the Female World a new Sort of Sin, call'd the *Flats*, that was follow'd not only in *Lucian's* Time, but is practis'd frequently in *Turkey*, as well as at *Twickenham* at this Day.[84]

Felicity Nussbaum speculates that "[t]his parallel drawn between women of Twickenham and Turkey very likely alludes to Lady Mary Wortley Montagu, who lived in Twickenham after her husband purchased a house in 1722."[85] Montagu had described the beauty and solidarity of Turkish women in her

"Friendship so curst" 315

Turkish Embassy *Letters*, and is here, according to Nussbaum, being implicated in the homoerotic practices associated with the Turkish bath and seraglio.[86]

The fear that women in England are carrying on in like manner crops up again in the section of *Satan's Harvest Home* entitled "Reasons for the Growth of Sodomy," a polemic ostensibly about men, but unable to refrain from remarks about women:

> But of all the Customs *Effeminacy* has produc'd, none more hateful, predominant, and pernicious, than that of the Mens *Kissing* each other. This *Fashion* was brought over from *Italy*, (the *Mother* and *Nurse* of *Sodomy*); where the *Master* is oftner *Intriguing* with his *Page*, than a *fair Lady*. And not only in that *Country*, but in *France*, which copies from them, the *Contagion* is diversify'd, and the Ladies (in the *Nunneries*) are criminally *amorous* of each other, in a *Method* too gross for Expression. I must be so partial to my own *Country-Women*, to affirm, or, at least, hope they claim no Share of this *Charge*; but must confess, when I see two Ladies *Kissing* and *Slopping* each other, in a *lascivious Manner*, and *frequently* repeating it, I am shock'd to the last Degree.[87]

Women kissing in the presence of others is a sign not only of foreign contagion, but of the criminal amorousness endemic to Italy and France. Despite the defensive disavowal of the applicability of criminal amorousness to his own Country-Women – in a manner not unlike Jane Sharp more than half a century earlier – the associations let loose in this passage indicate that the discourse has moved into an altogether different register. With the conceptual link made between the public kissing of women and the Italian bugbear, sodomy, with the use of "lascivious" to describe the apparently horrifying spectacle of "two Ladies Kissing and Slopping each other," and with the phobic inclusion of the fact that women might kiss and slop not once, but repeatedly, same-sex kissing is refigured as public sex.

The same year, another anonymous publication entitled "The Sapho-An" took upon itself the task of warning young men of, as its subtitle says, the "pleasures which the fair sex enjoy with each other":

> Know, whilst you idle thus away your time,
> Women in secret joys consume their prime,
> Some fav'rite maid, or handy young coquette
> Steals the rich prize you vainly strive to get;
> Of them be cautious, but the artful prude
> Watch most, for she will thoughtless girls delude...
> Your lovely nymph, in private, quench'd her flame
> With some experience'd, well-known crafty dame.[88]

With the threat to a woman's chastity embodied by "some fav'rite maid," "handy young coquette," or "well-known crafty dame," and with the name of Sappho linked to the English Ann in public, vernacular obscenity, the terms of female friendship become indistinguishable from the terms of tribadism.

As the knowing references to Sappho in several of the above texts suggest, sexual satire of the early and mid-eighteenth century not only draws on the tradition of Sappho herself, but melds that tradition with more sexually explicit ancient rhetorics. In chapter 5, I briefly discussed the Renaissance Sappho in the context of Harriette Andreadis's contention that Sappho was the "chief exemplar" of "lesbianism as we know it" in the seventeenth century.[89] By the mid-seventeenth century, the hyperphallic images found in Martial and Lucian accompanied the more ambiguously rendered Sappho (represented as pining for both men and women, and as such both celebrated and decried) in English vernacular texts. In 1656, for instance, R. Fletcher translated much of Martial, including "Ad Bassam tribadem Epig. 91" which addresses the tribade Bassa thus:

> Cause amongst males thou nere was seen to be
> Nor as unchast no fable feigned thee,
> But all thy offices discharged were
> By thy own sex, no man intruding there,
> I grant thou seem'dst *Lucretia* to our eye,
> But (o mistake!) *Bassa* th'art out ont, fie.
> Two twatts commit the fact, and dare it can,
> While a prodigious lust supplies the man,
> Th'hast made a riddle worth the *Thebane* guile,
> Where no man is, adultery bred the while.[90]

In a Shakespearean play, when a male character (Othello, Claudio, Leontes) accuses a female (Desdemona, Hero, Hermione) of appearing to be one thing but being something else, his meaning is quite specific: she is a whore. The deceit of a Bassa, who can "discharge" the "offices" of the masculine sex is simply outside of this Shakespearean field of reference. By means of Martial, Fletcher returns to the question that had vexed Brantôme – whether two women together can commit adultery – but arrives at a completely different answer. His assertion that "adultery" is "bred the while" is underscored by the graphic nature of his description: "Two twatts commit the fact."

Such erotic explicitness is further amplified in Ferrand Spence's 1685 translation of Lucian's dialogue between the two courtesans, Cleonarium and Leaena. This dialogue details the erotic exploits of "that Rich Lady of *Lesbos*," Megilla, who, along with her "Wife," Demonassa, had invited Leaena into their bed. In Leaena's description: "they began to toy, kissing me as Men are wont, not barely applying the Lips, but opening the Mouth, biting and pressing my Bosom, with all other Testimonies of a violent Passion, whereat I was strangely amaz'd, as not being able to guess the matter." When Leaena asks Megilla if she is a hermaphrodite or has had a sex change, Megilla replies that neither is the case; rather, she possesses "all the Passions and Inclinations of Men, and something

"Friendship so curst"

that will serve instead of Manhood."[91] With the increase in such translations and the rise of an English market in obscenity, the image of women "kissing . . . as Men are wont," along with "all other Testimonies of a violent Passion" become available to both titillate and satirize.

As noted in chapter 2, titillation often was the aim of pseudo-medical texts. This was certainly true of *Tractatus de Hermaphroditis: Or, a Treatise of Hermaphrodites* (1718), a collection of obscene anecdotes about "masculine women."[92] Disingenuously calling his work "an innocent Entertainment for all curious Persons, without any Views of inciting Masculine-Females to Amorous Tryals with their own Sex,"[93] the anonymous author romps through a series of sexual adventures of aristocratic ladies in Italy, each episode more sexually explicit than the preceding one. Although he admits in his Preface that the "Intrigues of my HERMAPHRODITES are indeed very amazing," he also assures the incredulous "that many Lascivious Females divert themselves one with another at this time in this City, is not to be doubted." After surveying the medical literature on hermaphrodites, including old chestnuts about the role of the clitoris in female pleasure, the author turns to his real topic:

Women well furnish'd in these Parts [the clitoris] may divert themselves with their Companions, to whom for the most part they can give as much Pleasure as Men do, but cannot receive in any proportion the Pleasure themselves, for want of Ejaculation, the Crisis of Enjoyment to the Male in the Intrigues of *Venus*. I am inform'd that Diversions of this nature are frequently practis'd by robust and lustful Females, who cannot with any prospect of safety to their Reputations, venture upon the Embraces of a Man, though they are never so strongly enclin'd. The unnatural Pleasures of this kind are finely illustrated in the following Song, written by Mr. ROWE, which I take it will not be improperly inserted in this Place.

Rowe's song follows:

    While SAPPHO, with harmonious Airs,
        Her dear PHILENIS charms,
    With equal Joy the Nymph appears,
        Dissolving in her Arms.
    Thus to themselves alone they are,
        What all Mankind can give;
    Alternately the happy Pair
        All grant, and all receive.
    Like the Twin-Stars, so fam'd for Friends,
        Who set by Turns, and rise;
    When one to THETIS Lap descends,
        His Brother mounts the Skies.
    With happier Fate, and kinder Care,
        These Nymphs by Turns do reign;
    While still the Falling, does prepare
        The Rising, to sustain.

> The Joys of either Sex in Love;
> In each of them we read,
> Successive each, to each does prove,
> Fierce Youth and yielding Maid.[94]

As is appropriate for a work that testifies to the delights of "Amorous Tryals" in order to entice, sell, and arouse, Rowe's song – and the narrative that follows – does not condemn female homoeroticism. It partakes of neither the persuasive cajoling of polite discourse nor the satiric offensiveness of the scandalmonger. Rather than see in such a "happy Pair" "dissolving" in each other's arms a severe carelessness toward men, Rowe presents these pastoral "Nymphs" as experiencing a "happier Fate, and kinder Care." Twin-stars, they are privy to the doubled delights to be experienced in the temporal and spatial alterations between the positions of "Fierce Youth and yielding Maid." Rather than Brantôme's assertion that female–female sex is "merely the apprenticeship to the great business with men,"[95] Rowe presents this happy pair as able to grant and receive "What all Mankind can give." In keeping with the title, *Tractatus de Hermaphroditis*, Rowe's song manipulates an image of the hermaphrodite to authorize its vision of a mutual and symmetrical sexuality which partakes of the "Joys of either Sex in Love."

The equivocal image of the hermaphrodite authorizes a happy jostling together in Rowe's song of the rhetorics of friendship and eroticism, innocence and licentiousness. In this it has much in common with Aphra Behn's lyric of thirty years before, "*To the fair* Clarinda, *who made Love to me, imagin'd more than Woman*" (1688).[96] Behn's poem begins with an apostrophe to the beloved which defines the central problem posed by Clarinda as one of naming: "Fair lovely Maid, or if that Title be / Too weak, too Feminine for Nobler thee, / Permit a Name that more Approaches Truth: / And let me call thee, Lovely Charming Youth." Is Clarinda a maid or youth? Or, as the verse enumerates the possibilities, nymph or swain? Cloris or Alexis? Aphrodite or Hermes? Insofar as Behn draws from a tradition of the hermaphrodite or androgyne that is at once allegorical and material, philosophical and medical,[97] Roberta Martin suggests that the poet deploys "a trope of a radical gender indeterminacy that escapes social censor and legal detection by slipping the traces of language and playing in the interstices of meaning made possible by changing definitions of gender and sexuality in the seventeenth century."[98] I would qualify this assessment by suggesting that it is less that the binary sex/gender/sexuality system is *subverted* by Behn's use of indeterminacy than that it has yet to be concretely formed. Coyly asserting that this "bright Nymph" who "betrays us to the Swain" was sent for pity to the female sex so that "we might Love, and yet be Innocent," Behn's speaker, like Orinda, uses the absence of a mature phallus to women's erotic advantage.[99] Although she asserts that "For sure no Crime with thee we can commit," she quickly equivocates in the next line: "Or if we shou'd – thy Form excuses it." Playfully keeping open the question of what kind of crime might be committed by two women with the use of an elliptical dash, the persona adopts a tone of mock innocence: "For who, that gathers fairest Flowers believes / A Snake lies hid beneath the Fragrant Leaves." Is the "Snake" that lies "hid" a diminutive penis or an enlarged clitoris? Since the title suggests that Clarinda is "*imagin'd* more than woman" and not, in fact, an actual hermaphrodite (however much her bodily charms might combine those of Hermes and Aphrodite), Behn clearly is laying claim to the pleasures of female–female eroticism under the auspices of the hermaphrodite's doubled body.

Behn's deployment of the hermaphrodite as a poetic figure for a woman's female love object was in some respects riskier than Philips's regendering of classical *amicitia*. Unmarried and associated with the disreputable stage, Behn was regularly celebrated and condemned as a woman who combined masculine wit with feminine softness. Those who approved lauded her: "With all the thought and vigour of our sex / The moving softness of your own you mix." Those who disapproved did so in rabid terms: "since her Works had neither Witt enough for a Man, nor Modesty enough for a Woman, she was to be look'd on as a Hermaphrodite, & consequently not fit to enjoy the benefits & Priviledges of either Sex..."[100] Behn was skirting on thin ice, and she probably knew it. But the use of the hermaphrodite was far more canny – and radical – than simply appropriating for a love poem the figure to which Behn herself was compared. The hermaphrodite at this point in the history of medical and literary discourses could not help but carry an erotic signification. To this most sexualized of vocabularies, Behn conjoined the literary discourse of erotic friendship, in a move that would come to mirror the transformation of (and the consequences for) the rhetoric of chaste innocence as it increasingly came under scrutiny.

Behn clearly was cognizant of the discourse concerning sodomy. She was intimate – probably in love with – John Hoyle, who was indicted on charges of buggery in 1687.[101] One of her literary mentors, for whom she wrote an elegy, was the notorious Earl of Rochester, who versified sodomy as yet one libertine pleasure among many. Behn had used the homoerotic resources of the pastoral in "Our Cabal" to describe the intimacy of "Mr. J. H." and "Mr. Ed. Bed" ("But all the Love he ever knew, / On *Lycidas* he does bestow: / who pays his Tenderness again, / Too Amorous for a Swain to a Swain") as well as in "To Amintas. Upon Reading the Lives of some of the Romans," where she explicitly characterizes the charm Hoyle held for both men and women: "For neither sex can here thy fetters shun."[102] Indeed, the pastoral served capaciously to articulate not only Behn's own desire for "Amintas," but provided the ground for the poetic expression of an equally passionate investment in Clarinda. Within the scope of Behn's *oeuvre*, then, we can begin to catch glimpses of a discourse that would further connect, as did *Satan's Harvest Home*, female–female desire to the more public discourse about sex among men.

In contrast to the playful indeterminacies exploited by Behn and Rowe, the figure depicted in *Tractatus de Hermaphroditis* is decidedly not a hermaphrodite. Despite the title, this text depicts neither real bodies with doubled genitalia nor fantastical bodies that change or merge through the force of desire. Rather, "masculine females" are masculine only in the sense that they enjoy sex with women; they are, in short, "Lascivious Females." They do not necessarily cross-dress, appear masculine, or pursue other masculine activities; they are beautiful women who desire and seduce other beautiful women. In thus employing an old term (hermaphrodite) to forge a new social category (masculine females), *Tractatus de Hermaphroditis* silently elides the other term (tribadism) that had been used to explain the existence of such women. Indeed, the "masculine female" both derives from the discourse of tribadism while departing significantly from it: none of these "masculine females" are monstrous or grotesque; although they may be "well furnish'd in these Parts," none have enlarged clitorises; and all of them are represented as sexually desirable.

As this licentious tract attempts to develop a new paradigm for phenomena previously understood as either hermaphroditism or tribadism, the lineaments of a debate about the relationships among women's bodily morphology, erotic desire, and behavior begin to emerge. Is the "masculine female" a category of gender or a category of eroticism? A phenomenon of the body or desire? Having discarded the central premise of Renaissance Galenism – that bodies, emotions, and behaviors map transparently onto one another – medical doctors in the eighteenth century were less inclined to view female–female eroticism as a function of anatomical aberration, whether hermaphroditism or clitoral hypertrophy. (Sex transformation, as we have seen, already had been discredited.) Their skepticism had the further effect of delegitimizing the philosophical discourse regarding the erotic androgyne. Behn deployed the figure of the hermaphrodite to metaphorize female–female desire at the moment it was losing currency in medical circles as a viable mode of explanation. Indeed, if *Tractatus de Hermaphroditis* appears to be a last gasp in this medical tradition, the death knell of this strategy is sounded by *A Mechanical and Critical Enquiry Into the Nature of Hermaphrodites* (1741) by James Parsons, doctor and member of the Royal Society.[103] His *Enquiry* begins as a scholarly attempt to debunk the common belief – common, that is, outside of scientific circles – that hermaphrodites exist. Any such double being would contradict what Parsons sees as the laws of Nature. Within his repudiation of hermaphroditism, however, hovers the ghostly image of the tribade.

Hermaphrodites, Parsons insists, are nothing other than women with enlarged clitorises or, as he terms them, "macroclitorides." This idea was not particularly revolutionary; it had been debated at least since Nicolas Culpeper and was soon to receive official accreditation with R. James's *Medical Dictionary* (1745), which asserts that "all the Histories related to Hermaphrodites" are "merely imaginary," the subjects so construed being "mere Women, whose *Clitoris* was grown to an exorbitant Size, and whose *Labia Pudendorum* were preternaturally tumid."[104] But Parsons goes one step further: an enlarged clitoris, he declares, has no necessary relation to erotic behavior. With this assertion, it would appear, two centuries of anatomical (and legal) confusion and conflation come to a halt.

Contextualizing the *Enquiry* in relation to prior medical views of the tribade, Theresa Braunschneider demonstrates that Parsons's replacement of the hermaphrodite with the "macroclitoride" disarticulates female–female eroticism from its prior link to an excessive bodily morphology: for Parsons, any woman, whatever her erotic proclivities, could be marked by clitoral hypertrophy; an enlarged organ is neither cause nor effect of female–female sex.[105] Such sex, Parsons contends, is a commonsense alternative to the threat of pregnancy outside of wedlock. It thus is a choice that any woman could make.

Understood during the sixteenth and seventeenth centuries as a peculiar manifestation of bodily morphology, gender inversion, and homoerotic desire, the tribade embodied an ontological problem: as such, her erotic desire required either supernatural explanation or medical intervention. When, however, the tribade, along with the hermaphrodite, was subjected to increased scrutiny under changing medical regimes, she became irrelevant to medical discourse, which deemed her not a medical but a behavioral problem. Her exceptionalism, always defensively reinscribed in seventeenth-century medical texts, gave way to typicality.[106] This shift in the terms of the tribade's intelligibility was replicated in contemporaneous literature and obscenity. For whereas the term "tribade" was retained in many literary and obscene works (and indeed, is still in use today), the fundamental transformation in the discourse of medicine – that female homoeroticism is a choice freely available to any woman – was reflected in these other discourses as well. During this same period, the discourse of "impossibility" associated with female–female eroticism became newly inflected with a discourse of propriety. In the seventeenth century, the impossibility imputed to female homoeroticism derived from its position outside of Nature; in the eighteenth century, the notion of impossibility was articulated in terms of concerns about proper behavior and manners. As women writers began to assert the superiority of female bonds; as male poets began to bemoan the exclusivity of female friends and to insert themselves forcibly into female dyads; as medical writers disarticulated homoerotic desire from the double nature of

322   The renaissance of lesbianism

the hermaphrodite; and as hack writers capitalized on the pornographic potential of "masculine females" cavorting on the Continent and corrupting English maids, the traits associated with the tribade were reconfigured and the meaning of homoeroticism transformed.

These changes in the cultural discourse of female homoeroticism suggest that the picture painted by social historians of a crisis in gender relations that began around 1550, peaked around 1650, and passed by 1700, is based on a very selective view of what counts as both a "crisis" and "gender relations."[107] If one focuses on discourses about male–female and female–female eroticism (as well as, one might note, male–male eroticism), one is struck by the increasing anxiety articulated in the late seventeenth and early eighteenth centuries. This period witnessed the inauguration of a regime of domestic heterosexuality and a corresponding sexualization of female chastity; profound changes in medical understandings of female anatomy, including the rejection of hermaphroditism and clitoral hypertrophy as modes of explanation for female sexual deviance; an increase in women's participation in the public sphere, including a chorus of voices contesting the sexual double standard, arguing for women's equality and freedom of marital choice, and proposing lifelong singleness as the condition best suited to women's aspirations; and the material circulation of a variety of vernacular texts, from travel narratives and marital advice books to stageplays and obscenity, all of which depicted erotic matters in increasingly graphic terms. If these are not aspects of a gender system in crisis, what is?

That these suspicions and protocols began to make their presence felt prior to what we might think of as the self-articulations of a self-conscious "sapphist" (such as Anne Lister in the early nineteenth century), suggests that in historical terms, erotic identities are less an emanation of personal desire than an effect of particular social arrangements and discursive formations.[108] That the discourse Lister found most useful to help forge her own sexual subjectivity was classical literature, especially Martial and Ovid, should therefore come as no surprise. Cannily using literary references as a way to ascertain other women's erotic knowledge (and availability), renaming one of her lovers Kallista (Greek for "most beautiful" but probably a reference to Calisto as well), Lister inhabited the ambivalent interstices between female friendship and perversion that were her inheritance from the erotic landscape of the late seventeenth century.[109]

The beginnings of a consolidation of domestic heterosexuality predated the articulations of suspicion regarding chaste female friendship. Discourses of companionate marriage had been promulgated through prescriptive literature for a century before Waller's lyric. This raises an interesting temporal disjunction in discursive domains. From Shakespeare's plays to Waller's poem, the structural trajectory of literary works proceeds first by articulating homoeroticism, then by negating it through masculine intrusion or marital closure. As in Van Dyck's *Mirtillo Crowning Amarillis*, the production of heteroeroticism seems to depend on a prior homoeroticism. (One might not be inaccurate in seeing in the narrative structure of eighteenth-century pornography the dramatic structures of *A Midsummer Night's Dream* or the visual hierarchies of Van Dyck's painting.) In broader historical terms, however, the reverse seems to be true. It is only after the consolidation of domestic heterosexuality as a dominant cultural ideology that "sapphism" would be produced out of the materials of loving friendship and tribadism.

With this historical shift in mind, we are in a better position to understand the indifference to the causes of tribadism within the old regime of impossibility. To identify specific causes and to adduce patterns of causality would be to admit, beyond the occasionally aberrant instance, the social efficacy of possibility itself. Once female–female sex becomes more than a monstrous specter, once it becomes more generally suspected as a genuine possibility – able to infiltrate even the most innocent, beauteous, loving pair of friends – its causality becomes identified (by James Parsons, among others) as a fit object of investigation.

From Iphis to Orinda to little A———n, the ideological distance traversed within the tradition of a "friendship so curst" could not be greater.[110] The differences can be summarized by the following shifts: From the expression of lament by a desiring female subject to the condemnation of female intimacy by men. From accepting as self-evident Nature's decrees to voicing a skeptical view of Nature or finding a way to manipulate Nature for one's own ends. From invoking the magical fantasy of sex transformation to rejecting such fantasies in the name of greater female freedom. From a governing logic of innocuousness and impossibility to a governing logic of suspicion and possibility. From the insignificance attributed to chaste female love to the erotic significance associated with a range of female social types: tribades, masculine females, macroclitorides, female husbands, tommies, sapphists, lesbians. These latter figures are born not only of particular configurations of "metonymic masculinity," class pretensions, and racial difference, as described by Lanser, but of the ongoing negotiation of the terms of Nature, friendship, anatomy, and obscenity.

I conclude the diachronic argument of *The Renaissance of Lesbianism* by suggesting that the interweaving of discourses of chaste female friendship with those of tribadism can be understood as one measure of the growing threat of the unnatural *within* the seemingly natural. By the turn of the eighteenth century, women's same-sex erotic proclivities were certainly deemed unnatural, but they were not judged, as in Iphis's plaintive cry, to be outside of Nature. To translate this into a more modern idiom: the convergence of the figures of tribade and friend can be seen as one effect of the growing interest in apprehending the *abnormal* within, and distinguishing it against, the putatively *normal*. It hardly seems coincidental that during this period the paradigm of the natural and the unnatural – underpinned by ideas of the miscellaneous but nonetheless hierarchical order of human and animal life within a Christian cosmos – began a slow and intermittent slide to a more scientific, biologically based concept of normality and its deviations. Although the *Oxford English Dictionary* cannot be relied on to prove the evolution of these concepts, it does provide a useful chronology. The word "norm," according to the *OED*, has been common since about 1855. Meaning a "standard, model, pattern, type," "norm" is the Anglicized form of "norma," which the *OED* charts as first appearing in 1676 in Sir Matthew Hale's *The Primitive Origination of Mankind*: "Again, will they suppose it a *Norma*, Rule, or Law of a most excellent frame and order."[111] The word "normal," however, has a longer history, derived first from the language of mathematics. Meaning "Right (angle), rectangular," "normal" appears first in 1650 in John Bulwer's *Anthropometamorphosis*, that bizarre treatise obsessed with the multitude of deviations (and artificial changes) wrought upon the human body: "those determined bounds of the hair, which are called by our Barbars the Normal Angels."[112] Thomas Blount's 1656 edition of *Glossographia* defines "normal" as "right by rule, made by the square or Rule," a definition which the *OED* uses to support an early meaning of "constituting, conforming to, not deviating or differing from the common type or standard; regular, usual (common since c. 1840)." The adverb "normally" has an even earlier provenance, used in books of surgery to refer to "in a regular manner; regularly," as in a translation of Jacques Guillemeau's *Frenche Chirurgerye* (1597), "therunto are many things required, which I heere normallye & rightlye will prosecute,"[113] and in a translation of Oswald Gabelkover's *Boock of Physicke* (1599), "applye the same on his Breste, 3 or 4 nightes normallye after other."[114] Together, these terms, derived from the language of mathematics, surgery, and physic, begin to gesture toward a new regime of intelligibility for human bodies and behaviors, governed not so much by understandings of Nature, but by concepts of standards and deviations. Parsons, for instance, consistently uses a lexicon of standards and deviations (including the terms "standard," "deviation," "ordinary," "distortion," and "perfection") to articulate his refusal to believe in gender ambiguity. Yet, the discourse of normality did not do away with the concept of Nature. Rather, the discourse of normality incorporated the moral corruption associated with the unnatural in such a way as to mystify its own operations of power.

One hinge for this movement from one discursive regime to another, I want to propose, can be located in the negotiation of Nature, friendship, and innocence in Katherine Philips's verse. Intertwining the materials of classical *amicitia* and the Platonic love celebrated by the *précieuses* with a specifically female homoerotic inheritance, Philips rescues female–female love from the elegiac cast imposed on it by Renaissance forms of thought. Elegiac as her verse often is, it also demonstrates that the energies of a female homopoetics need not be confined to a gesture of farewell. As my final chapter will argue, it is not so much Philips's self-articulation as a desiring subject that renders her crucial to the history of *lesbianism*. Rather, in her strategic revision of the terms of Nature, we can catch a glimpse of how female friendship would become, despite Philips's own intentions, less innocent, less obviously chaste, more suspect, more in need of defense. Before Philips, intense female intimacy was rarely in danger of social condemnation; after Philips, such intimacy was rarely completely free from it.

8 The quest for origins, erotic similitude, and the melancholy of *lesbian* identification

> In the past few decades it has proved difficult to make connections across ideological barriers; perhaps we can make them across time instead. Celibate friends, SM dykes, women who get mistaken for men whether they like it or not, singles and couples and threesomes, separatists, prostitutes, in-your-face activists, respectable closet-cases, those of us who also like orgies or weddings or study groups or men or domestic bliss: we can all find our origins here.[1]

In this final chapter, I propose that it is in that great and imperfect theory of psychoanalysis that we might find tools helpful to the project of theorizing *lesbian* history. Lest this proposal lead my readers to a collective groan, let me immediately clarify that I see in Freudian psychoanalysis two autonomous, though often intertwined, analytical projects: the assertion of grand developmental narratives, the veracity and explanatory power of which are compromised by their embeddedness within the normalizing systems they seek to explain; and the elucidation of certain complex psychic mechanisms, the hermeneutic subtlety and utility of which are unsurpassed. I do not believe that Freud's developmental narratives (the Oedipal complex and the alternative schemas he created to accommodate women) provide anything like an accurate representation or assessment of individual psychic history, although in certain respects they illustrate vividly the workings of patriarchal ideology within modernity. Thus, except for discussing in chapter 5 the ways in which Freud's explication of *lesbian* pathology derives from prior knowledges, I have not relied on psychoanalysis to scrutinize female sexuality. My use of psychoanalysis, rather, has been limited to deploying certain interpretative tools – the concept of psychic displacement (and with it, the corresponding concepts of the unconscious, repression, and projection) and the understanding of desire and anxiety as mutually constitutive – to analyze phenomena such as the medical appropriation of the Venus *pudica* and the cultural reinvention of the tribade. The belatedness of psychoanalysis, so often invoked among historical scholars to deauthorize its applicability to earlier eras, is precisely what renders it useful to my project, for psychoanalysis carries within itself the vestiges of its own engagement with early modern culture.[2]

It is with this recursive relationship between psychoanalysis and the Renaissance in mind that I turn to several psychic mechanisms – identification, introjection, mourning, and melancholy – in order to analyze, in psychic and historical terms, the relation between contemporary *lesbians* and the homoerotic figures I have analyzed in this book. By invoking identification, I do not mean to condone the ways in which that concept has been used, by Freud and his successors, to normalize the paths of desire or the workings of gender.[3] Nor do I mean to set myself apart as analyst, as if I were not implicated in the desires, transferences, and wish-fulfillments of other scholars; the previous chapters should have made clear the extent of my psychic and intellectual investments in a historicizing project. Nonetheless, because I believe that one aim of lesbian history is to probe the contingency and incommensurability of contemporary identities, it is with the help of psychoanalysis that I conclude my genealogy.

Since this chapter considers the quest for origins, it seems fitting to return to the opening of *The Renaissance of Lesbianism* and the notion of "practicing impossibilities" from John Lyly's *Gallathea*. In this play performed by boy actors before Queen Elizabeth, Cupid addresses his audience of aristocratic ladies with his impish scheme to confound Diana's virgin nymphs: "I will make their pains my pastimes, and so confound their loves in their own sex that they shall dote in their desires, delight in their affections, and practice only impossibilities" (2.2.6–9). Having traced the tradition of the *amor impossibilis*, I now want to track the enactment of impossibilities in Lyly's play. How are impossibilities practiced? At the level of plot, the answer is linear: first comes attraction to the other "boy's" beauty (2.1); then arrives self-awareness of passion (2.4 and 2.5) which, due to suspicion about the other's gender, leads to dismay (3.2); then comes an agreement to enjoy flirtation despite suspicion (4.4); and finally comes the climactic "revelation" of the girls' gender, and then the promise of marriage and consummation (5.3). Except for the equanimity with which each girl decides to indulge in her "mistaken" love and Venus's intervention on behalf of their affection, this could be any of a number of Renaissance crossdressing comedies.

But these exceptions make Lyly's play different. It is more thoroughly and frankly homoerotic in plot, structure, and character than *As You Like It* or *Twelfth Night*. Rather than seek to confirm the inappropriate nature of female–female desire through differences of status or state (think of Rosalind and Phebe in *As You Like It*, for instance), Lyly makes clear that to practice impossibilities is first, possible, and second, a matter of loving another who looks, behaves, and feels amazingly, if perplexingly, like the self. To practice impossibilities means to experience and confront the attraction of a love caused and defined by similarity rather than difference. Gallathea and Phyllida are depicted throughout in terms of their mirroring resemblance: they not only look like one another; they identify with one another. Their affinity is enhanced throughout by Lyly's masterful (albeit didactic) use of rhetorical parallelism, in which phrases of equal length (*isocolon*) and symmetrical grammatical elements (*parason*) structure the lovers' dialogue. For instance, after both characters secretly have soliloquized their distress over their predicament, first Phyllida wonders aloud, "I fear me he is as I am, a maiden," and then Gallathea says, "I fear the boy to be as I am, a maiden" (3.2.29–32). When, in response to Diana's admonition in the "unveiling" scene that they "leave these fond, fond affections," Gallathea asserts, "I will never love any but Phyllida. Her love is engraven in my heart with her eyes"; her pledge is seconded by Phyllida: "Nor I any but Gallathea, whose faith is imprinted in my thoughts by her words" (5.3.125–30). When Venus asks the pair if their love is "unspotted, begun with truth, continued with constancy, and not to be altered till death?" Gallathea vows, "Die, Gallathea, if thy love be not so," while Phyllida proclaims, "Accursed be thou, Phyllida, if thy love be not so" (5.3.136–40). Upon Venus's offer to transform one of the pair into a boy, Phyllida proclaims, "I am content, so I may embrace Gallathea," to which Gallathea replies, "I wish it, so I may enjoy Phyllida" (5.3.148–49). If the play's investment in presenting these lovers as coequal in everything makes for rather stilted dramatic action (suited more for a schoolboys' grammatical exercise than lively stage dialogue), the characters' linguistic symmetry nonetheless communicates effectively the mimetic nature of their mutual desires. As Gallathea puts it, in a punning remark that redoubles the effect of the personal pronoun: "Aye me, he is as I am, for his speeches be as mine are" (3.2.36–41). Such equipoise is not even disrupted by the play's close, for Venus's offer of a sex change leaves unspecified which character will be transformed.[4] So intent is this play on celebrating similitude that the endowment of physical difference necessitated by patriarchal marriage – the phallus – is deferred beyond the dramatic frame.

When Cupid remarks that he will "confound their loves in their own sex," Venus's son invokes the multiple meanings of *confound* listed in the *OED* for this period: "To defeat utterly, discomfit, bring to ruin, destroy, overthrow, rout, bring to nought"; "to discomfit, abash, put to shame, ashame"; "to throw into confusion of mind or feelings; so to surprise and confuse (a person) that he loses for the moment his presence of mind, and discernment what to do"; and "to throw (things) into confusion or disorder." In addition to this mêlée of confusion, shame, and destruction, a further meaning of *confound* was available to Lyly: "To mix up or mingle so that the elements become difficult to distinguish or impossible to separate." Treating as identical that which ostensibly is separate is not only the aim of Cupid's antics, but of the play as well.

The erotic similitude that rhetorically and thematically structures *Gallathea* relies upon the terms first offered by its Ovidian source, but neither Caxton's translation of 1480 nor Golding's translation of 1567 evince as strong an investment in it as does Lyly's play. Sandys's 1626 translation, however, renders the moment of mutual infatuation of Iphis and Ianthe in terms that expand into an all-encompassing range of likeness: "Like young, like beautifull, together bred, / Inform'd alike, alike accomplished: / Like darts at once their simple bosoms strike; / Alike their wounds, their hopes, ô far unlike!"[5] The reiteration of likeness in the figuring of their mutual love suggests that it is born not only out of bodily resemblance – both young, both beautiful, both female – but of educational experience and social accomplishment. Their similarities extend beyond the mere accident of physical form, making the emotional wounds that they experience in "their simple bosoms" affectively identical. Yet, their hopes differ because in Ovid's tale only one of the pair is crossdressed; thus, she alone is burdened with the unhappy knowledge of the *impossibilis* of their *amor*.

This language of erotic similitude is, by now, familiar. It is present, for instance, in what I take to be an emblematic instance, Helena's reminiscence of her affection for Hermia:

> We, Hermia, like two artificial gods,
> Have with our needles created both one flower,
> Both on one sampler, sitting on one cushion,
> Both warbling of one song, both in one key,
> As if our hands, our sides, voices, and minds
> Had been incorporate. So we grew together,
> Like to a double cherry, seeming parted,
> But yet an union in partition;
> Two lovely berries moulded on one stem;
> So, with two seeming bodies, but one heart. (3.2.203–12)

The multiple ways in which two become one – the reiteration of the word "both," the "incorporation" of their hands, sides, voices, and minds, the image of a double cherry, the final conflation of two bodies in one heart – assert a mimetic identification which it is the business of the play to disrupt and redirect toward gender and erotic difference.

As a defining trope of female homoerotic desire in the early modern period, the rhetoric of erotic similitude presumes the inevitability of likeness, equality, mutuality, and reciprocity when women express intense affection and longing for one another. Appropriated from the discourses of classical *amicitia* and Christian marriage, this rhetoric of similitude has, like chaste female friendship, been read until recently as necessarily devoid of eroticism – any physical desire is presumably "elevated" to a spiritual plane. My reading of Philips in the previous chapter should clarify, however, that the eroticism of this rhetoric is not contained by its articulation as spiritual longing.

In advancing this argument, I am extending the insights of Jeffrey Masten, whose book, *Textual Intercourse*, demonstrates the existence of an early modern collaborative male writing practice suffused with homoeroticism. Challenging the critical insistence that male–male desire in the early modern period necessarily takes the form of age- or status-hierarchy, Masten argues that both homoeroticism and collaboration depend upon and profit from the perception of similarities among men. At one moment, Masten extends his analysis to Emilia and Flavina in Shakespeare and Fletcher's *The Two Noble Kinsmen*, describing how their "emulous and collaborative friendship" depends on erotic similitude.[6] Indeed, Emilia banishes the specter of difference in her reminiscence: "What she [Flavina] lik'd / Was then of me approv'd, what not, condemn'd, / No more arraignment" (1.3.64–66). Liking, or desire, demands likeness, or similitude. Emilia then describes how "[t]he flowre that I would plucke / And put betweene my breasts, (O then but beginning / To swell about the blossome), she would long / Till she had such another, and commit it / To the like innocent cradle, where phoenix-like / They died in perfume" (1.3.66–71). Here, the rapturous expression of a passion that Emilia calls "fury innocent" in the Quarto (1.3.78; amended to "seely innocent" or "ev'ry innocent" by modern editors) depends upon the likeness of the two adolescent bodies: the possibility of each plucking identical flowers and placing them between identical "cradles," the two breasts that themselves are only beginning "to swell about the blossome." Not only are the two girls alike, but their breasts, each one like its counterpart and each pair of breasts like the other girl's, are likened to the flowers that they pluck. With the erotic energy of this reminiscence mediated through a floral circuitry, this passage locates erotic similitude at the literal heart of their relationship.[7]

Flavina and Emilia, Helena and Hermia, Iphis and Ianthe, Gallathea and Phyllida – these are the couples who, throughout this book, have given a face, voice, and presence to early modern *lesbianism*. Having illuminated their presence, however, I now want to submit the terms of their representation to scrutiny: what manner of *lesbianism* is this? If these characters impart to us a conceptual trace of a distant past, what can we glean from the expressions on their faces – faces that, in revealing their love for one another, seem to look so obsessively toward a mirror?

By broaching this question, I mean to invoke, as well, a reminder that the rhetoric of erotic similitude was not the only rhetoric representing female–female desires during the early modern period. The tribade's desires are interpreted precisely through a presumption of erotic difference – that which obtains between two women, only one of whom typically possesses (allegedly) an enlarged clitoris or dildo. Together, these representations bequeath to us two contradictory yet complementary logics of what it means for a woman to desire another woman. According to the rhetoric of erotic similitude in Renaissance literature, homoerotic desire enacts a similitude so extreme that all difference is banished from the circle of female intimacy. According to the discourse of tribadism in early modern medicine and travel literature, such desire involves a difference so perverse that it can only be conceptualized as an imitation of masculinity. The opposed logics of similitude and imitation govern the intelligibility of each homoerotic figure I have analyzed thus far: the adolescent friend, the chaste nymph, the lamenting lover, the crossdresser, the tribade. The former logic, however, has had a greater impact on the methods of historiography. To conclude my investigation of the way the past impinges on the present, this chapter examines the workings and the ramifications of the ethos of similitude. I first attend to the workings of similitude in contemporary discussions of queer and lesbian history, as they are manifested in two interrelated phenomena, historical continuism and psychic identification. I then turn to the genre of Renaissance lyric, that supposedly self-expressive mode, to analyze why similitude has had such a compelling hold on *lesbian* engagements with the past.

Historical inquiry implicitly is organized around the tension between continuity and change, identity and difference, although the emphases generally tilt toward one or the other.[8] According to Judith Bennett, the field of women's history most recently has privileged transformation as a more compelling paradigm than continuity. Suggesting that a preference for seeking evidence of transformation stems from a variety of disciplinary, developmental, political, and personal needs that deserve reexamination, Bennett argues that historians of women need to move beyond the model of transformation to recognize the adaptability of patriarchal structures or, as she puts it, the "patriarchal equilibrium" that works to maintain the status of women during periods of social, economic, and political change.[9] "[T]he *forms* of patriarchal power might have changed more than its *degree*," she argues; thus, we need to "study change in women's experiences without thereby positing transformation in women's status."[10]

I agree with Bennett that the forms of patriarchal power have been highly adaptable and durable. I question, however, whether a model of transformation currently dominates all fields of women's history. Within the subdiscipline of lesbian history, the search for historical foremothers has been, and continues to be, a primary motivation, and the logic of temporal continuity – and the related issue, similitude – has served as a governing paradigm. One of the most astute arguments for historical continuism is that made by Bernadette Brooten, who asserts in *Love Between Women: Early Christian Responses to Female Homoeroticism* that ancient Mediterranean texts demonstrate a coherent pre-Christian concept of erotic orientation. Whereas many things have changed since the pre-Christian era, one thing, she argues, has remained constant: the "long-term structures of male dominance and female subordination that so strongly characterize women's experience of sexuality."[11] Because Brooten views the censure of erotic love between women as tied to these long-term structures, and because she views patriarchal domination as definitive, she argues that "we can expect a lack of major turning points" in the history of female homoeroticism.[12]

David Halperin has critiqued Brooten for allowing a modern conception of *lesbianism* to "permeate the interior space" of her analysis, arguing that she "organizes her material around the modern concept of homosexuality, redescribes the [historical] phenomena in terms of it, and implies that sexuality and sexual orientation are more or less objective phenomena, independent of human perception, rooted in some transhistorical reality."[13] Despite this objection, Halperin concedes Brooten's point about periodization. Invoking Gayle Rubin's influential work on the transhistorical subordination of women, he agrees that lesbian history may be characterized by fewer turning points than that of male homosexuality:

The massive, universal or near-universal fact of male dominance, the corresponding kinship structures, the sexual division of labor, and the traffic in marriageable women that results from it mean, in particular, that women must submit to compulsory heterosociality, which denies them a social existence apart from men, whereas men are permitted various forms of homosociality so long as they have occasional sex with women. The dominating feature of women's sexual lives is not so much heterosexual desire as the inescapability of sexual relations with men.[14]

It is a mistake, I want to suggest, to assume that the fact of male domination, no matter how transhistorical, necessarily yields a greater continuity in the meaning of female homoeroticism than in male homoeroticism. Whereas certain long-term structures of gender domination (religious and state authorization of male–female marriage, the centrality of biological reproduction to social organization, and the privileging of phallic definitions of sexual practices) have been historically constant, their specific relationships to female–female desire have not. Just as the forms of patriarchy change in relation to other social forces (the influence of the Reformation on the family and corresponding reconfigurations of public and domestic labor are two examples), so too do erotic ideologies and arrangements mutate with the emergence of new discourses and social formations. It is certainly possible that despite such changes in form, the degree of constraint remains constant. Nonetheless, to assume that patriarchal culture utterly frames the experience of women is to grant masculinist discourses too much power. It is possible to keep structural influences on women's existence (gender ideologies, marital arrangements, reproductive imperatives) in the frame of analysis, without assuming that they *are* the frame. After all, some women did manage to elude precisely the feature that Halperin contends is inescapable: sexual relations with men.

Other theoretical issues at stake in Brooten's study and Halperin's rejoinder have been elucidated by Louise Fradenburg and Carla Freccero, who explicitly link historical continuism to the question of similitude in their introduction to *Premodern Sexualities*. Much as feminists have used psychoanalysis to trouble the doctrines of Freud, they deploy Foucaultian genealogy against Foucault's own commitment to what they call "alteritism" – the insistence on the radical incommensurability of past and present sexualities.[15] Critiquing alteritism as itself a form of essentialism, Fradenburg and Freccero defend the pleasures that historians and literary critics take in making identifications across time and place, in claiming people and practices of the medieval past as, for instance, gay or *lesbian*. Their diagnosis of the problem includes the charge that "a belief in the absoluteness of cultural and/or historical difference ... has, for many students of modernity, come to signify the essence of our contemporaneity. We are modern insofar as we know that we are incommensurably different from our past and from other cultures."[16] Insofar as alteritism stabilizes modern identities, and scruples against anachronism inhibit historical understanding, they suggest that positing "the power of the past to disrupt and remake the present is not necessarily to adopt a naive continuism."[17]

The question then becomes how to postulate a continuism that is not naive. What would a *sophisticated* continuism look like? Unfortunately, the answer is not clear. Fradenburg and Freccero instead articulate a further question: "What has to be asked is whether the observation of similarities or even continuities between past and present inevitably produces an ahistoricist or universalizing effect."[18] Although this is an excellent question, for it suggests the possibility of dissociating the *apprehension* of similarities and continuities from their possible *effects*, this methodological advance is stymied when universalizing effects are upheld as potentially subversive: "if we are to honor Foucault's insistence on the unpredictability of political strategies, we should not discount the oppositional potential even of grand narratives and continuist histories."[19]

Continuist histories are linked to similitude through Fradenburg and Freccero's use of the mirror as a central trope in their argument. Viewing oneself in the reflections of the past, they maintain, is a primary pleasure in the queering of history, and the "opposition between transhistoricist perspectives which seek, in the past, the allure of the mirror image, and historicist perspectives that 'accept' the difference of past from present, is itself highly ideological."[20] In championing the *jouissance* of identification, they argue that "one of the central challenges queer perspectives offer to historicist practice is their insistence that the purpose of recognizing pleasure's role in the production of historical discourse is not necessarily to launch yet another renunciation of such pleasure."[21] Correlating identification across time with pleasure, and resistance to identification with ascesis or a foreclosure of pleasure, they celebrate as *particularly queer* the pleasures of the mirror.

But is this pleasure genuinely queer, that is, resistant? Or is the pleasure of identification yet another emanation of the similitude that, since the Renaissance at least, has been a primary means of representing female homoeroticism? Why is it that identification is associated with pleasure, while forgoing identification in the name of historical alterity is correlated with an austere asceticism? Does opposition to collapsing the past into the present necessarily evacuate pleasure from the historical enterprise? Why is pleasure conceived only as the singular, ego-confirming gratification of the mirror? And what is it that would make the "allure of the mirror image" acceptable as a form of historicist practice? As these questions imply, I want to trouble Fradenburg and Freccero's opposition between identification as pleasure, on the one hand, and alterity as ascesis, on the other. These broad binaries are positioned unnecessarily as mutually exclusive. To echo Carolyn Dinshaw: "our choices as queer historians are not limited simply to mimetic identification with the past or blanket alteritism."[22] As she puts it, "[a]ppropriation, misrecognition, disidentification: these terms that queer theory has highlighted all point to the alterity within mimesis itself, the never-perfect aspect of identification. And they suggest the desires that propel such engagements, the affects that drive relationality even across time."[23] Whereas Dinshaw's impulse is to foster queer community by "touching" the medieval past, to make "new relations, new identifications, new communities with past figures who elude resemblance to us but with whom we can be connected partially by virtue of shared marginality, queer positionality,"[24] my impulse is to analyze the desires that propel such identifications. Such desires, while deeply felt and potentially productive, can obscure the ways that historical difference can provide us with critical resources and understandings otherwise unavailable.

One understanding that a perspective attuned to alterity enables is that the terms by which the relation between the homoerotic past and the present is structured are themselves products of a historical process. Two different conceptual issues tend to be conflated in the trope of the mirror: first, structures of psychological affect (identification, pleasure, confirmation), and second, methodological procedures and historical arguments (the assertion of historical continuism; the processes by which one pursues historical inquiry). Affect and procedure both depend on a homology between similitude and identification: to be similar is to identify with and as; to identify is to do so on the basis of perceived resemblance. I want to disjoin these two issues in order to hypothesize that the desire to view oneself in the mirror, however enabling personally, need not be the procedural ground of lesbian history. The correlation forged by Fradenburg and Freccero between pleasure and the mirror, I shall argue, not only enacts a disavowal of alterity, but reactivates the historical relations of homoeroticism to processes of mimetic identification. Similitude, identification, the mirror – these concepts are not only central to modern discourses of homosexuality,

The quest for origins 335

they are some of the principal historical materials out of which the discourse of homosexuality emerged.

To anatomize these ontological and epistemological issues, I turn now to the critical procedures involved in the attempt to identify as *lesbian* early modern women and texts. By "identify" I mean to invoke two processes that are related to the conflation of psychological affect and critical method described above: the effort to discover/recover/reclaim *lesbians* in the past, and the desire to invest those women with identities *like our own*. To identify is thus to embark on a process of mimetic identification (to identify is to identify *with*) that is as much psychic as historical. That such discoveries and investments are endemic to the field of lesbian scholarship is evinced not only in the work of Brooten, Fradenburg and Freccero, but, as chapter 5 suggested, in that of Harriette Andreadis and Terry Castle as well. Such identifications extend to Emma Donoghue's utopian desire, quoted in my epigraph, that the history of British *lesbian* culture since the Restoration might provide contemporary *lesbians* with a sense of their origins. Donoghue uncovered an impressive array of texts about female erotic intimacy to which I am indebted. Nonetheless, even though she is wary of "The Great Paradigm Shift" as the central question for lesbian history, her narrative implicitly treats eighteenth-century figures as straightforward precursors to contemporary *lesbians*, tacitly tracing a direct line of descent from Aphra Behn to Radclyffe Hall: "we can all find our origins here."[25] Scholarship on seventeenth-century women writers has been particularly invested in identifying *lesbians* as part of its reclamation of the female voice. It is to this body of work that I address the following questions. How does such an identification occur? By what inclusions and exclusions, claims and counter-claims? What historical and psychic exigencies operate on our identification of *lesbian* writing and writers in this period?

Consider the articulations of desire in the following three Renaissance lyrics written during a seventy-year period:

> Go gentle wreath, and let her know,
> I love her when I say not so.
> By my pains with thee she'l finde
> How oft she hath been in my minde.
> To thy fabrick hand and head
> Joyntly have contributed;
> And whilst others speak her fair,
> 'Tis I that have her to a hair.
> Go and be at her command,
> For alwaies thou wilt be at hand;
> Warm the blood which from that part
> Takes secret marches to her heart;
> The endlesse circularity,

Will shew loves perpetuity.
The subtile web, and secret twining,
Is like love with love combining:
Learn then by her pulse to know,
Whether she's in health or no;
And convey news to me,
By some kinde sympathy:
  Tell her then, that wearing me,
She's not without a part of me.

I Did not live until this time,
  Crown'd my felicity,
When I could say without a crime,
  I am not thine, but Thee.
This Carcass breath'd, and walkt, and slept,
  So that the World believ'd
There was a Soul the Motions kept;
  But they were all deceiv'd.
For as a Watch by art is wound
  To motion, such was mine:
But never had *Orinda* found
  A Soul till she found thine;
Which now inspires, cures, and supplies,
  And guides my darkned Breast:
For thou art all that I can prize,
  My Joy, my Life, my Rest.
No Bridegrooms nor Crown-conquerors mirth
  To mine compar'd can be:
They have but pieces of this earth,
  I've all the World in thee.
Then let our Flames still light and shine,
  And no false fear controul,
As innocent as our Design,
  Immortal as our Soul.

. . . Thy body is a naturall *Paradise*,
  In whose selfe, unmanur'd, all pleasure lies,
Nor needs *perfection*; why shouldst thou than
  Admit the tillage of a harsh rough man?
Men leave behinde them that which their sin showes,
  And are, as theeves trac'd, which rob when it snows.
But of our dallyance no more signes there are,
  Then *fishes* leave in streames, or *Birds* in aire.
And betweene us all sweetnesse may be had;
  All, all that *Nature* yields, or *Art* can adde.
My two lips, eyes, thighs, differ from thy two,
  But so, as thine from one another doe;
And, oh, no more; the likenesse being such,

> Why should they not alike in all parts touch?
> Hand to strange hand, lippe to lippe none denies;
>   Why should they brest to brest, or thighs to thighs?
> Likenesse begets such strange selfe flatterie,
>   That touching my selfe, all seemes done to thee.
> My selfe I embrace, and mine owne hands I kisse,
>   And amorously thanke my selfe for this.
> Me, in my glasse, I call thee...

Which, contemporary scholarship might tempt us to ask, is the *lesbian* love poem? Which lyric gives voice to *lesbian* desire? Can we put a gendered face on the enunciators of these discourses? Does the final poem, with its explicit images of the body, seem more likely to have been written by a woman who actually experienced desire for another woman? This excerpt, from the sixty-four-line elegy, "Sapho to Philaenis," was penned by John Donne, more often known for his witty and seductive heterosexual love poetry.[26] The degree to which it succeeds as an impersonation of *lesbian* desire has been a matter of debate. Janel Mueller, for instance, argues that "Sapho to Philaenis" celebrates and represents accurately *lesbian* love: "Donne really undertakes to imagine the pleasures, sustenance, and ideological implications by which lesbianism, as a mode of loving and being, resists patriarchal disposition and diminution of women."[27] Elizabeth Harvey, conversely, argues that the elegy's "transvestite ventriloquism" masquerades as a sympathetic "giving voice" to *lesbian* desire while actually silencing women's voices and managing Donne's anxious intertextual relationship to Ovid.[28] Paula Blank celebrates Donne's poem for its commitment to exploring the impossibility of desire and the use of Sappho's *lesbianism* to figure that impossibility.[29] As the burgeoning bibliography attests, the status of "Sapho to Philaenis" as a "lesbian love poem" is contested on the basis of contradictory readings of its masculine signature, its feminine persona, its intertextual erotics, and critics' presuppositions about the meaning of *lesbian* desire.[30]

The first poem, in contrast, has not, to my knowledge, been subjected to analysis. Entitled "A copie of Verses made by a Lady, and sent to another Lady, with a bracelet made of her own hair," it is of uncertain authorship and provenance, published anonymously in 1655 in John Cotgrave's miscellany, *Wits Interpreter, The English Parnassus*, a self-improvement anthology aimed at elite male readers hoping to perfect their skills as gentlemen.[31] Cotgrave's collection, as Arthur Marotti puts it, is a "hodgepodge"; it includes a primer on logic, model letters, dialogues for particular social situations, examples of wit, humor, and practical jokes, and (mostly Cavalier) poetry.[32] Although many of the (mostly unascribed) texts included in this anthology were filched from commonplace books kept by university students, I have been unable to find evidence of this verse's existence prior to its publication by Cotgrave. Its unknown origin invites certain questions. Was it written by a man? A woman? Is it an authentic expression of desire or a purely literary performance? Is it satiric or bawdy ("'Tis I that have her to a hair")? Why did Cotgrave include it in a book intended for elite male readers?

It is the second poem, "To My excellent Lucasia, on our Friendship. 17th July 1651" that we know was written by a woman, Katherine Philips, who experienced a passionate love for the addressee, Anne Owen. Composed between 1652 and 1654, but not published until after Philips's death, "To My excellent Lucasia" is the poem most often anthologized to represent her *oeuvre*.[33] This process of anthologization, combined with the impulse of reclamation, has led to a change in titles for Philips: less often introduced as "The Matchless Orinda," she now holds the honorary title of "Seventeenth-Century Lesbian Poet" – to invoke the subtitle of Elaine Hobby's essay on Philips in her wittily named collection, *What Lesbians Do In Books*.[34]

It is not my intent to prove Philips's erotic attachments (as chapter 7 made clear, I support the homoerotic reading of her biography); to defend or condemn Donne's appropriations of Sappho's voice; or to claim a female signature for "A copie of Verses made by a Lady." I will not compare the relative aesthetic merits of these poems or subject them to close readings. Rather, I want to use these three verses to raise some questions about what constitutes an early modern "*lesbian* voice," "*lesbian* author," and "*lesbian* writing." With their varying relations to an actual female signature, these poems can help us scrutinize the appeal of biographical gender and sexuality as critical touchstones, and can help us unpack the implicit relations between identity and textuality, subjectivity and poetic voice. Like the passages previously discussed from Ovid, Lyly, Shakespeare, and Fletcher, these poems inscribe and exploit a rhetoric of erotic similitude. With their help, we can understand more precisely the cultural work this rhetoric performs.

If we strategically suspend attention to the individual complexities of these poems, and focus instead on their commonalities, that is, if we read them together *as a rhetoric*, they reveal several interrelated assumptions. First, thematized through tropes of similitude, homogeneity, and mimetic identification, female–female desire is a matter of the physical likenesses present within the female gender. These similarities override and cancel out possible differences (of age, status, appearance, language), just as the correspondences of two female bodies are mirrored by the bilateral symmetries of the individual body: two lips, two arms, two thighs. Women who desire women reflect one another's bodies and desires in a receding play of mirrors, an "endlesse circularity" of "love with love combining." Second, this state of gender similitude magnifies the possibilities for unity, with the world contracted into an ever smaller, more intensely experienced microcosm: "I've all the world in thee." Of course, the unification of lovers and the idealization of sexual congress as a private, blissful state are staples of heterosexual love poetry, most notably that of Donne, who in "The Sun Rising" famously apostrophizes: "This bed thy center is, these walls thy sphere." These homoerotic verses, however, exploit the heightened possibilities for unity provided by gender similitude, celebrating the "secret twining" of two twin bodies that are also like themselves. Third, although the modes of address in these poems vary subtly, in each one the distance between "I" and "thee" is transited so easily that difference is erased: "I am not thine, but Thee." Fourth, in thus inhabiting the body and soul of the beloved, the lyric speaker enters an alternative sociality, a fantasy of elsewhere, in short, paradise, where she discovers not only all the pleasures to be had on earth, but heaven. Although this too is a common enough trope, here the invocation of paradise is contrasted to more mediated delights; compared to the totality of "sweetnesse" available to be enjoyed by women, the bridegroom as well as the conquering monarch possess but feeble fragments. Fifth, in this private realm of pleasure, knowledge of the beloved is magically conveyed, either through "kinde sympathy," whereby physical distance is overcome by the telepathic understanding immanent in women's amatory reciprocity, or through the communication of detachable body parts (a bracelet of hair), in an erotic synecdoche of part for whole. Physical distance disappears through a communion of body parts. Sixth, women's erotic innocence, purity, gentleness, and pleasure are conceived in explicit opposition to the difference, friction, and reproductive after-effects of heteroeroticism. The "tillage of a harsh, rough man," a sin which leaves indelible traces (semen, pregnancy), is contrasted to "our dallyance" which leaves "no signes." The productivity of *lesbian* love is limited to the production of love itself or to its aesthetic memorialization in bracelets of hair or the lyric poem. Seventh, the appeal of exploring bodily orifices and interiors gives way to surface pleasures: the contact of breasts and thighs, the sensuousness of a bracelet worn on the wrist. This erotics of bodily surfaces compounds the image of the female body as a mirror, with homoerotic desire fundamentally a captivating play of reflective surfaces: "Me, in my glasse, I call thee." Eighth, the combination of similitude and unity renders female–female desire solipsistic and self-absorbed. In loving the other, the lover loves herself; in touching herself, the lover touches the other: "touching my selfe, all seemes done to thee." Notwithstanding the insertion of Donne's masculine difference through the ghostly verbal pun, female bodies are mirrors, and the economy within which desire circulates is a closed circle, signified by the "glasse" or missive wreath made of the lover's hair. Finally, in the contraction of all experience into the state of love, in the enclosure of desire in the circumference of a circle, in the pleasure of viewing a twin or mirror image, these poems reject the world in favor of a utopian union of two, and only two. Notwithstanding Philips's frequent use of political imagery to mediate the intensities of her society of friendship, the political world is imaged as rough, rude, and angry – and tacitly is regulated to the world of men. With the mutual love between women represented as secluded, harmonious, protected, and safe, heteroeroticism implicitly signifies hierarchy, contention, artificiality, factionalism, and violence.

There is a certain charm to these expressions of paradisical love, desire, and pleasure, and, particularly in the contemporary context of homophobia, a certain satisfaction involved in willing the rest of the world to disappear. The desire to see similarities, particularly in the context of seduction or before the work of a relationship begins, is hardly unusual – or, I dare say, limited to *lesbians*. I suggest, however, that we resist momentarily the charms of these poems in order to examine the implications of their vision of female–female desire.[35] Granted, I have done some interpretative violence by collapsing their differences, ignoring many of their individual nuances, and bracketing the individual poetic voice.[36] Nor does my reading situate the poems in the literary lineages they mine and appropriate: Ovidianism, Neoplatonism, and Cavalier love poetry. I am aware, as well, that one could submit them to a deconstructive reading which, by elucidating how figures undo their own logic, might transform surface monovocality into a more hermeneutically satisfying polysemy. The rhetoric of similitude, for instance, could be shown to be inhabited by dissimulation; the rhetorical use of parallelism could be shown to yield subtle difference as well as symmetry.

Nevertheless, these poems thematically invite us to concentrate on surfaces, on mirror images, on similitudes. In doing so, we can see the paradox they produce: they figure love between women as utopian in its possibilities for unity, pleasure, and merger, and absolutely inconsequential in its social effects. Granting the possibility of amatory pleasure at the expense of any possible difference such pleasure might generate, the hypostasis of two women gazing in a mirror extends to a paralysis of politics and even signification. This innocuousness does not mean that these poems are not doing political work; rather, the political work they perform is to depoliticize *lesbian* desire, to place it safely outside the realm of social relevance.

Such, at least, is the thematic function of these poems. But what of their mode of address? The lyric, as countless critics have argued, is predicated on the supposition of a lyric voice. Rather than an authentic manifestation of self-presence, the concept of lyric voice depends on a rhetorical figure: personification. The figure of the lyric voice has specific implications for a reading of these three poems, for lyric personification counts on processes of identification for its success.[37] By consistently fashioning their lyric voice through the terms of erotic similitude, these poems redouble the effects of identification. Accomplishing through lyric means the rhetorical results of Lyly's isocolon and parason, they imply that the primary stake in representing female–female eroticism is the meaning and process of identification.

Given the pervasiveness of this rhetoric of erotic similitude as well as what I am arguing are its ideological effects, what is the role of the female signature in its construction? Is it true, as Donald Stone asserts about male-authored love poems in which a female speaker expresses her love for another woman that "[t]he sentiments expressed belong resolutely to the storehouse of commonplaces repeated over and over in the Renaissance in verse addressed to women by men, thus lending no little support to the contention that the portrayal of women loving women would enter an entirely new phase when the author was herself a woman"?[38] Have we, with the publication of *Poems: By the Incomparable, Mrs. K. P*, moved into "an entirely new phase" in the articulation of female–female desire?

In the last chapter I argued that Philips's verse functioned as a symptomatic hinge between the rhetoric of innocuous chaste friendship, which governed understandings of female–female desire in the Renaissance, and the rhetoric of suspect intimacies, which became a primary mode of intelligibility by the late eighteenth century. Philips's intervention in the tradition of the *amor impossibilis* performed a pivotal role in developing a "subjectivity effect" of and for female homoerotic verse: not only did she develop an array of thematizations and tones out of the tradition of homoerotic lament, including duplicity, betrayal, and frustration, but her intervention in the construction of Nature boldly authorized her homoaffiliations. Claiming for Philips a productive role in the history of *lesbian* representation, however, is not the only critical step that we might take, for the productivity and "subjectivity effect" of Philips cut two ways. Even as her poetry conveys the impression of immediacy, spontaneity, and desire, it is, after all, a representation; and as such, it does not venture beyond the presumption of similitude that organizes conceptions of female desire in her culture: that love between women is love in a mirror.

The rhetoric of erotic similitude in which Philips participates promulgates an aggregate image which, through its discursive repetitions, has the effect of a collective production of "truth" about female–female desire. This "truth," a discursive construction, no doubt enabled the affective and literary horizons of certain early modern women, from "Philo-Philippa" to Lady Mary Chudleigh. At the same time, it very well may have eclipsed the horizons of other women who did not fit its criteria. Insofar as the erotic practices of crossdressers, female husbands, and tribades depend not on an enactment of similitude but of difference, these lyrics deny the modes of homoaffectivity such women represent. Championing particular gratifications – for instance, to kiss, to caress, to merge – these criteria implicitly abnegate other pleasures: the desire to penetrate or be penetrated, to experience passion divorced from spiritual devotion, to love for a day or a year rather than eternally, to wear (or be seduced by a body wearing) masculine clothing. Effacing differences of status, age, language, gender self-conception, and body type, the rhetoric of erotic similitude consolidates a homogenization of *lesbian* affect and erotic practice that, while authorizing certain pleasures, satisfactions, and possibilities, forecloses others, consigning those homoerotically desiring women existing outside of its defining terms to unintelligibility and abjection.[39]

The rhetoric of erotic similitude thus not only functions as a governing criterion for representations of *lesbian* desire, it also fosters a normative female–female desire – what we might call a *homo-normativity* of early modern culture. By coining the term "homo-normativity," I mean to offer a general principle that can guide our efforts to interpret *lesbianism* in the early modern period: that female homoerotic desire prior to the reign of erotic identity gains cultural intelligibility through a regime of representation that abjects in direct proportion to what it enables. And yet, however powerful this homo-normative criterion is, it is not monolithic or fixed, and does not altogether determine representations. Homo-normativity does not exist at the behest of a totalizing and causal Symbolic order, phallogocentrism, or heteropatriarchy, but as a specific and contestable mode of enunciation; it could be resisted, altered, and refigured. That it was not resisted – that women writers colluded with rather than defied its conventions – vexes the exceptionalism often conferred upon an author such as Philips, an exceptionalism that positions her simultaneously in terms of alterity (her poetic identity is distinct from that of men) and exemplarity (she represents the Renaissance *lesbian*). Such critical appraisals forget that when Philips appropriates Donne, she immerses herself in an ever-receding vocal series: Donne had imitated Ovid, who had imitated Sappho, whose own fragmentary traces provide a compelling metaphor for the instabilities of the lyric voice itself. Once we set aside the logic of exceptionalism, the question posed by Philips's *oeuvre* has less to do with the nature of the consciousness or expressions of the *lesbian* subject, than with the continuing hold of homo-normativity on *lesbian* desire.

Just as the identification of *lesbian* authorship occurs by means of a rhetorical figure, the speaking voice, so too is modern *lesbian* identity constructed by figures of (and about) speech. "To speak is to possess meaning, to have access to the language which defines, delimits and locates power. To speak is to become a subject. But for women to speak is to threaten the system of differences which gives meaning to patriarchy."[40] Thus asserts Catherine Belsey, in a formulation that could be taken as a manifesto for the project of feminist and lesbian scholarship for much of the past thirty years: to speak is to be a subject; to be a subject is to possess a voice; to be a speaking female subject is to threaten patriarchy. As Belsey herself is aware, one of the most important tasks of feminist theory has been to come to terms with the post-structuralist challenge to such humanist assumptions, from the deconstruction of the sovereign subject to the "political promise of the performative."[41] With the equivalence of subject, speech, and agency destabilized, feminist theory has had to develop a viable theorization of agency on other terms. Not surprisingly, the trope of speech continues to structure new conceptualizations: ventriloquism has emerged as a figure for the scope of agency, while re-citation has become one of agency's modes of counter-mobilization.

Notwithstanding these theoretical advances, two critical activities that have motivated much feminist and lesbian scholarship (especially approaches to *lesbian* writers in the early modern period) have proven recalcitrant to deconstruction: giving voice and coming out. The effort to give voice has organized the projects of feminist history and literary criticism in general, and early modern scholarship in particular. To come out has been a crucial political and psychic rallying point for gay men, *lesbians*, and queers within modernity. Coming out is itself a form of giving voice, insofar as it is a performative speech act.[42] As rhetorical figures, both giving voice and coming out are conceived in terms of a correlation between speech and agency, on the one hand, and silence and disempowerment, on the other – a correlation that constitutes the subject as desirous of full articulation and in control of its lexicon and syntax. Both acts presume the feasibility of self-presence and self-meaning, and both depend upon a faith in authentic self-expression, as is made manifest by the logic structuring these statements: an authentic subject is expressed through her voice; a stable erotic orientation is expressed through coming out. Because coming out is presumed to convey a "moment of truth" in one's self-conception and social relations, coming out stories tend to be developmental, structured by such narrative conventions as the pre-history (the closet), a quest for the subject's real desire (homoaffiliation), an epiphany of self-recognition (typically figured through sexual contact), and then either self-condemnation (internalized homophobia) or self-acceptance (gay and proud). It is in the nature of such developmental narratives to invite an interpretative stance that already knows what it is looking for and how to find it. In the words of Julie Abraham, in the process of reading coming out stories, "all we need to learn is that the protagonist is a lesbian. It is very difficult, once the recognition of lesbianism has been achieved, to question what 'lesbian' might mean, or to explore the development of a self-consciously lesbian life beyond the point of coming out."[43]

Abraham is particularly interested in the narrative dead-end such stories enact. I want to turn the issue around and ask, what about the historical preconditions of coming out? For to come out presumes the prior existence of the closet. As a subjective and material architecture of privacy, secrecy, and shame, the closet has functioned as the hallmark of modern homosexual interiority, enforcing its own epistemology: "relations of the known and the unknown, the explicit and the inexplicit around homo/heterosexual definition."[44] Often functioning under the aegis of the "open secret," the closet is tied irrevocably to what, in the nineteenth century, became known as "the love that dare not speak its name."

Rhetorics of unspeakability and prohibition structured medieval and Renaissance articulations of sodomy: *peccatum mutum*, the mute sin, the crime not fit to be mentioned among Christians. This discursive history of unspeakability would seem to authorize the effort to locate the closet in early modern cultural formations, and indeed, the closet has been claimed as a specifically Renaissance topos. Alan Stewart, for instance, has explored the epistemology of the early modern writing closet, demonstrating that it is replete with erotic and political transactions among secretaries and masters, while Nicholas Radel has more radically suggested, on the basis of representations of male–male desire in Renaissance drama, that before there was a homosexual, there was a closet waiting for him.[45] Elaine Hobby argues that it is the closet that prevents Philips from articulating her *lesbianism* more explicitly, while Emma Donoghue presumes that "the pressures of a seventeenth-century closet" motivate Philips's insistence on her sexual purity.[46] Elizabeth Harvey characterizes the representation of *lesbianism* in the male-authored Renaissance lyric as part of a centuries-long tradition of censorship, while Elizabeth Wahl's reading of "invisible relations" depends explicitly on the "open secret": knowledge that is "implicitly recognized though never openly acknowledged except through circumlocution and double entendre."[47]

But was there, in fact, an early modern closet? To what extent did sodomy, tribadism, and passionate friendship exist under a regime of censorship and unspeakability? And did each of these forms of homoeroticism exist in similar relation to privacy, secrecy, self-knowledge, and disclosure? We can begin to answer these questions by taking up the most sophisticated case made for the early modern closet to date: Richard Rambuss's provocative suggestion that we might find in "the libidinal structures of the prayer closet" an antecedent to modern gay affects and identities.[48] Rambuss demonstrates that post-Reformation architectural spaces designed for private prayer enabled the circulation of male homoerotic desire, which was granted an intense means of expression in the poetry of religious devotion. Whereas the masculinity of God and Christ may not have afforded women a space in which to explore *their* homoerotic longings – at least not directly[49] – the affinities between early modern religious expression and certain forms of male homoerotic desire charted by Rambuss are utterly compelling.

Nonetheless, I want to suggest that, in contrast to the closet of modernity, the early modern prayer closet is not suffused by the affects of guilt and fear. Even within the lyric, that most privatized of genres fashioned on the imaginary basis of a solitary speaker speaking to himself, the rhetoric is not one of secrecy or shame. On the contrary, any shame expressed within the tropological prayer closet indicates not the status of homoerotic desire, but the status of the subject's worth in relation to God. And, although the rapture of a man at prayer might be experienced and recorded privately, its textual manifestations are proclaimed publicly, whether by circulation in manuscript collections or publication in books. As Steve Patterson says of representations of male homoerotic friendship in Renaissance drama, they "do not traffic in shame; nor do they invariably deflect same-sex desire onto a female decoy. The protestation of love between friends was public and straightforward – and perhaps this difference helps explain why modern critics, accustomed to the homosexual tropes of the clinic and the closet, have debated whether amity could in fact *be* homoerotic."[50] So too with representations of female homoeroticism: even when texts thematize a desire for seclusion, enclosure, and safety, they do so without the burden of guilt or shame implied by censorship.[51]

All of this leads me to suggest that in the early modern period, female homoerotic desire is rendered neither through the affects of the closet, nor the narrative of coming out, nor the unique voicings of an exemplary subject. Rather than find its condition of possibility in a logic of secrecy and disclosure, privacy and exposure, giving voice and coming out, early modern *lesbian* desire takes form within a mutually constitutive dynamic of articulation and abnegation. By this I mean that whenever certain aspects of homoerotic desire are articulated, other forms of that desire are tacitly negated – sometimes foreclosed, sometimes renounced, sometimes sacrificed to a too-easy intelligibility (the intelligibility of the monstrous, the unnatural, the abject, in short, the tribade). As Foucault and Butler have argued, conditions of intelligibility are most effective when they are least evidently operations of power, when their procedures simply replicate the "normative." Although invoking normativity in this context might seem to imply that the divide of homo- and heterosexual preexists the rhetoric of erotic similitude and its constitutive exclusions, in fact, the reverse is true: it is through the interaction of articulation and abnegation that the intelligibility of female–female desire is produced. This dynamic provides the constitutive framework for *lesbianism* prior to the regime of the closet. Female homoeroticism in the early modern period thus is not "the love that dare not speak its name." Rather, it is the love whose very intelligibility is purchased at the cost of differences within the rhetorics and representations of *lesbian* desire.

In my discussion of the rhetoric of erotic similitude, I have specifically avoided the word *narcissism*, because this psychoanalytic concept is itself a product of the discourse I have been analyzing.[52] Far from offering an interpretative framework within which to read the deployment of erotic similitude, Freud's theory of narcissism emerges out of the prior concepts of resemblance, symmetry, and sympathy which governed the terms of female–female desire. In the early modern period, Ovid's story of Narcissus was interpreted as a morality tale: unable to distinguish between himself and an image reflected in a pool, Narcissus pines and drowns; his tragedy is born of a pride and self-absorption so acute as to prove fatal. According to Sandys's translation and commentary:

"This fable... presents the condition of those, who adorned by the bounty of nature, or inriched by the industry of others, without merit, or honour of their own acquisition, are transported with selfe-love, and perish, as it were, with that madness."[53] Robert Burton concurs in *The Anatomy of Melancholy*; diagnosing one of the causes of melancholy to be "philautia" or "self-love," he maintains that it stems "from an over-weening conceit wee have of our good parts, own worth... for which, *Narcissus*-like, we admire, flatter, & applaud our selves, & think all the world esteems so of us."[54]

Freud appropriated Ovid's myth within the context of a discussion of the etiology of homosexuality, transforming Narcissus into a split figure of two forms of erotic aim, one purportedly normal, the other supposedly perverse: primary narcissism, a salutary mode in which the infant takes itself as love object, and secondary narcissism, a neurotic absorption in an other who is modeled on the self: "We have discovered, especially clearly in people whose libidinal development has suffered some disturbance, such as perverts and homosexuals, that in their later choice of love-objects they have taken as a model... their own selves. They are plainly seeking *themselves* as a love-object, and are exhibiting a type of object-choice which must be termed 'narcissistic.'"[55] Such modeling, for Freud, occurred under the auspices of gender affinity since, in his work, gender difference stands for difference *tout court*. Enshrining gender similitude as the fundamental factor in homosexual object choice, Freud elided the question of differences within each gender because he assumed gender identification and desire to be mutually exclusive in the normal oedipal complex. Despite the differences Freud proposes in the male and female oedipal journeys, the constitutive import of narcissism is as evident in Freud's writing on female as male homosexuality.[56] Indeed, Freud's intervention in sexological discourses had the effect of translating *inversion* (a paradigm structured by difference) into *homosexuality* (a paradigm structured by similitude), a translation that occurred by means of the concept of narcissism.[57] Narcissism within psychoanalysis thus depends on the symptomology of an already pathologized homosexuality, even as the theory of narcissism purports to be an explanation of homosexuality. Such recursivity in the theory of homosexuality recapitulates in structural terms the thematic mirroring evinced in the rhetoric of erotic similitude.

The problem of similitude continues to vex the psychological "treatment" of *lesbians* as well as feminist reformulations of Freud.[58] Annamarie Jagose, for instance, notes that in Luce Irigaray's use of the *lesbian* body, the

> emphasis on female homosexuality as a relationship of sameness... ensures a representation of female homosexuality as indistinguishable from autoeroticism and the pre-Oedipal merging with the maternal body... [I]n order to posit a sameness between women, in Irigaray's writing difference between women is disavowed. Female homosexuality, then, articulates relations of mimeticism between women structured by

trajectories of identification rather than desire. Female homosexuality is predicated on a relation with the self, or an object indistinguishable from the self, and is primarily located *outside the workings of desire*.[59]

Likewise, Judith Roof argues that feminist theories of women's writing and reception tend to "use lesbian sexuality as a metaphor for an originary feminine economy while denying the material lesbian."[60] The *lesbian* functions as a trope rather than a mode of possible existence, and is consistently conflated with the maternal body as a figure of imaginary origins: "The fact that this materno-lesbian precursory space obsessively reappears in feminist theoretical writing about both writing and reading, even when the writers are consciously aware of the impossibility of an originary moment, confirms the allure cast not only by the potential power promised by origins, but also – and perhaps more poignantly – by the imagined edenic economy of women together."[61]

We have seen how "the imagined edenic economy of women together" functioned in the early modern period as an elegiac imaginary, authored primarily by men who sought to segregate such female affiliations in an impossible space. But, as Jagose and Roof make clear, female theorists, critics and creative writers reenact this sequestering of *lesbian* possibility by locating it in a pastoral or pre-oedipal elsewhere. Suzanne Raitt argues, for instance, that Virginia Woolf and Vita Sackville-West shared a nostalgia for "a maternal femininity which was apparently lost, and which could be re-created only in the secret space of lesbian sexual pleasure." As seductive as this fantasy may have been, Raitt makes clear, the "idea that lesbian energy originated in a past golden age, either pastoral or pre-Oedipal, meant that it could be deployed as often to resist change, as to encourage it."[62] In their different ways, each of these critics notes that the "allure" of origins, including the association with similitude and a pastoral time and place, seems to captivate certain *lesbians*. Why are origins so alluring? Roof posits one reason:

the quest for origins reflects the urge to have what one cannot have that sustains desire in a tension between the threat of lack represented by no more desire and the specter of power promised by its fulfillment. Origins are alluring because their imagined pattern of joinder and multiplicity opposes the alienating singularity that enables the operation of binary oppositions – because they promise both fullness and the power to change all representations beyond the origin itself. Origins configured as women together appear to be the place of difference without sexual difference, difference without opposition.[63]

Within the context of this theoretical discussion, the rhetoric of erotic similitude takes on an additional dimension and urgency. The questions of similitude (the continuity of *lesbians* across time) and origins (when did *they* become like *us*?), which I have gathered under the rubric of identification, are not solely historical. For the mirroring, elegiac, and pastoral erotics that comprise this rhetoric pose the question of similitude as *the* constitutive question of *lesbianism*: what is *lesbianism*, and where does it come from? Such questions, both ontological and epistemological, have generated an uneasy alliance among psychoanalysis, feminist theory, and *lesbian* writing: despite their attitudes toward normalization, each of these discourses agrees that modern *lesbianism* not only emerged out of the concept of narcissism, but is a prime example of narcissism, whether such narcissism is termed pastoral, the pre-oedipal, or the pleasures of the mirror. As a distinctively modern identity, *lesbianism*, we might say, was born and named under the sign of similitude. Thus, as a conceptual tool, narcissism fails to offer much analytic purchase on *lesbian* desire, either for early or post-modernity. Rather than employ narcissism to read Renaissance figurations retroactively, then, I propose that we harness the early modern rhetoric of erotic similitude to fashion a genealogy of the link between narcissism and *lesbianism*. For although Michael Warner, in his brilliant unpacking of Freud's (il)logics, posits that "the theorization of homosexuality as narcissism is itself a form of narcissism peculiar to modern heterosexuality,"[64] it might be more historically accurate to say that the conflation of homoeroticism with narcissism – what Warner calls homo-narcissism – has *its* origins in the Renaissance rhetoric of erotic similitude.

Thus far, the rhetoric of erotic similitude has been deployed in my argument to provide analytical purchase on the notions of early modern *lesbianism* and *lesbian* authorship, to problematize the identification of a *lesbian* past that transparently maps onto the *lesbian* present, and to suggest that this identification both derives from and generates a specular structure in which are caught not only images from the past but our own *lesbian* faces. This enclosed specularity, I have argued, has at least four effects: it elides the historical alterity of erotic discourses and practices; it imposes an unwarranted form of exceptionalism onto certain early modern women; it resurrects the psychoanalytic misapprehension of *lesbianism* as the product of narcissism; and it obscures the extent to which contemporary discourses – like narcissism and identification – are themselves epiphenomena of early modern regimes of representation. The logic of similitude has not only governed the representation of women's intimacies, it also has functioned as a *de facto* method of interpretation: what was, in the early modern period, a conventional rhetorical trope, a literary conceit, has become in contemporary criticism an unwitting analytical maneuver, an unexamined methodology.

The fact that a mimetic structure of desire is a primary means by which contemporary critical relations to early modern women are mediated results not only in a critical impasse, but a psychic one. In one of the founding theoretical texts of gay historiography, *One Hundred Years of Homosexuality*, David Halperin gestured toward the problem of psychic investments when he advocated the need to "suspend our projects of identification (or disavowal, as the case may be) long enough to devise an interpretation of erotic experiences ... that foregrounds the historical and cultural specificity of those experiences."[65] This suspension of identification is precisely what *lesbian* historiography has avoided. Thus, before we take up the implied invitation of Fradenburg and Freccero to cherish our identifications, it behooves us to examine how the psychic impulses of identification (and disavowal) operate in our historical attachments to Renaissance *lesbian*s. To invoke identification in the psychoanalytic sense is to bring to the fore the construction of the subject through the experiences of loss and mourning. According to Freud, a common response to the loss of a love object is to identify oneself with it, and through such identification, to replace it from within. Identification registers the attempt to replace what one has lost with a viable substitute which, once introjected, helps the subject to consolidate her own sense of self. As "the detour through the other that defines a self," in the words of Diana Fuss, identification is absolutely necessary to psychic health.[66] At the same time, Fuss's *Identification Papers* also makes clear that inherent within the process of identification is violence, for "[h]ow can the other be brought into the domain of the knowable without annihilating the other *as other*?"[67] It cannot, she answers: "*every* identification involves a degree of symbolic violence" and "any identification is purchased through a set of constitutive and formative exclusions."[68]

Not all attempts at identification work smoothly. Both mourning and melancholia, in Freud's terms, enact a refusal to relinquish the lost object, which results in "profoundly painful dejection, cessation of interest in the outside world, loss of the capacity to love, inhibition of all activity."[69] The difference between the two is that in mourning, the loss of object is conscious – the mourner knows what she has lost – whereas "melancholia is in some way related to an object-loss which is withdrawn from consciousness."[70] Thus, "[i]n mourning it is the world which has become poor and empty; in melancholia it is the ego itself."[71] The conscious loss of the object can be healed: "when the work of mourning is completed the ego becomes free and uninhibited again."[72] But when "an *identification* of the ego with the abandoned object" transforms "an object-loss" into "an ego-loss,"[73] the result is melancholia, which "behaves like an open wound, drawing to itself cathectic energies ... from all directions, and emptying the ego until it is totally impoverished."[74]

In the revision of Freud instigated by Nicolas Abraham and Maria Torok, successful mourning involves not only conscious recognition of the loss one has sustained, but the *introjection* of the object (and the desires attached to it). Introjection in their work refers to an ongoing process of acquisition and extension of the self. Under its auspices, the lost object continues to live as part of the mourner's ego, broadening and enriching it; in turn, the successful mourner is able to name her loss, put an end to her dependency on the missing object, maintain a relationship to the outside world, and recognize in it a diversity and difference from herself.[75] Unsuccessful mourning or melancholy occurs when the ego incorporates not only the lost object, but the prohibitions surrounding it.[76] Incorporation denotes a fantasy in which the melancholic embodies the object, revitalizes it as an *imago*, and withdraws all libido from the external world. Refusing to mourn, in a state of psychic retreat, the ego's relations to the outside world become stilted and disaffected, with the libido fixated secretly on the lost object encrypted within.

So why am I waxing psychoanalytic, especially so late in a book that has been tilted more toward a historical mode of inquiry? Two questions salient to our response to the *lesbian* past arise from invoking identification and these antithetical mechanisms, introjection and incorporation. What has been lost and what is being excluded? I suggest that, in the dynamic between the alterity of the past and the needs of the present, the figure of the early modern *lesbian* functions as an identificatory relay: contemporary *lesbians* transit certain psychic projects through her textual traces. The effort to identify early modern *lesbians* is not so much a case of individual misrecognition as a collective melancholic response to the culturally disavowed trauma of historical elision.[77] Despite the common invocation of how homosexuals have been "hidden from history," there has been little investigation into the effects on the collective *lesbian* psyche of the systematic denial of historicity.[78] In Abraham and Torok's terms, suffering that is not recognized by others leads to incorporation rather than introjection.[79] In the face of a suffering that is unacknowledged as such by the culture of heterosexuality, rather than mourning our disconnection from women of the past and allowing them to exist autonomously through their textual traces, we have disavowed our mourning and encrypted the pain of that disavowal within our own critical procedures. In the words of Judith Butler, "to refuse a loss is to become it."[80] Given that each *lesbian*'s personal history of negation is magnified by the cultural denial of the history of *lesbianism*, such a response is understandable and, at the level of the individual psyche, potentially productive. On a cultural and methodological level, however, it ensures a continued melancholic identification with, and dependence upon, the terms of erotic similitude, in a paralyzing enactment of queer trauma.

In making this assessment of the melancholy of *lesbian* identification as a form of cultural trauma, I echo the methodological moves of Wendy Brown, who in *States of Injury* "examine[s] ostensibly emancipatory or democratic political projects for the ways they problematically mirror the mechanisms and configurations of power of which they are an effect and which they purport to oppose."[81] Brown finds that certain "images of freedom perform mirror reversals of suffering without transforming *the organization of the activity through which the suffering is produced* and without addressing the *subject constitution that domination effects*."[82] A similar mirror reversal, I submit, keeps historical scholarship on *lesbianism* locked into a debilitating engagement with the past. Like those "wounded attachments" – infelicitous formulations of identity rooted in injury – adduced by Brown, contemporary attachments to the early modern *lesbian* recycle and resuscitate a recursively melancholic logic. While seeking "to redress the pain and humiliation consequent to historical deprivation," this logic "sustain[s] the psychic residues of these histories," and "inadvertently redraw[s] the very configurations and effects of power that [it] seek[s] to vanquish."[83]

The melancholic attachment to the past not only recapitulates queer trauma; it also recapitulates the logic of homo-narcissism. When Freud argued that the melancholiac's original "object-choice had been effected on a narcissistic basis," he implied that melancholia is at root a problem of similitude.[84] If we pose the question of *lesbian* melancholia in terms of homo-narcissism, however, we need not buy into Freud's pathology of *lesbian* desire; rather, we can move beyond the mutual imbrication of *lesbian* identification and the mirror.[85] In particular, my analysis of the melancholy of *lesbian* identification has some affinities with Butler's proposal that gender and sexuality are melancholic effects. Insofar as gender is produced through identification, Butler argues, "masculinity" and "femininity" are the result of prohibitions that demand the loss of certain attachments while concurrently demanding that they not be avowed or grieved. Heterosexuality, too, is "purchased through a melancholic incorporation of the love that it disavows."[86] The results, she suggests, are dire: "where there is no public recognition or discourse through which such a loss might be named and mourned, then melancholia takes on cultural dimensions of contemporary consequence."[87]

Whereas Butler emphasizes the melancholia of heterosexuality, my inquiry seeks to understand the ways in which *lesbianism* enacts its own logic of melancholia. It is not that individual *lesbians* refuse to grieve connections to the past, but that the dominant culture preempts the very possibility of grief through its continual denial of a *lesbian* past and attenuation of a viable *lesbian* future. The experience of historical negation is exacerbated by the extent to which every generation of *lesbians* is faced with creating and sustaining for the future a culture that acknowledges, supports, and values erotic diversity. We know how heterosexuality reproduces itself; it does so, systematically, if imperfectly, not only through the melancholic disavowals adduced by Butler, but through such institutions as "Inheritance, Marriage, Dynasty, Family, Domesticity, and Population." It is by means of these "institutional pseudonyms," to quote Eve Sedgwick, that "heterosexuality has been permitted to masquerade so fully as History itself."[88] But though *lesbians* bear in our psyches the marks of heterosexuality's intermittent failure to reproduce itself, we are only beginning to realize how we might materially produce *over generations* a *lesbian*-affirmative culture.

Thus, to the extent that we identify mimetically with Renaissance *lesbians*, we not only seek to bridge an epistemological gap in historical knowledge and refute the pretensions of heterosexist history, but we also attempt to fill an existential gap in our own self-knowledge as *lesbians*. Performing a compensatory mediation between our own situation and those of historical subjects and texts, the identification of and with Renaissance *lesbians* authorizes retrospectively our own subjectivities and sexualities while occluding the distinctiveness of the situation of early modern women and discourses about them. In this regard, "Katherine Philips: Seventeenth-Century Lesbian Poet" functions as a stabilizing mirror, compensating for the fact that, despite the categories we inhabit, our knowledge of ourselves as individuals as well as within group identities is vexed, uncertain, in continual and oft-times painful negotiation. Quite simply, we do not know who and what "we" are, or how we might go about defining ourselves beyond the reaction formations conceived under the influence of heterosexism and homophobia. As a response to this epistemological and existential impasse, the act of identifying early modern *lesbians* functions as a technique for producing the truth about *lesbian* identity at the same time that it disavows the impossibility of attaining a secure definitional status. (In this limited respect, the attempts of *lesbians* to secure an identification with the past have something in common with the infant caught in the Lacanian mirror stage: in misrecognizing the mirror image for the Real, the infant is at once deluded and affirmed.) In disavowing the gap between self and other, *lesbians* perform a salutary act, one that consolidates our sense of identity, but which, as an act of historical consciousness and recovery, is founded precisely on a faultline that has yet to be adequately explored.

It has been one aim of this book to delineate how such faultlines came into existence – through what historical exclusions, deformations, splittings, and displacements. One way, I have argued, is through the seemingly "innocent" process of identifying *lesbians* in the early modern period. Such identification condenses a number of psychic and political projects: it is a collective act of historical memory, a means of opening lines of transmission of desire and culture, and a technique for stabilizing modern *lesbian* subjectivity. Whereas remembrance and transmission are crucial to the projects of queering history and culture, such a queering need not take place under the self-confirming auspices of the mirror. What we need is some way to transit imaginatively and affirmatively across time and culture without collapsing the distance: to introject the past, rather than incorporate or "encorpse" it as a likeness of ourselves.[89]

The psychoanalytic understanding of introjection and incorporation offers us a paradigm for "working through" the impasses of our scholarly and psychic alignments, inviting us to sever our "wounded attachments" by confronting the ritualistic and overdetermined character of our mimetic desires. My goal has not been to jettison identity, but to take it so seriously that its contradictions are exposed. By attempting to bring difference – historical, epistemological, and psychological – into dialogue with certain forms of connectedness, I have attempted to privilege neither continuism nor alterity (even as I have insisted that the tribade is not a butch and that the rhetoric of erotic similitude is not *lesbian* feminism). The issue is not whether "we" are or are not like early modern women, but how the discursive conditions of early modern England contribute to our current epistemological and existential impasses. It may be that as long as political and social enfranchisement is predicated on a foundation of individual rights, those rights will most efficaciously be articulated in terms of identities. (It may equally be the case that there is no necessary relation between a discourse of rights and predication of identities.) At the very least, we need to consider whether the historical representation of eroticism prior to a regime of identities may provide us with alternative modes of conceptualization. One way to confront, while also affirming, our identifications with the past is to perform a genealogy. As a history of the present, genealogy doesn't provide us with the security of teleology, but with cultural contradictions, faultlines, roads taken and not taken. I do not mean to overestimate the liberating effects of genealogy – demonstrating the production of a discourse of mimetic identification, not to mention a discourse of abjection, doesn't automatically free us from either. But the genealogical stance is a necessary critical position for *lesbians* at this moment, for it is from this standpoint that we can look simultaneously backward and forward, using our retrospection to imagine and produce a *lesbian*-affirmative future.

This book has been motivated not only by the attempt to more accurately historicize *lesbianism*, but to use history to contribute to the contemporary theorization of *lesbian* identity and the problem of *lesbian* representation. Believing that the epistemological question of future possibility cannot be generated solely from within the logic of similitude, it advocates a move beyond identity as a way to grapple with the impasses of (in)visibility, (im)possibility, and (in)significance. Insofar as this book has been written in the conviction that desire is a resource for historical engagement and future imagining, it is because desire takes us outside of ourselves, challenging us to meet and engage with an other. The other may possess similarities to ourselves but, if we are willing to forego mimetic idealizations, is not ourselves. According to Freud, the etiology of homosexuality inheres in the subject's conflation of identification and desire: the *lesbian* wants to be what she also wants; she wants the woman she also wants to be.[90] In closing, I hypothesize that whereas Freud was wrong about the relation between identification and desire in the individual *lesbian* subject, we might be able to make use of his mistake to diagnose and transform a historical symptom. What if we were to disrupt at a methodological level the conflation that psychoanalysis reads into the individual? What if we used the psychoanalytic understanding of the separate functions of identification and desire to force a wedge into the psychic structures that mediate our relations to the past? What if we approached the works of Katherine Philips (and other early modern women whose traces are waiting for us in the archives) not as subject *to* our identifications, but as objects *of* our desire? What if we reappropriated the tradition of homoerotic elegy and lament, and actively mourned the losses of *lesbian* history? Recognizing the extent to which our desires for these representations constitute them as objects, we might be able to enact our engagements with them as productive of something *else*. For my aim – expressed, I hope, throughout this book – is not *dis*identification, which would be just another form of disavowal. Rather, my desire is to enjoy the pleasures of queering history, while appreciating a past that both is, and is not, our own.[91]

Afterword

With the publication over the past decade of essays and, increasingly, monographs on female homoeroticism in the early modern period, it perhaps can be said that *lesbianism* in the Renaissance is no longer invisible. New texts have been brought to our attention and our understanding of well-known texts has been re-oriented. My own archival experience indicates that the materials treated in this book represent only the tip of the iceberg. As scholars continue to share their discoveries, the evidence will alter our understandings of the past as well as the tools deemed appropriate to investigate it. Undoubtedly, gaps in my own study will only grow more obvious over time. It is with an awareness of this probability that I want to conclude *The Renaissance of Lesbianism* by hazarding a few final questions and speculations.

Thus far, scholarship on early modern female–female desire has tended to stress either the recovery of long-forgotten texts (Poem XLIX is a stunning example) or the act of interpretation. Often such recuperative projects and hermeneutic activities are framed explicitly by questions of historicity (the applicability, for instance, of identity categories to prior erotic regimes) or questions of evidence (how do we know homoeroticism when we see it?). But other questions and assumptions, often only tacitly acknowledged and thus under-theorized, also significantly affect the nature of our work. To return to some of the questions broached in my Introduction: Is our aim to offer nuanced readings of literary texts? To develop a repertoire of homoerotic imagery? To construct a canon of *lesbian* works and thus a homoerotic literary history? To extrapolate homoerotic presences from biographical information and thereby fashion a canon of *lesbian* authors?

Or, are our goals more deliberately historical? If so, do we intend to provide a detailed synchronic picture or to chart a diachronic chronology of representations of female intimacy? How should the temporal, geographical, national, and linguistic parameters of such histories be defined, and how do those chosen parameters affect larger periodizations? In defining our object of inquiry, do we claim for female homoeroticism an independent social status or do we strive to demonstrate its embeddedness in, and mutual constitutiveness with, other social formations (heterosexuality, domesticity, status and rank, nationality, race)? Finally, what does the relative lack of conversation between work on female–female desire and the significant body of scholarship on male homoeroticism say about our field?[1] Is *lesbian*-oriented historiography and literary criticism best done in dialogue with women's history? With the history of male–male sexuality? With both? What do our answers to this question imply for the contemporary dialogue and tension between feminism and queer theory?

The Renaissance of Lesbianism has followed its own path in negotiating these questions. I have argued that, under the auspices of a renaissance of divergent discourses circulating in England, a symptomatic break in the representation of female homoeroticism occurred over the course of the seventeenth century, leading to what I have called the cultural perversion of *lesbian* desire. This process of perversion provided some of the primary materials out of which modern identity categories were fashioned. I also have argued, however, that early modern representations are decisively, indeed, definitively estranged from modern conceptual categories, and further, that the history of representations I have charted does not take the form of a teleology. Rather than attempt to forge links between the tribade, the tommy, the invert, and the butch, I have focused on certain conceptual axes that, within the temporal parameters of two centuries, organized the meanings of tribadism and female friendship. Nonetheless, there is no question that the two figures with which my book is principally concerned appear uncannily similar to subsequent emanations of homoerotic desire. Figures that, since the foundational work in lesbian history, have been treated as prototypical for the nineteenth century (the passing woman and the romantic friend), as fundamental to the pathologizing discourses of sexology and early psychoanalysis (the invert and the pervert), and as vital to twentieth-century self-definitions (butch and femme), seem to have been cut from much of the same cloth as the early modern tribade and friend. Whereas the accent thus far has been to query the terms of such identifications, I want to end by considering, albeit briefly and without moving too far beyond my expertise, why such apparent resonances reassert themselves.

The courageous work of Carroll Smith-Rosenberg and Lillian Faderman brought to the fore the importance of romantic friendships to the culture of nineteenth-century Britain and North America. "The female world of love and ritual," as Smith-Rosenberg characterized this phenomenon, included a wide spectrum of female bonds and passions present within family and friendship networks, which typically were expressed through a heavily romanticized idiom.[2] Such intense emotional connections, normatively embedded in structures of household and kinship, effectively were pathologized or, in Faderman's term, "morbidified," by the sexological and psychoanalytic apparatus emerging in the late nineteenth century.[3] Subsequent work by Marylynne Diggs and Martha Vicinus has demonstrated an earlier social investment in pathologizing at least some aspects of female friendship; this revised chronology, according to Vicinus, complicates the romantic friendship model by showing that romantic friendships "existed on a continuum that included acceptance, tolerance, discrimination, and outrage."[4]

Throughout the 1980s and early 1990s, the "romantic friendship thesis" was criticized for allegedly buying into the very desexualization of female bonds that these historians sought to historicize.[5] Fueled by the feminist sex wars (in which anti-pornography advocates were positioned against sex-affirmative liberationists), such critiques tended to deploy genital sexuality as a trump card over other expressions of desire. Terry Castle, for instance, founded her approach to *lesbianism* in the eighteenth and nineteenth centuries on the self-evident nature of *lesbian* sex:

What did women do who happened to desire one another before the crucial nomenclature appeared? According to the most extreme proponents of the sexological model, they mainly sat around doing needlework, pressing flowers into albums, and writing romantic letters to one another. If they ever got into bed together, it was strictly platonic: a matter of a few cuddles and "darlings" and a lot of epistemic confusion.[6]

With the access we now have to the range of female intimacies articulated across time, perhaps we can move beyond the sex/no sex formulation of this debate. For surely one of the problems that contributes to (and is obscured by) this controversy is that the *a priori* bifurcation of genital sex from "cuddling" does not adequately account for the complexity of meanings textualized in our cultural heritage.[7] Recognizing that there exists a range of possible erotic acts left unarticulated by recourse either to the genitals or to tropes of needlework and flower pressing, we need not promote definitions of eroticism whose own intelligibility relies on an insidious, and increasingly discredited, regime of visibility. I have attempted to expose the frangible nature of that regime by focusing on the specific incoherences that have governed the intelligibility – and lack of intelligibility – of female–female desire. These incoherences, replete with significations not only of eroticism but gender, perform ideological work that is both historically locatable and connected conceptually to some of the axiomatic rubrics of feminist and queer theory (e.g., similarity/difference, minoritizing/universalizing, materiality/immateriality).

With structural incoherences reframed and their constitutive agency acknowledged, we are in a better position to forgo other tired binaries (acts/identities, continuism/alterity) that thus far have organized our field, and to direct our energies to accounting for the apparent resemblances linking various manifestations of *lesbianism* across time. Such resemblances shimmer unsteadily and unevenly, moving closer or receding depending on what one is looking for. Within the frame of a particular set of identifications, for instance, a *lesbian* drag king might claim as historical precursor the passing woman of eighteenth-century narrative and ballads; but if she were to submit herself to the narrative conventions structuring the discourses of gender passing in say, Henry Fielding's *The Female Husband*, she quickly would find that the gulf of history is wide.[8] Indeed, it is here, in the leaps of *temporal passing*, that what we might call "epistemic confusion" is most likely to occur.

Rather than reiterate such identifications, it may be more profitable to begin to trace specific cycles of salience – by which I mean those discrete yet recurring moments when certain definitional elements crop up as particularly meaningful to understandings of eroticism. The evidence of the early modern period suggests that discrete features of *lesbian* representation acquired more importance as others declined. By the end of the eighteenth century, for instance, the figure that arguably had the most potential to signify transgressively had almost disappeared from the discourse that first gave her prominence: "A figure of intense medical interest in the seventeenth century, the tribade wanes as a focus of attention in medical discourse during the eighteenth century – in fact it ceases almost altogether to be an object of medical attention."[9] Why did the tribade slip away as an object of medical curiosity, only for some aspects of her identity to reemerge later, and in much different form, in the invert of sexology? The differences between the two, of course, are considerable. No longer diagnosed routinely through the presence of a hypertrophic clitoris, the tribade's monstrous abuse was refigured in the nineteenth century as the hypervirility of the mannish woman, whose masculine characteristics imbue not only her physical nature, but her very soul. And in the milieu of modern consumer culture, it would appear that souls must be clothed. After the 1928 obscenity trial of Radclyffe Hall, sartorial expressions of female masculinity were appropriated by *lesbians* bent on enacting their own subcultural forms; the closely cropped hair, starched shirts, jackets, ties, cigarette lighters, and monocles of post-war "Modern Girl" fashion became stylized markers of elite *lesbian* masculinity, a form of invert chic.[10]

The chaste female friend likewise was reconstituted as something both akin and alien to the innocent adolescent of Renaissance drama. By the late eighteenth century, under the auspices of a culture of manners, sensibility, and taste, the idioms of chastity and innocence seem to have been channeled into the twin virtues of propriety and sentiment. Fictionally immortalized by that hypervirtuous exemplar of moral womanhood, Samuel Richardson's Clarissa, the "particular friend" of the Enlightenment appears to be both libidinally attached to,[11] and tragically barred from, those female intimacies that might protect her from the worst abuses of patriarchy. What Clarissa lacked, we might observe, is precisely the access to the "female world of love and ritual" that, during the next century, subsisted hand-in-glove with the Victorian ideology of female passionlessness. Bolstered by a socio-economic investment in women's domesticity and the separation of spheres, the expectation of women's disinterest in heterosex paradoxically fostered the fervid expressions of love and desire among girls and women characterized by Smith-Rosenberg as "socially acceptable and fully compatible with heterosexual marriage."[12]

Why do certain figures of eroticism (and gender) become culturally salient at certain moments? Why do suspicions of deviant behavior sometimes seep in to the most innocuous-seeming of friendships and why at other times are such friendships immune from suspicion?[13] Each instance, my study has maintained, requires an investigation attuned to its historical specificity. At the same time, a tentative postulate might prove useful to future investigations: it would seem that certain axes of social definition, and the ideological faultlines they subtend, have been endemic features of erotic discourse since at least the early seventeenth century. Emerging at certain moments, silently disappearing from view, and then reemerging in another guise as particularly relevant (or explosively volatile), these recurrent explanatory logics seem to underlie the organization, and reorganization, of erotic life. Nonetheless, the forms these axes take, their specific manifest content, the discourses in which they are embedded, and the angle of relations between them all are subject to change. Social preoccupations come into and out of focus, political exigencies are reconfigured, discourses converge and the points of contact between them shift – and in the process, discourses themselves are altered. It is because of the ongoing power of these meta-categories of definition, and the ideological issues that they carry in their wake, that chaste femme love looks like an avatar of romantic friendship from one perspective, but from another angle, does not.

Like the periodic moral panics first adduced by Gayle Rubin and Jeffrey Weeks,[14] such cycles of salience may be linked temporally and conceptually to moments of social crisis which have their source in anxieties peripheral to eroticism (such as fears about changing gender roles, nationalist or racist fears of contamination, and broad concerns about morality or social discipline). The ideological function of body parts is one case in point. We can see the afterlife of the metonymic logic analyzed in chapter 5 in the determination of sexology to discover the sources and symptoms of behavioral aberrations in particular bodily morphologies. Like the tribade's enlarged clitoris, the essentialized characteristics attributed to the invert attest to a will to discover in the body an explanatory mechanism for its own deviations. From this perspective, the quest, during the age of genetics, for a "gay gene" (supposedly manifest in a specific gene on the X chromosome or in the hypothalamus, and symptomatized by such physical variations as the length of one's fingers and the size of one's ear lobes) reiterates the persistent desire to pin the mystery of homoeroticism onto a discrete physical essence. With psychoanalysis now largely in disrepute (or considered too expensive a therapy for all but the elite), the explanatory power of minuscule physical entities has again gained the upper hand. And if, as Siobhan Somerville suggests, "the current effort to re-biologize sexual orientation and to invoke the vocabulary of immutable difference" has its own origins in the "historically coincident" and "structurally interdependent" discourses of nineteenth-century sexology, comparative anatomy, and scientific racism,[15] then the production of anatomic essentialism out of the contact between travel narration and anatomy seems all the more important to acknowledge.

I am not proposing that we create static models (e.g., the model of bodily morphology), under which all historical variants would be gathered, organized, and codified. To offer the tribade and the friend, for instance, as the Ur-figures of lesbian history would be as mistaken as to insist on the transhistorical nature of *lesbianism*. To do the history of sexuality is not to turn a blind eye to perennial features of the erotic system, but neither is it too quickly to assume homology when not every facet repeats. Why do certain figures appear to adumbrate, echo, or reference one another? Which characteristics of their social formation actually recur? Why do these formations become saturated with meaning and then fade from view? What social forces help to create an interest in bodily or expressive acts among women, and through which discursive domains are such knowledges circulated? Based on my limited reading in other periods, it would seem that some of the factors regularly impinging on such matters are the relative credibility and prestige accorded to religious, scientific, medical, and legal discourses in the articulation of sexual knowledge; cultural assessments of appropriate and inappropriate sexual knowledge, including women's access to sexual language, the names of body parts, and medical taxonomies;[16] variations in gender performance and the stylizations of dress; the composition of familial, marital, and household arrangements; and the historically contingent relation between erotic acts and the emotions.[17]

Further, which material technologies help to enable the articulation of erotic concepts and definitions? During the eighteenth century, for example, the print media was pivotal to the dissemination of an epistemology of suspicion. Newspapers, scandal sheets, published trial records, the rise of the novel and the female novelist – all of these provided a material opportunity for the voicing of suspicion. Additionally included in our scrutiny of material technologies should be the role of earlier texts in influencing subsequent articulations of erotic knowledge. As made palpable by Anne Lister's references to reading Martial and Ovid, the ways that social agents appropriated and deployed prior rhetorics to legitimize their own desires and practices (or to delegitimize those of others) has been thus far an under-appreciated aspect of how the past was able to *be queer*.

The Renaissance of Lesbianism approached these questions from within the boundaries of a historically discrete study. Insofar as the trend in histories of *lesbian*-identified figures seems to involve locating them more firmly within their social context,[18] we can look forward to a more densely textured picture of what it meant for women to love and desire other women at particular times in specific communities. What will make such historical locations even more valuable, I want to suggest, will be the ability to analyze them in light of those perennial axes of social definition that accord to the history of *lesbianism* a certain consistency and eerie familiarity. Indeed, as gaps in our knowledge are filled, it might be possible to fashion a synoptic account of multiple linkages, forged from a variety of angles, between historical regimes – without losing sight of each regime's specificity, complexity, relative coherence, and incoherence.

Heretofore, our ability to forge such interpretative nexuses has been attenuated by the implicit historicist protocol that finds points of connection (or rupture) only in the historical period immediately preceding one's own object of inquiry. Even in scholarship attuned to discursive contradictions and struggles over representation, there is a tendency to assume that earlier eras are internally homogenous, somehow less complex, than one's own. Two examples from a valuable anthology on the cultural contexts of sexology must stand for a much broader trend. In a fascinating essay on the libel trial brought by Maud Allan against a newspaper publisher for linking her dance performances in Oscar Wilde's *Salome* to an alleged "Cult of the Clitoris," Lucy Bland provides some historical context: "From [the] late eighteenth century through into the early twentieth century, one of the most consistent medical characterizations of the anatomy of the lesbian was the claim of an unusually large clitoris . . . By the late nineteenth century, a number of sexologists were questioning some of these assumptions."[19] Likewise, describing the import of the late nineteenth century for the construction of homosexuality, Rita Felski remarks, "[s]exuality was no longer simply a question of particular acts, but was expressed in appearance, personality and even bodily structure."[20] Such statements, operating as received wisdom, mistakenly imply that the phenomena they describe are *new*. As we have seen, skepticism about linking same-sex behavior to enlarged clitorises was expressed in medical discourse as early as James Parsons; as a "medical characterization," the link between enlarged clitorises and *lesbianism* was hardly historically "consistent." What is of interest is why, at particular moments, a mode of explanation already discredited would reassert itself, and further, how it is possible that scholars can presume that when the invert arrives on the sexological scene, she carries with her no prehistory, no historiographic baggage, at all.

It is to the quiet yet insidious force of the "no longer simply" in Felski's formulation, however, that my final words turn. For if my book holds any interest or value for scholars working in other periods and fields, my hope is that it will be in the demonstration that there is nothing simple or pre-given about the erotic arrangements of *any* historical period. That passionate, desiring, erotic female conduct could be read through the defamations of the monstrous, the unnatural, the transgressive, *but at certain moments was not*, is my affirmative response, in an early modern key, to the essential early insights of those lesbian scholars whose work has enabled mine.

Notes

INTRODUCTION: "PRACTICING IMPOSSIBILITIES"

1. John Lyly, *Gallathea and Midas*, ed. Anne Begor Lancashire (Lincoln: University of Nebraska Press, 1969), 2.2.6–9. The play, which was performed by Paul's Boys at a private playhouse from 1584 to 1588, was also performed before the Queen at Greenwich, probably on New Year's Eve 1587/1588. In a paper written for a Shakespeare Association of America seminar in 1994, "Practising Impossibilities: The Censure and Approval of Women's Erotic Knowledge in John Lyly's *Gallathea*," Fiona McNeill also uses "practicing impossibilities" as a title and conceptual rubric, focusing on the play of recognition and misrecognition within the drama.
2. *A Critical Edition of Sir Richard Fanshawe's 1647 Translation of Giovanni Battista Guarini's Il Pastor Fido*, eds. Walter F. Staton, Jr. and William E. Simeone (Oxford: Clarendon Press, 1964); Alison McNeil Kettering, *The Dutch Arcadia: Pastoral Art and its Audience in the Golden Age* (Montclair, NJ: Boydell Press, 1983).
3. I am grateful to Kim Hall for bringing this painting to my attention. The painting was executed at the behest of the Prince of Orange, just prior to Van Dyck's appointment in England as court painter to Charles I. See *Anthony Van Dyck* (Exhibition catalogue, National Gallery of Art, November 1990–February 1991), eds. Arthur K. Wheelock, Jr., Susan J. Barnes, and Julius S. Held (Washington D.C.: National Gallery of Art, 1990).
4. A further question arises once one folds awareness of the tribade into the discursive context of Van Dyck's painting. Given the racialized rhetoric that I explore in chapter 5, it may not be stretching too far to see in the black huntress's face and gesture a resistance to heterosexual coupling. This is not to suggest that all African women signified tribadism to western Europeans in the early modern period. Nonetheless, her singularity further raises the issue of otherness within this purported heterosexual idyll. On the Renaissance use of a racialized aesthetic, see Kim F. Hall, *Things of Darkness: Economies of Racial Difference in Early Modern England* (Ithaca, NY: Cornell University Press, 1995). She also provides a brief reading of Van Dyck's painting in "Object into Object?: Some Thoughts on the Presence of Black Women in Early Modern Culture," in *Early Modern Visual Culture: Representation, Race, and Empire in Renaissance England*, eds. Peter Erickson and Clark Hulse (Philadelphia: University of Pennsylvania Press, 2000), pp. 346–79. See also Erickson's discussion of this painting in his Epilogue to the same volume (pp. 380–89), where he comments on the nymphs' "unmistakable

ardor" and the "complex intermediary role" of the black nymph, whom he reads as "an adherent of a Diana-like female band" (p. 383). I thank both authors for sharing their manuscripts with me.
5. I am grateful to Patricia Simons for bringing these paintings to my attention.
6. These entries are written, respectively, by Louis Crompton, David Lorenzo Boyd, and Claude Summers in *The Gay and Lesbian Literary Heritage*, ed. Claude Summers (New York: Henry Holt, 1995), pp. 598, 220, 222, 224, emphases mine. George Rousseau makes no references to early modern lesbianism in his entry on "English Literature: Restoration and Eighteenth Century," pp. 228–35.
7. Rudolf Dekker and Lotte Van de Pol, *The Tradition of Female Transvestism in Early Modern Europe* (New York: St. Martin's Press, 1989), p. 57.
8. In using this term, I am picking up on, and in chapter 7 I will extend, the significance of Terry Castle's brief reference to lesbianism prior to 1900 "as an absence, as chimera or *amor impossibilia* – a kind of love that, by definition, cannot exist," in *The Apparitional Lesbian: Female Homosexuality and Modern Culture* (New York: Columbia University Press, 1993), pp. 30–31. According to the classicists I have consulted, there is no grammatical or historical justification for the use of "impossibilia"; since "amor" is the nominative singular of the masculine noun, the correct adjectival form is "impossibilis." I thank David Halperin and Ralph Williams for their help in clarifying this matter.
9. On discourses of female homoeroticism in earlier periods, see Bernadette Brooten, *Love Between Women: Early Christian Responses to Female Homoeroticism* (Chicago and London: University of Chicago Press, 1996); Judith M. Bennett, "'Lesbian-Like' and the Social History of Lesbianisms," *Journal of the History of Sexuality* 9:1–2 (2000):1–24; Jacqueline Murray, "Twice Marginal and Twice Invisible: Lesbians in the Middle Ages," in *Handbook of Medieval Sexuality*, eds. Vern L. Bullough and James A. Brundage (New York and London: Garland, 1996), pp. 191–222; and Karma Lochrie, "Presumptive Sodomy and its Exclusions," *Textual Practice* 13:2 (1999): 295–310.
10. Jacob Burckhardt, *The Civilization of the Renaissance in Italy* (1860), trans. S.G.C. Middlemore (New York: MacMillan, 1904); Erwin Panofsky, *Renaissance and Renascences in Western Art* (Stockholm: Almquist and Wiksell, 1960).
11. Joan Kelly, "Did Women Have a Renaissance?" rpt. in *Women, History, and Theory: The Essays of Joan Kelly* (Chicago: University of Chicago Press, 1984), pp. 19–50.
12. The discourse and social effects of patriarchal authority were marked by regional, national, and, in particular, religious differences. A useful overview is that of Merry E. Wiesner in *Women and Gender in Early Modern Europe* (Cambridge: Cambridge University Press, 1993).
13. David Underdown, "The Taming of the Scold: The Enforcement of Patriarchal Authority in Early Modern England," in *Order and Disorder in Early Modern England*, eds. Anthony Fletcher and John Stevenson (Cambridge: Cambridge University Press, 1985), pp. 116–36. See also Susan Amussen, *An Ordered Society: Gender and Class in Early Modern England* (Oxford: Basil Blackwell, 1988). The issue of a crisis in gender relations is a contested one. In *Birth, Marriage and Death: Ritual, Religion, and the Life-Cycle in Tudor and Stuart England* (Oxford: Oxford University Press, 1997), David Cressy argues that gender

"created recurrent strains, though rarely so acute as to suggest a sex-gender system in crisis," p. 10. Laura Gowing concurs, arguing that "the model of 'crisis' that historians have sometimes applied to gender relations in the period c.1560–1640 is an unhelpful one" (*Domestic Dangers: Women, Words, and Sex in Early Modern London* [Oxford: Clarendon Press, 1996], p. 28). But, as Gowing herself notes, "Gender is *always* in contest: gender relations seem to be continually renegotiated around certain familiar points" (p. 28, her emphasis). Frances E. Dolan hits the nail on the head in her *Whores of Babylon: Catholicism, Gender, and Seventeenth-Century Print Culture* (Ithaca, NY and London: Cornell University Press, 1999) when she says that a "social order that depends on both heterosexuality and misogyny is a social order divided against itself" (p. 131). As Anthony Fletcher, *Gender, Sex, and Subordination in England, 1500–1800* (New Haven and London: Yale University Press, 1995), also suggests, insofar as patriarchy is an unstable and artificial formation, it is always a system in crisis; what is at stake is how those instabilities manifest themselves at particular moments in time.

14. On conduct literature, see Suzanne Hull, *Chaste, Silent, and Obedient: English Books for Women, 1475–1640* (San Marino, CA: Huntington Library, 1982); and Edmund Tilney, *The Flower of Friendship: A Renaissance Dialogue Contesting Marriage c. 1568–73*, ed. Valerie Wayne (Ithaca, NY: Cornell University Press, 1992), and Wayne, "Advice for Women from Mothers and Patriarchs," in *Women and Literature in Britain, 1500–1700*, ed. Helen Wilcox (Cambridge: Cambridge University Press, 1996), pp. 56–79.

15. Lyndal Roper, *Oedipus and the Devil: Witchcraft, Sexuality, and Religion in Early Modern Europe* (London and New York: Routledge, 1994), p. 38.

16. See Margaret Hannay, ed., *Silent but for the Word: Tudor Women as Patrons, Translators, and Writers of Religious Works* (Kent, OH: Kent State University Press, 1985); Katherine Henderson and Barbara F. McManus, eds., *Half Humankind: Contexts and Texts of the Controversy about Women in England, 1540–1640* (Urbana: University of Illinois Press, 1985); Frances E. Dolan, "'Gentlemen, I Have One Thing More to Say': Women on Scaffolds in England, 1563–1680," *Modern Philology* 92:2 (1994): 157–78, and *Dangerous Familiars: Representations of Domestic Crime in England, 1550–1700* (Ithaca, NY: Cornell University Press, 1994); and Jean Howard, *The Stage and Social Struggle in Early Modern England* (London and New York: Routledge, 1994), and "Women as Spectators, Spectacles, and Paying Customers," in *Staging the Renaissance: Reinterpretations of Elizabethan and Jacobean Drama*, eds. David Scott Kastan and Peter Stallybrass (London: Routledge, 1991).

17. Elizabeth Wahl's comparative study of French and English materials, *Invisible Relations: Representations of Female Intimacy in the Age of Enlightenment* (Stanford, CA: Stanford University Press, 1999), appeared in print just as I was completing my typescript. Although we differ in many particulars (discussed in later chapters), and the temporal frame of her work begins where mine concludes, many of our insights are compatible. As was true of the previously published essays by Harriette Andreadis, "The Erotics of Female Friendship in Early Modern England," in *Maids and Mistresses, Cousins and Queens: Women's Alliances in Early Modern England*, eds. Susan Frye and Karen Robertson (New York and Oxford: Oxford

University Press, 1999), pp. 241–58, "Sappho in Early Modern England: A Study in Sexual Reputation," in *Re-Reading Sappho: Reception and Transmission*, ed. Ellen Greene (Berkeley: University of California Press, 1996), pp. 105–21, and "The Sapphic-Platonics of Katherine Philips, 1632–1664," *Signs: Journal of Women in Culture and Society* 15:1 (1989): 34–60, her recent book, *Sappho in Early Modern England: Female Same-Sex Literary Erotics, 1550–1714* (Chicago: University of Chicago Press, 2001), focuses primarily on the later half of the seventeenth century. Emma Donoghue's comprehensive *Passions Between Women: British Lesbian Culture, 1668–1801* (New York: Harper Collins, 1993) likewise begins at the end of my period, as does Lisa Moore's *Dangerous Intimacies: Toward a Sapphic History of the British Novel* (Durham, NC: Duke University Press, 1997). Lillian Faderman, *Surpassing the Love of Men: Romantic Friendship and Love Between Women from the Renaissance to the Present* (New York: Morrow, 1981), has a brief chapter on Renaissance materials (mostly French) and Castle's *The Apparitional Lesbian* is mostly concerned with the late eighteenth century. Jonathan Goldberg's elegantly argued *Desiring Women Writing: Renaissance Examples* (Stanford, CA: Stanford University Press, 1997) is more concerned with female authorship than homoeroticism. For an overview of work, including that on male homoeroticism, see my bibliographic essay, "Recent Studies in Homoeroticism, 1970–1999," *ELR: English Literary Renaissance* (Spring 2000): 284–329.

18. Eve Kosofsky Sedgwick, *Epistemology of the Closet* (Berkeley and Los Angeles: University of California Press, 1990), pp. 58–59.
19. I am reiterating the idiom of Rudolph M. Bell's *How to Do It: Guides to Good Living for Renaissance Italians* (Chicago and London: University of Chicago Press, 1999), which focuses on the discourse of sexual advice for marital couples.
20. Personal communication.
21. Leo Bersani, *Homos* (Cambridge: Harvard University Press, 1995), esp. chapter 3.
22. As these models were developed by Sedgwick in *Epistemology of the Closet*, the minoritizing explanation views modern homosexuals as a distinct, relatively fixed minority; the universalizing explanation maintains that homosexual desire is a psychic and physical potential shared by everyone. Sedgwick argues that these two modes of explanation are always constitutively interrelated. Even the supposedly coherent "homosexuality as we conceive of it today" is "a space of overlapping, contradictory, and conflictual definitional forces" (p. 45). By insisting on a recognition of the role of discursive incoherence and historical simultaneity in the manufacture of competing interpretative paradigms, Sedgwick diagnosed a systemic crisis in modern homo/hetero definition.
23. See Brooten, *Love Between Women*; Faderman, *Surpassing the Love of Men*; Castle, *The Apparitional Lesbian*; Adrienne Rich, "Compulsory Heterosexuality and Lesbian Existence," *Signs: Journal of Women in Culture and Society* 5:4 (1980): 631–60; and Catharine Stimpson, "Zero Degree Deviancy: The Lesbian Novel in English," *Critical Inquiry* 8:2 (1981): 363–79.
24. See Judith Butler, "Imitation and Gender Insubordination," in *Inside/Out: Lesbian Theories, Gay Theories*, ed. Diana Fuss (New York and London: Routledge, 1991), pp. 13–31; David A. Miller, *Bringing Out Roland Barthes* (Berkeley: University of California Press, 1992), especially pp. 23–24; and David Halperin, *Saint Foucault:*

Towards a Gay Hagiography (New York and Oxford: Oxford University Press, 1995).

25. Some of the most useful concepts proposed by queer theory are: the analytical separation of sexuality from gender; the performative nature of erotic signification; the heterogeneity, contingency, and excess of erotic desires; and the instabilities *within* heterosexual practices that render them potentially resistant to normativity. On the theoretical and political meanings of *queer*, as well as the range of interpretations performed under this rubric, see Teresa de Lauretis, "Queer Theory: Lesbian and Gay Sexualities: An Introduction," *differences: A Journal of Feminist Cultural Studies* 3:2 (1991): iii–xviii; Eve Kosofsky Sedgwick, *Epistemology of the Closet,* and *Tendencies* (Durham, NC: Duke University Press, 1993); Judith Butler, "Critically Queer," *GLQ: A Journal of Lesbian and Gay Studies* 1:1 (1993): 17–32, *Gender Trouble: Feminism and the Subversion of Identity* (London and New York: Routledge, 1990), and *Bodies that Matter: On the Discursive Limits of "Sex"* (New York and London: Routledge, 1993); and Annamarie Jagose, *Queer Theory: An Introduction* (New York: New York University Press, 1995). On the analytical separation of sexuality from gender, see Gayle Rubin, "Thinking Sex: Notes for a Radical Theory of the Politics of Sexuality," in *Pleasure and Danger: Exploring Female Sexuality*, ed. Carole S. Vance (Boston: Routledge and Kegan Paul, 1984), pp. 267–319, as well as Sedgwick, *Epistemology of the Closet*, pp. 27–30. On whether this analytical separation has led to the privileging of (male) sexuality over (female) gender, with queerness operating as a default for a (white) male priority, see Biddy Martin, *Femininity Played Straight: The Significance of Being Lesbian* (New York and London: Routledge, 1996); and Judith Butler, "Introduction: Against Proper Objects," *differences: More Gender Trouble: Feminism Meets Queer Theory* 6:2–3 (1994): 1–26. On the relationship between queer theory and gay/lesbian studies, see Lisa Duggan, "The Discipline Problem: Queer Theory Meets Lesbian and Gay History," *GLQ: A Journal of Lesbian and Gay Studies* 2:3 (1995): 179–90.

26. Ed Cohen, "Are We (Not) What We are Becoming? Gay 'Identity,' 'Gay Studies,' and the Disciplining of Knowledge," in *Knowledges: Historical and Critical Studies in Disciplinarity*, eds. Ellen Messer-Davidow, David Shumway, and David Sylvan (Charlottesville and London: University Press of Virginia, 1993), pp. 397–421; citation p. 410.

27. Jonathan Goldberg, Introduction to *Queering the Renaissance* (Durham, NC and London: Duke University Press, 1994), pp. 1–14; citation p. 2. For this reason, I reserve the use of the term "erotic identity" to refer to modern identity categories (invert, lesbian, homosexual) which suture subjectivity to the direction or orientation of erotic desire. I correspondingly resist using heterosexuality as a generic term and reserve its applicability to modern formations of desire which depend on the combination of sexual acts, emotional affects, and personal identity, and which no longer necessarily depend on the transmission of property through marital affiliation.

28. Jeffrey Masten, *Spelling Shakespeare, and Other Essays in Queer Philology* (forthcoming). See also Carla Freccero, "Practicing Queer Philology with Marguerite de Navarre: Nationalism and the Castigation of Desire," in Goldberg, ed., *Queering the Renaissance*, pp. 107–23; and Patricia Parker, *Shakespeare From*

the Margins: Language, Culture, Context (Chicago and London: University of Chicago Press, 1996).

29. I am indebted to Jeffrey Masten for first suggesting to me that *friend* might be the salient, indeed obvious, term for my analysis of these female affects.

30. I have been guided in this effort by this assertion by David Halperin in *One Hundred Years of Homosexuality and Other Essays on Greek Love* (New York and London: Routledge, 1990): "The real issue confronting any cultural historian . . . is, first of all, how to recover the terms in which the experiences of individuals belonging to past societies were actually constituted and, second, how to measure and assess the differences between those terms and the ones we currently employ," pp. 28–9.

31. Two important exceptions that have influenced my work are Philippa Berry, *Of Chastity and Power: Elizabethan Literature and the Unmarried Queen* (London and New York: Routledge, 1989); and Theodora Jankowski, "'Where there can be no cause of affection': Redefining Virgins, Their Desires, and Their Pleasures," in *Feminist Readings of Early Modern Culture: Emerging Subjects*, eds. Valerie Traub, M. Lindsay Kaplan, and Dympna Callaghan (Cambridge: Cambridge University Press, 1996), pp. 253–74, "Pure Resistance: Queer(y)ing Virginity in William Shakespeare's *Measure for Measure* and Margaret Cavendish's *The Convent of Pleasure*," *Shakespeare Studies* 26 (1998): 218–55, and "'The Scorne of Savage People': Virginity as 'Forbidden Sexuality' in John Lyly's *Love's Metamorphosis*," *Renaissance Drama* 24 (1993): 123–53.

32. In "Lesbian History: All Theory and No Facts or All Facts and No Theory?" *Radical History Review* 60 (1994): 57–75, Martha Vicinus challenges lesbian history's emphasis on visibility, empiricism, and identity by investigating the relationship between the protocols of historical research (e.g., rules of evidence, empirical truth claims, the search for causality) and the aims of anti-foundationalist theory. Most historically oriented scholars of *lesbianism* have resisted entertaining either questions of ontology or the theoretical implications of historical difference; the deconstruction of identity associated with queer theory would seem to undermine the very foundations of lesbian history, an endeavor largely defined as a positivist project to recover the presence of *lesbians* in the past. Vicinus's point is not to use "sexy" theory to trump "old fashioned" history or to use "solid" history to trump "ludic" theory, but to employ a theorized historicism and a historicized theory. Extending her methodological aim beyond ascertaining empirically "what women did in bed," Vicinus proposes that a recognition of the "definitional uncertainty" that "is at the core of lesbian studies" legitimizes a move beyond a paradigm that privileges the visual as the sign of the sexual. In "'They Wonder to Which Sex I Belong': The Historical Roots of the Modern Lesbian Identity," rpt. in *Lesbian Subjects: A Feminist Studies Reader*, ed. Martha Vicinus (Bloomington and Indianapolis: Indiana University Press, 1996), pp. 233–59, Vicinus presents a typology of figures from the late seventeenth and eighteenth centuries as antecedents to the modern *lesbian*: the transvestite, the crossdressed actress, the free woman who is an occasional lover of women, and the romantic friend. If Vicinus's search for the "roots of modern lesbian identity" implies a more straightforward teleology than I believe is the case, her engagement with the terms of visibility nonetheless demonstrates the payoff of attending equally to history and theory and, more importantly, of attending to their potential effects on one another.

33. For a related argument focused on cinematic constructions of *lesbianism*, see my essay, "The Ambiguities of 'Lesbian' Viewing Pleasure: The (Dis)Articulations of *Black Widow*," in *Body Guards: The Cultural Politics of Gender Ambiguity*, eds. Julia Epstein and Kristina Straub (London and New York: Routledge, 1991), pp. 305–28.
34. David Halperin, entry on "Homosexuality" in the *Oxford Classical Dictionary*, 3rd edn., Simon Hornblower and Antony Spawforth, eds. (Oxford and New York: Oxford University Press, 1996), pp. 720–23; citation pp. 722–23.
35. On the centrality of male homoeroticism within the mythographic creativity of the Renaissance, see Leonard Barkan, *Transuming Passion: Ganymede and the Erotics of Humanism* (Stanford, CA: Stanford University Press, 1991), and *The Gods Made Flesh: Metamorphosis and the Pursuit of Paganism* (New Haven: Yale University Press, 1986); and James Saslow, *Ganymede in the Renaissance: Homosexuality in Art and Society* (New Haven: Yale University Press, 1986).
36. See Bruce Smith, *Homosexual Desire in Shakespeare's England: A Cultural Poetics* (Chicago: University of Chicago Press, 1991); Gregory Bredbeck, *Sodomy and Interpretation: Marlowe to Milton* (Ithaca, NY: Cornell University Press, 1991); Jonathan Goldberg, *Sodometries: Renaissance Texts, Modern Sexualities* (Stanford, CA: Stanford University Press, 1992); and Mario DiGangi, *The Homoerotics of Early Modern Drama* (Cambridge: Cambridge University Press, 1997).
37. Alan Bray, *Homosexuality in Renaissance England* (London: Gay Men's Press, 1982); and "Homosexuality and the Signs of Male Friendship in Elizabethan England," in Goldberg, ed., *Queering the Renaissance*, pp. 40–61.
38. In this respect, Bray's argument has some affinities with Lorna Hutson's *The Usurer's Daughter: Male Friendship and Fictions of Women in Sixteenth-Century England* (Routledge: London and New York, 1994). Reading Renaissance humanist idealizations of male friendship against themselves, Hutson stresses the ongoing instrumentality of Ciceronian *amicitia* as it was (re)interpreted in the sixteenth century. As a form of symbolic capital that establishes credit and trust, representations of familiar "service" serve important social functions. In addition to fostering social advancement, the establishment of alliances between men is dependent upon, and productive of, the exchanges of women as gifts of alliance.
39. Jeffrey Masten, *Textual Intercourse: Collaboration, Authorship, and Sexualities in Renaissance Drama* (Cambridge: Cambridge University Press, 1997); and George Haggerty, *Men in Love: Masculinity and Sexuality in the Eighteenth Century* (New York: Columbia University Press, 1999).
40. Haggerty, *Men in Love*, p. 14.
41. Alan Sinfield, *Faultlines: Cultural Materialism and the Politics of Dissident Reading* (Berkeley: University of California Press, 1992), and *Cultural Politics – Queer Reading* (Philadelphia: University of Pennsylvania Press, 1994).
42. Heinrich Kramer and James Sprenger, *Malleus Maleficarum* (1487), trans. Montague Summers (1928) (New York: Dover, 1971), p. 41.
43. The phrase "Eve's culpable flesh" is Margaret R. Miles's in *Carnal Knowing: Female Nakedness and Religious Meaning in the Christian West* (Boston: Beacon Press, 1989), p. 117. I thank Ray Clemens for alerting me to the existence of the female-headed serpent, which apparently was invented in the thirteenth century.

In *The Gothic Idol: Ideology and Image-Making in Medieval Art* (Cambridge: Cambridge University Press, 1989), Michael Camille briefly discusses this image, calling it "an embodiment of the duplicitous desire of the mirror, and perhaps even lesbian love" (p. 91). See also Henry Ansgar Kelly, "The Metamorphoses of the Eden Serpent During the Middle Ages and Renaissance," *Viator* 2 (1971): 301–28; and Nona C. Flores, "'Effigies Amicitiae . . . Veritas Inimicitiae': Antifeminism in the Iconography of the Woman-Headed Serpent in Medieval and Renaissance Art and Literature," in *Animals in the Middle Ages: A Book of Essays*, ed. Nona C. Flores (New York and London: Garland, 1996), pp. 167–95.

44. Ruth Mazo Karras, *Common Women: Prostitution and Sexuality in Medieval England* (New York and Oxford: Oxford University Press, 1996).
45. Gowing, *Domestic Dangers*, p. 2.
46. Jyotsna Singh, "The Interventions of History: Narratives of Sexuality," in *The Weyward Sisters: Shakespeare and Feminist Politics*, eds. Dympna Callaghan, Lorraine Helms, and Jyotsna Singh (Oxford: Basil Blackwell, 1994), pp. 7–58; citation p. 33.
47. *Ibid.*, pp. 13–14.
48. Patricia Crawford, *Women and Religion in England, 1500–1720* (London and New York: Routledge, 1993).
49. Roper, *Oedipus and the Devil*, pp. 41 and 43.
50. On female homoeroticism in Roman poetry, see Judith Hallett, "Female Homoeroticism and the Denial of Roman Reality in Latin Literature," *Yale Journal of Criticism* 3:1 (1989): 209–27, who argues that Latin authors "hellenized," "anachronized," and "masculinized" the tribade in order to distance her from "present-day Roman behavior" (p. 210).
51. Underdown, "The Taming of the Scold," pp. 119–22.
52. Gowing treats the "language of sexual insult" in *Domestic Dangers* as necessarily about "the practices of illicit heterosexual sex" (p. 7), presumably because that is the nature of the evidence in the records of church courts where "ordinary women and men fought over sexual words and marital conduct" (p. 8). Nor does the charge of tribadism crop up in the language of defamation studied by L. R. Poos, "Sex, Lies, and the Church Courts of Pre-Reformation England," *Journal of Interdisciplinary History* 24:4 (1995): 585–607.
53. John Bishop's catalogue of practices "both before, after, and against nature" (50v) includes incest, bestiality, love of statues, and men who "against nature doe filthly abuse men, and women, women" (51v) in *Beautifull Blossomes, gathered by John Bishop* (London: 1577). Thomas Gainsford likewise mentions female–female contact in his *The Rich Cabinet Furnished with Varietie of Excellent Discriptions, Exquisite Charracters, Witty Discourses, and Delightful Histories, Devine and Morrall* (London 1616), 82v–83l: "Lechery is a filthinesse of such beastly varietie, that men may sinne with men, women with women: man may sinne by himselfe, by and with his owne wife, with beasts in abhominable prostitutions: with their own blouds and kindred in incestuous maner: with other mens wives in adulterous copulation: with all sorts in filthy licenciousnesse: and in all, both abuse GOD, and confound themselves in body and soule"; cited by Bruce R. Smith, "L[o]cating the sexual subject," in *Alternative Shakespeares*, vol. II, ed. Terence Hawkes (London and New York: Routledge: 1996), pp. 95–121; citation p. 104.

Another possible example is William Perkins, *Christian Œconomie*, trans. Thomas Pickering (London, 1609), which refers to sodomy in terms vague enough to include female–female contact (pp. 24 and 117–18).

54. The poem is published in the notes to W. Milgate's edition of *John Donne: The Satires, Epigrams, and Verse Letters* (Oxford: Clarendon Press, 1967), p. 212 (lines 11–14, 19–20). The author is assumed by most critics to be Thomas Woodward, who is responding to a letter from Donne. This verse letter is discussed by Stephen Orgel, "Gendering the Crown," in *Subject and Object in Renaissance Culture*, eds. Margreta de Grazia, Maureen Quilligan, Peter Stallybrass (Cambridge: Cambridge University Press, 1996), pp. 133–65; Elizabeth Harvey, *Ventriloquized Voices: Feminist Theory and English Renaissance Texts* (New York and London: Routledge, 1992); Janet Halley, "Textual Intercourse: Anne Donne, John Donne, and the Sexual Poetics of Textual Exchange," in *Seeking the Woman in Late Medieval and Renaissance Writings: Essays in Feminist Contextual Criticism*, eds. Sheila Fisher and Janet Halley (Knoxville: University of Tennessee Press, 1989), pp. 187–206; and George Klawitter, "Verse Letters to T. W. from John Donne: 'By You My Love is Sent,'" in Claude Summers, ed., *Homosexuality in Renaissance and Enlightenment England: Literary Representations in Historical Context* (New York: Harrington Park Press, 1992), pp. 85–102.
55. Ben Jonson, *Volpone*, in *The Workes of Benjamin Jonson* (London: 1616).
56. This poem, a version of the "Proludium" that originally had appeared in *The Passionate Pilgrim*, was included untitled in the collection, "The Forest," in the *Workes* of 1616, pp. 829–30.
57. Patricia Simons has uncovered the extent to which visual representations of the three Graces and the Judgment of Paris carry homoerotic meanings, and I thank her for bringing this to my attention.
58. "An Epigram on the Court Pucell" (XLIX), written in 1609, was published in *Under-wood: Consisting of Diverse Poems* (1640).
59. In "Early Modern Women and 'the muses ffemall,'" in *"The muses Females Are": Martha Moulsworth and Other Women Writers of the English Renaissance*, eds. Robert C. Evans and Anne C. Little (West Cornwall, CT: Locust Hill Press, 1995), pp. 173–79, Frances Teague briefly explores the ramifications for Renaissance women writers of the muses' gender, noting that "[t]he muse might be seen as the poet's lovers [*sic*] and the relationship between a woman and the muse as homoerotic, threatening, and shameful. But an alternate version existed in which women, divine and mortal, came together in mutuality to enjoy models for accomplishment and support for education" (p. 178).
60. Douglas Bruster, "Female–Female Eroticism and the Early Modern Stage," in *Renaissance Drama* 24 (1993): 1–32; and DiGangi, *The Homoerotics of Early Modern Drama*.
61. Michael Morgan Holmes, "The Love of Other Women: Rich Chains and Sweet Kisses," in *Aemilia Lanyer: Gender, Genre, and the Canon*, ed. Marshall Grossman (Lexington, KY: University Press of Kentucky, 1998), pp. 167–90.
62. The phrase is Julie Abraham's in "A Case of Mistaken Identity?" her review of Castle's *The Apparitional Lesbian* in *The Women's Review of Books* 11:10–11 (July 1994): 36–37.
63. Masten, *Textual Intercourse*, p. 7.

64. For nuanced accounts of both the pleasures and dangers of gay/*lesbian* identity politics, see Diana Fuss, *Essentially Speaking: Feminism, Nature, and Difference* (New York and London: Routledge, 1989), and ed., *Inside/Out: Lesbian Theories, Gay Theories* (New York and London: Routledge, 1991); Michael Warner, ed., *Fear of a Queer Planet: Queer Politics and Social Theory* (Minneapolis: University of Minnesota Press, 1993); Laura Doan, ed., *The Lesbian Postmodern* (New York: Columbia University Press, 1994); Lee Edelman, "Queer Theory: Unstating Desire," *GLQ: A Journal of Lesbian and Gay Studies* 2:4 (1995): 343–46; Judith Roof, "The Girl I Never Want to Be: Identity, Identification, and Narrative," in *A Queer World: The Center for Lesbian and Gay Studies Reader*, ed. Martin Duberman (New York and London: New York University Press, 1997), pp. 9–16; and Sally O'Driscoll, "Outlaw Readings: Beyond Queer Theory," *Signs: Journal of Women in Culture and Society* 22:1 (1996): 30–51.
65. My understanding of genealogy has been informed particularly by the following works of Foucault: *The Archaeology of Knowledge and the Discourse on Language*, trans. A. M. Sheridan Smith (New York: Pantheon, 1972); "Nietzsche, Genealogy, History," in *Language, Counter-Memory, Practice: Selected Essays and Interviews*, ed. Donald F. Bouchard, trans. Bouchard and Sherry Simon (Ithaca, NY: Cornell University Press, 1977), pp. 139–64; and *Power/Knowledge: Selected Interviews and Other Writings, 1972–1977*, ed. Colin Gordon, trans. Gordon, Leo Marshall, John Mepham, and Kate Soper (New York: Pantheon, 1980).
66. Jon Simons, *Foucault and the Political* (London and New York: Routledge, 1995), p. 27.
67. My coinage of "strategic historicism" adapts Diana Fuss's terminology of strategic essentialism in *Essentially Speaking*.
68. Having proposed in the first volume of *The History of Sexuality* (trans. Robert Hurley [New York: Random House, 1978]), that "The sodomite had been a temporary aberration; the homosexual was now a species" (p. 43), Foucault offered the birth of the homosexual in the late nineteenth century as one aspect of a "generalized discursive erethism" (p. 32) which produced "an *incorporation of perversions* and a new *specification of individuals*" (pp. 42–43). The incitement to discourse that characterizes modernity, he argued, gave rise to a medical understanding of homosexual identity (in sexology, psychiatry, and psychoanalysis), as well as a counter-discourse initiated by homosexuals themselves. "Sexuality" is the term Foucault reserves to describe a discursive formation in which erotic acts are rendered intelligible through the rubric of identity, or, as he puts it, the "truth of the subject." For the logjams that these debates have created in the study of early modern homoeroticism, one need only review the polemics that organize the interventions of the following work: Karma Lochrie, "Desiring Foucault," *Journal of Medieval and Early Modern Studies* 27:1 (Winter 1997): 3–16; Joseph Cady, "'Masculine Love,' Renaissance Writing, and the 'New Invention' of Homosexuality," in *Homosexuality in Renaissance and Enlightenment England: Literary Representations in Historical Context*, ed. Claude Summers (New York: Haworth Press, 1992), pp. 9–40, and "The 'Masculine Love' of the 'Princes of Sodom' 'Practising the Art of Ganymede' at Henry III's Court: The Homosexuality of Henry III and His *Mignons* in Pierre de L'Estoile's *Memoires-Journaux*," in *Desire and Discipline: Sex and Sexuality in the Premodern West*,

eds. Jacqueline Murray and Konrad Eisenbichler (Toronto: University of Toronto Press, 1996), pp. 123–54; Rictor Norton, *The Myth of the Modern Homosexual: Queer History and the Search for Cultural Unity* (London: Cassell, 1997), and *Mother Clap's Molly House: The Gay Subculture in England, 1700–1830* (London: Gay Men's Press, 1992); Claude Summers, "Homosexuality and Renaissance Literature, or the Anxieties of Anachronism," *South Central Review* 9 (1992): 2–23; and Simon Shepherd, "What's So Funny about Ladies' Tailors? A Survey of Some Male (Homo)Sexual Types in the Renaissance," *Textual Practice* 6:1 (1992): 17–30.

69. See Carolyn Dinshaw, *Getting Medieval: Sexualities and Communities, Pre- and Postmodern* (Durham, NC and London: Duke University Press, 1999); Louise Fradenburg and Carla Freccero, eds., *Premodern Sexualities* (London and New York: Routledge, 1996); and David M. Halperin, "How to do the History of Male Homosexuality," *GLQ: A Journal of Gay and Lesbian Studies* 6:1 (2000): 87–124; "Forgetting Foucault: Acts, Identities, and the History of Sexuality," *Representations* 63 (1998): 93–120; and "Lesbian Historiography Before the Name?" *GLQ: A Journal of Gay and Lesbian Studies* 4:4 (1998): 557–630.

70. Sedgwick, *Epistemology of the Closet*, p. 44. Motivating Sedgwick's irony is her suspicion that the identification of a precise moment of conception is impossible, as well as her belief that the search itself tends to displace attention from the contradictory forms of homosexuality in modernity. Just as we resist totalizing the meaning of same-gender desire historically, she argues, we must resist reifying understandings of *lesbianism* in the present. Nonetheless, Sedgwick's discussion is itself relatively ahistorical, deliberately bracketing historical questions in favor of an approach that maps the incoherence of modern homosexuality. Concerned with texts produced during the period which oversaw the systematic categorization of erotic identities, Sedgwick trumps the issue of historicity with her brilliant deconstruction of homosexual definition. Sedgwick's intervention, however, has not stopped the search for origins, as Halperin notes in "How to do the History of Male Homosexuality," p. 117.

71. Cameron McFarlane, *The Sodomite in Fiction and Satire 1660–1750* (New York: Columbia University Press, 1997), p. 12.

72. *Ibid.*, p. 13.

73. McFarlane, *ibid.*, points out that the search for the origins of the homosexual has carried with it specific protocols of historical inquiry: "historians have generally assumed a correlation between an identified group and personal identity and have thus sought evidence of 'homosexual subcultures'" (p. 10). McFarlane suggests that the assumed link between individual identity, group formation, and subcultural practices is a remnant of the debate between acts and identities, itself a vestige of the unresolved (and perhaps unresolvable) contradictions between social constructionism and essentialism.

74. Tim Hitchcock, *English Sexualities, 1700–1800* (New York: St. Martin's Press, 1997), p. 90. It is worth quoting Hitchcock at some length:

> The popularity of cross-dressing, when combined with the "one body" model of reproduction and women's bodies, suggests a highly physical and yet open and mutable set of categories within which both society and individual women could view lesbian behaviour.

Hermaphrodites and tribades were "normal", and if we can read a level of tolerance from the treatment of cross-dressers during much of the century, then they too were, at the very least, commonplace. These categories in turn would have the effect of pushing female sexuality in specific directions. Each of them gave credence to and placed emphasis upon quasi-heterosexual forms of love-making. The frequent mention of strap-on dildos and strongly gendered role-play within relationships amongst the few lesbians identified in the early part of the century would support this conclusion ... the intellectual categories available at the beginning of the century suggested that lesbian couples should in some ways mimic heterosexual sex. And precisely because early eighteenth-century sexual behaviour was characterised by a strong non-penetrative emphasis, heterosexuality retained at least a passing relevance for women who loved women.

By the end of the century, with both the growing importance of romantic friendship and the idea of the 'passionless' woman, a new category and a new identity had become available. This new romantic lesbianism had the very modern characteristic of defining itself in opposition to heterosexuality. In the process it is likely (although not really demonstrable) that sexual behaviour changed, that mutual masturbation became more important and gendered role-play less so. In part, this development must be seen as a reaction to the changing nature of heterosexuality. As heterosex became more penetrative and more sharply characterised by extreme forms of gendered division, the applicability of its models and examples to lesbian love fell away (pp. 90–91).

75. Randolph Trumbach, *Sex and the Gender Revolution: Volume One: Heterosexuality and the Third Gender in Enlightenment London* (Chicago and London: University of Chicago Press, 1998), p. 1. Many of Trumbach's methodological concerns are ones I share: to locate the history of homosexuality in relation to changing configurations of heterosexuality; to position systems of eroticism in relation to changing conceptualizations of gender, marriage, and reproduction; and to chart diachronic change in the interactions of each of these systems. Nonetheless, I have many objections to his work, including his notion of a third gender (which, to my mind, too seamlessly conflates gender and eroticism). Although Trumbach's book is sketchy on *lesbianism* (a promised "second volume of this study" will present "a full analysis of London's sodomites and sapphists"), an earlier essay presents what I take to be his major ideas: "London's Sapphists: From Three Sexes to Four Genders in the Making of Modern Culture," in Epstein and Straub, eds., *Body Guards*, pp. 112–41. Although our critiques follow different emphases, I am indebted to Theresa Braunschneider's exposition of the androcentrism of Trumbach's work in her forthcoming University of Michigan Ph.D. dissertation, "Maidenly Amusements: Narrating Female Sexuality in Eighteenth-Century England" (2002). Braunschneider argues that "London's Sapphists" ostensibly discusses female–female sexuality over the course of the eighteenth century in London, but in the end defines gender as a relationship to desire for men: eighteenth-century Englishmen defined themselves as masculine because they did not desire men sexually; women felt they were female because they did. It is particularly striking how reliance on Trumbach allows Michael McKeon to ignore female–female eroticism in his otherwise impressive account of the shifting relations among gender, class, and eroticism in "Historicizing Patriarchy: The Emergence of Gender Difference in England, 1660–1760," *Eighteenth Century Studies* 28:3 (1995): 295–322.

76. Trumbach, "London's Sapphists," p. 112.
77. *Ibid.*, pp. 114–15.
78. *Ibid.*, p. 112, emphasis mine. For other striking examples of his use of parallelism, see pp. 113 and 121.
79. Throughout his inventory of crossdressers, Trumbach puzzles over the precise nature of women's erotic acts: of women who married other women, "the use of a dildo cannot be proven"; of the marriage between Mary East and her wife, "[t]he question that is most difficult to resolve is the nature of their sexual relation, and whether there had been one at all" (*Ibid.*, pp. 122–23). Of Charlotte Charke, "it is in the end impossible to say whether she ever experienced what would have seemed to her to be sexual intercourse with another woman" (p. 125). Trumbach ends his section on crossdressers with a particularly convoluted assertion, which inverts his previous emphasis on crossdressers: "the majority of women who had sexual relations with women – and they must have been a very small libertine minority of all women – did not cross-dress, and did not even take on masculine airs" (p. 125). How one gets to "the majority of women who had sexual relations" with other women from an analysis of all those crossdressers for whom sexual contact is not provable is puzzling.
80. *Ibid.*, p. 134, emphasis mine.
81. The term "uneven developments" was brought to my attention by Mary Poovey's *Uneven Developments: The Ideological Work of Gender in Mid-Victorian England* (Chicago: University of Chicago Press, 1988), and my interest in its methodological efficacy has been spurred by the works-in-progress of Susan Lanser on the invention of sapphism and of Margaret Ferguson on women's literacy.
82. Norbert Elias, *The Civilizing Process: The Development of Manners*, trans. E. Jephcott (New York: Urizen Books, 1978).
83. Peter Stallybrass, "Transvestism and the 'Body Beneath': Speculating on the Boy Actor," in *Erotic Politics: Desire on the Renaissance Stage*, ed. Susan Zimmerman (London and New York: Routledge, 1992), pp. 64–83; and Stephen Orgel, *Impersonations: The Performance of Gender in Shakespeare's England* (Cambridge: Cambridge University Press, 1996).
84. These are allusions to the influential works of Lawrence Stone, *The Family, Sex and Marriage in England 1500–1800* (London: Weidenfeld and Nicholson, 1977); and Roger Chartier, ed., *The History of Private Life (Vol 3): Passions of the Renaissance*, trans. Arthur Goldhammer (Cambridge, MA: Harvard University Press, 1989).
85. Valerie Rohy, *Impossible Women: Lesbian Figures and American Literature* (Ithaca, NY: Cornell University Press, 2000), p. 5.
86. Annamarie Jagose, *Inconsequence: Lesbian Representation and the Logic of Sequence* (forthcoming, Ithaca, NY: Cornell University Press, 2002), n.p. I thank the author for sharing her work prior to publication.
87. *Ibid.*, n.p, emphasis mine.
88. *Ibid.*, n.p.
89. See, in addition to Butler, Elizabeth Meese, *(Sem)erotics: Theorizing Lesbian: Writing* (New York: New York University Press, 1992); Judith Roof, *A Lure of Knowledge: Lesbian Sexuality and Theory* (New York: Columbia University

Press, 1991), and *Come as You Are: Sexuality and Narrative* (New York: Columbia University Press, 1996).
90. Jonathan Goldberg, "The History That Will Be," in Fradenburg and Freccero, eds., *Premodern Sexualities*, pp. 3–21; citation p. 5.

1. SETTING THE STAGE BEHIND THE SEEN: PERFORMING *LESBIAN* HISTORY

1. William Shakespeare, *A Midsummer Night's Dream* (2.1.161–64). All Shakespeare quotations are taken from *The Complete Works*, ed. David Bevington, 3rd edn. (Glenview, IL: Scott, Foresman & Company, 1980).
2. Brenda Marshall, Review of *Twelfth Night, The Nashville Scene*, October 28, 1992.
3. Nan Gurley, *Letter to the Editor, The Nashville Scene*, November 4, 1992.
4. In addition to the exchange in *The Nashville Scene*, my thinking about the terms of *lesbian* performance in Shakespeare was stimulated by two invitations: that of Barbara Bowen to take part in a panel discussion at the New York "Queer Theater Conference" in April of 1995, and that of Margo Hendricks to present a paper at "Behind the Seen: Text, Translation, Performance, A Weekend with Shakespeare," in conjunction with the 1996 Shakespeare Santa Cruz Festival. I thank Barbara and Margo for those opportunities.
5. For the cultural capital of "Shakespeare," see Marjorie Garber in "Shakespeare as Fetish," *Shakespeare Quarterly* 41:2 (1990): 242–50.
6. Lynda E. Boose and Richard Burt, eds., *Shakespeare, The Movie: Popularizing the Plays on Film, TV, and Video* (London and New York: Routledge, 1997), pp. 2–3.
7. Lorraine Helms, "Acts of Resistance: The Feminist Player," in Callaghan, Helms, and Singh, *The Weyward Sisters*, pp. 102–56; citation pp. 131–32.
8. The Public Theater, New York (1995); Shakespeare Santa Cruz (1996).
9. For a brief critique of the 1991 Shakespeare Santa Cruz production see Margo Hendricks, "'Obscured by dreams': Race, Empire and Shakespeare's *A Midsummer Night's Dream*," *Shakespeare Quarterly* 47:1 (1996): 37–60.
10. In *The Wilde Century* (New York: Columbia University Press, 1994), Alan Sinfield notes how this performance's "dissident effect depended on the audience having some knowledge or intuition of how it was intended to work": "I found myself uncertain, from moment to moment, whether I was watching a boy, a girl, a girl playing a boy, or a boy playing a girl playing a boy... However, some of my friends were initially disappointed because they'd been expecting to whoop it up in a gay version; once they got the idea, they were delighted" (p. 201). In a personal communication, Sinfield adds that the Cheek By Jowl presentation of Celia was "a big revelation": "she is plainly in love with Rosalind. While Rosalind frolics around with her various beaux, Celia stands to one side looking anxious, upset, yearning."
11. Cornerstone Theater Company, "Twelfth Night, or As You Were," performed at the Sixth World Shakespeare Congress, April 10–21, 1996, reviewed in the *Los Angeles Times*, Friday, April 12, 1996 (pp. F1, F24, F25).
12. Jill Dolan, *Presence and Desire: Essays on Gender, Sexuality, Performance* (Ann Arbor: University of Michigan Press, 1993), pp.155–56.

13. For a classic statement on gay male drag, see Esther Newton, *Mother Camp: Female Impersonators in America* (Englewood Cliffs, NJ: Prentice-Hall, 1972).
14. On the tradition of using boy actors, see Orgel, *Impersonations*.
15. See Butler, *Gender Trouble*.
16. Susan Bennett, *Performing Nostalgia: Shifting Shakespeare and the Contemporary Past* (London and New York: Routledge, 1996).
17. According to Bruce Smith, in "I, You, He, She, and We: On the Sexual Politics of Shakespeare's Sonnets," in *Shakespeare's Sonnets: Critical Essays*, ed. James Schiffer (New York: Garland, 1999), pp. 411–29, Celia was played as the disappointed lover of Rosalind in Lawrence Boswell's 1997 Shakespeare Theater of Washington production of *As You Like It*, p. 411. In addition, Gay Gibson Cima describes the transformation of the friendship of Portia and Nerissa to that of lovers in "Strategies for Subverting the Canon," in *Upstaging Big Daddy: Directing Theater as if Gender and Race Matter*, eds. Ellen Donkin and Susan Clement (Ann Arbor: University of Michigan Press, 1993), pp. 91–105.
18. This would seem to be precisely the point of Carl Miller's blithe dismissal of historical difference in *Stages of Desire: Gay Theatre's Hidden History* (London and New York: Cassell, 1996), whose token chapter on female characters in Renaissance drama, entitled "Lesbian Double Cherries," puns its way through the plays of Lyly, Shakespeare, Fletcher, Heywood.
19. Goldberg, *Queering the Renaissance*.
20. Isabel Hull, *Sexuality, State, and Civil Society in Germany, 1700–1815* (Ithaca, NY and London: Cornell University Press, 1996), p. 31. Although focused on a Reformation-conservative society, Hull's description of the dominance of patriarchal marriage is an accurate portrayal of early modern English culture.
21. *Ibid.*, p. 9.
22. The differences between Catholic and Protestant views on sexuality in general are aptly summarized by Hull, who takes issue with James Brundage's assertion that "the post-Tridentine Roman Catholic attitude toward sex [was] more negative than that of Protestants, to the extent that it continued to associate sex with impurity and the generally sinful condition of humanity" (James Brundage, *Law, Sex, and Christian Society in Medieval Europe* (Chicago: University of Chicago Press, 1987), an assessment that she terms "accurate, but incomplete" (Hull, *Sexuality, State, and Civil Society in Germany*, p. 23).
23. In *Love Between Women*, Brooten provides a lengthy exegesis of Romans 1:26–27. On the invention of sodomy as a category within medieval theological discourse, see Mark Jordan, *The Invention of Sodomy in Christian Theology* (Chicago: University of Chicago Press, 1997).
24. For an early overview of European sodomy laws and their effects on women, see Louis Crompton, "The Myth of Lesbian Impunity: Capital Laws from 1270 to 1791," in *The Gay Past*, eds. Salvatore J. Licata and Robert P. Petersen (New York and London: Harrington Park Press, 1985), pp. 11–25. See also Faderman, *Surpassing the Love of Men*; and Judith Brown, *Immodest Acts: The Life of a Lesbian Nun in Renaissance Italy* (Oxford and New York: Oxford University Press, 1986). On English sodomy statutes and prosecutions of men, see Bredbeck, *Sodomy and Interpretation*; Smith, *Homosexual Desire in Shakespeare's England*; Goldberg, *Sodometries*; and Bray, *Homosexuality in Renaissance England*.

25. According to Karma Lochrie, "Presumptive Sodomy and its Exclusions," both Albert the Great and John Chrysostom refer to woman–woman sins against nature. Although Brundage minimizes the import of references to *lesbianism* in medieval canon law, he includes in his notes references to theological and penitential texts that condemn same-gender female acts in *Law, Sex, and Christian Society in Medieval Europe*. See also Allan Frantzen's reading of Anglo-Saxon penitential manuals in *Before the Closet: Same-Sex Love from Beowulf to Angels in America* (Chicago and London: University of Chicago Press, 1998), pp. 138–83.
26. Sir Edward Coke, *Third Part of the Institutes of the Lawes of England* (London: 1644). It would appear that Coke's reference to female bestiality is authorized by medical writing. In *Microcosmographia: A Description of the Body of Man* (London: 1615), Helkiah Crooke observes that "Vesalius hath observed that the prostate glandules are notoriously large & ful in Monkies; and indeed they are of al creatures the most lascivious, as we do not only read in authors, but have also seene by the great Baboons which were heere to be seene among us; for they would in a maner offer violence even to a woman. It is therefore a very wicked and inhumane thing for Gentlewomen to cherish them in their bosoms yea in their beds, as I have seene some doe with mine owne eies" (p. 209).
27. The only broadside that appears in the Bodleian Library Catalogue of Ballads to refer to female sodomy likewise offers an account of a woman executed for committing buggery with a dog: "A looking-glass for wanton Women By the Example and Expiation of *Mary Higgs*, who was executed on Wednesday, 18th of July 1637, for committing the odious sin of Buggery, with her Dog, who was hanged on a Tree the same day," set to the tune of "In Summer time" (printed between 1672 and 1696).
28. Cited in Elspeth King, *The Hidden History of Glasgow's Women* (Edinburgh: Mainstream Publishing Co., 1993), p. 31. I am indebted to Lynda Boose for this reference.
29. Crompton, "The Myth of Lesbian Impunity," p. 17.
30. Henri Estienne, *Apologie pour Herodote* (Paris: 1566), trans. as *A World of Wonders: Or an Introduction to a Treatise Touching the Conformitie of ancient and modern wonder*, trans. R. C. (London: 1607), p. 69. Estienne's basic thesis in this compendium of modern sins is that the transgressions of the ancient world are nothing compared to those of the modern age. Estienne judges this particular case of marriage between women as "not altogether so wicked" as a case of female bestiality with a dog, and uses it to affirm that: "By which examples we see that our Age may well boast, that (notwithstanding the vices of former times) it hath some proper and peculiar to it selfe. For this fact of hers, hath nothing common with that which was practiced by those famous strumpets, who in old time were called *Tribades*" (p. 69).
31. *Montaigne's Travel Journal*, trans. Donald M. Frame (San Francisco: North Point Press, 1983), p. 5. This case is discussed by Thomas Laqueur, *Making Sex: Body and Gender from the Greeks to Freud* (Cambridge, MA: Harvard University Press, 1990), p. 139; Katharine Park, "The Rediscovery of the Clitoris: French Medicine and the Tribade, 1570–1620," in *The Body in Parts: Fantasies of Corporeality in Early Modern Europe*, eds. David Hillman and Carla Mazzio (New York and London: Routledge, 1997), pp. 171–93; Katherine Park and Lorraine Daston,

"The Hermaphrodite and the Orders of Nature: Sexual Ambiguity in Early Modern France," *GLQ: A Journal of Lesbian and Gay Studies* 1:4 (1995): 419–38; and Stephen Greenblatt, "Fiction and Friction," in *Shakesperean Negotiations: The Circulation of Social Energy in Renaissance England* (Berkeley and Los Angeles: University of California Press, 1988), pp. 66–93.

32. Article 116 of the *Constitutio Criminalis Carolina* covered a vast imperial territory composed of heterogeneous political entities, stretching from Austria to Germany to the Netherlands to Savoy. See Helmut Puff, "Female Sodomy: The Trial of Katherina Hetzeldorfer (1477)," *Journal of Medieval and Renaissance Studies* 30:1 (2000): 41–61. Puff explores the ways in which the rhetoric of silence and unspeakability informed legal discourse on female sodomy in Germany, focusing on a "female husband" from Nuremberg, who was drowned in the Imperial city of Speyer in 1477. I thank him for sharing his forthcoming book typescript, *Narrating the Unspeakable: Sodomy in Reformation Germany and Switzerland, 1400–1600*, and for his helpful response to my summary of legal statutes and prosecutions.

33. Lyndal Roper, *The Holy Household: Women and Morals in Reformation Augsburg* (Oxford: Clarendon Press, 1989), pp. 257–58.

34. Puff, *Narrating the Unspeakable*.

35. William Monter, "Sodomy and Heresy in Early Modern Switzerland," in Licata and Petersen, eds., *The Gay Past*, pp. 41–55, esp. 46–47. Monter also mentions in a footnote a widow, Isabel Galandre, who was burned as a witch in 1623 at Neuchatel, but provides no explanation for why he calls her a *lesbian*. The 1647 Basel case of Elsbeth Hertner, who was accused of both sodomy and witchcraft, is discussed by Puff in *Narrating the Unspeakable*.

36. Dekker and Van de Pol, *The Tradition of Female Transvestism in Early Modern Europe*, pp. 58–60. They report several other Netherlands cases in which the wife was deceived by her "husband's" crossdressing (pp. 60–61).

37. On the execution of the Spanish nuns, see Crompton, "The Myth of Lesbian Impunity," p. 17. The legal gloss that declared female sodomy a capital crime was written by Gregorio López; his commentary was widely accepted in the sixteenth century. According to Mary Elizabeth Perry, *Gender and Disorder in Early Modern Seville* (Princeton: Princeton University Press, 1990), the two reports of women in Seville occur, respectively, in the addendum to the report for 1624 and in a report by Christóbal de Chaves. Nonetheless, "[t]he possibility of lesbianism evidently did not preoccupy these officials, who saw women as sexually dependent on men, for few commented on sexual activity between women" (p. 123).

38. In *Forbidden Friendships: Homosexuality and Male Culture in Renaissance Florence* (Oxford and New York: Oxford University Press, 1996), Michael Rocke, who reviewed "thousands of Florentine sodomy cases . . . from a period of nearly two centuries . . . found not a single case of sexual relations between women" (p. 258, note 23), despite the fact that Florentine laws often specified that they applied equally to men and women.

39. The investigation of Benedetta Carlini occurred from 1619 to 1623; see Brown, *Immodest Acts*.

40. Eve Levin, *Sex and Society in the World of the Orthodox Slavs, 900–1700* (Ithaca, NY and London: Cornell University Press, 1989). Crompton, however, notes that,

according to Gregory Karpovich Kotoshikhin, in *On Russia in the Reign of Alexis Mikailovich*, after 1645 women were burned alive for sodomy ("The Myth of Lesbian Impunity," p. 19).

41. See Richard Godbeer, "'The Cry of Sodom': Discourse, Intercourse, and Desire in Colonial New England," *William and Mary Quarterly*, 3rd ser., 52:2 (1995): 259–86, citation p. 268; Mary Beth Norton, *Founding Mothers and Fathers: Gendered Power and the Forming of American Society* (New York: Knopf, 1996), pp. 347–57; and Roger Thompson, "Attitudes towards Homosexuality in the Seventeenth-Century New England Colonies," *Journal of American Studies* 23 (1989): 27–40.

42. Kathleen Brown, "'Changed... into the fashion of man': The Politics of Sexual Difference in a Seventeenth-Century Anglo-American Settlement," *Journal of the History of Sexuality* 6:2 (1995): 171–193; Mary Beth Norton, "Communal Definitions of Gendered Identity in Seventeenth-Century English America," in *Through a Glass Darkly: Reflections of Personal Identity in Early America*, eds. Ronald Hoffman, Mechal Sobel, and Fredrika Teute (Chapel Hill and London: University of North Carolina Press, 1997), pp. 40–66.

43. Few men were prosecuted under sodomy statutes as well; I would argue, however, that the reasons for the paucity of prosecutions differ along gender lines.

44. Early modern English views on the humoral body – as well as recent scholarship on the body – are synthesized by Anthony Fletcher, *Gender, Sex, and Subordination in England*, pp. 30–82. Nancy Sirasi provides a helpful overview of medical theory and practice in *Medieval and Early Renaissance Medicine: An Introduction to Knowledge and Practice* (Chicago and London: University of Chicago Press, 1990). Interpretations of early modern literature in terms of humoral theory are provided by Michael Schoenfeldt, *Bodies and Selves in Early Modern England: Physiology and Inwardness in Spenser, Shakespeare, Herbert, and Milton* (Cambridge: Cambridge University Press, 1999); and Gail Kern Paster, *The Body Embarrassed: Drama and the Disciplines of Shame in Early Modern England* (Ithaca, NY: Cornell University Press, 1991). The historical contingency of the early modern medical paradigm is summarized beautifully by Steven Mullaney in his review of Paster's book in *Shakespeare Quarterly* 48:2 (1997): 242–46. Paster, he writes,

> convey[s] in graphic and concrete terms just how alien the humoral body is to our modern sensibilities, accustomed as we are to a more disembodied psychologizing about affective experience and to an entirely different set of assumptions about the body itself. We think of ourselves as self-contained units (and our sense of individuality and even individual autonomy derive from such assumptions), relatively opaque to the gaze of doctors and friends (unless opened up by scalpel or encounter group), and maintained by a circulatory system that is itself understood as closed and self-contained. The humoral body, by contrast, was "a semipermeable, irrigated container in which humors moved" (8) and metamorphosed, one into the other, whose constituent and multiple fluids were not only in dynamic balance (or imbalance) but were also "all reducible to blood... [and] entirely fungible... [O]pen and fungible in its internal workings, the humoral body was also porous and thus able to be influenced by the immediate environment" (9). The everyday functioning of internal organs was "tumultuous and dramatic" even in health, and, as Paster astutely notes, this aspect of humoral physiology "ascribes to the workings of the internal organs an aspect of agency, purposiveness, and plenitude to which the subject's own will is often decidedly irrelevant" (10).

In the modern age our feelings are intensely personal, signs of our individuality and indeed of our very selves; in the early modern period, "one's" feelings had a life all their own. (p. 243)

45. My contention in *Desire & Anxiety: Circulations of Sexuality in Shakespearean Drama* (New York and London: Routledge, 1992) that early modern masculinity was vexed by a fear of effeminization has been challenged by Debora Shuger ("Excerpts from a Panel Discussion," in *Renaissance Discourses of Desire*, eds. Claude Summers and Ted-Larry Pebworth [Columbia, MO and London: University of Missouri Press, 1993], pp. 271–72); and Lorna Hutson ("On Not Being Deceived: Rhetoric and the Body in *Twelfth Night*," *Texas Studies in Literature and Language* 38:2 [1996]: 140–74). Shuger takes me to task for importing a psychoanalytic narrative onto early modern persons, and for presupposing that erotic desire (the longing for union with the beloved) is sexual desire (genital arousal), while Hutson is concerned with my extrapolation of evidence from medical texts. Although a full response lies beyond the scope of this book, I will say that the insistence of medical writers that bodies can *only* metamorphose in one direction (from female to male) and not the other direction evinces a defensiveness unaccounted for by their theories. Noting this points to a fundamental difference in methodology: Hutson and Shuger take medical writers at their word; I examine their rhetoric, repetitions, and elisions. But, even if one limits oneself to reading only the surface of the text, the belief that "nature always strives for perfection" is contradicted explicitly by at least one popular medical writer, Juan Huarte, who, in explaining the properties of heat and cold, articulates the possibility that while the fetus is still in the womb,

    if when nature hath finished to forme a man in all perfection, she would convert him into a woman, there needeth nought els to be done, save only to turne his instruments of generation inwards . . . nature hath sundrie times made a male with his genetories outward, and cold growing on, they have turned inward, and it became female. This is knowen after she is borne, for she retaineth a mannish fashion, as well in her words, as in all her motions and workings.

    See *The Examination of Mens Wits* (1594), trans. Richard Carew, ed. Carmen Rogers (Gainesville, FL: Scholars' Facsimiles and Reprints, 1959), pp. 269–70. I thank Michael Schoenfeldt for calling Huarte's text to my attention.
46. Francesco Maria Guazzo, *Compendium Maleficarum: The Montague Summers Edition* (1608), trans. E. A. Ashwin (New York: Dover, 1988), pp. 57–59.
47. I am indebted to Susan Lanser for help with the French.
48. For the seventeenth-century English translation from which my quote is taken, see Thomas Johnson, *The WORKES of that famous Chirurgion Ambrose Parey Translated out of Latine and compared with the French* (London: 1634), p. 974. See also *On Monsters and Marvels*, trans. Janis Pallister (Chicago and London: University of Chicago Press, 1982), p. 31; and *Des Monstres et Prodiges: Edition Critique et Commentée*, Jean Céard (Geneva: Droz, 1971).
49. Crooke, *Microcosmographia*, p. 250.
50. Nicolas Culpeper, *A Directory for Midwives (Culpeper's Midwife Enlarged)* (London: 1656), pp. 22–23. Culpeper's *Directory for Midwives* of 1651 was subsequently enlarged, and appeared in seventeen editions under various names, and in varied size, from quartos to duodecimos, until 1777. This passage does not

appear in the first edition; I have used the editions of 1656, 1662, and 1671. As an apothecary, Culpeper was not experienced in midwifery.
51. Roper, *Holy Household*, p. 257.
52. The case of Marie le Marcis, originally recorded by French physician Jacques Duval in *On Hermaphrodites, Childbirth, and the Medical Treatment of Mothers and Children* (Rouen: 1603), has elicited a fair amount of recent analysis. See Park, "The Rediscovery of the Clitoris"; Park and Daston, "The Hermaphrodite and the Orders of Nature"; Laqueur, *Making Sex*, pp. 136–38; Greenblatt, "Fiction and Friction," pp. 73–75; and Patricia Parker, "Gender Ideology, Gender Change: The Case of Marie Germain," *Critical Inquiry* 19:2 (1993): 337–64.
53. At this point, I leave aside Aristotle and Hippocrates, and primarily depend on the model of physiology that tended to dominate English medical practice, Galen's physiology of the four humors. The Galenic view of reproductive anatomy did not go uncontested; rather, it is in part such contestation that gives rise to conflicting interpretations of female–female eroticism.
54. On the emergence of the female warrior ballads around 1600, and their rise in popularity over the course of the seventeenth century, see Dianne Dugaw, *Warrior Women and Popular Balladry, 1650–1850* (Cambridge: Cambridge University Press, 1989).
55. Vern L. Bullough and Bonnie Bullough, *Crossdressing, Sex, and Gender* (Philadelphia: University of Pennsylvania Press, 1993).
56. I appropriate this term from Judith Halberstam's *Female Masculinity*, a study of the range of women's masculine gender performances since the nineteenth century (Durham, NC: Duke University Press, 1997).
57. Excerpted in *Women's Worlds in Seventeenth-Century England: A Sourcebook*, eds. Patricia Crawford and Laura Gowing (New York and London: Routledge, 2000), p. 151.
58. Catalina de Erauso, *Lieutenant Nun: Memoir of a Basque Transvestite in the New World*, trans. Michele Stepto and Gabriel Stepto (Boston: Beacon Press, 1996).
59. Patricia Crawford and Sara Mendelson, "Sexual Identities in Early Modern England: The Marriage of Two Women in 1680," *Gender and History* 7:3 (1995): 362–77.
60. In *Women in Early Modern England 1550–1720*, eds. Sara Mendelson and Patricia Crawford (Oxford: Clarendon Press, 1998), Mendelson and Crawford speculate that Arabella Hunt, who went on to become a celebrated lutenist and soprano at the royal court, may have been the "Mistress Hunt" who appeared in John Crowne's court masque *Calisto* discussed in chapter 6, and also speculate that the *Hunt vs. Poulter* case inspired Aphra Behn's dialogue in *The False Count* (1682), when an elderly husband says of his wife's relationship to her sister and maid: "I have known as much danger hid under a Petticoat, as a pair of Breeches. I have heard of two Women that married each other – oh abominable, as if there were so prodigious a scarcity of Christian Mans Flesh" (pp. 248–49).
61. Anthony à Wood, *The Life and Times of Anthony à Wood* (London: Wishart, 1932), entry for July 10, 1694. Cited by Donoghue, *Passions Between Women*, p. 64. Donoghue also cites two entries in the Taxal marriage register that imply that local officials in the Parish of Presbury solemnized two marriages between women:

Hannah Wright and Anne Gaskill, September 4, 1707; and Anne Norton and Alice Pickford, June 3, 1708 (p. 65).

62. Peter Stallybrass and Ann Rosalind Jones, "Fetishizing Gender: Constructing the Hermaphrodite in Renaissance Europe," in *Body Guards*, Epstein and Straub, eds., pp. 80–111. In the case of Thomas(ine) Hall, a North American court overruled the testimony of several groups of women who had investigated the subject's anatomy; the court determined that s/he was a hermaphrodite and decreed that s/he dress as a man, with the addition of a head scarf and apron to denote his less-than-legal male status. See Brown, "Changed... into the fashion of man" and Norton, "Communal Definitions of Gendered Identity" and *Founding Mothers and Fathers*, pp. 183–97.
63. Daniel Boyarin, "Are There Any Jews in 'The History of Sexuality'?" in *Journal of the History of Sexuality* 5:3 (1995): 333–55.
64. Puff notes that in the late medieval period "northern European powers were more active than Mediterranean societies in penalizing 'female sodomy'" ("Female Sodomy," p. 49); Hull stresses that after the Reformation both Catholic and Protestant states enacted similar moral legislation and engaged in similar secular efforts at general sexual regulation (*Sexuality, State, and Civil Society in Germany*, p. 24).
65. Crawford and Gowing, eds., *Women's Worlds in Seventeenth-Century England*, p. 149.
66. Hull, *Sexuality, State, and Civil Society in Germany*, p. 51.
67. Scholarly recourse to a transhistorical homophobia, which psychologizes the appeal of gay oppression, and to theories of gay genocide, which unifies all such oppression under a systematic intentionality, thus are not useful analytical tools.
68. Puff, "Female Sodomy," p. 44.
69. Juan Luis Vives, *A Very Fruitful and Pleasant Book Called The Instruction of a Christian Woman* (1523), trans. Richard Hyrde (London, *c*. 1529); rpt. in Joan Larsen Klein, *Daughters, Wives, and Widows: Writing by Men About Women and Marriage in England, 1500–1640* (Urbana and Chicago: University of Illinois Press, 1992), pp. 97–122; citation p. 108.
70. Sixteenth- and seventeenth-century anatomists and midwives argue about the presence or absence of the hymen and its reliability as a signifier of virginity. Most anatomists agree that the hymen is not found in all virgins and that it can be broken through a variety of means other than sexual intercourse. In *The Workes*, Paré argues against the existence of the hymen (p. 938). Gabriele Falloppia thought he proved its existence in his *Observationes anatomicae* (Venice: 1561). Crooke views the hymen as a sure sign of virginity. Even when writers uphold the hymen as a sign of virginity, most recognize that this membrane might be broken by means other than phallic penetration, as evinced in Thomas Bartholin's list of eight ways in which the hymen may be harmed, including "If Virgins break it through wantonness with their fingers, or some other Instrument," *Bartholinus Anatomy; MADE from the Precepts of his Father* (London: 1668), p. 74. As this reference to an instrument indicates, the controversy about the hymen was associated with female masturbation and tribadism. In *A Directory for Midwives* (1656), Culpeper occupies middle ground:

> In Virgins these Caruncles or Knobs are joyned together by a thin and sinewy Skin, or *Membrana*, interlaced with many smal Veins, which hath a hole in the midst, through which the Menstrual Blood passeth, about the bigness of ones little finger, in such as are grown up,

this is that noted skin which is called *Hymen*, and is a certain note of Virginity where ever it is found, for the first act of Copulation breaks it. I confess much controversie hath been amongst Anatomists concerning this, some holding there is no such thing at all; others, that it is, but it is very rare; the truth is, most virgins have it, some hold al, I must suspend my own judgement til more yeers bring me more experience; yet this is certain, it may be broken without Copulation, as it may be gnawn asunder by defluxion of sharp humors, especially in young Virgins, because it is thinnest in them, as also by unskilful applying *Pessaries* to provoke the Terms, and how many wayes else God knows. (pp. 23–24)

Nonetheless, Culpeper's translation of Johannes Veslingus's Latin *The Anatomy of the Body of Man* (London: 1653), says: "Such Virgins as keep themselves from playing the wantons with themselves, from the use of *Venus* and other external injuries, have a fleshy skin that covers the passage, guarded with *Caruncles*, which Ancients called *Hymen*... this is but in few, and many Midwives tear it away for an unprofitable excrement" (pp. 29–30). In *The Midwives Book, Or the Whole Art of Midwifry Discovered* (London: 1671), Jane Sharp disputes that the hymen is not found in all maids: "doubtless that is false, else it could have been no proof of Virginity to the *Israelites*"; she then repeats Culpeper's judgment that it can nonetheless be broken before copulation (p. 48).

71. See, on Russia, Levin, *Sex and Society in the World of the Orthodox Slavs*, p. 204.
72. Orlin, *Private Matters and Public Culture in Post-Reformation England* (Ithaca, NY: Cornell University Press, 1994), p. 185.
73. Hull, *Sexuality, State, and Civil Society in Germany*, p. 44.
74. Margaret Hunt, "The Sapphic Strain: English Lesbians in the Long Eighteenth Century," in *Singlewomen in the European Past, 1250–1800*, eds. Judith M. Bennett and Amy M. Froide (Philadelphia: University of Pennsylvania Press, 1999), pp. 270–96; citation p. 281.
75. In *Women's Worlds in Seventeenth-Century England*, Crawford and Gowing include a nineteenth-century redrawing of a woodcut from the *Roxburghe Ballads* that depicts two women embracing in bed together (p. 150).
76. "[W]antonly" is inserted into the seventeenth-century translation of Paré; the French is more neutral.
77. In aristocratic courts, the gentlewomen of the Bedchamber, who closely attended the queen's needs, were the most highly esteemed of her attendants. See Pam Wright, "A Change in Direction: The Ramifications of a Female Household, 1558–1603," in *The English Court: From the Wars of the Roses to the Civil War*, ed. David Starkey (London and New York: Longman, 1987), pp. 147–72.
78. George Williamson, *Lady Anne Clifford: Her Life, Letters, and Work* (Kendal, UK: Titus Wilson & Son, 1922), p. 76.
79. *Ibid.*, p. 69. I thank Karen Newman for bringing this entry of Anne Clifford's diary to my attention.
80. In *Desiring Women Writing* Jonathan Goldberg briefly discusses this diary entry, remarking in a footnote, "[t]his is not the first time they slept together – an earlier incident is reported on p. 23 – but it is apparently the first time they had sex" (pp. 39 and 200, note 27).
81. Thomas Harman, *Caveat or Warening for Common Cursetors vulgarly called Vagabones*, in *Awdley's Fraternitye of Vacabondes, Harman's Caveat, Haben's*

Sermon, &c. (London: 1567), eds. Edward Viles and F. J. Furnivall, Early English Text Society, Extra Series No. 9 (London: Oxford University Press, 1898; reprinted Millwood, NY: Kraus Reprint Co., 1975), pp. 17–91, esp. pp. 22–23.

82. Daryl Palmer, *Hospitable Performances: Dramatic Genre and Cultural Performances in Early Modern England* (West Lafayette, IN: Purdue University Press, 1992), p. 112.
83. Pierre de Bourdeille, Seigneur de Brantôme, *Lives of Fair and Gallant Ladies*, trans. Alfred Richard Allinson (New York: Liveright Citadel, 1933), p. 128. Considerable variations mark the two English translations of Brantôme's text, including unmarked elisions and unexplained areas of non-translation. Despite its problematic use of the term "Lesbian" as an identity category and its avoidance of an early modern idiom, I have used the more complete 1933 translation, checked it against those passages translated by Wahl in *Invisible Relations* and, when necessary, included in the notes information from *The Lives of Gallant Ladies*, trans. Alice Brown (London: Elek Books, 1961).
84. Brantôme, *Lives of Fair and Gallant Ladies,* p. 130.
85. *Ibid.*, p. 131.
86. *Ibid.*, p. 132. The 1961 edition translates this as "she did keep this damsel at bed and board, and did guard her carefully" (*The Lives of Gallant Ladies*, p. 131).
87. Brantôme, *Lives of Fair and Gallant Ladies,* p. 135; The 1961 translation is "excuse may be made for maids and widows for loving these frivolous and empty pleasures, preferring to devote themselves to these than to go with men and come to dishonour"; "this alone will make no man cuckold" (*The Lives of Gallant Ladies,* pp. 133–34).
88. Brantôme, *Lives of Fair and Gallant Ladies,* p. 129.
89. *Ibid.*, p. 133.
90. *Ibid.*, p. 137.
91. Michel de Montaigne, "On three kinds of social intercourse," *The Complete Essays* trans. M.A. Screech (Penguin: New York and London, 1991), pp. 929 and 930; emphasis mine. [B] refers to an addition to the original text made by Montaigne in 1588.
92. Philip Stubbes, for instance, called crossdressed women, "Hermaphroditi, that is, Monsters of bothe kindes, halfe women, halfe men," in *The Anatomy of Abuses* (London: 1583), F5v.
93. For a more extended treatment of the homoeroticism in this scene and the play see my chapter, "The Homoerotics of Shakespearean Comedy," in *Desire & Anxiety*.
94. Although my arguments with Stephen Greenblatt's "Fiction and Friction" will be addressed in chapter 4, I agree with his general observation that erotic friction in *Twelfth Night* is analogous to verbal wit and that "[d]allying with words is the principal Shakespearean representation of erotic heat" (p. 90) – a contention perhaps even more apropos of *Much Ado About Nothing*.
95. It hardly seems coincidental that the Shakespeare play most often used to fuel *lesbian* plots in contemporary pornography is *Twelfth Night*. See Richard Burt, "Baroque Down: The Trauma of Censorship in Psychoanalysis and Queer Film Re-Visions of Shakespeare and Marlowe," in *Shakespeare in the New Europe*, eds. Michael Hattaway, Boika Sokolova, and Derek Roper (Sheffield: Sheffield Academic Press, 1994), pp. 328–50. In "The Love That Dare Not Speak

Shakespeare's Name: New Shakesqueer Cinema," in *Unspeakable ShaXXXspeares: Queer Theory and American Kiddie Culture* (New York: St. Martin's Press, 1998), pp. 29–75, Burt argues for a queer rather than a gay Shakespeare. See also Laurie Osborne, *The Trick of Singularity: Twelfth Night and the Performance Editions* (Iowa City: University of Iowa Press, 1996).

96. One indication of the popularity of *A Midsummer Night's Dream* is the number of productions worldwide, as listed in the World Shakespeare Bibliography. In the 1996 *Bibliography* (*Shakespeare Quarterly* 48:5), listed under 'Stage Productions' there are eighty-seven entries for the play (pp. 701–09), compared to twenty-nine, for instance, for *The Merchant of Venice* (pp. 690–93) and thirty-five for *As You Like It* (pp. 611–14). In the 1997 *Bibliography*, there are eighty-eight entries (*Shakespeare Quarterly* 49:5, pp. 689–99); in 1998 there are eighty-four (*Shakespeare Quarterly* 50:5, pp. 744–51); and in 1999, there are sixty-nine (*Shakespeare Quarterly* 51:5, pp. 726–32). In his "Shakespeare in Production" edition of the play, Trevor Griffiths notes that *A Midsummer Night's Dream* is "now safely ensconced as one of the three Shakespeare plays to be studied in schools as part of the English National Curriculum" (Cambridge: Cambridge University Press, 1996), p. 1.

97. For an influential reading of the heterosexual teleology of *A Midsummer Night's Dream*, see C. L. Barber, *Shakespeare's Festive Comedy: A Study of Dramatic Form and its Relation to Social Custom* (Cleveland, OH and New York: Meridian, 1959). In the Arden edition of the play, Harold Brooks summarizes the dominant critical opinion: "love and marriage is the [play's] central theme: love aspiring to and consummated in marriage, or to a harmonious partnership within it" (*The Arden Shakespeare* [London: Methuen, 1979], p. cxxx). As Louis Montrose remarks, "[s]uch romantically inclined idealizations of married love tend to downplay the authoritarian and misogynistic aspects" of the play, *The Purpose of Playing: Shakespeare and the Cultural Politics of the Elizabethan Theatre* (Chicago and London: University of Chicago Press, 1996), p. 110. Montrose's influential comments on the play, initially published as "*A Midsummer Night's Dream* and the Shaping Fantasies of Elizabethan Culture: Gender, Power, Form," in *Rewriting the Renaissance: The Discourses of Sexual Difference in Early Modern Europe*, eds. Maureen Quilligan, Margaret Ferguson, and Nancy Vickers (Chicago: University of Chicago Press, 1986), pp. 65–87 and "'Shaping Fantasies': Figurations of Gender and Power in Elizabethan Culture," *Representations* 1 (1983): 61–94, have been elaborated and nuanced in his book (all subsequent citations refer to the book). Recent editors, responding in part to Montrose's influence, increasingly have acknowledged the coercive aspects of the play; see, for instance, *The Norton Shakespeare (Based on the Oxford Edition)*, eds. Stephen Greenblatt, Walter Cohen, Jean Howard, and Katherine Eisamen Maus (New York: W. W. Norton, 1997).

98. Montrose, *The Purpose of Playing*, p. 117.

99. Dorothy Stephens, "Into Other Arms: Amoret's Evasion," in *The Limits of Eroticism in Post-Petrarchan Narrative: Conditional Pleasure From Spenser to Marvell* (Cambridge: Cambridge University Press, 1998), p. 37.

100. *Edmund Spenser: The Faerie Queene* (1590–1609), ed. Thomas P. Roche, Jr. (New Haven and London: Yale University Press, 1987), pp. 568–69 (Book 4, Canto 1, Stanzas 15–16).

101. Sir Philip Sidney, *The Countess of Pembroke's Arcadia*, ed. Maurice Evans (Harmondsworth, UK: Penguin, 1977), p. 245. In this context, it is interesting to note that in the *Old Arcadia*, Philoclea compares her fervent desire for the crossdressed Cleophila (Pyrocles) to just such sisterly love:

> Thus did Cleophila wade betwixt small hopes and huge despairs, whilst in the mean time the sweet Philoclea found strange unwonted motions in herself. And yet the poor soul could neither discern what it was, nor whither the vehemency of it tended. She found a burning affection towards Cleophila; an unquiet desire to be with her; and yet she found that the very presence kindled the desire. And examining in herself the same desire, yet could she not know to what the desire inclined. Sometimes she would compare the love she bare to Cleophila with the natural goodwill she bare to her sister; but she perceived it had another kind of working. Sometimes she would wish Cleophila had been a man, and her brother; and yet, in truth, it was no brotherly love she desired of her.

> See *The Countess of Pembroke's Arcadia (The Old Arcadia)*, ed. Jean Robertson (Oxford: Clarendon Press, 1973), p. 97. In "What? How? Female–Female Desire in Sidney's *New Arcadia*," *Criticism* 39:4 (1997): 463–49, Richard A. Levin perceptively focuses on the homoerotics of the passage in which Philoclea comes to recognize her love for Zelmane (the crossdressed Pyrocles), arguing that "No passage in early modern English literature is nearly as full and explicit dealing with a woman's sexual desire for a woman and the possibility of sexual activity between them" (p. 464). Although I disagree with some of his conclusions, I appreciate Levin's insistence on the homoeroticism of this representation as well as his generosity in sharing his work before publication. More recently, Kathryn Schwarz has analyzed the extent to which *The Arcadia* expresses through its use of transvestite Amazonian disguise the "conviction that desire between women is an erotic irrelevance and the fear that it is a sexual fall" (*Tough Love: Amazon Encounters in the English Renaissance* [Durham, NC, and London: Duke University Press, 2000], p. 200).

102. Orgel, "Gendering the Crown," in deGrazia, Quilligan, and Stallybrass, eds., *Subject and Object in Renaissance Culture*, citation p. 162.
103. Ludovico Ariosto, *Orlando Furioso* (1516/1532), trans. Guido Waldman (Oxford: Oxford University Press, 1974), pp. 300–01, Canto 25.42.
104. Agnolo Firenzuola, *Tales of Firenzuola*, trans. anonymously, 2nd edn. with intro. by Eileen Gardiner (New York: Italica Press, 1987), pp. 21–22.
105. *Ibid.*, p. 23.
106. Thomas Dekker, *Satiromastix* (London: 1602).
107. *The Antipodes* (London: 1640), was first performed in 1638. I am grateful to Jennie Evenson for bringing this play to my attention.
108. Richard Brome, *The Antipodes*, ed. Ann Haaker (Lincoln: University of Nebraska Press, 1966), p. 20.
109. *Three Renaissance Travel Plays*, ed. Anthony Parr (Manchester and New York: Manchester University Press, 1995), p. 232.
110. DiGangi, *The Homoerotics of Early Modern Drama*, p. 96. DiGangi is similarly focused on containment in his reading of William Goddard's *A Satirical Dialogue* (1615):

> Alas, alas, what pleasure and delight
> Takes one mayde with an other in the night?

> But smale god knowes it, for my owne part I
> Ne're tooke anie with whom I e're did lie.
> For love, noe revells in that bedd doth keepe
> Where one girle, by an others side doth sleepe.
> For trulye (sisters) there is none that can
> Give maydes delight in bedd, but a young man. (sig. CIV)

DiGangi argues, "By having the sister insist so strenuously on the futility of female–female sex, Goddard raises the possibility of just such 'pleasure and delight,' especially for the younger, less experienced, sisters. Yet any speculation about the 'revells' girls keep in bed might well be dispelled by the youngest sister's pornographic account of the man of her dreams... [which] seems to prove that only a young man is equipped to give sexual delight to a maid" (pp. 97–98).

111. The 1640 edition of *The Antipodes* is believed to have been derived from the author's papers, or a transcript of these, which were used as a theatrical promptbook. Haaker's edition, based on a collation of twenty-two of the twenty-three extant copies of Q1, makes the amendment silently (p. 20); she notes in her Introduction that "[t]he press variants are mainly concerned with changes in punctuation and a few in spelling and spacing" (p. xx). Parr's textual gloss quietly notes "she Q" (p. 232), as does the older edition of Charles Mills Gayley, *Representative English Comedies* (New York and London: Macmillan, 1914), p. 448.

112. If, as Andrew Taylor remarks in "Reading the Dirty Bits" (in *Desire and Discipline*, eds. Murray and Eisenbichler, pp. 280–95), we need to trace "the material traces," the "stains of spittle or semen" on the page as evidence of "dirty reading" (pp. 284, 287), so too do we need to attend to those marks that indicate readers' disavowals.

113. Henri Lefebvre, *The Production of Space*, trans. Donald Nicholson-Smith (Oxford: Blackwell, 1991); Doreen Massey, *Space, Place and Gender* (Minneapolis: University of Minnesota Press, 1994); David Bell and Gill Valentine, eds., *Mapping Desire: Geographies of Sexualities* (London and New York: Routledge, 1995).

114. Stallybrass, "Patriarchal Territories: The Body Enclosed," in Ferguson, Quilligan, Vickers, eds., *Rewriting the Renaissance*, pp. 123–42.

115. It must be noted that this was ideology, not reality. Crawford and Mendelson argue that during daylight hours, "women treated their dwellings as fluid and open expanses, from which they surveyed the passing scene and emerged at will. They also freely resorted to each other's houses, making use of neighbours' dwellings much like a series of linked female spaces." In this respect, the "male ideal of encloistered femininity was irrelevant to most women's behavior" (*Women in Early Modern England*, pp. 206 and 210).

116. See Ann Matter, "My Sister, My Spouse: Woman-identified Women in Medieval Christianity," *Journal of Feminist Studies in Religion* 2:2 (1986): 81–93.

117. John Bale, *The Actes of the Englishe Votaryes, Comprehending their Unchast Practyses and Examples of All Ages* (London: 1546).

118. *Erasmus on Women*, trans. Craig R. Thompson, ed. Erika Rummel (Toronto: University of Toronto Press, 1996); p. 31.

119. The term is Donoghue's, who discusses Marvell's poem in *Passions Between Women*, p. 225.

120. James Holstun was the first to examine the homoerotics of "Upon Appleton House," in "'Will You Rent Our Ancient Love Asunder?': Lesbian Elegy in Donne, Marvell, and Milton," *ELH: English Literary History* 54:4 (1987): 835–67; a more thorough examination is provided by Kate Chedgzoy, "For *Virgin Buildings* Oft Brought Forth: Fantasies of Convent Sexuality," in *Female Communities 1600–1800: Literary Visions and Cultural Realities*, eds. Rebecca D'Monté and Nicole Pohl (London: Macmillan, 2000), pp. 53–75. I thank the author for sharing her essay with me before publication. See also Dorothy Stephens, "Caught in the Act at Nun Appleton," in *The Limits of Eroticism in Post-Petrarchan Narrative*, pp. 178–209, esp. pp. 179–80.
121. The diverse opportunities for homoerotic identifications and affiliations enabled by Protestant women's religious experience also are suggested by the role of ecstatic prophecy in some dissenting sects, as well as by the intimate friendships enabled by women's missionary activity. Quakers Sarah Chevers and Katharine Evans, for instance, sustained each other, practically and spiritually, during and beyond imprisonment by the Maltese Inquisition in ways that they analogize explicitly to marriage, using the term "yoke fellow" and invoking the terms of the marriage ritual to describe their friendship. (Katharine Evans and Sarah Chevers, *A Short Relation of Cruel Sufferings* [London: 1662].) Like Catholic women, dissenters were also the subject of libelous attacks, often focused on alleged erotic indiscretions such as public nakedness. The religious slander that projects onto nuns and dissenters a dangerous leaning toward unnatural lust seems most appropriately examined within the context of religious and political controversy. On dissenting women's prophecy, see Phyllis Mack, *Visionary Women: Ecstatic Prophecy in Seventeenth-Century Women* (Berkeley: University of California Press, 1992). On the intimacy of Chevers and Evans, see *Her Own Life: Autobiographical Writings by Seventeenth-Century Englishwomen*, eds. Elspeth Graham, Hilary Hinds, Elaine Hobby, and Helen Wilcox (London and New York: Routledge, 1989), pp. 119, 125, and 130; and Rosemary Kegl, "Women's Preaching, Absolute Property, and the *Cruel Sufferings (For the Truths sake) of Katharine Evans & Sarah Cheevers*," *Women's Studies* 24 (1994): 51–83.
122. The extent to which Carlini's mystical experience can be understood as *lesbian* has been much debated. In her review of Brown's *Immodest Acts*, for instance, Mary R. O'Neil argues that "[t]he presumptively diabolical origin of Benedetta's sexual actions was more significant, in the categories of the culture in which she lived, than the question of whether she did her diabolical deeds with a man or a woman," *The Sixteenth Century Journal* 17:3 (1986), p. 392. While this undoubtedly is true, it does not follow, as O'Neil asserts, that analysis of Carlini's experience should be interpreted exclusively from within the history of religious culture. A more extended dismissal of homoeroticism is that of Caroline Walker Bynum, who likewise remarks in "The Body of Christ in the Later Middle Ages: A Reply to Leo Steinberg," in *Fragmentation and Redemption: Essays on Gender and the Human Body in Medieval Religion* (New York: Urzone, 1991), that Brown's book "mistakenly places the behavior it considers in the context of sexual orientation. But what contemporaries asked about the actions of Benedetta Carlini ... was not whether they had an erotic component directed toward a woman, but whether Benedetta Carlini suffered from demonic possession or practiced fraud" (p. 333, note 27).

To the extent that Brown applied a modern erotic category to Carlini, I agree with Bynum's critique. Nonetheless, her dismissal is more subtle than is suggested by her impatience with presentism. For despite emphasis in her own work on medieval women's agency, her criticism of Brown concedes too much weight to the discourses of power. Elsewhere Bynum asks whether medieval viewers of religious art viewed the body through the lenses of sexuality and her answer is that without categories of sexual orientation, such a mode of viewing was impossible. Accepting Foucault's division between erotic acts and erotic identities as axiomatic, she uses the absence of sexual identity as a means to discount the eroticism of the body, visual representation, spiritual acts, and human interaction in the medieval period. One might note here that Bynam's suspicion of historical anachronism is hardly unique to her, and has been employed, intentionally or not, by many others in such a way as to write female homoeroticism out of history.

123. On medieval female homoerotic mysticism, see Kathy Lazzavo, "Sobs and Sighs Between Women: The Homoerotics of Compassion in *The Book of Margery Kempe*," in *Premodern Sexualities*, eds. Fradenburg and Freccero, pp.175–198; Karma Lochrie, "Mystical Acts, Queer Tendencies," in *Constructing Medieval Sexuality*, eds. Karma Lochrie, Peggy McCracken, and James Schultz (Minneapolis and London: University of Minnesota Press, 1997), pp. 180–200.

124. Frances E. Dolan examines anti-Catholic sentiment and emphasizes the systems of support Catholicism provided women in *Whores of Babylon*. In "A Refuge from Men: The Idea of a Protestant Nunnery," *Past and Present* 117 (1987): 107–30, Bridget Hill examines the appeal of the idea of a nunnery in post-Reformation England. Arguing that the "idea of a 'Protestant nunnery' goes through something of a renaissance in the late seventeenth and early eighteenth centuries" (p. 117), Hill suggests that the rise in numbers of singlewomen and concerns about the inadequacy of female education created conditions for the emergence of small communities of "celibate" women engaged in religious retirement, learning, and the pursuit of good works as well as various proposals for such communities.

125. As Montrose notes, Theseus "represents the life of a vestal as a punishment, and it is one that fits the nature of Hermia's crime . . . [E]ach of these men claims a kind of property in her . . . Yet Hermia dares to suggest that she has a claim to property in herself" (*The Purpose of Playing*, p. 127).

126. Sylvia Gimenez, "The Vestal's Progress: Is Escaping the Bride-Bed Merely *A Midsummer Night's Dream*?" unpublished paper.

127. Montrose, "*A Midsummer Night's Dream* and the Shaping Fantasies of Elizabethan Culture: Gender, Power, Form," in Quilligan, Ferguson, and Vickers, eds., *Rewriting the Renaissance*, p. 71.

128. Schwarz, "Missing the Breast," in Hillman and Mazzio, eds., *The Body in Parts*, p. 158.

129. *Ibid.*

130. Schwarz, *Tough Love*, p. 177.

131. The Cole–Orton masque, performed on Candlemas Night (February 2) in 1618 at Coleorton Hall, Leicestershire, was published by Rudolf Brotanek, *Die Englischen Maskenspiele* (Vienna and Leipzig: Wilhelm *Braumüller*, 1902), pp. 328–37. It is briefly discussed by David Norbrook in *Poetry and Politics in the English Renaissance* (London: Routledge and Kegan Paul, 1984), pp. 250–51, and "The

Reformation of the Masque," in *The Court Masque*, ed. David Lindley (Manchester, University of Manchester Press, 1984), pp. 94–110. Douglas Bruster briefly discusses the Amazonian passage in "Female–Female Eroticism and the Early Modern Stage." More extensive historical treatment of the masque, including debate about its authorship, is given by Karen Middaugh, "'Virtues Sphear': Court vs. Country in the 1618 Masque at Coleorton," in *Subjects on the World's Stage: Essays on British Literature of the Middle Ages and the Renaissance*, eds. David Allen and Robert White (Newark: University of Delaware Press, 1995), pp. 280–94; and Philip Finkelpearl, "The Fairies' Farewell: *The Masque at Coleorton* (1618)," *Review of English Studies* 46:183 (1995): 333–51, and "The Authorship of the anonymous 'Coleorton Masque' of 1618," *Notes and Queries* 238: 2 (1993): 224–26.

132. Brantôme, *Lives of Fair and Gallant Ladies,* p. 135; "'tis much better for a woman to be masculine and a very Amazon and lewd after this fashion" (p. 134, 1961 edn.).
133. The phrase "traffic in women" was first coined by Emma Goldman in her critique of marriage as prostitution, and gained critical prominence through the work of Gayle Rubin in "The Traffic in Women: Notes on the 'Political Economy' of Sex," in *Toward an Anthropology of Women*, ed. Rayna Reiter (New York: Monthly Review Press, 1975), pp. 157–210.
134. Margo Hendricks, "Obscured by Dreams: Race, Empire, and Shakespeare's *A Midsummer Night's Dream*," *Shakespeare Quarterly* 47:1 (1996): 37–60; citation p. 53.
135. I am grateful to P. A. Skantze for bringing this to my attention.
136. In the University of Chicago (4th) edition of *The Complete Works of Shakespeare*, David Bevington glosses this as "a complimentary allusion to Queen Elizabeth as a votaress of Diana and probably refers to an actual entertainment in her honor at Elvetham in 1591" (New York: Harper Collins, 1992), an opinion repeated in the Norton Oxford edition. In the New Cambridge edition, R.A. Foakes (Cambridge: Cambridge University Press, 1984) remarks that this image "has often been interpreted as a compliment to Queen Elizabeth; it seems probable that Shakespeare had the queen in mind," and Stanley Wells in the Penguin edition likewise remarks that the vestal virgin is "usually assumed to refer to Queen Elizabeth" (London: Penguin, 1967). In the Oxford edition, Peter Holland glosses this speech as "Usually taken as an allusion to Queen Elizabeth," although he also cites objections to this view (Oxford: Clarendon Press, 1994), p. 163. Montrose's intervention in this identification of what others see as a topical allusion stresses the extent to which Queen Elizabeth presents

> an integral element of the play's dramaturgy and ideology ... Shakespeare's ostensible royal compliment may be seen as a complex mediation of the charismatic royal presence that pervaded late Elizabethan culture and as an appropriation of the cult of the Virgin Queen ... Shakespeare's playtext splits the triune Elizabethan cult image between the fair vestal, who is an unattainable *virgin*, and the Fairy Queen, who is represented as both an intractable *wife* and a domineering *mother*. Oberon uses one against the other in order to reassert masculine prerogatives. (*The Purpose of Playing*, p. 176)

137. Judith M. Bennett and Amy M. Froide, "A Singular Past," in Bennett and Froide, eds., *Singlewomen in the European Past*, pp. 1–37.
138. Amy Louise Erickson, *Women and Property in Early Modern England* (London and New York: Routledge, 1993). Erickson's examination of probate documents

also reveals that in the making of wills, women had a decided "preference for female legatees" – a preference that Erickson interprets not only as women's recognition of their shared economic vulnerability, but their "close ties of female friendship" (pp. 221–22).
139. Hunt, "The Sapphic Strain," p. 287.
140. On English communities, see Froide, "Marital Status as a Category of Difference: Singlewomen and Widows in Early Modern England," in Bennett and Froide, eds., *Singlewomen in the European Past*, pp. 236–69.
141. Throughout this discussion, I am indebted to the careful research and generosity of Alan Bray, whose forthcoming book *The Friend* (Chicago: University of Chicago Press) examines such same-sex monuments in more detail.
142. Jean Wilson, "'Two names of friendship, but one Starre': Memorials to Single-Sex Couples in the Early Modern Period," *Church Monuments: Journal of the Church Monuments Society* 10 (1995): 70–83, citation p. 83, note 39.
143. Joseph L. Chester, *The Marriage, Baptismal, and Burial Registers of the Collegiate Church or Abbey of St. Peter, Westminster* (London: Harleian Society, vol. X, 1876).
144. Wilson, "'Two names of friendship, but one Starre,'" p. 83, note 39.
145. *The Spectator*, ed. Donald F. Bond (Oxford: Clarendon Press, 1965), vol. I, pp. 462–63.
146. *Ibid.*, p. 466.
147. *Ibid.*, pp. 464–65.
148. *Ibid.*, p. 463, note 1.
149. Graham Parry, *The Golden Age Restor'd: The Culture of the Stuart Court, 1603–42* (Manchester: Manchester University Press, 1981), p. 40.
150. David Bergeron, "Women as Patrons of English Renaissance Drama," in *Patronage in the Renaissance*, eds. Guy F. Lytle and Stephen Orgel (Princeton: Princeton University Press, 1981), pp. 274–90.
151. Stephen Orgel, "The Royal Theatre and the King," in Lytle and Orgel, eds., *Patronage in the Renaissance*, pp. 261–73, citation p. 267. In 1633, the Puritan barrister William Prynne was prosecuted for treason for attacking the royal theatricals in *Histriomastix* in terms that suggested that any woman who performed was a "notorious whore." See David Norbrook, "The Reformation of the Masque," in Lindley, ed., *The Court Masque*, pp. 94–110.
152. Stephen Orgel and Roy Strong, *Inigo Jones: The Theater of the Stuart Court*, 2 vols. (London: Sothebey Parke Bernet and Berkeley: University of California Press, 1972).
153. G. E. Bentley, *The Jacobean and Caroline Stage* (Oxford: Clarendon Press, 1956), vol. IV, p. 549. Bentley's comment refers to an unnamed and now lost pastoral and masque, performed to a small audience at court in 1625/6, in which the queen, who was the principal actress, and her ladies took speaking parts. According to a letter from Henry Manners to Sir George Manners, "I heare not much honor of the Queene's maske, for, if they were not all, soome were in men's apparell."
154. Andrew Gurr, *Playgoing in Shakespeare's London* (Cambridge: Cambridge University Press, 1987); Richard Levin, "Women in the Renaissance Theatre Audience," *Shakespeare Quarterly* 40:2 (1989): 165–74; and Ann Thompson,

"Women/'women' and the stage," in *Women and Literature in Britain, 1500–1700*, ed. Helen Wilcox (Cambridge: Cambridge University Press, 1996), pp. 100–16.
155. Montrose, *The Purpose of Playing*, p. 144, emphasis mine.

2. "A CERTAINE INCREDIBLE EXCESSE OF PLEASURE": FEMALE ORGASM, PROSTHETIC PLEASURES, AND THE ANATOMICAL *PUDICA*

1. Paré, *The Workes of that Famous Chirurgion Ambrose Parey*, p. 886.
2. Perry, *Gender and Disorder in Early Modern Seville*, pp. 127–36.
3. For the medical controversy on the hymen, see chapter 1.
4. *Lieutenant Nun*, p. 28.
5. *Ibid.*, pp. 16–17.
6. My analysis differs from that of Perry, who emphasizes the sexual controls on women in early modern Seville, and sees in de Erauso a repudiation of her body as well as her identity as a woman (*Gender and Disorder in Early Modern Seville*, pp. 134–36).
7. T. E., *The lawes resolutions of womens rights: or, the lawes provision for woemen. A Methodicall Collection of such Statutes and Customes, with the Cases, Opinions, Arguments and points of Learning in the Law, as doe properly concerne Women* (London: 1632), sig. B3v.
8. The legal status of early modern women has been much debated. Rosemary O'Day, *The Family and Family Relationships, 1500–1900, England, France, and the United States* (London: Macmillan, 1994) and Erickson, *Women and Property*, emphasize the extent to which women enjoyed legal identities and protected their interests through legal means; Mendelson and Crawford nonetheless conclude that "the legal situation of the majority of women underwent serious erosion in early modern England" (*Women in Early Modern England*, p. 48).
9. Linda Polluck, "'Teach her to live under obedience': the Making of Women in the Upper Ranks of Early Modern England," *Continuity and Change* 4:2 (1989): 231–58, esp. p. 247.
10. O'Day, *The Family and Family Relationships*, pp. 148–49.
11. Sara Jayne Steen, *The Letters of Arbella Stuart* (New York and Oxford: Oxford University Press, 1994), pp. 66–70.
12. Martin Ingram, *Church Courts, Sex and Marriage in England, 1570–1640* (Cambridge: Cambridge University Press, 1987), pp. 219 and 230.
13. *Ibid.*, pp. 225–26.
14. *Ibid.*, pp. 230 and 237.
15. Cressy, *Birth, Marriage and Death*, p. 277.
16. Morris Palmer Tilley, *A Dictionary of the Proverbs in England in the Sixteenth and Seventeenth Centuries* (Ann Arbor: University of Michigan Press, 1950), p. 124. Cited in Cressy, *Birth, Marriage, and Death*, p. 277.
17. Cressy, *Birth, Marriage, and Death*, pp. 277–78.
18. Lawrence Stone, *Road to Divorce: England 1530–1987* (Oxford: Oxford University Press, 1990), pp. 57–58.
19. Foucault, *The History of Sexuality*, vol. I, p. 31.
20. Margaret Spufford, *Small Books and Pleasant Histories: Popular Fiction and its Readership in Seventeenth-Century England* (Athens: University of Georgia Press, 1981), p. 63.
21. Fletcher, *Gender, Sex, and Subordination in England*, p. 53.

22. *Ibid.*, p. 114.
23. Angus McLaren, "The Pleasures of Procreation: Traditional and Biomedical Theories of Conception," *Reproductive Rituals: The Perception of Fertility in England from the Sixteenth to the Nineteenth Century* (London and New York: Methuen, 1984), pp. 13–29; citations pp. 14 and 29.
24. See, in addition to those cited below, J. Wing, *The Crown Conjugal or, The Spouse Royal* (London: 1620).
25. Henry Smith, *A Preparative to Mariage* (London: 1591), The English Experience #762 (Norwood, NJ: Johnson; Amsterdam, Netherlands: Theatrum Orbis Terrarum, 1975), p. 56.
26. Patricia Crawford, "Sexual Knowledge in England, 1500–1750," in *Sexual Knowledge, Sexual Science: The History of Attitudes to Sexuality*, eds. Roy Porter and Mikuláš Teich (Cambridge: Cambridge University Press, 1994), pp. 82–106, citation p. 84.
27. Cressy, *Birth, Marriage, and Death*, p. 290.
28. William Perkins, *Christian Œconomie*, trans. Thomas Pickering (London: 1609), p. 111.
29. William Whateley, *A Bride Bush. or, A Direction for Married Persons* (London, 1623), p. 13.
30. *Ibid.*, p. 19.
31. *Ibid.*, pp. 19–20.
32. Ingram, *Church Courts, Sex and Marriage in England*, p. 145.
33. Norton, "Communal Definitions of Gendered Identity in Seventeenth-Century English America," in Hoffman, Sobel, and Teute, eds., *Through a Glass Darkly*, p. 61.
34. See Gail Kern Paster, "The Unbearable Coldness of Female Being: Women's Imperfection and the Humoral Economy," *ELR: English Literary Renaissance* 28:3 (1998): 416–40.
35. John Sutton, *Philosophy and Memory Traces: Descartes to Connectionism* (Cambridge: Cambridge University Press, 1998), p. 40; this term is appropriated by Sutton from modern cognitive science. I thank Gail Paster for bringing this aspect of Sutton's work to my attention.
36. Cited by David Hoeniger, *Medicine and Shakespeare in the English Renaissance* (Newark: University of Delaware Press, 1992), p. 165.
37. See Schoenfeldt, *Bodies and Selves in Early Modern England*.
38. Jacques Ferrand, *Laurie maladie d'amour, ou mélancholie érotique (The Disease of Love, or Erotic Melancholy)*, trans. as *A Treatise on Lovesickness* (1610/1623), eds. Donald A. Beecher and Massimo Ciavolella (Syracuse NY: Syracuse University Press, 1990), p. 4.
39. *Ibid.*, pp. 4–5.
40. The symptoms of greensickness (related to hysteria, but also known as chlorosis) were, among other things, facial discoloration, difficulty breathing, head pains, and heart palpitations. In *The Fourth Book of Practical Physick, Of Women's Diseases* (London: 1684), Nicolas Culpeper defines frenzie of the womb (womb hysteria) as "an immoderate desire of Venery, that makes women almost mad, or a Delirium from an immoderate desire of Venery... The immediate Cause is plenty of hot and sharp Seed against Nature" (pp. 115–16). In "Sexual Knowledge in England," Crawford reproduces the following ballad: "A Remedy for Greensickness": "A Handsom buxom Lass / lay panting in her bed / She lookt as green as grass /

and mournfully she said / Except I have some lusty lad / to ease me of my pain / I cannot live / I sigh and grieve / My life I now disdain" (p. 95).
41. Nicholas Fontanus, *The Womans Doctour, Or, An exact and distinct Explanation of all such Diseases as are peculiar to that Sex* (London: 1652), p. 6. This translation of *Syntagma medicum de morbis mulierum* was intended less for midwives or surgeons than women in general.
42. Nicolas Culpeper, *Practice of Physick* (London: 1655), p. 419; cited on p. 109 by Robert Martensen, "The Transformation of Eve: Women's Bodies, Medicine and Culture in Early Modern England," in Porter and Teich, eds., *Sexual Knowledge, Sexual Science*, pp. 107–33.
43. In *The Technology of Orgasm: "Hysteria," the Vibrator, and Women's Sexual Satisfaction* (Baltimore and London: Johns Hopkins University Press, 1999), Rachel P. Maines argues that genital massage to orgasm by a physician or midwife was a standard treatment for hysteria in the Western medical tradition, from the fifth century BCE to the early twentieth century. Pre- and early modern authors she cites on hysteria and its treatment include the Hippocratic corpus, Celsus, Aretaeus, Soranus, Galen, Äetius, Moschion, Rhazes, Avicenna, Ferrari da Gradi, Rueff, Paracelsus, Paré, Riverius, Burton, Claudini, Harvey, Highmore, Fonteyn, Culpeper, de Castro, Zacuto, Pechey, and Horst.
44. Whateley, *A Bride Bush*, p. 20.
45. By 1600, about 150 medical and related books written in England had been published in almost 400 editions. See Hoeniger, *Medicine and Shakespeare* (p. 35), who also provides a helpful overview of the status of English medical practice, including a detailed list of publication of surgeries, anatomies, and remedies by surgeons, physicians, and humanists. Hoeniger also observes that "most Tudor noblemen and gentlemen owned a few medical books, and it was common for them and their wives to take care of their own health after acquiring some medical skills" (p. 26). According to Jonathan Sawday, *The Body Emblazoned: Dissection and the Human Body in Renaissance Culture* (London and New York: Routledge, 1995), the number of anatomical texts published in England each year after the Civil Wars increased threefold (p. 232).
46. Paré, *The Workes*, p. 889.
47. Crooke, *Microcosmographia*, p. 199. *Microcosmographia* was largely a synthesis of continental anatomists; illustrations drawn from Vesalius and de Valverde contributed to its popularity.
48. Sirasi, *Medieval and Early Renaissance Medicine*, p. 188.
49. According to Brooten, the original Greek text of the physician Soranus of Ephesos (early 2nd century), *On Acute and On Chronic Diseases*, is lost; there is a fifth-century Latin translation by Caelius Aurelianus (*Love Between Women*, p. 147). Soranus also wrote a treatise on gynecology, *Gynaikeia* (in which he recommends clitoridectomy for enlarged clitorises); these sections of his text were preserved by two Latin writers, Mustio and probably Caelius Aurelianus (p. 163). On the differences between Soranus and Caelius Aurelianus, as well as a discussion of Soranus's reference to tribadism, see Brooten, *Love Between Women*, pp. 146–73. Trotula of Solerno may have been a woman; her text is translated as *The Diseases of Women* by Elizabeth Mason-Huhl (Los Angeles: Ward Ritchie, 1940). See also Helen Rodnite Lemay, "William of Saliceto on Human Sexuality," *Viator:*

Medieval and Renaissance Studies 12 (1981): 165–81; Beryl Rowland, *The Medieval Woman's Guide to Health: The First English Gynecological Handbook* (Kent, OH: Kent State University Press, 1981); and Audrey Eccles, *Obstetrics and Gynaecology in Tudor and Stuart England* (Kent, OH: Kent State University Press, 1982).

50. Danielle Jacquart and Claude Thomasset, *Sexuality and Medicine in the Middle Ages*, trans. Matthew Adamson (Princeton: Princeton University Press, 1988), p. 131.
51. Fletcher, *Gender, Sex, and Subordination in England*, p. 34. For the complexities of this "replacement" as refracted through the conflict between Aristotelian and Galenic views, see Ian Maclean, *The Renaissance Notion of Woman* (Cambridge: Cambridge University Press, 1980), pp. 28–46.
52. Crooke, *Microcosmographia,* p. 258.
53. *Ibid.*, pp. 216–17.
54. François Poulain de la Barre, *De l'égalité des deux sexes* (Paris: 1673); trans. A. L., *The woman as good as the man, of the equality of both sexes* (1677). Excerpted in Kate Aughterson, *Renaissance Woman: A Sourcebook: Constructions of Femininity in England* (London and New York: Routledge, 1995), pp. 289–90; citation p. 289.
55. Laqueur, *Making Sex*, pp. 65–68.
56. Park, "The Rediscovery of the Clitoris," p. 173.
57. Realdo Colombo, *De re anatomica* (Venice: 1559). According to C. D. O'Malley and K. F. Russell, *David Edwardes Introduction to Anatomy 1532 (A Facsimile Reproduction with English Translation and Introductory Essay on Anatomical Studies in Tudor England)* (Stanford, CA: Stanford University Press, 1961), *De re anatomica* was the most popular of the foreign anatomies in England until well after the beginning of the seventeenth century: "It was excellent for its time, not certainly the equal of the *Fabrica*, but on the other hand much cheaper to purchase, less bulky to hold, and not so detailed as to be confusing," p. 23.
58. Thomas Vicary, Chief Surgeon to Henry VIII, was the leading surgeon during Edward VI's reign. Vicary's treatise, which was the first English printed text devoted exclusively to anatomy, was published in 1548; it survives only in a version of 1577, available in facsimile by the Early English Text Society: *The anatomie of the body of man*, eds. Frederick Furnivall and Percy Furnivall (London: Oxford University Press, 1930). See p. 77. The 1585 edition, entitled *The Englishmans treasure. With the true anatomye of mans body*, was, according to Fletcher, the most widely read anatomy in England during the late sixteenth century. Vicary's text was copied from a fourteenth-century English manuscript based on Lanfranc, Henri de Mondeville, and Gui de Chauliac (rather than Vesalius and his contemporaries), and thus represented a retrogression in anatomical knowledge. However, as Fletcher notes on p. 36 (*Gender, Sex, and Subordination in England*), Vicary comes very close to claiming the discovery of the clitoris.
59. Park, "The Rediscovery of the Clitoris," pp. 176–77.
60. *Ibid.*, p. 177.
61. Laqueur, *Making Sex*, p. 64.
62. Eccles, *Obstetrics and Gynaecology in Tudor and Stuart England*, p. 34.

63. Crooke, *Microcosmographia*, p. 238.
64. *Ibid.*
65. Bartholin, *Bartholinus Anatomy* (1668). Caspar Bartholin's first edition appeared in 1611; the first Latin edition by Thomas appeared in 1641. According to Andreadis, *Sappho in Early Modern England*, the first English edition appeared in 1653, entitled *The Anatomical History of Thomas Bartholin*. For reasons of access, I have relied on the 1668 edition, which in all relevant respects corresponds to the editions of 1653 and 1665.
66. *Aristotles Master-Piece, Or The Secrets of Generation displayed in all the parts thereof* (London: 1684). This book, along with *Aristotles Complete Master-piece*, *Aristotle's last legacy* (c. 1690) and *Aristotles Experienced Midwife* (London: c. 1700), was aimed at a popular market. Focused on sexual activity, conception, and pregnancy, it is an unscholarly compendium of previous authors, especially Paré. Because of its market popularity, it has been likened to pornography by Roy Porter and Laqueur (who calls it "the most ubiquitous sex guide in the Western tradition," *Making Sex*, p. 64). However, it is a mistake to characterize it as more explicit or prurient than Crooke or Culpeper; indeed, it is a good deal more reticent than they about certain topics, including the clitoris and tribadism.
67. William E. Engel, *Mapping Mortality: The Persistence of Memory and Melancholy in Early Modern England* (Amherst: University of Massachusetts Press, 1995), notes that the colloquial term "yard" "comes from the Old English *gyrd*, meaning a stick, twig, or shoot; it also was used to designate a standard unit of English long measure," p. 254, note 55.
68. Bartholin, *Bartholinus Anatomy*, pp. 61–62.
69. Culpeper, *Directory for Midwives* (1675), p. 23.
70. *Aristotles Experienced Midwife*, n.p.
71. François Mauriceau, *The Diseases of Women with Child, and in Child-bed*, trans. Hugh Chamberlen (London: 1683), p. 11. According to Eccles, Mauriceau was "by far the most influential man-midwife of the day" and his were "really the first satisfactory textbooks in English," *Obstetrics and Gynaecology in Tudor and Stuart England*, p. 14.
72. Culpeper, *A Directory for Midwives*, p. 70.
73. Fontanus, *The Womans Doctour*, p. 4.
74. Crooke, *Microcosmographia*, p. 295.
75. Eccles, *Obstetrics and Gynaecology in Tudor and Stuart England*, p. 34.
76. Sharp, *The Midwives Book*, p. 45. Available in facsimile, ed. Randolph Trumbach (New York: Garland, 1985), and a new scholarly edition, ed. Elaine Hobby (New York and Oxford: Oxford University Press, 1999). There is some controversy about whether Sharp was, indeed, a woman (Hobby thinks she was); her midwifery was preceded in France by Louis Bourgeois, whose *Observations* was published fifty years earlier.
77. On the basis of demographic evidence, Henry Abelove, "Some Speculations on the History of 'Sexual Intercourse' During the 'Long Eighteenth Century' in England," in *Nationalisms and Sexualities*, eds. Andrew Parker, Mary Russo, Doris Sommer, and Patricia Yaeger (New York and London: Routledge, 1992), pp. 335–42, speculates that in the period between 1680 and 1830, there was a "remarkable increase in the *incidence* of cross-sex genital intercourse" (p. 337), an

increase which he relates to the reorganization and confinement of all other erotic acts into "foreplay."
78. Crooke, *Microcosmographia*, p. 238. For examples of erotic "itching" in early modern "pornography," see Aretino's sonnets and John Marston's "The Metamorphosis of Pygmalion's Image" (stanza 33).
79. Paré, *The Workes*, p. 886.
80. *Ibid.*, p. 889.
81. Laurent Joubert, *Popular Errors* (*Erreurs Populaires au fait de la médecine et régime di santé* [Bordeaux: 1578]), trans. Gregory David de Rocher (Tuscaloosa: University of Alabama Press, 1989), p. 110. Joubert had a great reputation as a surgeon, and his *Erreurs Populaires* was enormously popular, with nineteen editions appearing before 1600.
82. *Ibid.*, p. 117.
83. Crooke, *Microcosmographia*, p. 274. Crooke raises the issue of women who "say that they have no sense or inkling of pleasure at all." He negotiates around this by maintaining that "pleasure is not therefore conceived because the seede toucheth the orifice of the wombe, but because it runneth through the spermaticall vessells of the woman which are of exquisite sense, otherwise women with childe who ejaculate their seede not into the inward orifice, but into the middle of the necke of the wombe, should have no pleasure in such ejaculations; but it is manifest that they have greater pleasure after they bee with child then before, because their seed passeth a longer course" (p. 295). Thus, women who conceive without pleasure have ill-affected wombs (p. 286); "an impure, mucous and moyste woman may conceyve without pleasure, or any sense of titillation at all" (p. 295).
84. *The Penguin Book of Renaissance Verse 1509–1659*, ed. David Norbrook and H. R. Woudhuysen (London and New York: Penguin, 1993), pp. 253–63. Norbrook notes that "Nash his Dildo" is an alternative manuscript title as well as a title used in contemporary allusions (p. 785). The poem, probably written sometime before 1597, was well known by the late 1590s.
85. See Carol Cook, "'The Sign and Semblance of her Honor': Reading Gender Difference in *Much Ado About Nothing*," *PMLA* 101:2 (1986): 186–202.
86. Gabriel Harvey attacked the immorality of Nashe's writings by associating him with "Aretine," and Nashe invoked Aretino as the epitome of the satiric writer; see David C. McPherson, "Aretino and the Harvey–Nashe Quarrel," *PMLA* 84:6 (1969): 1551–58. David Frantz calls Nashe the "self-styled English Aretino" in *Festum Voluptatis: A Study of Renaissance Erotica* (Columbus: Ohio State University Press, 1989), p. 6. See also M. L. Stapleton, "Nashe and the Poetics of Obscenity: *The Choise of Valentines*," *Classical and Modern Literature: A Quarterly* 12 (1991/92): 29–48, who charts Nashe's imitation and satire of his literary predecessors.
87. Frantz, *Festum Voluptatis*, pp. 195 and 197.
88. Locating Nashe in a tradition of Italian pornography, Frantz argues that "Nashe is working in a tradition in which female masturbation with a dildo is one of the conventions confirming male fantasies about the sexual drive of females. While the poet may fail to satisfy this drive, the male reader is nevertheless amused, confident in his ability to satisfy Francis" (*ibid.*, p. 197). In contrast to this reading of masculine confidence, Ian Moulton, in "Transmuted into a Woman or Worse:

Masculine Gender Identity and Thomas Nashe's 'Choice of Valentines,'" *ELR: English Literary Renaissance* 27:1 (1997): 57–88, argues that phallic power is undermined by the poem's representation of male sexual dysfunction. Jonathan V. Crewe, *Unredeemed Rhetoric: Thomas Nashe and the Scandal of Authorship* (Baltimore: Johns Hopkins University Press, 1982), maintains that "the poem stages a radical dislocation and consequent loss of ontological security, not only for its speaker, but for love poetry as such" (p. 51), one effect of which is that "female masturbation emerges not simply as a legitimate subject of love poetry but its true and compelling subject – its secret subject" (p. 52).

89. Werner Von Koppenfels, "Dis-Covering the Female Body: Erotic Exploration in Elizabethan Poetry," *Shakespeare Survey* 47 (1994): 127–37; citation p. 136.

90. On the circulation of "Venus and Adonis" as a form of soft porn meant not only to thematize female sexual frustration, but to produce it among its female readers, see Richard Halpern, "'Pining Their Maws': Female Readers and the Erotic Ontology of the Text in Shakespeare's *Venus and Adonis*," *Venus and Adonis: Critical Essays* (New York and London: Garland, 1997), pp. 377–88; citation p. 382.

91. Henry Neville, *Newes from the New Exchange, or the Commonwealth of Ladies, Drawn to the Life, in their several Characters and Concernments... Printed in the year, of Women without Grace* (London: 1649), p. 2. Also relevant is the reference to "a brave *Woman-man-of mettle*, heigh for my Lady *Hungerford*. Since Sir *Edward* is in Heaven, the fittest *mate* for her upon Earth, must needs be *Annis-water Robbin*, For they may fit one another by turns, and be beholding to nobody" (p. 7). *Woman-man-of-mettle* is marginally glossed: "Supposed a Hermaphrodite." Another woman is described as a "*Leviathan*. Sure, none but *Goliahs* weapon can fit her *Scabbard*, nor can any hand but his with the *six fingers* sufficiently *feele* her; and he that will please her (which she abundantly loves) must convert a *Weavers beam* into a *dildo*" (pp. 10–11). See also the obscene lampoon, *Erotopolis, The Present State of Betty-Land* (London: 1684); also known as *The Kingdom of Love*, this work is sometimes attributed to Charles Cotton.

92. On seventeenth- and eighteenth-century obscenity, see Peter Wagner, *Eros Revived: Erotica of the Enlightenment in England and America* (London: Secker & Warburg, 1988); David Foxon, *Libertine Literature in England, 1660–1745* (London: New Hyde Park, 1965); Roger Thompson, *Unfit for Modest Ears: A Study of Pornographic, Obscene and Bawdy Works Written or Published in England in the Second Half of the Seventeenth Century* (Totowa, NJ: Rowman & Littlefield, and London: Macmillan, 1979); and Rachel Weil, "Sometimes a Scepter is Only a Scepter: Pornography and Politics in Restoration England," in *The Invention of Pornography: Obscenity and the Origins of Modernity, 1500–1800*, ed. Lynn Hunt (New York: Zone Books, 1993), pp. 125–53. Ian McCormick includes excerpts of obscene works in his *Secret Sexualities: A Sourcebook of 17th and 18th Century Writing* (London and New York: Routledge, 1997).

93. Figuring a woman's body as an instrument, particular a viol or fiddle, is a popular trope in late sixteenth- and seventeenth-century bawdy, especially in the genre of city comedy. In her chapter on *The Roaring Girl*, Jean Howard analyzes the viol as a trope of female autoeroticism in *The Stage and Social Struggle*; Fiona McNeill extends this avenue of research in "Gynocentric London Spaces: (Re)Locating Masterless Women in Early Stuart Drama," *Renaissance Drama* 28 (1997; published in 1999): 195–244.

94. John Cotgrave, *Wits Interpreter, The English Parnassus* (London: 1655), p. 229. I am grateful to Bruce Smith for sending me a copy of this poem.
95. "My Thing Is My Own," in *Wit and Mirth: OR, PILLS TO PURGE MELANCHOLY; BEING A Collection of the best Merry Ballads and Songs, Old and New*, ed. Thomas D'Urfey (London: 1700); republished in 1707, 1712, and 1719. The 1719 edition is published in facsimile by Folklore Publishers (New York: 1959), pp. 216–18. The song was also collected in *Songs Compleat, Pleasant and Divertive; Set to Musick, by John Blow, Mr. Henry Purcell, and other Excellent Masters of the Town* (London: 1719). These publications were geared toward male singing in pubs, their "catches" often scatological and bawdy. I thank Amanda Eubanks Winkler for tracing the publishing history for me. This song is available on the CD, "The Art of the Bawdy Song, The Baltimore Consort and the Merry Companions," Dorian Recordings, 1992.
96. Lynn Hunt, "Introduction: Obscenity and the Origins of Modernity, 1500–1800," in *The Invention of Pornography*, p. 30. For a view that positions the birth of "modern" pornography and pornographic culture in the nineteenth century, and links them to the overvaluing of both sex and representations, see Walter Kendrick, *The Secret Museum: Pornography in Modern Culture* (New York: Viking, 1987).
97. On Aretino's *Sonetti lussuriosi* (1524), see Lynne Lawner, *I Modi: The Sixteen Pleasures: An Erotic Album of the Italian Renaissance*, ed. and trans. Lynne Lawner (Evanston, IL: Northwestern University Press, 1988); and Paula Findlen, "Humanism, Politics, and Pornography in Renaissance Italy," in Hunt, ed., *The Invention of Pornography*, pp. 49–108. In line with her argument that Aretino's sonnets describe a gallery of courtesans, Lawner argues that the "female protagonists are equal to the men, just as articulate and in control"; "The women initiate lovemaking, give commands, express their tastes in the most intimate details, are not only as exuberant as the men but just as knowledgeable in technical matters" (pp. 36–37). Given this celebration of Aretino's ventriloquism, it seems important to note the rigid gender binaries that structure the erotic action: despite two engravings in which the woman sits on top, no woman is described in the sonnets as being on top; the clitoris (having yet to be "rediscovered") goes unmentioned and cunnilingus unexplored; and, despite the apparent interchangeability of the woman's vagina and anus, no man is penetrated or fellated. An obsession with the vagina and asshole limits female pleasure to vaginal penetration. For Aretino's presence and influence in England, see Frantz, *Festum Voluptatis*.
98. According to the *Trésor de la langue française*, the French term "pornographe" was first used to refer to writing about prostitution; see Hunt, ed., *The Invention of Pornography*, p. 13.
99. Kathryn Norberg, "The Libertine Whore: Prostitution in French Pornography from Margot to Juliette," in Hunt, ed., *The Invention of Pornography*, pp. 225–52; citation p. 225.
100. Imported texts translated into the vernacular that include scenes of lovemaking among women include Nicholas Chorier's *Aloisiae Sigaeae, Toletanae, Satyra Sotadica de Arcanis Amoris et Veneris*, also known as *The Seven Dialogues of Aloisa* or *Satyra Sotadica The Dialogues of Luisa Sigea* (first published in Latin in 1659/1660). It was translated into French as *L'Académie des Dames* (Paris: 1680) and into English as *The Seven Dialogues of Aloisa (Tullia and Octavia)* and *A Dialogue Between a Married Lady and a Maid* in 1684. Mild homoerotic

encounters are described in the dialogues between Agnes and Angelica in Jean Barrin's *Vénus dans la Cloître* (1683), translated as *Venus in the Cloister or The Nun in her Smock* (2nd edn., 1725). They also occur in the home-grown pornography of John Cleland's *Memoirs of a Woman of Pleasure (Fanny Hill)* (London: 1748), in which Fanny is seduced by Phoebe Ayres, and in the pseudo-medical *Rare Verities: The Cabinet of Venus Unlocked and Her Secrets Laid Open. Being a Translation of part of Sinibaldus his Geneanthropeia* (London: 1658). On the homoerotic content of obscene works in this period, see Donoghue, *Passions Between Women*, especially pp. 183–219; Moore, *Dangerous Intimacies*; Wahl, *Invisible Relations*, pp. 218–51; Susan Lanser, "'Queer to Queer': Sapphic Bodies as Transgressive Texts," in *Lewd and Notorious: Female Transgression in the Eighteenth Century*, ed. Katherine Kittredge (Ann Arbor: University of Michigan Press, forthcoming); and Harriette Andreadis, "Sappho in Early Modern England."

101. Cited in Findlen, "Humanism, Politics, and Pornography," in Hunt, ed., *The Invention of Pornography*, p. 76.
102. A later English poem written about a dildo, "Signior Dildo" by John Wilmot, the Earl of Rochester (written *c.* 1673; published 1703), focuses precisely on the possibility that virtually all ladies will find the dildo (likened to a "candle, carret, or thumb") irresistible, for this prosthetic instrument allows them to take responsibility for their erotic fates.
103. Robert Martenson, "The Transformation of Eve: Women's Bodies, Medicine, and Culture in Early Modern England," and Roy Porter, "The Literature of Sexual Advice Before 1800," in Porter and Teich, eds., *Sexual Knowledge, Sexual Science*, pp. 107–33 and 134–57; Roy Porter, "The Secrets of Generation Display'd: *Aristotle's Masterpiece* in Eighteenth-Century England," in *'Tis Nature's Fault: Unauthorized Sexual Behavior During the Enlightenment*, ed. Robert Maccubbin (London and New York: Cambridge University Press, 1987), pp. 1–21.
104. Thompson, *Unfit for Modest Ears*, p. 161. Thompson suggests that "misuse" by readers was only one cause of medical writers' concern; the other was that disreputable publishers would dress up their texts into "something positively titillating" (pp. 164–65).
105. In "The 1599 Bishops' Ban, Elizabethan Pornography, and the Sexualization of the Jacobean Stage," in *Enclosure Acts: Sexuality, Property, and Culture in Early Modern England*, eds. Richard Burt and John Michael Archer (Ithaca, NY, and London: Cornell University Press, 1994), pp. 185–200, Lynda Boose charts the relation between obscene literature and Jacobean drama, which she argues together introduce a new lexicon and new field of interrelated interests: scatology, phallic aggression (epitomized by the malcontent), and misogyny. She divorces Nashe from this emerging tradition, however, because his poem "is too jocular and invests too much self-mocking humor in exposing the comedies of male impotence ever to reach the dark depths and psychic defenses that underlie the pornographic" (p. 192).
106. Paré, *The Workes*, p. 887.
107. Crooke, *Microcosmographia*, p. 200.
108. *Ibid.*, pp. 287, 223, 239.
109. James McMath, *The expert midwife* (Edinburgh: 1694), p. 11.
110. Bartholin, *Bartholinus Anatomy*, p. 65.

111. Sharp, *The Midwives Book*, p. 52.
112. Crooke, *Microcosmographia*, p. 199.
113. *Ibid.*, p. 200.
114. Paré, *The Workes*, p. 887.
115. Joubert, *Popular Errors*, p. 110.
116. McMath, *The expert midwife*, p. 11.
117. Ferrand, *A Treatise on Lovesickness*, p. 312.
118. Poulain de la Barre, *The woman as good as the man*, p. 289.
119. Thomas Raynald, *The birth of mankind, otherwise named The Womans Booke* (1545). Raynald's textbook was an enlargement and revision of *The byrth of mankind* by Richard Jonas (1540), which was an English translation of Eucharius Röesslin's *Der swangern Frauwen und Hebammem Roszgarten* (1513), which was itself an adaptation of Soranus's classical midwifery. Raynald's innovative text, one of the earliest to be addressed to midwives, is notable for including woodcuts that illustrate the birth stool and the various positions of the fetus in the womb. *The birth of mankind* was published in thirteen editions before 1654. I thank Dr. Alex Tulskey, M.D. for allowing me to examine his 1604 edition of Raynald, from which my citations (no pagination) are taken unless otherwise noted. The best critical reading of Raynald is that of Janet Adelman, "Making Defect Perfection: Shakespeare and the One-Sex Model," in *Enacting Gender on the English Renaissance Stage*, eds. Viviana Comensoli and Anne Russell (Urbana and Chicago: University of Illinois Press, 1999), pp. 23–52.
120. Raynald, *The Birth of Man-kinde: Otherwise Named the Womans Booke* (London: 1626), pp. 12–13.
121. See Schoenfeldt, *Bodies and Selves in Early Modern England*. It is interesting in this regard that the closest Crooke comes to designating the intestines as a sewer is to refer to the "valve or membrane" of the "collick gut" as a "floud-gate" (*Microcosmographia*, pp. 107–08).
122. H. R. Hayes, *The Dangerous Sex: The Myth of Feminine Evil* (New York: Putnam, 1964).
123. Janet Adelman, *Suffocating Mothers: Fantasies of Maternal Origin in Shakespeare's Plays, Hamlet to The Tempest* (London and New York: Routledge, 1992).
124. These early modern expressions of anxiety have medieval roots. In "From 'Diseases of Women' to 'Secrets of Women': The Transformation of Gynecological Literature in the Later Middle Ages," *Journal of Medieval and Early Modern Studies* 30:1 (Winter 2000): 5–39, Monica Green traces the medieval linguistic transformation from a paradigm of disease to one of gender in vernacular gynecological texts: "The transformation of gynecological literature into repositories of 'women's secrets' gave an unsavory, misogynist taint to the whole enterprise of writing publicly about women's bodies" (p. 28).
125. John Banister, *The History of Man* (London: 1578). Cited in Fletcher, *Gender, Sex, and Subordination in England*, p. 35.
126. Cited by Adelman, "Making Defect Perfection," p. 28.
127. Raynald, *The Birth of Man-kinde* (1626 edn.), p. 11.
128. Culpeper, *The Compleat Midwife's Practice Enlarged* (London, 1680), p. 276.
129. Sharp, *The Midwives Book*, p. 5.

130. Paré, *The Workes*, p. 130. On Paré's trial, see Park, "The Rediscovery of the Clitoris," and Céard's introduction to *Des Monstres et Prodigés*.
131. Paré, *The Workes*, p. 982. In a striking continuation of the trope of speech, Paré concludes his discussion of bestiality with an attack on concealment of the crime, which "the conscious beasts could not utter, yet the generated mis-shapen issue hath abundantly spoken and declared, by the unspeakable power of God" (p. 982).
132. On Paré and Joubert, see Evelyne Berriot-Salvadore, "The Discourse of Medicine and Science," trans. Arthur Goldhammer, in *A History of Women in the West*, vol. III, eds. Natalie Zemon Davis and Arlette Farge (Cambridge, MA and London: Harvard University Press, 1993), pp. 348–88.
133. For this reference to Pineaus, see Olav Thulesius, *Nicholas Culpeper: English Physician and Astrologer* (New York: St. Martin's Press, 1992), p. 87.
134. Sawday, *The Body Emblazoned*, p. 225. Whether the College's motivation was moral or political, Crooke addressed the threat of censorship in terms of the charge of obscenity.
135. Crooke, *Microcosmographia*, Preface, n.p.
136. *Ibid.*, p. 197.
137. *Ibid.*
138. *Ibid.*
139. *Ibid.*, p. 199.
140. *Ibid.*, p. 200.
141. *Ibid.*, p. 216. The first three definitions in the *OED* for "pretermit" in this period are (1) To leave out of a narrative; not to notice, mention, insert, or include; to omit. (2) To allow to pass without notice or regard; to overlook intentionally. (3) To fail or forbear to do, use, or perform; to leave undone, neglect, omit.
142. Midwives played important social roles not only as healers but as expert witnesses in legal cases involving paternity, infanticide, sexual assault, and gender ambiguity. In addition to enforcing secular English laws, midwives could perform baptisms, thus assuming one of the powers of the clergy. The female dominance of midwifery was eroded with changes in licensing practices and the monopoly of the Chamberlain family on the forceps. It is too simple, however, to view the writings of Raynald and Culpeper, in particular, as unsupportive of midwives, for both were attempting to convey to women the means to compete with male midwives who had the benefit of anatomical instruction. See Adrian Wilson, *The Making of Man-midwifery: Childbirth in England, 1660–1770* (London: UCL Press, 1995); and Hilary Marland, ed., *The Art of Midwifery: Early Modern Midwives in Europe* (London and New York: Routledge: 1993).
143. Pointing out that Vesalius's and Valverde's illustrations "had been in circulation in England for the past fifty years or more, and that the production of syncretic works was, equally, hardly an innovation on Crooke's part," Sawday suggests that it is a mistake to judge "the objections of Crooke's fellow physicians as a combination of prudery and obscurantism" (*The Body Emblazoned*, pp. 225–26). Instead, Sawday argues, we must remember that the early years of the seventeenth century were particularly tense times for "theological sensitivity" and that there was, in this context, "an *ideological* stake in controlling the ever more detailed dissemination of public information on the operation of the reproductive body" (p. 226). Certainly this is true. But Sawday's conception of the ideological is too narrow,

for the clash of theology and state politics is not the only context within which problems of censorship should be analyzed.

144. For further discussion of the gendered anxieties evinced in anatomical illustration, see my "Gendering Mortality in Early Modern Anatomies," in *Feminist Readings of Early Modern Culture*, eds., Traub, Kaplan, and Callaghan, pp. 44–92.

145. Jacopo Berengario da Carpi, *Isagogae breves* (Bologna, 1522). Translated into English by H. Jackeson, *Mikrokosmographia; Or a Description of the Body of Man* (London: 1664).

146. Quoted in Glenn Harcourt, "Andreas Vesalius and the Anatomy of Antique Sculpture," *Representations* 17 (1987): 28–61, esp. p. 28.

147. Nanette Salomon, "The Venus Pudica: Uncovering Art History's 'Hidden Agendas' and Pernicious Pedigrees," in *Generations and Geographies in the Visual Arts: Feminist Readings*, ed. Griselda Pollock (London and New York: Routledge, 1996), pp. 69–87; citation pp. 70–71.

148. Ibid., p. 74.

149. Thomas Geminus, *Compendiosa totius anatomie delineatio (A facsimile of the first English Edition of 1553 in the version of Nicholas Udall)*, Introduction by C. D. O'Malley (London: Dawson's, 1959). In this text, Geminus used Udall's abridged English translation of Vesalius's *De Humani Corporis Fabrica* (1543). As the first English anatomy to use copper plates for its engravings, Geminus's book, first published in 1545, "exerted considerable influence," according to Charles Singer in *The Evolution of Anatomy* (New York: Alfred Knopf, 1925), p. 171. The second edition replaced Udall's translation of Vesalius with parts of Vicary's 1577 edition of *Anatomie of mans bodie*.

150. Salomon notes that "the pudica pose is the one classical trope which is maintained without a break throughout the medieval period. It was ... a perfect formulation for images of Eve as the embodiment of sin in general and female weakness specifically," "The Venus Pudica," p. 77.

151. Adam and Eve were depicted not only on anatomical title pages but in engravings of anatomy theaters where skeletons in their likeness were often positioned as architectural ornament. Extrapolating from an engraving of the Leiden anatomy theater to Inigo Jones's anatomy theater for the London Barber-surgeons on Monkwell Street, Sawday views all images of Adam and Eve within the anatomical project as "harbingers of death" (*The Body Emblazoned*, p. 77). In his work in progress, Duke Pesta examines the role of the anatomical Adam and Eve as *memento mori*.

152. Karen Newman briefly analyzes Crooke's title page in *Fashioning Femininity and English Renaissance Drama* (Chicago and London: University of Chicago Press, 1991), pp. 2–6 and 11–12.

153. Crooke, *Microcosmographia*, p. 237.

154. André Du Laurens (Andreas Laurentius), *Opera omnia anatomica et medica* (Frankfurt: 1627), p. 199.

155. Sharp, *The Midwives Book*, p. 33.

156. Not much work has been done on discourses of masturbation in the early modern period, and the extent to which medical advice authorized individual masturbation is difficult to say. Concerns about self-pleasure emerge only sporadically in the seventeenth century, usually in the context of tribadism. Jean Riolan's *Discourse sur les hermaphrodites ou il est demonstré contre l'opinion commune, qu'il ny'a*

point de vrays hermaphrodits (Paris: 1614), for instance, describes a noblewoman's clitoris that "had begun to enlarge from a young age, always having her hand upon it when she was in bed, and feeling so much pleasure there in touching it, that little by little, it increased in size" (p. 78); translation by Wahl, *Invisible Relations*, p. 28, who argues for the importance of discourses of masturbation in the surveillance of tribadism. Robert Burton mentions "the other uncleanness of self-defiling monks, scarce to be named" in his increasingly anti-Catholic *The Anatomy of Melancholy*, ed. Holbrook Jackson (New York: Vintage, 1977), p. 652 – a reference that could refer to masturbation, sodomy, or both. In "Masturbation, Credit and the Novel during the Long Eighteenth Century," *Qui Parle* 8:2 (1995): 1–19, Thomas Laqueur argues that masturbation, understood as a medical and moral problem, was invented in the early eighteenth century as part of a market revolution. With the publication of the anonymous *Onania; or the Heinous Crime of Self Pollution* (c. 1712), masturbation became associated with uncontrolled imagination and the excess of desire, including "the enjoyment of pornography, the capacity to fantasize over medical illustrations, and the engrossment in the longings of fictional characters" (p. 3). See also his essay "The Social Evil, the Solitary Vice, and Pouring Tea," in *Solitary Pleasures: The Historical, Literary, and Artistic Discourses of Autoeroticism*, eds. Paula Bennett and Vernon A. Rosario (New York: Routledge, 1995), pp. 155–61.

3. THE POLITICS OF PLEASURE; OR, QUEERING QUEEN ELIZABETH

1. Berry, *Of Chastity and Power*, p. 188.
2. See Frances Yates, *Astrea: The Imperial Theme in the Sixteenth Century* (London: Routledge and Kegan Paul, 1975); and Roy Strong, *Portraits of Queen Elizabeth I* (Oxford: Clarendon Press, 1963); *The Cult of Elizabeth* (London: Thames & Hudson, 1977); and *Gloriana: The Portraits of Queen Elizabeth I* (London: Thames & Hudson, 1987). Both Yates and Strong focus on the deployment of political allegories through examining compositional sources and deciphering abstract symbols. They read Elizabeth's iconography within the terms of the nationalistic cult of Elizabeth or the imperial myth of Virgo-Astrea, the just virgin, "empress of the world, guardian of religion, patroness of peace, restorer of virtue" (*Astrea*, p. 60). This national and imperial iconography, as well as its critical elucidation, depends on the reification of virginity. In addition, Strong's assertion that "[t]he primary purpose of a state portrait was, of course, not to portray an individual as such, but to invoke through that person's image the abstract principles of their rule" (*Gloriana*, p. 36), remains the primary interpretative lens through which Elizabeth's image is viewed. Thus, despite their invaluable unpacking of symbolic significance (of the rainbow, sieve, ermine, and serpent), and thematic analysis of visual exempla, Yates and Strong tend to read everything as iconographic except the body itself. In privileging abstract symbol over embodiment, their approach elides not only the body's placement in history, but the management and deployment of the body through symbolic discourses. In Strong's association of Astrea with Venus, the body of Gloriana is the abstract principle of love, an object, not subject, of multiple desires. Despite Elizabeth Pomeroy's attempt to place the portraits of Elizabeth within a historical context, her analysis remains focused on

aesthetic design in *Reading the Portraits of Queen Elizabeth I* (Hamden, CT: Archon, 1989).

3. Although I have been much influenced by Berry, I agree with Laurie Shannon, who in "Emilia's Argument: Friendship and 'Human Title' in *The Two Noble Kinsmen*," *ELH: English Literary History* 64 (1997): 657–82, charges that Berry's elucidation of "the associative aspects of a chastity figured by Diana's circle are never explored. Berry reads such plural instances in terms of female narcissism, or in terms of Elizabeth's female 'community' with her mother, Anne Boleyn, or in terms of a unified feminine sphere, by which the masculine is excluded or civilized. Where these categories fail, Berry defaults to a lexicon of 'ambiguity' rather than directly argue the implications of a self-specified, same-sex association that her texts would seem to offer" (p. 660).

4. For Elizabeth's manipulation of these idioms, see Louis Adrian Montrose, "The Elizabethan Subject and the Spenserian Text," in *Literary Theory/Renaissance Texts*, eds. Patricia Parker and David Quint (Baltimore: Johns Hopkins University Press, 1986), pp. 317–31; and "'Eliza, Queene of shepheardes,' and the Pastoral of Power," *ELR: English Literary Renaissance* 10 (1980): 153–82. For limitations on Elizabeth's ability to control her royal image, see Montrose, "Idols of the Queen: Policy, Gender, and the Picturing of Elizabeth I," *Representations* 68 (Fall 1999): 108–61. See also Carole Levin, *The Heart and Stomach of a King: Elizabeth I and the Politics of Sex and Power* (Philadelphia: University of Pennsylvania Press, 1994); Leonard Tennenhouse, *Power on Display: The Politics of Shakespeare's Genres* (New York and London: Methuen, 1986); and Leah Marcus, "Erasing the Stigma of Daughterhood: Mary I, Elizabeth I, and Henry VIII," in *Daughters and Fathers*, eds. Lynda Boose and Betty Flowers (Baltimore: Johns Hopkins University Press, 1989), pp. 400–07. Elizabeth's manipulation of the idioms of virginity and maternity was not as uniform as is suggested by the above critics. In *Elizabeth I: The Competition for Representation* (Oxford: Oxford University Press, 1993), Susan Frye challenges the evidential basis for the Amazonian image of Queen Elizabeth, particularly in regard to the speech attributed to her at Tilbury. In *Virgin Mother, Maiden Queen: Elizabeth I and the Cult of the Virgin Mary* (London: Macmillan, 1995), Helen Hackett argues that the view that Elizabeth replaced the Virgin Mary in England's national consciousness needs to be specified by attention to when and why such appropriations took place. In *Gender and Heroism in Early Modern English Literature* (Chicago: University of Chicago Press, 2002), Mary Beth Rose counters other scholars' construction of Elizabeth as a monarch who strategically emphasized her virginity and maternity. She argues that although "Elizabeth frames, as it were, the body of her speeches with self-legitimizing references to her virginity," she "refrains in her public rhetoric from identifying fervently and consistently with the roles of virgin and/or mother... After her early speeches on marriage and the succession... Elizabeth virtually gives up on emphasizing the trope of virgin mother as a salient aspect of her self-presentation" (pp. 31–34).

5. In her laudable attempt to counter psychological explanations for Elizabeth's reputedly irrational aversion to marriage, Susan Doran, in *Monarchy and Matrimony: The Courtships of Elizabeth I* (Routledge: London and New York, 1996), too narrowly interprets the marriage negotiations as exclusively political. Demonstrating the importance of evaluating each courtship within its political and diplomatic

context, and shedding light on the role of the Privy Council, she focuses on the intent and outcome of the individual matrimonial suits, and on dispelling criticism of the Queen. See also her "Why Did Elizabeth Not Marry?" in *Dissing Elizabeth: Negative Representations of Gloriana*, ed. Julia Walker (Durham, NC and London: Duke University Press, 1998), pp. 30–59. Doran's displacement of the erotic by the political can be seen as well in Hackett, who, while acknowledging the eroticism of medieval invocations of the Virgin Mary, says of the early courtly love discourse addressed to Elizabeth: "religious devotion to the Queen is a metaphor for erotic desire for her, which in turn is a metaphor for political loyalty to her" (*Virgin Mother, Maiden Queen*, p. 79).

6. Montrose, "The Elizabethan Subject and the Spenserian Text," p. 315.
7. Andrew Belsey and Catherine Belsey, "Icons of Divinity: Portraits of Elizabeth I," in *Renaissance Bodies: The Human Figure in English Culture, c. 1540–1660*, eds. Lucy Gent and Nigel Llewellyn (London: Reaktion, 1990), pp. 11–35; citation p. 33.
8. Susan Frye, "Of Chastity and Violence: Elizabeth I and Edmund Spenser in the House of Busirane," *Signs: Journal of Women in Culture and Society* 20:1 (1994): 49–78, citation p. 55.
9. For further readings of Elizabeth's portraits that focus on gender, see Susan P. Cerasano and Marion Wynne-Davies, "'From Myself, My Other Self I Turned': An Introduction" in *Gloriana's Face: Women, Public and Private, in the English Renaissance* (Detroit: Wayne State University Press, 1992), pp. 1–24; Julia Walker, "Bones of Contention: Posthumous Images of Elizabeth and Stuart Politics," in Walker, ed., *Dissing Elizabeth*, pp. 252–76; and Nanette Salomon, "Positioning Women in Visual Convention: The Case of Elizabeth I," in *Attending to Women in Early Modern England*, eds. Betty S. Travitsky and Adele F. Seeff (Newark: University of Delaware Press, 1994), pp. 64–95. For the function of jewels in the portraits, see William Carroll, "The Virgin Not: Language and Sexuality," *Shakespeare Survey* 46 (1993): 107–20.
10. As Hackett observes, her subjects repeatedly noted "her extraordinary power to move while remaining unmoved," *Virgin Mother, Maiden Queen*, p. 100.
11. For the statement to Sir Thomas Pope and the speech to the first Parliament, see Hackett, *Virgin Mother, Maiden Queen*, pp. 52 and 53; for the statement to the envoy, see J. E. Neale, *Queen Elizabeth* (London: Jonathan Cape, 1934), p. 143; for the 1576 speech to Parliament, see *Elizabeth I: Collected Works*, eds. Leah S. Marcus, Janel Mueller, and Mary Beth Rose (Chicago and London: University of Chicago Press, 2000), p. 170.
12. On the basis of the Queen's Public speeches, Mary Beth Rose implies that the Queen held a more divided attitude: "On the one hand she refers to virginity positively, if vaguely as a preference ... Far from committing herself to virginity, however, she declares her intention to renounce it" (*Gender and Heroism in Early Modern English Literature*, pp. 31–34). Rose usefully reminds us that it would have been less than viable for Elizabeth to publicly declare her intention to remain single while still a marriageable monarch. And Rose is certainly correct to caution that we cannot know Elizabeth's secret thoughts. Despite such declarations of intent, however, Elizabeth never did forsake the single life.
13. Peter Stallybrass, "Patriarchal Territories: The Body Enclosed," in *Rewriting the Renaissance*, eds., Ferguson, Quilligan, and Vickers, pp. 123–42; citation p. 129.

The analogy of body and land is a common enough trope, structuring, for instance, the "Ditchley" portrait of Elizabeth standing atop a map of her realm and a contemporaneous anonymous Dutch engraving (1598) of Elizabeth protecting Europe against Spanish aggressors.

14. By suggesting this possibility, I do not mean to lend support to a reading strategy that hunts for transhistorical genital images; see my critique of this methodology in "The Rewards of Lesbian History," *Feminist Studies* 25:2 (1999): 363–94.
15. William Allen, *An admonition to the Nobility and People of England and Ireland Concerninge the Present Warres made for the execution of his Holiness Sentence, by the highe and mightie King Catholike of Spaine* (Antwerp: 1588), sig. B3r; rpt. in *English Recusant Literature, 1558–1640*, vol. LXXIV, ed. D. M. Rogers (Menston, UK: Scolar Press, 1971), pp. xix, xxi. There is some question whether Allen authored the pamphlet or merely allowed it to be published in his name. I am grateful to Katherine Eggert for alerting me to Allen's text and sharing portions of her typescript, *Showing Like a Queen: Female Authority and Literary Experiment in Spenser, Shakespeare, and Milton* (Philadelphia: University of Pennsylvania Press, 2000).
16. John Stubbs, *The Discoverie of a Gaping Gulf whereinto England is Like to be Swallowed by an other French mariage, if the Lord forbid not the banes, by letting her Majestie see the sin and punishment thereof* (London: 1579).
17. Ilona Bell, "'Souereaigne Lord of lordly Lady of this land': Elizabeth, Stubbs, and the Gaping Gulf," in Walker, ed., *Dissing Elizabeth*, pp. 99–117, esp. p. 100.
18. Peter Erickson examines the way portraits of Elizabeth, especially the Garter portrait, participate in a "precursor phase" in the emergence of a racialized image of whiteness in "'God for Harry, England, and Saint George': British National Identity and the Emergence of White Self-Fashioning," in Erickson and Hulse, eds., *Early Modern Visual Culture*, pp. 315–45.
19. Paré, *The Workes*, pp. 889 and 886.
20. Luce Irigaray, *This Sex Which Is Not One*, trans. Catherine Porter and Carolyn Burke (Ithaca: Cornell University Press, 1985), citation p. 28. In drawing this connection, I am echoing Berry, *Of Chastity and Power*, whose discussion of Spenser's Belphoebe notes the function of "multiple fastenings, knots, and foldings of her costume: hymen-like boundaries which emblematize her refusal of any phallic attempt at the unravelling and decoding of her body. At the same time, these features of her clothing also hint at an alternative, many-faceted eroticism, whereby the female body is 'close enwrapped' within itself" (p. 160).
21. David Howarth, *Images of Rule: Art and Politics in the English Renaissance, 1485–1649* (Berkeley and Los Angeles: University of California Press, 1997), pp. 102–03.
22. Belsey and Belsey, "Icons of Divinity," p. 20.
23. Paré, *The Workes*, p. 1001.
24. My reading counters that of Belsey and Belsey, who interpret the mermaid as "a parody of the image of the Queen," an "alternative sexual identity" firmly opposed by the "disembodied" Elizabeth ("Icons of Divinity," p. 14).
25. The extent to which anatomical illustration and cartography function as mutually sustaining "scientific" strategies for depicting the human body in this period is explored in my forthcoming essay, "Anatomy, Cartography, and the New World Body."

26. Frye, *Elizabeth I*, remarks on the "assemblage of iconographic elements that claim the queen's chaste body as the center of the Ptolemaic universe while wrapping her in a mantle whose open mouths, ears, and eyes form a disquieting suggestion of vaginal openings combined with a sense of governmental surveillance" (pp. 102–03). See also Christopher Pye, *The Regal Phantasm: Shakespeare and the Politics of Spectacle* (London and New York: Routledge, 1990).
27. Joel Fineman, *The Subjectivity Effect in Western Literary Tradition: Essays Toward the Release of Shakespeare's Will* (Cambridge, MA: MIT Press, 1991), p. 229. Earlier, he had called attention to "the way the painting places an exceptionally pornographic ear over Queen Elizabeth's genitals, in the crease formed where the two folds of her dress fold over on each other, at the wrinkled conclusion of the arc projected by the dildo-like rainbow clasped so imperially by the Virgin Queen" (p. 228).
28. Daniel Fischlin, "Political Allegory, Absolutist Ideology, and the 'Rainbow Portrait' of Queen Elizabeth I," *Renaissance Quarterly* 50:1 (1997): 175–206; citation p. 185.
29. *Ibid.*, pp. 187 and 188. Fischlin perceptively reads the portrait's "capacity to transfix with both an erotics of ambiguity and an ambiguous erotics" (p. 185). However, he seems torn between viewing the phallus as "undercut" by the vaginal folds, and viewing the queen as "male by virtue of her grasp of its cylindrical shape as it descends into and merges with her anatomy" (p. 187).
30. Rob Content, "Fair is Fowle: Interpreting Anti-Elizabethan Composite Portraiture," in Walker, ed., *Dissing Elizabeth*, pp. 229–51; citation p. 234.
31. Christopher Lloyd, *The Queen's Pictures: Royal Collectors Through the Centuries* (London: National Gallery, 1991), p. 62.
32. I am grateful to Peter Erickson for this particular point, as well as for generously contributing his thoughts to my readings of Elizabeth's portraits.
33. Janet Arnold, *Queen Elizabeth's Wardrobe Unlock'd* (Leeds: W. S. Maney & Son, 1988), p. 12.
34. *De Maisse, A Journal of all that was Accomplished by Monsieur de Maisse, Ambassador, in England from Henry IV to Queen Elizabeth, Anno Domini 1597*, trans. and eds. George Bagshaw Harrison and R. A. Jones (Bloomsbury: Nonesuch Press, 1931), pp. 24–25, emphasis mine. Large extracts of the French text are reprinted in Lucien Anatole Prévost-Paradol, *Elisabeth et Henri IV (1595–1598): Ambassade de Hurault de Maisse en Angleterre au sujet de la paix de Vervins* (Paris: 1855). I have reproduced the italicized portions here: "Elle avait le devant de sa robe en manteau ouvert et luy voyoit-on toute la gorge et assez bas et souvent, comme si elle eust eu trop chaud, elle eslargissoit avec les mains le devant dudict manteau . . . sa gorge se montre assez ridée, autant que (la laissoit veoir) le carcan qu'elle portoit au col, mais plus bas elle a encore la charnure fort blance et fort déliée autant que l'on eust peu veoir" (p. 151).
35. *De Maisse, A Journal*, pp. 36–37, emphasis mine. "Une robe dessous de damas blanc, ceinte et ouveerte devant, aussy bien que sa chemise, tellement qu'elle ouvrait souvent cette robe et luy voyait-on tout l'estomac jusques au nombril . . . elle a cette façon qu'en rehaussant la teste elle met les deux mains à sa robe et l'entrouvre, tellement qu'on luy veoit tout l'estomac" (Prévost-Paradol, *Elisabeth et Henri IV*, p. 155).

36. Arnold, *Queen Elizabeth's Wardrobe Unlock'd*, p. 9.
37. Lisa Jardine, *Reading Shakespeare Historically* (London and New York: Routledge, 1996), p. 23, citing Montrose, "'Shaping fantasies.'" Insofar as Montrose uses the ambassador's account to underscore a reading of an erotic dream of the Queen inscribed in Simon Forman's diary, Jardine's effort to delineate the line between life and representation is well taken. Yet, Jardine also suggests that for the Catholic de Maisse, any "glimpses of female flesh – neck, throat, and (in veiled *décolleté*) suggestions beyond – cannot be accommodated to his version of female decorum" (*Reading Shakespeare Historically*, p. 23).
38. *Ibid.*, p. 164, note 16. Elizabeth's alleged erotic provocation, Jardine writes, "turns out to belong to the twentieth-century English translation of de Maisse's diary far more than to the original French, although one would still want to take note of Hurault de Maisse's difficulty with the breach of decorum (in his terms) of a woman of Elizabeth's age receiving him with anything other than a gown which entirely concealed her body." See also pp. 163–64, notes 13 and 14, where Jardine argues, for instance, that "'Gorge' here surely means 'throat' rather than 'bosom' (see Robert and Huguet dictionaries), since the elaborate choker necklace she wears largely conceals it." Other biographers have sought to disarm the threat of Elizabeth's alleged self-display by resorting to sexist characterizations of her flirtatiousness. Christopher Haigh, *Elizabeth I* (London and New York: Longman, 1988), remarks that "the new French ambassador was confused when the Queen received him in her dressing-gown and kept pulling it open, until he realised that he was supposed to peep admiringly down her front" (p. 86).
39. Montrose, "'Shaping Fantasies," p. 67; and Hannah Betts, "'The Image of this Queene so quaynt': The Pornographic Blazon 1588–1603," in Walker, ed., *Dissing Elizabeth*, pp. 153–84; citation p. 160.
40. Paul Hentzner, *A Journey Into England by Paul Hentzner in the Year 1548* (1747), rpt. Horace Walpole, trans. R. Bentley (Reading: 1807), p. 26.
41. Phyllis Rackin, "Dating Shakespeare's Women," *Shakespeare Jahrbuch* 134 (1998): 29–43; citation p. 31.
42. Although Phillip Stubbes does not mention the fashion of bare breasts in his *Anatomy of Abuses* (1583), his nineteenth-century editor, Frederick Furnivall, saw fit to include a woodcut of "Bare Breasts" from *The Roxburghe Ballads* which was used to illustrate, among others, the ballad "The Cruel Shrow." See *Phillip Stubbes's Anatomy of the Abuses in England in Shakespeare's Youth, A.D.1583*, ed. Frederic Furnivall (The New Shakespeare Society) (London: 1877–79), p. 21; and *The Roxburghe Ballads* (1877) p. 96.
43. *Canon Pietro Casola's Pilgrimage to Jerusalem In the Year 1494*, ed. Mary Margaret Newett (Manchester: Manchester University Press, 1907), p. 144.
44. Thomas Coryat, *Coryats Crudities* (London: 1611), p. 261. The quotation continues: "and many of them have their backes also naked even almost to the middle, which some do cover with a slight linnen, as cobwebbe lawne, or such other thinne stuff: a fashion me thinkes very uncivill and unseemely, especially if the beholder might plainly see them. For I beleeve unto many that have *prurientem libidinem*, they would minister a great incentive & fomentation of luxurious desires. Howbeit it is much used both in Venice and Padua."

45. In "An Explication of the Emblems of the Frontispiece," Ben Jonson ascribes sexual looseness to the Frenchwoman: "These be the three countries with their *Cornucopia*, / That make him as famous, as *Moore* his *Utopia*. / OR, Here France gives him scabs, Venice a hot Sunne, / And Germanie spewes on him out of her Tunne." A subsequent illustration in Coryat's travel narrative of Margarita Emiliana – "I have here inserted a picture of one of their nobler Cortezans, according to her Venetian habites, with my owne neare unto her, made in that forme as we saluted each other" – portrays a bare-breasted courtesan greeting the author (*Coryats Crudities*, p. 261).

46. Estienne, *A World of Wonders*, p. 10. Whether many Venetian women wore fashions that fully exposed their breasts, it is the case that Venetian courtesans often were depicted in bare-breasted fashions. When Albrecht Dürer drew his "Lady in a Venetian Dress Contrasted with a Nuremberg Lady" (1495), the woman's abundant breasts, which, though not fully bared, are nonetheless uplifted for provocative display, provide a major point of his nationalist fashion comparison.

47. Frère Antoine Estienne Mineur, *A Charitable Remonstrance Addressed to the Wives and Maidens of France Touching Their Dissolute Adornments* (Paris: 1585); trans. William Rooke (Edinburgh, privately printed, 1887), p. 7. Because his rhetoric is so over the top, I cannot resist quoting him at length. He describes their "habiliments" as

> false hair, pads, curls, plaits, earrings, ornaments, hair combs, tiaras, masks, visors, low-cut open bodices trimmed with braids and fringes, and what you call burnouses, chains, jewels, bracelets, collars of different kinds and shapes, feathers, fans, busks, high sleeves, dresses of velvet, satin, damask, and taffetas, quite loose, and cut down back and front, and squared below the arm-pits, enriched with excessive trimming, flouncings, and outrageous ruffs; silk drawers and vests, suggestive stockings of silk embroidered with divers colours, with clocks, with garters of the same material, Venetian shoes with high heels. (p. 10)

His polemic reaches a fevered pitch when he finally addresses "your abominable open dresses" (p. 19): "What shall I say to you with your breasts uncovered? What a dishonour it is to a christian woman, to be exposed and uncovered as many among you are, even in public places, and before the eyes of all the world, and, what is more abominable, in the holy temples! Oh execrable wantoness! Oh crime intolerable! Oh pernicious scandal!" Even the friar realizes that he has become carried away: "The love of God transports me and makes me thus leave off the subject I am dealing with, the purpose of which is to shew you that you ought not to appear with breasts uncovered. Coming back now whence I started, I warn you that true christians are never dressed in such a way, but only pagans" (p. 30). His subsequent biblical history lesson and review of the Church fathers ends with the remark:

> But you will tell me you are not naked. Well, how far you are from it. You could not be more so without profaning all modesty and exposing that great work which nature has wished to be commanded. For, tell me, I ask you, is there any part of the human body which more excites to carnal love than the breasts? If it is not so, why does the prophet, wishing to signify the great spiritual love which is between him and his spouse, make use of this word, breasts, in so many passages of the Canticles, unless for this reason that he had nothing more apt to show the flame of his spiritual love, than that by which the carnal lover is roused to acts of love above all others. (p. 32)

48. James Henke also cites J. B., *A View of the People of the World*, which medically diagnoses bare breasts as a cause of women losing the use of their hands "through a refrigeration of the originall of the Nerves," in *Gutter Life and Language in the Early "Street" Literature of England* (West Cornwall, CT: Locust Hill, 1988), pp. 170–71. The idea of bodily display seems to have influenced Inigo Jones's costume designs for some of the court masques performed for (and by) Anne of Denmark and Henrietta Maria. For costume designs for Ben Jonson's masque "Chloridia," performed February 22, 1631, see Stephen Orgel and Roy Strong, *Inigo Jones: The Theater of the Stuart Court*, 2 vols. (London: Sothebey Parke Bernet and Berkeley: University of California Press, 1973). Earlier designs show breasts and nipples under diaphanous fabrics: Oceana for Jonson's "Masque of Blacknesse" (1605), and Tethys or a Nymph, for Samuel Daniel's "Thethys Festival" (1610).
49. Letter from Charles North to his father, April 13, 1667, Bodleian MS. North. C. 4., fol. 146; cited by Sophie Tomlinson, "'My Brain the Stage': Margaret Cavendish and the Fantasy of Female Performance," in *Women, Texts and Histories, 1575–1760*, eds. Clare Brant and Diane Purkiss (London and New York: Routledge, 1992), pp. 134–63; citation p. 163, note 59.
50. John Bulwer, *Anthropometamorphosis; Man Transform'd; or, The Artificiall changling Historically presented, In the mad and cruell Gallantry, foolish Bravery, ridiculous Beauty, filthy Finenesse, and loathsome Loveliness of most Nations, fashioning and altering their Bodies from the mould intended by Nature* (London: 1653), pp. 314–15.
51. *Ibid.*, p. 315.
52. Joubert, *Popular Errors*, p. 224.
53. A long tradition of Christian allegory emphasized the maternal connotations of the breast. Devotional art since the fourteenth century recurrently focused on the image of the *Maria lactans*, a figure of nourishment, nurturance, and self-sacrifice, as well as, in the words of Leo Steinburg, *The Sexuality of Christ in Renaissance Art and in Modern Oblivion*, 2nd edn. (Chicago and London: University of Chicago Press, 1996), the assurance that "the God rooting at Mary's breast had become man indeed, and that she who sustained the God-man in his infirmity had gained infinite credit in heaven" (p. 15). As one of the primary themes in Christian iconography, the lactating Virgin influenced images of Charity suckling her father, mother, or children, as well as the female Virtues spouting milk as a symbol of fertility. Despite Caroline Walker Bynum's certainty, in "The Body of Christ in the Later Middle Ages: A Reply to Leo Steinberg" in *Fragmentation and Redemption*, that "medieval viewers saw bared breasts (at least in painting and sculpture) not primarily as sexual but as the food with which they were iconographically associated" (p. 86), by the mid-sixteenth century, the breast could not be viewed without reference to its erotic salience. See also Steinberg's critique of Bynum ("Ad Bynum," in *The Sexuality of Christ*, pp. 364–89): "the proposition that 'medieval viewers' regarded bared breasts rather as nutritive assets than as erotic is argued by making the breast of the nursing Madonna the type of all female breasts... since the Virgin is singular and her breast's status unique, it is entirely inappropriate to cite images of the *Maria lactans* as evidence of how 'medieval people' perceived female breasts... If we would know how 'medieval people' viewed breasts in life or image, we would do better to consult pictures of Eve, or of female clients at public baths; or study the naked damned in medieval *Last Judgments*" (pp. 381–82).

54. John Floyd, *The Overthrow of the Protestants Pulpit-Babels, Convincing their Preachers of Lying & Rayling, to make the Church of Rome seeme mysticall Babell* (1612); rpt. English Recusant Literature, vol. CXLIX, ed. D. M. Rogers (Menston, UK: Scolar Press, 1973). Floyd attempts to confute William Crashawe's *Sermon at the Crosse*, otherwise known as *The Jesuites Gospell* (1610). In his "Preface to the Gentlemen of the Innes of Court," Floyd takes up Crashawe's accusation that Catholics "compare [Mary's] *breasts and milke with the wounds and bloud of Christ*," charging that Crashawe

> doth likewise forget himselfe, saying, *that no extraordinary blessednesse doth belong to the wombe of the Virgin, none to her breasts* in this regard only, that they did breed, and feed the Sonne of God, that she whome we do so exalt, is *no more than another holy woman*, but *a believing Jew*. And giving further passage to his passions, he doth not only beate her sacred wombe and breasts into dust & wormes, by scoffing at her assumption into heaven but also carelessely casteth them out of his hart into a lower place then wormes & magots, by a foule comparison of them & her milke, with other womens; not excepting the most impurest Strumpet. (p. 28)

Floyd returns to this theme later in his Preface, accusing Crashawe of being "better acquainted with other womens breasts, then the Virgins," for he dares to think "it no sinne, for a man full of sinne, without any care or respect, to approach & touch them by imagination" (p. 54). That Crashawe learned this disrespect from "his Father *Luther*" is clear to Floyd, who refuses to "turne into English" Luther's "devout contemplations upon womens breasts, laps, armes, and bodyes ... but such as understand Latyn will not wonder, that such meditations brought him in the end to marry a Nunne" (p. 54).

55. In *A History of the Breast* (New York: Ballantine Books, 1997), Marilyn Yalom asserts that "Renaissance France and Italy made of the female nude, and especially of her breasts, the centerfold of high-culture eroticism... The meaning of the breast in Renaissance high culture was unequivocally erotic" (pp. 73–74). She distinguishes the artistic interest in exposing the female body on the Continent from the situation in Elizabethan England, where "there is an absence of nude bodies in the plastic arts, but no lack of breasts on the lips of poets" (p. 76). Yalom attributes this difference to religion ("the visual display of flesh that had thrived among the Catholic elite was more suspect in Protestant circles" [p. 76]), to culture ("too long, too entrenched was the tradition of Nordic-Christian hostility to sensual delight" [p. 82]), as well as to Elizabeth herself who was, according to Yalom, dedicated to "project[ing] an androgynous image ... a stiff and formal icon, rather than a flesh-and-blood woman" (p. 78).

56. Thomas Lodge, *Rosalynde* (1590); and Andrew Marvell, "To His Coy Mistress" (1681). For more examples, see Robert P. Merrix, "The Vale of Lillies and the Bower of Bliss: Soft-core Pornography in Elizabethan Poetry," *Journal of Popular Culture* 19:4 (1986): 3–16.

57. Robert Herrick, *Hesperides* (London: 1648).

58. Alastair Fowler, "Robert Herrick," *Proceedings of the British Academy* 66 (1980): 243–64; citation p. 245.

59. George Puttenham published *Partheniad* 7 in an example of his section on resemblance in Book 3, "Of Ornament," in *The Arte of English Poesie* (London: 1589), pp. 204–05.

60. In *Microcosmographia*, Crooke describes virgins' breasts becoming "hard and like pleasant Apples" (p. 157), and the nipple "very like a strewberry" (p. 159). He also notes their affinity with the womb; the breasts are two, he says, so "that like good handmaides they might serve their dame the womb" (p. 157).
61. See, for instance, Gordon Braden, *The Classics and English Renaissance Poetry: Three Case Studies* (New Haven: Yale University Press, 1978): "The emphasis on foreplay and nongenital, especially oral, gratifications, the fixation on affects (smells, textures) and details (Julia's leg), and the general voyeuristic preference of perception to action... are all intelligible as a wide diffusion of erotic energy denied specifically orgastic focus and release. What is missing in the *Hesperides* is aggressive, genital, in other words, 'adult' sexuality" (p. 223).
62. Nancy J. Vickers, "Diana Described: Scattered Women and Scattered Rhyme," in *Writing and Sexual Difference*, ed. Elizabeth Abel (Chicago: University of Chicago Press, 1982), pp. 95–109. Vickers exposes the Petrarchan catalogue of somatic attributes as a tropological dissection that, in fragmenting the female body into its constitutive beauty parts, secures male poetic identity by allowing the male poet to feel whole and coherent. The anatomical blazon is thus a compensatory mechanism for male poetic subjectivity.
63. I am referring here to the recent anthology, *The Body in Parts: Fantasies of Corporeality in Early Modern Europe*, eds. Hillman and Mazzio.
64. William Kerrigan, "Kiss Fancies in Robert Herrick," *George Herbert Journal* 14: 1–2 (1990/91): 155–71; citation p. 160.
65. *Ibid.*, p. 163.
66. *Ibid.*, p. 166.
67. *Eliza's Babes: Or the Virgins-Offering. Being Divine Poems, and Meditations* (London: 1652), p. 56.
68. Yalom, *A History of the Breast*, p. 86; *Kissing the Rod: An Anthology of Seventeenth-Century Women's Verse*, eds. Germaine Greer, Susan Hastings, Jeslyn Medoff, Melinda Sansone (London: Virago, 1988), p. 146.
69. Lillian Schanfield, "'Tickled with Desire': A View of Eroticism in Herrick's Poetry," *Literature and Psychology* 39:1–2 (1993): 63–83; citation p. 79.
70. David Lee Miller, *The Poem's Two Bodies: The Poetics of the 1590 Faerie Queene* (Princeton: Princeton University Press, 1988), p. 229.
71. *Edmund Spenser: The Faerie Queene* (1590), ed. Thomas P. Roche, Jr. (New Haven and London: Yale University Press, 1981), p. 379 (Book 2, canto 12, stanza 74, lines 6–8).
72. I was first alerted to the homoeroticism of this passage by Heather Findley, who mentioned it in a paper presented at the "Bodies and Pleasures in Pre and Early Modernity" conference, University of California, Santa Cruz, November 1995. In *The Limits of Eroticism in Post-Petrarchan Narrative*, Stephens makes a brief comparison between this episode and the relationship between Britomart and Amoret in the service of her argument about how the transitive nature of gender creates a "conditional erotics" of Spenser's verse (p. 37).
73. See Stephen Greenblatt's chapter on the bower of bliss in *Renaissance Self-Fashioning: from More to Shakespeare* (Chicago: University of Chicago Press, 1980).
74. Strong, *Portraits of Queen Elizabeth*, pp. 18–19.
75. Hentzner, *A Journey Into England*, p. 27.

76. Arnold, *Queen Elizabeth's Wardrobe Unlock'd*, p. 11.
77. That hands are an erotic emblem is clear from Barnabe Barnes's Sonnet 63 from *Parthenophil and Parthenope: Sonnettes, Madrigals, Elegies and Odes* (1593):

> Jove for Europaes love tooke shape of Bull,
> And for Calisto playde Dianaes parte
> And in a golden shower, he filled full
> The lappe of Danae with coelestiall arte,
> Would I were chang'd but to my mistresse gloves,
> That those white lovely fingers I might hide,
> That I might kisse those hands, which mine hart loves
> Or else that cheane of pearle, her neckes vaine pride,
> Made proude with her neckes vaines, that I might folde
> About that lovely necke, and her pappes tickle,
> Or her to compasse like a belt of golde,
> Or that sweet wine, which downe her throate doth trickle,
> To kisse her lippes, and lye next at her hart,
> Runne through her vaynes, and passe by pleasures part.

78. Frye, "Of Chastity and Violence," p. 49.
79. *Ibid.*, pp. 53–54.
80. Bennett, "'Lesbian-Like' and the Social History of Lesbianisms," pp. 9–10. Although Bennett readily admits the problems with using the term *lesbian*, she argues that the "refusal to use 'lesbian' defers to homophobia" (p. 12).
81. Jankowski, "Pure Resistance." One difference between my analysis and Jankowski's is the relative weight we each give to erotic activity; her deployment of the category "queer" threatens to empty virginity of eroticism, including both autoeroticism and female–female desire.
82. Bennett, "'Lesbian-Like' and the Social History of Lesbianisms," maintains that her hyphenated construction "both names 'lesbian' and destabilizes it": "the 'like' in 'lesbian-like' decenters 'lesbian,' introducing into historical research a productive uncertainty born of likeness and resemblance, not identity" (p. 14).
83. *Calendar of Letters and State Papers Relating to English Affairs, preserved principally in the archives of Simancas* (London: H. M. Stationary Office, 1892), vol. I, p. 364.
84. Levin, *The Heart and Stomach of a King*, p. 133. Elizabeth's remark is briefly discussed by Leah Marcus, *Puzzling Shakespeare: Local Reading and Its Discontents* (Berkeley and Los Angeles: University of California Press, 1988), who also makes the observation that Mary Queen of Scots had "joked that if only she or Elizabeth were a man, they could have married" (p. 97); and Constance Jordan, "Representing Political Androgyny: More on the Siena Portrait of Queen Elizabeth I," in *The Renaissance Englishwoman in Print: Counterbalancing the Canon*, eds. Anne M. Haselkorn and Betty S. Travitsky (Amherst: University of Massachusetts Press, 1990), pp. 157–76, who states, "[g]iven the prominence accorded her second male body in the world of diplomacy and courtiership . . . her reflections here are not as strange or as idiosyncratic as they would be were she not a queen regnant" (p. 160).
85. Susan Frye, Review of *The Heart and Stomach of a King*, in *Shakespeare Quarterly* 47:3 (1996): 339–40; citation p. 340.

86. Laurie Shannon, "Nature's Bias: Renaissance Homonormativity and Elizabethan Comic Likeness," *Modern Philology* (98) 2000: 183–210; citation p. 196.
87. *Ibid.*, pp. 196–97.
88. In addition to Tennenhouse, *Power on Display*, see Frank Whigham, *Ambition and Privilege: The Social Tropes of Elizabethan Courtesy Theory* (Berkeley: University of California Press, 1984); and Richard McCoy, *The Rites of Knighthood: The Literature and Politics of Elizabethan Chivalry* (Berkeley: University of California Press, 1989).
89. Catherine Bates, *The Rhetoric of Courtship in Elizabethan Language and Literature* (Cambridge: Cambridge University Press, 1992).
90. Frye, *Elizabeth I*, pp. 104–05.
91. Berry, *Of Chastity and Power*, p. 65.
92. Insofar as the figure of Elizabeth manifests an aristocratic autoeroticism that commands male and female gazes alike, Elizabeth solicits female identification *and* female desire: desire to be Elizabeth, to possess what she possesses; and desire for Elizabeth, to possess her, and in so doing, partake of her body and her power. According to Strong, the audience for royal paintings was large and diverse; he suggests that "most families of substance would probably have owned a portrait of the Queen" (*Portraits of Queen Elizabeth I*, p. 23) – whether an original or a copy. Cheap engravings of the monarch were hawked in the streets of London. Most of the portraits that reached the Continent were exchanged as diplomatic gifts in connection with Elizabeth's marriage negotiations (p. 24); the rage for miniatures of the Queen that developed in the later years of her reign was in part due to their suitability as courtship gifts. Portraits conveyed not only the Queen's royal image, but her sexual promise. With the exception of the miniatures and engravings of Levina Teerlinc, the portraits of Elizabeth were the creation of male artists; their intended audience primarily was aristocratic men. However, just as there is no necessary contradiction between male spectatorship and female self-assertion, there is nothing to suggest that pleasure in viewing these paintings was limited to men.
93. Montrose, *Purpose of Playing*, p. 160.
94. Yates, *Astrea*, pp. 77 and 87.
95. It would be useful, for instance, to examine Elizabeth's biography in light of the other female aristocrats and rulers who embarked on passionate same-gender liaisons before and after her reign. The "illustrious Margaret of Austria," for instance, who was reputed to have loved "the fair Laodamia Forteguerra," was portrayed by both Brantôme and Firenzuola in the 1540s as an exemplary lover of women. See Brantôme, *Lives of the Fair and Gallant Ladies*, p. 136; and Agnolo Firenzuola, *On the Beauty of Women* (1541), trans. Konrad Eisenbichler and Jacqueline Murray (Philadelphia: University of Pennsylvania Press, 1992), p. 17. According to Jacqueline Murray, "Agnolo Firenzuola on Female Sexuality and Women's Equality," *Sixteenth Century Journal* 22: 2 (1991): 199–213, Firenzuola's reference to Margaret of Austria is either to the aunt of Charles V, who spent the last twenty-six years of her widowed life refusing to marry and died in 1530, or to Margaret of Parma, Charles V's daughter, who though married twice, also had a long widowhood (p. 209). A half century after Elizabeth, Queen Christina of Sweden, whose aversion to marriage was widely acknowledged, abdicated her throne amid rumors of illicit female affections. Christina's ostensible reason for abdication was her conversion to Catholicism. On the rumors of illicit affections, see Georgina Masson,

Queen Christina (New York: Farrar, Straus, & Giroux, 1968), pp. 85–87. The purported erotic liaisons of elite women of the French court of Henri II (1547–59) and the English court of Charles II (1660–85) were all notorious in their day. See Antonia Fraser, *Royal Charles: Charles II and the Restoration* (New York: Alfred Knopf, 1979), pp. 341–43, on Charles II's mistress, Hortense Mancini, Duchesse de Mazarin, who "developed a passionate friendship" with Anne, Countess of Sussex, one of the King's daughters (p. 343). Saint Evremond apparently remarked, "Each sex provides its lovers for Hortense" (p. 342). Miss Hobart Hamilton, a lady of the Restoration court, was notorious for her passionate advances toward younger women; see Ivan Bloch, *A History of English Sexual Morals* (London: Francis Alden, 1936), pp. 422–25, and Wahl, *Invisible Relations*, pp. 215–17.

96. Goldberg, *Sodometries*, pp. 41–42.
97. *Ibid.*, p. 47. We might use Goldberg's destabilization of the links between gender and eroticism to query, for instance, the normalizing assumption embedded within the characterization of Elizabeth as a disembodied "iron maiden" – even when this appraisal is proffered from a supposedly feminist and anti-imperialist orientation, as in the essay by Belsey and Belsey, "Icons of Divinity," p. 35.
98. See Jordan, "Representing Political Androgyny," whose important discussion of Elizabeth's "androgyny" unfortunately bifurcates into female chastity and male sexuality.
99. Sir Robert Naunton, *Fragmenta Regalia, &c.*, in *The Harleian Miscellany* (London: 1810), p. 124.
100. Peter Stallybrass, "Boundary and Transgression: Body, Text, Language," *Stanford French Review* (Spring/Fall 1990): 9–23; citation pp. 10–11.
101. Mark Kishlansky, *A Monarchy Transformed: Britain 1603–1714* (New York and London: Penguin, 1996), p. 77.
102. *Ibid.*, p. 118.
103. See, for instance, Anthony Van Dyck's painting, "Charles I and Henrietta Maria with their Two Eldest Children, Charles, Prince of Wales, and Mary, Princess Royal" ("The Greate Peece") (1632), which hung in Whitehall. As Roy Strong remarks, "Charles and Henrietta are the first English royal couple to be glorified as husband and wife in the domestic sense," *Van Dyck: Charles I on Horseback* (New York: Viking, 1972), p. 70. The patriarchal authority of state portraits of James I and Charles I is discussed by Jonathan Goldberg, *James I and the Politics of Literature: Jonson, Shakespeare, Donne, and Their Contemporaries* (Baltimore and London: Johns Hopkins University Press, 1983). On the fusion of domesticity and courtly politics associated with Henrietta Maria, see also Sophie Tomlinson, "She That Plays the King: Henrietta Maria and the Threat of the Actress in Caroline Culture," in *The Politics of Tragicomedy: Shakespeare and After*, eds. Gordon McMullan and Jonathan Hope (London and New York: Routledge, 1992), pp. 189–207; and Erica Veevers, *Images of Love and Religion: Queen Henrietta Maria and Court Entertainments* (Cambridge: Cambridge University Press, 1989); Parry, *The Golden Age Restor'd*, and Howarth, *Images of Rule*.
104. Paul Hammond, "The King's Two Bodies: Representations of Charles II," in *Culture, Politics, and Society in Britain, 1660–1800*, eds. Jeremy Black and Jeremy Gregory (Manchester and New York: Manchester University Press, 1991), pp. 13–48; citation p. 13.

105. Louise de Kéroualle, Duchess of Portsmouth, was a French Catholic and was influential in public affairs.
106. See Rachel Weil, "Sometimes a Scepter is Only a Scepter: Pornography and Politics in Restoration England," in *The Invention of Pornography*, pp. 125–53; and Hammond, "The King's Two Bodies."
107. Oliver Arnold analyzed the vision of the Houses of Parliament as a map of England in a paper presented at the conference, "Paper Landscapes," Queen Mary and Westfield College, July 1997.
108. Hammond, "The King's Two Bodies," p. 41.
109. *Ibid*.
110. Informal notions of a binding marriage contract, verbal and written, public and secret, had, of course, been used earlier, and as "spousals" held considerable power within the ecclesiastical courts; I am referring here to the meaning of contract as a legally enforceable agreement between ostensibly free persons who are thereby brought together into relations of equality. Lockean notions of contract are widely acknowledged to have profoundly affected political theory and social reality, despite the fact that "Whigs would reluctantly espouse Locke's contract theory of the state but resolutely deny its applicability to the family" – a view that was contested by feminists such as Mary Astell and Mary Chudleigh. See Lawrence Stone, *Road to Divorce*, p. 17. For the elision of the "sexual contract" within contract theory, see Carol Pateman, *The Sexual Contract* (Stanford, CA: Stanford University Press, 1988).
111. Michael McKeon, "Historicizing Patriarchy," p. 296. The "foundering of patriarchalist political theory at the end of the seventeenth century" is not, according to McKeon, only a function of the succession crisis; it also represents "one outcome of a more general, early modern disenchantment with aristocratic ideology ... summarized as the set of related beliefs that birth makes worth, that the interests of the family are identified with those of its head, and that among the gentry, honor and property are to be transmitted patrimonially and primogeniturally, through the male line" (p. 297). The effect is a double separation: "The family is increasingly distinguished from the state, while the component members of the family are increasingly distinguished from each other" (p. 298).
112. Lois G. Schwoerer, "Images of Queen Mary II, 1689–95," *Renaissance Quarterly* 42:4 (1989): 717–48; citation p. 729. According to Schwoerer, Mary's declaration was functionally disingenuous, as she directed the government during her husband's frequent absences from England. Kishlansky, on the other hand, calls her "a willing cipher for her husband's programme" and, as regent during the king's absences, "controlled by a Council of Nine and managed by William's detailed directives" (*A Monarchy Transformed*, p. 301).
113. Carol Barash, *English Women's Poetry, 1649–1714: Politics, Community, and Linguistic Authority* (Oxford: Clarendon Press, 1996), p. 51.
114. Kishlansky, *A Monarchy Transformed*, pp. 316–17.
115. "A New Ballad: To the Tune of 'Fair Rosamond'" (1708), in *Poems on Affairs of State: Augustan Satirical Verse, 1660–1717*, vol. VII, ed. Frank H. Ellis (New Haven: Yale University Press, 1975), p. 309. The ballad continues to describe Masham's reputed crimes against the state for thirty-one more stanzas.

116. On Anne's relationships with Sarah Churchill and Abigail Masham, see Donoghue, *Passions Between Women*, pp. 158–64; Wahl, *Invisible Relations*, pp. 117–21; Ros Ballaster, "'The Vices of Old Rome Revived': Representations of Female Same-Sex Desire in Seventeenth and Eighteenth Century England," in *Volcanoes and Pearl Divers: Essays in Lesbian Feminist Studies*, ed. Suzanne Raitt (London: Onlywomen Press, 1994), pp. 13–36; and Kishlansky, *A Monarchy Transformed*, pp. 319–32. Analyses that claim Anne as a *lesbian* can be found in Kendall, "Finding the Good Parts: Sexuality in Women's Tragedies in the Time of Queen Anne," in *Curtain Calls: British and American Women and the Theater, 1660–1820*, eds. Mary Anne Schofield and Cecelia Macheski (Athens: Ohio University Press, 1991), pp. 165–76; Rose Collis, *Portraits to the Wall: Historic Lesbian Lives Unveiled* (London: Cassell, 1994), pp. 13–28; and Dennis Rubini, "Sexuality and Augustan England: Sodomy, Politics, Elite Circles, and Society," in *The Pursuit of Sodomy: Male Homosexuality in Renaissance and Enlightenment Europe*, eds. Kent Gerard and Gert Hekma (New York and London: Haworth Press, 1989), pp. 349–81 (which also draws attention to political pamphlets linking William to sodomy).

4. THE (IN)SIGNIFICANCE OF *LESBIAN* DESIRE

1. Shakespeare, *A Midsummer Night's Dream* (3.2.203–12).
2. Stephen Orgel, "Gendering the Crown," in De Grazia, Quilligan, and Stallybrass, eds., *Subject and Object in Renaissance Culture*, p. 162.
3. *Ibid.*, p. 162.
4. The classic scholarly study, Samuel Chew's *The Virtues Reconciled: An Iconographic Study* (Toronto: University of Toronto Press, 1947), offers no insight into the question that drives my investigation, but it does provide a useful catalogue of the appearance of this theme in literary and visual iconography.
5. In the apocryphal book of Second Esdras, the argument takes place between the angel Uriel (who argues for Justice) and the prophet Ezra (who pleads for Mercy).
6. King James (Authorized) version. In the Vulgate, Righteousness is replaced with Justice.
7. As Chew, *The Virtues Reconciled*, attests, the theme appears not only as brief allusions in a score of literary texts, but as five full allegorical treatments in the first decades of the seventeenth century.
8. *Civitates Orbis Terrarum: The Towns of the World, 1572–1618*, ed. R. A. Skelton, 3 vols. (Cleveland, OH: World Publishing Co., 1966).
9. Orgel, "Gendering the Crown," p. 160.
10. Built on the site of a medieval castle in Derbyshire, the buildings, planned by Robert Smythson and carried on by his dynasty of architects, were begun in 1608 and completed by 1640. The paintings in the Little Castle were executed between 1620 and 1630 under Cavendish's direction. Ben Jonson's *Love's Welcome to Bolsover* was performed there for the King and Queen in 1634. Cavendish married Margaret Lucas in 1645 while both were exiled in Paris; although she had not seen Bolsover in its guise as pleasure palace for royalty (its moveables were removed to Welbeck for safe-keeping and remained there after the War), she was assigned a life interest in Bolsover in 1662.

11. Timothy Raylor, "'Pleasure Reconciled to Virtue': William Cavendish, Ben Jonson, and the Decorative Scheme of Bolsover Castle," *Renaissance Quarterly* 52:2 (1999): 402–39; citations pp. 403, 402. I am grateful to the author for sharing his typescript prior to publication.
12. I am grateful to Gina Bloom and Flagg Miller for photographing the lunettes prior to my own visit to Bolsover Castle.
13. See *Hendrik Goltzius, 1558–1617: The Complete Engravings and Woodcuts*, vol. I, ed. Walter L. Strauss (New York: Abaris Books, 1977), pages 314–17. Goltzius's sequence ends with the embrace of Concord and Peace, a pair missing from the Bolsover design.
14. Raylor, "'Pleasure Reconciled to Virtue,'" quickly passes over the Marble Closet and takes no notice of the sensuality of the lunettes.
15. Hull, *Sexuality, State, and Civil Society in Germany*, p. 44, emphasis mine.
16. Debora Kuller Shuger, *The Renaissance Bible: Scholarship, Sacrifice, and Subjectivity* (Berkeley, Los Angeles, London: University of California Press, 1994), p. 53.
17. Giles Jacob, *A New Law Dictionary: Containing, The Interpretation and Definition of Words and Terms used in the Law; and also the Whole Law, and the Practice thereof, Under all the Heads and Titles of the same* (London: 1729), n.p. Jacob was a diligent compiler and popular author of eight other vernacular law books. *A New Law Dictionary* reached a tenth edition in 1782, and was reissued up to 1835.
18. The *Dictionary of Popular Biography*, vol. V, ed. George Smith (Oxford: Oxford University Press, 1964), p. 1003.
19. John Disney, Vicar of St. Mary's, *A View of Ancient Laws Against Immorality and Profaneness* (Cambridge: 1729), pp. 180–81. In 1708, Disney published an earlier essay, "An Essay Upon the Execution of the Laws Against Immorality and Profaneness."
20. Disney, *A View of Ancient Laws*, p. 180.
21. *Ibid.*, p. 5.
22. Disney, *ibid.*, continues: "And this Interpretation (a) *Selden* approves, and Bp. *Patrick* (b): and the ancient Versions render the words accordingly (c)," thereafter glossing "(a) Seldeni, Uxor Hebraica, (b) *Patrick* in locum and (c) *Walton* Biblia Polyglotta," p. 5.
23. *The New Oxford Annotated Bible (New Revised Standard Version)*, eds. Bruce Metzger and Roland Murphy (New York: Oxford University Press, 1991), p. 248. Likewise, in *The Schocken Bible, Vol. 1, The Five Books of Moses*, trans. Everett Fox (New York: Schocken, 1995): "There is to be no holy-prostitute of the daughters of Israel, there is to be no holy-prostitute of the sons of Israel." (23:18), p. 957.
24. See the discussion of the King James version by Bray, *Homosexuality in Renaissance England*, p. 14. Calvin used "sodomite" and "whore" apparently interchangeably, in an instance that could refer to women as well as to men: "*Whores* as they are, yea... vile and shamefull *Sodomites*, committing suche heinous and abhominable actes, that it is horrible to thinke of," a locution that implies that women can be sodomites and men can be whores (emphasis mine); see Tomson's 1579 translation of Calvin quoted in the *OED* entry for "sodomite."
25. On the ubiquity of male prostitution in Italy, see Rocke, *Forbidden Friendships*. Satirists of London male prostitution include Phillip Stubbes, *The Anatomie of*

Abuses (1583); John Marston, *The Scourge of Villanie* (1598); and Thomas Middleton, *Micro-Cynicon: Sixe Snarling Satires* (1599).
26. On anti-theatrical attacks that characterize boy actors as prostitutes, see Arthur Kinney, ed., *Markets of Bawdrie: The Dramatic Criticism of Stephen Gossen* (Salzburg: Institut für Englische Sprache und Literatur, 1974); and William Prynne, *Histrio-mastix: The Player's Scourge or Actor's Tragedy* (1632–33) (New York: Garland, 1974).
27. Shakespeare, *Troilus and Cressida* (5.1.15–17) and *Hamlet* (2.2.587–88).
28. Thomas Beard, *The Theatre of Gods Judgements: Or, A Collection of Histories out of Sacred, Ecclesiassticall and prophane Authors, concerning the admirable Judgements of God Upon the Transgressours of his commandements* (London: 1597), pp. 359–62.
29. Robert Burton, *The Anatomy of Melancholy*, trans. F. D Kessinger and P. J. S. Kessinger (Kila, MT: Kessinger: 1991), vol. II, p. 653. These passages were originally published in Latin.
30. Thomas Blount, *Glossographia: Or a Dictionary Interpreting all such Hard Words ... as are now used in our refined English Tongue* (London: 1656, 1661) and *Nomo-lexicon: a law-dictionary: Interpreting such difficult and obscure Words and Terms As are found either in Our Common Statute, Ancient or Modern Lawes* (London: 1670).
31. N. H., *THE LADIES DICTIONARY: Being a General Entertainment for the Fair Sex* (London: 1694).
32. Nor does the term "tribade" occur in vernacular dictionaries in this period, despite its use in medical texts. I make this claim after finding not a single entry for tribade in any of the following early modern dictionaries: John Baret, *An Alvaerie or Triple Dictionarie, in Englishe, Latin, and French* (London: 1574); John Bullokar, *An English Expositor: Teaching the Interpretation of the hardest words used in our language* (London: 1616, 1621, 1663, 1688); Thomas Cooper, *Thesaurus Linguae Romanae Et Britannicae* (London: 1565); Randle Cotgrave, *A Dictionarie of the French and English Tongues* (London: 1611); E. Coles, *An English Dictionary. Explaining the difficult terms that are used in Divinity, Husbandry, Physick, Phylosophy, Law, Navigation, Mathematicks, and other Arts and Sciences* (London: 1685); Edward Cocker, *Cocker's English Dictionary* (London: 1704); Claude Desainliens, *A Dictionary French and English (French Littelton)* (London: 1571); Edward Phillips, *The New World of English Words* (London: 1658); Thomas Elyot, *Dictionary (Bibliotheca Eliotae)* (London: 1538); John Rider, *Bibliotheca Scholastica* (London: 1589); John Florio, *A Worlde of Wordes* (London: 1598, 1611); and John Minsheu, *A Dictionary in Spanish and English* (London: 1599) and *Ductor in Linguas, the Guide into Tongues* (London: 1617).
33. Their silence is particularly important given the fact that the legal profession became more preoccupied with concrete definitions and prosecutable evidence over the course of the seventeenth century. In the words of Ingram, *Church Courts, Sex and Marriage in England*, a shift occurred "in legal philosophy and practice which militated against uncertainty or imprecision in legal processes. Increasingly the accent was on specific, readily definable offenses and on means of prosecution which depended on individual, ascertainable accusers and prosecutors" (p. 373).
34. Hull, *Sexuality, State and Civil Society in Germany*, p. 48, emphasis mine.

35. Margaret Hunt, "Afterword," in Goldberg, ed., *Queering the Renaissance*, pp. 359–77; citation p. 373.
36. See Mary Beth Rose, "Women in Men's Clothing: Apparel and Social Stability in *The Roaring Girl*," *ELR: English Literary Renaissance* 14:3 (1984): 367–91; Lisa Jardine, "'As boys and women are for the most part cattle of this colour': Female Roles and Elizabethan Eroticism," in *Still Harping on Daughters: Women and Drama in the Age of Shakespeare* (Brighton, Sussex: Harvester Press, 1983), pp. 9–36; Leah Marcus, "Shakespeare's Comic Heroines, Elizabeth I, and the Political Uses of Androgyny," in *Women in the Middle Ages and the Renaissance: Literary and Historical Perspectives*, ed. Mary Beth Rose (Syracuse: Syracuse University Press, 1986), pp. 135–53; Karen Newman, "Portia's Ring: Unruly Women and Structures of Exchange in *The Merchant of Venice*," *Shakespeare Quarterly* 38:1 (1987): 19–33; Phyllis Rackin, "Androgyny, Mimesis, and the Marriage of the Boy Heroine on the English Renaissance Stage," *PMLA* 102:1 (1987): 29–41; Howard, "Cross-Dressing, the Theater, and Gender Struggle in Early Modern England," in *The Stage and Social Struggle in Early Modern England*, pp. 93–128; and Dympna Callaghan, *Shakespeare Without Women: Representing Gender and Race on the Renaissance Stage* (London and New York: Routledge, 2000).
37. See Marjorie Garber, *Vested Interests: Cross-Dressing and Cultural Anxiety* (New York: Routledge, 1992); Catherine Belsey, "Disrupting Sexual Difference: Meaning and Gender in the Comedies," in *Alternative Shakespeares*, ed. John Drakakis (London: Methuen, 1985), pp. 166–90; Orgel, *Impersonations*; Tracey Sedinger, "'If Sight and Shape be True': The Epistemology of Crossdressing on the London Stage," *Shakespeare Quarterly* 48:1 (1997): 63–79; and Charles Forker, "Sexuality and Eroticism on the Renaissance Stage," *South Central Review* 7:4 (1990): 1–22.
38. I include my analysis of "The Homoerotics of Shakespearean Comedy" in *Desire & Anxiety* in this.
39. In this respect, my articulation of the problem echoes that of Jonathan Goldberg in *Sodometries* (pp. 107–21), who opposes the tendency to view crossdressed figures as "the privileged locus of homosexuality," arguing that a critical preoccupation with crossdressing can in fact obscure the workings of homoeroticism in Renaissance texts.
40. According to editor Trevor Griffiths, in *Shakespeare in Production: A Midsummer Night's Dream* (Cambridge: Cambridge University Press, 1996),

> Pope marked 198–210 with the asterisks he used to distinguish the best lines in Shakespeare (these are the only lines he marked in the *Dream*) and recent critics have pointed to the speech's thematic value. However, the theatre's verdict has been harsher and the later parts of the speech have often been filleted. Vestris was relatively conservative in losing only 211–14. Although Kean, Saker and Daly omitted 193–4 (Daly actually beginning at 195), once again reducing the amount of comment on the situation, *the main target has been the recollections of Hermia and Helena's shared childhood*. There are two main approaches to 203–14: Benson cut everything; Kean started the trend to cut all the sampler and song section (203–8) and the heraldic references (212–14, cut well into the twentieth century). Saker, Daly and Tree followed Kean's editing; Bridges Adams followed Benson. The end of the speech also suffered into the 1950s, with Devine following Phelps and other nineteenth-century

directors in cutting the last three passionate and generalising lines. Atkins made the longest cuts in the speech, removing 198–214 and 217–19. (p. 161, emphasis mine)

41. For a recent reading focused on Celia's affections, see Jessica Tvordi, "Female Alliance and the Construction of Homoeroticism in *As You Like It* and *Twelfth Night*," in Frye and Robertson, eds., *Maids and Mistresses, Cousins and Queens*, pp. 114–30.
42. Sarah Chevers and Katharine Evans likewise use marital rhetoric to describe their relationship, "The Lord hath joined us together, and woe be to them that should part us" in their narrative, *A Short Relation of Cruel Suffering* (1662).
43. For the importance of marital metaphors to this play and an astute reading of this passage, see Patricia Parker, *Shakespeare from the Margins*, pp. 83–115, esp. p. 103.
44. Holstun, "'Will You Rent Our Ancient Love Asunder?'"
45. *The Riverside Shakespeare*, ed. G. Blakemore Evans (Boston: Houghton Mifflin, 1974).
46. For perceptive readings of the textual crux, "dividual," see Masten, *Textual Intercourse*, p. 51; and Peter Stallybrass, "Shakespeare, the Individual, and the Text," in *Cultural Studies*, eds. Lawrence Grossberg, Cary Nelson, and Paula A. Treichler (New York and London: Routledge, 1992), pp. 593–610.
47. Laurie Shannon, "Emilia's Argument," p. 662. I am grateful to Professor Shannon for sharing her essay with me prior to publication. See also Dorothea Kehler, "Shakespeare's Emilias and the Politics of Celibacy," in *In Another Country: Feminist Perspectives on Renaissance Drama*, eds. Dorothea Kehler and Susan Baker (Metuchen, NJ: Scarecrow Press, 1991), pp. 157–78; Richard Mallette, "Same-Sex Erotic Friendship in *The Two Noble Kinsmen*," *Renaissance Drama* 26 (1995): 29–52; and Richard Abrams, "Gender Confusion and Sexual Politics in *The Two Noble Kinsmen*," in *Themes in Drama 7: Drama, Sex, and Politics*, ed. James Redmond (Cambridge: Cambridge University Press, 1985), pp. 69–76.
48. Shannon, "Emilia's Argument," p. 661.
49. *Ibid.*, p. 675. Mallettte, "Same-Sex Erotic Friendship," also notes the eroticism of this scene, pointing out that in contemporary performance, "the bawdiness of the servant is not usually shared by the mistress" (p. 34).
50. See Paul Alpers, *What is Pastoral?* (Chicago and London: University of Chicago Press, 1996), who argues that "[t]hough the pastoral elegy is a special kind, we can use it to define pastoral convention, because death is the ultimate form of the separations and losses that pervade pastoral poetry" (p. 91).
51. Frances Frazier Senescu, ed., *James Shirley's "The Bird in a Cage": A Critical Edition* (New York and London: Garland, 1980).
52. According to Martin Butler, *Theatre and Crisis, 1632–1642* (Cambridge: Cambridge University Press, 1984), Prynne's reference to actresses "was only one out of nearly fifty exceptions raised against *Histriomastix*"; Archbishop Laud brought Prynne before the Star Chamber "for his scandalously extravagant and inflammatory language against virtually the entire social order" (pp. 84–85). Kim Walker stresses the gendered components of Prynne's denunciation in the context of *The Bird in a Cage* in "*New Prison*: Representing the Female Actor in Shirley's *The Bird in a Cage* (1633)," *ELR: English Literary Renaissance* 21:3 (1991): 385–400.

53. The image of a bird in a cage is also used by Erasmus in his courtship colloquy to refer to the bondage that exists in marriage.
54. Tomlinson, "She That Plays the King: Henrietta Maria and the Threat of the Actress in Caroline Culture," in *The Politics of Tragicomedy*, eds. McMullan and Hope, esp. p. 196.
55. The oral pleasures invoked seem to play on the bawdy connotations of the buttery as a site of female eroticism. According to Mendelson and Crawford, dairying was "a well-known courtship venue: a popular saying referred to 'creampot love', defined as what 'young fellows pretend to dairy-maids, to get cream and other good things of them'" (*Women in Early Modern England*, p. 111). Fiona McNeill also makes provocative observations about the buttery in "Gynocentric London Spaces: (Re)Locating Masterless Women in Early Stuart Drama."
56. By conflating rape with seduction here, I intentionally reproduce the ideology of the play.
57. Cavendish's vexed relationship to her literary precursors is discussed by Laura Rosenthal, *Playwrights and Plagiarists in Early Modern England: Gender, Authorship, Literary Property* (Ithaca, NY and London: Cornell University Press, 1996). Rosenthal also perceptively reads Cavendish's representations of homoeroticism (in several plays) as part of her strategy to reimagine property relations. I am grateful to Rosenthal for suggesting to me the pervasiveness of female homoeroticism in Cavendish's works.
58. Margaret Cavendish, Duchess of Newcastle, *The Convent of Pleasure*, in *Playes, Never Before Printed* (London: 1668), from which my citations are taken. A new edition is available, ed. Anne Shaver, *The Convent of Pleasure and Other Plays* (Baltimore and London: Johns Hopkins University Press, 1999); Shaver argues that Lord Cavendish authored the final two scenes and the epilogue (p. 238). For discussion of the extent to which Cavendish's plays were meant to be read rather than performed, see Shaver's Introduction, which judges the term "closet drama" inappropriate for Cavendish's plays, as well as Sophie Tomlinson, "'My Brain the Stage,'" and Marta Straznicky, "Reading the Stage: Margaret Cavendish and Commonwealth Closet Drama," *Criticism* 37:3 (1995): 355–90.
59. Misty Anderson, "Tactile Places: Materializing Desire in Margaret Cavendish and Jane Barker," *Textual Practice* 13:2 (1999): 329–52. It is interesting to note, however, that a seduction poem that William Cavendish wrote to Margaret Lucas in the mid-1640s, "Love's Muster," could have provided the blueprint for the convent of pleasure. It begins, "I'le Muster Up my senses with delight; / My taste, my touch, my smell, Hearing, and sight, / All att one tyme; height's pleasure shall obtayne, / With gentle stroakes Upon my Ravisht Brayne," and continues to enumerate the various sensual pleasures (pictures, food, perfumes, music) with which he will seduce her. It concludes by privileging touch as the preeminent sense: "Now all the Senses att one tyme wee'll measure, / And fill them till they all runn o'er with pleasur; / And danse the hay with Various sweet delight: / Touch moves to hearing, hearinge moves to sight, / Sight turnes to smellinge, smelling then doth haste / To be converted to her Neyghbor Taste; / And thus they chainge, and danse so quick a Strayne, / And foot it all Upon the moving brayne. / Or Else t'wer nothing. Nerves, they are the strings / That to the senses all the Pleasure brings.

When touch is satisfi'd, thus t'is related, / Then all the rest of senses are abated: / So all the rest wayts of her pleasure still; / Likes or dislikes all following her will." William Cavendish, *The Phanseys of William Cavendish Marquis of Newcastle Addressed to Margaret Lucas and Her Letters in Reply*, ed. Douglas Grant (London: Nonesuch, 1956), pp. 56–57 (no. 42).

60. Rosenthal provides an excellent critique of Cavendish's class politics, where "subject positions become restructured as pleasure seekers and pleasure providers, elite women who experience the multiple delights of the convent and laboring women who provide those conditions for pleasure" (*Playwrights and Plagiarists*, pp. 93–94). At the same time, one might profitably link Cavendish's commitment to aristocratic pleasures based on female embodiment and her monarchical absolutism to the erotic absolutism of Queen Elizabeth discussed in chapter 3. See Catherine Gallagher, "Embracing the Absolute: The Politics of the Female Subject in Seventeenth-Century England," *Genders* 1 (1988): 24–39.

61. I take issue with Donoghue's characterization, "the play is a lesbian romance, made barely acceptable at the last minute by a contrived ending which heterosexualises the plot," *Passions Between Women*, p. 232. Within the conventions Cavendish inherited, the conclusion would hardly seem contrived; rather, it is the putative *naturalness* of the ending that a historically attuned reading allows us to unpack.

62. The categories of sexual crime (under the purview of both the ecclesiastical and secular courts) make clear that what defines female criminality is the disruption of marital reproduction: fornication (intercourse before marriage), adultery, bastard-bearing, and whoredom are less a matter of erotic acts than actions that threaten patriarchal reproduction.

63. The relationship between signification, embodiment, and value has been explored theoretically by Butler in *Bodies that Matter*.

64. To this extent, the problem is akin to the cognitive dissonance explored by Bray, *Homosexuality in Renaissance England*.

65. Shannon, "Nature's Bias," p. 196, note 48.

66. *Ibid.*, p. 191. Although I agree that heterosexuality is "very incompletely naturalized in the Renaissance" (p. 194), we diverge in the overall weight we give to the "likeness topos" which she argues is fundamental to Renaissance concepts of nature and "at the center of positive ideas about union" (p. 186).

67. It is important to recognize the difference between actual "familiar letters" and a published collection. Whether copied from originals or the creation of the compiler's brain, model letters were directed toward those who fancied that one day they might need a polished epistolary style. Actual "familiar" letters, on the other hand, had multiple social functions, as Alan Bray argues in *The Friend*. Circulating among friends, kept, copied, and shared, they communicated information; forged and expressed affectionate bonds; and perhaps more importantly, within "familiar" networks of patronage, functioned as material tokens of potentially influential social connections.

68. Gervase Markham, *Hobsons Horse-load of Letters: Or, a President for Epistles* (London: 1617), fol. M1 and M1v. I am grateful to Bruce Smith for providing me with a typescript of selections from Markham's text as well as his estimation of them.

69. *Ibid.*, fols. M2 and M2v.
70. Reprinted in Crawford and Gowing, eds., *Women's Worlds in Seventeenth-Century England*, pp. 236–37.
71. *Ibid.*, p. 237.
72. *Ibid.*

5. THE PSYCHOMORPHOLOGY OF THE CLITORIS; OR, THE REEMERGENCE OF THE TRIBADE IN ENGLISH CULTURE

1. Sigmund Freud, "Female Sexuality (1931)," in *Sexuality and the Psychology of Love*, ed. Philip Reiff (New York: Macmillan, 1963), pp. 194–211, esp. p. 194.
2. See Anne Koedt, "The Myth of the Vaginal Orgasm," in *Radical Feminism*, ed. Anne Koedt, Ellen Levine, and Anita Rapone (New York: Quadrangle, 1973), pp. 198–207; and Thomas Laqueur, "Amor Veneris, Vel Dulcedo Appeletur," in *Fragments for a History of the Human Body*, Part 3, ed. Michael Feher (New York: Urzone, 1989), pp. 90–131.
3. Freud, "Femininity" (1932), in *New Introductory Lectures on Psychoanalysis*, ed. and trans. James Strachey (New York: Norton, 1965), pp. 99–119, esp. p. 104.
4. The radical potential within psychoanalysis – and in particular its utility to gay/*lesbian* politics – is adduced by Jeffrey Weeks, *Sexuality and its Discontents* (London: Routledge and Kegan Paul, 1985); Dollimore, *Sexual Dissidence: Augustine to Wilde, Freud to Foucault* (Oxford: Clarendon Press, 1991); and Arnold I. Davidson, "How to Do the History of Psychoanalysis: A Reading of Freud's *Three Essays on the Theory of Sexuality*," *Critical Inquiry* 13:2 (1987): 252–77.
5. Foucault, *The History of Sexuality*, vol. 1; Faderman, *Surpassing the Love of Men*; Jeffrey Weeks, *Coming Out: Homosexual Politics in Britain from the Nineteenth Century to the Present* (London: Quartet Books, 1977).
6. Peter Hulme, *Colonial Encounters: Europe and the Native Caribbean, 1492–1797* (London and New York: Methuen, 1986), p. 1.
7. Laqueur, *Making Sex*. Although I critique Laqueur in the pages that follow, none of my analysis would have been possible without his ground-breaking book.
8. Laqueur, "Amor Veneris," p. 119.
9. The existence of competing medical paradigms during the seventeenth century is argued by Katharine Park and Robert A. Nye, "Destiny is Anatomy," Review of *Making Sex: Body and Gender from the Greeks to Freud* by Thomas Laqueur, *New Republic* (February 18, 1991): 53–7; Daston and Park, "The Hermaphrodite and the Orders of Nature"; Park, "The Rediscovery of the Clitoris"; Joan Cadden, *Meanings of Sex Difference in the Middle Ages: Medicine, Science, and Culture* (Cambridge: Cambridge University Press, 1993); and Heather Dubrow, "Naval Battles: Interpreting Renaissance Gynecological Manuals," *American Notes and Queries: A Quarterly Journal of Short Articles, Notes, and Reviews* 5:2/3 (1992): 67–71. Laqueur's gender bias is analyzed in general terms by Paster in *The Body Embarrassed*, and the results of the wholesale adoption of his views in Renaissance literary criticism is critiqued by Adelman, "Making Defect Perfection."
10. The term "visibilizing" is Barbara Maria Stafford's, *Body Criticism: Imaging the Unseen in Enlightenment Art and Medicine* (Cambridge, MA: MIT Press, 1991), and I use it here to suggest the activity involved in rendering an object visible.
11. Laqueur, "Amor Veneris," p. 119.

12. *Ibid.*, p. 118.
13. Greenblatt, "Fiction and Friction," p. 66, emphases mine. By means of this anecdote, Greenblatt positions his analysis of Shakespeare's *Twelfth Night*, which he views as a partial retelling of Montaigne's story, in relation to non-theatrical discourses. Greenblatt's analysis of the play, which emphasizes the extent to which theatrical representations partake of anxieties, generically male, about the body's instability, undergirds his claim that within the Renaissance imagination, transformations of identity occurred unidirectionally: from imperfect to perfect, from female to male. Greenblatt draws heavily from Laqueur, *Making Sex*, who refers to this case on p. 139.
14. Greenblatt, "Fiction and Friction," p. 67.
15. For a helpful distinction between desires and acts, see Smith, *Homosexual Desire in Shakespeare's England*.
16. Crooke, *Microcosmographia*, p. 238.
17. Butler, *Gender Trouble*.
18. Dollimore, *Sexual Dissidence*.
19. Jacques Derrida, *Of Grammatology*, trans. Gayatri Chakravorty Spivak (Baltimore and London: Johns Hopkins University Press, 1974).
20. For an analysis of the dildo as a fetish in contemporary *lesbian* culture, see Heather Findlay, "Freud's 'Fetishism' and the Lesbian Dildo Debates," in Corey Creekmur and Alexander Doty, eds., *Out in Culture: Gay, Lesbian, and Queer Essays on Popular Culture* (Durham, NC: Duke University Press, 1995), pp. 328–42. She argues that in answer to the question of whether dildoes represent penises, the answer is "yes, but," an affirmation/negation that makes use of the logic of the fetish for *lesbian* pleasure. For additional analyses of the *lesbian* use of dildoes, see Colleen Lamos, "The Postmodern Lesbian Position: *On Our Backs*," and Cathy Griggers, "Lesbian Bodies in the Age of (Post)Mechanical Reproduction," both in Doan, ed., *The Lesbian Postmodern*, pp. 85–103 and 118–33.
21. Laqueur, *Making Sex*, p. 136; see also pp. 137 and 279.
22. I explore the relations between anatomy, travel narration, and cartography in constructing a normative body in "Gendering Mortality in Early Modern Anatomies," in *Feminist Readings of Early Modern Culture*, eds., Traub, Kaplan, and Callaghan, pp. 44–92, and "Mapping the Global Body," in *Early Modern Visual Culture*, eds., Erickson and Hulse, pp. 44–92. Anthony Pagden, *European Encounters with the New World: From Renaissance to Romanticism* (New Haven: Yale University Press, 1993), provides a provocative account of the way in which tropes of "discovery" govern early modern science and, by implication, link anatomy to travel narratives: "The discoverer carries out with him his lexicon of names, his repertoire of classifications, his knowledge of the invisible isolines and parallels which link him to home. He returns with samples, exhibits, slaves. This itinerary, which is always invariable, is, as Descartes may have been the first to recognize, the same 'journey' which every scientist must make," pp. 30–31. Patricia Parker links anatomies and travel narratives, provocatively reading Renaissance discourses of the body through the racialized discourse of colonialism in "Fantasies of 'Race' and 'Gender': Africa, *Othello*, and Bringing to Light," in *Women, "Race" & Writing in the Early Modern Period*, eds. Margo Hendricks and Patricia Parker (London: Routledge, 1994), pp. 84–100.

23. The generic instability of both anatomy and travel writing is worth underscoring. What Mary Campbell, *The Witness and the Other World: Exotic European Travel Writing, 400–1600* (Ithaca, NY: Cornell University Press, 1988), says of early travel literature is equally true of early anatomy: "Knowledge was scarce, reverenced, and largely inseparable from the particular texts that transmitted it. At the same time, texts themselves were fluid: plagiarized, misquoted, mistranslated, interpolated upon, bowdlerized, epitomized, transformed, and transformable at every stage of their complex dissemination" (p. 140).
24. In this respect, Greenblatt's question, "What is the origin of boundaries that enable us to speak of 'within' and 'without'?" is crucial. See his meditation on the early modern construction of such boundaries, *Marvelous Possessions: The Wonder of the New World* (Chicago: University of Chicago Press, 1991), p. 121. Margaret Hodgen, *Early Anthropology in the Sixteenth and Seventeenth Centuries* (Philadelphia: University of Pennsylvania Press, 1964), describes cosmographers and compilers of travel narrators thus: "they were all in some degree geographers, absorbed in the minutiae of the distribution of man and his cultures on every continent and island of the world. All were conners of maps, disposed to think of the array of strange rituals, creeds, and theologies in spatial terms; as associated with certain already located peoples; as distributed geographically" (p. 218).
25. Denise Albanese, *New Science, New World* (Durham, NC: Duke University Press, 1996).
26. As Louis Montrose has noted, the identification of territory with the female virginal body provided explorers of the New World powerful justifications for their right to conquer and subject native inhabitants, while simultaneously providing an image of one's own nation as inviolable; see "The Work of Gender in the Discourse of Discovery," *Representations* 33 (1991): 1–41. Likewise, in *Sodometries*, Goldberg shows how the discourse of sodomy could be manipulated to rationalize European ascriptions of bestiality onto South American tribes, while occluding the very desires that constitute the colonial imaginary.
27. Hall, *Things of Darkness*.
28. The Western fascination with the seraglio is explained by Mohja Kahf, in *Western Representations of the Muslim Woman: From Termagant to Odalisque* (Austin: University of Texas Press, 1999), as a historically specific phenomenon linked to political, socio-economic, and cultural developments in the seventeenth century such as discourses of monarchical absolutism and the emergence of a division between public and private spheres.
29. Ogier Ghiselin de Busbecq, *The Life and Letters of Ogier Ghiselin de Busbecq*, eds. Charles Thorton Foster and F. H. Blackburne Daniell (London: Kegan Paul, 1881), pp. 228–29. I am grateful to Doug Bruster for alerting me to the existence of this passage. The first of de Busbecq's "Turkish Letters," written *c*. 1554, was published in Latin in 1581; the first edition of all four letters was printed in 1589. There were eleven further Latin editions in the seventeenth century, along with French, German, Bohemian, Flemish, and Spanish editions. The first "Englished" edition was printed in 1694. The quotation I cite is from the 1881 edition, and has been checked against the 1664 edition for accuracy.
30. Robert Withers, *The Grand Signiors Serraglio*, in *Purchase His Pilgrimes*, ed. Samuel Purchase, 2 vols. (London: 1625), vol. II, pp. 1580–1613; citation

pp. 1586–87. Purchase continued the work of the Elizabethan compiler Richard Hakluyt, collecting anecdotes, diaries, log-books, letters, maps, and histories, as well as publishing many narratives that Hakluyt had collected but was not able to publish before his death in 1616. Together, the work published by Hakluyt and Purchase represents the greatest compendium of travel narratives from the sixteenth and early seventeenth centuries in English. According to Godfrey Goodwin in his edition, *The Sultan's Seraglio: An Intimate Portrait of the Life at the Ottoman Court* (London: Saqi Books, 1996), Withers's text is a translation of a confidential document, "*Descrizione del Serraglio del Gransignore*," by the Italian ambassador to the Sultan, Ottaviano Bon. Its inclusion in Purchase is its first appearance in English. When it was published again in English in 1650 under the title *A Description of the Grand Signior's Seraglio, or Turkish Emperours Court*, it was again falsely attributed to Withers.

31. Withers, *Grand Signiors Serraglio*, p. 1590.
32. Jean-Baptiste Tavernier, *Nouvelle relation de l'intérieur du serrail du Grand Seigneur* (Paris: 1675), trans. as *A New Relation of the Present Grand Seignor's Seraglio*, in *THE SIX VOYAGES OF JOHN BAPTISTA TAVERNIER, BARON of AUBONNE; THROUGH TURKY, INTO PERSIA AND THE EAST-INDIES, For the space of Forty Years* (London: 1678), p. 88.
33. My interpretation of the sequence of Romans 1: 26–27 is based on Brooten, *Love Between Women*, p. 213.
34. According to Nabil Matar, *Turks, Moors, and Englishmen In the Age of Discovery* (New York: Columbia University Press, 1999), Edward Grimeston's *The History of the Imperiall Estate of the Grand Seigneurs Seraglio* (1635) suggests that women seek to avenge themselves on their sodomitical husbands by engaging in homoerotic contact (p. 123).
35. Nicholas de Nicholay, *The Navigations, Peregrinations, and Voyages, Made into Turkie* (Paris: 1567), trans. T. Washington (London: 1585), p. 60. De Nicholay's work was first brought to my attention by Mario DiGangi.
36. De Busbecq, *Life and Letters*, p. 231.
37. As de Busbecq narrates it, the Aga of the Janissaries "tells her that an old woman like her ought to know better than to attempt so mad a freak, and asks, if she is not ashamed of herself? She replies, 'Tush! you know not the might of love, and God grant that you may never experience its power.' At this the Aga could not restrain his laughter; and ordered her to be carried off at once, and drowned in the sea. Thus the strange passion of this old woman brought her to a bad end" (*ibid.*, p. 232).
38. Thomas Glover, *The Muftie, Cadileschiers, Divans: Manners and attire of the Turkes. The Sultan described, and his Customes and Court*, in Purchase, ed., *Purchase His Pilgrims*, vol. II, pp. 1293–306; citation p. 1299. Glover's text was published in other Purchase editions under the following title: *The Journey of Edward Barton Esquire, her Maiesties Ambassadour with the Grand Signior, otherwise called the Great Turke, in Constantinople, Sultan Mahumet Chan. Written by Sir Thomas Glover then Secretarie to the Ambassadour, and since employed in that Honourable Function by his Maiestie, to Sultan Achmet.*
39. Leo Africanus, *The History and Description of Africa and of the Notable Things therein Contained*, trans. John Pory (London: 1600), ed. Robert Brown, 2 vols. (London: Haklyut Society, 1896), vol. II, pp. 458–59. Africanus was a Spanish Moor born in Granada, educated in Fez, who lived much of his life in Italy

(he converted to Catholicism, then reconverted to Islam). He wrote his *History* in Arabic and translated it into Italian in 1526. It was collected by G. B. Ramusio for his collection *Navigationi e viaggi* (*Voyages and Travels*) (Venice: 1550) and thereafter translated into French and English. I am grateful to Kim Hall for alerting me to the existence of this passage and to her analysis of it in *Things of Darkness*. In Africanus's story, the logical trajectory that transforms "objective" description into a cautionary tale is the shift in focus from the wicked witch to the silly husband. The *OED* defines "silly" in this time period as (1a) deserving of pity, compassion, or sympathy; (1b) helpless, defenseless; (2) weak, feeble, frail, etc. (3) unlearned, unsophisticated, ignorant. The means by which the move is made from witch to husband is through the intermediary figure of the wife: the woman who, first assumed to be innocent and naive, is soon so "allured with the delight" of an all-female erotic practice that she is sending her husband out to bring her consort home. If the diviner of Fez is initially represented as a woman who commits "unlawful Venerie" with others of her own kind, Africanus's primary interest seems to be less the unnaturalness or unlawfulness of her desires than the potential corrupting influence of her "burning lust" which effects an inversion of male triangular traffic in women. According to Everett K. Rowson in "The Categorization of Gender and Sexual Irregularity in Medieval Arabic Vice Lists," in Epstein and Straub, eds., *Body Guards*, pp. 50–79, in Arabic, "sahq" is a "verbal noun literally meaning 'pounding, rubbing, shaving,'" and is the usual term to connote female–female sexual activity as well as female masturbation (p. 63).

40. Leslie P. Pierce, *The Imperial Harem: Women and Sovereignty in the Ottoman Empire* (Oxford and New York: Oxford University Press, 1993), p. vii.
41. Obscurity is not the normative rhetoric of travel narratives, as descriptions of clothing, planting methods, military operations, etc. are far more detailed. The vagueness here may be due partly to the lack of "eye-witness" authority, as men and foreigners would not have been allowed access to the harem or the women's bath. But I would suggest that such vagueness is also constitutive of the general discourse of sexuality in this period – contemporary assertions of sodomy are similarly ambiguous. It is precisely this vagueness that seventeenth-century anatomies (and legal discourse) will attempt to dispel.
42. Kathryn Babayan, "The *Aqâ'îd al-Nisâ'*: A Glimpse at Ṣafavid Women in Local Iṣfahani Culture," in *Women in the Medieval Islamic World: Power, Patronage, Piety*, ed. Gavin R. G. Hambly (New York: St. Martin's Press, 1998), pp. 349–81; citation p. 369. Babayan's main textual source is the Iranian cleric, Aqâ Jamâl Khwansârî (d. 1710), whose *Aqâ'îd al-Nisâ'* (*Beliefs of Women*) is a mocking satire on contemporary beliefs and rituals, written on the eve of a crackdown on social permissiveness; she also refers to mention of tribades in the *Voyages* of Jean Chardin.
43. Such a study would need to distinguish between the various empires and states of North Africa and the Middle East. And whereas the figural intertwining of the erotic and the exotic within an evolving racialized discourse of European colonialism is also worthy of its own analysis, such a project would best be pursued by situating erotic tropes within the complex political relations among the various state and mercantile powers, East and West, North and South.
44. Sharp, *The Midwives Book*, p. 45.
45. *Ibid.*

46. *Ibid.*, pp. 45–47.
47. Whether Sharp is referring to the East or West Indies (or both) is unclear. Her reference to "Negro Women" suggests the slave economy that was underway in the West Indies; but other authors tend to focus on Africa and Turkey as sites of tribadism. In terms of cultural displacement of disease, syphilis is a case in point; see my chapter on English discourses of syphilis in *Desire & Anxiety*.
48. Goldberg, "Introduction," *Queering the Renaissance*, p. 13.
49. Sharp, *The Midwives Book*, p. 53.
50. Eve Keller, "Mrs. Jane Sharp: Midwifery and the Critique of Medical Knowledge in Seventeenth-Century England," *Women's Writing: The Elizabethan to Victorian Period* 2:2 (1995): 101–11. I am grateful to Eve Keller for sharing her work prior to publication.
51. Crooke, *Microcosmographia*, p. 238. In 1610, Ferrand, *A Treatise on Lovesickness*, similarly asserted that the clitoris could be enlarged through passion and that it is "known to many other women who unhappily abuse this part called *fricatrices* by the Latins, *tribades* by the Greeks and *ribaudes* by the French – among whom Sudas and Muret place the learned Sappho" (pp. 230–31).
52. This translation of Falloppia's Paris edition of 1562 is that of Harriette Andreadis, "Sappho in Early Modern England," p. 114. The first edition of *Observationes anatomicae* was published in Venice in 1561.
53. André Du Laurens (Andreas Laurentius), *Historia anatomica humani corporis et singularum eius partium multis* (Paris: 1595); translated by Andreadis, "Sappho in Early Modern England," pp. 114–15.
54. Cited by Park, "The Rediscovery of the Clitoris," p. 175.
55. *Ibid.*, p. 176.
56. Campbell, *The Witness and the Other World*, p. 8.
57. *Ibid.*, p. 71.
58. *Ibid.*, p. 249.
59. As noted in chapter 2, references to the tribade (drawn from Leo Africanus) added to the second edition of Paré's *Des Monstres et Prodiges* (1575) were excised from the third edition (1579) due to harassment by the Faculty of Medicine. Paré was forced to replace his discussion of Leo Africanus with a much briefer citation about a recent sodomy conviction of two women set down by the jurist Jean Papon; eventually he removed the entire passage about female genitalia (Céard, *Des Monstres et Prodiges*, pp. 162–63). Park notes that Paré "had reassured his critics in the Faculty of Medicine that the deformity that allowed a woman to have sex with another woman was extremely rare – so much so, he wrote, 'that for every woman that has it, there are ten thousand who don't.' His successors had no such consolation" ("The Rediscovery of the Clitoris," p. 178). Paré's original discussion of genital enlargement concerns the labia, not the clitoris: "The Greeks call them nimphes, which hang and, in some women, fall outside the neck of the womb; and they lengthen and shorten like the comb of a turkey cock, principally when they desire coitus, and, when their husbands want to approach them, they grow erect like the male rod, so much that they can take pleasure from them, with other women." (Translation of Céard's edition provided by Adriane Stewart.)
60. Although medieval accounts of marvels regularly feature various monsters and amazons, none list tribades in their classifications. See John Block Friedman,

The Monstrous Races in Medieval Art and Thought (Cambridge, MA and London: Harvard University Press, 1981); and Lorraine Daston and Katharine Park, *Wonders and the Order of Nature, 1150–1750* (New York: Zone Books, 1998).

61. Susan Stewart, *On Longing: Narratives of the Miniature, the Gigantic, the Souvenir, the Collection* (Durham, NC and London: Duke University Press, 1993), p. xii.
62. *Ibid.*, p. xiii.
63. On the anatomical construction of bodily norms, see Nancy G. Sirasi, "Vesalius and Human Diversity in *De Humani Corporis Fabrica*," *Journal of the Warburg and Courtauld Institutes* 57 (1994): 60–88.
64. Bartholin, *Bartholinus Anatomy*, p. 76. In French this was rendered as *le mespris des hommes*. See Park, "The Rediscovery of the Clitoris," p. 186.
65. Bartholin, *Bartholinus Anatomy*, p. 77. According to Andreadis, "[t]he Latin of Caspar Bartholin clearly describes contemporary understanding of female same-sex sexual activity, but it does not include the anecdotal embellishments and example of Sappho added by the younger Bartholin" ("Sappho in Early Modern England," p. 116).
66. In *European Encounters*, Pagden argues that the conventional impulse of Western travel narration is to make the incommensurate seem commensurable.
67. Jean Riolan, *Anthropographia* (1618); cited by Park, "The Rediscovery of the Clitoris," pp. 178–79.
68. Culpeper, *The Compleat Midwife's Practice Enlarged* (London: 1656), p. 26.
69. In support of her argument that it is not until after the Restoration that the idea of female–female desire becomes problematic in England, Elizabeth Wahl maintains that "the tone of anxiety that pervades French discussions of clitoral hypertrophy in the seventeenth century is largely absent from English treatments of the subject during this period" (*Invisible Relations*, p. 30) – a contention that seems to me to be belied by the texts of Crooke and Bartholin.
70. Nicholas Venette, *Conjugal Love, or The Pleasures of the Marriage Bed* (New York: Garland, 1984), p. 19. Venette's book, also known as *The Art of Conjugal Love* and *Portrait of Love, Considered in the State of Marriage*, went through eight printings before his death in 1698; the 1750 English edition I quote is designated as the twentieth edition. For a comparison of Venette to the medical writers who preceded him, see Evelyn Berriot-Salvadore, "The Discourse of Medicine and Science," in *A History of Women in the West*, eds. Zemon Davis and Farge, esp. p. 386. The other popular (and frequently republished) text in this genre, *Aristotles Master-Piece* (1684), states merely that the clitoris "is the Seat of venerial Pleasure, being like a Yard in Situation, Substance, Composition, and Erection, growing sometimes out of the Body two Inches, but that rarely happens, unless thro' extream lust or extraordinary accident" (p. 105).
71. Thomas Gibson, *The Anatomy of Humane Bodies Epitomized* (London: 1682) is compiled from Alexander Read's work; citation p. 174.
72. Daniel Tauvry, *A New Rational Anatomy, Containing an Explication of the Uses of the Structure of the Body of Man and some other Animals, According to the Rules of Mechanicks* (London: 1701), p. 127. This English translation of the third Paris edition of *Nouvelle anatomie raisonnée* is part of a post-Harvey mechanistic

breed of scientific inquiry, the anatomical premises of which are summed up in the Author's Preface: "I consider Man's Body, as being a Statick, Hydraulick, and Pneumatick Machine; of which the Bones are the Levers and Supporters, the Muscles the Strings, the Lungs the Pumps: and the Vessels the Pipes, in which the Liquors have a perpetual Circulation" (n.p.).

73. My use of the term "abjection" loosely derives from (and implicitly revises) Julia Kristeva's psychoanalytic formulation of abjection as a primal power of loathing in *Powers of Horror: An Essay on Abjection*, trans. Leon S. Roudiez (New York: Columbia University Press, 1982). In Kristeva's schema of infant development, the mother must be abjected before the intervention of the symbolic can occur; this primal experience of disunity in the symbolic/paternal function is also played out on the cultural front. In this sense, abjection is the process of expelling that which is within both the desiring subject and the social order. My revision of the term is in the spirit of Judith Butler, who in *Bodies That Matter* defines abjection thus:

> Abjection (in Latin, *ab-jicere*) literally means to cast off, away, or out and, hence, presupposes and produces a domain of agency from which it is differentiated... [T]he notion of *abjection* designates a degraded or cast out status within the terms of sociality. Indeed, what is foreclosed or repudiated *within* psychoanalytic terms is precisely what may not reenter the field of the social without threatening psychosis, that is, the dissolution of the subject itself... [C]ertain abject zones within sociality also deliver this threat, constituting zones of uninhabitability which a subject fantasizes as threatening its own integrity with the prospect of a psychotic dissolution. (p. 243, note 2)

74. Park, "Rediscovery of the Clitoris," p. 185. In addition to reading French medical literature, Park refers to the passage from the *Apologie pour Hérodote* by French humanist Henri Estienne, quoted in chapter 1. I would argue, however, that Estienne's desire to separate penetration with a dildo from tribadism has more to do with his larger polemic about the moral degeneration of the modern age than with popular conceptions of tribadism. It may also indicate a national difference, as the French seem far more preoccupied than the English with women's use of dildoes.
75. Friar Ludovico Maria Sinistrari, "Sodomia," part of his *De Delictis et Poenis* (1700), translated as *Peccatum Mutum (The Secret Sin)*, ed. Montague Summers (Paris: 1958), item 7, p. 34. Sinistrari, a Franciscan theologian (1622–1701), also published *Demoniality*, trans. Montague Summers (London: Fortune Press, 1927).
76. Sinistrari, *Peccatum Mutum*, "Contents of Matters," number 22, p. 21.
77. *Ibid.*, item 11, p. 37.
78. *Ibid.*, item 13, pp. 38–39.
79. *Ibid.*, item 16, p. 42.
80. *Ibid.*, item 24, pp. 50–51.
81. *Ibid.*, "Contents of Matters," number 24, p. 21.
82. Theresa Braunschneider, "The Macroclitoride, the Tribade, and the Woman: Configuring Gender and Sexuality in English Anatomical Discourse," *Textual Practice* 13:3 (1999): 509–32.
83. James Parsons, *A Mechanical and Critical Enquiry into the Nature of Hermaphrodites* (London: J. Walthoe: 1741).
84. Braunschneider, "The Macroclitoride, the Tribade, and the Woman," p. 518.

85. See James T. Henke, *Renaissance Dramatic Bawdy (Exclusive of Shakespeare): An Annotated Glossary and Critical Essays* (Salzburg: University of Salzburg, 1974). According to Brooten, the "Greek term for 'intercourse,' *chresis*, literally means 'use' ... A man 'uses' or 'makes use of' a woman or a boy" (*Love Between Women*, p. 245), a meaning that is shown by Carol Kazmierczak Manzione to be true in early modern England in "Sex in Tudor London: Abusing Their Bodies with Each Other," in Murray and Eisenbichler, eds., *Desire and Discipline*, pp. 87–100.
86. Wahl initially overstates the extent to which medical writers proposed that masturbation caused clitoral hypertrophy (*Invisible Relations*, pp. 27 and 35), and then suggests that the causal link remained "an open question well into the eighteenth century" (p. 36).
87. Sinistrari, *Peccatum Mutum*, items 17 and 18, pp. 43 and 45.
88. In his first edition of *Des Monstres et Prodiges*, Paré describes labial excision as a remedy to women's abuse with other women: "Thus they make them very shameful and deformed being seen naked, and with such women one must tie and cut that which is superfluous, because they can misuse them, giving that the surgeon is careful not to cut too deeply for fear of a great flow of blood, or of cutting the neck of the bladder, for then afterward they will not be able to pass urine, but it would trickle out drop by drop." (Translated of Céard's edition by Adriane Stewart.) After this passage he refers to the "memorable story drawn from the *History of Africa*." Likewise, Crooke (who did recognize a difference between the clitoris and labia) discusses labial (but not clitoral) amputation:

> Sometimes, they grow to so great a length on one side, more rarely on both; and not so ordinarily in maidens as in women ... what through the affluence of humours, what through attrectation, that for the trouble and shame (being in many Countryes a notable argument of petulancie & immodesty) they neede the Chirurgions helpe to cut them off (although they bleed much and are hardly cicatrised) especially among the Egyptians, amongest whom this accident (as Galen saith) is very familiar. Wherefore in Maidens before they grow too long they cut them off, and before they marry.

This passage is printed with the marginal gloss: "The Egyptian women lascivious" (*Microcosmographia*, p. 237).
89. The entire passage from *The Fourth Book of Practical Physick* (London: 1662) reads:

> The *Aloe* or wings in the privities of a woman, are of soft spongy flesh, like a Cocks-comb in shape and colour; the part at the top is hard and nervous, and swells like a Yard in Venery, with much Spirit. This part sometimes is as big as a mans Yard, and such women were thought to be turned into men.
>
> It is from too much nourishment of the part, from the looseness of it by often handling.
>
> It is not safe to cut it off presently: but first use driers and discussers, with things that a little astringe; then gentle Causticks without causing pain, as burnt Allum, Ægyptiacum.
>
> Take *Ægyptiacum, Oyl of Mastich, Roses, Wax*, each half an ounce. If these will not do, then cut it off, or tie it with a Ligature of Silk or Horse-hair, till it mortifie.
>
> *Ætitus* teacheth the way of amputation, he cals it the *Nympha* or *Clitoris*, between both the wings: but take heed you cause not pain or inflammation. After cutting, wash with Wine, with Myrtles, Bays, Roses, Pomegranate flowers boyled in it, and Cypress-nuts, and lay on an astringent Pouder.

> Some excrescenses grow like a tail, and fill the privities: they differ from a Clitoris: for the desire of Venery is increased in that, and the rubbing of the cloaths upon it, cause lust, but in an Excrescence of flesh, they cannot for pain endure copulation, but you may cut off this better than a Clitoris, because it is all superfluous. (pp. 3–4)

According to the *OED*, a "discusser" is a medicine that disperses humors.

90. E. B., *The Chyrurgeons Store-house* (London: 1674), a translation of Johannes Scultetus, *Wundarztneyishes Zeughaufs* (Frankfurt: 1655 and 1666). The illustration of Figure 1 of Table XLI (p. 194) "teacheth how *Hierom. Fabritius ab Aquapendente*, with an instrument made for a Polypus, cuts off the unprofitable increasing of a Clitoris, which is a common disease amongst the Ægyptians and Arabians. A shews the Clitoris laied hold of with the pincers: B shews the body of the Clitoris cut off, and placed beyond the pincers" (p. 195).

91. In *Making Sex*, Laqueur argues that clitoridectomy was neither advocated nor practiced in England until the eighteenth century. This view is contradicted at the level of advice, if not at the level of surgical practice, by Paré, Bartholin, and Culpeper. The historical and ideological relationship between ritual circumcision and Western surgical practices is confused. Western genital amputation is not identical to culturally sanctioned ritual circumcision. But many Western authors use ritual practices to authorize their descriptions of tribades and the need for surgery, and such surgery would attempt to achieve some of the same ends: forcibly imposing, and thereby affirming, cultural sameness, constancy, and homogeneity.

92. Historicizing the production of anatomical essentialism provides a means of challenging modern regimes of identity formation which demand that people "choose" one of only two erotic "orientations" or seek to find the origin of such "choices" in biology. Indeed, the historical development of anatomical essentialism provides a perspective from which to view the current debate over genetic origins of homosexuality. That such debates do have a history seems to me to help dispel utopian visions of redemption through biology (whether figured through a belief that an appeal to genetics will herald an end to homophobia or an end to homosexuals). Rather than authorizing modern quests for a "gay gene," early modern anatomies provide a cautionary tale: insofar as the "cure" of clitoral hypertrophy was genital mutilation, and the punishment for tribadism (at least in some countries) was burning at the stake, the discourse of anatomy sounds from the distance of centuries a warning about the liberatory promises of bio-genetics.

93. See Park, "The Rediscovery of the Clitoris"; Brooten, *Love Between Women*; and Cadden, *Meanings of Sex Difference in the Middle Ages*.

94. See Brooten, *Love Between Women*.

95. Hallett, "Female Homoeroticism and the Denial of Roman Reality in Latin Literature." According to Andreadis, "Sappho in Early Modern England," as early as the eleventh century, Sappho's relations with her friends were represented as transgressive, a view elaborated in commentary in the Venetian editions of the *Heroïdes*. The first English edition of the *Heroïdes* was published in 1567 by George Turberville, with a Latin edition following in 1583. Andreadis's work thus provides a corrective to that of Joan DeJean, who argues in *Fictions of Sappho, 1546–1937* (Chicago: University of Chicago Press, 1989) that Sappho was not associated with lesbianism in England prior to the eighteenth century; rather,

Andreadis shows how varied were the discourses that surrounded Sappho and how significant were allusions to her erotic investments in women.
96. My characterization of the ancient logic of activity and passivity is drawn from the work of Brooten, *Love Between Women*, and Halperin, *One Hundred Years of Homosexuality*, both of whom stress the importance of this binary system for organizing the meanings of sexual activity.
97. I thank David Halperin for helping me to see that the tribade is not so much invented or discovered in this period as refashioned according to new cultural exigencies.
98. Andreadis, "Sappho in Early Modern England," pp. 117–19.
99. *Ibid.*, p. 120.
100. Ornella Moscucci, "Clitoridectomy, Circumcision, and the Politics of Sexual Pleasure in Mid-Victorian Britain," in *Sexualities in Victorian Britain*, eds. Andrew H. Miller and James Eli Adams (Bloomington and Indianapolis: Indiana University Press, 1996), pp. 60–78; citation p. 69.
101. *Ibid.*, p. 70.
102. Felicity A. Nussbaum, *Torrid Zones: Maternity, Sexuality, and Empire in Eighteenth-Century English Narratives* (Baltimore and London: Johns Hopkins University Press, 1995), p. 7. See also Bellie Melman, *Women's Orients: English Women and the Middle East, 1718–1918* (Ann Arbor: University of Michigan Press, 1992).
103. The stories and the "Terminal Essay" appended to *The Book of The Thousand Nights and a Night* (1885–88) (trans. Richard F. Burton [New York: Heritage Press, 1934]) provided an influential source of information about tribadism in the Middle East. The endnote to the story of the 329th Night, which mentions a handmaid kissing a lady's cheek, for instance, states:

> Wealthy harims, I have said, are hot-beds of sapphism and tribadism. Every woman past her first youth has a girl whom she calls her "Myrtle" (in Damascus). At Agbome, capital of Dahome, I found that a troop of women was kept for the use of the "Amazons" (*Mission to Gelele*, ii.. 73). Amongst the wild Arabs, who ignore Socratic and Sapphic perversions, the lover is always more jealous of his beloved's girl-friends than of men rivals. In England we content ourselves with saying that women corrupt women more than men do. (p. 1528)

The "Terminal Essay" theorizes the existence of an equatorial "Sotatic" zone where illicit sexuality runs rampant. The notes define "Mascula" as deriving "from the priapiscus, the overdevelopment of clitoris (the veretrum mulibre, in Arabic Abu Tartúr, habens cristam), which enabled her to play the man" and define "Saḥákah" as "Lesbianise" and "tribassare": "the former applied to the love of woman for woman and the latter to its mécanique: this is either natural, as friction of the labia and insertion of the clitoris when unusually developed, or artificial by means of the fascinum, the artificial penis (the Persian 'Mayájang'); the patte de chat, the banana-fruit and a multitude of other succedanea" (pp. 3855–56). On the complexities involved in the sexological development of a model of inversion, see Chauncey, "From Sexual Inversion to Homosexuality: Medicine and the Changing Conceptualization of Female Deviance," *Salmagundi* 58–9 (1982–83): 114–46; and on the colonial imaginary of sexology, see Lynda Hart, *Fatal Women: Lesbian Sexuality and the Mark of Aggression* (Princeton: Princeton University Press, 1994).
104. See the trial transcripts of 1810, *Miss Marianne Woods and Miss Jane Pirie against Dame Helen Cumming Gordon* (New York: Arno, 1975), "Speeches of the Judges,"

p. 8. See also Lillian Faderman's redaction of the trial in *Scotch Verdict: Miss Pirie and Miss Woods v. Dame Cumming Gordon* (New York: William Morrow, 1983), as well as Lisa L. Moore's critique of Faderman's treatment in *Dangerous Intimacies*, pp. 78–83.
105. For sophisticated readings of this problem, see Jonathan Goldberg's Introduction and Margaret Hunt's Afterword to Goldberg, ed., *Queering the Renaissance*. As Hunt points out, the definition of the "subject" has hardly been available to women on the same terms that it has been to men.
106. I would argue that the psychomorphology of the tribade has more in common with current discourses of transgender and intersexuality than with butch affect and style. For the relationship between transgender and butch affect, see Halberstam, *Female Masculinities*. On intersexuality, see Anne Fausto-Sterling, *Myths of Gender: Biological Theories about Women and Men* (New York: Basic Books, 1985); and Alice Domurat Dreger, *Hermaphrodites and the Medical Invention of Sex* (Cambridge, MA and London: Harvard University Press, 1998), and ed., *Intersex in the Age of Ethics* (Hagerstown, MD: University Publishing Group, 1999). See also Sandy Stone, "The Empire Strikes Back: A Posttranssexual Manifesto," in Epstein and Straub, eds., *Bodyguards*, pp. 280–304; and Julia Epstein, "Either/Or – Neither/Both: Sexual Ambiguity and the Ideology of Gender," *Genders* 7 (1990): 99–142.
107. Castle, *The Apparitional Lesbian*, p. 8.
108. *Ibid.*, p. 62.
109. *Ibid.*, pp. 9 and 15. In her presumption that identities and languages transparently map on to one another, Castle associates an unproblematic identity with clarity of style and mass comprehension. When she asserts, for instance, that the lesbian "is not a nonsense," she endorses the coercions of clarity, implying that a theory that submits identity categories to scrutiny is manifestly absurd, and this absurdity is manifest in its syntax and prose style.
110. The claims to such knowledge have been problematized searchingly by Sedgwick in *Epistemology of the Closet* (see especially Axiom 5), and Butler in "Imitation and Gender Insubordination" in Fuss, ed., *Inside/Out*, and in *Bodies that Matter*.
111. Andreadis, "Sappho in Early Modern England," p. 105.
112. *Ibid.*, p. 120.
113. *Ibid.*, pp. 106 and 117.
114. *Ibid.*, p. 117.
115. Yopie Prins, *Victorian Sappho* (Princeton: Princeton University Press, 1999), p. 4.
116. *Ibid.*, p 7.
117. *Ibid.*, p. 17.
118. *Ibid.*, p. 20.
119. "Sappho survives as exemplary lyric figure precisely because of that legacy of fragmentation; the more the fragments are dispersed, the more we recollect Sappho as their point of origin" (*ibid.*, p. 8). In her ambivalent review of *Victorian Sappho* in *The London Review of Books* (30 September, 1999): 18–21, Terry Castle uses identity politics to cast Prins's deconstruction of the Sapphic signature as anti-*lesbian*. Castle assumes that because Prins resists a telos of literary history that culminates in Sappho-as-*lesbian*, she necessarily delegitimates *lesbianism*. To my mind, Prins's attempt to unpack the historicity of identifications which attempt to stabilize identity "in the name of Sappho" is congruent with *lesbian* theorizing.

120. Barbara Creed, "Lesbian Bodies: Tribades, Tomboys and Tarts," in *Sexy Bodies: The Strange Carnalities of Feminism*, eds. Elizabeth Grosz and Elspeth Probyn (London and New York: Routledge, 1995), pp. 86–103; citation pp. 93–94.
121. The need to reassert the pleasures of the vagina and penetration is advocated by Jane Gallop in *Thinking Through the Body* (New York: Columbia University Press, 1988).
122. Paula Bennett, "Critical Clitoridectomy: Female Sexual Imagery and Feminist Psychoanalytic Theory," *Signs: Journal of Women in Culture and Society* 18 (1993): 235–59; citation pp. 256–57.
123. Cotgrave, *A Dictionary of the French and English Tongues* (1611).
124. Andrea Dworkin, *Intercourse* (New York: Macmillan, 1987); Catharine MacKinnon, *Feminism Unmodified: Discourses on Life and Law* (Cambridge and London: Harvard University Press, 1987).
125. Rich, "Compulsory Heterosexuality and Lesbian Existence"; Audre Lorde, "Uses of the Erotic: The Erotic as Power," in *Sister Outsider* (New York: Crossing Press, 1984), pp. 53–59.
126. Vanita, *Sappho and the Virgin Mary: Same-Sex Love and the English Literary Imagination* (New York: Columbia University Press, 1996).
127. Irigaray, *This Sex Which Is Not One*, p. 28. See also *Speculum of the Other Woman*, trans. Gillian G. Gill (Ithaca, NY: Cornell University Press, 1985).
128. Irigaray, *This Sex Which Is Not One*, p. 90.
129. Critiques of Irigaray are legion, for the essentialism with which she was associated comprised a crucible for feminist theory in the 1980s. For two early influential critiques of Irigaray's essentialism, see Ann Rosalind Jones, "Writing the Body: Toward an Understanding of *l'Écriture féminine*," in *The New Feminist Criticism: Essays on Women, Literature, and Theory*, ed. Elaine Showalter (New York: Pantheon, 1985), pp. 361–77; and Toril Moi, *Sexual/Textual Politics: Feminist Literary Theory* (London and New York: Methuen, 1985).
130. Diana Fuss, *Essentially Speaking: Feminism, Nature, and Difference* (London: Routledge, 1989). Fuss's reassessment of essentialism as a strategy that one risks in order to advance certain political claims, as well as her analysis of the mutually implicated dynamic between essentialism and anti-essentialism, are helpful in reading Irigaray. Jane Gallop, "Lip Service," in *Thinking Through the Body*, pp. 92–99, is particularly good at demonstrating how Irigaray's *poiesis* of female sexuality "is always figurative, can never be simply taken as the thing itself" (p. 98). For defenses of Irigaray, see Margaret Whitford, *Luce Irigaray: Philosophy in the Feminine* (New York: Routledge, 1991); and Carolyn Burke, Naomi Schor, and Margaret Whitford, eds., *Engaging With Irigaray: Feminist Philosophy and Modern European Thought* (New York: Columbia University Press, 1994), particularly Carolyn Burke, "Irigaray Through the Looking Glass" (pp. 37–56), and Naomi Schor, "This Essentialism Which Is Not One: Coming to Grips with Irigaray" (pp. 57–78).
131. Gallop, *Thinking Through the Body*, p. 96, emphasis mine.
132. Irigaray, *This Sex Which Is Not One*, p. 24.
133. *Ibid.*, p. 218.
134. This is the basis of an important critique by Annamarie Jagose, "Irigaray and the Lesbian Body: Remedy and Poison," *Genders* 13 (1992): 30–42, who argues that Irigaray problematically relies "on a concept of *exteriority . . . as the very condition*

of female homosexuality" (p. 33). According to Jagose, Irigaray's construction of femininity is even more insidious than this, for its ultimate goal is not the elaboration of a *lesbian* politics, but a "renegotiation of an emancipated heterosexuality across the repressed and unrepresentable body of the female homosexual" (p. 38). In "The Hetero and the Homo: The Sexual Ethics of Luce Irigaray," in *Engaging With Irigaray*, pp. 335–50, Elizabeth Grosz offers a more generous reading of Irigaray's advocacy of a "*tactical homosexuality* modeled on the corporeal relations of the preoedipal daughter to her mother" (p. 338); what is crucial is Irigaray's commitment to "*the right to choose for oneself*" (p. 339). Grosz thus deems Irigaray less a *lesbian* theorist – a position which Grosz seems to equate with a prescriptive morality – than someone maintaining a critical difference "from all existing modes of sexual relation" (p. 335).

135. On feminist heterosexuality, see Joan Cocks, "Power, Desire, and the Meaning of the Body," in *The Oppositional Imagination: Feminism, Critique, and Political Theory* (London and New York: Routledge, 1989). Investigating feminist alternatives to a wholesale condemnation of heterosexual relationships, Cocks demonstrates the lack of fit between subjective desire and ideology, and imagines a range of possible subject and power positions within sexual relations.

136. I would argue that it is her reliance on metonymy that authorizes Irigaray's by now notoriously problematic conflation of male homosexuality and male patriarchal homosociality as "an economy of the same" in her coinage "hom(m)osexuality." See Fuss, *Essentially Speaking*, p. 111; Jagose, "Irigaray and the Lesbian Body," pp. 36–37; and Craig Owens, "Outlaws: Gay Men in Feminism," in *Men in Feminism*, eds. Alice Jardine and Paul Smith (London and New York: Routledge, 1987), pp. 219–32.

137. My thinking about legitimation as a metanarrative has been enhanced by Roof's "Lesbians and Lyotard: Legitimation and the Politics of the Name," in Doan, ed., *The Lesbian Postmodern*, pp. 47–66.

138. Interestingly, Fuss praises Irigaray's logic of metonymy because it displaces conventional linguistic hierarchies that privilege metaphor over metonymy. While I agree that metonymy might, at certain historical moments, have some advantages over metaphor, it is not clear to me that this has been the case historically with the *lesbian* body.

139. Butler, *Bodies that Matter*, p. xi.
140. *Ibid.*, p. 14.
141. *Ibid.*, p. 81.
142. See, in addition to Irigaray and Butler, Roof, *The Lure of Knowledge*; and Fuss, *Identification Papers* (New York and London: Routledge, 1995).

6. CHASTE FEMME LOVE, MYTHOLOGICAL PASTORAL, AND THE PERVERSION OF *LESBIAN* DESIRE

1. Pier Francesco Cavalli, *La Calisto*; libretto by Giovanni Faustini (Venice: 1651).
2. Douglas Bush, *Mythology and the Renaissance Tradition in English Poetry* (New York: W. W. Norton, 1963). Bush's view of the erotics of this synthetic mode is ambivalent: "Pastoral and mythological poems shade into each other, for pastoral writing in both prose and verse was drenched with mythology, and the mythological poem obviously owed much to the pastoral. In both is an artificial Arcadian scene, exhaustively described, inhabited by artificial nymphs and swains

and mythological figures, also – especially the nymphs – exhaustively described, and of course there is interminable sensuous or sensual love-making" (pp. 74–75).
3. See Lynn Enterline, *The Rhetoric of the Body from Ovid to Shakespeare* (Cambridge and New York: Cambridge University Press, 2000); and Goran Stanivukovic, ed., *Ovid and the Renaissance Body* (Toronto: University of Toronto Press, 2001).
4. M. Morgan Holmes, "Pastoral," in Summers, ed., *The Gay and Lesbian Literary Heritage*, pp. 536–39.
5. In addition to Smith, *Homosexual Desire in Shakespeare's England*, Bredbeck, *Sodomy and Interpretation*, Goldberg, *Sodometries*, and DiGangi, *The Homoerotics of Early Modern Drama*, see the Ph.D. dissertations of Stephen Whitworth, "The Name of the Ancients: Humanist Homoerotics and the Signs of Pastoral" (University of Michigan, 1997), and Frederick Greene, "Subversions of Pastoral: Queer Theory and the Politics and Poetics of Elegy" (University of California, Santa Barbara, 1997). Greene's emphasis on literary form, while not directly pertinent to the use of pastoral conventions that concern me, shares a kindred interest in the ways pastoral resists the closure of erotic plots, the stabilization of identities, and the production of absence and loss.
6. As Lisa M. Walker says in "How to Recognize a Lesbian: The Cultural Politics of Looking Like What You Are," *Signs: Journal of Women in Culture and Society* 18:4 (1993): "[b]ecause subjects who can 'pass' exceed the categories of visibility that establish identity, they tend to be regarded as peripheral to the understanding of marginalization" (p. 868).
7. See, in particular, Joan Nestle, ed., *Persistent Desire: A Femme–Butch Reader* (Boston: Alyson Publications, 1992); Sally R. Munt, ed., *Butch/Femme: Inside Lesbian Gender* (London and Washington: Cassell, 1998); Laura Harris and Elizabeth Crocker, eds., *Femme: Feminists, Lesbians, and Bad Girls* (New York and London: Routledge, 1997); and Elizabeth Kennedy and Madeline Davis, eds., *Boots of Leather, Slippers of Gold: The History of a Lesbian Community* (New York: Routledge, 1993). In *Femininity Played Straight*, Biddy Martin notes that in the influential work of Teresa de Lauretis ("Sexual Indifference and Lesbian Representation," *Theatre Journal* 40:2 [1988]: 155–77) and Sue-Ellen Case ("Toward a Butch–Femme Aesthetic," *Discourse* 11:1 [1988–89]: 55–73), femmes are analyzed solely in terms of a butch–femme dynamic, a perspective that not only reinscribes the centrality of the butch to modern conceptions of *lesbianism*, but reveals an anxiety that femme *lesbians* are indistinguishable from straight women (pp. 71–94). The presumption, in the words of Walker, that the "femme's adaptation of what has been historically defined as a 'feminine' sexual style is tacitly constructed as evidence of her desire to pass for straight and not of her desire for other women" (and correlatively, that the butch is "the authentic lesbian") ("How to Recognize a Lesbian," pp. 882 and 881), is given quintessential expression in Radclyffe Hall's *The Well of Loneliness*; see Esther Newton, "The Mythic Mannish Lesbian: Radclyffe Hall and the New Woman," *Signs: Journal of Women in Culture and Society* 9:4 (1984): 557–75.
8. See Sheila T. Cavanagh, *Wanton Eyes and Chaste Desires: Female Sexuality in "The Faerie Queene"* (Bloomington: Indiana University Press, 1994).
9. Jane Davidson Reid, ed., *The Oxford Guide to Classical Mythology in the Arts, 1300–1990s*, 2 vols. (New York and Oxford: Oxford University Press, 1993). Volume I lists over one hundred writers and artists who have made use of the

Calisto myth in words, music, or visual image; in addition to many paintings, there have been several operas and a ballet. The majority of these treatments occurred from the early seventeenth to the mid-eighteenth century. Kathleen Wall, *The Callisto Myth from Ovid to Atwood: Initiation and Rape in Literature* (Kingston, Ont. and Montreal: McGill-Queen's University Press, 1988), discusses classical and Renaissance versions of this myth, as well as nineteenth- and twentieth-century versions, from a heterosexual perspective.

10. Berry, *Of Chastity and Power*; Simons, "Lesbian (In)Visibility in Italian Renaissance Culture."

11. According to Reid, *The Oxford Guide to Classical Mythology in the Arts*, the classical sources are Ovid, *Metamorphoses* 2.409–531; *Fasti* 2.155–92; Apollodorus, *Biblioteca* 3.8.2–9.1; Pausanias, *Description of Greece* 1.25.1, 8.3.6–7, 8.4.1, 10.9.5; Hyginus, *Fabulae* 177; *Poetica astronomica* 2.1; *Astronomy* 4 (p. 281). For a brief discussion of the variants of the myth, including who changes Calisto into a constellation (Jove, to disguise his transgression; Diana, to punish the flouting of chastity; Juno, out of jealousy), see *The Myths of Hyginus*, trans. and ed. Mary Grant (Lawrence: University of Kansas Press, 1960).

12. Along with the sixteenth-century compendia of continental mythographers (Lilius Gregorius Gyraldus, Vincenzio Cartari, and Natalis Comes) and dictionaries of mythology, there were Latin editions of the *Metamorphoses*, often appended with commentaries, published in England and the Continent. Calisto's story is retold in John Gower's *Confessio amantis* (c. 1390). In 1480 William Caxton prepared for the press, but probably never printed, a translation of the *Metamorphoses*; see *The Metamorphoses of Ovid translated by William Caxton 1480*, 2 vols. (New York: George Braziller, 1968), vol. I, n.p. The story of Calisto appears in Caxton's translation of Raoul Lefevre's *The Recuyell of the Historyes of Troye* (Bruges: c. 1474) as well.

13. For general treatments of Ovid in the Renaissance, see Lee T. Pearcy, *The Mediated Muse: English Translations of Ovid 1560–1700* (Hamden: Archon Press, 1984); Jean Seznec, *The Survival of the Pagan Gods: The Mythological Tradition and its Place in Renaissance Humanism and Art*, trans. Barbara F. Sessions (New York: Pantheon Books, 1953); and John Glenn, *A Critical Edition of Alexander Ross's 1647 Mystagogus Poeticus, or the Muses Interpreter* (New York: Garland Press, 1987).

14. For the sake of consistency, although Calisto is often spelled Callisto, I have used the one spelling throughout; I use Jove or Jupiter depending on how he is named in the text; and Arcas is sometimes spelled Archas.

15. *The. XV. Bookes of P. Ovidius Naso, entytuled Metamorphosis, translated oute of Latin into English meeter* (London: 1567) in *Shakespeare's Ovid Being Arthur Golding's Translation of the Metamorphoses*, ed. W. H. D. Rouse (London: Centaur Press, 1961) (lines 530–45).

16. Caxton's version is likewise not very expansive: Jupiter "approached unto her and embraced and kissed her more freely than a maid oughte to do and came near her than Diane was wonte to do... he embraced her in his armes and cast her down upon the grasse and there took her maidenhood from her."

17. Calisto is the constellation of the Great Bear, also known as Septentrio. It does not move from its place, nor does it set, attributed to the fact that Tethys, wife of the

Ocean and foster mother of Juno, forbids its setting in the Ocean out of solidarity with the wronged wife. In Golding's version, Calisto's stellification causes the ongoing consternation of Juno, who complains: "how passing is my powre: / I have bereft hir womans shape, and at this present howre / She is become a Goddesse" (*Shakespeare's Ovid*, p. 53 [lines 646–48]).

18. George Sandys, *Ovid's Metamorphosis Englished, Mythologized, and Represented in Figures* (1632), eds. Karl K. Hulley and Stanley T. Vandersall (Lincoln: University of Nebraska Press, 1970), p. 91. The first five books appeared in 1621, the complete translation in 1626, and the commentary in 1632.
19. In *Ovid's Metamorphosis Englished: George Sandys as Translator and Mythographer* (New York and London: Garland Press, 1985), Deborah Rubin notes that this passage is morally inconsistent: Calisto is both "the deceived innocent and the guilty fallen woman" (p. 155).
20. As Bush remarks, "the moralized Ovid enjoyed a prolonged euthanasia" (*Mythology and the Renaissance Tradition in English Poetry*, p. 78).
21. Because Calisto's son Arcas plays a role in the royal lineage of England, Calisto's story appears in the genre of historical verse epic. William Warner, *Albion's England, Or Historical Map of the Same Island* (1586), began as a treatment of mythological and English legends, but as augmented and revised, it ran up to the reign of James I in editions of 1589, 1592, 1596, 1597, 1602, 1606, and 1612. His treatment of the Calisto tale is based on Caxton.
22. In *Mythology and the Renaissance Tradition in English Poetry*, Bush remarks that Heywood follows Warner, including the use of verbal correspondences (p. 66).
23. Heywood, actor, playwright, translator, wrote over two hundred works, including three contributions to the controversy over women. In *Images of Women in the Works of Thomas Heywood* (Salzburg: Salzburg Studies in English Literature, 1974), Marilyn L. Johnson describes Heywood as "middle-of-the-road" on the question of women's equality (p. 27).
24. Thomas Heywood, *The Golden Age* (London: 1609), n.p.
25. Thomas Heywood, *Troia Brittanica: Or, Great Britaines Troy* (London: 1609).
26. From Shakespeare's "procreation" sonnets, Heywood appropriates the argument of usury and use – "Hoord not (quoth he) unto your selfe such Treasure, / Nor let so sweet a flower ungathered vade" – as well as the language of copying: "Nature her selfe hath tooke from you fit measure / To have more beautious Creatures by you made, / Then crop this flower before the prime be past, / Loose not the Mould that may such fayre ones cast" (stanza 53). He also merges the rhetoric of anti-Catholicism with royal duty:

> Let not a Cloyster such rare beauty smother,
> Y'are Natures mayster-peece, made to be seene;
> (Sweet) you were borne, that you should beare another,
> A Princesse, and discended from a Queene,
> That you of Queenes and Princes might be mother.
> Had she that bare you still a virgin beene,
> You had not been at all: Mankind should fade,
> If every Female, liv'd a spotlesse mayde. (stanza 54)

27. Heywood's logic is that the "Infant-soules that should have beene enrold / In Heavens predestin'de booke, begot of you, / Are by your strangenesse, to oblivion sold, / You might as well your hands in blood imbrew" (stanza 56).
28. Thomas Heywood, *The Escapes of Jupiter* (Oxford: Oxford University Press, 1976).
29. Between Heywood's first and second rendition of the story, the anonymous W. N. published *Barley-breake, or a Warning for Wantons* (London: 1607). This verse narrative, which mines aspects of Ovid and Warner, is, as its subtitle suggests, a cautionary tale. As an eclectic, wild mix of pastoral and Jacobean tragedy, it employs the Calisto story as an inset tale as part of its attempt to discipline errant women. Having witnessed his daughter Euphema's immodest behavior during a kissing game of barley-break, the shepherd Old Elpin calls her away. The next day, while watching their sheep, he narrates the story of Jupiter's youthful rape. Euphema pays him no heed, allows herself to be seduced by Streton, becomes pregnant, leaves home, and is soon abandoned. Returning to her father, she witnesses his spontaneous death at the sight of her. Euphema stabs herself over his corpse, and Streton finds himself pursued and murdered by a flock of angry birds. Because *Barley-breake* is primarily a tale of *impudicia*, not much of it is relevant to my discussion. Nonetheless, its representation of the seduction of Calisto by the crossdressed Jove reveals a similar understanding of the acceptability of female bodily contact during the rape scene:

    > Soone sate [Jove] downe the faire Calisto by;
    > As who would say, Let's rest: for walkes are weary.
    > Where laughing, they claspe eithers ivory hands,
    > Proove strength of armes, as maids will being merry,
    > Clip wrests, draw lots, meat wastes with silken bands.
    > And now although the game began in sport,
    > The silly Nymph rude earnest doth sustaine:
    > It's vaine to strive, or use the womens arte,
    > Screeke out, or struggle, prayers are but vaine. (pp. 14–15)

30. *La Calisto* was first recorded by Raymond Leppard in 1970/75 in a modernized, historically inaccurate, and full orchestral version after the modern revival at Glyndebourne in 1970. The recording by Bruno Moretti in 1988 is more faithful to Faustini's original autograph score, and it is this libretto, augmented with an English translation provided by Beverly Ballaro, that I have used. I have also consulted the 1993 recording by René Jacobs.
31. According to the *New Grove Italian Baroque Masters* (New York and London: W. W. Norton, 1984), Cavalli composed nearly thirty operas for Venetian houses, and his operas were a "mainstay of the repertory as opera gained a firm footing even in many smaller Italian towns during the 1650s and 1660s" (p. 144). Nonetheless, *Calisto* was not much of a success; there were only eleven performances, and its use of gods and goddesses was deemed old-fashioned. For analyses of Cavalli, in which, unfortunately, this opera does not much figure, see Ellen Rosand, *Opera in Seventeenth-Century Venice: The Creation of a Genre* (Berkeley: University of California Press, 1991), and Jane Glover, *Cavalli* (New York: St. Martin's Press, 1978).

32. See Wendy Heller, "Chastity, Heroism, and Allure: Women in the Opera of Seventeenth-Century Venice," Ph.D. dissertation (Brandeis University, Massachusetts, 1995).

33. GIOVE IN DIANA: Hor l'amarezza De la dimora, Homai ristora Con la dolcezza De baci tuoi.
    CALISTO: Quanti ne vuoi Te ne darà, Ten porgerà, Devoto il labro, Che d'invocare Hà per costume Sempre il tuo Nume.
    GIOVE IN DIANA: In ricovero più ombroso, In loco pìu frondoso, Al mormorar, che fà l'humor cadente Di trovata Sorgente Più limpida di questa, A' baciarsi le bocche Partiam, seguace amata.
    A DUE: A baciarsi andiam, sì, sì. Sien del Dì Liete al core Tutte l'hore, Col goderle in dolci paci. Non s'indugi, à baci, à baci.

    Leppard's translation is a bit freer, but evokes the full sensuality of this passage:

    JOVE: Now that you see me in bitter sadness, restore my comfort with all the rapture of your sweet kisses.
    CALISTO: I'll give as many as you could wish. I offer you my lips, my two lips that adore you.
    JOVE: We'll find somewhere more shady and somewhere far more leafy; and there beside the softly murmuring waters of a fountain that's even more cystalline than this is let us relish our kisses at once, [at once, at once,] my dearly loved handmaid.
    TOGETHER: Let us kiss and kiss again [and again]. Let us fill hours of leisure full of [full of] pleasure by enjoying the sweetest, [the sweetest,] sweetest blisses. Let us not delay our kisses, our kisses, [our kisses, kisses] not delay. (pp. 7–8)

34. According to the liner notes in Jacobs's CD, "Jove's part is noted in the bass clef, that of 'Jove as Diana' in the soprano clef (rising to high G, which gives the baritone a top G, impossible for even a good falsetto baritone). Could the part of 'Jove as Diana' have been sung by the real Diana? This is not only possible, but even probable, since the true and the false Dianas never meet; but it is not very satisfactory from a theatrical point of view. One can imagine that Cavalli chose this expedient because he could not find a baritone who was capable of singing falsetto well enough" (p. 29).

35. "De la tua bocca i favi Sì grati, e sì soavi... celesti rubini."

36. Kerrigan, "Kiss Fancies in Robert Herrick," pp. 160–61.

37. Irigaray, *This Sex Which Is Not One*. Later in the opera, when Diana and Endymion admit their mutual love, they sing a duet that reiterates the oral imagery and eroticism of kissing.

38. "Fonti limpide, e pure Al vostro gorgoglio La mia Divina, et Io coppia diletta, e cara Ci bacieremo à gara. E formeremo melodie soavi, Quì dove con più voci Eco risponde, Unito il suon de baci, al suon de l'onde."

39. See Simons, "Lesbian (In)Visibility in Italian Renaissance Culture."

40. The use of "nymphae" as a term for the lips of the vagina apparently derives from Galen; its use in anatomical texts is thoroughly conventional. See Paré, *The Workes of that famous Chirurgion Ambrose Parey*, Culpeper, *A Directory for Midwives*, Venette, *Conjugal Love*, and *Aristoteles Master-piece*. The first reference in a dictionary to the nymphae as "a little excrescene, or peece of flesh, in the middest of a womans privities" occurs in Randle Cotgrave's *A Dictionarie of the French and English Tongues* (1611). Thomas Elyot's *Dictionary* (1538) defines "nymphae" as "goddesses of the waters, or spirits, being conversaunt aboute waters, elfes,

women of the fayrie. sometyme the Muses be so called. also yonge bees, as sone as they have receyved their fourme." Thomas Cooper's *Thesaurus Linguae Romanae Et Brittanicae* (1565) defines "nymphae" as "A bride or new married wyfe" and "Young bees before they flee." Thomas Blount's *Glossographia* (1656) defines a "nymph" as "a Bride or new married Wife. Hence those Virgin Goddesses of the Woods, mountains and waters had this name, as the Napaee, Oreades, Dryades, Hamadryades, Naiades, Nereides, &."

41. Crooke, *Microcosmographia*, pp. 237–38.
42. Sharp, *The Midwives Book*, pp. 33–34.
43. See Nicola Zingarelli, *Vocabulario della lingua italiana* (Bologna: N. Zanichelli, 1956): "Piccole labbra della vagina," p. 1018.
44. Given that Thomas Bartholin maintained that earlier anatomists were referring to the clitoris when they used the term "nymphae," one might argue as well that the nymphae has an even greater erotic signification.
45. CALISTO: Giubilo immenso, e caro Le dolci labra tue Nel petto mi stillaro. Fur pure, oh Dio, soavi Quei baci, che mi desti ò Dea cortese Mà la mia bocca il guiderdon ti rese...
   DIANA: Taci lasciva, taci. Qual, qual delirio osceno L'ingegno ti confonde? Come immodesta, donde Profanasti quel seno Con introdur in lui sì sozze brame? Qual meretrice infame Può de tuoi, dishonesta, Formar detti peggiori? Esci de la foresta, Né più trà i casti, e verginal miei chori Ardisci conversar putta sfrenata: Dal senso lusinghier contaminata Và, fuggi, e nel fuggir del piede alato T'accompagni il rossor del tuo peccato.
46. "Nel vago seno accolta Abbracciata, Fui baciata... Mi condusse In antro dilettoso, E mi baciò più fiate Come se stato fosse il vago, il sposo."
47. "Alfin la tanto rigida, Quella, ch'è delle vergini L'imperatrice, e Satrapa, E' come l'altre femine Soggette al senso fragile."
48. "O Rè de l'Universo Ricreata mi sento Al tuo divino accento... Eccomi Ancella tua. Disponi a tuo piacere, Monarca de le sfere, Di colei, che creasti; Che con frode felice, ò mio gran Fato Accorla ti degnasti Nel tuo sen beato."
49. "Il Ciel rida A' contenti De la fida Al gran Dio de gl'elementi."
50. "Questi falsi sembianti, Con gl'arnesi mentiti Signor deponi, che di vaghe in vece Troverai di mariti." This conflation of anti-theatrical anxiety and fear of sodomy is widespread in English discourse as well.
51. GIOVE IN DIANA: Non è negato il bacio à casto labro. Bocca pura, e pudica Può baciar senza biasmo, La Pastorella amica.
    GIUNONE: Sì, mà ne gl'Antri lecito non gl'è Condur le semplicette, e farle poi Un certo dolce che, Come fatto provar gl'havete voi.
52. JUNO: Altro, che baci, dì, V'intervenne, vi fù Trà la tua Diva, e te?
    CALISTO: Un certo dolce che, Che dir non tel saprei.
53. "Vignettes of Royal Collections and Collectors from Queen Elizabeth to Queen Victoria," in *The Queen's Pictures: Royal Collectors Through the Centuries*, ed. Christopher Lloyd (London: National Gallery Publications, 1991), p. 33. I am grateful to Patricia Simons for bringing this comment to my attention.
54. Eleanore Boswell, *The Restoration Court Stage, 1660–1702, With a Particular Account of the Production of 'Calisto'* (Cambridge, MA: Harvard University Press, 1932), p. 208.

55. I have followed the dating of Andrew R. Walkling, who provides a detailed analysis of the performers and expenditures and situates the masque in the context of courtly politics in "Masque and Politics at the Restoration Court: John Crowne's *Calisto*," *Early Music* 24 (1996): 27–62.
56. *Ibid.*, p. 52.
57. Carol Barash, *English Women's Poetry*, p. 47.
58. *Ibid.*, p. 48.
59. James A. Winn recognizes the homoerotic quality of Crowne's masque, but minimizes its effect on the audience in *"When Beauty Fires the Blood": Love and the Arts in the Age of Dryden* (Ann Arbor: University of Michigan Press, 1992), pp. 236–44, especially pp. 239–40.
60. Elizabeth J. Bellamy, "Waiting for Hymen: Literary History as 'Symptom' in Spenser and Milton," *ELH: English Literary History* 64:2 (1997): 391–414. In her reading of the chastity of Amoret in *The Faerie Queene* and of the Lady in *Comus* as static and stalled, Bellamy interprets chastity as the return of the repressed of literary history, and charts a corresponding emergence of bourgeois marital chastity as an episteme.
61. John Crowne, *Calisto: Or, The Chaste Nimph* (London: 1675) in *The Dramatic Works of John Crowne: With Prefatory Memoir and Notes*, eds. J. Maidment and W. H. Logan, 4 vols. (Edinburgh and London: William Patterson and H. Hotheran, 1873–74), vol. I, p. 237.
62. Bellamy, "Waiting for Hymen," p. 401.
63. Mikhail Bakhtin, *Rabelais and His World*, trans. Hélène Iswolsky (Bloomington: Indiana University Press, 1984).
64. For a useful discussion of the asymmetry of shame in butch and femme identities, see Munt's Introduction to *Butch/Femme*, pp. 1–11.
65. Castle, *The Apparitional Lesbian*, p. 62.
66. Dollimore, *Sexual Dissidence*.
67. Orlin, *Private Matters and Public Culture*.
68. Because Stone's *The Family, Sex, and Marriage in England* has proven, for good or ill, to be a touchstone for subsequent work, it is worth summarizing his periodization of family structure. He posits that the sixteenth-century English family was characterized by marriages that were "arranged by parents and kin for economic and social reasons, with minimal consultation of the children." Under the pressure of Reformation ideology and new property relations, this form of family was replaced in the early seventeenth century by a more restricted "nuclear family," which was less permeable to the influence of extended kin and more dedicated to emotionally strong ties. Although parents still retained the choice of spouses, a right of veto was conceded to resistant children. After the revolutionary 1640s and 1650s, financial and property interests gave way to personal affection as the principal criterion of spousal choice, heralding the emergence of what Stone calls the "closed domesticated nuclear family." As Stone maps these shifts, they indicate a movement from family relations characterized by emotional distance and deference to those structured, by the early eighteenth century, by "affective individualism." Other proponents of change include Edward Shorter, *The Making of the Modern Family* (New York: Basic Books, 1975); Randolph Trumbach, *The Rise of the Egalitarian Family* (New York: Academic Press, 1977);

John Gillis, *For Better, For Worse: British Marriages, 1600 to the Present* (New York and Oxford: Oxford University Press, 1985); and, to a lesser extent, O'Day, *The Family and Family Relationships*.

69. A helpful overview of the debates is provided by Michael Anderson, *Approaches to the History of the Western Family, 1500–1914* (London and Basingstoke: Macmillan, 1980).

70. The infelicities of Stone's account are amply documented by Alan Macfarlane in his lengthy review essay in *History and Theory* 18 (1979): 103–26, wherein he faults Stone's assumptions and in certain respects demolishes his use of evidence. Stone's dependence on aristocratic and gentry sources, his characterization of sixteenth-century family life as cold and unyielding, and his description of evolutionary changes proceeding from the top to the bottom of the social scale have been rejected by most historians writing in his wake. See Peter Laslett, *The World We Have Lost* (New York: Charles Scribner's Sons, 1965); and Alan Macfarlane, *Marriage and Love in England: Modes of Reproduction, 1300–1840* (Oxford and New York: Basil Blackwell, 1986).

71. Ralph Houlbrooke, *The English Family, 1450–1700* (London and New York: Longman, 1984), pp. 15–16.

72. In his Afterword to *The Friend*, Bray analyzes the political and professional undercurrents to these controversies, arguing that some of the rifts are a function of contemporary social policies regarding the family. I would add that the tendency among historians to emphasize continuity seems more of a backlash against Stone than is warranted. As O'Day remarks, "[t]he severe criticism levelled at the 'affective' school of family history ... has unfortunately deflected interests away from family relationships" (*The Family and Family Relationships*, p. 268).

73. One need not subscribe to Stone's binary characterization of family and village life at 1600 and 1800, accept his schematic teleology, or turn a blind eye to his mishandling of textual sources in order to credit the belief that expectations of intimacy between spouses increased over this time. Indeed, the insistence of Macfarlane and Laslett that marital relations did not change at all seems as wrongheaded as Stone's programmatic insistence that they underwent a revolution. In particular, Macfarlane's reading in *Marriage and Love in England* of medieval romance, Renaissance poetry, and Restoration drama as evidence for the timelessness of family forms and meanings is particularly misguided; beyond its bracketing of the very different social milieus of these literary forms, his interpretation takes no cognizance of generic and tonal differences.

74. The confusion between family and household is of particular concern to O'Day, *The Family and Family Relationships*, who faults demographic historians for their use of "entirely census-derived descriptions" which fail to adequately account for the complexity of family interactions (p. 25).

75. See Margo Todd, *Christian Humanism and the Puritan Social Order* (Cambridge: Cambridge University Press, 1987); Kathleen Davis, "The Sacred Condition of Equality – How Original were Puritan Doctrines of Marriage?" *Social History* 5 (1971): 563–79; and Edmund Leites, "The Duty to Desire: Love, Friendship, and Sexuality in Some Puritan Theories of Marriage," *Journal of Social History* 15 (1982): 383–408. In *Of Chastity and Power*, Berry suggests that in addition to the influence of Puritan and humanist discourses, English culture also assimilated

an idealized concept of marriage from French and Italian Catholic conduct books directed toward an aristocratic audience.
76. I am thinking particularly of Cressy's *Birth, Marriage and Death*, which in every other respect is a model of careful scholarship.
77. Keith Wrightson, *English Society, 1580–1680* (London: Hutchinson, 1982), pp. 83–84. Wrightson's rank-based analysis of courtship is well founded, providing greater socio-economic specificity to our understanding of family formation. But by locating his treatment of the family within the section of his book on "enduring structures," he implies that whereas comprehensive changes took place within the social order of rank, property, and labor – especially a growth in social inequality throughout the sixteenth and seventeenth centuries – those marriage patterns *that matter* remained fairly static: "In general marriage confirmed social distinctions, and the process of family formation both faithfully reflected, and served to perpetuate the social order: its privileges, its obligations, its opportunities, its constraints and its injustices" (p. 88). Indeed, in order to deny the possibility of diachronic change in affective relations, Wrightson cautions that "an apparently greater emphasis on emotional considerations toward the end of our period might be in part an illusion created by better documentation in the form of diaries and letters. In any case, it must be remembered that emotions are not generated in a social vacuum. They could be aroused where an individual had, as it were, *learned* to love, in accordance with the values of his or her day and station in life" (p. 87, emphasis in original).
78. The question of personal correspondence is a complex one. There is no question but that letters between husbands and wives demonstrate a change in rhetoric as the seventeenth century progresses, in part because the "increasing readiness of members of the propertied classes to write rather than dictate letters made possible a new epistolary privacy." But did the new epistolary privacy simply encourage "a loosening of formalities, a fuller expression of intimate feelings and a more discursive treatment of personal pleasures," as Houlbrooke suggests, or did the new experience of privacy actually intensify conjugal feeling? (Houlbrooke, *The English Family*, p. 4).
79. *Ibid.*, p. 118.
80. *Ibid.*, p. 119.
81. Wayne, "Advice for Women from Mothers and Patriarchs," in Wilcox, ed., *Women and Literature in Britain*, p. 68.
82. Erickson, *Women and Property in Early Modern England*, p. 7.
83. Crawford and Gowing, *Women's Worlds in Seventeenth-Century England*, p. 164.
84. Mendelson and Crawford, *Women in Early Modern England*, p. 432.
85. Fletcher, *Gender, Sex and Subordination*, pp. 407 and 412.
86. *Ibid.*, p. 400.
87. *Ibid.*, p. 395.
88. *Ibid.*, pp. 393 and 394.
89. Rebecca Ann Bach, "Early Modern England Without Heterosexuality," paper presented at the Shakespeare Association of America (1998).
90. See also Dympna Callaghan, "The Ideology of Romantic Love: The Case of *Romeo and Juliet*," in Callaghan, Helms, and Singh, eds., *The Weyward Sisters*, pp. 59–101, who explores "the emergent construction of romantic love as mutual heterosexual

desire leading to a consummation in marriage, a union of both body and spirit," stressing that much of this ideology's effectiveness inheres in the fact that it centers "on women's subjective experience" (p. 60). Locating the "hegemonic ideology of romantic love" alongside "some of the definitive conditions of nascent modernity," she argues that the "Puritan doctrine of marriage requires nothing less than that women are endowed with desiring subjectivity, which can then be actively solicited and controlled by the social order" (pp. 72 and 79).

91. Catherine Belsey, "The Serpent in the Garden: Shakespeare, Marriage and Material Culture," *The Seventeenth Century* 11:1 (1996): 1–20; citation p. 1.
92. *Ibid.*, p. 17.
93. Belsey's argument is this: "Part of the project of the early modern romance of marriage was to bring desire in from the cold: to moralize and domesticate a destabilizing passion, confining it within the safety of the affective family ... Desire is fearful, possessive, proprietary, beyond the pleasure principle" (*ibid.*, pp. 16–17). Insofar as Belsey's primary analytical lens is a Lacanian interpretation of desire – as predicated on lack and thus perennially troubled by the instabilities of signification – the questions she poses are rather different from mine.
94. Belsey, "Love as Trompe-L'oeil: Taxonomies of Desire in *Venus and Adonis*," *Shakespeare Quarterly* 46:3 (1995): 257–76; citation pp. 266–68.
95. *Ibid.*, p. 271.
96. Tilney, *The Flower of Friendship: A Renaissance Dialogue Contesting Marriage*, ed. Wayne, lines 440–44. As Wayne points out, marital love for Tilney is a process by which two bodies become one heart: the man's. This advice, including Tilney's trope of theft, is repeated in the Puritan conduct book by John Dod and Robert Cleaver, *A Godlie Forme of Householde Government* (London: 1598): "The husband ought not to bee satisfied that he hath robd his wife of her virginitie, but in that he hath possession and use of her will."
97. Dorothy Leigh, *The Mother's Blessing: Or, The godly Counsaile of a Gentlewoman not long since deceased, left behind her for her Children* (London: 1616); this mother's advice book went through fifteen editions by 1630.
98. Robert Crofts, *The Lover: or, Nuptiall Love* (London 1638), sigs. A7v–A8r.
99. Belsey, "Love as Trompe-L'oeil," p. 273.
100. William Harvey, ANATOMICAL EXERCITATIONS, *Concerning the* GENERATION *of Living Creatures: To which are added Particular Discourses of Births, and of Conceptions, &c.* (London: 1653). See Eccles, *Obstetrics and Gynaecology in Tudor and Stuart England*, pp. 33–41; Hilda Smith, "Gynecology and Ideology in Seventeenth-Century England," in *Liberating Women's History: Theoretical and Critical Essays*, ed. Bernice A. Carroll (Urbana: University of Illinois Press, 1976), pp. 97–114; and Nancy Tuana, "The Weaker Seed: The Sexist Bias of Reproductive Theory," in *Feminism and Science*, ed. Nancy Tuana (Bloomington and Indianapolis: Indiana University Press, 1989), pp. 147–71.
101. *Aristotle's Master-Piece*, p. 3, emphasis mine.
102. *Ibid.*, p. 96.
103. See O'Day, *The Family and Family Relationships*.
104. On the growing emphasis on maternity, see Ruth Perry, "Colonizing the Breast: Sexuality and Maternity in Eighteenth-Century England," in *Forbidden History:*

The State, Society, and the Regulation of Sexuality in Modern Europe, ed. John Fout (Chicago and London: University of Chicago Press, 1992), pp. 107–37.

105. Corresponding shifts in both France and the colonies occurred later. According to Wahl, in France both the Catholic respect for virginity and "the aristocratic ethos of *galanterie* prevented the idea from achieving much influence until well into the eighteenth century" (*Invisible Relations*, p. 88). In *Domestic Revolutions: A Social History of American Family Life* (New York: Macmillan, 1988), Susan Kellogg and Steven Mintz stress the extent to which colonial marriage was an economic affair, often governed by considerations of kinship and politics. Focusing on the Puritan structure of the household as an economically productive, educational, and religious unit, they contrast it explicitly to English households: "The disciplined Puritan family of the New World was quite different from the English family of the sixteenth and seventeenth centuries that had been left behind. In fact, it represented an effort to re-create an older ideal of the family that no longer existed in England itself" (p. 7). The movement toward a more companionate, privatized mode (with greater emphasis on childrearing and the confining of sexual activity within marriage) seems to have been initiated in North America first by the Quakers in the Delaware Valley in the eighteenth century, and only thereafter migrating into New England and the Chesapeake Bay. Also, see their entry "Family Structures" in the *Encyclopedia of American Social History*, eds. Mary Cayton, Elliott Gorn, and Peter Williams, 3 vols. (New York: Charles Scribner's Sons, 1993), vol. III, pp. 1925–44.
106. Vanita, *Sappho and the Virgin Mary*, pp. 28–29.
107. For an exploration of this dynamic within postmodern culture, see Hart, *Fatal Women: Lesbian Sexuality and the Mark of Aggression*, especially pp. 91–103.
108. Gillis, *For Better, For Worse*, maintains that "[f]riendship was often as consuming as a love affair, and therefore a major psychological reason why both men and women approached marriage so late and so ambivalently, knowing full well that this meant an end to so many well-developed and emotionally sustaining associations of the very long years of bachelor and spinsterhood" (p. 34). In this homosocial context, courting took the form of "innocent polygamy": ritualized games and behaviors that "permitted young people to show an interest without committing them to a more binding relationship" (p. 23). The transition from country dancing and kissing games to keeping company, night visiting, and betrothal was, Gillis argues, a difficult one for many people, as "their culture did not prepare them for the abrupt change from being a friend to becoming a lover" (p. 39).
109. Two exceptions to this conceptual bifurcation are Hitchcock, *English Sexualities, 1700–1800* and Trumbach, *Sex and the Gender Revolution*, both of whom critique historians for exactly this problem and attempt to place eighteenth-century discourses of homosexuality in relation to heterosexuality.
110. Peter Stallybrass, "Character Assassination," presented at the 1992 Modern Language Association conference; and Butler, "Imitation and Gender Insubordination," in Fuss, ed., *Inside/Out*.
111. Although I am making a historical point here, it corresponds to Butler's theoretical and political point in *The Psychic Life of Power: Theories in Subjection* (Stanford, CA: Stanford University Press, 1997) that the tendency within gay and *lesbian*

identity to "disavow a constitutive relationship to heterosexuality" attributes to heterosexuality "a false and monolithic status," while also missing "the political opportunity to work on the weakness in heterosexual subjectivation" (p. 148).

112. Howarth, *Images of Rule*, remarks of the Queen's probable reaction:

> Never can she have been made angrier by visual imagery than when she discovered herself starring in the title role in a horror version of the story of Diana and Calisto. The intention of the Dutch rebels in casting her as Diana in a print issued in Holland with an accompanying text in Dutch was to establish Elizabeth as the champion of their cause . . . Rarely can there have been such a mismatch between an image and its source . . . Elizabeth cannot have relished this encouragement to her subjects to dwell upon her gross, corporeal nature. As a woman who had been forced to perform the difficult contortion of turning her status as a Virgin Queen into a positive source of strength, she must have found the crude and explicit reference to the fate of Calisto powerfully repugnant. (pp. 111 and 114)

113. According to Reid, *Oxford Guide to Classical Mythology*, Boucher depicted Jupiter (and or Diana) and Calisto at least eight times. Erica Rand, "Lesbian Sightings: Scoping for Dykes in Boucher and *Cosmo*," *Journal of Homosexuality* 27:1/2 (1994): 123–39, interprets Boucher's "Jupiter in the Guise of Diana and the Nymph Callisto" (1757), as perpetuating rather than subverting a heterosexual norm.

7. "FRIENDSHIP SO CURST": *AMOR IMPOSSIBILIS*, THE HOMOEROTIC LAMENT, AND THE NATURE OF *LESBIAN* DESIRE

1. Hester Lynch Thrale Piozzi, *Thraliana: The Diary of Mrs. Hester Lynch Thrale (Later Mrs. Piozzi), 1776–1809*, ed. Katherine C. Balderston, 2 vols. (Oxford: Clarendon Press, 1942), vol. I, p. 356, diary entry of 1778.
2. Blount, *Glossographia* (1661).
3. Blount, *Nomo-lexicon* (1670).
4. N. H., *The Ladies Dictionary* (1694).
5. The "Flats" is referred to in the anonymous *Satan's Harvest Home, or the Present State of Whorecraft, Adultery, Fornication, Procuring, Pimping, Sodomy, And the Game at Flatts . . . And other Satanic Works daily propagated in this good Protestant Kingdom* (1749). Published in *Hell Upon Earth: Or the Town in an Uproar and Satan's Harvest Home*, ed. Randolph Trumbach (New York: Garland, 1985), p. 18. In "'Queer to Queer': Sapphic Bodies as Transgressive Texts," in Kittredge, ed., *Lewd and Notorious*, as well as her unpublished work, Susan Lanser has speculated that "singular," "whimsical," "whimmy" and possibly "queer" all functioned as code words for sapphism.
6. Thrale Piozzi, *Thraliana*, vol. II, p. 949.
7. Susan Lanser, "Befriending the Body: Female Intimacies as Class Acts," *Eighteenth Century Studies* 32:2 (1998–99): 179–98; and "Sapphic Picaresque, Sexual Difference, and the Challenges of Homo-adventuring," in *Textual Practice* 15:2 (2001): 251–68.
8. As Lanser argues, British nationhood in this period was particularly imbricated in a pro-natalist domesticity which, in a sense, rendered "heteropatriarchy" a national project. In addition to charting the emergence of sapphic figures, Lanser also analyzes the construction of the spinster which, interestingly enough, was not associated with homoerotic bonds in this period. See her "Singular Politics: The

Rise of the British Nation and the Production of the Old Maid," in Bennett and Froide, eds., *Singlewomen in the European Past*, pp. 297–323. In answering the question, "why does the old maid *not* get discredited as a tribade or sapphist?," Lanser argues that "to acknowledge the possibility of homosexual desire in the 'old maid' would dismantle and expose the entire system of old-maid ideology, in which the singlewoman's physical and moral deficiencies rest on the presumption of her heterosexual desire – on the presumption that she wants a man and cannot get one and as a result has become the miserable person she is" (pp. 314–15).

9. Wahl, *Invisible Relations*, p. 11. In its broad outlines, Wahl's historical argument correlates with my own. Her schema, however, reproduces a binary model of eroticism (sexualized = genital, idealized = non-genital), that I have tried to avoid by highlighting the eroticism within chastity. She also privileges French models both temporally and analytically, granting to French medicine, the Platonic love cult of the *précieuses*, and pornography an originating force and influence on English culture: "Not until the return of the Stuart monarchy from its exile in France brought about an accompanying resurgence of the influence of French culture, did the idea of female–female desire and homosexual practice begin to take on the features of an 'open secret' in England as well as in France" (p. 31). Although the *précieuses* certainly had an impact on Cavendish and Philips, Wahl's more general contention is contradicted by the number of indigenous English texts alluding to female–female desire prior to the Restoration, which Wahl argues are implicit or "coded" (p. 49).

10. The function of the term "impossible" parallels another word that, as Patricia Parker has shown, is intimately tied to erotic relations in the early modern period: *preposterous*. Rescuing the term from the discursive realm of the merely ridiculous, Parker has demonstrated its linguistic role in the articulation and policing of sexuality. According to the anatomist William Harvey, for instance, "The male woos, allures, makes love; the female yields, condescends, suffers. The contrary is preposterous" ("Gender Ideology, Gender Change," p. 362, note 54). Perhaps more important than its use to indicate the inversion of heterosexual gender roles, "preposterous" and its variants are used to describe the arsy-versy, back-for-front logic of sodomy; see Parker, *Shakespeare From the Margins*.

11. Susan Lanser, "*Hic Lesbias*: Sexual Representation and Enlightenment Politics," unpublished paper.

12. I thus would take issue with Tim Hitchcock's claim that it was in the eighteenth century that "a clearer set of boundaries between the 'natural', i.e., penetrative and heterosexual, and the 'unnatural' were promulgated to a wide audience" (*English Sexualities*, p. 2). Prior to the eighteenth century, he argues, "[n]on-heterosexual sex outside the context of marriage was certainly a heinous sin, but it was not a perversion of 'nature'" (p. 5).

13. See John Boswell, *Christianity, Social Tolerance, and Homosexuality: Gay People in Western Europe from the Beginning of the Christian Era to the Fourteenth Century* (Chicago: University of Chicago Press, 1980); Jordan, *The Invention of Sodomy in Christian Theology*; Warren Johansson and William A. Percy, "Homosexuality," in *Handbook of Medieval Sexuality*, eds. Vern L. Bullough and James A. Brundage (New York and London: Garland, 1996), pp. 155–89; Vern L. Bullough, "The Sin against Nature and Homosexuality," in *Sexual Practices*

and the Medieval Church, eds. Vern L. Bullough and James A. Brundage, eds. (Buffalo, NY: Prometheus, 1982), pp. 55–71. In *Getting Medieval*, Carolyn Dinshaw notes that the Middle English *kynde* derives from the Old English *cynd*, which she connects to "nature": both of these concepts, she implies, draw "on concepts of abstract Nature and the natural order of things as well as on concepts of origin, generation and generativity, birthright, natural bodily disposition and individual character, and a group with its commonalities" (p. 6).

14. Quoted in Camille, *The Gothic Idol*, p. 92, emphasis mine.
15. The Old French *Roman de Silence* (late thirteenth-century), which describes the chivalrous exploits of a transvestite heroine who resists homoerotic advances, also focuses on the meaning of Nature. See Kathleen M. Blumreich, "Lesbian Desire in the Old French *Roman de Silence*," *Arthuriana* 7:2 (1997): 47–62; and Valerie R. Hotchkiss, *Clothes Makes the Man: Female Cross Dressing in Medieval Europe* (New York and London: Garland, 1996), esp. chapter 7.
16. *The Boke of Huon of Bordeaux*, ed. Sidney L. Lee, trans. Lord Berners, *Early English Text Society*, series 2, vol. XL, pp. 720–29. A medieval play, *Miracle de la file d'un roy*, presents the moment of disclosure thus:

> There is no need to speak further of this.
> Put yourself at ease,
> Because everything you have told me here
> I promise you carefully to conceal,
> And I will show you such honor
> As a woman must show her husband
> In all matters, I swear this upon my soul,
> Nor will I ever hold you less dear.

See Robert L. A. Clark and Claire Sponsler, "Queer Play: The Cultural Work of Crossdressing in Medieval Drama," *New Literary History* 28 (1997): 319–44, p. 325; and Diane Watt, "Behaving like a Man? Incest, Lesbian Desire, and Gender Play in *Yde et Olive* and its Adaptations," *Comparative Literature* 50:4 (1998): 265–85.

17. Ludovico Ariosto, *Orlando Furioso*, trans. Guido Waldman (Oxford: Oxford University Press, 1974), Canto 25, p. 300.
18. *Ibid.*, Canto 25, p. 301.
19. In addition to texts discussed in this chapter, the story of Iphis and Ianthe is retold in John Gower's *Confessio Amantis* (*c*. 1390), Barnabe Rich's *Farewell to the Military Profession* (1581), Thomas Heywood's *Gynaikeion* (1624), and John Dryden, *Ovid's Metamorphoses in Fifteen Books* (1717). In the view of Karma Lochrie, *Covert Operations: The Medieval Uses of Secrecy* (Philadelphia: University of Pennsylvania Press, 1999), pp. 213–16, and Dinshaw, *Getting Medieval*, pp. 10–11, Gower's translation of Ovid's tale seems to open up the textual possibility that female–female desire is natural. See *Confessio Amantis*, Book 4, lines 451–505 in *The Complete Works of John Gower*, ed. G. C. Macaulay (Oxford: Clarendon Press, 1901), pp. 313–15.
20. Golding, *Shakespeare's Ovid*, lines 53–63.
21. Sandys, *Ovid's Metamorphosis Englished*, p. 421.
22. Sidney, *The Countess of Pembroke's Arcadia*, p. 243.

23. *Ibid.*, pp. 239–40.
24. Lyly, *Gallathea* (4.4. 37–43).
25. The Egyptian goddess Isis was most commonly associated with Demeter, but she became a pantheistic power, identified also with Aphrodite (Venus), Hera, Semele, Io, Tyche, and others.
26. Most critics read the central conflict in *Gallathea* as that between lust and chastity, or between the earthly and divine Venus. In *The Tudor Play of Mind: Rhetorical Inquiry and the Development of Elizabethan Drama* (Berkeley and Los Angeles: University of California Press, 1978), Joel Altman argues that this conflict is accommodated in "chaste love" (p. 214).
27. Sir Richard Maitland and Alexander Arbuthnot, *The Maitland Quarto Manuscript*, ed. William A. Craigie (Edinburgh and London: W. Blackwood, 1920). This poem was brought to my attention by Jane Farnsworth, "Voicing Female Desire in 'Poem XLIX,'" *SEL: Studies in English Literature* 36:1 (1996): 57–72. Farnsworth suggests that Mary Maitland, the daughter of the man who compiled the manuscript, may have written the poem.
28. The main critical text on this tradition is Laurens J. Mills, *One Soul in Bodies Twain: Friendship in Tudor Literature and Stuart Drama* (Bloomington: Principia Press, 1937), who reads the glorification of male friendship in such authors as Erasmus, Elyot, Lyly, Sidney, Bacon, and Montaigne, defends them against charges of homosexuality, and does not mention female friendship; indeed, the attitude toward women in this book is made clear in the index, which confines its treatment of "Woman" to the following list: "Woman accuses husband of preferring his friend to her; demands that lover kill his best friend; falls in love with wooer for friend; recognizes prior rights of friendship; resents being given to lover's friend; woman's curiosity leads to broken friendship and tragedy" (pp. 469–76).
29. See Jonathan Culler, "Apostrophe," in *The Pursuit of Signs: Semiotics, Literature, Deconstruction* (Ithaca, NY and London: Cornell University Press, 1981), pp. 135–54.
30. According to several critics who have looked at the manuscripts, William Cavendish wrote parts of the play, including much of Madame Mediator's speech.
31. Rosenthal, *Playwrights and Plagiarists in Early Modern England*, p. 96.
32. See also *The Blazing World*, where Cavendish imagines a platonic union between her beloved Empress and herself within the confines of the body of the Duke.
33. Cavendish, *The Presence*, in *Plays, Never Before Printed*, p. 80.
34. Cavendish, *Assaulted and Pursued Chastity* from *Nature's Pictures* (London: 1656) in *The Blazing World and Other Writings*, ed. Kate Lilley (New York and London: Penguin, 1994), p. 49.
35. In *Whores of Babylon*, Dolan explores the possibility that during Henrietta Maria's reign as queen consort, "some Catholics were able to advocate, perhaps even experience, women's command and women's community, however briefly" (p. 102).
36. *Letters From Orinda to Poliarchus* (London: 1705) (Letter #13, July 30, 1662), p. 58. Poliarchus was the pastoral name for Philips's closest friend at court, Charles Cotterell, Master of Ceremonies to Charles II, whom she tried to marry to Anne Owen after Anne was widowed at age twenty-one.

37. Philip Webster Souers, *The Matchless Orinda* (Cambridge, MA: Harvard University Press, 1931).
38. For treatments of Philips as seventeenth-century poet and cultural figure, see Elizabeth Hageman, "The Matchless Orinda," in *Women Writers of the Renaissance and Reformation*, ed. Katharina Wilson (Athens: University of Georgia Press, 1987), pp. 566–608; Dorothy Merwin, "Women Becoming Poets: Katherine Philips, Aphra Behn, Anne Finch," *ELH: English Literary History* 57:2 (1990), 335–55; Kate Lilley, "True State Within: Women's Elegy 1640–1740," in *Women, Writing, History, 1640–1740* eds. Isobel Grundy and Susan Wiseman (London: Batsford, 1992), pp. 73–92; and Paula McDowell, "Consuming Women: The Life of the 'Literary Lady' as Popular Culture in Eighteenth-Century England," *Genre* 26:2–3 (1993): 219–52.
39. For readings of Philips and female homoeroticism, see Wahl, *Invisible Relations*, chapter 3; Andreadis, "The Sapphic-Platonics of Katherine Philips, 1632–1664"; Elaine Hobby, "Katherine Philips: Seventeenth-Century Lesbian Poet," in *What Lesbians Do In Books*, eds. Elaine Hobby and Chris White (London: The Women's Press, 1991), pp. 183–204, and *Virtue of Necessity: English Women's Writing, 1646–1688* (London: Virago Press, 1988), pp. 128–42; Celia Easton, "Excusing the Breach of Nature's Laws: The Discourse of Denial and Disguise in Katherine Philips' Friendship Poetry," *Restoration* 14 (1990): 1–14; Mary Libertin, "Female Friendship in Women's Verse: Towards a New Theory of Female Poetics," *Women's Studies* 9:3 (1982): 291–308; Ellen Moody, "Orinda, Rosania, Lucasia *et aliae*: Towards a New Edition of the Works of Katherine Philips," *Philological Quarterly* 66:3 (1987): 325–54; Arlene Stiebel, "Not Since Sappho: The Erotic in Poems of Katherine Philips and Aphra Behn," in Summers, ed., *Homosexuality in Renaissance and Enlightenment England*, pp. 153–73, and "Subversive Sexuality: Masking the Erotic in Poems by Katherine Philips and Aphra Behn," in Summers and Pebworth, eds., *Renaissance Discourses of Desire*, pp. 223–36. Two recent dissertations focus almost exclusively on the homoeroticism of Philips's poetry: Susan Hardebeck, "'If Soules No Sexes Have . . .': Women, Convention and Negotiation in the Poetry of Katherine Philips" (Ph.D. dissertation, Northern Illinois University, 1996); and Jennifer Lange, "'Hearts Thus Intermixed Speak': Erotic 'Friendship' in the Poems of Katherine Philips" (Ph.D. dissertation, Bowling Green State University, 1995).
40. Virginia Jackson, "Dickinson's Figure of Address," in *Dickinson and Audience*, eds. Martin Orzech and Robert Weisbuch (Ann Arbor: University of Michigan Press, 1996), pp. 77–103, contests "the definition of lyric poetry as privacy gone private" (p. 78) by examining the structure of address in Emily Dickinson's poetry, "in which saying 'I' can stand for saying 'you,' in which the poet's solitude stands in for the solitude of the individual reader – a self-address so absolute that every self can identify it as his own" (p. 79). She argues that this logic of address, which "converts the isolated 'I' into the universal 'we' by bypassing the mediation of any particular 'you'" (p. 80) is in fact a product of "post-Romantic theories of the lyric" (p. 81).
41. See, for instance, Susan Stewart, "Preface to a Lyric History," in *The Uses of Literary History*, ed. Marshall Brown (Durham, NC: Duke University Press, 1995), pp. 199–218, who attempts to "think dialectically regarding relations between lyric

and history by paying attention to lyric as a structure of thought mediating the particular and the general" (p. 200). Virginia Jackson and Yopie Prins in "Lyrical Studies," *Victorian Literature and Culture* 27:2 (1999): 521–30, have suggested that Cultural Studies has avoided the lyric because "lyrics have been misunderstood as the personal subjective utterances of historical subjects" which are instead "performative effect(s)" (p. 529). See also Prins, *Victorian Sappho*; I thank Yopie Prins for discussing with me the critical tradition of the lyric subject, voice, personification, and identification. For previous work that deconstructs the conflations between voice, persona, and author as formal, linguistic properties of the lyric, see Jonathan Culler, "The Modern Lyric: Generic Continuity and Critical Practice," in *The Comparative Perspective on Literature: Approaches to Theory and Practice*, eds. Clayton Koelb and Susan Noakes (Ithaca, NY and London: Cornell University Press, 1988), pp. 284–99; Barbara Johnson, *The Critical Difference: Essays in the Contemporary Rhetoric of Reading* (Baltimore: Johns Hopkins University Press, 1980); and the following essays in *Lyric Poetry: Beyond New Criticism*, eds. Chaviva Hošek and Patricia Parker (Ithaca, NY and London: Cornell University Press, 1985): Herbert F. Tucker, "Dramatic Monologue and the Overhearing of Lyric," pp. 226–43, Jonathan Culler, "Changes in the Study of the Lyric," pp. 38–54, and Paul de Man, "Lyrical Voice in Contemporary Theory," pp. 55–72.

42. Joel Fineman, *Shakespeare's Perjured Eye* (Berkeley and Los Angeles: University of California Press, 1986); and *The Subjectivity Effect in Western Literary Tradition*. In Fineman's account of poetic subjectivity, insofar as it is "[b]uilt up on or out of the loss of itself, its identity defined as its difference from itself, a hole opens up within the whole of poetic first-person self-presence. This 'hole' within the 'whole' ... inserts into the poet a space of personal interiority, a palpable syncope, that justifies and warrants poetic introspection. This accounts for the strong personal affect of Shakespeare's lyric persona, what is called its 'depth'" (*The Subjectivity Effect*, p. 111).

43. Fineman argues that Shakespeare's sonnets progress from visionary idealization and homologous attraction in the epideictic poems to the young man to linguistic doubleness and heterogenous desire in the poems addressed to the "dark lady." This movement from an admiring sameness to a denigrated difference is read as a developmental transition, with the dark lady poems installing not only a novel Shakespearean subjectivity, but "the dominant and canonical version in our literary tradition of literary subjectivity per se" (*The Subjectivity Effect*, p. 105).

44. Paula Blank, "Comparing Sappho to Philaenis: John Donne's 'Homopoetics,'" *PMLA* 110 (1995): 358–68. The specular similitude of Philips would thus seem more akin to the homogenizing visual imagery that pervades the "ascetic" homosexual desire which Fineman reads in Shakespeare's sonnets to the young man; but Fineman would, I think, argue that such homopoetic desire, caught, as it is, in the terms of specularity, is debarred from enacting a novel subjectivity. My argument here counters Fineman's dismissal of eroticism from the purview of Shakespeare's homoerotic poetry, an issue I have addressed in more detail in "Sex Without Issue: Sodomy, Reproduction, and Signification in Shakespeare's Sonnets," in Schiffer, ed., *Shakespeare's Sonnets*, pp. 431–52.

45. Usually translated as "On Friendship," the Penguin edition of *The Complete Essays* translates "*De l'amitié*" as "On affectionate relationships," pp. 205–19, citation

p. 210. The inserted [A] and [C] refer to the original editions of 1580 and 1592/5. My understanding of the erotic energies animating the texts of Montaigne is much indebted to Jeffrey Masten's analysis of what he calls their "language of equitable jouissance" in *Textual Intercourse*, p. 35.
46. Montaigne, "*De l'amitié*," pp. 213 and 212.
47. *Ibid.*, p. 209.
48. *Ibid.*
49. Bray, *The Friend*.
50. Montaigne, "*De l'amitié*," p. 210.
51. Feminist scholarship is just beginning to excavate these alliances; see Frye and Robertson, eds., *Maids and Mistresses, Cousins and Queens*; Crawford and Gowing, eds., *Women's Worlds in Seventeenth-Century England*; and Crawford and Mendleson, eds., *Women in Early Modern England*.
52. The chapter "Of Amity, and the love of Inclination, and Election" in *The Compleat Woman* (1639) diagnoses the dangers of amity in remarkably ungendered terms. *A Discourse of Friendship* (1667), composed by the portrait painter Mary Beale for her friend Elizabeth Tillotson, explores the possibility of turning one's husband into one's friend.
53. As Souers explains,

> Her family and her friends were two different parts of her life; they represented two irreconcilable points of view, and, what is even worse, two political parties. With a husband who was one of Cromwell's tools, an uncle who was a zealous dissenting minister, an aunt who was the wife of Oliver St. John, and a mother who was the wife of Philip Skippon, she was joined indissolubly to the Parliamentarians. Yet her friends were all Royalists. Lucasia was allied to the Owens, who suffered much in the early years of the war; Rosania was the wife of a man whose honors after the Restoration were too numerous to have been bestowed on a supporter of the Commonwealth; Cartwright was an out-and-out Cavalier, and so were Lawes and Birkenhead, Vaughn and Taylor. (*The Matchless Orinda*, p. 79)

54. *Poems (1667) By Katherine Philips*, Intro. Travis Dupriest (Delmar, NY: Scholars' Facsimiles, 1992); all subsequent citations are from this edition. The 1664 unauthorized edition included 74 poems; the 1667 edition, which includes 116 poems and five translations, was entitled *Poems By the most deservedly Admired Mrs. Katherine Philips The Matchless Orinda. To which is added Monsieur Corneille's Pompey & Horace, Tragedies. With several other Translations out of French.*
55. Montaigne, "*De l'amitié*," pp. 211–12.
56. Wahl, *Invisible Relations*, p. 147.
57. "Friendship's Mystery: To My Dearest Lucasia."
58. Warren L. Chernaik, *The Poetry of Limitation: A Study of Edmund Waller* (New Haven and London: Yale University Press, 1968), p. 61.
59. Wahl, *Invisible Relations*, p. 156.
60. Barash, *English Women's Poetry*, pp. 55–100; citation p. 73. Comparing manuscript versions to published lyrics, Barash attempts to place some distance between Philips and her poetic persona, and traces changes in the poet's conception of friendship over the course of her career, as the friend-as-political-ally becomes the confidante who becomes the woman-with-whom-one-is-in-love. Her reading reveals less a trajectory of "the love affair" than an astute articulation of the

differences between the poems addressed to Lucasia and Rosania: "The relationship with Lucasia evolves more ritualistically than the relationship to Rosania, and is contrasted with rather than mapped onto heterosexual conventions of courtly love" (pp. 70–71). As this final clause suggests, however, one problem with Barash's otherwise insightful analysis is that she views Orinda under the guise of the male courtier, reading all of the poems as if they are addressed from a male poet to female beloved – unless and until something in the poem, like a female pronoun, gives the homoeroticism away. Assuming that male impersonation is the only available poetic stance, Barash reinscribes female–female eroticism as pseudo-heterosexual. Caught between respect for historical alterity and an under-theorized notion of *lesbian* possibility, Barash says "[this] is not to say that Katherine Philips was not in love with Anne Owen, or that that is not a question that matters. But it is important to situate relationships between women in terms of the social codes within which they would have had meaning to the participants" (p. 78). Barash implies that "in love with" a woman would not have been intelligible to Philips, forgetting that Orinda treats her friendships *as* love affairs which surpass marriage in their intensity. The homoerotic readings of both Barash and Wahl rely on the narrative implicit in the manuscript versions of the poems.

61. *Ibid.*, p. 92.
62. *Ibid.*, p. 93.
63. This pressure to choose heterosexuality is analyzed by Theresa Braunschneider's chapter on the "reformed coquette" of eighteenth-century fiction in her University of Michigan Ph.D. dissertation," Maidenly Amusements (2002).
64. Wahl, *Invisible Relations*, p. 152.
65. Barash, *English Women's Poetry*, pp. 98–99.
66. Wahl, *Invisible Relations*, p. 158.
67. Barash, *English Women's Poetry*, p. 99.
68. *Ibid.*
69. The concepts of coding, masking, and disguise are present in many of the essays cited above; see, in particular, Hobby, "Katherine Philips"; Stiebel, "Not Since Sappho" and "Subversive Sexuality"; and Easton, "Excusing the Breach of Nature's Laws."
70. Although our positions are very similar, there is an important difference between my reading of Philips's verse as a "hinge" and Wahl's construction of Philips as occupying "a peculiarly liminal position" (p. 168). Because she views the importation of French pornography and medical texts after the Restoration as decisive in changing the discourse about sexual relations among women, Wahl views Philips's poetry as less of an agent in that change than I do.
71. For a useful reading of Philo-Philippa's poem, see David Robinson's Ph.D. dissertation, "To Boldly Go Where No Man Has Gone Before: The Representation of Lesbianism in Mid-Seventeenth and Early Eighteenth-Century British and French Literature" (University of California, Berkeley, 1998).
72. *Collection of the Most Choice and Private Poems, lampoons &c, from the withdrawing of the late King James 1688 to the year 1701, collected by a person of quality* (Brotherton Collection of Manuscript Verse, Leeds Library).
73. *The Ladies Dictionary*, pp. 196–97. See also Thomas Blount, *The Academy of Eloquence* (London: 1670), whose entry on "friendship" reads thus: "As Passion hath well been said to be Friendship run mad; so Friendship may be properly stiled

Sober Passion, as having all the spirit and cordiality of the wine of love, without the offensive fumes and vapors of it."

74. Lanser, "Queer to Queer," n.p.
75. Ballaster, "'The Vices of Old Rome Revived,'" p. 31. In "Separating the Inseparables: Female Friendship and Its Discontents in Eighteenth-Century France," *Eighteenth-Century Studies* 32:2 (1998–99): 215–31, Christine Roulston similarly argues that by the mid-eighteenth century in France, the notion of "inseparable friendships" between women had become a considerable focus of anxiety. Whereas romantic friendship "was a legitimate social paradigm for women of the aristocracy and the bourgeoisie, it was also one that could be delegitimated at strategic moments" (p. 217). Charting the use of the term "inseparable" to describe female friends in the novels of Rousseau and Laclos, as well as in the revolutionary obscenity directed against Marie-Antoinette, Roulston argues that the meaning of female inseparability changed once women became powerful participants in the public sphere.
76. Edmund Waller, *Poems &c.* (London: 1645), pp. 41–42. There are over twenty "Sacharissa" poems, most of them considered poems of actual courtship. See "Beauty's Sovereignty: Waller's Cavalier Lyrics," in Chernaik's *The Poetry of Limitation*, pp. 52–114. This particular poem is little discussed in scholarship on Waller, whose work is mostly considered in terms of his courtly panegyric and Cavalier *carpe diem* lyrics.
77. According to the moralizing seventeenth-century mythographer, Alexander Ross, the doves who draw Venus's chariot "shew the sincerity and want of gall, quarrelling, or malice in love." See Glenn, *A Critical Edition of Alexander Ross's 1647 Mystagogus Poeticus*, p. 55.
78. "On the Friendship between two Ladies. Words out of Waller, Sett by Mr. W. I," in *Mercurius Musicus: Or, The Monthly Collection of New Teaching Songs* (London: Henry Playford, 1699). I thank Amanda Eubanks Winkler for this reference. Many of Waller's lyrics were set to music by Henry Lawes, which gave them a far greater circulation than they would otherwise have had.
79. A similar poem, circulating in France in the early seventeenth century, "*Deux belles s'ayment tendrement*" by Saint-Pavin, a French libertine poet, constructs female homoeroticism as self-deluded, insufficient, and wasteful:

> Two beauties love each other tenderly,
> They have an interest one for the other,
> And from the same dart which wounds them
> They suffer equally.
> Without complaining about their torment
> Both of them sigh ceaselessly,
> Sometimes the lover plays the mistress,
> Sometimes the mistress is the lover;
> Whatever they do to please one another,
> Their hearts cannot be satisfied,
> They waste their best days;
> Innocents who delude themselves
> Search in vain in their loves
> For the pleasures that they refuse us.   (translation by Adriane Stewart)

As Wahl notes in her reading of this poem, the final line "serves to undermine . . . the comforting assertion of the essential insufficiency of lesbian desire by betraying an underlying anxiety that lesbian sexuality constitutes a rebuff to male sexual potency" (*Invisible Relations*, p. 63).

80. R. [Robert] and J. Dodsley, *Collection of Poems in Six Volumes by Several Hands* (London: J. Hughs, 1758), vol. V, p. 275. This poem was included in the manuscript, "A Collection of verses upon several occasions by several hands, begun March 26th 1732."
81. Delarivier Manley, *The New Atalantis*, ed. Rosalind Ballaster (New York: Penguin, 1992), p. 154.
82. *Ibid.*, p. 161.
83. " An Ode to Myra," was included in the first edition *of The Toast, An Epic Poem in Four Books. Written in Latin by Frederick Scheffer, Done into English by Peregrine ODonald, Esq.* (Dublin: 1732), pp. 82–86; citation p. 53. For a summary of the entire poem, a key to the persons represented, and the personal motivations of its author, see David Greenwood, *William King, Tory and Jacobite* (Oxford: Clarendon Press, 1969), pp. 40–73. Although King accuses the Countess of performing unnatural acts with Lady Allen, it is worth speculating whether his "little A———n" could also be a veiled reference to Queen Anne.
84. *Satan's Harvest Home*, p. 18.
85. Nussbaum, *Torrid Zones*, p. 142.
86. Montagu's letters were written 1717–18, but published in 1763.
87. *Satan's Harvest Home*, pp. 51–52.
88. *The Sapho-An. An heroic poem of three cantos, in the Ovidian stile, describing the pleasures which the fair sex enjoy with each other. Found amongst the papers of a lady of quality, a great promoter of Jacobitism* (London: 1749).
89. Andreadis, "Early Modern Sappho," p. 117.
90. R. Fletcher, *Ex otio Negotium. Or, Martiall his epigrams Translated. With Sundry Poems and Fancies* (London: 1656).
91. "A Dialogue Between Cleonarium and Leaena," in *The Dialogues of the Courtizans*, in *Lucian's Works Translated from the Greek*, trans. Ferrand Spence, 4 vols. (London: 1684–85), vol. IV, pp. 304–06.
92. *Tractatus de Hermarphroditis: Or, A Treatise of Hermaphrodites* (London: 1718) was printed by E. Curll in Fleet-street, a publisher prosecuted by the government for obscenity. According to Susan Lanser and Theresa Braunschneider (personal communication), there is no compelling reason to accept the common attribution of Giles Jacob, as it is very different from his other published work. The text is bound with Johann Heinrich Meibom's *A treatise of the use of flogging in venereal affairs*, and includes an engraving of a woman flogging a kneeling man, his buttocks prominently on display, while another woman, seated on her bed, fondles her own breast. Meibom's *Treatise* is listed in the National Union Catalogue as having its first (Latin) edition, *De Usu Flaborum*, in 1629. According to Roger Thompson in *Unfit for Modest Ears*, this treatise on flagellation – which advocates the theory that heat in the loins produces erections (hence the usefulness of flogging) – was popular from the early seventeenth century, reaching its height of popularity in the late the eighteenth century in Paris.
93. In his opening, the author defends himself against charges of obscenity in language drawn from anatomical investigation: "as it is my immediate Business to trace every

Particular for an ample Dissertation on the Nature of *Hermaphrodites*, (which obliges me to a frequent Repetition of the Names of the Parts employ'd in the Business of Generation) so, I hope, I shall not be charg'd with Obscenity, since in all Treatises of this Kind it is impossible to finish any one Head compleatly, without pursuing the Methods of Anatomical Writings," *Tractatus de Hermaphroditis*, p. 2.

94. *Ibid.*, pp. 17–18.
95. Brantôme, *Lives of Fair and Gallant Ladies*, p. 131.
96. Aphra Behn, *Poems Upon Several Occasions* (London: 1684), pp. 33–44; and *Lycidus, or the Lover in Fashion* (London: 1688), pp. 175–76.
97. For these different discourses about the hermaphrodite, see Stallybrass and Jones, "Fetishizing Gender: Constructing the Hermaphrodite in Renaissance Europe," in Epstein and Straub, eds., *Body Guards*.
98. Roberta C. Martin, "'Beauteous Wonder of a Different Kind': Aphra Behn's Destabilization of Sexual Categories," *College English* 61:2 (1998): 192–210; citation pp. 207–08. Barash likewise argues that Behn's speaker transgresses gender boundaries, turning "a grammatical either/or into a sexual both/and" in *English Women's Poetry* (p. 129), but disputes the attempt by Bernard Duyfhuizen ("'That which I dare not name': Aphra Behn's 'The Willing Mistress,'" *ELH: English Literary History* 58 [1991]: 63–82) to draw further homoerotic potential out of Behn's poetry; whereas Duyfhuizen argues that this ostensibly heterosexual love poem exists in a variant that is frankly homoerotic, Barash asserts that "there is no way to read female–female erotic address from the poem itself" (p. 125).
99. Wahl makes the point that the "singular 'I' who opens the poem" expands to a plural "we" that extends "the possibility of lesbian desire to a community of women" (*Invisible Relations*, p. 57).
100. Quoted in Sara Heller Mendelson, *The Mental World of Stuart Women: Three Studies* (Brighton: Harvester Press, 1987), p. 176.
101. See Ruth Salvaggio, "Aphra Behn's Love: Fiction, Letters, and Desire," in *Rereading Aphra Behn: History, Theory, and Criticism*, ed. Heidi Hutner (Charlottesville and London: University Press of Virginia, 1993), pp. 253–70.
102. Behn, *Lycidus*, pp. 161–63.
103. James Parsons, *A Mechanical and Critical Enquiry into the Nature of Hermaphrodites* (1741). According to Donoghue, *Passions Between Women*, the edition of 1745 includes a fold-out featuring "a huge centrefold-style engraving of the vulva of a 'hermaphroditical' Angolan woman sold into slavery in America" (p. 34).
104. Ballaster, "'The Vices of Old Rome Revived,'" p. 19.
105. Braunschneider, "The Macroclitoride, the Tribade, and the Woman," perceptively locates Parsons's "tolerance" within the shift to two incommensurate genders and suggests that the repudiation of the hermaphrodite and the unveiling of the macroclitoride set the stage for the further medical elision of female erotic pleasure.
106. See also Giovanni Bianchi, *The True History and Adventures of Catherine Vizzani*, probably translated by John Cleland (London: 1751), which makes clear that women intent on erotic adventure with other women are quite typical, both psychologically and anatomically: "The *Clitoris* of this young Woman was not pendulous, nor of any extraordinary Size, as the Account from Rome made it, and as it is said, to be that of all those Females, who among the *Greeks*, were called *Tribades*, or who followed the Practices of *Sappho*" (pp. 43–44). The title page continues: *A YOUNG Gentlewoman a Native of Rome, who for many Years past in the Habit*

of a Man; was killed for an Amour with a young Lady; and found on Dissection, a true Virgin. With curious Anatomical REMARKS *on the Nature and Existence of the* HYMEN. See Carolyn Woodward, "'My Heart so Wrapt': Lesbian Disruptions in Eighteenth-Century British Fiction," *Signs: Journal of Women in Culture and Society* 18:4 (1993): 838–65.

107. For social historians' views, see Dolan, *Domestic Familiars*, pp. 17–18.
108. See the diary of Anne Lister, *I Know My Own Heart: The Diaries of Anne Lister 1791–1840*, ed. Helena Whitebread (London: Virago Press, 1988). Excerpts from Lister's diaries also have been reprinted (New York: New York University Press, 1992). On Lister, see Anna Clark, "Anne Lister's Construction of Lesbian Identity," *Journal of the History of Sexuality* 7:1 (1996): 23–50; Castle, *The Apparitional Lesbian*; and Halberstam, *Female Masculinity*.
109. Jagose's remarks on Lister are particularly astute: "Nowhere is the ambivalent nature of female friendship as it pitches between purity and perversion more productively exploited than when Lister, that imperturbable sexual pragmatist, feigns the former in order to cinch the latter" (Introduction, *Inconsequence*, n.p.).
110. We can also see the lineaments of this shift in Jane Barker's miscellaneous romance, *A Patch-Work Screen for the Ladies* (1723). Barker depicts the choice of a woman spurned by her husband to remain loyal to her husband's female servant as "unaccountable"; the judgment of unaccountability seems based as much on the transgressions of class as on affective bonds between women. See *The Galesia Trilogy and Selected Manuscript Poems of Jane Barker*, ed. Carol Shiner Wilson (Oxford and New York: Oxford University Press, 1997); and Kathryn King, "The Unaccountable Wife and Other Tales of Female Desire in Jane Barker's *A Patchwork Screen for the Ladies*," *The Eighteenth Century* 35:2 (1994): 155–72.
111. Sir Matthew Hale, *The Primitive Origination of Mankind, considered and examined according to the light of nature* (London: 1677), p. 344.
112. Bulwer, *Anthropometamorphosis*, p. 55.
113. Jacques Guillemeau, *The French Chirurgerye, or all the manualle operations of Chirurgerye*, trans. A. M. (Dorte: 1597), p. 50.
114. Oswaldus Gabelhouer (Oswald Gabelkover), *The Boock of Physicke*, trans. A. M. (Dorte: 1599), p. 102.

8. THE QUEST FOR ORIGINS, EROTIC SIMILITUDE, AND THE MELANCHOLY OF *LESBIAN* IDENTIFICATION

1. Donoghue, *Passions Between Women*, p. 24.
2. An influential argument against the use of psychoanalysis is articulated by Stephen Greenblatt, "Psychoanalysis and Renaissance Culture," in Parker and Quint, eds., *Literary Theory/Renaissance Texts*, pp. 210–24. For sophisticated defenses of the applicability of psychoanalysis, see Dollimore, *Sexual Dissidence*; Timothy Murray and Alan K. Smith, eds., *Repossessions: Psychoanalysis and the Phantasms of Early Modern Culture* (Minneapolis and London: University of Minnesota Press, 1998); and Carla Mazzio and Douglas Trevor, eds., *Historicism, Psychoanalysis and Early Modern Culture* (London and New York: Routledge, 2000).
3. On Freud's use of identification in the psychoanalysis of homosexuality, see my *Desire & Anxiety*; Weeks, *Sexuality and its Discontents*; Charles Bernheimer

and Claire Kahane, eds., *In Dora's Case: Freud–Hysteria–Feminism* (New York: Columbia University Press, 1985); Fuss, *Identification Papers*; Butler, *Bodies that Matter*; and Teresa de Lauretis, *The Practice of Love: Lesbian Sexuality and Perverse Desire* (Bloomington and Indianapolis: Indiana University Press, 1994).

4. At the allegorical level of character, the promise of sex transformation unifies Venus (who promises phallic pleasures) with Diana (chaste love).
5. Sandys, *Ovid's Metamorphosis*, p. 421. The Oxford verse translation, *Metamorphoses*, trans. A.D. Melville, intro. and notes E. J. Kenney (New York: Oxford University Press, 1986), amplifies the importance of a shared education: "Equal in age they were, equal in looks, / And both from the same masters had received / The first instruction of their early years; / And so it was that both their simple hearts/ Love visited alike and both alike / Were smitten – but their hopes how different!" (p. 221).
6. Masten, *Textual Intercourse*, p. 51.
7. As Laurie Shannon points out,

   Emilia's narrative does not suggest that likeness was the source of the friendship. Instead, sameness seems to have been, in a way, its goal, as the two copy one another, adopting the other's patterns and striving for resemblance. Flowers, bodily ornament – conventional female signs – are circulating, here, between women themselves. Even the casual actions and careless habits of dress of one become the serious ambition of the other. ("Emilia's Argument," p. 671)

   In addition, as Peter Stallybrass notes ("Shakespeare, the Individual, and the Text," in Grossberg, Nelson, and Treichler, eds., *Cultural Studies*), Emilia's imagery, "(the cradle, the phoenix, the plucked flower) conjures up the antithesis of the innocence she proclaims" (p. 605).

8. See Fredric Jameson, "Marxism and Historicism," in *The Ideologies of Theory: Essays 1971–1986, Vol 2: The Syntax of History* (Minneapolis: University of Minnesota Press, 1988).
9. Judith Bennett, "Theoretical Issues: Confronting Continuity," *Journal of Women's History* 9:3 (1997): 73–94; citation p. 83. Bennett credits Sandy Bardsley for the term "patriarchal equilibrium."
10. *Ibid.*, pp. 75 and 82.
11. Brooten, *Love Between Women*, pp. 23–24.
12. *Ibid.*, p. 24.
13. Halperin, "Lesbian Historiography Before the Name?" citations pp. 562 and 564.
14. *Ibid.*, p. 573.
15. Fradenburg and Freccero, *Premodern Sexualities*, p. xviii.
16. *Ibid.*, p. xv.
17. *Ibid.*, p. xix.
18. *Ibid.*
19. *Ibid.*, p. xvii.
20. *Ibid.*, p. xix.
21. *Ibid.*, pp. xvii–xviii.
22. Dinshaw, *Getting Medieval*, p. 34.
23. *Ibid.*, p. 35.

24. *Ibid.*, p. 39.
25. Insofar as Donoghue multiplies her quest for origins, she implies that history helps us to value the diversity of gender styles and erotic practices both in the past and present. The problem is that she implies that multiple origins can compensate for the lack of continuity and affinity among contemporary *lesbians*. This impulse, of course, is not limited to *lesbians*. The emotional stakes in the search for identificatory models are aptly expressed by filmmaker Derek Jarman, whose attempts to intervene in the normalizing narratives of the British cultural past could be taken as a queer desideratum: "Without our past our future cannot be reflected, the past is our mirror." Open letter to *The Independent*, May 20, 1993, protesting against the planned closure of Bart's hospital, where he was being treated for HIV-related conditions; cited by Kate Chedgzoy, *Shakespeare's Queer Children: Sexual Politics and Contemporary Culture* (Manchester: Manchester University Press, 1995), p. 216, note 1.
26. "Sapho to Philaenis" probably was written in the 1590s; it circulated in manuscript and was published in the posthumous edition of Donne's *Poems* in 1633. I quote from the John T. Shawcross edition of *The Complete Poetry of John Donne* (Garden City, NY: Doubleday, 1967).
27. Janel Mueller, "Lesbian Erotics: The Utopian Trope of Donne's 'Sapho to Philaenis,'" in Summers, ed. *Homosexuality in Renaissance and Enlightenment England*, pp. 103–34 (citation p. 104), recasts some material from her earlier "Troping Utopia: Donne's Brief for Lesbianism in 'Sapho to Philaenis,'" in *Sexuality and Gender in Early Modern Europe: Institutions, Texts, Images*, ed. James Grantham Turner (Cambridge: Cambridge University Press, 1993), pp. 182–207.
28. Elizabeth Harvey, "Ventriloquizing Sappho: Ovid, Donne, and the Erotics of the Feminine Voice," *Criticism* 31:2 (1989): 115–38:

    what appears to be Donne's generous bestowing of language and independence on Sappho, in direct contrast to Ovid's violations of her, turns out to be an act of colonization... the otherness of a classical text (Ovid's) and the otherness of woman (Sappho) are domesticated and re-shaped into an image of the self, a process that is mediated both by ventriloquism and by voyeurism. (p. 126)

    James Holstun opened the question of male poets' appropriation of the female voice via Donne's construction of *lesbianism* as a "tautology," a "mute autocosm" in "'Will You Rent Our Ancient Love Asunder?': Lesbian Elegy in Donne, Marvell, and Milton."
29. Blank, "Comparing Sappho to Philaenis: John Donne's 'Homopoetics,'" rigorously takes up the terms of similitude in the service of a Lacanian reading of desire. Dismissing Holstun's argument about the tautological idiom of the poem as a projection of autoeroticism onto *lesbianism*, she argues that "difference emerges as the only inviolable, invariable feature of erotic experience with an other" (p. 359). Sappho's desire is doomed to failure because it is based on a homopoetics that rhetorically creates sameness through comparisons, a sameness that cannot be sustained, even within the poem. This interpretation of the poem, satisfying on the linguistic level, seems insufficiently attentive to its own political context, for in attempting to resist the equation between sameness and narcissism, Blank's privileging of a Lacanian invocation of the other elides the specificity of *lesbian*

desire. Barbara Correll, "Symbolic Economies and Zero-Sum Erotics: Donne's 'Sapho to Philaenis,'" *ELH: English Literary History* 62:3 (1995): 487–507, comes close to Blank in asserting that the "'failure' that Donne sees paralyzing women's same-sex love and undermining signification . . . is also the failure of difference that haunts other poetic works in the Donne canon" (p. 490). For both Correll and Blank, the poem's crisis of signification is primarily a matter of writing, for which *lesbianism* is simply a useful signifier. The attempt to link Donne's lyric to other poems negotiating the play of sameness and difference is also the motive of C. Annette Grisé's "Depicting Lesbian Desire: Contexts for John Donne's 'Sapho to Philaenis,'" *Mosaic* 29:4 (1996): 41–57.

30. Wahl partially throws in her lot with Mueller, arguing that the poem "conveys a deeply rooted ambivalence toward lesbian desire, expressing both an attraction to its utopian promise of plenitude as well as the fear that this promise may prove an illusion and dissolve into barren autoeroticism" (*Invisible Relations*, p. 53). In "The Sapphic Voice in Donne's 'Sapho to Philaenis,'" *Renaissance Discourses of Desire*, eds. Summers and Pebworth, pp. 63–76, Stella Revard likewise judges Donne as "sympathetic," having made the attempt to "fathom the love of woman for woman that inspired" Sappho's lyrics by "looking through Sappho's eyes" (p. 76). The issue of male control over female subjectivity is the focus of Cecilia Infante in "Donne's Incarnate Muse and His Claim to Poetic Control in 'Sapho to Philaenis,'" in *Representing Women in Renaissance England*, eds. Claude Summers and Ted-Larry Pebworth (Columbia: University of Missouri Press, 1997), pp. 93–106. William West, in "Thinking with the Body: Sappho's 'Sappho to Philaenis,' Donne's 'Sappho to Philaenis,'" *Renaissance Papers* (1994): 67–83, asserts that Donne revalues as positive the female body, surface, and narcissism. Bruce Woodcock also finds of "Sapho to Philaenis" that "[u]nder the veil of female homoeroticism . . . is in fact an invitation to male narcissism or homoeroticism"; the poem "can be read as a surreptitious invitation to the male reader to *enjoy* himself by enjoying *himself*," in "'Anxious to amuse': Metaphysical Poetry and the Discourse of Renaissance Masculinity," in *Writing and the English Renaissance*, eds. William Zunder and Suzanne Trill (London: Longman, 1996), pp. 51–68; citation pp. 63–64.

31. *Wits Interpreter, The English Parnassus. Or, A sure Guide to those Admirable Accomplishments that compleat our English Gentry, in the most acceptable Qualifications of Discourse, or Writing. In which briefly the whole Mystery of those pleasing Witchcrafts of Eloquence and Love are made easie* (London: 1655), p. 46. I am grateful to Bruce Smith for alerting me to the existence of this poem, sending me a copy, and explaining what is known of its provenance. According to Smith, most of the poems that eventually made their way into print are to be found in many of the university manuscript anthologies, but this one is not. It is not cited in the first-line index of manuscripts in the Bodleian, Folger, Houghton, or British Libraries; and Adam Smyth's on-line index of poetry in miscellanies cites it as occurring only in *Wits Interpreter*.

32. Arthur F. Marotti, *Manuscript, Print, and the English Renaissance Lyric* (Ithaca, NY and London: Cornell University Press, 1995), p. 276. According to Marotti, *Wits Interpreter* "was aimed at a social and intellectual elite, and took satiric aim at the self-improvement books produced for the lower classes" (pp. 270–71).

33. See the *Norton Anthology of Literature by Women: The Tradition in English*, eds. Sandra Gilbert and Susan Gubar (New York: Norton, 1985); *The Penguin Book of Homosexual Verse*, ed. Stephen Coote (London: Penguin, 1983); *The New Oxford Book of Seventeenth-Century Verse*, ed. Alastair Fowler (Oxford: Oxford University Press, 1991); *The Penguin Book of Renaissance Verse*, eds. Norbrook and Wouduysen; *Chloe Plus Olivia: An Anthology of Lesbian Literature from the Seventeenth Century to the Present*, ed. Lillian Faderman (New York: Penguin, 1994); *Poems Between Women; Four Centuries of Love, Romantic Friendship, and Desire*, ed. Emma Donoghue (New York: Columbia University Press, 1997).
34. Elaine Hobby, "Katherine Philips: Seventeenth-Century Lesbian Poet," in Hobby and White, eds., *What Lesbians Do In Books*, pp. 183–204. For similar invocations of Philips as *lesbian*, see Andreadis, "The Sapphic Platonics of Katherine Philips, 1632–1664"; Arlene Stiebel, "Not Since Sappho: The Erotic Poems of Katherine Philips and Aphra Behn"; Faderman, *Surpassing the Love of Men*, pp. 65–73; and Donoghue, *Passions Between Women*, pp. 109–50.
35. Blank and Correll argue, for instance, that the tropes of Donne's heterosexual love poetry are congruent with the rhetorics of "Sapho to Philaenis"; I would argue, however, that even when heterosexual relations are described through similitude, the sexually differentiated body is figured as a necessary impediment to full isomorphism.
36. "Sapho to Philaenis," for instance, includes a recognition of difference that intrudes upon and momentarily disrupts the utopian fantasy of sameness desired by Sappho. The poem begins as a lament over not only lost love but lost poetic powers. It moves to the unhappy recognition that the beloved is not the self, but separate; interestingly enough, it uses the image of the mirror to figure that difference: "When I would kiss, tears dim mine eyes, and glasse." The similitude Sappho celebrates seems to be wishful thinking.
37. In the words of Yopie Prins (elucidating the deconstructive theories of Paul de Man and Jonathan Culler): "Lyric reading predicated on the figure of the voice creates the possibility of identification of and with a speaker, in order to defend against readings that could make lyric less intelligible, more resistant to the recuperation of a lyric subject," *Victorian Sappho*, p. 19.
38. Donald Stone, entry on "French Literature: French Literature Before the Nineteenth Century" in Summers, ed., *The Gay and Lesbian Literary Heritage*, p. 291.
39. By foregrounding the overdetermined nature of these poems, I am not dismissing scholarly efforts to find textual evidence of women's participation in the writing of *lesbian* love. Such archival work remains crucial to the compilation of a literary and cultural tradition; we need scholars attentive to a range of erotic valences combing the archives for texts that have passed unnoticed or unappreciated by earlier researchers. Nor do I mean to diminish the import of women's literary production or to suggest that lived experience does not influence literary creation. We cannot eliminate all references to authorial gender in our discussion of these poems if we aim to do justice to the meanings of *lesbianism*. At the same time, by de-emphasizing, at least momentarily, the coincidence of individual author and textual mode, by thinking less about the subject of the lyric and more about lyrical subjectivity, we can begin to understand better the terms by which *lesbian*

desire was granted cultural intelligibility. The impulse for my reading strategy is, precisely, strategic, motivated by the realization that, with only a very few exceptions (Anne Lister, perhaps, among them), individual women's biographies do not, at this point, provide us with much information about the meaning of *lesbianism* prior to the advent of erotic identities.

40. Catherine Belsey, *The Subject of Tragedy: Identity and Difference in Renaissance Drama* (London and New York: Methuen, 1985), p. 191.
41. Judith Butler, *Excitable Speech: A Politics of the Performative* (New York and London: Routledge, 1997), p. 161.
42. As Julia Creet remarks in "Anxieties of Identity: Coming Out and Coming Undone," in *Negotiating Lesbian and Gay Subjects*, eds. Monica Dorenkamp and Richard Henke (New York and London: Routledge, 1995), pp. 179–99, coming out is

    a process of signification, of naming or categorizing feelings that had previously existed. A single utterance will not suffice, for new situations demanding the revelation of identity are encountered constantly. The story of coming out is itself a narrative of development . . . and the repetitive act of coming out (or "being out") is performative, that is, it (re)creates and maintains identity, not just discloses it. (p. 182)

    Butler introduces an important caveat to this notion, however, in her discussion of the deployments of declarations of "coming out" in the context of the "Don't ask, don't tell" policy of the U. S. military: "The declaration that is 'coming out' is certainly a kind of act, but it does not fully constitute the referent to which it refers; indeed, *it renders homosexuality discursive, but it does not render discourse referential*" (*Excitable Speech*, p. 125).
43. Julie Abraham, "A Case of Mistaken Identity?" citation p. 36.
44. Sedgwick, *Epistemology of the Closet*, p. 3.
45. In "Fletcherian Tragicomedy, Cross-dressing, and the Constriction of Homoerotic Desire in Early Modern England," *Renaissance Drama* 26 (1995): 53–82, and "Homoeroticism, Discursive Change, and Politics: Reading 'Revolution' in Seventeenth-Century English Tragicomedy," *Medieval and Renaissance Drama in English* 9 (1997): 162–78, Nicholas Radel argues that Stuart tragicomedy functions as "prohibitory drama" that constructs a nascent division between male homoeroticism and heteroeroticism, and thus opens space for an ideology of the closet and homophobia.
46. Donoghue, *Passions Between Women*, p. 111.
47. Wahl, *Invisible Relations*, p. 117.
48. Richard Rambuss, *Closet Devotions* (Durham, NC and London: Duke University Press, 1997).
49. Holmes, "The Love of Other Women: Rich Chains and Sweet Kisses," suggests that women could mediate their homoerotic affiliations through Christ.
50. Steve Patterson, "The Bankruptcy of Homoerotic Amity in Shakespeare's *Merchant of Venice*," *Shakespeare Quarterly* 50:1 (1999): 9–32; citation p. 28.
51. Or if they do imply censorship, it is done in terms of Butler's reconfiguration of censorship as a continual foreclosure, that is, as a preemptive process that draws lines between permissible and impermissible speech, and hence "produces discursive regimes through the production of the unspeakable," *Excitable Speech*, p. 139.

52. In contrast to most critics who examine the trope of the mirror in Renaissance literature, my interest is not subjectivity *per se*, but the implication of the mirror in a discourse of homoerotic desire. Most critics focus on a Freudian, Lacanian, or Kristevan theory of primary narcissism, and by implication, the splitting of the subject in the mirror stage. Neglecting the implications of narcissism for object choice, they privilege instead issues of the ego, subjectivity, and gender. For the individual subject, the internal distance figured by the mirror is an enabling, even necessary, condition of identity formation. But for erotic relations, the mirror signifies just one among many possible modes of relation.
53. Sandys, *Ovid's Metamorphosis*, p. 160.
54. Robert Burton, *The Anatomy of Melancholy* (Oxford: 1624) (2nd edn.), p. 108.
55. Sigmund Freud, "On Narcissism: An Introduction" (1914), in *The Standard Edition of the Complete Psychological Works of Sigmund Freud*, ed. James Strachey, 24 vols. (London: Hogarth Press, 1953–1974), vol. XIV, pp. 73–102; citation p. 88.
56. See Freud, "The Psychogenesis of a Case of Female Homosexuality" (1920), *Standard Edition*, vol. XVIII, pp. 145–74; "Female Sexuality" (1931), *Standard Edition*, vol. XXI, pp. 221–43; "Femininity" (1933), *Standard Edition*, vol. XXII, pp. 112–35; "Fragment of an Analysis of a Case of Hysteria" (1905), *Standard Edition*, vol. VII, pp. 1–122.
57. See Chauncey, "From Sexual Inversion to Homosexuality."
58. For the extent to which the conflation of gender and sexuality continues to preoccupy clinical psychoanalysis, see Adria E. Schwartz, *Sexual Subjects: Lesbians, Gender, and Psychoanalysis* (New York and London: Routledge, 1998).
59. Jagose, "Irigaray and the Lesbian Body: Remedy and Poison," p. 35.
60. Roof, *A Lure of Knowledge*, p. 173.
61. *Ibid.*, p. 128.
62. Suzanne Raitt, *Vita and Virginia: The Work and Friendship of Vita Sackville-West and Virginia Woolf* (Oxford: Clarendon Press, 1993), p. 16.
63. Roof, *A Lure of Knowledge*, pp. 127–28.
64. Michael Warner, "Homo-Narcissism: or, Heterosexuality," in *Engendering Men: The Question of Male Feminist Criticism*, eds. Joseph Boone and Michael Cadden (London and New York: Routledge, 1990), pp. 190–206; citation p. 202.
65. Halperin, *One Hundred Years of Homosexuality*, p. 2.
66. Fuss, *Identification Papers*, p. 2.
67. *Ibid.*, p. 4.
68. *Ibid.*, p. 9. Fuss's salutary examination of identification is in the service of an engagement with identity politics, which she says "needs to come to terms with the complicated and meaningful ways that identity is continually compromised, imperiled, one might even say *embarrassed* by identification" (p. 10).
69. Freud, "Mourning and Melancholia" (1917), *Standard Edition*, vol. XIV, pp. 243–58; citation p. 244.
70. *Ibid.*, p. 245. The distinction between mourning and melancholy is attenuated in "The Ego and the Id" (1923), *Standard Edition*, vol. XIX, pp. 12–66, in which Freud returns to melancholia to examine the processes of identification by which the ego is constituted.
71. Freud, "Mourning and Melancholia," p. 246.
72. *Ibid.*, p. 245.
73. *Ibid.*, p. 249.

74. *Ibid.*, p. 253.
75. Nicolas Abraham and Maria Torok, *The Shell and the Kernel*, vol. I, ed., trans., intro. Nicholas T. Rand (Chicago and London: University of Chicago Press, 1994).
76. Writes Torok, *ibid.*:

    [I]ncorporation is born of a prohibition it sidesteps but does not actually transgress. The ultimate aim of incorporation is to recover, in secret and through magic, an object that, for one reason or another, evaded its own function: mediating the introjection of desires. Refusing both the object's and reality's verdict, incorporation is an eminently illegal act; it must hide from view along with the desire of introjection it masks; it must hide even from the ego . . . Installed in the place of the lost object, the incorporated object continues to recall the fact that something else was lost: the desire quelled by repression. Like a commemorative monument, the incorporated object betokens the place, the date, and the circumstances in which desires were banished from introjection: they stand like tombs in the life of the ego (p. 114). The magical "cure" by incorporation exempts the subject from the painful process of reorganization. When . . . we ingest the love-object we miss, this means that we *refuse to mourn* and that we shun the consequences of mourning even though our psyche is fully bereaved. Incorporation is the refusal to reclaim as our own the part of ourselves that we placed in what we lost; incorporation is the refusal to acknowledge the full import of the loss, a loss that, if recognized as such, would effectively transform us. In fine, incorporation is the refusal to introject loss. (p. 127)

77. Limits to the analogy I am making include the fact that the melancholy of *lesbian* identification does not stem from ambivalence as does melancholia, and thus does not involve the kind of self-reproach Freud diagnoses as central to this disorder; nor does the process of severing attachment to the lost object require the redirection of rage against it.
78. Martin Duberman, Martha Vicinus, and George Chauncey Jr., eds., *Hidden from History: Reclaiming the Gay and Lesbian Past* (New York: New American Library, 1989).
79. The importance of a second party "witnessing" a subject's trauma is a central insight as well of the cultural study of memory, which suggests that memory is as much a cultural as individual phenomenon. See Shoshana Felman and Dori Laub, eds., *Testimony: Crises of Witnessing in Literature, Psychoanalysis and History* (New York: Routledge, 1992), who argue that traumatic memories need to be legitimized and narratively integrated in order to lose their hold over the subject.
80. Butler, *The Psychic Life of Power*, p. 187.
81. Wendy Brown, *States of Injury: Power and Freedom in Late Modernity* (Princeton: Princeton University Press, 1995), p. 3.
82. *Ibid.*, p. 7.
83. *Ibid.*, pp. xii, 29, and ix.
84. Freud, "Mourning and Melancholia," p. 170.
85. In this I am inspired by Warner, "Homo-Narcissism: or, Heterosexuality," who demonstrates the conceptual contradictions inherent to the concept of homosexuality as narcissism.
86. Butler, *The Psychic Life of Power*, p. 139.
87. *Ibid.* I differ from Butler, however, insofar as she maps the constitution of gender directly onto the constitution of sexuality, arguing, via Freud, that the "heterosexual matrix" is that which *produces* gender: the constructions of femininity or

masculinity "proceed through the accomplishment of an always tenuous heterosexuality" (p. 135). Although she acknowledges that there are ways of experiencing gender and sexuality that "do not presume that gender is stabilized through the installation of a firm heterosexuality" (p. 136), her theory of gender subversion throughout depends on the assumption that gender is an effect of sexuality. Although she states her intent to invert the pervasive assumption that sexuality proceeds from and expresses gender, her prioritization of sexuality *as causal*, and thus her reinvigoration of a teleological mode of explanation, are not explained sufficiently.
88. Sedgwick, *Tendencies*, pp. 10–11.
89. I am invoking here the terminology of Abraham and Torok, who describe incorporation in terms of encorpsing and the crypt.
90. This conflation of identification and desire, axiomatic in the psychoanalytic understanding of *lesbianism*, is constitutive of homo-narcissism. Queer theorists have shown that Freud's conflation operates according to a specious logic in which homoerotic desire is aligned "naturally" with identification and similitude, while heterosexuality becomes the privileged signifier of desire and difference. See Leo Bersani, *The Freudian Body: Psychoanalysis and Art* (New York: Columbia University Press, 1986); Butler, *Bodies that Matter* and "Imitation and Gender Insubordination," in Fuss, ed., *Inside/Out*; Warner, "Homo-Narcissism: or, Heterosexuality," in Boone and Cadden, eds., *Engendering Men*; and Fuss, *Identification Papers*, p. 45.
91. This formulation was suggested to me by Theodore Leinwald, to whom I am grateful.

AFTERWORD

1. Although I have engaged at different points with this scholarship, a few more words may be said. In many respects, the relations between chaste female friendship and tribadism seem to correlate with what we know of male friendship and sodomy in the early modern period – with several important provisos. Whereas a discourse of sodomy had been available to the Christian West through the Catholic church since the late eleventh century, it was only after the reintroduction of a discourse of tribadism to Western Europe in the sixteenth century that the threat of tribadism was widely disseminated. Second, the social hierarchies that female friendship maintained were qualitatively different from those hierarchies that organized orderly bonds among men. Third, even at the end of the seventeenth century, an accusation of tribadism in England would have had little of the apocalyptic force, and probably would have set off none of the juridical mechanisms, of a public charge of male–male buggery. It also seems that one of the dominant patterns of male homoeroticism – age and status inequality – may not have figured centrally in women's erotic relations during this time. Much research is yet to be done on the erotic involvements between women of different social classes, but it appears that social and bodily hierarchies, while occasionally present, seem less definitive to the overall organization of female–female desire. In her study of the relations between mistresses and gentlewomen companions of the eighteenth century, Betty Rizzo argues that women as frequently played the role of domestic tyrant as benevolent friend. She also notes, however, that even for relationships

circumscribed by the economic inequalities of employer and "humble companion," it remains the case that "equality and altruism are ideals more attractive, even more imaginable, to people used to thinking of themselves as politically inferior rather than superior" (Betty Rizzo, *Companions Without Vows: Relationships Among Eighteenth-Century British Women* [Athens, GA and London: University of Georgia Press, 1994], pp. 1 and 23). The textual materials I have analyzed suggest that an expectation of equality informed most representations of female erotic liaisons.

2. Smith-Rosenberg, "The Female World of Love and Ritual."
3. Faderman, *Surpassing the Love of Men* and *Odd Girls and Twilight Lovers: A History of Lesbian Life in Twentieth Century America* (New York: Columbia University Press, 1991).
4. Marylynne Diggs, "Romantic Friends or a 'Different Race of Creatures'? The Representation of Lesbian Pathology in Nineteenth-Century America," *Feminist Studies* 21:2 (1995): 1–24; and Martha Vicinus, "Lesbian Perversity and Victorian Marriage: The 1864 Codrington Divorce Trial," *Journal of British Studies* 36 (1997): 70–98; citation p. 71. Diggs and Vicinus also insist that, in the words of Vicinus, the modern *lesbian* "existed before she was identified by sexologists" (p. 71), thus countering Faderman's over-emphasis on the power of sexology and psychoanalysis. See also Vicinus, "Distance and Desire: English Boarding School Friendships, 1870–1920," rpt. in *Hidden from History*, eds. Duberman, Vicinus, and Chauncey, pp. 212–29.
5. In *Dangerous Intimacies*, Moore, for instance, takes Faderman to task for her anodyne notion of romantic friendship, which discounts the presence of carnality among such friends. Faderman's work is far more vulnerable to this charge than is that of Smith-Rosenberg, who specifically grounds romantic friendship within "the relationship along the spectrum of human emotions between love, sensuality, and sexuality" ("The Female World of Love and Ritual," p. 53).
6. Castle, *The Apparitional Lesbian*, p. 8.
7. Even in the historically nuanced work of Andreadis, *Sappho in Early Modern England*, and Wahl, *Invisible Relations*, a sexual/asexual binary is defined in terms of genital practices; although they argue that women who hoped to retain access to the idealized, respectable mode of relation must protect themselves from the aspersions cast by the specter of sexualization, they reinscribe the binary as definitive of eroticism itself.
8. For an astute analysis of such narrative conventions, see Braunschneider, "Maidenly Amusements."
9. Braunschneider, "The Macroclitoride, the Tribade, and the Woman," p. 513.
10. Laura Doan, "Passing Fashions: Reading Female Masculinities in the 1920s," *Feminist Studies* 24:3 (1998): 663–700.
11. On the intimacy between Clarissa and Anna Howe, see the final chapter of Braunschneider's "Maidenly Amusements."
12. Smith-Rosenberg, "The Female World of Love and Ritual," p. 53.
13. Familial and social opposition, of the sort experienced, for instance, by Eleanor Butler and Sarah Ponsonby, clearly created the need for subterfuge. Their contemporary, Anna Seward, complained that her correspondence with Elizabeth Cornwallis had to be conducted secretly: "It is hard that our attachment to each

other should be a secret, the disclosure of which must involve as much distress and misery to both of us as if we were of a different sex, and our intercourse guilty" (quoted in Mavor, *The Ladies of Llangollen*, p. 90).

14. Rubin, "*Thinking* Sex," in *Pleasure and Danger*, ed. Carole Vance; Jeffrey Weeks, *Sex, Politics and Society: The Regulation of Sexuality Since 1800* (New York: Longman, 1981).
15. Siobhan B. Somerville, "Scientific Racism and the Invention of the Homosexual Body," in *Sexology in Culture: Labelling Bodies and Desires*, eds. Lucy Bland and Laura Doan (Chicago: University of Chicago Press, 1998), pp. 60–76; citations pp. 73 and 62.
16. Laura Doan, "'Acts of Female Indecency': Sexology's Intervention in Legislating Lesbianism," in Bland and Doan, eds., *Sexology in Culture*, pp. 199–213.
17. Suzanne Raitt, "Sex, Love and the Homosexual Body in Early Sexology," in Bland and Doan, eds., *Sexology in Culture*, pp. 150–64.
18. In addition to the recent work of Bray, Lanser, and Vicinus, see Jill Liddington, *Female Fortune: Land, Gender and Authority: The Anne Lister Diaries and Other Writings, 1833–36* (London: Rivers Oram Press, 1998).
19. Lucy Bland, "Trial by Sexology?: Maud Allan, *Salome* and the 'Cult of the Clitoris' Case," in Bland and Doan, eds., *Sexology in Culture*, pp. 183–98; citation p. 184.
20. Rita Felski, "Introduction," in Bland and Doan, eds., *Sexology in Culture*, pp. 1–8; citation p. 4.

Subject index

Endnotes are indexed only when they include a substantive discussion.

Numbers in italics refer to illustrations.

abjection, 33, 432 n.73; of female body, 105, 120, 122, 123; of tribades, 210, 216, 226, 228, 342, 345; of femmes, 257–58
abuse, 141, 182, 235; of clitoris, 7, 188, 206, 210, 213–14
actors, 36–7, 175–76; actors, boy, 39, 169, 238; *see* crossdressing; performance
acts vs. identities, 28, 32, 357
adolescence, 19, 20, 52, 174, 281, 307, 358
adultery, 41, 144, 167, 251, 259, 316
advice, erotic, 96, 103; *see* conduct literature
Africa, 7, 198, 201, 202, 203, 206, 212, 217
agency, female, 10, 61, 72, 79, 139, 174, 213, 263, 342–43; female erotic, 66–67, 103, 125, 131, 137, 195, 216; *see* pleasure, erotic; voice, female
allegory, 162; of chastity, 232, 255–57; Christian, 234, 251, 411 n.53; in Cavendish, 296; *see* virtues, allegorical
alterity, historical, 26–28, 32, 353; alteritism, 333–34
Amazonia/Amazons, 65–67, 76, 172–74
America, North, 43–44, 82–83, 449 n.105; South, 49, 77–78, 215
amicitia/amitié/amity, 8, 18–19, 289, 298–300, 313, 319, 324, 329, 368 n.38, 453 n.28; *see* friendship, female–female
amor impossibilis, 6, 33, 279, 281–90, 327, 363 n.8
anatomical illustrations, 7, 88, 90, *91*, *92*, *113*, *119*, *120*, *121*; anatomist anatomized in, *123–24*; classical antique in, 112, *114*, *115*, *116*, 117; clitoris in, 88, 90, 91, 92, 209; self-demonstrating corpse in, *123*
anatomical *pudica*, 33, 77, 117–24, 125, 130, 131
anatomy, dissection in, 86, 88, 198; relation to cartography, 132–33; relation to conduct literature, 83, 143; relation to travel literature, 197–98, 203, 208, 216; sexual, 45, 51, 77, 215–16, 249–50; *see* clitoris; hermaphrodite; medicine
anatomy texts, 7, 19, 45, 51, 84–96, 125, 190, 191–92, 194; censorship of, 104–11, 117; female imperfection and perfection in, 86–87, 93, 106, 120, 204; transmission of, 86, 88, 129; tribade in, 204–20; *see* clitoris; tribade/tribadism; medicine
androgyne/androgyny, 46, 50, 153, 320; *see* hermaphrodite/hermaphroditism
aphrodisiac, 94, 98
arousal, erotic, 85–86, 88, 93–95, 99, 102, 131; *see* pleasure, erotic
astrology, 8, 47, 83
authorship, female, 341, 465–66 n.39
autoeroticism, 124, 225–26, 285; *see* masturbation

ballads, 23, 48, 80, 156–57
bath, 18; Diana's nymphs bathing, 243, 248–49, *271*, 275; Turkish (*hannam*), 200–03, 315
bawdy, 60, 61, 67, 80, 96, 99, 170, 173, 177, 237
bed, 52; bedfellow, 60, 237, 241, 245; marriage, 80, 81, 268; female sharing of, 19, 52–54, 58–61, 170–71
bestiality, 42, 164–66, 168
bigamy, 49, 50
bisexuality, 14, 189
blazon, 144–45, 246
body, 10, 16, 17, 22–24, 83–96, 99, 111, 117; as matter, 22, 122; classical, 257; grotesque, 206–07, 257; mapping of, 190, 197–98, 217, 220; morphology of, 46, 270, 321, 359, 360; one sex, 191–92; two-sex, 192; *see* anatomy; humoralism

472

body politic, 127–30, 132–33, 154–57; *see* identity, national
Bolsover Castle, 160–62
breasts, 85, 86, 117, 224; bare, 75, 140–41; in poetry, 143–49; meaning of, 141, 143; nipples of, 95, 141, 143–45; relation to genitals, 143, 145; role in Calisto's seduction, 235, 238, 241–42
buggery, 7, 164–65, 168; female, 276–77, 309; *see* sodomite/sodomy
butch, 17, 39, 230, 353, 356

cartography, 128, 132, 197–98
castration, 222–23; anxiety, 66
censorship, 104, 108–12, 344, 430 n.59; *see* secrecy
chaste femme love, 17–18, 20, 33, 230–31, 250, 257–58, 308, 341; relation to *amicitia*, 300; threat to marriage, 269, 270; *see* femme–femme love; friendship, female–female; tribade/tribadism, relation to female friend
chastity, 17–18, 100, 112, 117, 358; as affective bond, 173, 182–83; erotic potential of, 55, 58–62, 69, 102, 125–38, 148–54, 230–32, 235, 237, 269, 322, 325; fetishization of, 252–57; ideology of, 15, 22, 23, 51–52, 61, 77–78, 187; internalization of, 264; marital, 81; Elizabeth I's motto of, 156; *see* chaste femme love; virginity
childbirth, 105–07, 109, 178; *see* generation; reproduction
Civil Wars, 26, 33, 99, 154–55, 164, 170, 259, 264
Classical (Greek and Roman) literature, 7–9, 24–25, 54–55, 229–30, 231-32, 316; women's appropriation of, 322, 360
clitoris, 34, 102, 104, 107, 109, 122, 124, 219; circumcision/clitoridectomy, 203, 212, 216, 219, 434 n.90 and n.91; description of, 89–93; enlarged, 7, 17, 26, 45–47, 50, 193, 203, 205–20, 317, 361; homology with penis (female yard), 89–93, 188–91, 193, 209, 210, 214, 222; illustrations of, 88, 90, *91*, *92*, 209; macroclitoride, 20, 213, 277, 321, 323; rediscovery of, 10, 16–17, 87–93, 125, 190, 192, 197; relation to breasts, 145; relation to genitalia, 129, 133, 138, 150, 223–26; relation to vagina, 188–89; rubbing of, 195, 211, 222; tentigo, 88, 90, 129, 205; *see* reproduction, relation to clitoris; tribade/tribadism
clothing, 358, 360; eroticism of Elizabeth's, 126–27, 130–37, 139–41, 149–50; Herrick's eroticism of, 143, 146, 149; *see* crossdressing; masculinity, female

closet, coming out of the, 33, 307, 343–45, 466 n.42; epistemology of the, 170, 343
colonialism, 20–21; in anatomy, 197–98, 203, 204, 208, 219, 225, 227; in literature, 68, 76; in psychoanalysis, 190, 220; in travel literature, 197–98, 203
concealment, strategy of, 112–24, 125, 148–50, 190
conduct literature, 9, 22–24, 80-3, 125, 259, 264, 266–67
continuism, historical, 28, 32, 331–34, 353, 357; relation to similitude, 333
convent, 62–65, 76, 77; rules of, 8, 64; *see* nuns
courtier, 101, 126, 244
court, ecclesiastic, 23, 41–44, 64, 77; legal, 23, 31, 41–44; royal, English, 69, 75–76, 152, 153, 175; royal, French, 54
courtship, 79–80, 151, 174; of Elizabeth I, 126; plot, 57, 58, 69, 181; relation to royal court, 152
crimen contra naturam, 42, 165–66, 168, 206, 280; *see* nature; sodomite/sodomy
crossdressing, in society, 29–30, 42–44, 47–51, 77–78, 79, 279, 341; in drama, 5–6, 27, 39, 169–81, 236–39, 287–88, 290–91, 327; in Cavalli's opera, 247–48, 252; in Cavendish's plays, 177–80; in pastoral paintings, 1, *2*, *3*, *4*, *5*, 272, *273*, *274*; in prose romance, 58–59, 239–44, 245–47, 281–82, 286–87, 292–94; in Shakespearean drama, 56, 75, 170, 177; in translations of Ovid, 232, 234, 283–86
cuckoldry, 54–55, 97
cunnilingus, 63, 145

deconstruction, 183, 196, 222, 340, 342–43
desire, erotic, 5–8, 10, 13, 19, 78, 96; separation of licit from illicit, 218, 269, *see* heterosexuality; homoeroticism; identification; love; lust
dictionary, 7, 164–65, 167–68, 221, 223, 249, 276–77, 300–10, 324, 420 n.32
différance, 196; *see* supplementarity
dildo, 30, 42–44, 50, 52, 55, 96–98, 100, 103, 182, 193–97, 212, 426 n.20; *see* prosthesis
disclosure, strategy of, 112, 114, 126, 148–50
donna con donna, 54–55
double standard, sexual, 23, 95, 261, 264, 322
drag, 39–40, 76; *see* crossdressing
drama, 64–65; comedy, 5–6, 24, 97, 98, 327–30; female homoeroticism in, 59–62, 67–69, 74–76, 164, 236–39, 287–88, 290–91; heterosexual closure of, 174–75, 177, 180, 182, 229, 291, 297; ideological

drama (*cont.*)
  power of, 36–37; Shakespearean, 56–58, 167–75; tragedy, 24

editing, textual, 61–62
effeminacy, 29–30, 45, 67, 68, 167, 240, 315; *see* masculinity
elegy, 126; containing strategy of, 172–75, 178; relation to pastoral, 175, 229, 308; in Philips's verse, 302–08, 324; *see* lament, homoerotic
Enlightenment, 167, 192, 220, 221, 270, 277, 280, 358
episteme, 191–92
epistolary correspondence, 7, 79, 184–87, 288, 299, 424 n.67, 447 n.78
eroticism, as category of analysis, 21; healthful benefits of, 83–86, 96; pleasures of, *see* pleasure, erotic
eroticism/erotic acts, 28, 32, 41–44, 47, 50, 52–53, 223; *see* arousal, erotic; cunnilingus; foreplay; kissing; masturbation; orgasm; penetration; positions, erotic; sodomite/sodomy
essentialism, 333; anatomical, 208, 220, 224, 228, 359–60, 434 n.92; gender, 195, 225, 437 n.130; of *lesbianism*, 220–21

family, 40–41; agent in historical process, 268; analogy to nation, 155–56; historiography of, 28, 33, 259–66; *see* heterosexuality; marriage; patriarchy
faultlines, ideological, 22, 28, 52, 61, 79, 96, 98, 143, 352, 359
female masculinity, *see* masculinity, female
femininity, 11, 182, 183, 214; *see* femme; gender
feminist/lesbian criticism and theory, 10, 28, 38, 103, 144–45, 204, 220–28, 348, 357; reclamation of Philips, 295
femme, 20, 356, 439 n.7
femme–femme love, 170–83, 230, 257–58; *see* chaste femme love; chastity, erotic potential of; friendship, female–female
fetish/fetishism, 128, 150; of Herrick, 143–47
figure, rhetorical, 13, 20
film, *see* performance, film
foreplay, 94
France, 141; ambassador of, 139–140; censorship in, 109; clothing styles, 142; eroticism among the elite, 54–55; influence on English court, 254; pornography in, 102; sexual practices in, 29, 193–94, 315; sodomy in, 42, 45, 47, 48, 51
fraud, sexual, 47, 48, 49

friction, erotic, 25, 57, 93, 213; fricatrice/confricatrice, 17, 25, 201, 205, 206, 208, 210; *see* clitoris, rubbing of; rubster; tribade/tribadism
friendship, female–female, 8, 11, 15, 17–19, 26, 31, 34, 37, 53, 57–75, 147; association with tribadism, 218, 231, 321–22; censure of, 256, 458 n.75; literary representations of, 56–62, 170–81, 280–316; men's exclusion from, 310–13; romantic, 29, 218, 221, 277–79, 356–59; similarity to modern *lesbianism*, 356, 360; *see* amicitia/amitié/amity; chaste femme love; femme–femme love; marriage, relation to friendship
friendship, male–male, 8, 18, 345; *see* amicitia/amitié/amity
funeral monuments, 70–74

gender, 11, 22–24, 216; clothing as signifier of, 140; instability of, 153, 169, 182, 196, 215; equality, 87, 96; imitation, 50, 195–97, 214, 216, 220, 227; relations, 9–10, 20, 29–31, 40–41, 44, 96, 322; relation to sexuality, 468–69 n.87; roles, 50, 137, 153, 182; *see* femininity; identification, gender; masculinity, female; patriarchy
genealogy, 13, 28, 32–34, 227, 327, 353
generation, 15, 106, 110; *see* reproduction
genitalia, 46, 77, 84, 95, 104, 117, 122, 357; covering of, 112, 114, 115–20, 125, 133; display of, 127, 129, 131–38; male aversion to, 79, 104–07, 120–22; sink of the body, 105, 107, 129; *see* clitoris; hymen; labia; penis; uterus; vagina
Germany, 24, 42–43, 51, 141, 142, 162–63, 204
greensickness, 84, 94, 393–94 n.40
gynecology, appropriation by male practitioners, 112, 204; *see* anatomy; anatomy texts; medical texts; midwifery texts

hannam, *see* bath, Turkish
harem, *see* seraglio
health, 223, 225, 227; *see* eroticism, healthful benefits of
hermaphrodite/hermaphroditism, 12, 30, 45, 46–47, 49–51, 109, 167, 215; causes of, 46–47; disbelief in, 278, 320–22; legal charges of, 276; representations in literature, 56, 57, 317–20; *see* androgyne/androgyny; transformation, sex; tribade/tribadism, relation to hermaphroditism
heterosexuality, 3, 11, 12, 22, 26, 27, 40, 75, 218; compulsory, 269; domestic, 218,

265–69, 294–95, 305, 322; eroticism within, 79–86, 93–103, 223, 358; historical construction of, 153–54, 259–70; presumed naturalness of, 261; producing gender, 468–69 n.87; relation to homoeroticism, 180–81, 218, 258–59, 269–70; relation to patriarchy, 224, 227, 331–32; regulation of, 163; reproduction of, 351; resistance to, 150–52; *see* identity, erotic; marriage, companionate; modernity, erotic categories of
historicism, strategic, 28, 31–32
historiography, of gender, 191–92; of homosexuality, 12, 14, 28–32, 348–49, 371–72 n.68, 469 n.1; of *lesbianism*, 3, 11–12; 26–35, 219–28, 270, 327, 331–35, 348–49, 353–54, 355–61, 367 n.32; of marriage and the family, 259–65, 269; of women, 9–10, 12, 331
Holy Roman Empire, 42–43, 193
homoeroticism, female, *see* femme–femme love; friendship, female–female; heterosexuality, relation to homoeroticism; homosexuality; marriage, female–female; sodomite/sodomy, female; tribade/tribadism
homoeroticism, male, *see* buggery; homosexuality; sodomite/sodomy
homonormativity, 183, 342
homophobia, 36, 51, 182, 220, 247, 340
homosexuality, as term, 277; etiology of, 346, 353; latent, 157; modern, 33, 40, 189–92, 214, 219, 335, 361; *see* identity, erotic; modernity, erotic categories of
homosociality, male, 68
hortus conclusus, 62
household, 18, 22, 40, 72, 184, 261; architecture of, 259; female-headed, 70; as physical space of, 52–53
humanists/humanism, 23, 31, 81, 141, 223, 259
humoralism, 44–45, 83–96, 107, 125, 213–14, 217, 320, 379–80 n.44; *see* medicine, Classical (Greek and Roman)
hymen, 51–52, 77–78, 93, 253, 382–83 n.70; *see* virginity

identification, 33, 68–69, 222, 228; cross-gender, 123; gender, 77, 153, 189; mimetic (as mirror image), 19, 330, 333–34, 338–42, 352; of *lesbians*, 27, 327, 335, 350; pleasures of, 333–35; relation to desire, 153, 353–54, 469 n.90; psychoanalytic theory of, 349–51; with *lesbians*, 27–28, 335, 352; *see* gender roles; similitude, erotic
identity, erotic, 13–16, 20, 26, 28–31, 32, 34, 39, 76, 225–28, 366 n.27; historical development of, 197, 214, 218, 220, 231, 353; politics of, 27–28, 38, 353, 436 n.119, 467 n.68; regulatory function of, 220; *see* modernity, erotic categories of
identity, national, 12, 22, 154–55, 198, 278; *see* nationalism
imagination, role in eroticism, 82, 90, 176–77
imperialism, 128, 132–33, 158
impossibility, 3, 11, 19, 33–34, 253, 278, 321, 323, 353; practicing impossibilities, 5–7, 22, 327; *see amor impossibilis*
impotence, 82, 86, 97–98, 122
impudicia, 257, 271; *see* modesty
incorporation, 146, 204; psychoanalytic concept of, 350, 352, 468 n.76
infertility, 86
(in)significance, 19, 33, 64, 163–64, 174–75, 181–84, 186–87, 197, 229–31, 271, 275, 308, 323, 353
intercourse, 96, 100, 104–07, 145, 153, 224; *see* heterosexuality, eroticism within; penetration; sexuality, phallic definitions of
intersexuality, 220, 436 n.106
introjection, 327, 349–50, 352
invert/inversion, 20, 29, 214, 219, 270, 321, 346, 356
Italy, 54, 64; anatomists of, 88, 129; art of, 249; clothing styles of, 141, *142*; mock wedding games in, 52; opera of, 247; pornography of, 102; sexual practices of, 85, 315; sodomy in, 43, 48, 211

jewels, 139, 143, 144, 150, 224; pearls, 127, 129–33, 136, 137, 144, 150

kissing, female–female, 1–3, 13, 18, 19, 59, 60–62, 291, 316–17; censure of, 315; in Calisto narratives, 231–33, 235, 238, 241–42, 246, 247–48, 250, 252; visual depictions of, 1, *2*, *3*, *4*, *5*, 162
kissing, male–female, 85, 144–45
kinship, 259; kinswomen, 52, 53; voluntary, 299–300
knowledge, erotic, 10, 60–61, 78–79, 89, 100, 102, 360; scientific, 117, 122–24, 270, 360

labia, 88, 90, 205, 210, 223–27, 321; excision of, 216, 433 n.88, 433–34 n.89; relation to nymphs, 248–50; *see* clitoris; genitals; vagina
lament, homoerotic, 19, 280–96, 323, 354
law, 7, 12, 22, 41–44, 78, 164–69, 182
libertinism, 19, 99, 102
literacy, female, 7, 21

locus amoenus, 62, 173, 301
love, 1, 5, 6, 19, 31, 83–84, 94; courtly, 239–40, 300; Platonic, 83, 296, 297; romantic, 261–62, 264–68, 447–48 n.90; *see* chaste femme love; femme–femme love; heterosexuality
lust, 7, 17, 63, 93–94, 143, 182, 199, 220; equated with femininity, 22–25, 96, 214, 215, 268; relation to the humors, 46, 54–55, 215; separation from love, 266–68

manuscript culture, 7, 345
marriage, age of, 79; annulment of, 82–83; companionate, 8, 125, 155, 259–65, 269; contract, 155, 416 n.110; debt, 82; divorce, 82–83, 167, 159; dynastic, 259, 299; elopements, 79; eroticism within, 80–83, 262, 265–69; escape from/resistance to, 62, 69, 125, 173, 185; female–female, 18, 37, 40, 45, 47, 48, 151–52, 193, 200; female appropriation of, 172; female subordination within, 261–63; heterosexual/patriarchal, 11, 18, 22, 40–41, 62, 78, 174; metaphor for monarchy, 154–56; non-Western, 198; premarital sex, 79–80; rates of, 69–70; regulation of sexuality within, 163; relation to friendship, 295, 305–06, 309–13; representations of, 178, 185; *see* family; heterosexuality, domestic; reproduction
marvels, 45, 206–07
masculinity, female, 20, 45–51, 67, 77–78, 196–97, 358; Elizabeth's performance of, 153; relation to sapphism, 277–79, 317–21, 323; *see* gender, imitation
masturbation, 84, 95, 99–100, 124, 137, 195, 219, 403–04 n.156; *see* autoeroticism
masque, court, 66–67, 75, 254–57
maternity, 156, 268; *see* childbirth; pregnancy
medicine, Arabic, 85–86, 205, 217; Classical (Greek and Roman), 17, 44, 47, 85–86, 88, 205, 217; history of, 33, 85–86; medical examination, 46–47, 49; medical texts, 12, 17, 31, 44–47, 79, 83–96, 103–24, 125, 264, 267–68, 324; relation to obscenity, 79, 103–04, 122–24; *see* anatomy texts; humoralism; midwifery texts; misogyny, of medical texts
medieval references to female homoeroticism, 8, 42, 168, 217
melancholy, 33; love, 83, 240; of *lesbians*, 350–52; virgin's, 60; *see* psychoanalysis, melancholy in
metamorphosis, 175, 232; *see* transformation, sex

metaphor, 20, 189, 225
metonymy, 20, 190–91, 210, 223–28, 255, 359
midwifery, texts, 19, 106–09, 203–04, 210; midwives, 49, 84, 85, 108–09, 112, 203–04, 402 n.142; *see* anatomy texts; medicine
minoritizing concepts, 13, 215, 357, 365 n.22
misogyny, 22–23, 38, 78, 96, 98, 122; of medical texts, 89, 104, 107, 112, 122, 204
modernity, 8, 14, 326; erotic categories of, 26–27, 192, 218, 231, 266, 270, 356
modernization, emotional, 263, 269; theatrical, 38–40
modesty, 15, 112, 117, 125, 128, 133, 138, 187; *see impudicia*
molly, 29–30; house, 18; *see* effeminacy
monarchy, 154–57, 158, 415–16 n.95; *see* court, royal
mythology, 18, 20, 229–32; in visual arts, 18, 161, 271–75; the graces, 25; the muses, 24–25; *see* nymphs; pastoral(ism)

narcissism, 226, 256, 345–48, 467 n.52; *see* psychoanalysis
nationalism, 128–29, 132–33, 158–60; *see* identity, national
nature, 79, 85, 87, 117–18, 141, 142, 323–24; in literature, 178; Nature's secrets, 79, 108, 111, 122; Nature's veil, 111–13, 280; relation to *amor impossibilis*, 279–95; in Philips's verse, 300–08; the unnatural, 123, 157, 323–24; *see crimen contra naturam*; sodomy; tribade/tribadism
Netherlands, 29, 43, 116
New Historicism, 28, 265
New World, 198; *see* America
normality/normativity, 207, 323–24, 345
nudity, 112, 114, 138, 147, 161–62, 198, 274–75, 412 n.55; *see* breasts, bare
nuns, 43; 62–65, 75, 77, 215–16; in Calisto narratives, 234, 247; *see* convents
nymphae, 443–44 n.40; *see* labia
nymphs, 1–5, 18, 125, 254, 301, 317–18; *see* Calisto

obscenity, 7, 12, 19, 78–79, 89, 96–103, 109–110, 117, 125; charge against Calisto, 250; projected onto women, 108, 122; prosecution for, 358; relation to medicine, 79, 103–04, 122–24, 218, 321; satiric, 26, 31, 155, 156–57, 271–72, 314–17, 323; *see* pornography
opera, 11, 17, 247–48, 250–53
orality, 143–47, 248, 423 n.55
origins, quest for, 28, 335, 463 n.25

orgasm, 77, 83–86, 90, 93–95, 106, 223; demise of two–seed theory, 267–68; female ejaculation, 25, 89, 90, 93, 94, 191; male, 268; simultaneous, 96; treatment for hysteria, 394 n.43; vaginal, 190; *see* clitoris, homology with penis; pleasure, erotic
Ottoman empire, 198, 201

passing women, 40, 48–51, 356, 357–58; *see* crossdressing
pastoral(ism), 1–6, 7, 12, 17–19, 20, 178–80, 275, 291, 318, 319; in Philips's verse, 295–96, 301–05, 3008; relation to elegy, 175, 229, 230, 308; relation to female body, 248–50; relation to green world, 175
pastorals, theatrical, 75, 175
patriarchy, 18, 40–41, 51, 69, 78, 80–81, 174; crisis in, 9–10, 155–56, 181, 263–64, 322, 363–64 n.13, 417 n.111; female subordination within, 23, 125, 169, 202, 227, 261, 310, 331–32; heteropatriarchy, 278; historical changes in, 155–56, 331–32; relation to body politic, 155–56; relation to reproduction, 181, 332; tribade's relation to, 195; sexual equality within, 80, 125; *see* gender, relations; marriage
penetration, phallic, 42, 52, 85, 94, 95, 130, 144, 165; absence of, 253; metaphors of, 298; *see* intercourse; penis
penetration, among women, 13, 30, 182, 193–97, 211–13; vaginal, 189, 220, 223; disavowal of, 165; *see* dildo; tribade/tribadism
penis, 45, 47, 49, 52, 85, 87, 95, 100, 103, 111, 287; homology with clitoris, 90–93, 191, 193; homology with uterus, 90–91, 191; insufficiency of, 98–99, 122–23; metaphors of, 155, 204; penis envy, 189; size of, 196; *see* impotence
performance, contemporary theatrical, 36–40, 56, 57; film, 38–39; gender, 196
periodization, historical, 12, 192, 260, 270, 355
Persia, 203
perversion, 33, 231, 257–58, 270, 279, 322, 356
phallus, 34–35, 99, 129, 133, 143, 189, 226, 328; desire for, 196–97; displacement of, 223–26; female appropriation of, 137, 170; *lesbian*, 227; violence of, 224; phallic stage, 189; *see* sexuality, phallic definitions of
pleasure, erotic, 15, 81, 85, 88–98, 99–103, 129–37, 223–26; as compensation for childbirth, 105–07; lack of, 397 n.83

poetry, 24, 25; *carpe diem*, 292, 311–12, 313; Cavalier, 304, 310–12, 340; epideictic, 144, 147, 297; love lyric, 56–57, 288–90, 295–308, 335–38; lyric, 17, 143–49, 222, 296–97, 308–13, 340, 344; narrative, 58–59, 63–64, 147–49, 239–44, 281–83, 286–87; obscene, 96–102; subjectivity effect in, 296–97, 341; *see* ballads; obscenity
polymorphous perversity, 143–47, 150, 152, 189
pornography, 218, 323, 357; development of, 99, 102–03; *see* obscenity
Portugal, 45
positions, erotic, 42–44, 165; *see* eroticism/erotic acts
postmodernism, 40, 76; *see* post-structuralism
post-structuralism, 32, 342; *see* deconstruction
précieuses, 154, 279, 324
pregnancy, 54, 85, 97, 100, 105–06, 156–57; bridal, 79; cause of Calisto's banishment, 233, 236, 238, 243–44
print culture, 8, 21, 122, 360
privacy, 52, 79, 259–60; as pornographic convention, 102; relation to the closet, 343–44
prosecution, legal, 41–44, 47, 49–51, 193, 277; *see* court, legal; law; sodomite/sodomy
prosthesis, 31, 33, 77, 100, 122, 124, 194, 227; *see* dildo; supplementarity
prostitution, 23–24, 50, 76, 96, 102–03, 140, 141–43; courtesan, 102; male, 167; *see* whore
psychoanalysis, 33, 144–45, 188–91, 220, 222–23, 356; feminist, 226–28; melancholy in, 327, 349–51; narcissism in, 345–48; used to theorize lesbian history, 326–27, 348–54; Lacanian, 35, 352; *see* Freud
psychomorphology, 33, 191, 207, 214, 216, 218, 220, 222, 227
pudica, 133; *see* anatomical *pudica*; Venus *pudica*

queer, criticism, 38; philology, 15; theory, 14, 28, 33, 333–34, 357, 366 n.25

race/racialization, 2, 12, 14, 20–21, 217, 362 n.4; in anatomy texts, 208, 219; in literature, 68, 69; scientific racism, 360
rape, 26, 93, 167, 231; literary representations of, 177; of Calisto, 232–38, 241–43, 245–47, 255
Reformation, 24, 63, 125, 164, 259, 332, 344
religion, Catholicism, 43, 62–64, 104, 130, 139–40, 143; Christianity, 22–23, 26, 31, 41, 117, 331; conflict over, 126; dissenting

religion (*cont.*)
  beliefs, 50, 264, 268, 388 n.121; Fall of Man, 22–23, 117; image of serpent, 22, 116; Judaism, 49; Muslim, 7, 198–203; Protestantism, 9, 23, 24, 63, 81–82, 130, 140, 143, 147, 344
Renaissance, meaning of, 7–11, 36–37, 126
reproduction, 11, 15, 62, 75, 78, 95–96, 98, 122, 125, 132; relation to clitoris, 89, 93–96; relation to marriage, 181, 189; *see* generation
Restoration, 19, 102, 154–55, 164, 254, 264, 268, 305, 335
romance, genre of, 7, 243–44; *see* crossdressing, in prose romance
rubster/ribaude, 17, 208, 221; *see* clitoris, rubbing of; friction, erotic; tribade/tribadism
Russia, 43, 52

sadomasochism (SM), 13, 300
Sahacat, 201, 206
sapphism/sapphist, 20, 30–31, 221–22, 224, 231; narratives, 10; production of, 277–79, 322–23; sapphic platonics, 300; *see* Sappho
satire, 313–14; *see* obscenity, satiric
scopophilia, 143; *see* voyeurism
Scotland, 42, 51
secrecy, 33; open secret, 33, 279, 343–44; relation to the closet, 343–44
separatism, gender, 63, 66–67, 182, 234, 247, 251
seraglio, 199–202, 315
sermons, 9, 23, 24
servants/service, 18, 52, 57
sexology, 189, 219–20, 356, 359–60, 361
sexuality, phallic definitions of, 15, 34–35, 61, 129, 133, 144–45, 332; *see* heterosexuality; phallus; visibility
similitude, 311; erotic, 19, 33, 184, 327–31, 338–42, 345–48; *see* identification, mimetic (as mirror image)
sin, 23, 165–67, 211–13
singlewomen, 69–70, 75, 310, 322
Societies for the Reformation of Manners, 18, 165, 167
sodomite/sodomy, 7, 18, 22, 29–30, 63, 110, 158, 167, 344; female, 42, 166, 181, 193–94, 276–78, 369–70 n.53; definition of, 42, 46; legal definition of, 164–66, 168, 276–77; prosecution of, 41–44, 47, 49, 51, 319; relation to monarchs, 154; Sodom, 306; theological definition of female, 211–13; *see* buggery; court, legal; *crimen contra naturam*; law; prosecution, legal; statutes, legal

space, 62–65, 76, 198, 202; female-governed, 175–80
Spain, 43, 45, 49, 51, 77–78, 129, 193, 204; Armada, 126–28
status, social (class, rank), 12, 14, 40, 48, 262, 469–70 n.1; aristocratic and gentry, 20–21, 54, 180, 184; middling, 9, 20–21, 52, 76; the poor, 53–54
statutes, legal, 36, 41–44, 164–65; *see* buggery; courts, legal; law; prosecution, legal; sodomite/sodomy
subject, category of the, 27, 220, 270; history of the, 33
substitution, 98, 100
supplementarity, 194–97
Switzerland, 43
Symbolic, the, 226, 342

tactility, 131, 143, 179, 225
terminology, 13–16, 201
theater, contemporary, 27; early modern, 7, 10, 75, 141, 274, 319; early modern audience of, 37–8, 75–6; *see* actors; performance
theology, 8, 22, 122, 167–68, 280; *see* religion, Christianity
tommy, 20, 30, 277
torrid zone, 219
transformation, sex, 45–47, 49–51, 93, 109, 215–16, 320, 323; relation to *amor impossibilis*, 279, 281–95, 297, 308
transgender, 436 n.106
transgression, erotic, 20, 22, 32, 196, 206, 209, 216, 257; meanings of, 154, 182, 183, 187; transgressive reinscription, 196
transexuality, *see* transformation, sex
transvestism, *see* crossdressing
travel narratives, 7, 19, 141, 142, 197–203; appropriation by anatomy, 203, 206, 208, 217, 220, 360; relation to anthropology, 198
trial, legal, 219, 276, 358; *see* court, legal; law; prosecution, legal
tribade/tribadism, 8, 15, 29, 192–97, 200, 341; abjection of, 210, 216, 226–28, 342, 345; as transgression, 22, 181, 196, 257–58; causes of, 45–47, 213–15, 323; definition of, 16–17; differences from modern *lesbianism*, 220–23, 356, 358; dramatic use of, 57; literary references to, 24–26; medical description of, 45, 203–20; prosecution of, 193–94; relation to female friend, 20, 231, 250, 257–58, 277–79, 322–25, 330–31; relation to hermaphroditism, 45–47, 49–51, 320–22; relation to sodomy, 168, 193–94, 199–200, 202; similarity to modern

Subject index

lesbianism, 356, 360; *tribas*, 17, 201, 217; visual representation of, 158–60
Turkey, 7, 198–203, 314–15

universalizing concepts, 13, 215, 357, 365 n.22
uterus, 87, 90–93, 104–07; illustrations of, 90, 91; *see* womb

vagina, 45, 49, 50, 90–93, 102, 104–07, 137; relation to breast, 145; relation to clitoris, 188–89, 223; *vagina dentura*, 107
Venus *pudica*, 112, 117, 132; *see* anatomical *pudica*
viol/violin, as erotic metaphor, 99, 101–03
virtues, allegorical, 66, 137–38, 146; the "Virtues Embracing," 160, *161*, *162*, *163*, 182
virgin/virginity, 5, 102; Elizabeth I's, 125–30, 140, 150–51; health of, 93; relation to women's social status, 51–52, 77–78; revirgination, 24; vestal, 65, 69, 76; virgin knot, 126–27, 129, 132, 133; virgin's melancholy, 60; *see* chastity; chaste femme love; nuns

visibility, 15, 19, 62, 69, 76, 221, 357; relation to invisibility, 3, 5, 11, 33–35, 36, 37, 353, 355; as problem of narrative, 34; *see* disclosure, strategy of; sexuality, phallic definitions of
visual arts, 1, *2*, 3, *4*, *5*, 17–18, 32, *118*, 158–60, *161*, *162*, 248, *249*, 253–54, 270; *see* Calisto, artistic representation of; Elizabeth I, Queen of England, portraits of
voice, female, 10, 224–26, 337–38, 342–43, 345; lyric, 340, 342; *see* agency, female
votaress, 65, 69, 76, 152
voyeurism, 98, 143, 148–50, 161–62
vulva, *see* labia; vagina

whore, 23, 24, 25, 26, 166–67, 316; dichotomy with virgin, 126; accusation against monarchs, 156, 175; *see* prostitution
widows, 65, 69–70, 72–76, 80, 93, 151; *see* household, female-headed
witchcraft, 22–23, 24, 26, 45; African, 201; persecution of, 22, 43
womb, suffocation of, 84, 94; wandering, 93; *see* uterus

Name and title index

Fictional characters and titles are listed alphabetically, rather than under the author's name. Endnotes, including those referring to scholars, are indexed only when they include a substantive discussion.
Numbers in italics refer to illustrations.

Abraham, Julie, 343
Abraham, Nicholas, 349–50
Achilles, 167, 289
Acteon, 245, *249*, 271
Actes of the Englishe Votaryes (Bale), 63
Acrasia (*The Faerie Queene*), 148–49
Adam (Genesis), 116–17
"Ad Bassam tribadem Epig. 91" (Fletcher), 316
Adelman, Janet, 107
Adonis, 99, 229
Africanus, Constantinus, 86
Africanus, Leo, 109, 201, 203, 205, 208
"Against Pleasure" (Philips), 306–07
Aguecheek, Sir Andrew (*Twelfth Night*), 36, 56
Albion's England (Warner), 234, 236–67, 243
Albucacis, 205
Alcmena, 244
Alexis, 318
Allan, Maud, 361
Allen, William, 129–30
Allied Virtues (Goltzius), 161, *163*
Amarillis Crowning Mirtillo (Breenbergh, Van Loo), 3, *4*, *5*
Amarillis, 1, *2*, 3, *4*, *5*, 323
Amigoni, Jacopo, 272, *273*
Amity, Queen of (*Assaulted and Pursued Chastity*), 293–94, 296
Amores (Ovid), 229
Amoret (*The Faerie Queene*), 58
Amorett ("On the Friendship betwixt Sacharissa and Amorett"), 310
"Amor Veneris, Vel Dulcedo Appeletur" (Laqueur), 188, 191
Amour, King of (*Assaulted and Pursued Chastity*), 293–94, 296
Anatomia del corpo humano (Valverde), 117, *119*, *123*, *124*

Anatomy of Humane Bodies Epitomized (Gibson), 210
Anatomy of Melancholy, The (Burton), 346
Anderson, Misty, 179
Andreadis, Harriette, references to Sappho, 221–22, 300, 316; homoerotic representations, 10, 217, 218, 335; sexual/asexual binary, 470 n.7
Anne, Jacobean Queen of England and Scotland, 75
Anne of Denmark, Queen of England and Scotland, 7, 156–57, 254, 277, 310
Antipodes, The (Brome), 60–62
Anthropometamorphosis (Bulwer), 141, 143, 324
Antiquarum Staturarum Urbis Romae (de Calivari), *118*
Antonio (*The Merchant of Venice*), 39
Antonio (*Twelfth Night*), 36
Aphrodite, 318, 319
Apollo, 162
Apollodorus of Athens, 232
Apparitional Lesbian, The (Castle), 220–21
Arcas/Archas, 233, 244
Aretino, Pietro, 104, 110, 399 n.97
Ariosto, Ludovico, 59, 280, 282
Aristotles Master-Piece, 90, 396 n.66
Armada portrait of Queen Elizabeth (Gower), 126–33, *127*, 145, 150, 155
Armour, Margaret, 42, 51
Arnold, Janet, 138–39, 150
Artegall (*The Faerie Queene*), 58
"Articles of Friendship" (Philips), 304
Amussen, Susan, 263
Assaulted and Pursued Chastity (Cavendish), 292, 294, 295
Astell, Mary, 264, 310

Name and title index

Aston, Herbert, 185–86
Astrea, 125; *see* Elizabeth I; Gloriana
Astrea (*The New Atalantis*), 313
As You Like It (Shakespeare), crossdressing in 57; female friendship in, 310; femme–femme love in, 170–71, 174; homoeroticism in, 327; modern production of, 39; setting of, 245
Atlas of England and Wales (Saxton), *159*, 160
Athena, Pallas, 25, 160
Atlanta, 237, 245
Aurelianus, Caelius, 205
Avicenna (Abu Ali al-Husayn ibn Abd Ala ibn Sīnā), 88, 205
Awbrey, Mary (Rosania), 301, 302, 304

Babayan, Kathryn, 203
Bach, Rebecca, 266
Bacon, Sir Francis, 280
Bagot, Margaret, 79
Bale, John, 63
Ballaster, Ros, 310
Banister, John, 108
Barash, Carol, 254, 300, 305, 306–08, 456–57 n.60
Barbara (*The Antipodes*), 60–61
Barley-breake, or a Warning for Wantons, 442 n.29
Barnfield, Richard, 229
Barre, Poulain de la, 87, 106
Bartholin, Caspar, 90
Bartholin, Thomas, discussion of female anatomy, *92*, 93 208–09, 210, 211–14, 216; female reproductive equality, 87, 105; rubster reference, 221; Sappho reference, 217
Bartholinus Anatomy (Caspar and Thomas Bartholin), 90, *92*, 93
Barnes, Barnabe, 414 n.77
Bassa ("Ad Bassam tribadem Epig. 91"), 24, 316
Bassanio (*The Merchant of Venice*), 39
bawd (*Assaulted and Pursued Chastity*), 292–93
Beard, Thomas, 167–68
Beaumont, Sir Thomas, 66
Behn, Aphra, 7, 10, 317–20, 335
Bell, Ilona, 130
Bell, Susanna, 50
Bellamy, Elizabeth, 254, 257
Bellona, 160
Belsey, Andrew, 127, 131
Belsey, Catherine, 127, 131, 266, 267, 342, 448 n.93
Bennett, Judith, 151, 331

Bennett, Paula, 223
Bennett, Susan, 39
Berry, Philippa, 125, 152, 405 n.3, 407 n.20
Betts, Hannah, 140
Bible, the, anatomies' citation of, 209; artistic representation of, 133; friendship in, 289; marital love in, 81; Psalms, 160; Romans, 42, 165–66, 200, 208
Bird in a Cage, The (Shirley), 170, 175, 176–78
Birth of mankind, The (Raynald), 103, 106–07, 108–09
Bland, Lucy, 361
Blank, Paula, 297, 337, 455 n.44, 463–64 n.29
Blount, Thomas, 168, 276, 324
Boleyn, Elisabeth, 43
Bond, Donald, 74
Boock of Physicke (Gabelkover), 324
Book of Common Prayer, The, 133, 171, 290
Book of the Thousand Nights and a Night, The (Burton), 219
Bordone, Paris, 271
Boose, Lynda, 400 n.105
Boucher, François, 272, *274*
Bourchier, Lady Frances, 53
Bovey, Katharina, 72–74; funeral monument of, *73*
Bradamant (*Orlando Furioso*), 59, 282, 286
Braden, Gordon, 413 n.61
Braithwaithe, Richard, 141
Brantôme, Pierre de Boudeille, Seigneur de, antique homoeroticism in, 54–55, 67; gossip about women, 103, 202; status of female–female sex, 316, 318
Braun, Georg, 160
Braunschneider, Theresa, 213, 321, 460 n.105
Bray, Alan, 18, 19, 299
Breenbergh, Bartholomeus, 3
Bride Bush, A (Whateley), 81–83, 267
Britomart (*The Faerie Queene*), 58
Brome, Richard, 60
Brooten, Bernadette, 331–32, 335
Brown, Judith, 388–89 n.122
Brown, Wendy, 350–51
Brundenell, Frances, Countess of Newburgh, 314
Bruster, Douglas, 26
Bulstrode, Celia, 25
Bulwer, John, 141, 143, 324
Burckhardt, Jacob, 9
Burton, Richard, 219, 435 n.103
Burton, Robert, 7, 168, 346
Busbecq, Ogier Ghiselin de, 198–99, 200, 219
Bush, Douglas, 229

Butler, Judith, 196, 226–27, 345, 350–51, 449–50 n.111, 466 n.42, 466 n.51, 468–69 n.87
Bynum, Caroline Walker, 388–89 n.122, 411 n.53

Callaghan, Dympna, 447–48 n.90
Calisto, 18, 231–58, 270, 300, 301, 322; artistic representation of, *271*, *272*, *273*, *274*, 275
Calisto, La (Cavalli and Faustini), 247–48, 250–52, 257
Calisto: Or, The Chaste Nimph (Crowne), 254–57
Calivari, Giovanni Battista de, *118*
Cambridge Group for the History of Population and Social Structure, 260
Campbell, Mary, 206–07
Carlini, Benedetta, 64, 388–89 n.122
Carpi, Jacopo Berengario da, 112, *113*
Carracci, Annibale, 271
Carravagio, Michelangelo Merisi da, 11
Casola, Pietro, Canon, 141
Cassiana (*The Bird in a Cage*), 176–77
Castle, Terry, 220–01, 335, 357, 436 n.109, 436–37 n.119
Catharine ("Virgo misogamos"), 63
Catullus, Gaius Valerius, 229
Cavalli, Pier Francesco, 247–48, 250–52, 254, 257
Caveat or Warening For Common Cursetors (Harman), 53
Cavendish, Margaret, Duchess of Newcastle, critiques of men, 185; extreme décolleté of, 141; female–female relationships, 7, 170, 177–80, 297, 313; proto-feminism of, 264, 295; views of Nature, 280, 290–94, 301
Cavendish, Sir Charles, 160
Cavendish, William, Duke of Newcastle, 141, 160–62
Caxton, William, 283, 328
Celia (*As You Like It*), 39, 171, 174, 182, 187, 307, 310
Cesario/Viola (*Twelfth Night*), 36, 39
Chamberlain, Hugh, 94
Charles (*As You Like It*), 171
Charles I, King of England and Scotland, 75, 154, 305
Charles II, King of England and Scotland, 154–55, 253–54
Chaucer, Geoffrey, 98
Cheek by Jowl, 39
Chernaik, Warren, 304
Chirugie françoise (Daléchamps), 205
"Chloe to Artimesa. 1700," 308–10

"Choise of valentines, The" (Nashe), 96–9, 102, 103, 104, 397–98 n.88
Christ, as redeemer, 160; brides of, 62, 126; female desires routed through, 26; feminine attributes of, 22, 64; marital love model, 81; masculinity of, 344
Christian Œconomie (Perkins), 81
Chudleigh, Lady Mary, 341
Churchill, Sarah, Duchess of Marlborough, 156–57
Chyrurgeons Store-house (Scultetus), 216
Citherea ("On the Friendship betwixt Sacharissa and Amorett"), 311
Civilization of the Renaissance in Italy, The (Burckhardt), 9
Civitates Orbis Terrarum (Braun and Hogenberg), 160
Clarinda ("*To the fair* Clarinda, *who made Love to me, imagin'd more than Woman*"), 318, 320
Clarissa (*Clarissa Harlowe*), 358
Claudio (*Much Ado about Nothing*), 316
Cleland, John, 103
Cleonarium (Lucian), 316
Clifford, Lady Anne, 53
Cloris, 318
Cohen, Ed, 14
Coke, Sir Edward, 42, 165, 168, 276
Cole–Orton masque, 66–67
Colombo, Realdo, 16, 88–90, 109
Compendiosa totius anatomie delineatio (Geminus), *116*–17
Compleat Midwife, The, 103
Complete Midwife's Practice Enlarged (Culpeper), 209
Comus (Milton), 257
Conjugal Love, or The Pleasures of the Marriage Bed (Venette), 209–10
Content, Rob, 137
Convent of Pleasure, The (Cavendish), 170, 177–80, 290–91, 296
"Copie of Verses made by a Lady, and sent to another Lady, with a bracelet made of her own hair, A," 337–38
Cornerstone Theater Company, 39
Correll, Barbara, 464 n.29
Coryat, Thomas, 141, *142*
Coryats Crudities (Coryat), 141, *142*
Cotgrave, John, 99, 337–38
Cotgrave, Randle, 223
"Court Pucell, The" (Jonson), 25
Coverley, Sir Roger de, 74
Cowen Orlin, Lena, 52
Crawford, Patricia, 81, 263
Creed, Barbara, 222

Creet, Julia, 466 n.42
Cressida (*The History of Troilus and Cressida*), 26
Cressy, David, 80, 81
Crofts, Robert, 267
Crooke, Helkiah, discussion of clitoris, 89–90, *91*, 93, 194–95, 205, 208, 210, 213; female anatomy, 117, *120*, *121*, 122–23; female pleasure, 95; female reproductive equality, 86–87; nymphae, 249; sex transformation, 45; use of other texts; 206; views of Nature, 85, 104, 110–12
Crowne, John, 7, 254–57, 259
Cullen, Countee, 11
Culpeper, Nicholas, discussion of clitoris, 209, 210, 216; hermaphrodites, 46, 321; female–female contact, 84–85; female reproductive equality, 87; reader of, 109; relation to obscenity 103
Culpepper's Midwife (Culpeper), 103
Cupid, 160; in Cavendish's *Assaulted and Pursued Chastity*, 293; in Hoadley's "On the Friendship of two young Ladies," 312; in Lyly's *Gallathea*, 5–6, 327–28; in Sandys's *Metamorphoses*, 285; in Shakespeare's *A Midsummer Night's Dream*, 36, 65, 69; in Waller's "On the Friendship betwixt Sacharissa and Amorett," 311
Cynthia, 233, 244

Daléchamps, Jacques, 205
Danaë, 176, 244
Daphne, 162
Darnley portrait of Queen Elizabeth, 133, *135*, 145
David, King, 289
De Delictis et Poenis (Sinistrari), 211
De Humani Corporis Fabrica (Vesalius), 86, *114*, *115*
Deitzsch, Agatha, 43
Dekker, Thomas, 59
"De l'amitié" (Montaigne), 298
Demetrius (*A Midsummer Night's Dream*), 39, 64, 68–69
Demonassa (Lucian), 316
De re anatomica (Colombo), 88–89
Derrida, Jacques, 196
Desdemona (*Othello*), 26, 316
Des Monstres et Prodiges (Paré), 45, 109
Devereux, Lady Frances (née Howard), 66, 79
Devereux, Lord Robert, Third Earl of Essex, Viscount Hereford, 79
Diana, 18, 229, 231–32, 234, 301, 304; in Cavalli and Faustini's *La Calisto*, 247–48, 250–53; in Crowne's *Calisto: Or, The Chaste Nimph*, 254–56; in Golding's *Metamorphoses*, 232–33, 234; in Heywood's *The Escapes of Jupiter*, 244–45, 247; in Heywood's *The Golden Age, Or the Lives of Jupiter and Saturn, with the Deifying of the Heathen*, 237–39, 245; in Heywood's *Troia Brittanica: Or, Great Britaines Troy*, 240–41, 243–44; in Lyly's *Gallathea*, 5, 287–88, 327–28; in Ovid's *Metamorphoses*, 232, 250, 252; in Sandys's *Metamorphoses*, 233, 234, 238; in Shakespeare's *The Two Noble Kinsmen*, 173; in the visual tradition, 248, *249*, *271*–2, *274*–75; in Warner's *Albion's England*, 234–36, 237, 238–39
Diana Discovering the Pregnancy of Calisto (Titian), *271*
Diderot, Denis, 280
DiGangi, Mario, 26, 61, 386 n.101
Diggs, Marylynne, 356
Dinshaw, Carolyn, 334
Directory for Midwives, A (Culpeper), 216
Discoverie of a Gaping Gulf, The (Stubbs), 130
Disney, John, 165–68
Dissection des parties du corps humain, La (Estienne), 88
Ditchley portrait of Elizabeth I, 155
Dolan, Jill, 39
Dollimore, Jonathan, 196, 258
Donella (*The Bird in a Cage*), 176–77, 182
Donne, John, use of Ovid, 342; female–female desire, 7, 172, 337, 338; idealization of sex, 339; lyric seduction, 143, 313; metaphysical conceits of, 296; tribadism, 24, 158
Donoghue, Emma, 102–03, 335, 344
Doran, Susan, 405–06 n.5
Dudley, Robert, Earl of Leicester, 153
Duke Senior (*As You Like It*), 245
Du Laurens, André, 117, 205, 210
Duval, Jacques, 47
Dworkin, Andrea, 224, 227

Eccles, Audrey, 89
Echo, 248
Eclogues (Virgil), 229
Edelstein, Barry, 36
Egeus (*A Midsummer Night's Dream*), 68
"Elegy 16: To His Mistress Going to Bed" (Donne), 313
Eliza (anonymous poet), 147
Elizabeth I, Queen of England, alleged sexual profligacy of, 128, 129; artistic representations of, 158, 271, 404–05 n.2, 415 n.92; breasts of, 138–40; erotics of court, 69, 79; female circle of, 125, 152,

Elizabeth I (*cont.*)
   153; hands of, 130, 131, 151; portraits of, *127*, *134*, *135*, *136*, *145*, 159; theater affinity, 75, 149, 327; rule of, 7, 160, 243, 254; virginal eroticism of, 110, 125–40, 144, 147, 150–6, 157, 226, 230, 253; virginity of, 125–29, 153–54, 405 n.4, 406 n.12; *see* Astrea; courtship; Gloriana; marriage, female–female
Elizabeth I and the 3 Goddesses (attributed to Hans Eworth or Joris Hoefnagel), 137, *138*
Emilia (*The Two Noble Kinsmen*), 172–75, 182, 187, 307, 330
Endymion, 251, 252
Epistemology of the Closet (Sedgwick), 11, 170
Epitome (Vesalius), 112, *114*, *115*–16
Epyre, King of, 239, 244
Erasmus, Desiderius, 63
Erauso, Catalina de, 48–49, 51, 77, 124, 152
Erickson, Amy, 263
Erreurs populaires (Joubert), 95, 110
Escapes of Jupiter, The (Heywood), 244
Estienne, Henri, 42, 88, 141, 410 n.47
Eubulus ("Virgo misogamos"), 63
Eugenia (*The Bird in a Cage*), 176
Euripedes, 232
Eve (Genesis), 7, 22–23, 105, 147; as anatomical figure, 116–17
Expert midwife, The (McMath), 105

Fable of Diana and Acteon (Parmigianino), 249
Faderman, Lillian, 211, 356, 470 n.5
Faithful Shepherd, The (Fanshaw), 1; *see Il Pastor Fido*
Fairie Queene, The (Spenser), 58–9, 147–49
Falloppia, Gabriele, 16, 88–89, 109, 205, 210
Fanshaw, Sir Richard, 1
Faulds, Elspeth, 42, 51
Faustini, Giovanni, 247
Felski, Rita, 361
Female Husband, The (Fielding), 358
Ferrand, Jacques, 83–84, 106
"Fiction and Friction" (Greenblatt), 193
Fielding, Henry, 358
Filmer, Sir Robert, 155–56
Fineman, Joel, 137, 297, 455 n.42, n.43, n.44
Fiordispina (*Orlando Furioso*), 59, 282, 284, 286
Firenzuola, Agnolo, 59
Fischlin, Daniel, 137
Flavina (*The Two Noble Kinsmen*), 172–74, 307, 330

Fletcher, Anthony, 80–81, 86, 95, 263–65
Fletcher, John, use of erotic similitude, 330, 338; female–female desire, 7, 170, 175, 177; homoerotic lament, 172–73, 180
Fletcher, R., 316
Flower of Friendship, The (Tilney), 267
Floyd, John, 143, 412 n.54
Fontanus, Nicholas, 84–85
Fool (*The Presence*), 292
Foucault, Michel, appearance of "homosexual," 192, 214, 371–72 n.68; archaeology of, 191; conditions of intelligibility, 345; erotic desire, 80; genealogy, 28, 333
Fourth Book of Practical Physick (Culpeper), 216
Fowler, Alistair, 144
Fowler, Constance, 185–86
Fradenburg, Louise, 332–35, 349
Francis ("The choise of valentines"), 96–98
Frantz, David, 98
Freccero, Carla, 332–35, 349
Frenche Chirurgerye (Guillemeau), 324
"Fresh Cheese and Cream" (Herrick), 145
Freud, Sigmund, developmental taxonomies of, 144, 218; heterosexual imperative of, 188–91; lesbian identity, 220, 223, 326–27; narcissism, 345–46, 348–49, 351, 353; *see* psychoanalysis
Friend, The (Bray), 299
"Friendship in Embleme, or the Seal. To my dearest Lucasia" (Philips), 305
Frye, Susan, 127, 137, 150–52, 405 n.4
Furies, the, 251
Fuss, Diana, 225, 349, 437 n.130

Gabelkover, Oswald, 324
Galenus, Claudius, 44, 84
Gallathea, 5–6, 287, 327–28, 330
Gallathea (Lyly), 5–6, 287, 327–29
Gallop, Jane, 225, 437 n.130
Ganymede, 18, 167, 170, 171
Gay and Lesbian Heritage, The (Summers), 3
Geminus, Thomas, *116*–17
Gentleman's Journal: Or the Monthly Miscellany, The, 48
Gerard of Cremona, 86
Gibson, Thomas, 210
Gillis, John, 269, 449 n.108
Gimenez, Sylvia, 65
Glasgow Presbytery, 42, 51
Gloriana, 125, 138; *see* Astrea; Elizabeth I
Glossographia (Blount), 168, 276, 324
Glover, Thomas, 200–01
Goldberg, Jonathan, 14, 35, 152–53, 204

Name and title index

Golden Age, The (Heywood), 236–37, 241, 244–45
Golding, Arthur, 232–34, 283, 288, 328
"Go, Lovely Rose" (Waller), 311–12
Goltzius, Hendrik, 161
Goneril (*King Lear*), 26
Gosson, Stephen, 141
Gouge, William, 80–81
Gower, George, *127*
Gowing, Laura, 24, 262
Graces, the, 25
Greenblatt, Stephen, 193–95, 426 n.13
Greer, Germaine, 147
Grosz, Elizabeth, 437–38 n.134
Guarini, Giovanni Battista, 1
Guazzo, Francesco Maria, 45
Guillemeau, Jacques, 324
Guyon (*The Faerie Queene*), 148–49

Hackett, Helen, 405 n.4
Haggerty, George, 19
Hale, Sir Matthew, 324
Hall, Radclyffe, 335, 358
Hall, Thomas/Thomasine, 44, 49
Hallett, Judith, 217
Halperin, David, 17, 332, 348
Halpern, Richard, 99
Hamlet, 64, 167
Hamlet (Shakespeare), 64
Hammon, Mary, 44
Hammond, Paul, 154, 155
Happy, Lady (*The Convent of Pleasure*), 177–80, 290, 296, 302
Harman, Thomas, 53–54
Harvey, Elizabeth, 337, 344, 463 n.28
Harvey, William, 267
Hayes, H. R., 107
Helena (*A Midsummer Night's Dream*), homoerotic desire, 39, 68, 76, 170–72, 174, 182, 187, 290, 329, 330; heterosexual desire, 58, 65, 307
Helms, Lorraine, 38
Hendricks, Margo, 68
Henke, James, 141
Hentzner, Paul, 140, 150
Henri IV, King of France, 139
Henrietta Maria, Queen of England and Scotland, 75, 154, 175, 295
Henry V (Shakespeare), 38
Henry VIII, King of England, 154
Hercules, 161, 162
Hereford, Earl of; *see* Lord Robert Devereux
"Hermaphrodite, The" (King), 314; *see* "The Toast"
Hermaphroditis, 229

Hermes, 256, 318, 319
Hermia (*A Midsummer Night's Dream*), homoerotic desire, 68, 76, 158, 170–72, 174, 329, 330; heterosexual desire, 58, 64–5, 307
Hermione (*The Winter's Tale*), 26, 316
Hero (*Much Ado about Nothing*), 316
Heröides (Ovid), 217, 221, 229
Herrick, Robert, 143–47, 149, 313
Hertner, Elsbeth, 43
Hesperides (Herrick), 143–44
Hetzeldorfer, Katherina, 51
Heywood, Thomas, 7, 236–39, 242–44, 246–47, 252, 257, 292
Hill, Fanny, 102
Hippolyta (*A Midsummer Night's Dream*), 65, 67
Hippolyta (*The Two Noble Kinsmen*), 67, 172
Historie of Man, The (Banister), 108
History and Description of Africa (Africanus), 201
History of Sexuality, The (Foucault), 80
Histrio–mastix (Prynne), 175
Hitchcock, Tim, 29, 372–73 n.74, 449 n.109
Hoadley, John, 281, 312–13
Hobby, Elaine, 300, 338, 344
Hobsons Horse-load of Letters (Markham), 184–85, 186
Hogenberg, Franz, 160
Hollingsworth, Ralph, 50
Holmes, Michael Morgan, 26
Holstun, James, 172–74
Holy Roman Empire, Constitutions of, 42
Homer, 244
Houlbrooke, Ralph, 260, 262
House of Lear (Jackson), 39
Howard, Frances; *see* Devereux, Lady Frances
Howarth, David, 131, 450 n.112
Hoyle, John, 319
Hull, Isabel, 41, 50, 52, 62, 162–64, 168–69, 180
Hulme, Peter, 190
Humorous Lovers, The (Cavendish), 141
Hunt, Arabella, 49, 276, 381 n.60
Hunt, Margaret, 52, 169
Hunt vs. Poulter, 49, 50, 276
Huon de Bordeaux, 281, 282
Hutson, Lorna, 380 n.45
Hyginus, Gaius Julius, 232

Ianthe, 18, 230, 276, 278, 280, 330; in Caxton's *Metamorphoses*, 283; in Golding's *Metamorphoses*, 284; in Philips's "To the Excellent Orinda," 308; in Ovid's *Metamorphoses*, 283; in Sandys's *Metamorphoses*, 285, 329

Ide (*Yde et Olyve*), 281–82, 286
Identification Papers (Fuss), 349
Idylls (Theocritus), 229
Il Pastor Fido (Guarini), 1; *see The Faithful Shepherd*
Iphis, 18, 230, 276, 278, 280, 286, 287, 290, 300, 301, 323, 330; in Caxton's *Metamorphoses*, 283; in Golding's *Metamorphoses*, 283–84; in Ovid's *Metamorphoses*, 283; in Philips's "To the Excellent Orinda," 308; in Sandys's *Metamorphoses*, 284–86, 329
Ingram, Martin, 79–80
Institutes of the Lawes of England (Coke), 165, 276
Intelligence, Lady (*The New Atalantis*), 313
Invisible Relations (Wahl), 10
I ragionamenti (Firenzuola), 59
Irigaray, Luce, 131, 224–26, 227, 248, 346
Iris, 66
Isabella (*Measure for Measure*), 64
Isis, 284, 287
Isogogae breves (da Carpi), 112, *113*

Jackson, Reginald, 39
Jackson, Virginia, 296
Jacob, Giles, 164–65, 167–68, 277
Jacquart, Danielle, 86
Jagose, Annamarie, 34, 346–47, 437–38 n.134
James I, King of England and Scotland, 48, 79, 141, 154
James II, King of England and Scotland (Duke of York), 254
James, R., 321
Jankowski, Theodora, 151
Jardine, Lisa, 139–40, 409 n.37 and 38
Jarman, Derek, 463 n.25
Johnson, Elizabeth, 44
Johnson, Thomas, 85, 109
Jonathan (friend of King David), 289
Jones, Inigo, 75
Jones, Lady Catharine, 70, 72
Jones, Richard, Viscount and Earl of Ranelagh, 72
Jonson, Ben, 7, 25–6
Joosten, Maeyken, 43
Josselin, Ralph, 79
Joubert, Laurent, 95, 106, 110, 143
Jove, 231; in Cavalli and Faustini's *La Calisto*, 247–48, 251–3; in the Cole-Orton masque, 66; in Crowne's *Calisto*, 255; in Golding's *Metamorphoses*, 232, 234; in Heywood's *The Golden Age*, 239; in Heywood's *Troia Brittanica*, 239–44; in Ovid's *Metamorphoses*, 232, 234; in Sandys's *Metamorphoses*, 233–34; in the visual tradition, 272, *274–75*; in Warner's *Albion's England*, 234–36, 239; see Jupiter
Joyless, Martha (*The Antipodes*), 60–2
Juana, princess of Spain, 151
"Julia's Petticoat" (Herrick), 146
Julius III, Pope, 160
Juno, 137; in Cavalli and Faustini's *La Calisto*, 251–52; in the Cole–Orton masque, 66; in Crowne's *Calisto*, 256–57; in Golding's *Metamorphoses*, 232–33; in Jonson's *Volpone*, 25; in Ovid's *Metamorphoses*, 234; in Sandys's *Metamorphoses*, 234; in Shakespeare's *As You Like It*, 171; in Warner's *Albion's England*, 234, 236
Jupiter, 249; in Cavalli and Faustini's *La Calisto*, 250; in Crowne's *Calisto*, 255–56; in Heywood's *The Escapes of Jupiter*, 244–47; in Heywood's *The Golden Age*, 236–38, 245; in Heywood's *Troia Brittanica*, 243, 245, 292; in Sandys's *Metamorphoses*, 238; in Shirley's *The Bird in a Cage*, 176–7; in the visual tradition, 271–72, *273*; in Warner's *Albion's England*, 234–36, 239; *see* Jove
Jupiter and Calisto (Amigoni), *273*
Jupiter and Calisto (Rubens), *273*

Keller, Eve, 204
Kelly, Joan, 9
Kendall, Captain Charles, 70
Kendall, Mary, 70–72, 75; funeral monument of, *71*
Kéroüalle, Louise Renée de, Duchess of Portsmouth, 254
Kerrigan, William, 145, 248
King, William, 314
Kirk Session, 42
Knidian Aphrodite (Praxiteles), 112–14
Koedt, Anne, 188

LaBoëtie, Etienne de, 298
Ladies Dictionary, The, 168, 277, 309–10, 313
Ladies Library, The (Steele), 72
Ladies of Llangollen, 279
Lady (*Comus*), 257
Lanser, Susan, 103, 278, 279–80, 310, 323, 450 n.5, 450–51 n.8
Lanyer, Aemilia, 26
Laqueur, Thomas, 88, 188, 191–93, 195, 219, 222, 278, 403–04 n.156
Laslett, Peter, 260
Lavinia (*I ragionamenti*), 59
Law Dictionary (Blount), 168, 276

Lawes resolutions of womens rights, The (T. E.), 78
Leaena (Lucian), 316
Lear, King (*King Lear*), 26
Le Beau (*As You Like It*), 171, 310
Leigh, Dorothy, 267
Lely, Sir Peter, 253
le Marcis, Marie/Marin, 47
l'Estage, Françoise de, 42
Leontes, King (*The Winter's Tale*), 316
Letters (Montagu), 315
Levin, Carole, 151
Levin, Richard A., 386 n.101
Lewis, C. S., 266
Linfea, 251
Lister, Anne, 322, 360
Lloyd, Christopher, 137
Lodge, Thomas, 143
Lorde, Audre, 224
Love Between Women (Brooten), 331
Lover: or, Nuptiall Love, The (Crofts), 267
Lucia (*I ragionamenti*), 59
Lucian, 24, 54, 55, 314, 316
Lucasia (Anne Owen, Lady Dungannon), 300, 301–03, 305–07, 338
"Lucasia, Rosania, and Orinda parting at a Fountain, July 1663" (Philips), 301
Lucretia, 316
Luther, Martin, 63
Lycaon, King, 234, 239, 244
Lyly, John, 5–6, 7, 178, 287–88, 327–29, 338, 340
Lysander (*A Midsummer Night's Dream*), 58, 65, 68, 74–5, 171

Macfarlane, Alan, 260, 446 n.70, 446 n.73
McKeon, Michael, 417 n.111
MacKinnon, Catherine, 224, 227
Maclean, Ian, 86
Madame Mediator (*The Convent of Pleasure*), 291
Magalotti, Lorenzo, 253
Maisse, André Hurault de, 139–40, 149–50
Maitland Quarto Manuscript, The (Maitland), 288–90, 297, 355
Making Sex (Laqueur), 191–92
Malleus Maleficarum, 23
Malvolio (*Twelfth Night*), 39
Mandeville, Bernard, 310
Maniére, Catherine de la, 42
Manley, Delarivier, 313
Markham, Gervase, 184–85, 288
Marlowe, Christopher, 11, 229
Marotti, Arthur, 337

Mars, 25, 160, 162
Martensen, Robert, 103
Martialus, Marcus Valerius, 8, 54, 67, 217, 229, 322, 360; "Ad Bassam tribadem Epig. 91" of, 24, 316
Martin, Roberta, 318
Marvell, Andrew, 7, 63, 143, 172, 313
Mary, the Virgin, 64, 126, 143, 146
Mary, Princess of Orange, 156
Mary II, Queen of England and Scotland, 254–55
Masham, Abigail, 156–57
Massachusetts General Court, 43
Masten, Jeffrey, 13, 15, 19, 27, 329–30
Maurier, Giovanni Michiel, Seigneur de, 150
Mazo Karras, Ruth, 23
McFarlane, Cameron, 29, 372 n.73
McKay, Claude, 11
McKeon, Michael, 155–56, 278
McLaren Angus, 81, 95
McMath, James, 105, 106
Measure for Measure (Shakespeare), 64
Mechanical and Critical Enquiry Into the Nature of Hermaphrodites, A (Parsons), 320
Medical Dictionary (James), 321
Megilla (Lucian) 24, 316
Melville, Herman, 11
Mendelson, Sara, 263
Men in Love (Haggerty), 19
Merchant of Venice, The (Shakespeare), 39, 57
Mercury, 252, 256
Metamorphoses (Ovid), 229, 232, 283; *see* Caxton, Golding, Sandys
Michelangelo (Buonarroti), 11, 18
Microcosmographia (Crooke), sex transformation, 45, 208; sexual reproduction, 85–7, 110–02, *120*, *121*; clitoris, 89–90, *91*, 194–95, 205
Midsummer Night's Dream, A (Shakespeare), 64, 180; colonialism in, 67–69; femme–femme love in, 170, 174; homoeroticism in, 37, 39, 57–8, 62, 65, 69, 74–76, 152; pornographic structure of, 323
Midwives Book, The (Sharp), 203
Miller, David, 148
Milton, John, 257
Minerva, 137
Mineur, Antoine Estienne, 141
Mirtillo, *1*, *2*, *3*, *4*, *5*, 323
Mirtillo Crowning Amarillis (Van Dyck), *1*, *2*, *3*, 18, 323
Moore, Lisa, 470 n.5
Monsieur Take-Pleasure (*The Convent of Pleasure*), 291

Montagu, Lady Mary Wortley, 314–15
Montague, Walter, 175
Montaigne, Michel de, 42, 55, 193, 286, 298–300
Montrose, Louis, 57, 65, 76, 126–29, 139–40, 150, 152, 385 n.97, 405 n.4
Moscucci, Ornella, 219
Mother's Blessing, The (Leigh), 267
Mueller, Janel, 337
Mullaney, Stephen, 379–80 n.44
"My Thing is My Own," 100–02, 103
"Myth of the Vaginal Orgasm, The" (Koedt), 188

Naomi, 289
Narcissus, 345–46
"Nashe his Dildo"; *see* "The choise of valentines"
Nashe, Thomas, 96–99, 100, 103, 104, 122, 141, 158
Navigations, Peregrinations, and Voyages, Made into Turkie (de Nicholay), 200
Neptune, 178, 287
Neville, Henry, 99
New Atalantis, The (Manley), 313–14
New Arcadia, The (Sidney), 59, 158, 185, 286
Newes from the New Exchange (Neville), 99
New Law Dictionary, A (Jacob), 164–65, 167, 277
New Rational Anatomy (Tauvry), 210
New Relation of the Present Grand Seignor's Seraglio, A (Tavernier), 199–200
Newton, Isaac, 280
New York Public Theater, 39
Nicholay, Nicholas de, 200, 202, 217
Norberg, Kathryn, 102
Norman, Sara, 44
Norton, Mary Beth, 82
Nussbaum, Felicity, 219, 314, 315
Nymphe, 254, 256–57

Oberon (*A Midsummer Night's Dream*), 39, 67–69, 76
Observationes anatomicae (Falloppia), 88
"Ode to Myra, An" (King), 314
Of Domesticall Duties (Gouge), 80
Olivia (*Twelfth Night*), 36, 56–57, 177
Olyve (*Yde et Olyve*), 281–82, 286
Omphale, 162
One Hundred Years of Homosexuality (Halperin), 348
"On the Friendship betwixt Sacharissa and Amorett" (Waller), 310–12
"On the Friendship of two young Ladies" (Hoadley), 312–13

Opera Omnia Anatomica Et Medica (Du Laurens), 117
Ophelia (*Hamlet*), 64
Orgel, Stephen, 59, 158, 160, 162
Orinda (Katherine Philips), 295, 297, 302, 304–05, 318, 323; in "Lucasia, Rosania, and Orinda parting at a Fountain, July 1663," 301; in "Orinda to Lucasia parting October 1661. at London," 303; in "To My excellent Lucasia, on our Friendship. 17th July 1651," 336; in "To my Lucasia," 303; in "To the Excellent Orinda," 308; in "Wiston Vault," 300; *see* Philips, Katherine
Orlando Furioso (Ariosto), 59, 282
Orsino (*Twelfth Night*), 36, 39, 56–57
Othello (*Othello*), 316
"Our Cabal" (Behn), 319
Overthrow of the Protestants Pulpit-Babels, The (Floyd), 143
Ovid, *Amores* of, 229; authorizing function of, 8, 18, 202, 276, 278–79, 286; in Cavalli and Faustini's *La Calisto*, 250, 252; in Donne's "Sapho to Philaenis," 337, 342; *Heröides* of, 217, 221; homoeroticism in, 3, 338; in Lister's diary, 322, 360; *Metamorphoses* of, 229, 230, 231, 234, 237, 247, 270, 280, 283, 329; Narcissus myth in, 345–46; in Nashe's "The choise of valentines," 98; in Philo-Philippa's "To the Excellent Orinda," 308; in Shakespeare's *As You Like It*, 171; in Shakespeare's "Venus and Adonis," 99; in Sidney's *The New Arcadia*, 286–87
Ovide Moralisé, 251
Owen, Anne, Lady Dungannon (Lucasia), 300, 301–03, 305–07, 338
Oxford English Dictionary, 277, 324

Palmer, Daryl, 53
Pamela (*The New Arcadia*), 59
Panofsky, Erwin, 9
Papon, Jean, 42
Paré, Ambroise, female genitalia, 104, 194, 216; female reproduction, 85, 105, 132; obscenity of, 109–10; sex transformation, 45, 53, 206; sexual activity, 94–95, 267
Park, Katharine, 87, 88, 192, 205, 211
Parker, Patricia, 451 n.10
Parliament, Acts of, 42
Palmer, Barbara Villiers, Countess of Castlemaine and Duchess of Cleveland, 253–54
Palmer (*The Faerie Queene*), 149
Paris, 25, 137, 149
Parmigianino, Francesco Mazzola, *249*
Parsons, James, 213, 320–21, 323, 324, 361

"Parting with Lucasia: A Song" (Philips), 302–03
Passions of the Mind, The (Wright), 83
Paster, Gail Kern, 379–80 n.44
Patterson, Steve, 345
Patriarcha (Filmer), 155–56
Patroclus (*The History of Troilus and Cressida*), 167, 289
Paul, the Apostle, 42, 166
Pepys, Samuel, 144
Pérez de Montalván, Juan, 77
Perithous, 289; *see* Pirithous
Perkins, William, 81
Pescas, 256–57
Phaeton, 232, 250
Phebe, 232
Phebe (*As You Like It*), 170, 174, 327
Philenis, 317
Philenzo (*The Bird in a Cage*), 176–77
Philips, Katherine, 7, 10, 344, 352, 354; "Against Pleasure," 306–7; *amicitia* of, 296–300, 305–08, 319, 324, 329; "Articles of Friendship," 304; erotic similitude of, 338, 341–42; female–female love, 170, 309–10; "Friendship in Embleme, or the Seal. To my dearest Lucasia," 305; "Lucasia, Rosania, and Orinda parting at a Fountain, July 1663," 301; Nature, 280–81, 301–02, 304, 325; "Orinda to Lucasia parting October 1661. at London," 303; "Parting with Lucasia: A Song," 302–03; *Poems: By the Incomparable, Mrs. K. P.*, 296, 307, 308, 341; "Retir'd Friendship. To Ardelia, A," 304; Society of Friendship of, 295, 300, 305, 339; "To Mr. Henry Lawes," 302; "To Mrs. M. A. at Parting," 302; "To Mrs. M. Awbrey," 304; "To My excellent Lucasia, on our Friendship. 17th July 1651," 338; "To my Lucasia," 301, 303; "To my Lucasia in defense of declared friendship," 306; "Wiston Vault," 300; *see* Orinda
Philip II, King of Spain, 129
Philip IV, King of Spain, 51
Philoclea (*The New Arcadia*), 59, 286–87
Philo-Philippa ("To the Excellent Orinda"), 308, 310, 341
Phyllida, 5–6, 287, 327–28, 330
Pierce, Leslie, 201
Pineaus, Severinus, 110
Pirie, Jane, 219
Pirithous (*The Two Noble Kinsmen*), 172; *see* Perithous
Pitati, Bonifazio de', 271
Pliny the Elder (Gaius Plinius Secundus), 206, 286

Poem XLIX; *see The Maitland Quarto Manuscript*
Poems: By the Incomparable, Mrs. K. P. (Philips), 296, 307, 341
Politic Would-be, Lady (*Volpone*), 25
Polykleitos, 112
Pope, Mary, 72, 74
Pope, Sir Thomas, 128
Porter, Roy, 103
Poulter, Amy (a.k.a. James Howard), 49, 51, 276
Practical Part of Love, The 103
Practice of Physick (Culpeper), 84
Praxiteles, 112–14
Premodern Sexualities (Fradenburg and Freccero), 333
Preparative to Mariage (Smith), 81
Presence, The (Cavendish), 291–92
Primaticcio, Francesco, 249
Primitive Origination of Mankind, The (Hale), 324
Princess (*The Presence*), 291–92
Prince(ss) (*The Convent of Pleasure*), 178–79, 180, 290–91
Prins, Yopie, 222, 436–37 n.119
Profitable Treatise on the Anatomie of Mans Body (Vicary), 88
Prynne, William, 75, 175, 176, 177
Puck (*A Midsummer Night's Dream*), 69
Puff, Helmut, 51
Puttana errante, La, 102
Puttenham, George, 144
Pyrocles (*New Arcadia*), 286

Queen Elizabeth's Wardrobe Unlock'd (Arnold), 138–39
Queering the Renaissance (Goldberg), 40

Rackin, Phyllis, 140
Radel, Nicholas, 344, 466 n.45
"Rainbow" portrait of Elizabeth I, 134–37, *136*, 145
Raitt, Suzanne, 347
Rambuss, Richard, 344
Raylor, Timothy, 160–61
Raynald, Thomas, 106–07, 108
Recuiel des dames (Lives of Fair and Gallant Ladies) (Brantôme), 54
Reflections on Marriage (Astell), 310
Regan (*King Lear*), 26
Renaissance and Renascences in Western Art (Panofsky), 9
"Retir'd Friendship. To Ardelia, A" (Philips), 304
Reulin, Anna, 43

Revard, Stella, 464 n.30
Rich, Adrienne, 224, 225, 227
Richard III (Shakespeare), 38
Richardson, Samuel, 358
Riolan, Jean, 47, 209
Rohy, Valerie, 34
Romano, Guilio, 110
Romans, Letter to the (the Apostle Paul), 42
Romeo and Juliet (Shakespeare), 38
Roof, Judith, 347
Roper, Lyndal, 9, 24
Rosalind (*As You Like It*), 39, 170–71, 174, 307, 310, 327
Rosania (Mary Awbrey), 301, 302
Rose, Mary Beth, 405 n.4, 406 n.12
Rosenthal, Laura, 291
Roulston, Christine, 458 n.75
Rowe, 317–18, 320
Rubens, Peter Paul, 272, *273*
Rubin, Gayle, 332, 359
Ruth, 289
Ryther, Augustine, *159*

Sacharissa ("On the Friendship betwixt Sacharissa and Amorett"), 310
Sackville-West, Vita, 347
Saint-Pavin, 458 n.79
Salamacis, 229
Salome (Wilde), 361
Salomon, Nanette, 114
"Sapho-An, The," 315–16
"Sapho to Philaenis" (Donne), 337–38
Sappho, appropriations of, 63; as poetic exemplar, 221–22, 314, 315–16, 317, 338, 342; sapphism, 54, 197, 200, 202, 208, 210, 217; *see* sapphism/sapphist
Sappho in Early Modern England (Andreadis), 10, 218
Sandys, George, 7, 232–34, 238, 284–86, 288, 329, 345
Satan's Harvest Home, 314–15, 320
Satiromastix (Dekker), 59–62
Sawday, Jonathan, 110, 402–03 n.143
Saxton, Christopher, 158, *159*, 160, 162
Schanfield, Lillian, 147–48
Schwarz, Kathryn, 66
Scrots, William, 131, 133, *134*
Scultetus, Johannes, 216
Sebastian (*Twelfth Night*), 36, 57
Sedgwick, Eve Kosofsky, 11, 14, 29, 170, 351, 365 n.22, 372 n.70
Seely, Maria, 50
Seldon, John, 166
Semele, 244

Sensuality, Prince of the Kingdom of (*Assaulted and Pursued Chastity*), 292–94, 296
Seymour, Sir William, 66
Shakespeare Stanta Cruz, 39
Shakespeare, The Movie (Boose and Burt), 38
Shakespeare, William, 7, 64, 140; anti-feminist invective, 26; audiences of, 75; cultural appropriations of, 38–40; female intimacies in works of, 37, 170, 179, 180, 202, 338; in *A Midsummer Night's Dream*, 65, 68–69, 152; in *As You Like It*, 310; in *The Two Noble Kinsmen*, 67, 172–73, 175, 177, 330; homoeroticism in works of, 11, 36, 322; lyric subjectivity of, 296–97
Shannon, Laurie, 151, 173, 180, 405 n.3, 462 n.7
Sharp, Jane, on female anatomy, 105, 117, 120, 122, 250; female reproduction, 87, 94; on male anatomy, 204; midwifery of, 109; on tribadism, 203–04, 210, 213, 219, 315
Shepherd's Paradise, The (Montague), 175
Shirley, James, 7, 170, 175–78, 189
Shorter, Edward, 262
Shuger, Debora, 164, 380 n.45
Sidney, Lady Mary, Countess of Pembroke, 59
Sidney, Sir Philip, 59, 158, 185, 280, 286, 288, 296, 386 n.101
Silva, Guzman de, 151
Silver Age, The (Heywood), 244
Simons, Jon, 28
Simons, Patricia, 248
Sinfield, Alan, 22, 28
Singh, Jyotsna, 23
Sinistrari, Ludovico, 211–16
Sirasi, Nancy, 85–86
Smith, Henry, 81
Smith-Rosenberg, Caroll, 356, 359, 470 n.5
Salerio (*The Merchant of Venice*), 39
Solanio (*The Merchant of Venice*), 39
Somerville, Siobhan, 359
Soranus, 8, 86, 205
Spectator, The (Addison and Steele) 72
Spence, Ferrand, 316
Spenser, Edmund, 7, 18, 58–59, 98, 147–50, 229, 296
Spufford, Margaret, 80
Staggins, Nicholas, 254
Stallybrass, Peter, 128, 154
States of Injury (Brown), 350
Steele, Richard, 72, 74
Steinberg, Leo, 411 n.53
Stevens, Dorothy, 58
Stewart, Alan, 344
Stewart, Susan, 207

Stone, Donald, 341
Stone, Lawrence, 80, 260, 262, 445–46 n.68, 446 n.70, 446 n.73
Strabo, 206
Strong, Roy, 137, 404–05 n.2
Stuart, Lady Arbella, 53, 79
Stubbs, John, 130
"Suite de l'entretien" (Diderot), 280
Summers, Claude, 3
"Sun Rising, The" (Donne), 339
Sutton, John, 83

Tassi, Agostino, 271
Tauvry, Daniel, 210
Tavernier, Jean-Baptiste, 199–200
Tennessee Repertory Theater, 36
Textual Intercourse (Masten), 19, 329
Theatre of Gods Judgements (Beard), 167–68
Theatre Rhinoceros, 39
Theocritus, 229
Thersites (*The History of Troilus and Cressida*), 167
Theseus, 289; *see* Theseus, Duke
Theseus, Duke (*The Two Noble Kinsmen*), 172–74; *see* Theseus
Theseus, Duke (*A Midsummer Night's Dream*), 64–5, 67–8, 180; *see* Theseus
Thetis, 317
Thimelby, Katherine, 185–86
This Sex Which Is Not One (Irigaray), 224–25
Thomasset, Claude, 86
Thompson, Roger, 103
Thrale Piozzi, Hester, 276, 278, 279
Tilney, Edmund, 267
Titian, *271*
Titiana (*A Midsummer Night's Dream*), 65, 67–69, 76
Titus Andronicus (Shakespeare), 38
"To a Lady in Retirement" (Waller), 311–12
"To Amintas. Upon Reading the Lives of some of the Romans" (Behn), 319
"Toast, The" (King), 314; *see* "The Hermaphrodite"
"To His Coy Mistress" (Marvell), 313
Tomalin ("The choise of valentines"), 96–98, 122
Tomlinson, Sophie, 176
"To Mr. Henry Lawes" (Philps), 302
"To Mrs. M. A. at Parting" (Philips), 302
"To Mrs. M. Awbrey" (Philips), 304
"To My excellent Lucasia, on our Friendship. 17th July 1651" (Philips), 338
"To my Lucasia" (Philips), 301, 303
"To my Lucasia in defense of declared friendship" (Philips), 306

Torok, Maria, 349–50
"To the Excellent Orinda" (Philo-Philippa), 308
"*To the fair* Clarinda, *who made Love to me, imagin'd more than Woman*" (Behn), 318
"To the Virgins, to make much of Time" (Herrick), 146, 313
Tractatus de Hermaphroditis, 317–18, 320
Travellia/Affectionata (*Assaulted and Pursued Chastity*), 292–94
Troia Brittanica (Heywood), 239–45, 292
Trotula of Salerno, 86
Trumbach, Randolph, 29–31, 262, 373 n.75, 374 n.79, 449 n.109
Twelfth Night (Shakespeare), 36, 39, 56–57, 75, 177, 327
Two Gentlemen of Verona, The (Shakespeare), 57
Two Noble Kinsmen, The (Fletcher and Shakespeare), 67, 170, 172–75, 177, 330

Underdown, David, 9, 24, 263
"Upon Appleton House" (Marvell), 63
"Upon Julia's Breasts" (Herrick), 145–46
"Upon Julia's Clothes" (Herrick), 146–47
"Upon Sibilla" (Herrick), 146
"Upon the Nipples of Julia's Breast" (Herrick), 144
Urban XIII, Pope, 51
Uxor Ebraica (Seldon), 166

Valverde de Humoso, Juan de, 117, *119*, *123*, *124*
Van Breugel, Cornelia Gerrits, 43
Van der Heyden, Pieter, *272*
Van Dyck, Anthony, 1–2, 18, 323
Vanita, Ruth, 224, 269
Van Loo, Jacob, 3
Venette, Nicholas, 209–10
Venus, 160, 162; in *Tractatus de Hermaphroditis*, 317; in Hoadley's "On the Friendship of two young Ladies," 312; in Jonson's *Volpone*, 25; in Lyly's *Gallathea*, 287–88, 327–28; in Sidney's *The New Arcadia*, 59; the Venus *pudica*, 117, *118*; in the Judgment of Paris, 137, *138*; in Ovid, 171, 229; *see* Venus *pudica*
"Venus and Adonis" (Shakespeare), 99
Vesalius, Andreas, 86, 89, 90, 112, *114*, *115*–16
Vicary, Thomas, 88, 90
Vicinus, Martha, 356–57, 367 n.32, 470 n.4
Vickers, Nancy, 413 n.62
Victorian Sappho (Prins), 222
View of the Ancient Laws Against Immorality and Profaneness, A (Disney), 165–66

"Vine, The" (Herrick), 145
Viola/Cesario (*Twelfth Night*), 36, 56–57, 177; *see* Cesario
"Violin, The," 99–100, 102, 103
Virgil, 18, 229
Virgin Unmask'd (Mandeville), 310
"Virgo misogamos" ("The Girl with No Interest in Marriage") (Erasmus), 63
Vives, Juan Luis, 51
Volpone (Jonson), 25

Wahl, Elizabeth, 10; argument regarding historical shift, 278, 279, privileging of French models, 451 n.9; reading of Philips, 300, 306, 308, 344, 457 n.70; sexual/asexual binary, 451 n.9, 470 n.7
Wale, Bertelminia, 43
Walkling, Andrew, 254
Waller, Edmund, 7, 310–13, 322
Warner, Michael, 348
Warner, William, 7, 234–39, 252, 257, 259
Wayne, Valerie, 263, 448 n.96
Weeks, Jeffrey, 359
West, William, 464 n.30
Whateley, William, 81–85, 267

What Lesbians Do In Books (Hobby), 338
Whitman, Walt, 11
Wilde, Oscar, 361
William III, King of England and Scotland (Prince of Orange), 156, 254
Wilmot, John, Earl of Rochester, 99
"Wiston Vault" (Philips), 300
Withers, Robert, 199–200
Wits Interpreter, The English Parnassus (Cotgrave), 99, 337
Woman as good as the man, The (Barre), 87
Woman's Doctour, The (Fontanus), 84
Wood, Anthony à, 49
Woods, Marianne, 219
Woolf, Virginia, 347
Wright, Thomas, 83
Wrightson, Keith, 262, 447 n.77
Wundarztneyishes Zeughaufs (Scultetus), 216

Yalom, Marilyn, 137, 412 n.55
Yates, Francis, 137, 152, 404–05 n.2
Yde et Olyve, 281–82

Zelmane (*New Arcadia*), 286–87
Zeus, 18
Zimmern, Froben Christop von, 46

Cambridge Studies in Renaissance Literature and Culture

General editor
STEPHEN ORGEL
Jackson Eli Reynolds Professor of Humanities, Stanford University

1. Douglas Bruster, *Drama and the market in the age of Shakespeare*
2. Virginia Cox, *The Renaissance dialogue: literary dialogue in its social and political contexts, Castiglione to Galileo*
3. Richard Rambuss, *Spenser's secret career*
4. John Gillies, *Shakespeare and the geography of difference*
5. Laura Levine, *Men in women's clothing: anti-theatricality and effeminization, 1579–1642*
6. Linda Gregerson, *The reformation of the subject: Spenser, Milton, and the English Protestant epic*
7. Mary C. Fuller, *Voyages in print: English travel to America, 1576–1624*
8. Margreta de Grazia, Maureen Quilligan, Peter Stallybrass (eds.), *Subject and object in Renaissance culture*
9. T. G. Bishop, *Shakespeare and the theatre of wonder*
10. Mark Breitenberg, *Anxious masculinity in early modern England*
11. Frank Whigham, *Seizures of the will in early modern English drama*
12. Kevin Pask, *The emergence of the English author: scripting the life of the poet in early modern England*
13. Claire McEachern, *The poetics of English nationhood, 1590–1612*
14. Jeffrey Masten, *Textual intercourse: collaboration, authorship, and sexualities in Renaissance drama*
15. Timothy J. Reiss, *Knowledge, discovery and imagination in early modern Europe: the rise of aesthetic rationalism*
16. Elizabeth Fowler and Roland Greene (eds.), *The project of prose in early modern Europe and the New World*
17. Alexandra Halasz, *The marketplace of print: pamphlets and the public sphere in early modern England*
18. Seth Lerer, *Courtly letters in the age of Henry VIII: literary culture and the arts of deceit*
19. M. Lindsay Kaplan, *The culture of slander in early modern England*
20. Howard Marchitello, *Narrative and meaning in early modern England: Browne's skull and other histories*

21. Mario DiGangi, *The homoerotics of early modern drama*
22. Heather James, *Shakespeare's Troy: drama, politics, and the translation of empire*
23. Christopher Highley, *Shakespeare, Spenser, and the crisis in Ireland*
24. Elizabeth Hanson, *Discovering the subject in Renaissance England*
25. Jonathan Gil Harris, *Foreign bodies and the body politic: discourses of social pathology in early modern England*
26. Megan Matchinske, *Writing, gender and state in early modern England: identity formation and the female subject*
27. Joan Pong Linton, *The romance of the New World: gender and the literary formations of English colonialism*
28. Eve Rachele Sanders, *Gender and literacy on stage in early modern England*
29. Dorothy Stephens, *The limits of eroticism in post-Petrarchan narrative: conditional pleasure from Spenser to Marvell*
30. Celia R. Daileader, *Eroticism on the Renaissance stage: transcendence, desire, and the limits of the visible*
31. Theodore B. Leinwand, *Theatre, finance, and society in early modern England*
32. Heather Dubrow, *Shakespeare and domestic loss: forms of deprivation, mourning, and recuperation*
33. David Posner, *The performance of nobility in early modern European literature*
34. Michael C. Schoenfeldt, *Bodies and selves in early modern England: physiology and inwardness in Spenser, Shakespeare, Herbert, and Milton*
35. Lynn Enterline, *Rhetoric of the Body from Ovid to Shakespeare*
36. Douglas A. Brooks, *From Playhouse to Printing House: Drama and Authorship in Early Modern England*
37. Robert Matz, *Defending Literature in Early Modern England: Renaissance Literary Theory in Social Context*
38. Ann Jones and Peter Stallybrass, *Renaissance Clothing and the Materials of Memory*
39. Robert Weimann, *Author's Pen and Actor's Voice: Playing and Writing in Shakespeare's Theatre*
40. Barbara Fuchs, *Mimesis and Empire: The New World, Islam, and European Identities*
41. Wendy Wall, *Staging Domesticity: Household Work and English Identity in Early Modern Drama*
42. Valerie Traub, *The Renaissance of Lesbianism in Early Modern England*
43. Joe Loewenstein, *Ben Jonson and Possessive Authorship*